Successful Manager's Handbook

Successful Manager's Handbook

Development
Suggestions
for
Today's Managers

Brian L. Davis   Carol J. Skube
Lowell W. Hellervik   Susan H. Gebelein
James L. Sheard

Published by

Personnel Decisions International

Offices throughout North America, Europe, and Asia

Book Design: Peter Seitz and Associates, Inc.
Cover Design: The Kuester Group
Cartoons: John Bush
Editorial Services: Joan E. Kremer and Marsha K. Drew
Production: Publication Support Services, Inc.

This book is bound by the otabind process so that
it will lie flat when opened. The spine gap is a
feature of the otabind method.

The PROFILOR is a registered trademark of Personnel Decisions International

1996 Edition, First Printing

Copyright 1992 by
Personnel Decisions International

Printed in the United States of America.

ISBN 0-938529-03-X

Contents

Successful organizations do not just *happen* — and they do not just *stay* successful. Great organizations are made up of individually successful people who do the right things at the right time in the right circumstances. The managers of these organizations are leaders who work with their people to create clear direction and vision, build effective teams, focus on customer needs, and practice sound business management.

At Personnel Decisions International we are convinced that these skills can be learned. Good managers can become even better ones through the proper use of experiences, relationships, education, and training. These four avenues of development allow individuals to enhance their strengths and overcome their limitations.

Since our founding in 1967, we have been committed to helping managers grow and develop into the kinds of great managers that create success — individually, within their teams, and for their organizations. It was out of this mission that the first edition of this handbook came, the award-winning *Improving Managerial Effectiveness*, published in 1984.

At the same time that we've been helping our clients through the process of assessing and developing individuals and organizations, we've also learned much from them. One result is that we have seen skills, such as championing change, fostering teamwork within and across organizations, and focusing on customer needs and quality, become as important as the core management skills, such as planning and organizing. We have also recognized the increasing importance of continually developing ourselves and our organization as our challenges become greater and greater.

These and other insights are among the new developments that are incorporated into this *1996 Edition* of the *Successful Manager's Handbook*. This new edition focuses on what it takes to be a successful and effective manager as we complete this decade and move into the 21st century. Like the award-winning first edition, *Improving Managerial Effectiveness* (1984), and the second, third, and fourth editions, *Successful Manager's Handbook* (1986, 1989, 1992), this expanded edition provides specific ways in which managers can develop new skills and fine-tune existing ones. It contains on-the-job tips and development suggestions and lists of books and public seminars that can help you develop your skills. Included in the development recommendations are specific actions you can take on your job now or in developmental assignments.

You will find it most helpful to first read the introductory chapter, Using This Handbook, which contains an overview of managerial development, recommendations for creating useful development plans, and suggestions for following through on your development plans. Then you can use the Contents listing to identify the specific sections that interest you.

This Handbook is organized around Personnel Decisions' Wheel of Managerial Success, which represents the nine core *factors* that we have found to be critical to managerial success. Each of these core factors — Administrative Skills, Communication Skills, Interpersonal Skills, Leadership Skills, Motivation Skills, Organizational Knowledge, Organizational Strategy Skills, Self-Management Skills, and Thinking Skills — is covered in its own chapter. Within each chapter are sections covering each of the specific skills, or *dimensions*, that comprise the factor. By organizing the handbook in this manner, it can be used with The PROFILOR® or as a stand-alone aid to your managerial growth and development.

The PROFILOR® management model, which is described in Using This Handbook, is a useful tool for determining the key skills you need now and in the future to be an effective manager in your organization. It can also help you promote an understanding of management, develop a common language about management that can increase communication, and demonstrate the need for change. The PROFILOR® is part of The PROFILOR® Family of 360-degree assessments, which also includes the Executive Success Profile, The PROFILOR® for Individual Contributors, The PROFILOR® for Internal Consultants, and The PROFILOR® for Teams.

The *Successful Manager's Handbook* is a result of our work in management assessment, growth, and development. Our orientation is an outgrowth of our backgrounds as organizational and behavioral psychologists, innovators in the area of assessment and development, and practical business-directed professionals, as well as our work with clients — companies and organizations located throughout the world. By using the principles and ideas presented in this handbook, you can create your own development plans, as well as guide others toward attainable development.

We believe you will find the *Successful Manager's Handbook* to be immediately useful and a source of reference for the future. We also encourage your feedback and your help in compiling the future editions of this work.

The Editing Team
Successful Manager's Handbook

ACKNOWLEDGE-MENTS

The Editing Team wants to recognize and thank those who also helped to make this edition possible. The *Successful Manager's Handbook* (1996 Edition) is a result of true partnerships within PDI and with our client companies. Thank you for your help.

Fran Duncan
Bonnie Anderson
Karen Schwichtenberg
Gwen Stucker
Victor Gonzales
Ellen Kruser
Gregory Duncan
Joy Hazucha
Dawn Beeson
Lee White
Carolyn Carr

Val J. Arnold
Kate Briggs
Maggie Broucek
Stephanie K. Butler
Lynn Clark
Carole Coffey
Marilyn Condon
Kay Lillig Cotter
Beth Erickson
Keith M. Halperin
Kenneth L. Hedberg
David M. Heine
Cay Shea Hellervik
Ray S. Hibbs
Katherine E. Holt
Sandra J. Johnson
David G. Lee
Suzanne E. Lewis
Elizabeth H. Mackall
Cynthia E. Marsh
Fernando A. Mendez
David B. Peterson
Joanne K. Pfau
Louis N. Quast, Jr.
Peter M. Ramstad
Karis Rieke Gust
Elaine B. Sloan
Carol Sommers
Julie H. Sturek
Lois M. Tamir
A. Dale Thompson
Keith D. Wilcock
PDI client partners

USING THIS HANDBOOK

Continual development of your skills is essential to survive in today's marketplace. Competitive pressure and fundamental changes will remain the hallmark of the business environment. Thus, the need for new and upgraded skills will continue. Lifelong learning is not simply an educational concept; it is a business necessity. Organizations have found that they are successful only when their employees have the skills necessary to meet both current and future needs. To ensure that your organization keeps pace with the competition and continues to evolve and grow, you must place a high priority on developing your people.

You may have found that, although you are committed to the principles of continuous improvement, it has been difficult to come up with new and challenging ideas for your development. For example, you may have experienced situations such as the following:

- You are creating a development plan for yourself and want to do more than simply list training courses out of the company catalog.

- The "360-degree feedback" you received from your manager, peers, and direct reports helped you identify some development needs, and now you want some clear ideas about your next steps.

- You have seen some managers in your organization advance and successfully take on increased responsibility and others plateau or derail. You want to be a part of the former, rather than latter, group of managers.

- What was formerly valued and emphasized in your organization has changed, and you want to ensure that your skills will support your success in the new environment.

Furthermore, if you are like most managers, you will likely face one or all of the following situations at some point in your career:

- You are coaching someone who has high potential for advancement, and you need ideas for improving identified development needs.

- You are writing a performance appraisal and want suggestions for helping the person to develop particular skills.

- You are coaching a seasoned employee and need new ideas for ways to fine-tune his or her skills and effectively challenge him or her.

- You are mentoring a team member and want to ensure that you are providing helpful and accurate guidance.

These two themes — developing oneself and developing others — form the core of this Handbook.

This Handbook is like having a management development consultant at your side to provide advice on development activities specifically suited to you and others that you are coaching. It offers a collection of on-the-job development suggestions and stretch experiences in a format that is easy to understand and use. The Handbook also lists public seminars and their providers, and books related to each skill area.

To get the most from this tool, it is helpful to first read this introductory chapter, which outlines key development concepts, presents steps for creating a development plan, and offers suggestions on how to use this Handbook for writing development plans.

Keys to Growth and Development

The most important key to your successful growth is your own sense of personal responsibility for your development. You are responsible for planning and managing your development progress. For effective development to occur, you will need a plan that is tailored to your development needs and includes ways to get continued feedback.

Others can help by encouraging, supporting, and guiding your development efforts. You can grow on your own, yet your efforts can be significantly enhanced with the support of others who can provide ongoing feedback and encourage accountability. Help can come from many sources — your manager, a colleague, a mentor or coach, or even others outside your organization.

Additional keys to success in improving managerial performance include:

- An accurate assessment of current strengths and weaknesses

- A written development plan focusing on increasing strengths and improving weak areas

- Specific behavioral goals

- A plan tailored to your learning style

- Ongoing feedback on progress

- Recognition of improvement

Using PDI's "Development FIRST" Model*

From our experience of helping managers develop their skills, we have identified the following five steps to help you proactively drive your development and establish a cycle of continuous learning:

1. *Focus* on priorities: Identify your critical issues and goals.

2. *Implement* something every day: Stretch your comfort zone daily.

3. *Reflect* on what happens: Extract maximum learning from your experiences.

4. *Seek* feedback and support: Learn from others' ideas and perspectives.

5. *Transfer* learning into next steps: Adapt and plan for continued learning.

Notice that these five steps alternate between an inward and an outward focus. Effective development involves both a reflective process, as well as action and interaction with others during the course of the five steps. Once you have consolidated your experiences in the final step, you then cycle back to the beginning to focus on your next priority for learning.

STEP ONE: FOCUS ON YOUR PRIORITIES

Analyze Your Skills Portfolio

Before you can effectively focus your developmental efforts, you must analyze your current skills portfolio. Conduct a skills assessment to identify your current strengths and development needs, as well as the skills you will need to be effective in the future. As you assess your strengths and weaknesses, use your own knowledge of your skills, but also get input from others. Research has found that most people can more accurately assess their own skills when they solicit feedback from others.

In addition, it is useful to assess important skills based on a model. If you evaluate yourself solely on your personal opinion of

---

* *Development FIRST*, David B. Peterson, Ph.D., and Mary Dee Hicks, Ph.D., Personnel Decisions International, 1995.

what makes an effective manager, you may overlook some critical skills important for your job. Using a model of effective managerial performance will ensure that you address the total range of skills necessary for success.

Personnel Decisions International has developed The PROFILOR® Family that provides models of skills needed to be effective in various positions, levels, and organizations. These models were developed through many years of experience in management assessment and development and identify the most critical dimensions of effectiveness in various positions. One model of managerial effectiveness is presented at the end of this chapter — The PROFILOR®.

To assess your skills, review this management model. Then rate yourself on the skills you've chosen from the model. Ask for feedback from others to check the accuracy of your ratings.

Another option for obtaining comprehensive feedback on your skills from others is to use a multi-rater, or "360-degree feedback," instrument. For information about The PROFILOR® Family of feedback instruments developed by Personnel Decisions International, contact Client Relations, Personnel Decisions International, 2000 Plaza VII Tower, 45 South Seventh Street, Minneapolis, MN 55402-1608, 800/633-4410 or 612/339-0927.

Also based on The PROFILOR® model is the DevelopMentor™ software system developed by Personnel Decisions International. The DevelopMentor™ walks the user through an assessment of development needs and the creation of a development plan, including objectives, on-the-job action items, resources, developmental assignments, criteria for success, and so forth.

The system can also be used to coach others on their development. The coaching part of the software parallels the individual system. The coach can create coaching plans, make additions to an individual's development plan, and provide on-the-spot coaching assistance.

The DevelopMentor™ contains an extensive knowledge base of information for individuals and one for coaches. The contents of the *Successful Manager's Handbook* are also included.

Determine Your Goals

Once you have completed an assessment of your skills, the next step is to determine the areas in which you want to develop. To do this, first determine the skills critical to your current job. Then identify the skills that will be important in the future based on your career goals and your organization's business vision and strategies. Choose the skills to be developed, taking into account both your skills assessment and the importance of those skills now and in the future.

Focus on the skills that have the greatest priority. Leverage your strengths, as well as develop your weaker areas. Genuine progress on your two or three most important goals is far more rewarding than negligible progress on a dozen less critical fronts.

Write specific objectives for each goal. Determine whether you need:

- More information and knowledge

- Practice in applying the knowledge or skills (for example, handling group conflict or problem solving in ambiguous situations)

- Increased priority on using the skills you have

Write your objectives to specifically address the need. For example, one manager might write as an objective, "to increase my priority on acknowledging people's feelings and preferences," while another might choose, "to increase my skill at using participative decision making with my team."

Development is an ongoing process rather than an event. Approach your goal setting with this in mind. Limit your focus and avoid trying to develop too much at one time. As you address the areas you currently have targeted for development, you will want to revise and update your goals to meet changing needs and conditions.

Create a Plan

If you are serious about your development, you need a plan. Think of your development as you would any other project or business plan. Many of the same elements are required — goals, action steps, people involved, time frames. It is critical to use a format that makes sense to you so you will actually *use* it. (A sample development plan is shown at the end of this section.)

Consider the following questions when you are preparing your development plan:

- Based on your priorities, what are your two or three most important development objectives?

- What is the personal and organizational rationale that will keep you motivated to achieve each objective?

- What action steps will you take on each priority?

- What is your timetable? What milestones will mark your progress?

- What resources do you need (such as feedback from others, budget for training, or time from your coach)?

- How will you enlist the support of others?

- What are the most likely barriers and how will you overcome them?

- How will you measure success?

Be sure to tailor your development plan to your needs and your learning style. For example, if you learn best by seeing something done rather than by reading about it or simply being thrown into the situation, your plan should reflect that. If you listen to audiocassettes during a long commute, use these for getting new information. If you need to put a higher priority on using a skill, make that behavior a priority.

When you are doing development planning with your people, respect their learning styles. If they do not know how they learn, help them discover their style by talking with them about how they have learned things previously.

Draw from the following range of development activities to meet your particular developmental needs:

- Use on-the-job opportunities, including:
  - Improving a process or procedure that is inefficient or out of date
  - Starting something new — product, plant start-up, or new service
  - Representing your manager at meetings or functions
  - Coaching someone who is weak in an area in which you excel
  - Managing new projects
  - Making presentations
  - Taking on special assignments that challenge you
  - Offering to follow up on certain items generated in meetings
  - Volunteering to lead a task force or committee

      - Transferring to a different job, function, or business to gain experience
      - Interviewing your counterparts in other organizations about their "best practices," and summarizing what you learn at a staff meeting

- Learn from off-the-job experiences, including:
  - Joining and/or leading community groups
  - Trying a new skill in a volunteer organization
  - Making presentations to civic organizations

- Model others who are competent at a skill, which involves:
  - Watching them in action
  - Asking them how they handle certain situations
  - Asking what lessons they have learned about being effective
  - Trying some of these ideas yourself
  - Discussing what you tried, and asking for additional ideas

- Take formal courses, such as:
  - Workshops and training courses
  - Seminars
  - Adult education classes

- Read books, articles, and manuals.

- Conduct research, which involves:
  - Searching for information and materials in a certain area
  - Asking questions and seeking information from other people
  - Consulting with friends, managers, associates, spouse, or others who can give advice in the area of concern

- Practice, which involves:
  - Identifying a skill or behavior that needs improvement
  - Trying out the behavior away from work in a similar situation
  - Practicing the behavior in the actual work situation

- Use the *Successful Manager's Handbook*. This Handbook is particularly valuable for identifying development activities because it contains specific development suggestions for 39 management skill areas, utilizing a full range of developmental methods. The explanation (see page 9) on Using the Handbook provides more detailed ways in which it can help you identify development activities.

STEP TWO: IMPLEMENT SOMETHING EVERY DAY

Development is most effective when it is treated as a continuous process, rather than as an "event" that happens periodically. Strive to make development a part of your daily discipline. Even five minutes a day, if used wisely, can make a tremendous difference in your development.

Look for on-the-job situations that will stretch your comfort zone and move you toward your development goals. Since time is in such short supply, attempt to link your development goals and action steps with something you are already doing. Take time each morning to determine how you can capitalize on the day's activities (e.g., meetings, conversations, or problem solving) to further your development.

Taking intelligent risks and venturing into the unknown results in true learning and change. If you know how you will fare before you start, you probably won't learn much. Attempt to separate what you are *learning* from how you are *performing*. Ask, "What have I just learned?" instead of, "How did I just do?" As you try new things, negotiate realistic expectations about how much you will accomplish and what standards you need to meet while you are learning.

STEP THREE: REFLECT ON WHAT HAPPENS

Reflecting on your progress can keep you motivated, provide opportunities to recognize your successes, and help you determine when and how to revise your current development goals and objectives. Build progress checks into your overall development process by doing the following:

- Get regular feedback from others on how you are doing.

- Schedule time to periodically compare your actual accomplishments with the objectives in your plan.

- To increase your accountability for your goals, discuss your development objectives and progress with your manager and others.

- Keep a log to track progress in the area you are working to develop.

- As you progress toward your goals, take time to congratulate yourself.

Using the Handbook

The *Successful Manager's Handbook* is organized into 9 chapters that altogether contain 39 sections. These 9 chapters correspond to the 9 factors of our management model, and the 39 sections relate to the 39 management skills. The development recommendations are categorized into these chapters and sections.

Information in each skill area includes valuable tips for improving performance, detailed on-the-job activities, recommended readings, and suggested seminars.

You can use this Handbook in at least three ways:

- To find helpful information about an entire factor. If you are interested in development suggestions for the whole range of skills in a particular factor, turn to the first page in that chapter. You will see the skills included in that factor, and then you can review the suggestions for these skills.

- To locate suggestions for developing specific skills. If you know the particular skill you want to develop, turn to the specific section that addresses that skill, and read the suggestions provided.

- To find a specific suggestion. If you are using The PROFILOR®, turn to the specific page referenced in your feedback report to find the suggested activity.

When you use this Handbook, it is useful to:

1. Skim all of the suggestions in a skill area.

2. Study those most relevant to your need.

3. Then tailor the suggestions to fit your own situation.

Rather than leaving the opportunity to monitor your learning to chance, create time for reflection. Natural cycles for reflection include the following:

- *Daily doses*. Find a time each day to reflect on what you have learned (for example, your commute to or from work, a quick reflection as you plan the next day, and so forth).

- *Periodic reviews*. Consolidate your lessons over a span of time. Cycles like weeks, months, or even the seasons provide a natural rhythm for review.

- *Major events*. Reflect whenever something significant happens (for example, you complete a big assignment, you tackle a crisis, and so forth).

- *Midpoints*. Take stock at the halfway point in large projects. You have some experience behind you and still have opportunities to make a difference if you change your approach.

STEP FOUR: SEEK FEEDBACK AND SUPPORT

Effective development rarely happens in a vacuum. Rather, it occurs through a continuous process of feedback and the involvement of others. Regular feedback is important for a variety of reasons. Feedback can:

- Tell you if you are on course and how to correct if you veer off.

- Sustain your motivation.

- Let you see yourself as others see you.

- Be central to your development partnership with others.

As you solicit feedback, think about what information will be helpful. If you are just beginning to work on something, you may want fairly broad feedback on what you have done. As you advance, specific detail may be most helpful. Let others know what kind of feedback would most benefit you so they can focus their observations on the key areas where you need information.

Get feedback from a variety of people, including two or three people from whom you can seek regular feedback. Be opportunistic; seek feedback from anyone who has the opportunity to observe you and who you expect will be honest with you. Let others know that you are serious about wanting feedback. Then be sure to follow through by adapting your behavior in response to the feedback you receive.

In addition to feedback, you may need the help and support of others in a variety of different areas. Others can help in many ways. They can:

- Encourage you to try new things and give you the freedom to make mistakes.

- Offer you assignments or responsibilities that require you to try new things.

- Provide moral support so you can express your fears and concerns openly.

- Allow time for you to focus on development activities.

- Give you sage advice and counsel to gather new ideas and critically examine your knowledge and assumptions.

You can get help and support from a wide variety of people. While the involvement of your manager is important, include the following in your learning and development:

- Colleagues, peers, and direct reports

- A team leader or member

- Human resources staff

- Role models

- A mentor or coach

STEP FIVE: TRANSFER LEARNING INTO NEXT STEPS

It is important to take periodic breaks to reflect on where you have been and where you are now. Natural times to reflect occur when you have accomplished an objective, when you are stuck, or when you have changed responsibilities.

Many managers write and work development plans but do not acknowledge to themselves that change has occurred. Yet, it's important to celebrate the accomplishment of a development objective. Personal recognition reinforces the idea of development, builds self-confidence and feelings of personal worth, and provides renewed energy for your continued growth. In addition, subtle changes may be hard for others to see and acknowledge to you.

You may wish to continue your development by attaining the next level of mastery on a skill. If you see a payoff for mastery, consider the following strategies:

- Seek experience in new, complex situations.

- Spend time with the gurus and experts.

- Pursue learning in related areas and search for the synergies, connections, and parallel ideas.

- Teach others as a way to deepen your expertise.

If your development efforts have not been successful so far and you are not sure what to do next, consider the following recommendations:

- Complete training that is directly related to development goals.

- Prepare and regularly review a development plan, especially with your manager.

- Seek feedback from a variety of people on a regular basis.

- Consistently spend time and effort on your development.

- Analyze the barriers to your development, and work to remove them.

You may be in a situation where you are ready to apply your new knowledge and skills to your next development priority. Acknowledge and conclude this phase of your development by taking stock of your new capabilities, determining which development strategies and tactics worked the best, and recharging your batteries in preparation for future challenges and opportunities.

Helping Others to Develop

The same principles and steps you use for your own development also work for others. As a manager, part of your job is to help your people develop. Therefore, you will want to help them by:

- Assessing and providing feedback on their skills.

- Helping them determine future skill needs based on their career goals.

- Assisting in identifying developmental activities and experiences.

- Giving them access to resources and people for growth.

- Providing ongoing feedback and coaching.

- Giving recognition for growth.

- Challenging them to continually grow and learn.

You can share this Handbook with your people so they can get ideas for their own development.

We are confident that you will find this a helpful resource for your development and the development of your staff. We look forward to hearing your comments and suggestions. The *Successful Manager's Handbook*, like learning, is a continuous effort for improvement and enhancement.

Sample Development Plan

Building on Strengths

Please record the strengths you have chosen for greater utilization, your specific objectives and action plans, the involvement of others you require, and your target date for completion.

STEP 1: **Strengths Targeted**	STEP 2: **Action Plans**	STEP 3: **Involvement of Others**	STEP 4: **Target Dates**
STRENGTH: Foster Teamwork Objectives: • Involve others. • Promote teamwork among groups.	1. Conduct a debriefing with customer focus team to find if I've missed anyone necessary to the discussion on new quality standards. 2. Keep a list, based on findings, of interested people to be involved in discussions. 3. Each time I meet with my staff, ask about problems in coordination with other groups. 4. Develop and conduct study to determine teamwork issues among groups; feedback information to team.	customer focus team none staff H.R. person, staff, team leaders	7/15 7/15 ongoing; eval qtrly 10/15
STRENGTH: Coach and Develop Objectives: • Increase my skill in identifying strengths and development needs.	1. Volunteer to be trained as an assessor for in-house development centers. 2. Participate in training for assessment. 3. Serve as an assessor in two centers. 4. Use assessment skills with my own staff for career development discussions.	boss assessment staff boss staff	7/1 8/15 Sept.-Dec. Nov.-Dec.
STRENGTH: Analyze Issues Objectives: • Coach others to understand complex concepts and relationships.	1. Give feedback to staff that this is a development need for them. 2. Agree to work with them on this. If anyone does not see the need, have that person track the effect. 3. Have them present their analysis of issues, including factors involved, possible consequences, alternative views and anticipated side effects. 4. Give positive reinforcement of improvements.	Sara and James James and/or Sara Sara and James Sara and James	7/20 8/1 ongoing; eval qtrly ongoing; eval qtrly

Addressing Development Needs

Please record the development needs you have chosen for improvement, your specific objectives and action plans, the involvement of others you require, and your target date for completion.

STEP 1: **Development Needs Targeted**	STEP 2: **Action Plans**	STEP 3: **Involvement of Others**	STEP 4: **Target Dates**
DEVELOPMENT NEED: Display Organizational Savvy Objectives: • Know what battles are worth fighting.	1. Ask for feedback about when I have misjudged this: What did I do? What were the consequences? 2. Write negative and positive consequences on a notecard; read each morning. 3. Identify when others are telling me (verbally or non-verbally) that I'm pushing too hard. 4. Ask my boss or peer to develop a less alienating way to have my point heard. Feedback information to team. 5. Simply back off.	boss, trusted peer none none boss, peer none	8/15 eval mthly ongoing ongoing ongoing; eval qtrly
DEVELOPMENT NEED: Leverage Networks Objectives: • Establish networks with people in the industry.	1. Talk with boss about best industry organizations. 2. Determine how to get involved in the organization. 3. Identify ways in which that involvement can be useful. 4. Use network to bring in information and points of view from others outside the company.	boss none none industry organizations	7/1 1/30 March ongoing; eval qtrly
DEVELOPMENT NEED: Empowerment Objectives: • Increase the latitude I give others to manage their responsibilities. • Empower others with more authority.	1. Shadow managers known for empowering others. 2. Based on these observations, ask for additional feedback from direct reports. 3. Listen to tape on delegation. 4. Determine three things I can do differently. 5. Ask for feedback after I have begun implementing changes.	peers direct reports none direct reports direct reports	8/15 9/15 9/15 9/15 10/15

The **PROFILOR**® Wheel

The PROFILOR®
Skills Dimensions

Administrative Skills

Establish Plans
Develops short- and long-range plans that are appropriately comprehensive, realistic, and effective in meeting goals; integrates planning efforts across work units.

Structure and Staff
Recruits and hires the right people for permanent and temporary assignments; builds a strong team with complementary strengths; provides for staff continuity; forms the right structures and teams.

Develop Systems and Processes
Identifies and implements effective processes and procedures for accomplishing work.

Manage Execution
Assigns responsibilities; delegates and empowers others; removes obstacles; allows for and contributes needed resources; coordinates work efforts when necessary; monitors progress.

Work Efficiently
Allocates one's own time efficiently; handles multiple demands and competing priorities; efficiently processes paperwork; manages meetings effectively.

Communication Skills

Speak Effectively
Speaks clearly and expresses self well in groups and in one-to-one conversations.

Foster Open Communication
Creates an atmosphere in which timely and high-quality information flows smoothly between self and others; encourages the open expression of ideas and opinions.

Listen to Others
Actively attends to and conveys understanding of the comments and questions of others; listens well in a group.

Deliver Presentations
Prepares and delivers clear, smooth presentations; carries self well in front of a group.

Prepare Written Communication
Conveys information clearly and effectively through both formal and informal documents; reviews and edits written work constructively.

Interpersonal Skills

Build Relationships
Relates to people in an open, friendly, accepting manner; shows sincere interest in others and their concerns; initiates and develops relationships with others as a key priority.

Display Organizational Savvy
Develops effective give-and-take relationships with others; understands the agendas and perspectives of others; recognizes and effectively balances the interests and needs of one's own group with those of the broader organization.

Leverage Networks
Identifies and cultivates relationships with key stakeholders representing a broad range of functions and levels; uses informal networks to get things done; builds strong external networks with people in the industry or profession.

Value Diversity
Shows and fosters respect and appreciation for each person whatever that person's background, race, age, gender, disability, values, lifestyle, perspectives, or interests; seeks to understand the worldview of

others; sees differences in people as opportunities for learning about and approaching things differently.

Manage Disagreements
Brings substantive conflicts and disagreements into the open and attempts to resolve them collaboratively; builds consensus.

Leadership Skills

Provide Direction
Fosters the development of a common vision; provides clear direction and priorities; clarifies roles and responsibilities.

Lead Courageously
Steps forward to address difficult issues; puts self on the line to deal with important problems; stands firm when necessary.

Influence Others
Asserts own ideas and persuades others; gains support and commitment from others; mobilizes people to take action.

Foster Teamwork
Builds effective teams committed to organizational goals; fosters collaboration among team members and among teams; uses teams to address relevant issues.

Motivate Others
Encourages and empowers others to achieve; creates enthusiasm, a feeling of investment, and a desire to excel.

Coach and Develop Others
Accurately assesses strengths and development needs of employees; gives timely, specific feedback and helpful coaching; provides challenging assignments and opportunities for development.

Champion Change
Challenges the status quo and champions new initiatives; acts as a catalyst of change

and stimulates others to change; paves the way for needed changes; manages implementation effectively.

Motivation Skills

Drive for Results
Drives for results and success; conveys a sense of urgency and drives issues to closure; persists despite obstacles and opposition.

Show Work Commitment
Sets high standards of performance; pursues aggressive goals and works hard to achieve them.

Organizational Knowledge

Use Financial and Quantitative Data
Establishes realistic budgets; uses financial and quantitative information effectively to manage.

Use Technical / Functional Expertise
Possesses up-to-date knowledge in the profession and industry; is regarded as an expert in the technical/functional area; accesses and uses other expert resources when appropriate.

Know the Business
Shows understanding of issues relevant to the broad organization and business; keeps that knowledge up-to-date; has and uses cross-functional knowledge.

Organizational Strategy Skills

Manage Profitability
Emphasizes the need to contribute to the organization's profitability; makes decisions that enhance the organization's financial position.

Commit to Quality
Emphasizes the need to deliver quality

products and/or services; defines standards for quality and evaluates products, processes, and/or services against those standards; manages quality.

Focus on Customer Needs
Anticipates customer needs; takes action to meet customer needs; continually searches for ways to increase customer satisfaction.

Promote Corporate Citizenship
Fosters wise use of scarce resources; works on community issues relevant to the business; devotes time and effort to future resources.

Recognize Global Implications
Seeks to understand issues, trends, and perspectives of various cultures and countries; recognizes that what works in one's own country will not necessarily work in another; addresses cultural and geographic differences in strategies and approaches.

Self-Management Skills

Act with Integrity
Demonstrates principled leadership and sound business ethics; shows consistency among principles, values, and behavior; builds trust with others through own authenticity and follow-through on commitments.

Demonstrate Adaptability
Handles day-to-day work challenges confidently; is willing and able to adjust to multiple demands, shifting priorities, ambiguity, and rapid change; shows resilience in the face of constraints, frustrations, or adversity; demonstrates flexibility.

Develop Oneself
Learns from experience; actively pursues learning and self-development; seeks

feedback and welcomes unsolicited feedback; modifies behavior in light of feedback.

Thinking Skills

Think Strategically
Considers a broad range of internal and external factors when solving problems and making decisions; identifies critical, high pay-off strategies and prioritizes team efforts accordingly; uses information about the market and competitors in making decisions; recognizes strategic opportunities for success; adjusts actions and decisions for focus on critical strategic issues (for example, customers, quality, competition).

Analyze Issues
Gathers relevant information systematically; considers a broad range of issues or factors; grasps complexities and perceives relationships among problems or issues; seeks input from others; uses accurate logic in analyses.

Use Sound Judgment
Makes timely and sound decisions; makes decisions under conditions of uncertainty.

Innovate
Generates new ideas; goes beyond the status quo; recognizes the need for new or modified approaches; brings perspectives and approaches together, combining them in creative ways.

For additional information on other competency models developed by Personnel Decisions International, call 800/633-4410.

ADMINISTRATIVE SKILLS

ADMINISTRATIVE SKILLS

When Ed Jones took over a new division, his staff was impressed by his leadership abilities. Ed quickly and accurately assessed problems and made sound decisions.

As the months went by, however, Ed's staff became less enthusiastic. Because Ed lacked the necessary administrative skills, his decisions were not effectively implemented. His inability to develop effective processes for project completion, to form organizational structures that capitalized on the complementary strengths of his staff, and to structure his own time made it difficult for his staff members to perform their responsibilities effectively. As a result, everyone's productivity suffered.

As this case illustrates, an effective manager possesses a balance of leadership and administrative skills — leadership skills to identify what to do, and administrative skills to get things done.

This chapter stresses the administrative aspect of management. It presents development activities in the following areas to help you structure your efforts and those of others to attain maximum productivity:

Establish Plans: Develops short- and long-range plans that are appropriately comprehensive, realistic, and effective in meeting goals; integrates planning efforts across work units.

Structure and Staff: Recruits and hires the right people for permanent and temporary assignments; builds a strong team with complementary strengths; provides for staff continuity; forms the right structures and teams.

Develop Systems and Processes: Identifies and implements effective processes and procedures for accomplishing work.

Manage Execution: Assigns responsibilities; delegates and empowers others; removes obstacles; allows for and contributes needed resources; coordinates work efforts when necessary; monitors progress.

Work Efficiently: Allocates one's own time efficiently; handles multiple demands and competing priorities; efficiently processes paperwork; manages meetings effectively.

ESTABLISH PLANS

Plans are nothing; planning is everything.

— Dwight D. Eisenhower

Many managers give lip service to the importance of planning, but when time is short, they abandon planning in favor of getting started on the "real" work. This is a shortsighted approach. Work performed without adequate planning often falls short of the desired goals or misses them entirely. In the long run, the required rework at the end of the project takes much more time than it would have taken to plan adequately — living proof of the variation on Murphy's Law: "There's never time to do it right, but always time to do it over."

The work of establishing plans includes developing both long- and short-range plans that are appropriately comprehensive, realistic, and effective in meeting goals. Managers begin the planning process by developing strategic plans and then continue by breaking down these plans into annual, monthly, weekly, and daily plans. Effective planners also integrate their planning efforts across work units, as well as anticipate problems and develop contingency plans.

This section divides the broad range of necessary planning skills into three parts:

Part 1: Developing General Planning Skills

- Understanding Your Organization's Strategic Vision
- Developing Action Plans to Support Your Organization's Strategic Vision
- Preparing Long-Range Plans
- Establishing Goals and Objectives
- Assessing Resource Needs
- Making Plans That Are Realistic

Part 2: Improving Your Planning Skills

- Using Plans to Manage
- Balancing Planning Efforts with Day-to-Day Demands
- Involving Others in the Planning Process
- Coordinating Across Units
- Consulting with Skilled Planners

Part 3: Engaging in Proactive Planning
- Doing Preventive Planning
- Planning for Contingencies: Identifying Risk
- Planning for Contingencies: Absences

Valuable Tips

- Identify the three to five critical success factors that you and your group must accomplish to achieve your goals. Then develop plans to achieve them.

- Set aside "quiet time" each day for reviewing plans and updating planning activities.

- To balance attention to detail with broader planning, ask for feedback to ensure that you are not stressing one area over the other.

- Build your annual department goals and objectives around the strategic plan. Then develop monthly, weekly, and daily plans to accomplish your strategic goals and objectives.

- Have employees submit an annual work plan for your review. Ask them to include specific objectives, priorities, and timetables.

- Seek opportunities for assignments requiring strategic planning.

- Study the long-range plan for your company or division and consider its implications for your department.

- Break large projects into several smaller steps, with deadlines for each step. Ask for feedback regarding the adequacy of your project plan.

- Set definite deadlines with your manager when taking on tasks.

- Add more details to your plans.

- Ask your manager to let you know of instances when your planning could be more effective.

- Request assignments that require careful planning and attention to detail.

- After your plan is developed, ask others to identify potential problems. Then determine your contingency plans.

- Make it a habit to do an environmental scan when doing strategic planning.

- If your specialty is strategy, use your team and peers to help develop tactics.

PART 1

**Understanding
Your Organization's
Strategic Vision**

Developing General Planning Skills

An organization's strategic vision defines what the organization wants to be and where it wants to go. An effective strategy guides the decisions that affect the direction of the organization. An organization's operating philosophy is on the opposite end of the same continuum; it defines how the organization is run.

In order to develop successful plans, it is necessary for managers both to understand their organization's strategic vision and to incorporate that vision into their plans and day-to-day operations. Consider the following steps:

1. Become comfortable articulating your organization's vision and strategic direction. To clarify and increase your understanding in this area, ask yourself questions such as:

    *   What is the organization's strategic vision?

    *   What does that mean for me and my unit?

    *   What are the future opportunities?

    *   What talents and resources will I need to accomplish my part?

2. Ask for whatever information you need to understand the strategy and direction.

3. Link your operational plans with the organization's vision and strategic direction.

4. Plan for ongoing review and updates to ensure that your departmental plans support your organization's strategic vision.

**Developing Action
Plans to Support
Your Organization's
Strategic Vision**

Sometimes the best-engineered strategic planning falls by the wayside because managers do not develop concrete action plans for accomplishing strategic goals. Or, some managers get lost in the day-to-day details and lose sight of the big picture, the strategic vision of the organization. Action plans are essential for implementing and monitoring strategy. The following suggestions can help you develop effective strategic action plans:

1. Ensure that your group's goals and your own "mesh" with the strategic goals of the organization. If there is a mismatch, revise the goals so that they will support the broader goals of the organization.

2. Rank these goals in priority order. The top two or three goals should be those that will have the greatest impact on achieving corporate strategic goals.

3. Define your goals and the roles of your staff in achieving them. Can you or your group accomplish the goal alone? If so, how? If not, whose support — and what type of support — will you need? Get input from those whose support you will need to determine the degree to which they are willing and able to give it.

4. Determine key results areas and identify the steps required to achieve these results. Include any anticipated obstacles to achievement and specify how you will handle them.

5. Develop objective measures of success that will tell you when you have reached an objective or goal.

6. Put all of this into a format that is clear, accessible, and easy to update. Be flexible, and be prepared to change your action plans if internal or external factors alter the company's strategic direction.

Preparing Long-Range Plans

The best way to develop long-range planning skills is to actually create long-range plans. The following four-step process will help you construct these plans:

1. Identify a departmental objective that requires a long-range plan. Take the responsibility for creating this plan. Also specify a date by which you intend to complete the plan. This will help ensure that you complete your project in a timely way.

2. Create your plan. Following are the topics or sections that are included in most long-range plans:

   - Goals
   - Deadlines
   - Tasks and subtasks
   - Organization of subtasks into order of importance
   - Budget
   - Required resources
   - Constraints
   - Implementation process (target dates, assignment of personnel, monitoring techniques, and so forth)

3. Review your completed plan with your manager to assess its completeness and accuracy.

4. Consider using a software planning tool to organize and monitor the work.

Some management positions require less long-range planning than others. Even if your current responsibilities do not include planning, it's important to work on attaining long-range planning skills. Although you may not need these skills at the moment, they will most likely be required for managerial advancement. Discuss with your manager the possibility of assuming responsibility for the planning of projects that are outside your immediate job area or becoming a member of a project team that is involved in long-range planning.

Establishing Goals and Objectives

Most businesspeople acknowledge the importance of planning and goal setting. Sometimes, however, time pressures get in the way. Setting aside time to identify and develop your business goals and strategies is the first step in improving your ability to plan and manage effectively.

Once you have developed business strategies, you can translate them into clear objectives and tactics. Consider the following suggestions:

- Once you and your people have developed your vision and mission, work with them to formulate strategies, specific objectives, and tactics to accomplish the objectives.

- Review your department's strategies, objectives, and tactics for compatibility with the organization's strategic plans.

- Identify colleagues who appear to have well-defined strategic plans. Ask what process they used to develop objectives and tactics.

- Ask your direct reports to submit an annual work plan for your review and then use their ideas to construct an operational plan for the department.

- Plan an off-site retreat with your direct reports to brainstorm and choose the most viable tactics for reaching objectives.

- Communicate your department's business strategies and objectives to peers in other departments. Seek input on objectives and tactics that might affect them.

Assessing Resource Needs

When you are implementing a new plan, project, or system, it is necessary to make realistic estimates of required resources in order to achieve the desired goals efficiently. You can't expect others to carry out your directions successfully without adequate resources. Without timely access to resources of all types, delays will occur. To ensure that you have adequately assessed your resource needs, follow this process:

1. Review strategies already implemented and compare resources required on a like-sized project. If your previous budgets were off target, determine why, and make appropriate adjustments.

2. Make a list of all resources and supplies that will be required to implement the project or strategy. Gain input from others.

3. For each resource, identify when it will be needed, the different ways it can be obtained, and what acceptable substitutes exist.

4. When preparing estimates for human resources needs, identify cross-training opportunities to utilize resources in other departments.

5. Be realistic about your resources. For instance, if three different tasks need to be accomplished on a computer and only one computer is available, either find additional computers to use or build in extra time to complete that phase of the project.

6. Establish systems to measure and monitor the productivity of various resources. This will enable you to more accurately estimate your resource needs in the future.

Making Plans That Are Realistic

Unrealistic plans can create more problems than they solve. For example, an impossible schedule set by one department may eventually affect the schedules of many other departments, causing inefficient use of resources, late introduction to the marketplace of an advertised product, and a general sense that things are out of control.

As a result, it's essential that managers include techniques for evaluating project plans as a part of the planning process. Following are suggested "reality checks" you can perform to ensure that your project plans are realistic:

*   After developing a plan, have a trusted peer play devil's advocate by confronting you with all of the possible things that could go wrong. Make changes to address any problems you may have overlooked.

- In addition to evaluating individual plans, be sure to evaluate how one plan affects all of the others. Get into the habit of keeping a calendar large enough to chart all of your projects simultaneously. Keeping track of the overall picture is the best way to avoid overcommitting yourself. It also provides a quick reference for monitoring the availability of resources and time.

- Invite the various people or groups affected by the plan to contribute to its construction. When the plan is complete, ask each person to review it one last time to evaluate how realistic it is.

PART 2
Using Plans to Manage

Improving Your Planning Skills

All too often, managers develop elaborate plans only to have them collect dust on a shelf or in a file drawer. To be an effective management tool, a plan must be continually monitored and updated. Your goals and objectives must be a part of your monthly, weekly, and daily plans or they will become victims of the daily crises and interruptions that inevitably fight for your time. It's important to spend some time every day working toward accomplishing your goals.

Evaluate and update your plan on a regular basis. If your plan is detailed and specific, it should be quite simple to manage by:

- Using target dates for various phases of the project. Be sure that expectations, latitude, and due dates are clear and agreed upon with others.

- Delegating responsibility (and appropriate decision-making authority) to the right person or people.

- Requesting status reports from your employees on their progress toward goals.

- Monitoring and following up on progress. By documenting performance against your plans (for example, budgeted vs. actual labor) you will be better able to evaluate results and develop realistic plans for future projects.

- Intervening and adjusting plans when necessary.

Balancing Planning Efforts with Day-to-Day Demands

Managers often allow day-to-day activities to capture their attention while planning and strategy fall by the wayside. Use the following suggestions to ensure that you carry out your plans and spend the time you need for planning:

- Keep a log to determine how you are spending your time. Evaluate your time allocations to ensure that you are giving proper time and attention to the "big plan." Consider delegating more.

- When you are faced with many demanding and competing priorities, ask yourself which are the most important ones and make them your first priority. When an urgent matter arises, determine how it fits into your daily plan (is it urgent and important, or simply urgent?) and act accordingly.

- Use the 80/20 rule, which states that 80 percent of the value of a group of items is generally concentrated in only 20 percent of the items. Simply put, the 80/20 rule means that you can be 80 percent effective by achieving 20 percent of your goals. If you have a daily "to-do" list of ten items, this means that you can generally expect to be 80 percent effective by successfully completing only the two most important items on your list.

- Use a software planning package or a Gantt chart to plan complex and multiple projects. These tools will help you keep track of what needs to be done. See the Develop Systems and Processes section for more information on Gantt charts.

Involving Others in the Planning Process

When making plans, involve your employees in the planning process right from the start. Why? *Because you need their experience, skills, and expertise.* Also, when people participate in planning something, they make a personal investment in reaching the goal. Try the following process to involve others:

1. List all of the individuals who can help with the plan. Obviously, you need to include the people affected by the plan. Also include all of the people who have information or feedback that would be helpful. Review your list with a colleague to make sure you have included everyone.

2. Ask each person for ideas on how to develop or improve the plan, and incorporate them whenever possible.

3. Review your plan with each individual on the list, gathering information on how the plan might affect him or her.

4. Take time to explain to each person how his or her piece of the plan fits into the overall picture.

By involving others in planning the project, you will get the information you need and strengthen their commitment and interest as well.

Coordinating Across Units

To ensure integrated and cooperative implementation, managers must coordinate planning efforts within and across work units. Consider the following guidelines to help you coordinate your planning efforts:

- Determine the support and coordination you will need from other work groups. Bring these groups into the planning process early to ensure cooperation and a workable plan.

- Even when you do not see a direct connection between your proposed plan and other work units, review your plan from their perspective to determine if they might see a relationship. Copy interested others on your plans; it is better to err on the side of overcommunicating.

- Ask your direct reports to submit a work plan for your review. Evaluate their plans for duplication of effort and resource availability, and then put these plans together to build a larger operational plan for your department.

- Initiate a six-month (midyear) review of progress against your annual plan. Revise your plans where necessary, and coordinate your revisions with your direct reports so they can focus more clearly on the strategic objectives.

Consulting with Skilled Planners

Individuals in your organization who are known for their planning skills may be able to help you improve your skills. Here are three ways you can learn from these people:

1. Observe the planning process. Ask your manager to help you become involved in various planning processes. Participate in these activities and observe the techniques of the skilled planners. Contribute to the proceedings when appropriate and ask your manager to provide feedback on your performance.

2. Review the written plans of skilled planners. Notice what they included in their plans and how they organized them. Find out how the plans were developed and who was involved in their development. And, finally, find out how the plans are used in the management process and whether they have proven effective.

3. Ask for advice on your plans. Review your plans with someone who can offer constructive suggestions for improvement. Ask the person to comment on both the content and format of your plans.

PART 3

Doing Preventive Planning

Engaging in Proactive Planning

Although there will always be unforeseeable circumstances that remain out of your control, in many cases you can successfully integrate preventive remedies into your plans.

1. Over the next month, keep a list of discrepancies between actual performance and objectives, recording the cause, corrective action, and final outcome.

2. At the end of this period, do the following:

   • Examine your list. Use hindsight to critically examine the extent to which these problems could have been prevented.

   • Classify the causes of the prevalent problems into broad categories. For example, lists of similar problems might suggest a common cause, such as a failure to attend to detail, poor communications, lack of initial involvement of others, and so forth.

   • Correct the pattern.

3. After a three-month period, repeat this process. You should find a decrease in the frequency of problems.

Planning for Contingencies: Identifying Risk

Identifying risk areas in the initial stages of planning is one way you can anticipate and prepare for potential problems.

Each time you begin work on a project or long-term assignment over the next three months, initiate the following process:

1. Prepare a breakdown of all tasks and critical decision points, and then determine the critical path of the project.

2. Analyze each component to detect areas of risk. Be a negative thinker for the moment; try to think of everything that could go wrong. For example:

   • Information required for effective planning might be unavailable.

   • A technical procedure new to employees might be required.

   • A service group that you use might be undergoing staffing problems.

3. Categorize potential problems into high- and low-risk areas.

4. Prepare several possible approaches for dealing with such problems should they occur.

5. Introduce safety factors into your planning for high-risk areas:

   • Consider allocating more time and/or funds to these phases.

   • Introduce tough control methods in the high-risk areas.

   • Ensure that you are kept fully informed of all developments, either through actual observation or written reports.

Planning for Contingencies: Absences

The absence of key people can cause bottlenecks in the work flow of an organization. To prevent such problems, it's important that you plan for your own absences and encourage your employees to do the same. To prepare for absences:

• Communicate your scheduled absences to all concerned individuals via memo, unit bulletin board, staff meeting, or other appropriate means. Encourage people who often need your help to request whatever assistance they may need from you before you leave.

• Delegate tasks as necessary to ensure that the work flow will continue without interruption or delay while you are gone.

• Inform concerned persons of resources and sources of assistance available during your absence. For example, let your team know which of your direct reports will attend meetings for you.

Evaluate how well your contingency planning is working. If you return from an absence to find that work has been delayed or stopped, examine your planning process to determine what additional or different planning steps you can take prior to future absences.

RECOMMENDED READINGS

The publications listed here were selected for their content and suitability to a managerial audience.

The New Project Management

Frame, Davidson J., San Francisco: Jossey-Bass, 1994
ISBN: 1-55542-642-5
The author, using his extensive business experience, establishes a set of core competencies that give the project manager a greater chance of success in today's complex business environment. The book takes the project manager through all steps and issues involved in successful project management.

Strategic Planning Plus

Kaufman, Roger, Newbury Park, CA: Sage Publications, 1992
ISBN: 0-8039-4804-2
The author discusses strategic planning at three levels — micro, macro, and mega — and describes in detail how to create a strategic plan to identify and meet the needs of your organization. The author provides guidance on how to identify the organization's direction, a six-step process for identifying and solving organizational problems, and methods for evaluating progress and revising strategic plans.

Forecasting, Planning, and Strategy for the 21st Century

Makridakis, Spyros G., New York: The Free Press, 1990
ISBN: 0-02-919781-3
Practical and straightforward, this book presents a nontechnical reassessment of forecasting, planning, and strategy. After presenting the myths and realities of forecasting, the author offers a complete analysis of the factors that influence short-, medium-, and long-term planning.

Manufacturing Renaissance

Pisano, Gary P., and Hayes, Robert H., Boston: Harvard Business School Press, 1995
ISBN: 0-87584-610-6
This collection of twenty *Harvard Business Review* articles explores how to gain a competitive advantage through a manufacturing strategy based on flexibility, responsiveness, innovation, and customer service. One article details how to reorganize the factory in order to achieve greater flexibility. Another describes four stages of manufacturing effectiveness culminating with the production process actually generating new opportunities for other functions.

Vision: How Leaders Develop It, Share It, and Sustain It

Quigley, Joseph V., New York: McGraw-Hill, 1993
ISBN: 0-07-051084-9
This book has been widely endorsed by recognized leaders for its approach to developing and implementing the vision and strategy of a business. The author provides a specific method for developing a company's strategic vision and putting it into practice.

Corporate Game: A Computer Adventure for Developing Business Decision-Making Skills

Rye, David E., New York: McGraw-Hill, 1993
ISBN: 0-07-911763-5
You're given a million dollars to launch a company and one year to make it successful. Rye's book and accompanying software program painlessly teaches economics, marketing, manufacturing, and how these disciplines interact.

Strategic Business Forecasting

Shim, Jae K.; Siegel, Joel G.; and Liew, C.J., Chicago: Probus Publishing, 1994
ISBN: 1-55738-569-6
These three top experts outline forecasting methods for all corporate and financial activities. You can learn to develop accurate projections for everything from profits to expenses to help ensure the long-term success of your company.

The Little Black Book of Project Management

Thomsett, Michael C., New York: AMACOM, 1990
ISBN: 0-8144-7732-1
This book teaches the project manager how to tackle a big project by defining it, breaking it down into more manageable segments, and seeing the project through to completion. Also included are methods of predicting and overcoming problems which may arise during the course of the project.

MRP II: Making It Happen - The Implementors' Guide to Success with Manufacturing Resource Planning (2nd ed.)

Wallace, Thomas F., Essex Junction, VT: Oliver Wight, 1990
ISBN: 0-939246-20-1
Manufacturing Resource Planning (MRP) is a proven set of tools for managing a manufacturing business. This book details how to implement MRP II to achieve better customer service, shorter delivery times, higher productivity, and lower purchase costs.

SUGGESTED SEMINARS

The seminars listed here were selected for their appeal to a managerial audience. The reputation of the vendor, the quality of their seminar offerings, and the specific seminar content were considered in the selection process.

Because of the dynamic nature of the seminar marketplace, some seminars may have been upgraded or replaced, and others may no longer be offered. Likewise, costs and locations may have changed since this listing was compiled. We recommend that you contact the vendor directly for updated and additional information.

Basic Project Management: Planning, Scheduling, and Control

This program provides information on how to effectively manage a project by employing effective skills in the following areas: controlling schedules, team building, implementation, computer support, and project follow-up.
Length: 4 days; Cost: $1,550
Locations: Call vendor
American Management Association
P.O. Box 319, Saranac Lake, NY 12983
Telephone: 800/262-9699

Strategic Planning

This program covers establishing a "climate" for planning; defining the corporate mission; defining key result areas that drive the business; conducting a situational analysis using both internal and external factors; identifying opportunities and threats in the key result areas; and implementation of the strategic plan.
Length: 3 days; Cost: $1,490
Locations: Call vendor
American Management Association
P.O. Box 319, Saranac Lake, NY 12983
Telephone: 800/262-9699

Strategic Marketing Management

This program is designed for experienced managers with significant marketing responsibility. Topics covered include: key elements of marketing strategy; processes of marketing analysis, planning, and control; organizational design as it relates to the marketing function; implementation of marketing plans; and the relationship of marketing to overall business and corporate strategy.
Length: 2 weeks; Cost: $9,000
Location: Boston
Harvard Business School
Executive Education Programs
Soldiers Field-Glass Hall, Boston, MA 02163-9986
Telephone: 800/427-5577

The Kerzner Approach™ to Project Management Excellence

This seminar teaches participants a step-by-step approach to developing a project plan. Topics include: providing project leadership, coordinating efforts with minimum paperwork, developing economic and feasible contingency plans, establishing a meaningful project budget, and determining proper, measurable milestones.
Length: 2 days; Cost: $895
Locations: Call vendor
International Institute for Learning, Inc.
110 East 59th Street, Suite 657, New York, NY 10022-1380
Telephone: 800/325-1533

Project Management

This hands-on, results-oriented program will assist managers in completing projects on schedule, within budget, and with the desired results by: clarifying project goals, specifying the needed resources, scheduling the project and assigning responsibility for completing tasks, monitoring and modifying the project during implementation, and evaluating the success of the project.
Length: 3 days; Cost: $1,095
Locations: Call vendor
Kepner Tregoe
Research Road, P.O. Box 704, Princeton, NJ 08542
Telephone: 800/537-6378

Project Management: Skills for Success

This seminar is designed for managers in technical environments. Participants in this seminar will learn how to: develop accurate project schedules and controls; estimate time, costs, and resources; and build and manage high performance project teams.
Length: 4 days; Cost: $1,995
Locations: Call vendor
Learning Tree International
1805 Library Street, Reston, VA 22090-9919
Telephone: 800/843-8733

Applied Strategic Planning

In this program, participants will learn about the various roles in the design and implementation of an organization's strategic plan; how a successful planning team focuses on establishing priorities, self-examination, and confronting difficult choices; new ways to develop criteria for making and evaluating operating decisions; and how to ensure ongoing successful implementation of strategic plans.
Length: 3 days; Cost: $875
Locations: Call vendor
University Associates
8380 Miramar Mall, Suite 232, San Diego, CA 92121
Telephone: 619/552-8901

Project Management: Planning, Scheduling, and Control

This workshop is designed to teach managers how to set up a project plan and notebook; estimate project costs, resources, and time; employ network scheduling and allocate time-critical resources; establish feedback systems for project control; and utilize project status reports.
Length: 3 days; Cost: $875
Location: Madison, WI
University of Wisconsin-Madison
Management Institute, Grainger Hall
975 University Avenue, Madison, WI 53706-1323
Telephone: 800/348-8964

STRUCTURE AND STAFF

As a manager or aspiring manager, you must be aware of the dynamic structure of your organization. Business demands and employee skills are constantly changing, and it is important to be responsive to these changes. Staying on top of them involves performing activities ranging from diagnosing structural problems to effective recruiting techniques.

Part 1: Developing an Effective Structure

- Analyzing Your Current Organization Structure
- Diagnosing Structural Problems by Surveying Employees
- Improving the Structure of Your Organization
- Improving the Span of Control in Your Organization
- Using Project Teams and Task Forces Effectively

Part 2: Staffing Effectively

- Staffing Your Team with Competent People
- Building a Team Whose Members Have Complementary Strengths
- Matching Individuals to Jobs
- Anticipating Long-Term Staffing Problems
- Identifying High-Potential Performers

Part 3: Recruiting Employees

- Evaluating Your Recruiting Efforts
- Improving the Interviewing Process
- Using Multiple Interviewers
- Increasing Your Interviewing Effectiveness
- Avoiding Common Rating Errors

Valuable Tips

- Draw your organization chart using several different possible structures, and decide which one would work best.

- Analyze how your organization structure will need to be different one, two, and five years from now.

- Keep abreast of changes in other parts of the organization that may affect the way your department should be structured.

- Ask people in other departments for input about how your department could be better structured to improve cooperation.

- Talk to people in similar departments to see how they are organized.

- Establish task forces for specific projects, and then disband them upon completion of the project.

- Develop job descriptions highlighting the knowledge, skills, and abilities required for each of the positions in your organization.

- Have others in your organization conduct interviews and rate candidates' predicted future performance on all areas of the job description. Then synthesize all independent ratings and discuss discrepancies.

- Identify the skills and work styles that will be necessary for your future plans and hire accordingly.

- If you use self-managed work teams, deliberately hire people who will work successfully in this environment.

- View recruiting competent people as your responsibility, not that of the human resources department.

- Develop a reference-check interview format to use with external candidates.

- Attend an interviewing workshop such as Selecting For Success® Interview Training public workshops offered by Personnel Decisions International.

- Interview candidates in a way that gets them to describe what they have done in the past in areas relevant to the job under consideration.

- Hire people who will complement your strengths and compensate for your weaknesses.

PART 1

Analyzing Your Current Organization Structure

Developing an Effective Structure

The way you structure your organization plays a large part in determining your success as a leader. Although there is no one correct way to structure an organization, the structure you choose will affect productivity, quality, customer satisfaction, employee morale, and budget. Following are some key steps in planning the structure for your organization:

1. Understand your department's business. Ask yourself:

   - What is my vision?

   - What is my mission?

   - What are my long- and short-term goals?

   If your organization does not have a vision and/or mission statement, consider developing one for your unit. Involve your people in the process.

2. Analyze the operations performed in your department. One way to do this is to draw a flowchart of the tasks that must be accomplished and the flow of information necessary to meet your goals.

3. Next, study your work unit's organization — who reports to whom and their responsibilities. Compare the current structure to your analysis of the work flow by asking yourself the following questions:

   - Does the chart reveal duplication of effort in any of the operational steps?

   - Are any employees performing functions not directly related to the accomplishment of departmental goals?

   - Does the work unit lack technical expertise that would help it attain its goals?

   - Does the department possess technical expertise it no longer needs?

   - Do individuals in the work unit have ready access to the information, expertise, or other resources needed to perform their functions?

   - Are too many or too few individuals available to carry the work load for any step of the process?

4. Research the structure of other work units in your organization, or other organizations within your company, such as sister divisions or departments in other plants. Find out how they are set up, and examine the ways in which they are satisfied or dissatisfied with their organization structure.

5. Review and revise your structure to ensure that it supports your mission and vision.

Diagnosing Structural Problems by Surveying Employees

If your organization is experiencing serious problems and you are unsure of the causes of these problems, consider conducting a survey of the key members of your staff to determine if structural problems exist. Following are important questions, listed by subject area, to include in your survey:

CLARITY OF RESPONSIBILITIES

- What is the main purpose of your job?

- Who might be unclear about your function and why do you think the confusion exists?

- What overlapping responsibilities exist between any part of your operation and any other part(s) of the division/ department? If there is overlap, identify where it is and the possible reasons for it.

- Who expresses confusion about who is responsible for certain tasks or functions? List their areas of confusion.

- Where does your work come from? Where does it go?

DECISION MAKING AND AUTHORITY

- What kinds of decisions:
  - Get stalled, and why?
  - Should you be making?
  - Should your manager be making?
  - Should your employees be making?
  - Are you asked for your input on?

- To what extent do you have sufficient authority to carry out your responsibilities?

ORGANIZATION STRUCTURE

- What is your satisfaction level with the organization structure beneath you? What would you like to see changed?

- If you could change the structure of any part of your organization, how would you change it?

- To whom do you directly report? Do you report to anyone else in any capacity? If so, explain the situation and your opinion of its effectiveness.

- Does anyone who reports directly to you also report to anyone else in any capacity? If so, explain the situation and your opinion of its effectiveness.

- To whom do you go with your problems, clarification on procedures, and technical advice?

SPAN OF CONTROL

- Do you feel that you supervise too many or too few people to be efficient and effective? If so, what could be done to remedy the situation?

- To what extent do you feel that your manager supervises too many or too few people to be efficient and effective? How could the situation be improved?

GENERAL

- Describe any ways (other than those already listed) in which the present organization structure makes it difficult for you to do your job.

Improving the Structure of Your Organization

An organization's structure needs to be dynamic. What once worked well may no longer serve the needs of the organization or its customers. Effective managers regularly review and adjust the structure of their organizations to meet shifting internal and external needs and the changing skills of employees. The following suggestions can help you review and improve the structure of your own organization:

- Design your structure with empowerment in mind. Whenever possible, create a structure where people do the "whole job."

- Ensure that your organization's structure is current, especially if you have just experienced a reorganization, downsizing effort, or heavy growth. Reevaluate job descriptions, reporting relationships, and lateral structure to account for current reality. Make necessary changes in a timely and responsive fashion.

- Try out innovative structures to stay current. Analyze the feasibility of a new structure, and then develop a "pilot" to evaluate its effectiveness. If it is successful, modify it as needed and implement it.

- Set up a team to evaluate the structure of the organization and make recommendations for changes.

- When developing a new product or initiating an interdepartmental project, reach down into the organization to find promising talent and create a cross-functional task force. Look for participants at varying levels of the organization.

- When working on recurring problems, staff the team with representatives from groups not previously involved. Use customers' input or representation; involve administrative support people; get new perspectives.

Improving the Span of Control in Your Organization

If managers are responsible for inappropriate numbers of people, management time may be used inefficiently. Other important tasks may be neglected because the manager must spend too much time dealing with employee problems, and employee time may be wasted because of inadequate control, poor guidance, and slow decision making.

Researchers have found that no standard rules exist for choosing an appropriate span of control; different spans are appropriate for different situations. However, the trend in many organizations is to "do more with less" and to think "lean." To analyze your situation, consider the following factors:

- Manager's level in the organization. High-level managers are often responsible for strategic planning and complex problem solving, thus leaving less time for close supervision of direct reports.

- Manager's experience level. Experienced managers can often accomplish tasks faster than inexperienced managers, and therefore can handle more direct reports.

- Similarity of the functions the manager supervises. If the functions being supervised are similar, less knowledge is required on the part of the manager. Also, more employees will be doing the same types of work and therefore will be available to assist each other, enabling the manager to handle more direct reports.

- Geographic proximity of the functions supervised. When functions are geographically separated, more time is spent traveling, mailing documents, making phone connections, and so forth, thus reducing the available time for supervision.

- Complexity of the functions supervised. Complex functions often require more supervision, which serves to lower the number of direct reports.

- Direction needed by employees. Employees with lower levels of competence or experience require more supervision than do those with higher levels.

- Degree to which functions or tasks must be coordinated. Functions that require a great deal of coordination may require more managerial time, again reducing the available time for supervision.

- Amount of supervision required for vendors and other people who do not formally report to the manager. If the manager must supervise a number of vendors, distributors, or franchisees, for instance, less time will be available for working with direct reports.

You could also ask the other managers in your organization to evaluate their own situations using these factors. Then compare your assessment with theirs and work together to arrive at appropriate spans of control.

Using Project Teams and Task Forces Effectively

Employees closest to the work are the people most likely to have sound suggestions for improvements in how the work gets done. It makes good sense, then, to include people from all levels of the organization on project teams and task forces. To assemble and use project teams and task forces wisely:

- Use project teams and task forces when you need input from others on a specific problem or focus. Keep in mind the problem or opportunity as you determine the composition of the team.

- Invite employees who raise issues or problems to participate on a task force that will generate the solutions. Involve employees in task forces that are set up to address issues raised through employee opinion surveys or other feedback instruments.

- Involve members at the lower levels of the organization when developing new products or services. Draw on their experience with customers, manufacturing processes, and materials management. Include engineers and designers along with marketing and salespeople.

- Clearly define the purpose of the task force and its authority. The task force can then determine specific goals and objectives within this overall purpose and work to achieve those objectives. Determine with the task force what it needs from you to get the job done.

- Provide task force training in managing meetings, group process skills, problem-analysis strategies, and conflict resolution.

- When a project team or task force has completed its mission, recognize its work, and dissolve the group. Modify and/or reunite successful task forces to work on related issues.

PART 2

Staffing Your Team with Competent People

Staffing Effectively

Remember the saying, "You can only be as good as your people." Top-notch talent is not only desirable, but essential. Keep in mind, too, that your organization's reputation for training and development can be a critical factor in attracting high-caliber talent. The best people want to go where they know their effort and achievements will be met with new and better opportunities.

Set a personal standard for hiring the best, developing them fully, and letting them take advantage of opportunities. To recruit and attract good people:

- Know the job that you are hiring for. Do a complete job analysis to get a clear picture of the experience and skills you need for the position. Also consider what additional criteria you need for total team functioning.

- Know the kinds of employees who are successful in your organization. If you are deliberately hiring outside the profile of people who usually are successful, be prepared to support the person. Change agents cannot survive without support.

- Enlist the assistance of your best performers in recruiting others. Train them in interviewing skills.

- When you are filling a position, ask trusted, competent people to make referrals to you.

- Sponsor a conference in your field. Invite bright, effective people to contribute. Get to know them.

- Be proactive as you review unsolicited resumés. If you get resumés from people who look good, talk to them even if you have no opening at the time. If they turn out to be good, keep in touch.

- Build relationships with placement officers at colleges and universities, which are good sources of talent.

- Look for talent inside your organization before or while you look outside. Consider talent both in your department and in other areas of the organization. However, don't "settle" for an internal person who can't do the job.

- Be willing to invest the training time in someone who has potential.

- Actively participate in professional organizations that provide opportunities for you to meet talented professionals.

Building a Team Whose Members Have Complementary Strengths

Successful teams are made up of members whose strengths are complementary. Staffing your team requires a clear understanding of your staffing needs and any "talent gaps." To build a team with complementary skills:

1. Define the team in terms of the knowledge, skills, and abilities required to accomplish the work. Chart the current strengths and weaknesses of individuals in your group against this. Identify critical gaps you may need to fill.

2. Review your strategic plan and your understanding of your group's future challenges. Analyze the mix of people on your team and identify missing skills or perspectives.

3. Once the needs are identified, develop your existing staff to meet those needs and hire people who will add to the team as a whole, not just to the specific job.

4. Each time you recruit a new team member, take a fresh look at your organization structure and the key roles that must be staffed to achieve your business objectives. Outline the critical requirements for each role in terms of the specific skills and experience necessary for success.

Avoid the following two traps that many managers fall into:

- Hiring in your own image. Hiring employees who are mirror images of yourself is likely to result in a team with limited skill sets and points of view. For example, if you are very precise, methodical, and timely and you hire people who are that way, too, your team may lack flexibility and responsiveness to change.

- Not hiring the best. This is usually not a conscious decision, but many managers do not hire someone smarter or more talented than they are because they fear they will be overshadowed or have difficulty managing the employee.

Matching Individuals to Jobs

The positions you design and the people you choose to fill them represent a dynamic challenge in today's environment, where "doing more with less" and continuous improvement are quickly becoming the norm in many organizations.

The best performers are typically those employees with the skills and interests that closely match those required by the positions they hold. In addition, high performing employees have the desire to learn more, work hard, and take on additional responsibility. To improve your skills in matching individuals to jobs, try these steps:

1. Identify the signs of poor matches in your department. Examples of these signs include resignations, terminations, substandard performance, excessive absenteeism, and excessive interpersonal conflict.

2. Review each situation that signaled a poor match over the past year, and look for the reason for the mismatch. Were there skills an individual needed but did not have? Problematic personal styles? Skills the individual had but didn't use?

3. As you analyze these situations, look for a pattern. For example, are your employees' skills consistently underutilized or consistently lacking in particular areas?

4. Develop strategies for preventing employee-position mismatches by changing your selection or placement procedures. For example, if your past employees have been overqualified for their jobs, modify your selection standards.

5. If mismatches occur in the future, evaluate the reasons for them and, if possible, take steps to remedy them.

Anticipating Long-Term Staffing Needs

One of your responsibilities as a manager is to staff your team with competent people today and in the future. To ensure your team's competency and effectiveness in the long term, anticipate the staffing needs and challenges you are likely to face down the road. Consider the following suggestions:

- Draw an organization chart of your division or department. Ensure that all members of your team are represented. Include reporting relationships. Determine the likelihood of positions being opened as a result of promotions, lateral moves, resignations, and additions to staff.

- Examine strategic business objectives and identify staffing issues related to achieving these objectives. For example, you have been a technically driven organization and you plan to become more market focused: What does that mean regarding whom you hire and promote?

- Review business forecasts and strategic plans, and assess the current operating effectiveness of your work unit to identify staffing problems and to project staffing needs for the future.

- Identify high-potential performers and poor performers.
  - Develop accelerated action plans for your "high potentials" and link them into programs that exist for other high potentials in the organization.
  - Address the issues of your problem performers. Develop plans for improvement, and let them know the consequences if they don't improve.

- Identify employees, within your department and in other parts of the organization, whom you consider to be "back-ups" to replace employees, including yourself, who may be promoted, make lateral moves, leave the organization, and so forth.

- If your organization has a succession-planning process, link your succession-planning information with that of the entire organization.

- Talk with knowledgeable human resource managers and with other managers to get their perceptions of the performance of your team members and of the back-up candidates you have identified.

- Develop the skills of your back-up candidates. Coach the candidates and give them on-the-job assignments that will help them prepare for future promotions.

- Keep your departmental succession-planning information current and use it for managing your area.

- Identify if and when changes in demographics will affect your business. Realistically, what are the implications of these changes for your organization?

Identifying High-Potential Performers

The long-term success of your organization requires that you identify people with high potential for executive management. Furthermore, changing business demands, the organization's growth, and changes in its business strategy also require that this process of identifying and developing high-potential performers be a dynamic one.

You can identify and groom high-potential management candidates at each of three levels: entry, middle, and executive level. The following suggestions can help you do this at each level:

- When identifying candidates at the *entry* level, look for those who have the basic skills and talents required for executive management. These basic ingredients usually include strong conceptual skills and learning ability; basic interpersonal effectiveness, including an orientation of self-awareness and concern for others; strong motivation to be a leader; and a drive for achievement.

  To help you determine the potential of individuals, you can use such vehicles as structured interviews, testing, assessment centers, and job simulations.

  Seed your organization with these high-potential performers. Then develop their skills and track their development on an ongoing basis.

- When identifying candidates at the *middle* level, look for those with developed skills, not just talent. Does the person have strong problem-solving, decision-making, and strategic-thinking skills? Does he or she have a history of leading? Of making things better or different? Does the person develop strong working relationships within the organization? Has his or her achievement drive broadened to enjoy achievement through and with others?

  To help you identify high-potential performers at this level, carefully evaluate their work history and use assessment strategies and career discussions with them. Find out not only their strengths and weaknesses, but also their career interests. Keep in mind that some high-potential performers have the interest and skills for high-level functional positions, while others are more suited for general management. You can use Personnel Decisions' models of managerial effectiveness to help you in your assessment of high-potential management candidates.

To help you develop high-potential people at this level, give them job assignments that will challenge and further develop their skills. In developing these individuals, give them experiences that will focus on the management area for which they are best suited — functional management or general management. For example, if your organization is planning to diversify or to become more international, build in experiences that will help your high-potential performers gain skills in those areas. Also consider your organization's strategies for the future and see that your candidates develop the skills needed to carry out those strategies.

- At the *executive* level, a candidate will have already solidified his or her skills in either functional or general management. Look for people who have demonstrated high levels of skills in these kinds of management positions.

To develop high-potential performers at this level, your strategy depends on the type of management for which you are developing the individual.
- For general managers, focus development efforts on acquiring a breadth of general management experience, with versatility in business situations as the key. Provide experiences in managing a startup, fixing a business in trouble, downsizing a business, and so forth.
- For functional managers, focus on developing the individual's depth in his or her particular function.

Organizations have found that developing high-potential general management candidates within the organization is critical. General management requires in-depth knowledge of the organization's businesses and is quite specific to that organization. As a result, general management experience and skills may transfer less easily between organizations. Functional executive managers, on the other hand, can successfully transfer that experience from one organization to another, and even to a different industry.

PART 3

Evaluating Your Recruiting Efforts

Recruiting Employees

Recruiting plays a significant role in the success of your staffing program. If you are in a position to evaluate the effectiveness of your program, conduct or, if appropriate, ask your human resource organization to conduct, the following analysis:

1. Gather the following types of information about the effectiveness of your program:

   - What is the cost per hire? (Find this figure by dividing the cost of each recruiting source by the number of hires. Also, divide the total cost of your entire recruiting program by the total number of hires. This analysis will tell you whether a given source is cost effective.)

   - What is the time lapse from identification of the need for candidates to the hire date? (This analysis will tell you whether your recruiting process is efficient.)

   - How many hires are produced from each source? (This analysis, combined with cost information, will tell you whether a given recruiting source is productive.)

2. Analyze the data you've collected. Establish a rank order of recruiting sources based on overall effectiveness of the sources.

3. As a general rule, concentrate your recruitment efforts on the sources that provide the best candidates at the lowest cost in the shortest time. However, for strategically important positions or jobs requiring a unique combination of background and skills, increased recruiting costs can be dollars well spent.

Improving the Interviewing Process

Although the interview is often the primary mechanism for obtaining information about applicants, many interviewers spend more time telling applicants about the job than finding out about the applicants. As a result, many interviewers make hiring decisions that are based more on "gut feeling" than on objective data.

The following procedure will help you obtain better information during the interviewing process:

1. Be aware of the principle, "If you don't know what you're looking for, you're not likely to find it." Before you interview, determine the specific requirements of the job to be filled, including the knowledge, skills, and other competencies needed to perform the job effectively.

I WANT TO BE OPEN MINDED ABOUT THIS INTERVIEW, SO TRY NOT TO CALL ME "DAD."

2. Prepare an interview guide. Include questions that you will ask all candidates applying for a position. Research has shown that the use of a standard outline improves the reliability and validity of hiring decisions.

3. Realize that the best predictor of future performance is past performance in similar positions. Therefore, emphasize questions that probe a candidate's past behavior in areas related to the job for which you're interviewing. Recent and long-standing behavior has much greater validity than old and sporadic behavior. Avoid asking questions that are based on hypothetical circumstances, that inquire about the candidate's attitude, or that rely too heavily on the candidate's stated goals; these questions most often generate hypothetical "textbook" answers the candidates know you want to hear. Effective questions include:

- What is the most difficult decision you have made in the last six months?

- Tell me about your most challenging customer-service situation and how you handled it?

- Give me an illustration of the most successful team accomplishment your management team has had, and describe your role in its achievement.

4. Create a comfortable environment for your candidate by being on time, spending a few minutes chatting informally to put the candidate at ease, and avoiding interruptions.

5. Take notes during the interview to be sure that you can evaluate the candidate based on facts (rather than unclear recall) when the time comes to make the final hiring decision.

6. Try to get additional information about the candidate to confirm your conclusions. Reference checks and the conclusions of other interviewers can substantiate or contradict your own findings. If other interviewers disagree with your conclusions, consult with them and review the data they have collected. You may discover that you have obtained different information. You may also discover areas in your own questioning that could be improved.

Using Multiple Interviewers

Many organizations have more than one person interview each candidate. The use of multiple interviewers helps reduce individual biases and neutralizes the impact of rating errors. It also makes more efficient use of interviewer time and permits the collection of in-depth information.

The following guidelines can help make the multiple interviewing process more effective:

1. Assign responsibility for coordinating the process to one individual. Typically, this is someone from the human resources department.

2. Give each interviewer a copy of the job description or a list of knowledge, skills, abilities, and other qualifications necessary to perform the job. This will ensure that interviewers know what to look for when they interview.

3. Assign each interviewer different dimensions of the job so that each can focus on a specific area. For example, one person could obtain information on technical skills, another could assess people skills, and a third could investigate project-management skills. Build in some overlap so there is more than one perspective on each skill area.

4. Have each interviewer use a standard outline containing questions that focus on the candidate's past behavior and accomplishments in the area being evaluated. Also, decide which interviewer will tell the applicant about various aspects of the job and organization so interviewers don't repeat or contradict one another.

5. After the interview, have each interviewer rate the candidate on the dimension he or she was assigned.

6. Compare the independent ratings and look for a consensus. If there is a discrepancy among ratings or if the position being filled is very important, have the interviewers get together to discuss the candidate and arrive at a consensus.

Increasing Your Interviewing Effectiveness

Interviewing is a skill that improves with practice. Consider the following suggestions to improve your interviewing effectiveness:

• Aim for an 80/20 applicant/interviewer talk ratio.

• Learn to differentiate good information from "sizzle." Good information usually contains specific behaviors that the candidate has engaged in, while "sizzle" information sounds good, but means little, and serves to falsely inflate your evaluation of a candidate.

- Be comfortable with silence after you have asked a question. This will allow the candidate to think and take initiative.

- Display energy and show enthusiasm for the job for which you are interviewing candidates.

- Videotape yourself doing an interview (not a real one!). Watch the tape yourself and with others. Solicit feedback on how you can improve your skills.

In addition, avoid the following ineffective types of questions:

- Questions that can be answered with "yes" or "no." These questions begin with "did," "should," "would," "are," "will," etc. Instead, use open-ended questions that start with "what," "how," "give me an example," "describe," etc.

- Leading questions. These questions tell candidates what they should have done and are highly prone to falsified responses. The leading question, "You must have had to put in a lot of extra hours to get everything done on time, huh?" can be adapted to "What did you do to handle the situation?" to elicit a more meaningful response.

- Threatening questions. For example, the question, "Why didn't you just put in some overtime?" may be perceived as threatening. These questions affix blame onto the candidate and imply that he or she did the wrong thing. Such questions are likely to put candidates on the defensive, and may inhibit their responses during the rest of the interview.

- Questions about philosophies, beliefs, and opinions. An example of such a question is, "In your opinion, what qualities are essential to effective leadership?" Candidates tend to respond to these questions by giving "canned" answers designed to tell you just what you want to hear. This information tends to be misleading and may confound your perception and rating of the candidate.

- Run-on or multiple-choice questions. These questions tend to give the candidate hints about what to say and may be confusing to the candidate.

Avoiding Common Rating Errors

It is human nature to "commit" the following rating errors when evaluating candidates. However, developing an awareness of common rating errors is the first step in avoiding them, and will result in more accurate selection decisions on your part.

- First-impression effect. This error occurs when the candidate is evaluated during the first four minutes of the interview. Such an evaluation is based on first impression data (smile, eye contact, handshake, and so forth). This first impression is weighted too heavily and carries into the entire interview.

- Contrast effect. This error occurs in comparing two or more candidates. If an interviewer sees a very weak person first, the second candidate the interviewer sees, who may be average, will be rated higher than average due to the contrast between the first and second candidates.

- Blind-spot effect. In this case, an interviewer may not see certain types of deficits because they are just like his or her own. For example, the interviewer who prefers "the big picture" may not appreciate a detail-oriented person.

- Halo effect. The halo effect occurs when a candidate is strong in one dimension, and the interviewer then views him or her as being strong in all dimensions of the evaluation.

- High-potential effect. In this situation, the interviewer judges the candidate's credentials rather than his or her past performance, experience, and other behaviors.

- Dramatic-incident effect. Here, the interviewer places too much emphasis on one specific behavior area. One specific problem may wipe out years of good work in the eyes of the interviewer.

RECOMMENDED READINGS

The publications listed here were selected for their content and suitability to a managerial audience.

Corporate Lifecycles

Adizes, Ichak, Englewood Cliffs, NJ: Prentice-Hall, 1990
ISBN: 0-13-174426-7
The author describes the behavior of an organization throughout various stages in its "life cycle" and provides tools for analyzing the changes in behavior during an organization's growth. The author also introduces a process for changing organizational behavior, as well as organizational cultures and their performance.

Extraviewing: Innovative Ways to Hire the Best

Bell, Arthur H., Burr Ridge, IL: Irwin Professional Publishing, 1992
ISBN: 1-55623-571-2
Bell's book can help you implement structured hiring techniques based on a plan, not a hunch. Hire the best candidates who will shine in their jobs and blend in with the team.

Benchmarking Staff Performance

Fitz-Enz, Jac, San Francisco: Jossey-Bass, 1993
ISBN: 1-55542-573-9
Drawing on his experience and numerous examples, the author shows how to plan and implement a staff benchmark project from identifying the internal functions to target for continuous improvement to selecting and contacting appropriate benchmark organizations. The author also points out the potential problems and conflicts that may result from a benchmarking project and how to respond to them.

Human Value Management

Fitz-Enz, Jac, San Francisco: Jossey-Bass, 1990
ISBN: 1-55542-228-4
This book provides human resource managers with tools and techniques for playing a more integral role in their company's growth and development. The author shows how to focus human resource management to proactively support an organization's goals.

Behavior Description Interviewing

Janz, Tom; Hellervik, Lowell; and Gilmore, David C., Newton, MA: Allyn & Bacon, 1986
ISBN: 0-205-08597-0
Behavior description interviewing improves on traditional approaches by systematically probing what applicants have done in the past in situations similar to those they will face on the job. This book is written for interviewers from many backgrounds who want to make the best, most scientific hiring decisions within the structure of an interview.

The New Leaders: Guidelines on Leadership Diversity in America

Morrison, Ann M., San Francisco: Jossey-Bass, 1992
ISBN: 1-55542-459-7
This book covers: why diversity at the management level is important to organizations; the barriers operating today that keep women and people of color out of the executive suite; the practices used by progressive organizations to achieve diversity; and the elements of these practices that make them effective. The author also describes a step-by-step approach to designing and carrying out a diversity strategy.

Cross-Functional Teams

Parker, Glenn M., San Francisco: Jossey-Bass, 1994
ISBN: 1-55542-609-3
Parker's book shows how teams comprised of individuals from different departments can achieve success, especially when the task is complex and requires speed, creativity, and special customer attention. Also included are suggestions on how to lead, appraise, reward, and best utilize cross-functional teams.

Liberation Management

Peters, Tom, New York: Fawcett Columbine, 1994
ISBN: 0-449-90888-7
Peters holds that in the "new economy" the most important work will be "brainwork." He shows how successful companies are replacing old hierarchical business structures with networks of small, autonomous, project-oriented teams.

Personnel Selection in Organizations

Schmitt, Neal; Borman, Walter C.; and Associates, San Francisco: Jossey-Bass, 1992
ISBN: 1-55542-475-9
This book presents the tools, developed through extensive study and research, for measuring and connecting the skills, knowledge, and abilities of individuals with specific job requirements. Ensuring that the most capable individuals are hired to fill specific work requirements should be the goal of every company and this book provides techniques for accomplishing this.

Team-Based Organizations	**Shonk, James H.,** Burr Ridge, IL: Irwin Professional Publishing, 1992 ISBN: 1-55623-703-0 The benefits of effective teamwork are well documented. Shonk's book will help you decide whether or not teaming is right for your company. It will then help you determine what types of teams to create, how to support them, how to make the conversion to teamwork, and how to manage the team-based organization once it's up and running.
Organizational Capability	**Ulrich, Dave, and Lake, Dale,** New York: John Wiley & Sons, 1990 ISBN: 0-471-61807-1 The authors go beyond the premise that the people of a company are its most important asset by introducing a concept they call "organizational capability." This concept is meant to help organizations realize their potential for competing from the inside out. Based on the authors' extensive research and first-hand experience with clients, this book offers both a strategic overview of organizational capability and precise guidelines for putting it into action.

SUGGESTED SEMINARS	The seminars listed here were selected for their appeal to a managerial audience. The reputation of the vendor, the quality of their seminar offerings, and the specific seminar content were considered in the selection process.

Because of the dynamic nature of the seminar marketplace, some seminars may have been upgraded or replaced, and others may no longer be offered. Likewise, costs and locations may have changed since this listing was compiled. We recommend that you contact the vendor directly for updated and additional information.

Interviewing Skills

This program uses videotaped practice sessions and personalized feedback to teach the basics of interviewing. The program also includes how to measure candidates' qualifications against job requirements and how to identify the best candidate.
Length: 1 day; Cost: Call vendor
Locations: Call vendor
Communispond, Inc.
300 Park Avenue, 22nd Floor, New York, NY 10022
Telephone: 212/486-2300

Beyond Teams

This workshop will equip participants with concepts and applications to help them establish the most effective organizational structures and the most effective use of teams. Topics include: the importance of accountability in hierarchical systems; "effectiveness" versus "outputs" as the criterion for measurement; the ways to organize work; whether a team is appropriate or not; and naturally occurring managerial layers.
Length: 5 days; Cost: $4,350
Location: Bedford, MA
Levinson Institute, Inc.
404 Wyman Street, Suite 400, Waltham, MA 02154
Telephone: 800/290-5735

Selecting For Success® Interview Training

This workshop teaches the critical skills needed in interviews to get in-depth information from candidates, and make the best hiring decisions. Topics include: predicting future performance, avoiding common interviewing errors, structuring and controlling interviews, and coordinating interview results with others involved in the hiring process.

Length: 2 days; Cost: $575

Locations: Call vendor

Personnel Decisions International
2000 Plaza VII Tower, 45 South Seventh Street
Minneapolis, MN 55402-1608
Telephone: 800/633-4410

Interviewing: A Strategic Approach

This seminar is designed to provide participants with knowledge and skill in interviewing. Specifically, the seminar focuses on: developing and using predictive questioning techniques; taking the needed actions to protect an organization from liability as a result of a discrimination suit; utilizing techniques for forming judgments from interviewing data; and enhancing personal communication style in interviewing.

Length: 3 days; Cost: $1,470

Location: Ann Arbor, MI

University of Michigan Business School
Executive Education Center
Ann Arbor, MI 48109-1234
Telephone: 313/763-1000

DEVELOP SYSTEMS AND PROCESSES

Structuring effective systems and processes will help you eliminate inefficiencies and roadblocks. It will also help you clarify work procedures, set up appropriate communication channels, and standardize work processes. This section focuses on the development of your management skills in these areas:

- Analyzing the Work Flow
- Aligning the System
- Using Tools to Standardize Work Processes
- Improving Work Procedures
- Eliminating Interference
- Improving Work Flow by Changing Office Layout
- Improving Efficiency through the Use of Technology

Valuable Tips

- Look for new technology that can increase your department's efficiency.

- Ask yourself what could be eliminated without losing production capacity.

- Read a book on process-flow analysis and apply the principles to your department.

- If your group uses expensive equipment, explore the possibility of adding additional shifts to utilize it to a greater degree.

- Clarify the steps and procedures to be used in accomplishing key tasks in your department.

- Challenge your team to identify tasks or procedures that should be streamlined.

- Look for ways to reduce the duplication of effort in your department.

- Detail each step that must occur from the time work enters your department until it leaves your department. Eliminate unnecessary steps.

- Look at the physical layout of your department to see how it might be changed to improve communication or enhance efficiency.

- Ask your people what trends they have noticed in the problems with which they typically deal.

- Identify problems resulting from lack of attention to detail, and establish procedures to ensure that they don't recur.

- When managing complex or multiple projects, use a flowchart to track and distribute the work load over time.

Analyzing the Work Flow

Organizational structures are dynamic. A structure that worked well at one time under certain conditions may no longer be effective or efficient. As the demands on your unit, the skills of your employees, and the external environment change, so must the structure of your unit.

With your team, periodically review the structure of your department to determine whether it continues to facilitate, and not hinder, getting the work done. Involving your team in this analysis is critical.

1. List your work unit's goals.

2. Use your team to analyze the operations performed in your department. Draw a flowchart of the processes and tasks that must be accomplished, along with the information the unit needs to meet its goals. Identify both the formal processes and the way things really are done. Chart the decision makers and the key communication points. Include people both inside and outside your work unit who are involved in the process.

3. Next, study your work unit's current structure, such as who reports to whom and what their responsibilities are.

   • How did it come to be structured the way it is today?

   • Which elements of this design no longer serve a purpose?

   • Was the structure built around the capabilities of managers or employees who are no longer with the organization?

4. Identify what is working and what is not.

   • Identify bottlenecks and recurring problems.

   • Note places where the formal process is circumvented.

   • Highlight internal and external customer-service problems.

   • Examine the level at which decisions are made.

   • Identify duplication of effort.

   • Include what is working well. Examine why.

5. Ask the team to troubleshoot the problem areas and make recommendations.

6. Research the structures of other work units in your organization, such as related divisions or departments. Find out how their work processes are set up, what works well and what doesn't, and why.

7. Continue to clarify responsibilities and procedures through team meetings and other communication vehicles.

Aligning the System

To accomplish the vision and mission of the organization, you must ensure that your systems support them. To help you assess and improve the alignment of your systems to the mission, use the following technique:

1. Examine the following systems to determine if they are aligned with your mission:

   - Leadership style

   - Decision-making style

   - Problem-solving style

   - Training and development

   - Performance planning and appraisal

   - Reward systems

   - Information systems

2. For each system, ask yourself, "Does this system support, block, or create obstacles to achieving the mission?" For example, assume the goal is to improve customer service by making products available fast; however, the lack of a good information system may prevent you from supplying materials to manufacturing quickly enough to accomplish the goal.

3. Determine what needs to be done to create or align the systems to support the mission.

Using Tools to Standardize Work Processes

If you standardize your work processes, you will not have to "reinvent the wheel" for each new project or for different kinds of situations. Instead, you can modify the process to fit each new initiative. Meeting guidelines, problem-solving models, quality-improvement models, models for troubleshooting complaints, and planning tools are typically useful tools to have.

A good working tool:

- Contains accurate, consistent information.

- Explains procedures in easy-to-read terminology so employees can clearly understand and follow the directions.

- Allows employees at all levels to follow the process.

- Accommodates changes and updates.

- Is cost effective.

Some effective tools for standardizing your work processes include the following:

- Flowcharts, which convey the relationships of one process or person to another via visual descriptions of work cycles. Flowcharts are treelike diagrams that represent the work flow among process components. Standard symbols (such as circles and squares) are used to identify tasks, and lines are used to represent relationships.

  Flowcharts are especially effective when the process relationships are complex and when several tasks occur simultaneously. Using flowcharts, you can identify critical paths that will allow you to track progress.

- Gantt charts, which are graphic representations of the time relationships in a project. A Gantt chart works particularly well for projects that involve simple, repetitive tasks, projects that will not go through many process changes, and projects for which the plan needs to be communicated simply and directly to others. Gantt charts do not work well if the various steps are highly interdependent.

  A sample Gantt chart is pictured below. Actual start and completion dates and amount of progress on the project can be tracked on the chart in different colors.

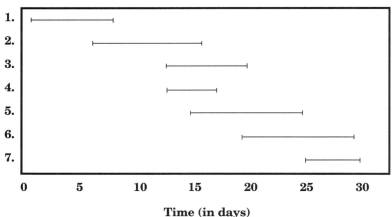

Project Steps

Time (in days)

- Project planning worksheets, which provide overall snapshots of projects. A project planning worksheet breaks a project into specific tasks and steps, estimates the time required and the cost involved for each task or step, and identifies the person or group responsible for carrying the task through to completion.

- Meeting guidelines, which provide a model for conducting meetings. The model may be one that has been agreed upon by the group or one established for the whole organization as a way to make meeting time more productive.

As a manager, it is useful for you to determine whether your group has the standardized processes it needs to consistently meet objectives or quality standards.

Improving Work Procedures

As you critically analyze your routines, you can eliminate or modify inefficient procedures and systems by creating new approaches. Use the following steps to generate and analyze new alternatives. While it is productive to do this on an individual level, it is also critical that you work with your team and create new approaches as a group.

1. Identify procedures that you and your team find outdated, overly time-consuming, or difficult to complete.

2. Find out the purpose of the procedure.

3. Evaluate the procedure in detail, critiquing each step. Determine whether the step is necessary and if it could be eliminated or combined with another step to save time.

4. Generate as many alternate procedures as possible that would meet the same objective.

5. Review your potential alternatives. It may be possible to combine the best elements of several alternatives to obtain one superior solution.

6. Set up a system to evaluate how well your solution really works. Continue to evaluate it for improvement.

Set aside time during regularly scheduled staff meetings to discuss changes and improvements to your unit's work processes and procedures. During these sessions, encourage employees to challenge decisions on procedures they feel have become outdated. Stress the need to make continuous improvements in the work process, and solicit ideas for change.

Refer to the Champion Change and the Innovate sections of this Handbook for additional information and ideas on improving work procedures.

Eliminating Interference

Time inefficiencies interfere with accomplishing desired objectives. Inefficiencies and roadblocks are common, particularly when working on complex tasks. The first and most important step in dealing with such issues is to find out where your time is really going. To do so, follow this procedure:

1. During the next week, log all of your major time wasters or problems that come up. Ask your direct reports to do the same.

2. After a week, analyze your logs both individually and as a group by asking:

   - How is time spent?

   - Is time wasted by people or events, and are they internal or external?

   - How can these problems be controlled or eliminated?

3. Implement action plans to remove the inefficiencies identified in the previous step.

4. A few weeks after implementing your action plan, start another log of your time to determine if the changes have been made and whether they have been helpful.

When confronted with roadblocks and inefficiencies that are complex or involve different functions or teams, pull together a cross section of people involved in the process (for example, customers, salespeople, suppliers, designers, manufacturers, and distributors). Follow these steps:

1. Ask the team to identify the work flow from the beginning to the end.

2. Note the process, people involved, common problems, and stress points.

3. Next, highlight the critical path that will help you set priorities on which issues to address.

4. Finally, determine priorities to work on, resources needed, appropriate people, and so on.

Refer to the Work Efficiently section of this Handbook for additional suggestions.

Improving Work Flow by Changing Office Layout

Professional office designers study offices to determine the most effective layout of furniture and equipment. You can apply their techniques on a less-sophisticated level to eliminate inefficiencies in your work area.

1. Draw a diagram of your current office layout, then trace work flow and travel patterns on this diagram by determining who walks where to get what or to talk to whom. You may want to trace the flow of a particular job, such as the flow of a product through a plant.

2. After you have determined the current flow, ask yourself the following questions to determine if the current work flow and placement of workstations, machines, files, desks, and so forth, are as efficient as possible:

    *   Are equipment and supplies located near those who need them most often?

    *   Are the workstations of people who must communicate frequently placed close together to facilitate communication?

    *   Are high-traffic or noisy areas located far enough away from areas where people require quiet in order to concentrate?

    *   Is the office arranged to minimize tiring work conditions, such as poor ventilation, fumes, dust, or poor lighting?

3. Change the layout of the work area to eliminate the problems you identified.

Improving Efficiency through the Use of Technology

Technological improvements that are well planned can significantly increase efficiency. In many cases, the cost of technology is quickly paid back through productivity increases. To help your department maximize productivity and efficiency through current technology, consider the following suggestions:

*   Purchase new technology. Tasks that are performed by hand can often be partially or totally performed more efficiently and more accurately by machines. For example, a voice mail phone system may eliminate some of your organization's current receptionist duties and may make it easier to communicate with some people who are currently difficult to reach.

*   Update existing equipment. Evaluate your existing equipment to see whether it needs to be updated. Analyze the resulting productivity gains to see if they would offset the cost.

- Replace old equipment. Obsolete and malfunctioning equipment results in downtime and can impede the work flow. Evaluate the age and efficiency of your equipment to determine whether it is time to replace it.

- Purchase additional equipment. If your employees waste time by waiting in line to use equipment, a cost-benefit analysis may show that you could save money by adding an additional machine. For example, if you have many computer programmers attempting to use one printer, you may save expensive payroll dollars by buying another printer.

- Lay out your office more efficiently. Evaluate your current office layout. Visit other organizations to see how they lay out office space and use technology. Based on what you learn, change your own office layout to increase efficiency.

- Brainstorm opportunities with your team. Periodically, gather your team together to identify ways your team can take advantage of current technology to increase productivity.

RECOMMENDED READINGS

The publications listed here were selected for their content and suitability to a managerial audience.

Breakthrough Process Redesign

Adair, Charlene B., and Murray, Bruce A., New York: AMACOM, 1994
ISBN: 0-8144-5031-8
The authors provide a clear, concise guide to total quality improvement. Their method integrates redesign with customer value, corporate goals, leadership, and innovation.

Business Process Benchmarking

Camp, Robert C., Milwaukee: ASQC Quality Press, 1995
ISBN: 0-87389-296-8
Benchmarking should be used to improve business processes and not only to solve narrow operational problems. Camp offers a ten-step plan adapted for evaluating processes and also shows managers how to establish, support, and sustain benchmarking. Six case studies and seven appendices on resources conclude this detailed and authoritative guide.

Process Innovation

Davenport, Thomas H., Boston: Harvard Business School Press, 1993
ISBN: 0-87584-366-2
The author contends that in today's competitive market it is no longer sufficient to simply formulate business strategy, rather it is necessary to also design the processes that will implement the strategy. This idea of process innovation combines technology and management to enhance productivity.

Management of Information Technology

Frenzel, Carroll W., Boston: Boyd & Fraser, 1992
ISBN: 0-87835-508-1
Frenzel examines issues involved in information technology from all levels of management. The book deals with various aspects of management: information asset management, people management, long- and short-range planning, and managing expectations. Also included are examples of how new technology is currently influencing business and industry.

Reengineering the Corporation

Hammer, Michael, and Champy, James, New York: HarperBusiness, 1993
ISBN: 0-88730-640-3
In the current business environment of global competition, companies must abandon outdated notions of how the work is done and ensure that processes and procedures are efficient and effective. This book provides a roadmap for the reengineering journey, showing how to focus on your larger objectives, not on minute tasks.

Integrated Process Design and Development

Shunk, Dan L., Burr Ridge, IL: Irwin Professional Publishing, 1992
ISBN: 1-55623-556-9
The author contends that to be successful all areas of a company must work together as an integrated whole. This book provides a plan for combining people and technology into one smoothly integrated organization.

SUGGESTED SEMINARS

The seminars listed here were selected for their appeal to a managerial audience. The reputation of the vendor, the quality of their seminar offerings, and the specific seminar content were considered in the selection process.

Because of the dynamic nature of the seminar marketplace, some seminars may have been upgraded or replaced, and others may no longer be offered. Likewise, costs and locations may have changed since this listing was compiled. We recommend that you contact the vendor directly for updated and additional information.

Work Improvement Through Redesign and Simplification

In this workshop participants will learn to streamline processes to eliminate unnecessary work; reduce cycle time, errors, and duplication of work; and learn the causes of problems before trying to solve them.
Length: 2 days; Cost: $1,435
Locations: Call vendor
American Management Association
P.O. Box 319, Saranac Lake, NY 12983
Telephone: 800/262-9699

Project Management

This hands-on, results-oriented program will assist managers in completing projects on schedule, within budget, and with the desired results by: clarifying project goals, specifying the needed resources, scheduling the project and assigning responsibility for completing tasks, monitoring and modifying the project during implementation, and evaluating the success of the project.
Length: 3 days; Cost: $1,095
Locations: Call vendor
Kepner Tregoe
Research Road, P.O. Box 704, Princeton, NJ 08542
Telephone: 800/537-6378

Introduction to Process Management

This workshop presents a set of tools for identifying, analyzing, improving, and managing the processes that impact quality, cycle time, cost, productivity, customer focus, and organizational structure, from the authors of *Improving Performance: How to Manage the White Space on the Organization Chart.*
Length: 1 day; Cost: $450
Locations: Call vendor
Rummler-Brache Group
163 Washington Valley Road, Suite 103, Warren, NJ 07059
Telephone: 908/469-5700

MANAGE EXECUTION

Managing execution includes delegating and coordinating work. Skilled and effective delegators give work to staff members using a method that capitalizes on their strengths and helps overcome their weaknesses. The manager's responsibility is to ensure that the employee has the appropriate direction and authority to execute the work. With new employees, delegation means patiently explaining the steps and clearly defining the end product. With more experienced employees, delegation means backing away and trusting their judgment and abilities.

This two-part section provides guidelines for effectively managing the execution of work within your group. Included are suggestions for:

Part 1: Developing Effective Delegation Skills

- Increasing Your Willingness to Delegate
- Identifying Tasks for Others to Do
- Determining to Whom to Delegate
- Conveying Clear Expectations for Assignments
- Assigning the Appropriate Degree of Authority
- Monitoring the Progress of Others

Part 2: Improving Your Ability to Manage Execution

- Delegating Assignments to the Lowest Appropriate Level
- Using Situational Leadership to Improve Delegation
- Empowering Others to Manage Their Responsibilities
- Avoiding Upward Delegation
- Being Accessible to Provide Assistance or Support
- Coordinating Work with Other Groups

Valuable Tips

- Delegate to the lowest level possible.

- Evaluate the work load of each of your employees. If work does not seem to be evenly distributed, redistribute responsibilities.

- Set aside time each week to meet with employees and review progress on work.

- Set up an information source, such as a weekly progress report, that will allow you to monitor the progress and success of your employees.

- Don't second-guess your people; ask them to explain.

- Use delegation as a way of helping a key employee learn a function important for his or her promotion.

- When an employee comes to you with a problem about his or her work, ask how he or she plans to handle the problem.

- Identify responsibilities you are personally handling that could be handled by each of your employees, and delegate accordingly.

- Find ways to individualize delegation to meet the needs and abilities of each person (for example, an employee new to a task may need more detailed instructions).

- Ask several people in positions similar to yours what kinds of tasks they typically delegate.

- Spend more time face-to-face with your employees finding out how things are going.

- Have your people set their own deadline dates and then hold to them — except on rare occasions when slippage is clearly justified.

- If due dates are missed, schedule new dates with your people.

- Create a tickler file and use it as a means of following up on assignments. Ask your secretary to help.

- If a delegated assignment does not meet your expectations, don't redo it yourself. Show your employee what needs to be changed and have him or her rework it.

- When presenting an issue to an employee, ask for his or her plan to address it. Then let the person proceed to create and "own" the solution.

- Show at least as much care and concern for the person you are delegating to as you have for the project itself.

- Always coordinate the work of your area with the areas affected by it.

- Touch base regularly with the groups that service your area and with those you serve. Ask what you can do to make things run more smoothly.

- As you work with your employees, coach them on managing execution with others in the organization.

- Keep your electronic calendar up to date so others will know how and where to reach you.

- Ask others to use e-mail to keep you informed of progress they are making on projects. Set up check-in times during the project planning stage.

- Investigate ways to use electronic calendars to evenly distribute projects and individual work loads.

- When leaving a voice mail message, slowly and clearly enunciate numbers or things that must be written down by the listener. This will eliminate errors and save the person having to listen to the message repeatedly.

PART 1

Increasing Your Willingness to Delegate

Developing Effective Delegation Skills

It's not uncommon for managers to resist delegating the work they once did themselves. However, to be an effective and successful manager, it is essential that you delegate work to others.

To increase your willingness to delegate, first determine the reason for your resistance, then identify ways to overcome it. Common reasons for managers' reluctance to delegate include:

- Insufficient time to explain the task or train someone to do it. While this is sometimes an acceptable reason for not delegating short-term projects, more often it is not. The time you spend teaching employees tasks will save you time and effort in the long run. This sharing of knowledge is an investment in time that pays off in many ways.

- Desire for perfection. If you feel that you are the only person who can do certain tasks well enough, be careful; this is a danger sign. It's often unlikely that you are the only person who can do them. Start by delegating parts of these tasks, and coach employees to help them perform to your satisfaction.

- Personal satisfaction and/or reward from task accomplishment. If you enjoy a task or receive recognition from others when you perform it, you may tend to reserve it for yourself when you could be delegating it. It is difficult to give up work you really like. Learn to achieve satisfaction from other parts of your job — such as coaching others, doing strategic work, and so forth.

- Lack of confidence in employees' abilities. If you lack confidence in an employee's abilities, carefully evaluate what the employee can and cannot do. You may want to check your impressions with others, because people sometimes pigeonhole other people based on one or two vivid events. Then delegate work the person can do, and provide coaching as the work proceeds.

- Fear of failure. Many managers are concerned that if mistakes are made, the consequences will be disastrous. Identify the possible risks with the employee. If the risks are really large, ask that contingency plans be made. Ultimately, you need to be willing to take responsibility for your employees' mistakes on delegated tasks to help them grow and develop.

Identifying Tasks for Others to Do

In order to delegate, a manager must take the time to identify activities or projects that can be accomplished by others. To determine which of your activities would be best to delegate, follow these guidelines:

1. List all the activities for which you are currently responsible. Then classify each activity as a task that:

   • You must retain and perform yourself

   • You can share with your people

   • You can delegate to your people

   The following chart will help you structure your analysis.

Task	Retain	Share	Delegate
1.			
2.			
3.			
4.			

2. Now, return to your task list and examine those items that you have retained. Are you holding on to any tasks unnecessarily? Could you further develop your staff by passing along some of these duties?

Determining to Whom to Delegate

Assigning tasks to employees who possess the required skills to perform those tasks leads to greater efficiency in your work unit. In addition to freeing your time for other tasks, delegating serves as a vehicle to develop your staff and add variety to their jobs.

To choose the appropriate employee to whom to delegate a task, use the following guidelines:

1. Explain to your employees that you will delegate responsibilities to help them build on their strengths and overcome their weaknesses.

2. When you have a task or project to delegate, begin by considering any employee who:

- Currently has the optimal skills to execute the task
- Has a high level of interest in the area, or has asked to do similar work
- Has a need to further develop in this particular area
- Has the time to do it

3. Next, narrow your list of prospective delegatees by considering the dynamics of the task:

   - Its visibility and importance
   - Its interaction with other projects, people, and resources
   - Its complexity
   - The amount of "teaching" time you have available

4. Once your list of employees is narrowed to a manageable level, select the best person for the task. Assign tasks in a way that allows your employees to capitalize on their strengths and, at the same time, address their development needs.

When delegating, it's easy to assign too much work to experienced workers and too little to those who require more assistance. It's important to remember that each employee needs sufficient responsibilities to challenge his or her abilities. Help employees to strike a comfortable balance that leaves them neither overworked nor underchallenged.

From time to time, meet with individual employees to solicit feedback on your delegation practices. Seek answers to questions such as:

- Is the timing of delegated tasks compatible with employees' regular schedule of tasks?
- Have delegated assignments been challenging without being too much of a "stretch"?
- Has the amount of delegated work been appropriate — neither too much nor too little?

Take note of comments that indicate areas in which you could improve your delegation practices. Incorporate these comments into assignments you can make in the future.

Conveying Clear Expectations for Assignments

Employees can waste valuable time if they don't have clear direction for the work they are performing. In the worst cases, they may produce results that bear little or no resemblance to the desired outcome. Such experiences are frustrating to both you and the employee.

When delegating, it's important that your direction is clear and that the employee understands your expectations. To provide clear objectives when delegating, follow these guidelines:

1. After deciding who will do the assignment, determine how much involvement the employee should have in deciding the specifics of the assignment. Experienced employees should be highly involved in determining timing, methods, amount of help required, and so forth.

2. For each project or task you wish to delegate, write a clear statement of its purpose and its goal. Also identify:

   - When it is to be completed

   - Any specific instructions or guidelines the employee needs in order to execute the work

   - The level of authority the employee has

   - Any interim progress reports required

   - What final reports are required

3. Discuss the assignment with the employee and answer any questions. Don't end the discussion until you're certain that the employee fully understands your expectations.

4. At the end of the discussion, ask the employee to describe the assignment in his or her own words. This will help you to determine whether you have mutual agreement about the assignment.

5. Check with the employee periodically during the project to ensure that he or she is proceeding without difficulty. Sometimes, questions arise during the course of a project and employees are reluctant to ask for assistance because they don't want to appear incompetent.

6. During the course of the project, keep track of any instances of unclear or inadequate direction. Note the cause of each misunderstanding so that you can improve your direction on future assignments. You may wish to initiate discussions with employees to obtain feedback on your direction and guidance.

Assigning the Appropriate Degree of Authority

Empowering others with the appropriate level of authority goes hand-in-hand with managing execution. Employees will not feel that they have the authority to proceed on their own if they must go to you for approval at every stage of an assignment.

To determine the degree of authority to delegate, follow these steps:

1. Create a chart that shows the task, the delegatee, and the degree of authority you are giving the person:

   • Proceed without approval

   • Proceed, but inform me of your actions

   • Obtain approval before proceeding

   Your chart should look something like this:

Task	Delegatee	Proceed without Approval	Proceed but Inform	Obtain Approval
1.				
2.				
3.				
4.				

   Indicate the degree of authority you wish to give the employee by checking the appropriate column. Then examine each assignment to determine if you are retaining authority unnecessarily.

2. When you assign these responsibilities to your staff members, discuss the degree of authority you wish him or her to assume. Strive to delegate the appropriate amount of authority, in other words, enough to "stretch" your people.

3. Look for assignments for which employees can take complete authority. These will save you the most time in the long run.

4. Hold periodic discussions with individual employees to determine whether you have given them the appropriate level of authority. Try to assess whether you are assigning too much or too little authority. Take notes on employees' comments and consider their concerns when making future assignments.

Monitoring the Progress of Others

An important part of delegation, especially in the beginning, is checking the progress being made on assignments. It's not enough to simply establish a final deadline; employees may not realize they are running behind until it's too late to finish the job. The following guidelines offer a good way to check people's progress without creating more work for yourself than you saved by delegating:

- Ask employees to write action plans and produce progress reports. Have your employees give a copy to you and keep one for themselves; this will ensure that you both know what is expected. Depending on the person's experience level, you may want to be involved in the planning process to ensure that the progress reports are acceptable.

- Establish due dates for interim reports, working with your employees, and keep a copy of these reports in your file.

- Ask your employees to schedule time and prepare for update meetings with you.

- Establish the expectation that you want to hear about problems before they mushroom. When you are told about problems, concentrate on how the employee plans to handle it. Do not "shoot the messenger" or become the "problem solver."

- Set aside time to work with employees who require personal attention.

Keep in mind that employees will require different levels of your attention and involvement depending on their experience levels. If your monitoring and follow-up show that performance is not meeting planned goals, try the following:

- If the discrepancy is minor, alert the people who are working on that phase of the project and ask them to find ways to get back on track.

- If the discrepancy is major, invite the people working on the project to discuss the situation with you and to work out a plan to get back on track. You may need to make recommendations for restructuring the work or obtaining additional resources to meet the original goals.

- To keep your team on track, give consistent feedback. Feedback is essential for monitoring progress; it not only helps employees correct mistakes before they become serious problems, but also reinforces positive behaviors and encourages the development of desirable work habits.

- Give feedback in a timely manner.
- Give both positive and negative feedback, when each is appropriate.
- Communicate the fact that you are willing to provide feedback. This will encourage employees to consult you.

Refer to the sections in this Handbook titled Develop Systems and Processes and Work Efficiently for additional methods and tools for effective follow-up.

PART 2

Delegating Assignments to the Lowest Appropriate Level

Improving Your Ability to Manage Execution

Managers often retain activities that can best be accomplished by others at a lower level in the organization. Effective managers move decision making and responsibility to the lowest possible level. Use the following process to assess and improve your present pattern:

1. For one month, write down a list of assignments, problems, and decisions that your group needs to handle. Then identify the members of your team who are assigned to each responsibility. Indicate the degree of authority the person has in doing the work. For example:

    A = Makes decisions and does the work; lets you know the outcome.

    B = Makes decisions; tells you before he or she actually does it.

    C = Makes recommendations; the two of you then decide upon the course of action.

    D = Comes to you with recommendations and you make the final decision.

    E = Carries out the project after you tell him or her exactly what to do.

2. Analyze your results by asking yourself questions such as:

    • Do I give A-type authority to only one or two people?

    • Am I making all of the decisions?

    • Can I assign any work to someone at a lower level?

    • Do I overmanage by giving people who don't need help ideas about solutions or about how to proceed?

    • Do I check everything before my people can act?

3. Improve your delegation by considering the following suggestions:

- When you decide to delegate a task, look for an appropriate employee beginning at the lowest level of your organization. Work your way up until you find someone. Realize that if the employee does not work directly for you, you will need to work through his or her manager.

- Determine whether you can break the task into components and assign portions to employees in lower-ranking positions.

- Consider forming a small committee or task force of employees at lower levels in the organization to execute certain tasks.

- Talk with the people to whom you typically delegate. Ask them which tasks from you they have further delegated.

- Identify the people to whom you currently are uncomfortable delegating work. Then make a plan for developing these people.

- Give advice and make changes in others' work wisely and sparingly. Too much of either trains people not to think on their own and does not allow people to learn from their mistakes.

Using Situational Leadership to Improve Delegation

Employees with different skill and experience levels need varying degrees of supervision. The model, Situational Leadership, developed by Paul Hersey and Kenneth Blanchard, asserts that the effective manager varies the amount of structure and support he or she provides based on the developmental level of the employee.

When an employee is new to the job, clear direction and instruction are needed. On the other hand, a technical expert on the job for ten years needs little direction and instruction regarding the job. This same employee may need encouragement and support, however, if he or she is nervous about making a key presentation to executives.

Development level is determined, according to Hersey and Blanchard, by skills and experience for the specific task and by the degree to which the employee is committed to or in agreement with the desired outcome. An experienced person who disagrees with how the work should be done will need more direction than one who agrees with the method and goal.

To use the model of Situational Leadership when delegating work, first determine:

- The skill level of the employee for the work

- The employee's commitment to the goal

When the skill level is low, provide direction and instruction. As the employee gains skills and experience, provide less direction and more encouragement and support until both of you are confident that the employee can make appropriate decisions with only minimal supervision.

Effective managers work with employees to determine the amount of direction and help employees want. The following tips can help you determine when to supervise and coach:

- Use the Situational Leadership model to determine employees' development levels, and supervise accordingly.

- Ask your employees if you provide enough, too much, or too little direction and support.

- When you and an employee disagree, use the Situational Leadership model to discuss your respective views.

- Give the employee the "benefit of the doubt."

- Realize that the mark of an experienced manager is the ability to allow employees to make mistakes and learn from them.

- For employees who want more help than you have given, ask them what they want and respect this need.

Empowering Others to Manage Their Responsibilities

Seasoned managers and employees can usually handle their own responsibilities with little help from their manager. Managers who "keep" too much responsibility are often seen as overcontrolling and lacking in respect for others. The following suggestions will allow you to give your employees enough "breathing room" so they can manage their own responsibilities:

- When you establish goals with your people on an annual basis, ask them the level of involvement they want from you. Ask what you can do to be helpful. Repeat this request as often as possible.

- When you are updated on projects and there are problems, encourage your employees to also present you with solutions.

- Let your staff go forward with their ideas unless you have a major problem with the way they plan to handle them. Keep in mind that learning from mistakes is one of the most effective and common ways for people to develop their abilities.

- When your employees come to you with problems or opportunities, ask for their recommended plan of action. This keeps the responsibility in their hands.

- Resist the temptation to strive for perfection. On most delegated tasks, the importance of the learning process should take precedence over the importance of minute, less vital details.

Avoiding Upward Delegation

Upward delegation refers to cases in which an employee, with the manager's explicit or implicit acceptance, gives the manager a task to complete. For example, if an employee told his manager that he didn't know how to complete the last section of a report, the manager might be busy at the time and say, "Just leave it here; I'll finish it." Most likely, this employee will require help with his next report, too.

If an employee has problems doing a delegated task, talk about the assignment, ask for the employee's ideas for solving the problem, and suggest ways to accomplish the task. If it's obvious that the task is too difficult for the employee, assign it to someone else. Ordinarily, you shouldn't take the task back. If you do, you're right back where you started in terms of your work load, with even less time to complete the task.

Being Accessible to Provide Assistance or Support

One of your primary management responsibilities is to make yourself available to employees to answer their questions and address their concerns. When the press of daily activities tends to make you unavailable:

- Update your calendar regularly. Give your staff access to your calendar so they can arrange a time to meet with you.

- Coordinate your schedule with your secretary and set up times when you will check in at the office, either by phone or in person. Let your staff know that your secretary has this information.

- Set up regular meetings (for example, weekly, monthly, quarterly) to answer employees' questions and to get the information that will keep you abreast of their work.

- Take time to contact employees periodically, particularly those you do not see daily. These need not be formal meetings. Taking time to talk with people, even informally, conveys a nonverbal message of support. Also, your employees will be less likely to view you as an "absentee manager."

Coordinating Work with Other Groups

Confusion within an organization and inefficiencies in getting things done may be due to lack of coordination among work groups. If coordination is a problem in your area, consider the following suggestions:

- Realize that your area is not an island. Make it a habit to consider others with whom you need to coordinate on projects. Train your people to think of how their actions will affect others and how to involve and inform them. Take into account the people on your team, other teams in the organization, your customers, and your suppliers.

- Ensure that managers and supervisors at every level have a clear understanding of their responsibilities and have the authority and effective procedures for carrying them out. Recognize that it is critical that they also understand the responsibilities of others.

- Communicate effectively with your peers. Managers on the same level, especially those in different groups and departments, must communicate effectively if an organization is to run smoothly. Is horizontal communication in your group blocked or hampered in any way? If so, what can be done to improve it?

- Designate certain people to act as liaisons to help you coordinate your activities more effectively. For example, product managers or customer representatives can serve as liaisons who communicate with various people and coordinate the various functions for particular products, clients, or projects.

- Consider forming a committee to improve coordination. Examples of such committees include:
  - General management committees, which make joint decisions across departments, set policies, and oversee the operations of the company as a whole
  - Special-area committees, which consist of managers with special areas of interest, such as salary determination, capital expenditures, and planning

- Multiple-level management committees, which facilitate vertical communication and coordination

Take care to ensure that committees are not overused or underused, and that all active committees continue to serve useful purposes.

RECOMMENDED READINGS

The publications listed here were selected for their content and suitability to a managerial audience.

People Smarts

Alessandra, Tony, and O'Conner, Michael J., San Diego: Pfeiffer & Company, 1994
ISBN: 0-89384-421-7
The authors introduce the "platinum rule": treat others the way they want to be treated and both parties win. Since everyone is unique, your goal is to adapt your approach to meet the different needs and priorities of the people you deal with. This book is helpful in identifying behavioral styles and learning how to adjust your behavior to increase trust, credibility, and cooperation.

The Empowered Manager

Block, Peter, San Francisco: Jossey-Bass, 1991
ISBN: 1-55542-265-9
This book is written for executives involved in running an organization and for managers caught in a bureaucratic mode of thinking. Block offers practical ways for executives and managers to take more responsibility for making positive changes in the organization and developing an entrepreneurial spirit in themselves and in members of their work teams.

HeroZ: Empower Yourself, Your Coworkers, Your Company

Byham, William C., and Cox, Jeff, New York: Harmony Books, 1994
ISBN: 0-517-59860-4
HeroZ is based on the premise that teamwork and participation are the best ways to unleash potential and achieve organizational success. It clearly shows, by using metaphor, how personal empowerment and quality principles lead to customer satisfaction.

Managing for Results

Drucker, Peter F., New York: HarperBusiness, 1993
ISBN: 0-88730-614-4
The author holds that a successful business operation focuses on opportunities rather than problems. This book combines economic analysis with entrepreneurial initiatives in order to show the manager or individual how to move his or her enterprise forward.

The Situational Leader

Hersey, Paul, Escondido, CA: Center for Leadership Studies, 1985
ISBN: 0-446-51342-3
The author provides a brief and succinct guide, based on the Situational Leadership model, that describes how to develop people and effectively utilize human resources. The author outlines a practical model to help managers meet the ongoing challenges faced by individuals in leadership situations.

Making Organizations Competitive

Kilmann, Ralph H.; Kilmann, Ines; and Associates, San Francisco: Jossey-Bass, 1990
ISBN: 1-55542-285-3
This book shows how managers can make their organizations more responsive, creative, and flexible by building strong strategic alliances among groups that traditionally have not seen each other as partners. The authors offer practical techniques for coordinating competitive policies among diverse functions within an organization, establishing collaborative relationships with outside companies, and forging productive relationships between groups that have traditionally been adversarial.

Cross-Functional Teams

Parker, Glenn M., San Francisco: Jossey-Bass, 1994
ISBN: 1-55542-609-3
Parker's book shows how teams comprised of individuals from different departments can achieve success, especially when the task is complex and requires speed, creativity, and special customer attention. Also included are suggestions on how to lead, appraise, reward, and best utilize cross-functional teams.

Teaming Up

Ray, Darrel, and Bronstein, Howard, New York: McGraw-Hill, 1995
ISBN: 0-07-051646-4
Beyond telling why teams are a good idea, this book directs organizations on how to implement and guide self-directed teams on a day-to-day, year-to-year basis. Based on research of the struggles and successes of a wide range of organizations, the authors describe how to: prepare for self-directed work teams, design the teams for self-direction, and implement the new system for success now and in the future.

SUGGESTED
SEMINARS

The seminars listed here were selected for their appeal to a managerial audience. The reputation of the vendor, the quality of their seminar offerings, and the specific seminar content were considered in the selection process.

Because of the dynamic nature of the seminar marketplace, some seminars may have been upgraded or replaced, and others may no longer be offered. Likewise, costs and locations may have changed since this listing was compiled. We recommend that you contact the vendor directly for updated and additional information.

The Changing Role of the Manager

This course will help managers meet the challenge of leading in a participative work environment. Participants will learn to identify skills, systems, and processes needed to build a participative work environment; negotiate across organizational boundaries; resolve conflicts; and manage personal and organizational resistance to change.
Length: 3 days; Cost: $995
Locations: Call vendor
Association for Quality and Participation
801-B West 8th Street, Cincinnati, OH 45203
Telephone: 800/733-3310

Situational Leadership II® for Managers

This seminar introduces Ken Blanchard's Situational Leadership II® principles. The seminar uses a variety of case studies, instruments, and video programs to help participants gain insight into their leadership style and learn how to use the Situational Leadership II® model to improve their managerial effectiveness.
Length: 3 days; Cost: $895
Locations: Call vendor
Blanchard Training and Development
125 State Place, Escondido, CA 92029
Telephone: 800/728-6000

Facilitative Leadership: Tapping the Power of Participation

In this seminar, participants learn how to: encourage team participation by focusing on process, results, and relationships; appropriately involve people in problem solving and decision making; design meetings, project plans, and change strategies that people support and understand; and develop a personal plan for continuously improving themselves as leaders.
Length: 3 days; Cost: $1,125
Locations: Call vendor
Interaction Associates, Inc.
600 Townsend Street, Suite 550, San Francisco, CA 94103
Telephone: 415/241-8000

Emerging Leaders

This program, designed for current and future leaders, addresses the evaluation, building, and sustaining of leadership excellence. Participants will assess and develop their leadership excellence with regard to four areas: personal, people, business, and work.
Length: 5 days; Cost: Call vendor
Location: Call vendor
Personnel Decisions International
2000 Plaza VII Tower, 45 South Seventh Street
Minneapolis, MN 55402-1608
Telephone: 800/633-4410

Leadership Through People Skills

This seminar is designed to teach participants the practical skills it takes to become leader-managers, turn vision into reality, empower people with the freedom to act competently and confidently, and manage in all directions — upward with the boss, laterally with coworkers, and downward with direct reports.
Length: 3 1/2 days; Cost: $1,245
Location: St. Louis
Psychological Associates, Inc.
8201 Maryland Avenue, St. Louis, MO 63105
Telephone: 800/345-6525

Delegation and Team Effort: People and Performance

This program introduces the skills necessary for effective delegation and team leadership. Participants learn to manage in the team environment; design high performing teams; create a context for high performing teams; and overcome roadblocks to effective delegation.
Length: 5 days; Cost: $3,400
Location: Ann Arbor, MI
University of Michigan Business School
Executive Education Center, Ann Arbor, MI 48109-1234
Telephone: 313/763-1000

Effective Management Techniques

This seminar includes the following topics: functions of a manager; delegation, the key to effective management; how to develop a productive organizational climate; clear-cut authority and effective decision making; and spurring change and inspiring motivation through delegation.
Length: 3 days; Cost: $1,250
Location: Nashville, TN
Vanderbilt University
Owen Graduate School of Management, Executive Programs, 401 21st Avenue South, Suite 100
Nashville, TN 37203
Telephone: 615/322-2513

WORK EFFICIENTLY

In today's increasingly competitive marketplace, managers must effectively juggle many priorities, efficiently complete large volumes of work, and be increasingly responsive to get the job done, keep costs low, and produce quality products. A manager's ability to work efficiently directly affects the attainment of these goals, regardless of his or her level in the organization.

This section covers strategies for three key areas of working efficiently — managing your time, expediting the flow of paperwork, and conducting effective meetings.

Part 1: Managing Your Time

- Determining Priorities
- Dealing with Higher-Priority Tasks First
- Reducing Excessive Interruptions
- Reducing Job Overload
- Overcoming Procrastination
- Responding to Phone Calls and Written Requests
- Assessing Your Daily Accomplishments

Part 2: Expediting the Paperwork Process

- Processing Paperwork Efficiently
- Eliminating Unnecessary Memos
- Improving Documentation
- Organizing an Effective Filing System
- Handling Paperwork by Organizing Your Desk
- Creating More Efficient Office Space

Part 3: Managing Meetings

- Setting Up Meeting Facilities
- Preparing an Effective Agenda
- Organizing Your Meeting
- Managing Your Meeting

Valuable Tips

- Record due dates for assignments on your calendar.

- Organize your files so that others can easily locate items when you are out of the office.

- Use hanging folders for files requiring fast and easy access.

- Archive or throw away infrequently used files.

- Have your secretary maintain a day file for all of your written correspondence.

- Sort your in-basket according to priority, and work on high-priority items first. Skim or throw away low-priority items.

- Have your employees represent you at meetings when appropriate.

- Schedule your time more carefully, being sure to include time for administrative details.

- Set aside time in your weekly calendar for follow-up procedures in your work.

- Before leaving work each evening, list the things that need to be done the next day.

- In order to facilitate the planning and organizing of your work week, limit it to 40 hours.

- Set your own deadlines for tasks, and reward yourself when you have met them.

- Take time to just sit still and plan, organize, and attend to detail.

- Monitor how you spend your time for a week. Use the insights to adjust your schedule so it is in line with your job priorities.

- Delegate all filing tasks to your secretary.

- Take a course in time management.

- Schedule "quiet time" every day for work requiring uninterrupted thinking and planning.

- Return phone calls early in the day or near the end of the day to increase your chances of getting through.

- Use a daily planning tool.

- Look at time as a financial investment and monitor how you spend it.

- Be more careful about scheduling foreseeable events on your weekly calendar.

- Have someone trace the flow of paperwork to assure efficiency and avoid duplication.

- Assign a "process observer" for meetings to help keep the group functioning effectively.

- Publish the agenda for meetings in advance, and advise people of any required preparation.

- Assure that your meetings start and end on time. Don't wait for "latecomers."

- Try to limit your meetings to one-and-a-half hours. Set up another meeting if more time is required.

- Avoid time-wasting "telephone tag" by using voice mail to communicate exactly why you called and what you need. The other person will then be able to knowledgeably respond to you or your voice mail.

- If you cannot remember to change the specific greeting on your voice mail, develop a generic one to use for most occasions. Only change the message if you will be out for an extended time or will be unable to retrieve your messages.

- In your voice mail message, always give the caller the option and the procedure to use to reach a "live" person.

- When reading your electronic mail, don't automatically print out a copy of everything. Save paper by only printing out those messages you need in paper form.

- Be selective when routing electronic mail. Send copies of messages only to those who need to receive them.

- Use voice mail, e-mail, and your fax machine to more efficiently communicate with those in different time zones.

PART 1

Determining Priorities

Managing Your Time

Do you sometimes feel immersed in unimportant details at the expense of high-priority tasks? To determine whether you are using your time wisely, complete the following exercise:

1. For the next week, keep a detailed record of how you spend your time. Each day, write down the tasks you perform and how much time you spend on them.

2. On a separate sheet, list your primary job responsibilities according to importance and the amount of time they should receive.

3. Compare your lists to determine whether you are devoting the bulk of your time to your high-priority work.

4. Adjust your schedule and priorities as necessary to ensure that your daily work aligns with your major job responsibilities.

5. Periodically repeat this exercise to ensure that the allocation of your time and energy is in line with your strategy and objectives.

Dealing with Higher-Priority Tasks First

Do you often reach the end of the day feeling as if you have done a lot, but accomplished very little? Charles Hobbs, a noted expert on time management, suggests that many people tend to confuse urgent matters with truly vital ones, resulting in the accomplishment of urgent "trivialities" rather than high-payoff tasks.

Hobbs suggests creating a prioritized to-do list by grouping daily tasks into three categories:

- Vital (high payoff) tasks

- Important (yet less vital) tasks

- Tasks with limited payoff

For each of these three lists, prioritize the items by asking yourself the following questions:

- Which of these tasks will be of most benefit to the organization?

- Which tasks do organizational or departmental priorities suggest are most important?

- Which of these tasks does my manager consider most important?

- What are the consequences of not completing these tasks today?

- If I have time to complete only three or four of these tasks today, which should I plan to do?

- Which of these tasks would I feel best about finishing and getting off my desk?

When you've prioritized all three lists, create a to-do list, focusing on the most vital tasks first. When an urgent matter arises, determine how it fits into your daily plan (is it urgent and vital, or simply urgent?) and act accordingly.

Reducing Excessive Interruptions

The nature of managerial work involves frequent interruptions. As you rise in the organization, the amount of time you can spend without interruptions will probably decrease. However, too many interruptions may be a major source of that "where has the day gone?" feeling at the end of the day. To help minimize interruptions, follow this procedure:

1. For one week, keep a log of who interrupts you and the reason for each interruption.

2. Using your analysis of your log and a chart with two columns labeled "Reasons for Interruptions" and "Possible Solutions," implement a plan that will help you handle each of those situations in the future. Here's an example:

Reasons for Interruptions	Possible Solutions
People stop by to socialize; they interrupt me because of my accessibility.	Decrease my accessibility. Close my office door when I don't want to be interrupted. Establish set times when I am available for impromptu talks.
Individuals are insecure about making decisions on their own because of lack of experience or confidence, so they come to me more often than necessary.	Establish programs to help these individuals develop their skills and increase their confidence.
People who could make decisions on their own are coming to me for approval.	Delegate more authority. Analyze the topics discussed during the interruptions to determine which areas could be delegated.
People have questions about coordination of staff members' duties.	Schedule more frequent staff meetings.
People lack information.	Establish a better means of disseminating information with better project plans, more informational memos, and more discussion at staff meetings.

3. After you have implemented your plan, keep another log of your interruptions for a week to determine if they have decreased.

4. When people come to your door, stand up and greet them at the door before they have a chance to sit down in your office. This way, you can limit the length of the conversation to a greater degree.

5. If you are too busy, tell people and let them know when you can talk. Be sure you are available at that time. People will often ask if the time is convenient after you use this technique.

Reducing Job Overload

Job overload usually means poor performance in the short term, and exhaustion and burnout in the long term. When people are overloaded with work, both the people and the organization suffer.

To determine if you are overloaded, analyze your job performance the way you would analyze an employee's performance. Do you meet deadlines? Do you accomplish what you say you will accomplish? If your analysis shows that you are trying to do too much, the suggestions that follow can help you reduce your work load:

- Concentrate on your most important objectives. Delegate the less important tasks to others or let them go undone.

- Delegate routine tasks that do not require your involvement.

- Look ahead and divide your work load into time stages to make it more manageable. Determine what should be done tomorrow, next week, next month, and next year, and plan accordingly.

- Schedule time for essential work. If appointments tend to fill your calendar, leaving no time for other important tasks, block out time on your calendar for these tasks.

- When accepting assignments, be practical about the amount of work you take on versus the amount of time you have available.

Overcoming Procrastination

People procrastinate in different ways, to different degrees, and for different reasons. Many people habitually put off things they know they should be doing. The following tips are designed to help you get a start on overcoming procrastination:

- Make firm deadline commitments with your manager, employees, and customers, and note them on your calendar to force yourself to start the projects.

- If you procrastinate on follow-up tasks, block out time on your weekly schedule and dedicate it to following up.

- If you put off projects that seem too difficult or overwhelming, make a list of the small, easy tasks involved in the project and do these tasks first. Their momentum may carry over into the more difficult tasks.

- If you find a particular project unpleasant, consider delegating it, or do the most interesting tasks involved in the project first. Let the momentum of these tasks carry over into the less interesting tasks.

- Tell yourself you'll work on a project for a half hour to see how it goes (knowing that you can handle it for a short period of time). By the end of the half hour, you may have found that the task isn't so difficult or distasteful after all.

- Establish ways to reward yourself along the way — for example, a coffee break after writing the introduction to a report or a change of pace after completing a major project.

- Think differently about undesirable tasks. Instead of focusing on your dislike for the task, focus on the sense of accomplishment you'll feel after finishing the task.

- Simply do the undesirable task first to get it out of the way.

- Ask your staff to give you feedback about how your procrastination impacts them. If that input concerns you, write it down on a note card and keep it in sight on your desk as a reminder.

Responding to Phone Calls and Written Requests

Returning phone calls and responding to written correspondence are important, yet often cumbersome, responsibilities for most managers. To become more efficient, follow these guidelines:

- Schedule time on your calendar each day to return phone calls. Between 8:00 and 9:00 in the morning and 4:30 and 5:30 in the afternoon are often good times to catch people in their offices.

- If you return a phone call and the person is out or unavailable, schedule a telephone appointment with him or her and record this appointment on your calendar.

- Use voice mail effectively:
  - If possible, change your outgoing message to let callers know if you are in or when you will be returning calls.
  - Check your voice mail often and respond to messages promptly.
  - When you are returning calls and reach someone's voice mail, speak distinctly, leaving a short, concise message.
  - Receive the full benefit of this technology by leaving a message that explains the substance of why you are calling. Often, answers can be left on your voice mail without the need of playing "telephone tag."

- If an administrative person answers your phone, work with that person to ensure that he or she takes clear, complete, and accurate phone messages. In many cases the question can be answered at this point, or referred to a more appropriate person.

- Develop a system whereby your administrative person schedules all phone messages into your electronic or paper calendar for your reference.

- Respond to notes and memos by writing your response directly on the correspondence. Make a copy for your files if necessary. Or, if it will save you time and documentation is not necessary, use the telephone to respond to written requests.

- If you have an electronic mail system, use it to respond quickly to people. This often cuts down on paper correspondence. You can send messages across time zones or overseas to be accessed quickly during working hours.

- With your administrative person, develop a system for written requests you receive by having him or her screen your in-basket for urgent requests, and prioritizing the remaining correspondence appropriately. Learn to differentiate between what is important, what is urgent, what can be delegated, and what can be ignored.

Assessing Your Daily Accomplishments

To help you more accurately predict the time required for various short-term tasks and show you which tasks are taking the majority of your time, complete this exercise:

1. At the beginning of each day, plan — in detail — the work you expect to complete that day. List the tasks according to priority, and determine the amount of time you expect to spend on each.

2. At the end of the day, review your list to determine how much of the work you accomplished and how long it took to accomplish it.

If your analysis reveals a considerable discrepancy between what you planned to accomplish and what you actually accomplished, look for reasons for the discrepancy. Too many interruptions? Procrastination? Plan and problem-solve accordingly.

PART 2

**Processing
Paperwork
Efficiently**

Expediting the Paperwork Process

To be an effective administrator, it's essential to recognize and attend to important details while ignoring unimportant details. The following technique will help you develop a workable system for dealing with paperwork:

1. Each time you process paperwork, identify the papers that contribute to your most important objectives and responsibilities. These are the ones that count. Learn to handle them skillfully.

   - Glance through each piece quickly to get an initial understanding of its contents and impact.

   - Place the documents in the order of their importance.

   - Read carefully, highlighting or underlining key points that are important for you to stay aware of or that will influence future actions.

   - In the margin, cross-reference other documents that contain information relevant to this particular piece of paperwork.

   - Take action.

   - File the document where it will be easily accessible.

2. Eliminate as many of the remaining documents and keep as few papers as possible.

   - Take yourself off distribution lists if appropriate.

   - Whenever you are tempted to say, "I'm going to keep this just in case," you can probably throw the paper away or route it to someone else.

   - Practice the art of "wastebasketry" to avoid filing and retaining unnecessary information.

3. Adopt one of time management expert Alan Lakein's basic rules: Handle each piece of paper only once. If you pick up a piece of paper, don't put it down without doing something that will help move it on its way.

4. Use the telephone rather than generate paperwork for someone else.

Eliminating Unnecessary Memos

Although some memos are necessary, informal surveys reveal that employees in most organizations spend far more time writing and reading memos than is advisable — and at great cost to the organizations. To determine whether the memos you and your people write promote efficiency, periodically ask yourself the following questions:

- Are the messages short and to the point? If not, make your memos more concise.

- Would a phone call or brief personal visit be a more effective method of communication? Memos involve one-way communication; phone calls and discussions allow people to read each other's reactions, ask questions, and clear up misunderstandings immediately.

- Does the memo describe a task that could be done in less time than it takes to write the memo?

- Are formal, typed memos sent when handwritten, short-form memos or notes would suffice? Is electronic mail appropriate?

- Time management specialist R. Alec Mackenzie recommends that you take an occasional inventory to assess the efficiency of your department's memo-writing practices. Examine the memos written and received in a one-month period. How many could have been shorter? How many were unnecessary?

Improving Documentation

Information and decisions that are trusted to memory may easily be forgotten or unavailable for use when they are needed. To ensure the documentation and accessibility of information, consider the following suggestions:

- Keep a record of decisions made at meetings by asking someone to take notes of the proceedings. Organize the meeting minutes for future reference, and file them so that they can be readily located when needed.

- Document decisions reached by phone or in one-to-one meetings in the same way, and make certain they are filed for future reference. If appropriate, send a copy of the documentation to others involved with, or affected by, the decision so that everyone has a chance to react and make corrections if necessary.

Organizing an Effective Filing System

Poor filing systems waste time and can even stop the flow of work if they inhibit people from finding the needed information. Often, administrative personnel are the most competent people for setting up effective filing systems. Thus, you may want to team up with your secretary or set up a committee of administrative personnel to streamline your office files.

Following are guidelines to consider in designing a filing system:

- The system should be understandable to those who do not use it on a daily basis. This ensures that information can be retrieved even when the person in charge of the files is on vacation or leaves the organization.

- The folders used most often should be readily accessible.

- The filing cabinets should be placed near those who use them most often.

- Guidelines should be established regarding the length of time different types of files should be retained. Experts suggest that current operations files should include no more than one year's correspondence. However, your organization should determine its own policies based on the use and importance of its filed materials.

- A checkout system can be established to record who has the file.

Handling Paperwork by Organizing Your Desk

If your desk is covered with stacks of paper, you probably waste quite a bit of time sorting through the stacks as you look for documents you need to complete your work. To eliminate this problem, establish a filing system for organizing your paperwork.

Develop a categorization system that fits your needs. The following series of files comprises one system you can use or modify:

- A "review" file — for paperwork generated by others that must be reviewed in a timely way in order for work to progress. (For example, you might attend to this file in the early morning and late afternoon, when interruptions are minimal and interaction with others is not required to keep projects moving.)

- A "reading" file — for papers that do not require a response or carry associated deadlines. (This file is attended to in your spare time.)

- A "file" folder — for papers that have been processed and should be retained. (Give this folder to your secretary periodically for filing.)

- An "action item" file — for lists of tasks to be performed and for work in progress.

- A "delegate" file — for papers concerning activities that could be performed by others.

Creating More Efficient Office Space

The arrangement of your office furniture and items on your desk can either help or hinder your efficiency. To use your office space more efficiently:

- Arrange your office to maximize your working style. If being able to look out of a window enhances your creativity, allowing you to accomplish more, face your desk toward the window. If you are easily distracted by people walking past your office, position your desk to avoid this distraction.

- Eliminate time stealers. If a book or file you refer to once a day is across the room, or under something else, make it more accessible. The minutes you save can be spent more productively.

- Organize your desk top based on the frequency with which you use items.
  - Frequently used items, such as your calendar or computer, need to be right at hand.
  - Items, such as your phone, that are not constantly used need to be within reach.
  - Items that are used infrequently should not be on your desk. These things can be located so that you must get up from your desk to get them.
  - Keep in front of you only what you are currently working on, and remove all else.

PART 3

Managing Meetings

Research indicates that managers spend between 25 percent and 75 percent of their working hours in group meetings. Efficient, productive meetings are vital communication and decision-making forums. Inefficient, unproductive meetings waste valuable time.

Setting Up Meeting Facilities

When the logistics of setting up meetings are handled in advance, less time is wasted, and meeting initiators and leaders appear more competent. Important elements in setting up meetings include:

- Meeting time. Choose a time when all necessary facts and people are available. Also, select a time that will help ensure that the meeting ends at a logical time — just before lunch or quitting time, for example.

- Location. Select a location that is accessible to all who will attend.

- Room size. Select a room that is the appropriate size for your group — neither so large that participants can sit far away from the action and each other, nor so small that participants have insufficient room to write or sit comfortably.

- Ventilation and temperature. Ensure that the room is not too stuffy, drafty, hot, or cold.

- Equipment. Be sure that all necessary equipment is on hand and set up. Meeting time should not be wasted while someone looks for a flipchart or TV monitor. Check teleconference equipment to ensure that those joining via the telephone will hear and be heard.

- Furniture arrangement. If possible, set up the room to maximize group attention and participation. If the group is small, use a semicircular seating arrangement that exactly accommodates the number of people involved. If you must use rows, use more short rows rather than a few long rows so people aren't too spread out and the speaker's eye span will not have to be too wide.

- Seating. Encourage participants to sit close to the speakers and each other rather than spreading out across the room. This promotes equal participation.

You may wish to create a checklist of these points to use when setting up your meetings.

Preparing an Effective Agenda

Agendas are essential for conducting efficient meetings. They allow group members to prepare for meetings and ensure that all necessary items are addressed. When preparing agendas, check to see that you have taken the following steps:

1. State the purpose of the meeting at the top of the agenda. This helps participants determine whether they should attend.

2. State a definite start and stop time for the meeting.

3. Structure a content and process agenda. Determine the type of process and action desired on each agenda item. You are likely to have "information only," "discussion only," and "decisions required" items. This helps people prepare for the meeting and determines the goal to be attained in addressing each item.

The following example illustrates one way to structure an agenda.

Goal-setting Kickoff Meeting

September 15
10:00 - 11:30

Item	Process / Action	Time
1. New goal-setting guidelines	Presentation	10:00 - 10:15
2. Next year's corporate goals	Presentation	10:15 - 10:25
3. Next year's division goals	Discussion; assign responsibility to dept. heads	10:25 - 10:45
4. Next year's individual goals	Discussion; set dates for compl.	10:45 - 11:10
5. Process for completion/ review	Discussion; consensus	11:10 - 11:30
6. Adjourn		11:30

---

4. Establish priorities. Set priorities for each agenda item so that group members focus on addressing the most important items.

5. Determine the order of the agenda items. Most experts recommend placing the most important topics toward the beginning of the agenda; that way, if time runs out, the items left unaddressed are lower priority. However, you may wish to run through any informational items on your agenda at the beginning of the meeting to ensure that they are covered.

6. Establish time limits on items. Decide on an approximate amount of time to be spent on each agenda item. Enforce your

time limits on "information only" and "discussion only" items. On "decision required" items, acknowledge when the time limit has been reached; then ask the group to decide whether and how to continue with these items.

Organizing Your Meeting

Organizing the meeting in advance is just as important as arranging for the appropriate facility. Your attention to organizational considerations can greatly affect the efficiency of the meeting and the way in which others evaluate your meeting management skills. Over the next several months, pay special attention to the following steps required to organize a meeting:

- Prepare an agenda. (See the preceding suggestions for preparing an agenda.)

- Determine the necessary pre-meeting communication. Distribute the agenda well in advance of the meeting. This enables participants to gather materials and prepare their arguments.

- If people will be joining the meeting by teleconference, send or fax copies ahead of time of any overheads or handouts that will be used.

- Limit the number of participants. Invite only those people who are needed for decision making or who require the information that will be presented.

Managing Your Meeting

Managing meetings effectively takes practice. Over the next several months, take on the leadership of several meetings. Then, during the course of the meetings, refer to the following guidelines for practicing the principles of good meeting management. You may wish to take a copy of these guidelines with you to the meetings until you feel that they have become a natural part of your management style.

1. Manage your meeting before it begins. Distribute handouts, prepare flipcharts, or set up the first overhead. Place calls to all teleconference attendees so they will be on the line and ready when the meeting begins.

2. Start the meeting on time. When people expect meetings to start late, they arrive late. If, on the other hand, they must walk in after a meeting has started, they are more likely to arrive at future meetings on time.

3. Begin with a reminder of the time allotted for the meeting and with an assurance that the meeting will end on time.

4. Review the agenda and amount of time allotted to each item.

5. Appoint a recorder for the meeting who will take minutes and monitor the time. Have the recorder inform the group of the time remaining and whether the meeting is running behind schedule.

6. Express your concern to the group if the meeting is straying from the agenda or if specific items are taking longer to cover than originally planned. Come to a mutual agreement about whether the group should monitor itself to keep the discussion more limited.

7. If any group members are being disruptive, deal with the disruption by inquiring about their concerns, asking for their cooperation, or giving them feedback about their impact on the group.

8. At the end of the meeting, take a few moments to "process" the meeting. Discuss what went well, what problems came up, and what you can do about the ways in which the group works together. End the meeting on time.

9. Follow up by distributing copies of meeting minutes and reminders about assignments and deadlines to all persons who attended.

In addition to the steps above, use the following facilitation techniques to foster effective communication among the participants:

- Listen. Listening will influence the group's ability to achieve understanding and reach the decisions needed to meet its goals.

- Ask questions. Questions are an excellent tool for monitoring and facilitating discussions. Knowing how to ask the right questions can be more important than knowing the answers.

- Integrate contributions. Link various points of view and keep the group on target by identifying areas of understanding, agreement, and disagreement.

- Summarize. A periodic summary of key ideas or major points will help to keep the group focused and on track with the agenda.

RECOMMENDED READINGS

The publications listed here were selected for their content and suitability to a managerial audience.

Right on Time! The Complete Guide for Time-Pressured Managers

Bittel, Lester R., New York: McGraw-Hill, 1991
ISBN: 0-07-005585-8
This book describes time management skills to help managers evaluate whether personal and professional time is well spent or wasted, to budget their own time and that of their support staff wisely, and to establish time-saving organizational structures.

Effective Meetings

Burleson, Clyde, New York: John Wiley & Sons, 1990
ISBN: 0-471-50843-8
This is a comprehensive guide detailing how to prepare and conduct an effective meeting that will increase the productivity of all the participants. This book will show how to: prepare for the meeting, set goals for the meeting, use audiovisual equipment to enhance productivity, and inspire creative thinking.

First Things First

Covey, Stephen R.; Merrill, A. Roger; and Merrill, Rebecca R., New York: Simon & Schuster, 1994
ISBN: 0-671-86441-6
Here is a book on time management that goes beyond the simple quick fixes of behavioral engineering with the premise that where you're headed is more important than how fast you're going. Rather than focusing on time and things, it emphasizes relationships and results. This guide helps you manage your time by bringing balance to your life.

How to Run a Successful Meeting in Half the Time

Frank, Milo O., New York: Pocket Books, 1990
ISBN: 0-671-72601-3
This book is filled with proven strategies, tips, and step-by-step techniques to make meetings brief and productive. The author asserts that no meeting has to be boring, time-wasting, or unproductive, whether it is a one-on-one conversation, a gathering of ten people, or a conference with hundreds in attendance.

How to Get Control of Your Time and Your Life	**Lakein, Alan**, New York: NAL-Dutton, 1989 ISBN: 0-451-15802-4 The author, considered one of the top experts in time management, has created effective systems to help people determine the best use of their time so as to "gain control of their lives." Using practical wisdom and simple but effective rules, the book addresses a variety of topics, including how to build your willpower, how to work smarter, and how to "waste" time for pleasure and profit.
The Time Trap	**Mackenzie, Alec R.**, New York: AMACOM, 1990 ISBN: 0-8144-5969-2 Based on years of studying people's work habits, the author has laid out practical, easy-to-use tips and techniques for overcoming the problems of procrastination, interruptions, decision making, organization, and delegation. These suggestions can help you become more efficient at work and enable you to maximize your personal time for high priority activities.
Running a Meeting That Works	**Miller, Robert F.**, New York: Barron's, 1991 ISBN: 0-8120-4640-4 This concise handbook takes a facilitator through every step needed to have a successful and productive meeting. Some of the steps include: identifying the purpose of the meeting, preparing yourself and others, guiding the meeting, encouraging participation, knowing when to conclude a meeting, and assessing the meeting.

SUGGESTED SEMINARS

The seminars listed here were selected for their appeal to a managerial audience. The reputation of the vendor, the quality of their seminar offerings, and the specific seminar content were considered in the selection process.

Because of the dynamic nature of the seminar marketplace, some seminars may have been upgraded or replaced, and others may no longer be offered. Likewise, costs and locations may have changed since this listing was compiled. We recommend that you contact the vendor directly for updated and additional information.

Time Management

This seminar is designed to help individuals at all levels make the best possible use of time. Topics include: taking charge of your time clock, a systematic approach to time control, accomplishing more with fewer meetings, and getting your team involved in time management.
Length: 2 days; Cost: $1,085
Locations: Call vendor
American Management Association
P.O. Box 319, Saranac Lake, NY 12983
Telephone: 800/262-9699

Time and Stress Management

This seminar is designed for those who want to get maximum productivity from their time and are concerned about the effects of stress on their job performance and personal health. The techniques and concepts taught in this seminar enable participants to recognize the symptoms and effects of stress and to minimize their negative impact.
Length: 1 day; Cost: $350
Location: New York
Arthur Andersen & Company
1345 Avenue of the Americas, New York, NY 10105
Telephone: 212/708-8080

Basic Skills for Mastering Meetings

This seminar is designed to enhance skills for meeting leadership. Lectures, professional video presentations, and small group practice sessions demonstrate how to set up, conduct, and follow through on successful meetings.
Length: 1 day; Cost: $325
Locations: Call vendor
Interaction Associates, Inc.
600 Townsend Street, Suite 550, San Francisco, CA 94103
Telephone: 415/241-8000

Managing Management Time

Also known as "Get Them Monkeys Off Your Back," this program examines the causes and effects of time management problems and deals with the realities of managing other people's performance.
Length: 2 days; Cost: $525
Locations: Call vendor
William Oncken Corporation
18601 LBJ Freeway, Suite 315, Mesquite, TX 75150
Telephone: 214/613-2084

COMMUNICATION SKILLS

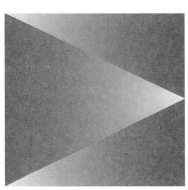

COMMUNICATION SKILLS

Effective communication skills form the foundation for successful management. They are so fundamental that we sometimes forget their significance or assume we are skillful. Communication skills enable you to lead others. You cannot lead without being able to communicate your ideas well. People will not go with you unless you have established with them your ability to lead. That requires trust which is a by-product of effective two-way communication.

Effective communication includes both speaking and listening, informing others, and fostering open communication. When you master these skills, you harness a great deal of power — the power to get things done through others.

Effective communication involves:

- Knowing who needs what information and communicating that information in a concise, timely way

- Choosing and effectively using the most appropriate communication medium — oral or written — for those who will receive the information and how it will be used

- Knowing how to listen effectively

- Helping others communicate effectively, to ensure that communication occurs among all organizational levels and with all needed people

This chapter presents development activities in the following five communication skills areas:

Speak Effectively: Speaks clearly and expresses self well in groups and in one-to-one conversations.

Foster Open Communication: Creates an atmosphere in which timely and high quality information flows smoothly between self and others; encourages the open expression of ideas and opinions.

Listen to Others: Actively attends to and conveys understanding of the comments and questions of others; listens well in a group.

Deliver Presentations: Prepares and delivers clear, smooth presentations; carries self well in front of a group.

Prepare Written Communication: Conveys information clearly and effectively through both formal and informal documents; reviews and edits written work constructively.

SPEAK EFFECTIVELY

Following are examples of four managers' speaking habits:

- Arnold likes to use the words he learned in a college linguistics course to impress others in meetings.

- When giving formal presentations, Claire provides a minimum of background information to avoid boring any higher-level employees who might be in attendance.

- Dirk avoids holding meetings because he claims he's "better at putting things in writing."

- Kari assumes that employees whose eyes dart around the room when she is speaking during meetings are shy or otherwise uncomfortable with maintaining eye contact.

Each of these managers is considered highly competent by their managers and employees alike. Yet each needs improvement in at least one facet of oral communication. Without the ability to communicate with clarity and conviction using the spoken word, even the most competent leader falls short of managerial excellence.

This section provides guidelines for improving your oral communication skills. It includes suggestions for:

- Getting Your Point Across When Talking

- Speaking Clearly and Concisely

- Speaking with Enthusiasm and Expressiveness

- Developing a More Informal Style of Speaking

- Speaking Effectively in Front of a Group

- Improving Your Speaking through Practice

- Increasing Your Awareness of Nonverbal Communication

Valuable Tips

- To prevent rambling, outline in your mind what you are trying to say and then stick to it.

- Ask the listener to summarize what you said. Explain that this will help you to know you spoke clearly.

- Paraphrase questions you are asked, both to be certain of the meaning and to give yourself time to think.

- Get a coworker to provide you with immediate feedback through a prearranged signal on a behavior you are trying to improve.

- Use lead-in phrases such as, "That's an interesting question," to show respect for the person and to give you time to organize your answer.

- Eliminate speech habits that may annoy others, such as talking too slowly, too rapidly, or too hesitatingly.

- For increased impact, learn to breathe from your diaphragm in order to project your voice.

- Deliberately use a new word every day in your discussions.

- If you have trouble with language usage, such as subject-verb agreement, have a colleague or a personal friend give you frequent feedback on it.

- When asked a tough question, allow yourself to pause for a moment to compose your answer instead of "shooting from the hip."

- Develop a flash card system to record new words and their meanings as you come across them in your daily reading. Aim for five words a day, and review them periodically.

- Seek feedback on your communication abilities from a friend or trusted peer.

- Become more animated in your style by using appropriate gestures and body language to "punctuate" your discussion.

- Work at varying your volume, pitch, and pace to emphasize your major points in discussions. It is easier for the audience to listen when the speaker's voice varies.

- Watch for nonverbal cues of disinterest or lack of understanding in others so you can clarify your point.

- Lean forward to show more intensity and commitment when presenting your point of view.

- Maintain a balanced stance. Keep your weight evenly distributed on both feet to prevent swaying and slouching.

Getting Your Point Across When Talking

Conveying your ideas clearly is important when you want to have an impact on others. If you tend to talk loudly, ramble, or use poor grammar, your message may get lost or lose its effect. To ensure that your message gets communicated:

- Think through the main idea you are trying to express. State the idea in a clear, concise statement.

- Organize supporting thoughts or facts in such a way that they lead to your main point.

- Once you have made your point, ask the listeners for their reactions to ensure that they have understood you accurately.

- If you find that you are still misunderstood, ask yourself:
  - What did I intend to communicate?
  - What did the other person think I said?
  - Did I provide sufficient and/or accurate information?
  - What did I say that would have clouded my main point?
  - Are there certain situations where I am often misunderstood?
  - Are there certain people with whom I often experience miscommunication problems?
  - What adjustments could I make that would improve my communication?

Use the answers to these questions to better understand miscommunication problems and to formulate strategies for improving communication.

Speaking Clearly and Concisely

One barrier to effective communication is verbosity. Some people believe that wordiness is a sign of knowledge or power, but it actually obscures the meaning of your key points and distracts the listener. In addition, many people are annoyed by verbosity and tend to tune out speakers whose speech is overly wordy.

If you believe or have been told that you tend to be wordy, there are several steps you can take to change that pattern. Some people only need to remind themselves regularly to be more concise. For many people, however, wordiness is a habit that can be difficult to break without assistance from others. During the next several months, use the following methods in your effort to become more concise:

- Ask a trusted coworker or your manager to tell you, during your discussions, if you are being redundant or if you have wandered off the topic. In addition, for group discussions or formal presentations, ask someone to use a predetermined signal to let you know if you are becoming too wordy. When you get the signal, condense what you are saying and get back on track.

- Pay attention to how others are reacting to your speech during discussions and meetings. If they begin to lose eye contact with you or get restless, assume that you may be straying from the topic or that your communication has grown redundant. Pause to ask yourself if you are being too wordy; if so, sum up what you are saying and end your speech, or go on to your next point.

- To determine whether your key points are clear, ask people to summarize what you have told them. This will give you an opportunity to find out if you are being too wordy and to restate your points if others have misunderstood you.

- Keep your answers to questions to less than one minute. Longer answers may come across as verbose.

- Ask your colleagues to let you know when you are speaking concisely as well as when you are being verbose.

Speaking with Enthusiasm and Expressiveness

Your speaking style directly affects your ability to be convincing. The manner in which you present your ideas has a major impact on how influential you are. One way of discovering how enthusiastic you sound is to record yourself and listen to how you come across to others. To learn from this technique, use the following suggestions:

- Record a meeting or presentation in which you must convincingly present your point of view. Choose situations that are long enough to allow you to become comfortable with the tape recorder's presence so that you use your typical speech patterns.

- Don't listen to the tapes immediately. Set them aside for at least one week.

- After a week, listen to the tapes and answer the following questions:
  - Did your tone of voice and inflection accurately reflect the meaning and importance of your words?
  - Did you speak too slowly or without variations in intonation?
  - Was your level of enthusiasm appropriate for the topic, the audience, and the setting?
  - Did you use words that would make your point "come to life"

(for example, analogies, metaphors, or examples, versus simply stating your point of view)?

- Based on your answers to these questions, determine areas in which you were dissatisfied with your communication style. In particular, focus on those areas that seem to affect how enthusiastic you sound. Create a development plan to improve your skills in the areas you identify. For example, you may decide that you need to speak more rapidly, use less jargon, express yourself more clearly, or change your style in some other way.

- During the next several months, incorporate the suggestions in your development plan into your speaking style.

Developing a More Informal Style of Speaking

Often, the good ideas suggested in a presentation go unnoticed because of the presenter's stiff, formal style. People find it much easier to understand ideas when they are presented in a natural, informal style.

Here are some tips for developing a more informal speaking style — particularly when you are making presentations. Follow these suggestions closely for the next three months.

- When you plan a presentation, imagine yourself talking to one person. If you were making the presentation to this person in private, how would you organize the presentation? How would you decide which topics to discuss and what supporting materials (for instance, examples, explanations, statistics, quotations) to use? Adopt the same style for your actual presentation.

- Use examples, comparisons, analogies, and metaphors to liven up your message. Also, make sure the presentation is applicable to your listeners, particularly when discussing highly abstract or technical topics.

- Be natural and use a conversational style.

- Use relaxation techniques to become as comfortable as you can.

- Enjoy yourself and the speaking process. Your listeners will pick up your sense of satisfaction and will enjoy themselves more, too.

- Follow recommendations on effective use of language, including the use of:

- Active rather than passive voice ("the committee debated the issue" rather than "the issue was debated by the committee")
- Verbs that describe action rather than existence ("jump," "run," and "fly" rather than "is")
- Short, simple words rather than complex words or jargon
- Short, clear sentences rather than long, rambling ones

Speaking Effectively in Front of a Group

Much of a manager's work is done in groups. Therefore, speaking effectively in a group is important. Actively seek opportunities to give presentations or facilitate group discussions. Take the following steps to make the most of each such development opportunity:

1. Find out what you can about the audience.

   - What is their knowledge of the topic?

   - What is their background? Do they share similar experiences and beliefs, or do they come from a variety of backgrounds?

   - What are they expecting?

2. Based on your research of the audience, determine the approach you will take. Decide how much background information you need to provide, what questions your presentation should answer, and the tone you should adopt (persuasive, informational, or other).

3. Outline your presentation by writing down all of the key points you wish to make and then organize them in the most effective way. When deciding on the content of your presentation:

   - Choose explanations and examples that are appropriate for your audience. If you have no way of determining the audience's knowledge of the topic, be prepared to present background information at the start of the presentation.

   - Use phrases such as "There are five methods of..." or "The four most popular approaches are..." to maintain a clear and logical flow in your speech.

4. Present your opinions forcefully and directly. Eliminate phrases like "it seems to me" and "it is likely," which tend to lessen the impact of what you have to say. Improve your vocabulary to increase your impact. Avoid big, long nouns and try, in particular, to develop your use of strong, punchy verbs.

Your greater mastery of language will make you a more credible speaker.

5. Illustrate your key points with specific, "real-life" examples from your own work and from situations familiar to your listeners.

6. Determine whether your presentation would benefit from the use of black or white boards, flipcharts, overhead transparencies, handouts, slides, or other visual aids.

7. Rehearse each presentation — particularly the first few. Rehearsing in front of a mirror enables you to see whether your gestures and facial expressions are appropriate.

8. Attempt to predict which topics in your presentation might draw questions and/or opposing views from members of your audience. Be prepared to answer the questions, defend your points, and cite your sources of information, if necessary. If you don't know the answer to a question, admit it and go on; don't pretend that you know the answer.

For additional tips in this area, read the Deliver Presentations section of this Handbook.

Improving Your Speaking through Practice

The best way to continue to develop your speaking abilities is to look for occasions to practice your skills. Consider the following suggestions:

- Seek out assignments that require you to make presentations to groups.

- Volunteer for membership on committees, task forces, and interdepartmental projects; these usually involve speaking opportunities.

- Whenever possible, offer to represent your manager at meetings. This will ensure that you are called on often to speak before the group.

- Pursue speaking opportunities in your community. You may wish to volunteer to speak as a representative of your company at meetings of community organizations.

- Assist other people in developing their speaking skills; often the "teacher" learns as much as the "pupil" does.

- Join a Toastmaster's Club and participate regularly.

Increasing Your Awareness of Nonverbal Communication

Consider all of the ways people say "no." The speaker of that one word can make the listener feel angry, rejected, sad, happy, hopeful, or any of a range of feelings in between. That's because it's not just *what* we say but *how* we say it that determines what we've communicated. We all send nonverbal messages through gestures, body posture, vocal patterns, and facial expressions as we talk and listen. Recognize that gestures and other nonverbal messages may have different meanings in other countries and cultures. A good communicator picks up the nonverbal messages sent by listeners and responds accordingly.

To improve your awareness of nonverbal communication, spend some time during the next several months performing the following activities.

1. During the next week, carefully notice the nonverbal messages being sent by *listeners* in a variety of speaking situations — casual conversations, group discussions, and formal meetings or presentations — in which you are just an observer. Look for nonverbal indications of the listeners' feelings, such as:

    *   Loss of eye contact with the speaker

    *   Listeners' postures (relaxed, tense, leaning forward)

    *   Facial expressions

    *   Hand motions (drumming, fidgeting, etc.)

    On the chart below, note the nonverbal behavior; the message that was communicated by the behavior; and your guess about the reason behind the nonverbal behavior.

BEHAVIOR	Message Communicated	Probable Causes

2. Next, concentrate on yourself. Take note of the nonverbal behavior of others directed to you when you are talking. For one week after each encounter you have, note the nonverbal behavior, the message sent to you, and the possible reasons for the behavior.

    This exercise will help you become more aware of nonverbal messages. You can then pay more attention to responding to nonverbal messages you receive.

RECOMMENDED READINGS

The publications listed here were selected for their content and suitability to a managerial audience.

You've Got to Be Believed to Be Heard

Decker, Bert, New York: St. Martin's Press, 1993
ISBN: 0-312-09949-5
In this book, Decker shows you what he has learned through experience and extensive research — how to effectively and confidently reach, persuade, and motivate with the spoken word. The key to personal impact is to win the emotional trust of your audience. This book gives examples and specific how-to exercises to help you build a foundation that will transform the way you speak and listen.

Conversationally Speaking

Garner, Alan, Los Angeles: Lowell House, 1991
ISBN: 0-929923-72-3
Garner's practical, concise book outlines strategies that teach the reader to start conversations, ask the kind of questions that promote conversation, avoid behavior that invites rejection, issue invitations that are likely to be accepted, achieve deeper levels of understanding, handle criticism constructively, resist manipulation, become more confident in social situations, and listen so that others will be encouraged to talk.

Persuasive Business Speaking

Snyder, Elayne, New York: AMACOM, 1990
ISBN: 0-8144-7722-4
The author offers straightforward advice for business speakers: be prepared, be brief, be interesting, and be seated. Her book provides a concise and complete guide for formulating a focused speech and projecting an executive image.

How To Think On Your Feet

Woodall, Marian K., New York: Warner Books, 1993
ISBN: 0-446-36413-4
This concise book provides techniques for improving the quickness and quality of responses to difficult questions. The author also provides guidance on how to quickly and clearly formulate answers, as well as improve the delivery of the communication.

SUGGESTED SEMINARS

The seminars listed here were selected for their appeal to a managerial audience. The reputation of the vendor, the quality of their seminar offerings, and the specific seminar content were considered in the selection process.

Because of the dynamic nature of the seminar marketplace, some seminars may have been upgraded or replaced, and others may no longer be offered. Likewise, costs and locations may have changed since this listing was compiled. We recommend that you contact the vendor directly for updated and additional information.

Effective Executive Speaking

Participants in this program are actively involved in evaluating their strengths and development needs, making an impromptu talk, building ideas, using visual aids, and answering questions. This program includes videotaping.
Length: 3 days; Cost: $1,260
Locations: Call vendor
American Management Association
P.O. Box 319, Saranac Lake, NY 12983
Telephone: 800/262-9699

Effective Communicating™

This program is designed to help participants improve their natural speaking style. Through discussion, individual coaching, and videotaped exercises, participants learn how to increase their personal impact, master the use of gestures and posture, and use their voice for more persuasive and interesting delivery.
Length: 2 days; Cost: Call vendor
Locations: Call vendor
Decker Communications, Inc.
44 Montgomery Street, San Francisco, CA 94104
Telephone: 415/391-5544

The Effective Presentations Seminar

This seminar teaches managers how to deliver clear, concise presentations through the use of video analysis of skills and accelerated training exercises. The program covers controlling tension, organizing and delivering messages, enhancing eye contact, and implementing visual aids.
Length: 2 days; Cost: Call vendor
Locations: Call vendor
Executive Speaking, Inc.
3036 Plaza VII Tower, 45 South Seventh Street
Minneapolis, MN 55402
Telephone: 612/338-5748

Communication Workshop: Learning by Doing

Through structured practice, participants learn how to improve communication, practice skills involved in communicating and listening, understand problems of organizational communication, explore the effect of stress on interpersonal communication, practice giving and receiving feedback, and gain greater awareness of one's own communication style and impact on others.

Length: 6 days; Cost: $1,245

Location: Bethel, ME

NTL Institute
1240 North Pitt Street, Suite 100
Alexandria, VA 22314-1403
Telephone: 800/777-5227

Speaking With Impact

This seminar allows the participant to gain feedback on his or her current skill level and teaches the participant to develop his or her unique speaking style. Participants learn to motivate their audiences and gain confidence in all aspects of public speaking.

Length: 2 days; Cost: $695

Locations: Call vendor

Personnel Decisions International
2000 Plaza VII Tower, 45 South Seventh Street
Minneapolis, MN 55402-1608
Telephone: 800/633-4410

Talk So People Listen

This program helps participants develop a more effective speaking style and feel more in control of both formal and routine speaking situations through extensive videotaping and individualized coaching and critiquing.

Length: 3 days; Cost: $1,400

Locations: Atlanta; San Francisco

Speakeasy, Inc.
3414 Peachtree Road N.E., Monarch Plaza, Suite 800
Atlanta, GA 30326
Telephone: 404/261-4029

Executive Communication

This program teaches participants to analyze and improve their styles of written and oral presentation. Topics include: analyzing your audience; organizing your material; structuring the communication; written communication issues; oral communication issues; and managing the communication of your employees.
Length: 5 days; Cost: $3,200
Location: Ann Arbor, MI
University of Michigan Business School
Executive Education Center, Ann Arbor, MI 48109-1234
Telephone: 313/763-1000

FOSTER OPEN COMMUNICATION

To build trust and solid working relationships with employees and others in the organization, it's important to be seen as someone who is committed to sharing information with others and who goes beyond communicating only what is necessary. Developing a climate in which you and your team are open with information — information exchanges between you and your people, between departments or divisions, and between team members — is critical in order to function effectively.

This section contains the following suggestions:

Part 1: Keeping Communication Channels Open

- Interacting with People Openly and Directly
- Encouraging Others to Express Contrary Viewpoints
- Providing Others with Open Access to Information
- Conveying Necessary Information to Others
- Making Sure That People Have No "Surprises"
- Keeping People Up-to-Date with Information
- Encouraging Employees to Share Information

Part 2: Keeping Your Manager Informed

- Evaluating Your Communication with Your Manager
- Providing Information to Your Manager
- Supplying the Appropriate Amount of Detail
- Establishing Communication with a New Manager

Valuable Tips

- Find out what your employees want to know.

- Encourage your staff to keep one another informed and share information.

- Establish a departmental bulletin board to keep people up-to-date on both personal and professional items of interest.

- Hold periodic staff meetings to share information about recent developments in the organization.

- In staff meetings, encourage two-way communication, solicit agenda items from employees, and allow employees time to raise issues.

- For the purpose of informal communication, hold monthly breakfast meetings that have no agenda.

- Keep your manager and employees up-to-date by submitting a monthly activity report for your area.

- Alert your manager to possible implications of events occurring either inside or outside of the organization. Don't assume that your manager is aware of these implications.

- Don't "shoot the messenger" of bad news.

- Ask your manager which key people you should keep informed.

- List the key organizational people upon whom your success depends, and make a special effort to keep them informed.

- Copy your manager on all correspondence to managers in the organization at his or her level or higher.

- Ask your manager about any perceived "surprises" in your area and then look for ways to avoid recurrences.

- Don't gloss over anything that goes wrong in your area. Report the situation as accurately as possible.

- Talk with peers or people in other departments about "communication breakdowns." Devise ways to avoid them.

- Always double-check all written communications before mailing; also ask yourself, "Who else should know about this?"

- Use the "informal organization" as a way of keeping others informed. Wander around, have coffee with people, ask them questions, and so on.

- At the end of every day, ask yourself what occurred that should be reported to other people.

- Return phone calls promptly.

- Make a point of updating the appropriate people even when nothing new has developed.

- Ask your secretary to suggest who should be copied on documents you produce.

- Appoint a "recorder" for the meetings you conduct and have the minutes distributed to the appropriate people.

- Promptly respond to notes, letters, and other requests so people know what you are doing about their communications.

- If they are available, use electronic aids (voice mail, electronic mail) to pass along information that doesn't require face-to-face exchange when you cannot do so in person or in writing.

PART 1

Interacting with People Openly and Directly

Keeping Communication Channels Open

Direct and open communication with others fosters trust, enhances information flow, and builds stronger relationships. Use the following guidelines to increase such communication:

- Let people know in a timely way about information that affects them. Respond as quickly as possible to any questions they may have.

- Be aware of the messages you send nonverbally. Communicate a positive, open message to people by facing them and making eye contact (or using other culturally appropriate gestures when in other countries or cultures).

- To help your employees and others develop their skills, convey positive and constructive feedback. Positive feedback lets people know what they are doing correctly and the behavior you appreciate. Constructive feedback informs people of their ineffective behavior and gives them an opportunity to compensate for or improve the behavior.

- If conflicting or mixed messages come up in conversation, confront the discrepancy and work with the other person to clarify the misunderstanding.

- When you receive vague messages, define the issues in concrete terms so that all parties are clear about what is being said.

- When you need to get a point across in a direct, yet nonaggressive, fashion, simply say what you think and feel without putting the other person down.

Encouraging Others to Express Contrary Viewpoints

How do you react when someone disagrees with your point of view? You may be tempted to assume that you've heard the argument before and counter it before the person has a chance to explain. You may scowl or tap your pen impatiently.

The next time someone disagrees with you:

1. Wait until the person has finished speaking, even if you're sure you understand the argument.

2. Restate the main points of the person's point of view and then really try to understand this perspective.

3. Ask the person to verify the accuracy of your restatement and to clarify it if necessary.

I WANT YOU TO BE COMPLETELY OPEN AND HONEST WITH ME.

4. Identify the points or goals with which you sincerely agree.

5. Then — and only then — state specifically which points you disagree with, and why.

While you may not change your position any more frequently by using this technique, people will feel that you have considered their input and that you understand their point of view.

Employees will feel more comfortable and are more likely to share information with you if you are approachable. For suggestions on how to increase your approachability, refer to the Build Relationships section of this Handbook.

Providing Others with Open Access to Information

To manage their own work effectively, employees need to have up-to-date information about what is happening in their area of responsibility and in the organization in general. Consider the following suggestions to help others get access to the information they need to do their jobs effectively:

- Encourage your people to identify the help they need to complete assignments and projects. Give them access to appropriate information and files, to other people in the organization, and to outside resources. It is your job as a manager to pave the way for your people to have access to appropriate individuals and resources in the organization.

- When disseminating information, share more of it than your direct reports or your peers absolutely need. People need to know what is going on in other functions in order to understand how their work affects the broader organization.

- Whenever possible, give others access to current information, such as attitude survey results, future trends of the organization, and other strategic information. This will help them understand what is currently going on and how they can be most helpful.

- Communicate to others your desire to provide open access to information.

Conveying Necessary Information to Others

The flow of information in an organization is its life force; to maintain and improve the vitality of the organization, information must freely flow upward, laterally, and downward.

The following information flow checklist can help you keep in mind the many types of information that should "keep moving" in all three directions.

Your Manager

___ Monthly status reports
___ Project progress reports
___ Work items behind schedule
___ Department/organization problems or concerns
___ Possible staffing changes
___ Communications with your manager's peers and managers
___ Vacation or travel plans
___ Successes of your people

Your Peers

___ Procedural or technical changes or innovations
___ Upcoming projects affecting them
___ Reorganizations within your department
___ Your department's mission, vision, and objectives

Your Employees

___ Company policy changes
___ Upcoming projects
___ Organizational events
___ Development opportunities
___ Changes to the organization's vision, mission, or strategies

Modify this checklist to meet your needs, adding any communication needs specific to your department or organization.

Making Sure That People Have No "Surprises"

Communicating only what people need to know is not communicating enough. To get more than minimal information flowing and to ensure that others get the information they need to manage at an optimal level, consider the following:

- Get to know people in other departments. Find out about their current priorities and problems and the direction they foresee for their groups. Look for areas in which your responsibilities overlap with theirs. If appropriate, discuss how you might establish a process for communicating with each other.

- Ask coworkers what kinds of information will help them perform their jobs more effectively.

- When you write or receive a memo, ask yourself who would be interested in its contents. Route the memo. Get into the habit of writing "FYI" (For Your Information) at the top of such memos. This indicates that you are routing the memo for informational purposes rather than action.

- If an upcoming change in another department will affect your department, share information with your employees before the grapevine does. Let them know what the change is and how it will affect your department. Encourage them to come to you with their questions and concerns.

- Build relationships in which you feel free to go to others with both positive and negative information.

- Analyze the communication problems you encounter and then work to find effective solutions. If the problem is seriously affecting your work or the work of your department, consider bringing in a trained facilitator to help overcome any obstacles that have arisen.

Keeping People Up to Date with Information

A lack of needed or helpful information can cause employees anxiety. By keeping them apprised of what is happening, you minimize the time they spend trying to find this information for themselves. Following are some guidelines for specific situations:

- When you must delegate an "action item" — a task with rigid time constraints — explain the reason for the deadline and its urgency.

- When you get an informational memo directed specifically to you, consider whether that information would be useful to your employees. If so, route the memo as is, or modify it to fit the circumstances and their needs. In this way, you can help keep employees aware of organizational events and decisions.

- If you route policy memos generated by someone else in the organization, help your employees understand the policies by:
  - Attaching a note explaining the thrust of the policies.
  - Highlighting the parts of the policies most relevant to them.
  - Explaining why and how the policies are being made or changed. If you don't know the reasons behind the policies, find out before routing the memos to your department.

- Establish a departmental bulletin board. Encourage people to post items of interest to others. Also use the bulletin board to announce personal or company events and activities.

- As you read technical, professional, or industry literature, think of others who may be interested in the information. You may want to route articles or post clippings on the bulletin board.

- Consider holding periodic department- or division-wide informational meetings. Invite your entire staff, including clerical and support personnel. Use this meeting to inform your employees of the organization's plans and goals and the progress they are making in helping to attain these goals. Ask your staff to comment on the organization and to offer suggestions for improvement.

Encouraging Employees to Share Information

If your people rely solely on you to obtain the information they need to effectively perform their responsibilities, you are likely to feel added pressure, and they will probably wind up with inadequate amounts of information. Helping your employees recognize and use fellow team members as information sources will increase both information flow and effective team functioning. Try the following suggestions to encourage information sharing:

- Take an active role in establishing a climate that encourages the exchange of ideas, constructive criticism, the latest departmental news, and open access to necessary information.

- Design your staff meetings so that you are not the sole disseminator of information. Actively involve other team members in giving updates on departmental news and sharing other relevant information. Encourage information sharing with each other in that setting and in their work areas.

- Encourage staff members to talk directly to one another. For example, if an employee approaches you with a problem that he or she is having with another employee, suggest that they first try to work out the conflict with one another.

- If people have a habit of going to you for information that can be easily obtained from other employees, redirect them to the appropriate resource instead.

PART 2

Evaluating Your Communication with Your Manager

Keeping Your Manager Informed

Managers differ in the amount of information they wish to receive from employees and the degree to which they wish to be consulted on decisions. The following exercise will help you determine the degree of upward communication you have established with your manager:

Does one or more of the following statements describe your communication with your manager?

1. You assume that your manager is uninterested in most of what goes on in your department.

2. You avoid giving your manager bad news.

3. You tend to wait for your manager's decision instead of voicing recommendations of your own.

4. You talk with your manager only at his or her request.

If any of these statements are true, there probably is important information that your manager should know but is not receiving from you. Such blocks in communication can impede an organization's progress toward its goals.

Providing Information to Your Manager

Most managers frown on surprises — and not only the unpleasant ones. Whatever the situation, they want to be informed in advance so they know what to expect and have a chance to prepare for it. Therefore, keeping your manager informed of your activities and major factors or occurrences that might affect him or her is an important part of your job. The following guidelines can help you ensure that you are providing enough information to your manager:

1. Ask your manager to identify the kinds of information he or she is most interested in receiving from you. Also ask about areas in which your manager wants immediate updates after you've taken action.

2. Try to prevent surprises by giving your manager information that may have negative implications for your work unit or important items that he or she is likely to hear from someone else if you don't pass it along.

3. As you attempt to increase the information you provide to your manager, check to ensure that you are providing the desired amount of information — not too much or too little — in each of the identified critical areas.

Supplying the Appropriate Amount of Detail

Although most employees make the mistake of supplying too little information to their managers, some have the opposite problem — they supply too much. Their reasons for doing so include:

- Assuming that the manager needs every technical detail to understand why a decision was made

- Assuming that details will impress the manager

- Being excited about the project, including the technical details

Because managers must manage their time in order to accomplish their tasks just as you must, it's important to use your judgment in deciding what information you should pass on.

Establishing Communication with a New Manager

Adjusting to a new manager, whether due to corporate reorganization or a move to a different company, takes some energy and effort on your part. The following procedure will help you establish communication guidelines for your new relationship:

1. Request a meeting to discuss your mutual expectations. Clarify the amount of authority your manager expects you to assume for your various responsibilities — whether you are to proceed on your own, proceed but inform your manager of what you are doing, or seek approval before proceeding.

2. Determine how your manager wants you to give him or her information (in writing, orally, with what frequency, and so on).

3. Establish a relationship in which you feel free to go to your manager with both positive and negative information. Although it is important that you be able to act independently, let your manager know when you are working on a major problem. Follow the rule of "no surprises" when communicating with your new manager.

RECOMMENDED READINGS

The publications listed here were selected for their content and suitability to a managerial audience.

People Smarts

Alessandra, Tony, and O'Conner, Michael J., San Diego: Pfeiffer & Company, 1994
ISBN: 0-89384-421-7
The authors introduce the "platinum rule": treat others the way they want to be treated and both parties win. Since everyone is unique, your goal is to adapt your approach to meet the different needs and priorities of the people you deal with. This book is helpful in identifying behavioral styles and learning how to adjust your behavior to increase trust, credibility, and cooperation.

Managing by Storying Around

Armstrong, David, New York: Doubleday, 1992
ISBN: 0-385-42154-0
Armstrong has taken one of the oldest forms of communication — storytelling — and turned it into a powerful management tool. His method is simple and timeless, yet effective, for imparting information from rules and training to policies.

The Human Touch

Arnold, William W., and Plas, Jeanne M., New York: John Wiley & Sons, 1993
ISBN: 0-471-57291-8
Arnold, the president of a leading medical center, stresses the crucial role of each individual in the organization and uses basic values, common sense, accessibility, and respect to increase productivity and profits. This account of providing person-centered leadership shows how to combine tough performance standards with the courage to be human.

Beyond the Trust Gap

Horton, Thomas R., and Reid, Peter C., Burr Ridge, IL: Irwin Professional Publishing, 1991
ISBN: 1-55623-269-1
The authors suggest that downsizings, mergers, and acquisitions have ruptured relations between managers and their employees and created a "trust gap." This book offers guidelines for regaining credibility with middle managers in order to develop the speed and productivity needed to succeed in the competitive world economy.

Credibility: How Leaders Gain and Lose It

Kouzes, James M., and Posner, Barry Z., San Francisco: Jossey-Bass, 1993
ISBN: 1-55542-550-X
In this book Kouzes and Posner, the leadership experts, show why leadership is fundamentally a relationship with credibility as the cornerstone. By providing rich examples, they show how leaders can encourage greater initiative, risk taking, and productivity by demonstrating trust in employees and resolving conflicts on the basis of principles, not positions.

I Wish I'd Said That

McCallister, Linda, Ph.D., New York: John Wiley & Sons, 1992
ISBN: 0-471-55551-7
The author describes in detail the six major styles of communication: Nobel, Socratic, Reflective, Magistrate, Candidate, and Senator. By identifying and recognizing these communication styles, you will learn how to control interactions without building resentment. Also provided is a Communication Style Profile test so you can identify your communication style and learn how to communicate more effectively.

SUGGESTED
SEMINARS

The seminars listed here were selected for their appeal to a managerial audience. The reputation of the vendor, the quality of their seminar offerings, and the specific seminar content were considered in the selection process.

Because of the dynamic nature of the seminar marketplace, some seminars may have been upgraded or replaced, and others may no longer be offered. Likewise, costs and locations may have changed since this listing was compiled. We recommend that you contact the vendor directly for updated and additional information.

Planning Communications to Support Organizational Objectives

This program enables participants to analyze and increase conceptual understanding of planned communications processes, and it provides training in specific skills needed to implement communication plans based on operating objectives.
Length: 2 days; Cost: $399
Locations: Call vendor
Gavin-Hodges Associates
Benjamin Fox Pavilion, Suite 700-37
Jenkintown, PA 19046
Telephone: 215/576-0606

Communication Workshop: Learning by Doing

Through structured practice, participants learn how to improve communication, practice skills involved in communicating and listening, understand problems of organizational communication, explore the effect of stress on interpersonal communication, practice giving and receiving feedback, and gain greater awareness of one's own communication style and impact on others.
Length: 6 days; Cost: $1,245
Location: Bethel, ME
NTL Institute
1240 North Pitt Street, Suite 100
Alexandria, VA 22314-1403
Telephone: 800/777-5227

Emerging Leaders	This program, designed for current and future leaders, addresses the evaluation, building, and sustaining of leadership excellence. Participants will assess and develop their leadership excellence with regard to four areas: personal, people, business, and work. Length: 5 days; Cost: Call vendor

Emerging Leaders

This program, designed for current and future leaders, addresses the evaluation, building, and sustaining of leadership excellence. Participants will assess and develop their leadership excellence with regard to four areas: personal, people, business, and work.
Length: 5 days; Cost: Call vendor
Location: Call vendor
Personnel Decisions International
2000 Plaza VII Tower, 45 South Seventh Street
Minneapolis, MN 55402-1608
Telephone: 800/633-4410

People Skills

This seminar teaches the participant the skills involved in listening, reaching agreement, confronting problems, and managing conflict. Private coaching in instant-replay video sessions helps participants develop their skills and monitor their progress.
Length: 4 days; Cost: $1,100
Locations: Cazenovia, NY; San Francisco
Ridge Associates, Inc.
5 Ledyard Avenue, Cazenovia, NY 13035
Telephone: 315/655-3393

Trust and Teamwork

This seminar teaches specific skills necessary to bring compassion and accountability to the workplace. Experiential in nature, the program focuses on creating a more collaborative, open, and trusting work environment. Participants will examine their own communication styles, learn to manage their credibility, create collaboration, and learn constructive confrontation skills.
Length: 2 days; Cost: $595
Locations: Call vendor
The Atlanta Consulting Group
1600 Parkwood Circle, Suite 200, Atlanta, GA 30339
Telephone: 800/852-8224

LISTEN TO OTHERS

Listening involves hearing the speaker's words, understanding the message and its importance to the speaker, and communicating that understanding to the speaker. Listening is a skill that underlies all management skills. It is key to developing and maintaining relationships, making decisions, and solving problems. Listening is such a part of our everyday lives, both at work and at home, that sometimes we take it for granted.

Aspects of listening covered in this section include:

- Evaluating Your Listening Skills
- Listening for the Total Message
- Interpreting Nonverbal Messages
- Using Nonverbal Attending
- Using Open-ended Probes to Encourage Communication
- Using Paraphrasing to Improve Communication
- Using Reflective Statements to Open Communication Channels
- Using Summary Statements to Increase Understanding
- Listening to People without Interrupting
- Listening Willingly to Others' Concerns
- Listening Willingly to Employees' Disagreements
- Clarifying What People Say
- Listening Well in a Group

Valuable Tips

- When talking with someone on the telephone, avoid sorting through your in-basket or doing other work.

- Don't put a caller on the speaker phone unless it is a conference call with others present in your office. Many people do not like the "public" nature of a speaker phone and may resent that you are doing things other than giving them your full attention.

- When listening, always follow this order: 1) hear, 2) understand, 3) interpret, and 4) respond; don't jump from "hear" to "respond" without making sure you understand.

- Focus your attention on understanding someone's meaning instead of formulating your response.

- Avoid interrupting people; wait until they have finished making their points.

- When disagreeing with someone, summarize what you think their position is before responding with your point of view.

- Ask open-ended questions to draw out a person's thoughts and feelings by using phrases beginning with "what," "how," "describe," "explain," and so forth.

- In meetings, paraphrase what others have said when clarification is necessary.

- Reschedule a conversation if you cannot give it your undivided attention.

- Attend to the feelings, as well as the content, of the message.

- Avoid close-ended questions that can be answered with a "yes" or a "no."

- Use your knowledge of nonverbal behavior to assess how a person is feeling.

- Maintain good eye contact without staring.

- Sit or stand squarely facing the other person. Lean forward to show interest.

- In intercultural situations, adapt your listening behaviors to ensure they are respectful of the other person's culture.

- Take a course in active listening.

- Practice using your listening skills at home and with friends.

- Look and *be* interested.

Evaluating Your Listening Skills

How well do you listen when someone else speaks? Complete the following evaluation exercise after you've had a:

- Conversation with an employee who has a problem

- Conversation with an employee who is passing on information

- Conversation with your manager

- Group problem-solving session in which you are very concerned about the decisions being made

- Group problem-solving session in which you are only mildly concerned about the decisions being made

- Negotiation session

- Casual conversation

- Discussion with a colleague

EVALUATION CHECKLIST *(Circle the appropriate response.)*

Did you frequently:

Interrupt?	**Yes/No**
Show impatience as you waited for the person to finish speaking?	**Yes/No**
Suggest solutions before the problem was fully explained?	**Yes/No**
Misinterpret what was said (hear what you wanted or expected to hear rather than what was meant) such that the speaker corrected your interpretation?	**Yes/No**
Demonstrate by your gestures (leaning back, looking bored, and so forth) that you were uninterested in what was being said?	**Yes/No**
Spend a great deal more time talking than listening?	**Yes/No**
Find that your mind often wandered to other subjects, causing you to miss what was being said?	**Yes/No**
Think about what you would say next rather than about what the speaker was saying?	**Yes/No**

If you answered yes to any of these questions, you may want to work on improving your listening skills.

Listening for the Total Message

Effective listening goes beyond hearing the words and facts the speaker communicates. It also includes processing the information to understand the total message. The following techniques can help you process a speaker's words:

- Listen for main thoughts or ideas. This is especially important when listening to people who include a lot of detail in their messages or who tend to ramble.

- Attempt to determine the speaker's frame of reference for what is said. What information forms the basis for the ideas?

- View the thoughts and ideas from the speaker's perspective. Why does that person think the way he or she does about a subject?

Interpreting Nonverbal Messages

When you are listening, pay attention to speakers' nonverbal messages as well as their verbal messages. This will help you understand the total message.

Nonverbal messages may include:

- Clenched fists (anger)

- Crossed arms (distance, resistance to negotiation)

- Hand on chin (thinking)

- Facial expressions (a variety of emotions, depending on the expression)

- Drumming fingers (impatience, boredom)

Nonverbal behavior can have a variety of meanings, which vary from culture to culture. Therefore, when you notice a particular nonverbal behavior, make a guess about the reason for the behavior and then check out your interpretation with the person. Ask what the person is thinking or feeling if you notice a behavior that is inconsistent with what you expect.

Using Nonverbal Attending

Nonverbal attending is behavior that lets the other person know you are listening. It is important because it:

- Sets a comfortable tone

- Encourages the other person to keep talking

- Shows concern and interest

- Signals the speaker that you are following the conversation

To improve your nonverbal attending, increase your use of the following behaviors when listening to others:

- Move from behind the desk.

- Maintain eye contact, unless it makes the other person uncomfortable.

- Lean forward slightly.

- Allow pauses — don't feel you must speak when the other person pauses to collect his or her thoughts.

- Smile when the speaker uses humor.

- Nod to indicate that you understand or agree.

- Avoid distractions such as answering the telephone.

When you are with a person from a different country or culture, be aware that nonverbal behaviors can have different meanings in different cultures. If possible, check out the practices of the culture before your conversation.

Using Open-ended Probes to Encourage Communication

An open-ended probe is a question that allows the other person to talk at length; it can't be answered with a "yes" or a "no." An open-ended probe begins with words such as "tell me about," "how," "explain," and "describe." This type of question:

- Provides an invitation to talk

- Encourages the other person to "open up"

- Allows the other person to expand on a topic in a comprehensive way

- Lets the other person know that his or her thinking matters to you

- Helps the other person vent anger and other negative emotions

The following are examples of open-ended probes:

Employee: I think it was a mistake to give Harry the assignment.

Manager: Tell me your concerns about Harry doing the job.

Peer:	That's the craziest thing I've ever heard! If you think that plan will work, you must be out of your mind!
Peer:	What makes you say that?

To increase your use of open-ended probes:

1. For a day, keep track of the number of open-ended probes you use in your discussions with others.

2. Over the next month, consciously work to increase the number of open-ended probes you use. If you are uncomfortable with this at first, you might want to begin by using it with an employee or peer with whom you have a good working relationship. Then, when you have gained confidence, try using open-ended probes with others.

Using Paraphrasing to Improve Communication

A paraphrase is a brief rephrasing of information given by the other person. It states the essence of the content in the listener's own words. Paraphrases involve information, ideas, facts, and opinions. Paraphrasing is important because it:

- Shows that you are listening and that you understand what the speaker is saying

- Ensures that your interpretation of the message is correct

- Allows the speaker to explore the issue more fully

Following is an example of paraphrasing:

Manager:	I can't figure out what to do with Sarah. She's bright, but she thinks she has the answer to everything. Usually she suggests something very different from what we're doing, or an idea that would require us to change our methods or work up a new gadget or form that would take time and money.
Peer:	You think her ideas are too far-fetched and would be difficult to implement.

To increase your use of paraphrasing:

1. For a week, keep track of the number of times you use paraphrasing each day during discussions with other people.

2. Over the next three months, increase the number of times you paraphrase speakers' comments. Begin by practicing with an employee or peer with whom you have a good working relationship. Then, when you have gained confidence, use paraphrasing with others.

Using Reflective Statements to Open Communication Channels

Reflective statements are short, declarative statements that repeat the speaker's emotions or feelings without indicating agreement or disagreement. Reflective statements are particularly useful in dealing with people's emotions or with conflict situations. These statements help open communication channels by:

*   Creating strong rapport

*   Causing the speaker to feel understood

*   Helping the speaker further explore the issue or topic

*   Helping the speaker vent emotions or "let off steam"

Following are examples of the effective use of reflective statements:

Manager: Since I've become a unit manager, I'm not sure how I'm doing. I don't know if I'm really in control. Sometimes I think I made the wrong decision in accepting this promotion.

Peer: You're worried about making it in your new position.

Employee: I'm stuck on the budget report, and I'll tell you why. I can't get any of the information from Thompson. I've asked him for the figures I need several times, but he keeps putting me off. I don't know if he's trying to sabotage me or what, but he's doing everything he can to create problems.

Manager: You're pretty ticked off at Thompson.

To increase your use of reflective statements:

1. For a week, keep track of the number of reflective statements you use each day when other people discuss subjects involving emotions and feelings with you.

2. Over the next three months, increase the number of reflective statements you use.

Using Summary Statements to Increase Understanding

A summary statement is a brief restatement of the core themes and feelings the speaker has expressed during a long conversation. The statement should not imply evaluation or agreement.

Summary statements increase understanding because they:

- Help the speaker identify the key elements of his or her situation.

- Show that you are making an effort to understand the speaker's point of view.

- Promote further discussion of the issue.

Following are examples of summary statements:

- "It sounds like your main concern is lack of cooperation from quality control."

- "As I understand it, Charlie, you think the problem with the first-line supervisors is their perception that they do not have enough responsibility and authority."

To develop your skill in using summary statements:

1. Practice by developing statements for discussions and speeches you see on TV or hear on the radio.

2. When you are comfortable that you can restate core themes and feelings in a natural manner, move on to using summary statements during meetings and discussions at work. Increase your use of these statements until you feel that you are using them regularly and appropriately.

Listening to People without Interrupting

One of the keys to being a good listener is allowing the other person to make his or her point before presenting your own. If you tend to interrupt others when they are speaking, try these guidelines:

1. Over the next month, ask others to count the number of times you interrupt them in various conversations, both one-to-one and in group settings.

2. Analyze each incident, asking yourself the following questions:

   • To whom was I talking?

   • What was the situation?

   • What was the topic of discussion?

3. If your analysis reveals that you tend to interrupt others only in certain situations (for example, when talking with a certain individual or about a certain issue), make an effort each time you are in that situation to curb your tendency to interrupt.

   If no pattern develops, just be aware that you need to become more patient with others, allowing them to finish speaking before asserting your point of view.

4. In your analysis, notice whether you are sitting forward when you interrupt. Try sitting back in your chair. It is more difficult to interrupt if your physical posture is more relaxed.

As you implement your new behaviors, seek feedback from others on whether your interrupting has decreased.

Listening Willingly to Others' Concerns

The last time you talked with a friend or colleague about work frustrations, were you looking for advice or just a willing listener? Chances are, you wanted a sounding board — someone to hear what you were saying and understand — not someone who would solve your problems for you.

Employees, managers, and coworkers occasionally need to express their concerns or frustrations about their work loads, specific projects, coworkers, or other job-related matters. They're likely to be looking for a sounding board, not someone to solve their problems.

On such occasions, you can be most helpful by simply listening and showing empathy, understanding, and encouragement.

In addition, you may want to analyze the balance between the amount of time you spend talking and the amount you spend listening. Although it feels great to command the attention of others, too much talking can isolate you from the communication you need to function in your role.

To analyze your talking-listening balance, use this technique:

1. Over the next two weeks, monitor your talking-listening ratio during conversations with others. You may want to use a tape recorder in meetings or discussions to determine your ratio.

2. Review your data and determine the trend. If you find that you talk more than 50 percent of the time, you will probably want to improve the ratio.

3. Use listening techniques to decrease your percentage of talking time and increase your percentage of listening time.

4. Continue to monitor your talking-listening ratio for an additional two weeks by spot-checking conversations or meetings to make certain that you are talking less than 50 percent of the time.

Listening Willingly to Employees' Disagreements

How do you react when an employee disagrees with your point of view? It can be tempting to assume that you've heard that argument before and to counter it before the employee has finished explaining. An employee who can express disagreement with management demonstrates the valuable quality of independent thinking. You can encourage this quality by listening willingly when your employees disagree with you.

A good way to show your willingness to listen to disagreements is to use summary statements. (Refer to the suggestions on using summary statements in this section for examples.) The next time an employee disagrees with you, try this approach:

1. Wait until the person is done speaking, even if you're sure you understand the argument.

2. Restate the main points of the employee's argument.

3. Ask the employee to verify the accuracy of your statement and to clarify it if necessary.

4. Then — and only then — state specifically which points you disagree with and why.

While you may not change your position any more frequently using this technique, employees will feel that you have considered their input and understand their point of view.

Clarifying What People Say

Listening is not a passive activity. To be most effective in listening to others, you must actively demonstrate that you understand what they have said. To do so, spend time during the conversation verbally confirming what you have heard.

- Take time during a conversation to respond to what the other person is saying. Be aware of any tendencies you have to "tune out" or daydream when someone else is talking.

- Use the paraphrasing and reflecting techniques described in this section as the primary means of demonstrating what you have heard.

- If you discover that you have misunderstood the speaker, use open-ended questions to ask the speaker to clarify what he or she intended to convey.

- Keep in mind that miscommunication occurs because of miscues from both the speaker and the listener. Try to remain nonjudgmental when dealing with miscommunication problems.

Listening Well in a Group

Being an effective listener in a group requires the same skills as listening one-on-one. However, people can easily fall into some additional pitfalls in group listening.

Examples of poor listening behavior in groups include:

- Having side conversations

- Doing paperwork

- Preparing your presentation

- Looking away from the speaker

To be more effective at listening in groups:

- In group situations, notice any tendencies you have to drift off or to do anything other than listen. When you find yourself not listening, begin instead to use appropriate listening skills such as:
  - Looking at the speaker
  - Asking relevant questions
  - Nodding
  - Leaning forward
  - Smiling when appropriate

- If you tend to become preoccupied, especially in large meetings, sit close to the speaker.

- Use the listening skill of summarizing to move discussions to closure or decision points.

- Use open-ended probes to generate interaction in the group or prompt a reaction to your statements.

- Observe your reactions to people who have side conversations or do paperwork while you are talking. This may sensitize you to the impact of your own behaviors.

- If the content of the discussion does not pertain to you or your area of responsibility, challenge yourself to find something to learn from the person or group doing the talking. You may watch how the speaker tries to influence others, the way a group member builds support for his or her position, or the way in which visual aids are used.

RECOMMENDED
READINGS

The publications listed here were selected for their content and suitability to a managerial audience.

Listen to Win

Bechler, Curt, and Weaver, Richard L., II, New York: Master Media Limited, 1994
ISBN: 1-571010-02-5
Listening can be one of management's least expensive and most effective tools, according to the authors. Their powerful, people-oriented book will help you learn to live with others, connect with them, get the best from them, and empower them.

A Briefing for Leaders

Dilenschneider, Robert L., New York: HarperBusiness, 1992
ISBN: 0-88730-467-2
This book sets forth the techniques and requirements for becoming a successful leader. Through actual case studies the author presents strategies and methods for becoming an effective leader, including learning how to listen, interpret, and analyze the communication that managers receive.

Bridging Differences: Effective Intergroup Communication

Gudykunst, William B., Newbury Park, CA: Sage Publications, 1994
ISBN: 0-8039-5646-0
This book is useful to anyone who works with people from different cultural and ethnic backgrounds. The author shows how stereotypes lead to ineffective communication, including misinterpretation of messages we receive from members of cultural and ethnic groups different from our own.

The Skilled Facilitator

Schwarz, Roger M., San Francisco: Jossey-Bass, 1994
ISBN: 1-55542-638-7
This book is a guide for all facilitators and managers on how to successfully lead a group toward creative resolution of the tasks before them. The book tells how to deal with all types of problems and situations that may arise in the course of group interaction.

SUGGESTED SEMINARS

The seminars listed here were selected for their appeal to a managerial audience. The reputation of the vendor, the quality of their seminar offerings, and the specific seminar content were considered in the selection process.

Because of the dynamic nature of the seminar marketplace, some seminars may have been upgraded or replaced, and others may no longer be offered. Likewise, costs and locations may have changed since this listing was compiled. We recommend that you contact the vendor directly for updated and additional information.

Effective Listening/ Better Results: Making Communication Work for You

This seminar organizes the best communication ideas and techniques into a simple, effective, easy-to-learn system. Participants will learn to use encouragement and praise to build rapport, separate message content from feelings, ask questions to expand knowledge and bring out new ideas, give directions effectively, and criticize performance rather than people.
Length: 2 days; Cost: $1,085
Locations: Call vendor
American Management Association
P.O. Box 319, Saranac Lake, NY 12983
Telephone: 800/262-9699

Communication Workshop: Learning by Doing

Through structured practice, participants learn how to improve communication, practice skills involved in communicating and listening, understand problems of organizational communication, explore the effect of stress on interpersonal communication, practice giving and receiving feedback, and gain greater awareness of one's own communication style and impact on others.
Length: 6 days; Cost: $1,245
Location: Bethel, ME
NTL Institute
1240 North Pitt Street, Suite 100
Alexandria, VA 22314-1403
Telephone: 800/777-5227

People Skills

This seminar teaches the participant the skills involved in listening, reaching agreement, confronting problems, and managing conflict. Private coaching in instant-replay video sessions helps participants develop their skills and monitor their progress.
Length: 4 days; Cost: $1,100
Locations: Cazenovia, NY; San Francisco
Ridge Associates, Inc.
5 Ledyard Avenue, Cazenovia, NY 13035
Telephone: 315/655-3393

Better Management Through Better Communication

This seminar focuses on writing with clarity, dynamic speaking, the power of listening, and the interpersonal process.
Length: 2 days; Cost: $1,250
Location: Nashville, TN
Vanderbilt University
Owen Graduate School of Management
Executive Programs
410 21st Avenue South, Suite 100, Nashville, TN 37203
Telephone: 615/322-2513

DELIVER PRESENTATIONS

Many professionals are apprehensive, and some are even terrified, at the prospect of speaking in front of an audience — *any* audience. Yet, the ability to give effective presentations to a variety of audiences is one of the hallmarks of a successful manager. It's likely that you are called upon to give presentations off and on throughout the year. Even if your presentations are infrequent, they often represent a high-impact communication opportunity. Unless you are already a seasoned speaker, you can benefit by learning to prepare and deliver presentations that are well organized, dynamic, and motivational.

This section contains two parts:

Part 1: Preparing an Effective Presentation

- Anticipating the Audience's Needs
- Putting Together the Presentation Draft
- Using Visual Aids Effectively

Part 2: Delivering the Presentation

- Communicating Your Attitudes Nonverbally
- Avoiding Distracting Mannerisms
- Developing Confidence and Poise
- Managing Anxiety
- Handling the Question-and-Answer Session

Valuable Tips

- Make an audiotape or videotape of your presentation and review it critically with a trusted colleague.

- When you are preparing for an important presentation, rehearse it on videotape to see how you come across.

- Pursue opportunities to give more presentations.

- Anticipate questions and prepare answers in advance.

- Concentrate on getting your message across, not on whether you are a good speaker, and you will be less nervous.

- Seek feedback on your use of gestures, grammar, vocal expressiveness, general delivery style, and visual aids during presentations.

- Remember that most people don't look as nervous as they feel.

- Keep in mind that visual aids should complement, not *be*, your presentation.

- Seek opportunities to give speeches through community or service organizations such as the Chamber of Commerce.

- Join groups or take classes in which you have to make regular presentations.

- Get some coaching from a professional speech trainer.

- Join a local Toastmaster's Club to become more comfortable speaking in front of groups.

- Make eye contact with people in the audience as you speak.

- Use note cards or an outline.

- Practice everything first — giving the presentation, using audiovisuals, relating stories, etc.

- Do "dry runs" with your people and ask for their feedback.

PART 1

Anticipating the Audience's Needs

Preparing an Effective Presentation

The first step in preparing for a presentation is to analyze the needs of the audience. You can then tailor your presentation to their interests and expectations.

As you analyze your audience, consider the following questions:

- What need or opportunity prompted the presentation?
  - What is the general purpose of the presentation (for instance, a ceremonial occasion, information, persuasion, entertainment)?
  - What kind of response or specific outcome do I want as a result of the presentation?

- Who, specifically, will be attending the presentation?
  - What are the relevant demographic characteristics (such as educational backgrounds, ages, gender) of audience members?

- What do audience members already know about the subject?
  - What has been their exposure to, or experience with, the particular subject I am addressing?
  - What background information is necessary for the group?

- What is the audience's attitude toward me, the presenter?
  - What is the level of my credibility?
  - How does the audience perceive my role in the meeting?

- What is important to the audience?
  - What do they want and need to know from my presentation?
  - Of the information I have, what do they most need to know?
  - How can I capitalize on the audience's interests and expectations to reach my objective?

- What are the physical arrangements?
  - When will I be presenting? How much time do I have?
  - How many people will be there?
  - How will the audience be seated?
  - What equipment is available for visual aids?

- How will I improvise if my best-laid plans fall through?
  - What if I have only a portion of the time that I expected?
  - What if the audiovisual equipment I counted on is not available?

Putting Together the Presentation Draft

One of the most time-consuming, yet critical, steps in giving a presentation is preparing the draft of your speech or presentation. Follow these steps when preparing your draft:

1. Do your homework. Research, collect, and review the relevant information for the presentation.

2. Formulate your main ideas. Main ideas are the key statements around which the presentation is built. Because main ideas provide your audience with a "road map" of where your presentation is going, be sure to state them clearly. Keep the following guidelines in mind:

   - State main ideas in simple, declarative sentences.

   - Express them as precisely and vividly as possible.

   - Include only one idea in each statement.

   - State all main ideas positively, if possible.

   - Use active verbs.

3. Include supporting material. While the main ideas provide the structure of the presentation, supporting material adds interest, clarity, persuasion, and impact. Vary the types of supporting data for each main idea. Examples of supporting material include the following:

   - Explanations

   - Examples

   - Anecdotes

   - Statistics

   - Comparisons/analogies

   - Quotations

4. Select a structure. The structure helps you organize your material, so your next step is to choose the kind of structure that best accomplishes your communication objective. The following list describes several common presentation structures:

   - Problem solution. The body of the message presents a problem, suggests a solution, and indicates the likely benefits if the proposed solution is put into effect.

- Classification. The important items are listed; each then becomes a major point in the presentation.

- Time order. Events are arranged in sequential order.

- Climax. Main points are presented in order of increasing importance.

- Simple to complex. Main ideas are arranged in order from the simplest to the most complex.

- Proposition support. Main points are stated and then backed up by supporting evidence.

5. Develop an introduction. This is where you grab the audience's attention. Begin with an item of interest to the specific audience. Provide some background information to indicate the importance of your subject matter. Include the purpose of your presentation and a brief summary of the main ideas. Several ways to open a presentation are:

- Use a dramatic statement.

- Ask a question that requires a response from the audience.

- Refer to a recent or well-known event.

- Tell a story from your own experience.

- Cite a quotation from an authoritative source.

6. Develop a conclusion. A conclusion gives the audience a feeling of completion. Briefly restate the substance of the presentation and focus the audience's attention on the desired response.

In the final stages of preparation, develop an outline that you can use to practice with and, if necessary, to actually deliver your presentation.

Using Visual Aids Effectively

Visual aids are indispensable for many presentations, yet few presenters use them to maximum advantage. Effective use of visual aids can enhance your effort to convey information by communicating ideas through sight as well as sound. Keep in mind, however, that visual aids are not a substitute for careful preparation, good organization, or expressive delivery. The following questions can help you select and use the most effective visual aids:

- What are my options? Learn about the different types of visual aids, such as slides, flipcharts/boards, overheads, and computer presentation software, and the advantages and disadvantages of each.

- What types of visual aids are best for this situation? The purpose, audience, and physical setting should determine what types of visuals to use. Ask, "How can I communicate my information in the clearest, most interesting, and most economical way, given the size of the audience and the facilities available?" The answer will help you decide whether to use visual aids, what types to use, and how many.

- Are the visual aids I'm planning well done? Good visual aids are:
    - Clear. Avoid complex and highly detailed visual aids. When you need to explain a subject in detail, use a series of simple visuals rather than a single complex visual.
    - Large enough. The audience member farthest from the presenter should be able to read the smallest part of the visual. Check the size in advance.
    - Accurate. Verify the accuracy and precision of charts, diagrams, and drawings, as well as their spelling.
    - Attractive. Audiences assume that sloppy visuals are evidence of sloppy preparation. Factors such as creativity, neatness, color selection, balance, and proportion can heighten your audience's attention and give you more credibility.
    - Appropriate in number. Visual aids are meant to *augment* your presentations. Too many visual aids are worse than too few.

- How should I use the visual aids? The keys to success in using visual aids include planning, preparation, and practice. For each visual aid you use, follow this sequence:
    - Plan where it fits in the presentation.
    - Prepare a transition to introduce the visual aid to the audience.
    - Describe its essential components, but don't read it verbatim.
    - Make your point.
    - Move smoothly into the next segment of the presentation.

In addition to integrating your visual aids with your verbal content, keep the following in mind:

- Before the presentation, make sure the visuals and equipment are in place, the equipment works properly, and that you know how to operate it.

- Avoid standing between the visual aid and your audience.

- Display the visual aid only when it relates to the point you are making.

- Speak to your audience, not to your visual aid.

- Maintain maximum eye contact with the audience.

- Resist the tendency to drop your voice level when using a visual aid.

PART 2

**Communicating
Your Attitudes
Nonverbally**

Delivering the Presentation

To deliver an effective presentation, you need to supplement your verbal message with nonverbal cues so that you clearly communicate what is important. Consider the following points about nonverbal behaviors as you give your presentation:

- Facial animation. Your face displays an instant picture of the attitudes and emotions you wish to convey. Vary your facial expression to match the content of your material. If you are excited, show it.

- Eye contact. Eye contact conveys your confidence and interest in the audience. Make eye contact with many members of the audience; avoid gazing exclusively at one person or at a spot above the heads of the audience.

- Vocal variety. A good speaking voice varies in pace, pitch, volume, and tone. While many people are not naturally endowed with melodious voices, most have the potential for a wide range of pitch and tone. A voice that has variety is more interesting to listeners.

- Gestures. Use gestures to emphasize and reinforce statements. Allow gestures to flow naturally from your message.

- Stance. In general, a relaxed stance and physical movements that complement and support your message are most effective. A rigid posture usually conveys nervousness, and random walking or other movements tend to be distracting.

- Dress/appearance. Your audience's willingness to listen to you may be based on its immediate impression of you. Choose attire that is consistent with the presentation purpose and is appropriate for the audience and setting.

Avoiding Distracting Mannerisms

When you speak, avoid unpleasant and annoying behaviors. Most audiences become annoyed when speakers:

- Use a monotone voice

- Mumble

- Repeat too much

- Appear unprepared

- Come across as vague or indefinite

- Frequently say "ah," "um," "like," or "you know"

- Mispronounce words

- Jingle change in their pocket

Seek feedback from trusted colleagues to see whether you are engaging in any of these annoying behaviors.

Developing Confidence and Poise

Ironically, presenters who are terrified by an audience experience the same physiological effects as presenters who are stimulated by an audience — they just use their energies differently. The best way to develop your confidence is to give several successful presentations. You can speed up this process by doing the following:

- Prepare thoroughly. Genuine confidence is the result of a thorough knowledge of your subject. If you are unprepared, you should be nervous!

- Practice by yourself and with a colleague. Periodically audiotape or videotape your practice sessions.

- Connect with your audience. If possible, build rapport with individual audience members before the presentation.

- Be committed to your ideas. You will convey to the audience a strong interest and belief in what you are saying.

- Relax. You will probably relax more readily if you avoid excess stimulants and nicotine. Also avoid looking over your presentation notes just before the delivery.

- Remain flexible. Don't take yourself too seriously; be open to conflict, be flexible, smile. If you sense that some members of the audience are "drifting" during the presentation, try these techniques:
  - Vary your vocal projection, pitch, and pace.
  - Make eye contact with these individuals.

- Ask a question.
- Use a visual aid.
- Refer to members of the audience or to a real-life situation.

- Be positive. Adopt a positive mental attitude; if you believe you can do it, you probably can.

Managing Anxiety

For many people, giving a presentation conjures up an image of cold, clammy hands, a dry throat, shaky knees, or a fluttering heartbeat — all symptoms that normally accompany fear. Use the following suggestions to reduce your level of anxiety:

- Dispel the notion that you need to eliminate anxiety before you can give a successful presentation. Channel this energy into improved concentration and expressiveness.

- Realize that anxiety decreases (but doesn't disappear) with experience, and that anxiety is not as noticeable to your listeners as it is to you.

- Engage in mental scanning. Before you present, visualize the actual room, the audience, and your position in the room. Mentally go over what you are going to do from the moment you open your mouth.

- Take five or six deep breaths just before presenting. Inhale and exhale for three or four counts each time.

- Come to grips with your fear of making a mistake. To think that a good presenter will not make a mistake is both untrue and unhealthy. The key is to regain control after the error occurs. If you pick up and go on, so will the audience.

Handling the Question-and-Answer Session

The question-and-answer session is an important part of many presentations. You can't be sure that you are getting your message across to your listeners until you get feedback from them. If you haven't covered a topic of concern to a listener, the question-and-answer session can provide your audience with the desired information. When handled well, this session can be an effective and meaningful part of the total presentation. Use the following guidelines:

- Be prepared and ready to respond to the issues related to the content of your material.

- Pause to think about the question. Sometimes answers are literally correct but ignore the larger issue of concern to the questioner.

- Answer concisely. Research shows that answers that last 10 to 40 seconds work the best. Shorter answers can seem too abrupt, and longer answers can seem too elaborate.

- Relate your answers to one or more key points in the presentation to reinforce your most important messages.

- Keep on track. Don't let the session get sidetracked into areas that are not relevant to your presentation objective. Instead, offer to deal with these questions at the conclusion of your presentation.

- Speak to the entire audience. By directing your answer to the entire audience rather than to a single listener, your audience's attention will be focused on you rather than on the questioner.

- Be honest. If you don't know, say so. Answering honestly will give you and your message more credibility.

- Provide a "capper." The question-and-answer session can distract from the main emphasis of your presentation. Avoid ending with an answer to a question. Instead, take the last few moments to restate your key points.

RECOMMENDED READINGS

The publications listed here were selected for their content and suitability to a managerial audience.

Make Presentations With Confidence

Buchan, Vivian, New York: Barron's, 1991
ISBN: 0-8120-4588-2
This book teaches you how to prepare for making a successful presentation by gathering facts, organizing thoughts, getting the audience's attention, and using charts, slides, and other visual aids. This book is designed to help prepare you to present your company's ideas and plans at meetings.

I Can See You Naked

Hoff, Ron, Kansas City, MO: Andrews and McMeel, 1992
ISBN: 0-8362-8008-3
This book provides countless techniques on how to make fearless and successful presentations in every possible situation. Some of the issues involved in making presentations include: what are the basic elements of an effective presentation, how to deal with nervousness, how to handle questions, how to make your presentation interesting, how to gear your presentation to a particular audience, and how to learn from your mistakes.

How to Prepare, Stage, and Deliver Winning Presentations

Leech, Thomas, New York: AMACOM, 1992
ISBN: 0-8144-7813-1
The author contends that even the best and most innovative ideas will not be accepted unless they are presented after sufficient preparation and with proper delivery. This book is a guide on how to effectively prepare your ideas, overcome nervousness, and successfully deliver your presentation.

How To Think On Your Feet

Woodall, Marian K., New York: Warner Books, 1993
ISBN: 0-446-36413-4
This concise book provides techniques for improving the quickness and quality of responses to difficult questions. The author also provides guidance on how to quickly and clearly formulate answers, as well as improve the delivery of the communication.

SUGGESTED SEMINARS

The seminars listed here were selected for their appeal to a managerial audience. The reputation of the vendor, the quality of their seminar offerings, and the specific seminar content were considered in the selection process.

Because of the dynamic nature of the seminar marketplace, some seminars may have been upgraded or replaced, and others may no longer be offered. Likewise, costs and locations may have changed since this listing was compiled. We recommend that you contact the vendor directly for updated and additional information.

Effective Executive Speaking

Participants in this program are actively involved in evaluating their strengths and development needs, making an impromptu talk, building ideas, using visual aids, and answering questions. This program includes videotaping.
Length: 3 days; Cost: $1,260
Locations: Call vendor
American Management Association
P.O. Box 319, Saranac Lake, NY 12983
Telephone: 800/262-9699

Visual Aids for Presentations: From Designing Tips to Delivery Techniques

This hands-on workshop offers a combination of lectures, practical demonstrations, and learn-by-doing exercises. Participants will create their own visual aids, develop a checklist of "how-to's," and receive feedback on delivery, content, and use of visual aids.
Length: 2 days; Cost: $1,085
Locations: Call vendor
American Management Association
P.O. Box 319, Saranac Lake, NY 12983
Telephone: 800/262-9699

Executive Presentation Skills

This program covers preventing nervousness, organizing the information of your speech, using visual aids, and handling questions effectively.
Length: 2 days; Cost: $1,150
Locations: Call vendor
Communispond, Inc.
300 Park Avenue, 22nd Floor, New York, NY 10022
Telephone: 212/486-2300

Effective Communicating™

This program is designed to help participants improve their natural speaking style. Through discussion, individual coaching, and videotaped exercises, participants learn how to increase their personal impact, master the use of gestures and posture, and use their voice for more persuasive and interesting delivery.
Length: 2 days; Cost: Call vendor
Locations: Call vendor
Decker Communications, Inc.
44 Montgomery Street, San Francisco, CA 94104
Telephone: 415/391-5544

The Effective Presentations Seminar

This seminar teaches managers how to deliver clear, concise presentations through the use of video analysis of skills and accelerated training exercises. The program covers controlling tension, organizing and delivering messages, enhancing eye contact, and implementing visual aids.
Length: 2 days; Cost: Call vendor
Locations: Call vendor
Executive Speaking, Inc.
3036 Plaza VII Tower, 45 South Seventh Street
Minneapolis, MN 55402
Telephone: 612/338-5748

The Open Program

This seminar enables participants to determine their own personal communication style through individualized exercises, practice presentations, and private videotape consultation. Participants learn to control nervousness, organize content, design effective visual aids, and demonstrate communication proficiency.
Length: 2 days; Cost: $1,195
Locations: Call vendor
Executive Technique
716 North Rush Street, Chicago, IL 60611
Telephone: 800/992-1414

Speaking With Impact

This seminar allows the participant to gain feedback on his or her current skill level and teaches the participant to develop his or her unique speaking style. Participants learn to motivate their audiences and gain confidence in all aspects of public speaking.
Length: 2 days; Cost: $695
Locations: Call vendor
Personnel Decisions International
2000 Plaza VII Tower, 45 South Seventh Street
Minneapolis, MN 55402-1608
Telephone: 800/633-4410

Plan for Results

Participants in this workshop will work individually and in small groups to learn how to plan their communications strategically and use visual aids effectively.
Length: 1 day; Cost: $500
Locations: Atlanta; San Francisco
Speakeasy, Inc.
3414 Peachtree Road N.E., Monarch Plaza, Suite 800
Atlanta, GA 30326
Telephone: 404/261-4029

Presentation Skills for Managers: Speaking with Clarity and Confidence

Through demonstration, practice, and feedback, participants in this workshop learn to manage "butterflies," establish rapport with their audience, structure presentations for clarity and impact, grab the audience's attention, and conclude with emphasis.
Length: 3 days; Cost: $895
Location: Madison, WI
University of Wisconsin-Madison
Management Institute, Grainger Hall
975 University Avenue, Madison, WI 53706-1323
Telephone: 800/348-8964

PREPARE WRITTEN COMMUNICATION

The following memo was sent by a division manager:

TO: ALL DIVISION A EMPLOYEES

RE: RESTRUCTURIZATION OF DIVISION A
DEPARTMENTS

The negative interface that transpired after the meeting held last Wednesday on our division's restructurization has caused an operational delay in the conversion of our facilities as desegnated. Consequently, future perimeters concerning the extensive redevelopement of the work force of Division A will be determined by those functionaly responsible for the implementation of the type of tasks discussed. The inclusion of input by other individuals will be at the sole desgretion of the aforementioned management personel.

The manager who wrote this memo had a message he wanted to get across to the employees in Division A. Did he succeed in conveying it?

Documents like this one — confusing, wordy, and full of typos, misspellings, and grammatical errors — are common in the business world. So is confusion on the part of their recipients, who can only scratch their heads and guess at the sender's meaning. Unfortunately, confusion resulting from written materials is less likely to be cleared up than are misunderstandings resulting from in-person communications.

The need for clarity, simplicity, and accuracy in written communications is obvious. This section can help you improve the effectiveness of your written communication skills.

Part 1: Building Basic Writing Skills

- Writing Clearly and Concisely
- Using Correct Grammar, Spelling, and Punctuation
- Using Technical Terms Appropriately
- Eliminating Unnecessary Detail
- Writing Reports
- Increasing Your Vocabulary

Part 2: Improving Your Writing Skills

- Improving Your Business Letters and Memos
- Writing Expressively
- Creating Effective Visual Aids
- Avoiding Miscommunication in Written Documents
- Reducing Procrastination When Writing Reports
- Reviewing the Written Work of Others

Valuable Tips

- When you are writing, consider the recipients. What do they know already? What can you tell them?

- Outline your memos and letters before beginning to write.

- When you write reports, summarize key points or conclusions on the first page and document them with more information on subsequent pages.

- Write like you speak to make your writing as readable as possible.

- Learn the writing style of your organization and follow it. For example, don't use "flowery" language (many adjectives and adverbs) when it is inappropriate.

- Have your secretary or assistant edit and proofread your correspondence for sentence structure and grammatical errors.

- Refer to a grammar/style reference book such as *The Little English Handbook* when in doubt about grammar.

- Keep a dictionary and thesaurus on hand to check spelling and word usage.

- Use a variety of sentence structures — simple, complex, and compound — to add interest to your writing.

- When you write for a nontechnical audience, have a nontechnical person identify jargon. Then either eliminate it or include a glossary defining the terms.

- Use charts and tables wherever possible to present numerical information.

- Use "action verbs" to add punch to your message.

- Eliminate weak words like "very," "interesting," "often," and other bland adjectives or adverbs.

- Keep paragraphs short. Make sure the content of a paragraph revolves around only one thought — the topic sentence.

- If you do a large amount of routine correspondence, standardize it as much as possible.

- If procrastination is a problem, start writing a rough draft early so you have time to revise it at least once.

- When allocating blocks of time for writing, set aside periods of one to one-and-a-half hours, rather than trying to do it in segments of 5 to 15 minutes.

- Develop a flash card system to work on your own common misspellings.

- Dictate correspondence, memos, and so forth, to save time.

- Seek immediate and specific feedback on reports you write.

- Take a second or third look at your memos before sending them.

- Use a grammar-checking software program on your computer to identify errors you frequently make, and use that feedback to focus your efforts to improve your writing.

PART 1

Writing Clearly and Concisely

Building Basic Writing Skills

One of the cornerstones of good written communications is the clear, concise expression of ideas or information. The following guidelines can help you achieve clarity and conciseness from the very start of the writing process:

1. Before you start writing, outline the key points or ideas you want to address in the order in which you want to present them.

2. Start by identifying the main topic of the piece and any supporting concepts you will be discussing. For example, you might begin by saying, "In summarizing the main points of the meeting, I will describe how they relate to our planning process."

3. In addition to introducing your topic before discussing it, be sure to end your piece with a summary statement that capsulizes the ideas and facts you've presented.

4. Consider the reader's needs. How much detail is needed? Is the entire piece likely to be read? (If not, open with an "executive summary," a page or less in length. This frees the reader from wading through unessential details before getting to the "meat" of the document.)

5. Write a first draft, and then review and revise it before composing the final version.

6. Ask someone else for feedback on your writing. Give your manager, a peer, or a friend the letter or report to read. Ask them, "What did you think I was trying to convey?" and "What parts don't you understand?" You will know your writing is improving when your readers' understanding of your ideas matches your intent.

Using Correct Grammar, Spelling, and Punctuation

Following is an excerpt from a memo written by a department manager:

> "We are checking into the feasibility of the program for it's applicability to our purposes. Upon reaching a decision you will be notified."

You probably understood what this manager was trying to say. However, the errors in spelling, punctuation, and sentence structure greatly reduce the impact and effectiveness of the message.

Correct use of the technical components of the language — including grammar, spelling, punctuation, and sentence structure — is essential for producing effective written communications. The following suggestions can help you improve your use of these components:

- Choose a grammar/style book that you will use as a guide in working on your written communication skills. (Corbett's *The Little English Handbook*, which addresses 50 areas that commonly cause problems for adult writers, is recommended.) Set a schedule for completing the book, and write a summary of each section's key points as you finish it. You might want to mark the sections that focus on your problem areas and check your writing against the guidelines offered in those sections.

- If your secretary edits your memos and reports, ask to have the next few typed verbatim (exactly as you dictate or write them). Examine these copies for errors you typically make — grammatical errors, poor sentence structure, and so on. You might also ask your secretary to compile a list of your most common writing errors. This list can help you pinpoint the areas you need to improve.

- If you use a computer in your writing process, obtain spell-checking and grammar-checking software programs to use on your writing. Such programs can serve you in two ways:
  - Identify spelling and grammatical errors that can be fixed before your final version is completed.
  - Point out errors you make frequently so that you can improve your skills in those areas. Also, a good grammar-checking program can actually teach you the rules you are breaking as it checks your writing.

Using Technical Terms Appropriately

What were your feelings as you read the sample memo in the introduction to this section? Did the buzzwords and complex terminology affect your comprehension? Memos that contain technical terms may seem perfectly clear to employees in technical positions, but they are likely to confuse and frustrate nontechnical employees.

When you are writing a memo to a diverse group of individuals, keep technical language to a minimum. The following guidelines will help you determine the appropriate, effective use of technical terminology:

- Identify your audience. If it consists primarily of individuals with technical expertise, the use of technical terms and concepts may be appropriate, even desirable. The more diverse the group, however, the fewer technical terms you should use.

- When you prepare a piece for wide distribution, have a colleague from another department read it before you send it. Ask the person to review the document for its use of technical terms and for the clarity of its message.

- If the use of technical terms is unavoidable in a document intended for wide distribution, you may want to:
  - Define the terms.
  - Use the terms in a context that makes their meaning apparent.

- If you communicate with certain departments on a regular basis, learn their jargon. Get a list of the terms commonly used by these groups, and occasionally use the words in your correspondence to them.

Eliminating Unnecessary Detail

Unnecessary detail wastes your time and the time of those to whom you are presenting your ideas. In addition, the impact of your message can be lost if the reader or listener must sift through unimportant data in order to determine the key points. To reduce extraneous detail, follow these guidelines:

- Before writing a memo or report to review a large amount of information, list the points that you really need to make. Then include this information in summary form and provide the detail in an addendum, or indicate in the report that the detail is available upon request.

- To develop more succinct writing, go over your memos and see if you can cover the same content in half the words.

- Learn more about your method of handling detail. Ask trusted colleagues to give you feedback on your concern with detail and to suggest ways in which you might eliminate excess detail in your writing.

- When you are writing a report, discuss the task with your manager. Ask which details you can bypass, and which are critical. When you finish the report, ask your manager to review it to determine if you included the appropriate amount of detail.

Writing Reports

Many managers need to write or edit reports that must communicate a lot of information clearly. The following guidelines will assist you in preparing reports that your audience understands and that communicate your important conclusions and recommendations. Keep in mind that these are specifically designed to help you improve your skill in writing reports that must convey more information than the average letter or memo.

1. Whenever possible, start your reports well in advance of their due dates. Map out enough time to write at least one rough draft. Most good writers produce quality pieces because they've taken the time to revise their documents.

2. Make a list of the points you want included in your report, and then create an outline. Check to see that each section flows logically into the next. You might experiment with several outlines, selecting the one that is likely to have the greatest impact on and be clearest to the reader.

3. Use headings and subheadings to indicate to the reader when a new idea begins. Examples of headings include "Background Information," "Conclusions," and "Recommendations." A table of contents listing the headings is recommended for reports that are longer than ten pages.

4. When you're ready to begin writing, make sure you have everything you'll need — your outline, resource notes, and any other information sources. Interrupting your writing to locate an article or notes from a meeting can break your train of thought.

5. Consider the needs and purposes of your audience throughout the writing cycle. Ask yourself what you want the reader to learn from the report, what he or she will do with the information, and what he or she already knows about the subject. This information will help you make decisions about the background data, terminology, and definitions you include in your report.

6. Edit your report. Delete unnecessary and redundant parts, sentences, or phrases, and simplify wordy and awkward passages. It's usually a good idea to keep your sentences and paragraphs short, and to avoid unnecessary jargon and long words.

7. Ask your manager or a qualified colleague to review your preliminary final draft and provide feedback. The factors needing attention include organization (order and flow of sections), transitions, suitability of language for the audience, and overall clarity.

Increasing Your Vocabulary

Increasing your vocabulary will enable you to use unfamiliar words correctly and add variety to your writing. Following are some suggestions for ways to increase your vocabulary:

- Keep both a thesaurus and a dictionary at your desk for easy reference when you come across a new word.

- Use a systematic process, such as the following, for building your vocabulary:

  1. Note unfamiliar words that you come across in your work and in outside reading. Write each word on one side of an index card. Look the word up in the dictionary and write its meaning on the reverse side. Prepare 10 or 15 of these cards.

  2. Check yourself on the meanings of these words once a day. When you think you have learned the meaning of a particular word, take the card out and add a new vocabulary card to your pile.

  3. Incorporate these new words into memos or reports whenever possible. However, be careful not to use words that may be too difficult for your readers to understand.

  4. Keep the vocabulary cards you have mastered in a separate file. At the end of a month, ask a colleague or a family member to test you on the accumulated cards. If you have forgotten any of these, add them once again to the pile of cards you review daily.

- Increase your exposure to new words by reading business-oriented publications such as *Business Week* or *Harvard Business Review*.

- Use the word-building section of *Reader's Digest* for the next few months.

PART 2

Improving Your Business Letters and Memos

Improving Your Writing Skills

Clarity, organization, and a sense of purpose in your business letters and memos are vital to getting and keeping the reader's attention. Follow these guidelines to write letters and memos that will be read and understood:

1. Open your letter or memo with a description of your subject and your purpose in writing about it.

2. State your conclusions, decisions, and recommendations. (If you anticipate a negative response to your conclusions, you may want to give the facts first, before your conclusions.)

3. Elaborate on the subject, providing only the details that are relevant to the purpose of your report. If you must include additional data or statistics to support your conclusions, put them in an easy-to-read table or graph that you can include in an appendix.

4. End your letter or memo with an offer to provide additional information or to take appropriate action if the reader wishes.

Writing Expressively

When you've mastered the skills of improving the organization, clarity, and grammatical accuracy of your materials, you're ready to work on putting "pizzazz" into your writing — to develop a style that's expressive. This touch is what compels the reader to keep reading. The following guidelines will help you develop a more expressive style of writing:

- Use the active voice whenever possible. Replace passive ("being") verbs with active verbs. Look at the following two ways of saying the same thing:
  - Managers are motivated by the idea of quality.
  - The idea of quality motivates managers.

  The active verb "motivates" is stronger and shorter than the passive verb "are motivated by." The active voice gives your sentences more punch and precision. You can make this type of change with any sentence written in the passive voice.

- Put the action you're talking about in the verb rather than in the noun, again for dynamism. Look at these two sentences:
  - His strategic planning is a reflection of the company's new values.
  - His strategic planning reflects the company's new values.

Instead of using the verb "is" or "are," try to pull the verb out of the noun (or adjective) that follows "is/are."

- Avoid opening your sentences with bland phrases like "It is" and "There are." Starting a sentence with the subject is a good way to ensure that it ends up in the active voice.

- Get into the habit of writing shorter sentences and paragraphs. Short sentences pack a stronger punch than do long, convoluted ones.

Creating Effective Visual Aids

Visual aids can help you illustrate and add impact to the key points in your written materials. Make sure, however, that the pictorial representation of your message is accurate and relevant. Following are guidelines for preparing effective visual aids:

1. Define the function of the visual aid.

2. Prepare samples of the various formats (tables, graphs, or charts) to determine which one would most effectively support your written document.

3. Determine the general message you want to convey with the visual aid, then jot down the specific key points to be addressed.

4. Develop the visual aid, referring to your notes to ensure accuracy and consistency.

5. Ask your manager or a skilled colleague to evaluate the usefulness and accuracy of your visual aid before you add it to your document.

6. Solicit feedback on your visual aid and ask for suggestions on how you might improve it.

Avoiding Miscommunication in Written Documents

Communication problems that result from written documents can serve a useful purpose. They can enable the writer to identify and correct errors and be more concise in the future. When you learn that one of your written pieces has missed its mark, follow this procedure:

1. Ask the recipient of the document to summarize its message, as he or she perceived it.

2. Determine the reason for the miscommunication by asking yourself the following questions:

   - Was insufficient information communicated?

- Was inaccurate information communicated?

- Was unnecessary detail included?

- Did the reader simply misinterpret the message?

3. After evaluating a number of your written materials, pinpoint any problem areas. Devote special attention to reducing errors in these areas in the future.

Reducing Procrastination When Writing Reports

Many people put off writing the first draft of a report because they have a difficult time deciding where to start. If you're one of these people, the following guidelines will give you some suggestions for getting started:

1. Begin by relaxing. Think about the topic at hand in a free association kind of way. Brainstorm and generate as many ideas as possible about the subject. Don't judge your thoughts or worry about organization at this step. Instead, simply jot down each of your ideas on a piece of paper.

2. Review your brainstorming list, looking for key ideas and topics that support or relate to your report's purpose. Identify the major ideas, then group the subpoints under those headings.

3. Using these major ideas, create a general outline. An outline can help you organize your ideas and structure your reports. Make sure that each section flows logically to the next; if necessary, add topics and ideas that improve the flow.

4. Using your outline, write your first draft by developing and expanding upon the ideas and topics you identified in the preceding step. Avoid "censoring" your writing during this step. Instead, capitalize on the momentum you have built in the previous steps by keeping your pen or pencil in motion.

5. Once you have completed this part of your draft, write an introduction and conclusion, both of which summarize the material you have covered.

Reviewing the Written Work of Others

Some managers tend to avoid giving employees specific feedback, both positive and negative, on their written work. Yet this feedback is essential for improving another's writing skills. Use the following guidelines to edit, review, and give feedback on the written work of others:

- Be positive and encouraging when editing a report or document. Be critical, but don't miss opportunities to give positive feedback.

- Before reviewing and editing the work of others, ask yourself these questions:
  - What should I be most concerned with — content, structure, or both? Big picture, details, or both? Creativity? Correct format?
  - At what level of expertise should this document be presented?

- Check your content questions with the original writer before modifying or editing the document. You may be making unnecessary or incorrect changes.

- Take a course on editing and text revision to improve your ability to pick up grammatical and structural mistakes in the work of others, as well as to improve your own writing.

RECOMMENDED READINGS

The publications listed here were selected for their content and suitability to a managerial audience.

The Little English Handbook

Corbett, Edward P. J., and Finkle, Sheryl L., Glenview, IL: HarperCollins, 1994
ISBN: 0-673-99323-X
This handbook is designed to serve as a guide on the basic matters of grammar, style, paraphrasing, punctuation, and mechanics of written prose. It addresses the most common and persistent problems encountered in the writing process. The book is well organized and annotated, and includes samples of letters, a resume, and a research paper.

The Business Grammar Handbook

Pancoast, Scott R., and White, Lance M., New York: Evans and Company, 1992
ISBN: 0-87131-709-5
Good writing skills are essential to success in business and as the authors emphasize, good grammar is a key element to quality writing. This handbook focuses on problems commonly found in business communication and shows how to correct them.

Persuasive Business Proposals

Sant, Tom, New York: AMACOM, 1992
ISBN: 0-8144-5100-4
The author begins with the basics by defining a proposal and the four essential elements of persuasion: Source, Message, Channel, and Receiver. Then he details the step-by-step process of writing winning proposals. Also included are hazards to avoid and concrete examples.

The Basics of Business Writing

Stuckey, Marty, New York: AMACOM, 1992
ISBN: 0-8144-7792-5
This book includes a system for breaking writing into manageable steps, instructions for organizing and refining business writings, and a four-step process for overcoming writer's block. It also includes discussions on grammar, punctuation, and commonly misspelled words, as well as examples of business writing formats.

The Perfect Memo!

Westheimer, Patricia H., Indianapolis: JIST Works, 1994
ISBN: 1-57112-064-5
Using "before" and "after" memos based on actual writing samples, the author shows how to dramatically improve in-house correspondence and how to use it to influence.

SUGGESTED SEMINARS

The seminars listed here were selected for their appeal to a managerial audience. The reputation of the vendor, the quality of their seminar offerings, and the specific seminar content were considered in the selection process.

Because of the dynamic nature of the seminar marketplace, some seminars may have been upgraded or replaced, and others may no longer be offered. Likewise, costs and locations may have changed since this listing was compiled. We recommend that you contact the vendor directly for updated and additional information.

Business Writing: When English is a Second Language

This comprehensive workshop is designed to improve the written communication skills of business and technical professionals at all levels who speak English as their second language.
Length: 3 days; Cost: $1,100
Locations: Call vendor
American Management Association
P.O. Box 319, Saranac Lake, NY 12983
Telephone: 800/262-9699

How to Sharpen Your Business Writing Skills

This is a practice-based program for all supervisors, managers, and professionals whose responsibilities involve written communications. Program content includes: how to write in a conversational manner; ways to grab the reader's attention; how to organize your writing; choosing the most effective formats for reports and proposals; and how to write persuasive memos.
Length: 4 days; Cost: $1,260
Locations: Call vendor
American Management Association
P.O. Box 319, Saranac Lake, NY 12983
Telephone: 800/262-9699

Effective Business Writing

This seminar is designed to help professionals who regularly write proposals, reports, or memos to become proficient in written communication. The seminar teaches participants the techniques necessary to express themselves clearly, concisely, and persuasively, and to organize their thoughts to their readers' frame of reference.
Length: 2 days; Cost: $650
Location: New York
Arthur Andersen & Company
1345 Avenue of the Americas, New York, NY 10105
Telephone: 212/708-8080

Write to the Top: Writing for Corporate Success	A practical, learn-by-doing seminar that offers techniques for improving writing speed and impact through a combination of individual attention, short lectures, individual and group exercises, and discussions. Length: 2 days; Cost: $495 Location: Lexington, MA **Better Communications** **1666 Massachusetts Ave., Suite 14, Lexington, MA 02173** **Telephone: 800/878-5440**
Speaking On Paper	This program has two objectives: to improve the organization, clarity, and tone of your memos, letters, and reports; and to enable you to write more efficiently and effectively. Length: 1 day; Cost: $450 Locations: Call vendor **Communispond, Inc.** **300 Park Avenue, 22nd Floor, New York, NY 10022** **Telephone: 212/486-2300**
Effective Reports, Proposals, and Memos	In this program, key concepts of the information mapping method are outlined. A proven approach to organizing information, refining your analysis and content, and applying the method back on the job are a few of the major topics discussed. Length: 2 days; Cost: $1,025 Locations: Call vendor **Information Mapping, Inc.** **300 Third Avenue, Waltham, MA 02154** **Telephone: 617/890-7003**
Persuasive Business Writing	Participants in this seminar will learn to: communicate concisely, clearly, and correctly; organize their ideas to achieve the greatest impact; edit for the most effective style and tone; and approach any writing task with confidence. Length: 2 days; Cost: $700 Location: Houston **Rice University** **Jesse H. Jones Graduate School of Administration** **Office of Executive Development, P.O. Box 1892** **Houston, TX 77251-1892** **Telephone: 713/527-6060**

INTERPERSONAL SKILLS

INTERPERSONAL SKILLS

Today's successful, respected manager knows that "people" skills are critically important business skills for a manager. By forming give-and-take relationships in which you strive to enhance understanding and mutual respect, acknowledge the needs and feelings of others, focus on the positive aspects of conflict, and see differences of others as necessary for building an effective team, you can create a healthy environment for productivity. In addition, you can foster personal and professional growth in colleagues, direct reports, bosses, and yourself.

This chapter presents suggestions for improving your interpersonal skills in the following major areas:

Build Relationships: Relates to people in an open, friendly, accepting manner; shows sincere interest in others and their concerns; initiates and develops relationships with others as a key priority.

Display Organizational Savvy: Develops effective give-and-take relationships with others; understands the agendas and perspectives of others; recognizes and effectively balances the interests and needs of one's own group with those of the broader organization.

Leverage Networks: Identifies and cultivates relationships with key stakeholders representing a broad range of functions and levels; uses informal networks to get things done; builds strong external networks with people in the industry or profession.

Value Diversity: Shows and fosters respect and appreciation for each person whatever that person's background, race, age, gender, disability, values, lifestyle, perspectives, or interests; seeks to understand the worldview of others; sees differences in people as opportunities for learning about and approaching things differently.

Manage Disagreements: Brings substantive conflicts and disagreements into the open and attempts to resolve them collaboratively; builds consensus.

BUILD RELATIONSHIPS

Being an expert in the technical aspects of management (delegating, planning, organizing, and so forth) is essential in order to keep things running smoothly. But building solid relationships with others in the organization is also critical, because, as a manager, you must rely on others to support you in achieving goals. The more you commit to developing and maintaining respectful, productive relationships with others, the larger the payoff in terms of motivation, commitment, and support.

To help you build more effective relationships, this section focuses on three primary areas:

Part 1: Improving Social Skills

- Obtaining Feedback on Your Interpersonal Style
- Reducing Tendencies to Dominate
- Becoming More Relaxed and Open
- Reducing Sarcasm
- Increasing Tolerance for Differing Points of View
- Increasing Your Sociability
- Experimenting with New Social Roles
- Making Small Talk

Part 2: Building Relationships

- Treating People with Respect
- Treating People Fairly
- Becoming More Approachable
- Developing Effective Working Relationships with Your Employees
- Taking a Personal Interest in Your People
- Developing Effective Working Relationships with Peers
- Communicating with Colleagues in Other Departments
- Considering People's Feelings When Making Decisions
- Adopting a More Accepting View of Others
- Increasing the Quality of Relationships

Part 3: Developing and Maintaining a Strong Relationship with Your Manager

- Developing an Effective Working Relationship
- Minimizing Defensiveness in Interactions
- Voicing Disagreement with Your Manager
- Increasing Feedback from Your Manager
- Giving Feedback to Your Manager

Valuable Tips

- Be less judgmental and evaluative in your day-to-day dealings with people.

- Check your common courtesies to others; for example, do you greet people in the morning, say "hello" in the halls, and say "thank you"?

- Listen to the input of your family and close friends. They often have insights about your style and personality that others may not share as openly.

- Apologize to people when you have hurt or ignored them.

- Focus on people's good qualities rather than on their deficiencies.

- Be aware of times when coworkers are hurting in their personal lives — death, illness, divorce, and so forth — and express your interest and concern in words, by a visit, or with a gift of flowers.

- Smile more!

- If you have taken some of your staff for granted, take the time to talk to them, take them to lunch, or otherwise extend yourself.

- Plan an occasional social event with coworkers, such as golf or a picnic. Get to know them outside of the workplace.

- Keep a calendar of birthdays, hire dates, and so forth, and recognize people on significant dates, either verbally or by sending cards or notes.

- Seek feedback from people you trust about your personal impact.

- When dealing with people, try out different strategies depending on the situation and the people involved.

- Learn about others by asking them about their interests.

- Learn to be less abrasive and tactless in your interpersonal relations by confronting the *issue* instead of the *person*.

- Work to become less sarcastic by having a trusted friend give you feedback whenever he or she hears you being sarcastic.

- Be more friendly, positive, and optimistic when you meet someone for the first time.

- Ask others directly how things are going for them.

- Make sure you are not giving off signals of manipulation or in other ways creating a climate of mistrust around you. In particular, don't use information unfairly to gain advantage.

- Try "management by walking around." For instance, get out into the work area and see what is going on. Do this frequently.

- Don't allow yourself to become so busy or self-centered that you fail to notice the needs and concerns of others.

- Look for small opportunities to build acquaintances with coworkers — coffee, lunch, and so forth.

- Ask if you can help when you see a colleague "in a bind" on a project or assignment.

- Compliment your coworkers for comments, ideas, or successes that you appreciate.

- Seek feedback from your manager regarding instances when you may have reacted without considering others' feelings.

- Seek feedback from your manager and trusted peers about situations when your behavior comes across as too self-serving.

PART 1

Obtaining Feedback on Your Interpersonal Style

Improving Social Skills

To improve your relationships with others, you must see yourself as others see you. But you may get little feedback about how others see you. As managers move higher and higher in organizations, they often receive less and less feedback. You may want to set up two or three situations in which you can solicit feedback on a regular basis. Following are suggestions for accomplishing this:

- Ask a respected colleague or manager with whom you regularly interact in one-to-one and group situations to serve as a feedback source. Ask for the person's impressions of your style and impact in a variety of situations.

- When conducting performance appraisal interviews, encourage an exchange of information by asking employees for feedback on your interpersonal style.

- Seek feedback from others on the behaviors you are trying to change. If possible, tape several discussions and review them with someone in a position to give you objective feedback. That person's feedback can help you determine which areas need improvement. An alternative is to obtain feedback on your interpersonal style using a "360-degree" feedback instrument available through Personnel Decisions International.

Reducing Tendencies to Dominate

At times, a person's enthusiasm about his or her ideas, or the desire to ensure that those ideas are heard and accepted, can be carried to the point where others feel that the person is abrasive, overbearing, or domineering.

To determine if you dominate discussions, either intentionally or unintentionally, answer the following questions after each of the next few discussions in which you participate.

EVALUATION CHECKLIST *(Circle the appropriate response.)*

Did you interrupt frequently to interject your opinions?	**Yes/No**
Did you restate your opinions often?	**Yes/No**
Were you very forceful in stating your opinions?	**Yes/No**

Did you speak often, thereby preventing others from having equal discussion time? **Yes/No**

Were you highly critical of the opinions of others? **Yes/No**

If you answered "yes" to any of these questions, consider the following suggestions when participating in future discussions:

- Make an effort to eliminate interruptions.

- Set a limit on the number of times you will voice the same opinion. For example, decide that you will restate your opinion only if it is apparent that the group did not hear or understand it the first time, or if you are asked to restate it.

- Present your viewpoints in less dogmatic or domineering ways. Use "I think" or "in my opinion," rather than global pronouncements, such as "obviously…" or "everyone knows…"

- Become aware of the proportion of discussion time you use; become sensitive to signals from others that they would like to speak.

- Refrain from immediate judgment and criticism of others' ideas. If criticism is required, deliver it in a way that demonstrates sensitivity to the feelings of others.

- Ask open-ended questions that encourage others to give their points of view.

In time, you will find that valuing others' contributions will increase your acceptance by the group and make others more willing to consider your ideas.

Becoming More Relaxed and Open

It's easier to work with people if they feel that you are comfortable with them. If you create an initial impression of extreme seriousness or intensity, people may be hesitant to open up and establish in-depth communication with you. Practice the following three steps to give the impression that you are relaxed and open in the presence of others:

1. When you are meeting someone for the first time, be quick to greet them, stand up, and shake hands.

2. Smile warmly at the person you are meeting.

3. Make small talk and use light humor in your initial conversation.

You may feel more comfortable practicing these behaviors in informal settings at first. Then seek out work-related group situations, such as meetings and conferences, in which you can practice letting down some of your interpersonal guardedness.

Reducing Sarcasm

Humor can be a lifesaver, especially in stressful situations. Sarcasm, however, can hurt and alienate people. It may even cause you to lose the support of others. The following guidelines can help you reduce your use of inappropriate or potentially hurtful sarcasm:

1. Identify those occasions in which you use sarcasm in a way that may offend others. Analyze the way in which you used your wit. Determine whether there were any instances in which your use of humor may have hurt others.

2. If you notice a pattern of sarcasm, work to change this behavior. In each situation, analyze the personalities of the people present to determine the appropriate use of humor.

3. Remind yourself that your goal is to retain your sense of humor while eliminating any tendencies to insult or hurt others.

Continue this development program until you feel comfortable with your use of humor.

Increasing Tolerance for Differing Points of View

When you feel strongly about an issue, it can be difficult to consider others' viewpoints objectively. Yet it's important to recognize others' contributions and to realize that their viewpoints are just as important to them as yours are to you. If you have difficulty acknowledging and accepting others' ideas, try the following exercise to increase your tolerance:

1. Ask a trusted coworker or supervisor to help you identify any patterns of rigid or intolerant behavior. Together, examine the probable effect of your words and actions on others. It's important that you remain as open and nondefensive as possible during these reviews.

2. With your "coach," analyze how others may have felt. Did they become angry, hurt, or obstinate? What made them feel that way, and what can you do in the future to minimize such negative reactions? Consider alternate approaches to these situations.

3. Consider role-playing each situation — having your coach play the role of the "injured party" while you experiment with more tolerant approaches. Ask for your coach's response to your new approaches.

4. When you are comfortable with your new style, apply it in work situations. With practice, you will develop a more objective, less judgmental attitude concerning others' viewpoints.

Increasing Your Sociability

The ability to meet new people and feel comfortable in social situations can be important to career advancement. If you have difficulty in social situations, you may want to develop your social skills. The following suggestions can help:

- Over the next month, set goals to take the initiative in forming social contacts, particularly in informal settings. For example, you might set goals related to speaking up more often, attending more social events, or meeting new people at these functions. Make an effort to become more involved.

- Broaden your circle of acquaintances. Introduce yourself to people you have wanted to meet but were too busy or too shy to talk to. Consider setting a goal to become acquainted with a certain number of people per week.

- Learn more about each of your acquaintances' interests. This is especially helpful if you have difficulty thinking of things to talk about; other people's interests often provide excellent opportunities for small talk.

Don't expect to become comfortable in social situations immediately; changes like this don't happen overnight. As time passes, however, you will find that you are beginning to enjoy social situations more and that they have become less threatening.

Experimenting with New Social Roles

Experimenting with new social behaviors can be difficult in work settings, yet practice is important. To gain practice in nonthreatening situations, consider the following suggestions:

- Take an active role in a selected civic or community service activity. This type of volunteer activity allows you to work with new people under minimal pressure. Plus, you don't have to worry about the effects of your behavior or actions on your long-term career growth.

- Set specific goals for each type of behavior you plan to try. Keep a record of new behaviors, your initial reactions to them, and your feelings about your progress over time.

As you become comfortable with your new behaviors, begin to practice them in the work setting.

Making Small Talk

Your ability to engage in small talk can help others feel more comfortable and can help establish cooperative relationships. Many people find it difficult to make small talk — to find something to say to people they don't know very well. Following are two simple methods for overcoming this problem:

- Listen for "free" information. Listen to people talk and notice the hints they give about their interests, likes, and dislikes. For example, in a casual conversation about the weather, people might mention that they can't wait to get home to the garden or out on the lake. You've learned two topics of interest to those people — gardening and boating.

  To practice using free information, follow these guidelines:
  - Over the next week, listen to a variety of conversations and note the information people give that could be used as a lead-in to small talk.
  - Use this information to formulate questions. For example, if a person mentioned that it's a great day for golf, you could find out about his or her interest in the game by asking such questions as, "How long have you played?" and "Do you play often?" You may want to practice this skill with a friend. Ask the friend to make a comment and then respond with a question.
  - Take care not to ask too many questions in rapid succession. Once you have asked some questions, reveal some information about yourself. Mention how you feel about the subject or offer some free information about your own interests.

- Prepare topics for discussion. Read through the newspaper or news magazines, or watch the news on television. Prepare a few opening and follow-up comments that you could use in making small talk. Practice including these comments in your conversations with others.

Remember that small talk does not have to be about personal interests. It can be about business as well.

Practice these methods for several weeks. You will probably feel awkward in the beginning, but as time passes, you will become increasingly comfortable asking questions of others, revealing information about yourself, and discussing current events.

PART 2

Treating People with Respect

Building Relationships

In their book *Leaders: The Strategies for Taking Charge*, Warren Bennis and Burt Nanus suggest that before managers can treat others with dignity and self-respect, they must possess or develop positive self-regard. To achieve positive self-regard, they say:

- Recognize your strengths and compensate for your weaknesses.

- Continue to work and develop your skills and talents.

- Learn to discern the fit between your strengths and weaknesses and your organizational needs.

Bennis and Nanus observed that once managers develop positive self-regard, they demonstrate positive "other-regard." Here are some guidelines to consider:

- Accept people as they are, not as you would like them to be. Try to understand what other people are like on their own terms.

- Treat those you are close to with the same courteous attention that you extend to strangers and acquaintances.

- Give people the benefit of the doubt.

- Be objective and nonevaluative in your day-to-day dealings with people.

- Confront issues, not people.

- Minimize sarcasm. Be aware of instances in which you might be perceived as insensitive.

- Foster an environment of openness and trust.

- Allow people to save face.

Treating People Fairly

Treating people fairly involves a wide range of behaviors — from the amount of work assigned and opportunities given that can be perceived as favoritism, to attempts to "help" people that can be perceived as discriminatory, to decisions that can be confusing and interpreted as unfair if others don't know the rationale behind them.

It is important to assign work equitably so your employees feel that you are treating them fairly. Equity does not mean equality; rather, it means using the same criteria for each person when assigning projects and tasks. It is appropriate to have better performers assigned to more challenging tasks. To examine your current assignment practices and beliefs:

1. Make a list of each employee's work assignments. Then analyze the distribution of these assignments. Consider the following:

   - The amount of work assigned to each employee. Is it too much or too little when compared with what you give to other employees?

   - The level of the assignments. What is the proportion of challenging work to mundane, or "dirty," work, and how does this ratio compare with that of other employees?

   - The way in which assignments are made. Are some employees allowed to become more involved than others in the decision-making process for assigning work?

2. Ask employees for their opinions of the current distribution of responsibilities, with specific reference to these factors.

3. Make appropriate changes.

4. If people believe they should have more challenging assignments, tell them what they must do to get them.

5. Examine your criteria for making assignments to ensure that you are not treating some people more carefully than others.

Your fair treatment of people goes beyond equitable assignments. It also involves your ability to:

- Avoid pressure to take sides in a dispute between or among employees.

- Give recognition to all who deserve it, especially the "average" performers.

- Monitor your tendency to favor certain employees (such as those with whom you socialize outside of work), and take steps to prevent favoritism.

- Explain the reasons for your decisions. When people understand the rationale behind the decision and feel as if they have been a part of the process, they are more likely to perceive you as being fair.

Becoming More Approachable

Approachable managers are more likely to be informed of both negative and positive information. This is an ideal position because it helps eliminate "surprises." Thus, becoming more approachable can help you manage more smoothly by preventing crises. The following suggestions will help you increase your approachability:

- If employees currently view you as unapproachable, determine what you do to give this impression. Is it that they never see you? Do you appear uninterested in their problems? Do you become angry when informed of problems? Consider switching roles and looking at yourself as your employees see you. Then make changes based on your analysis.

- Establish an open-door policy. This does not mean that you must be available at all times. It means setting aside regular blocks of time for discussing employee concerns and making sure that employees are informed of your new schedule.

- Be accessible. Consider moving closer to your employees' work area — their "turf" — to appear less remote and show your interest in day-to-day operations. Gradually increase the frequency of your informal, drop-in visits with employees. (A drastic change may cause them to think that you are unhappy with their work and want to check up on them.)

- If you invite employees to discuss problems, be prepared to respond nondefensively. A "shoot the messenger" reaction will put you right back where you started, regardless of how much time you set aside for discussions.

Stick with your program once you start it. Insincere attempts to appear approachable may worsen communication instead of improving it. For example, if you establish times when you will be available and then consistently schedule other events at these times, your employees may decide that you are not really interested in communicating with them and may view your efforts as a half-hearted experiment.

Developing Effective Working Relationships with Your Employees

You will enhance your relationships with your employees by showing:

- Sincere interest in them and what is important to them

- Respect for all, even for people with whom you disagree or do not understand

- Simple courtesy: saying "please" and "thank you"

- Respect for employees' ideas and experience by asking for their advice and involvement

- Recognition of their contributions

You can improve your relationships with your employees by soliciting their feedback. Because such a request can lead to awkward or otherwise uncomfortable communication, ask for the feedback in an informal, nonthreatening manner. Also, let employees know that your reason for requesting such information is to improve your working relationships with them. To solicit employees' feedback:

1. Arrange an individual, informal meeting with each employee to discuss your working relationship. Provide as nonthreatening an environment as possible for this meeting. Hold it in "neutral territory" — conference room, cafeteria — not in your office.

2. Ask the employee for comments on things you do that help the working relationship and for suggestions on how you might improve it. Be careful not to dominate the conversation, and try to respond to the employee's remarks in a nondefensive, honest way.

3. Don't promise more than you can deliver; remember, your follow-through will be the key to improving the relationship.

You may wish to explore other ways of soliciting employees' feedback on your relationships with them. Some employees may prefer to give anonymous feedback. Or, you may ask for feedback from a trusted peer who is in a position to observe your relationships with your employees.

Whatever plan or procedure you use to obtain feedback, your aim should be to generate goals for improving your working relationships with your employees. You may want to share your goals with them. After working toward your goals for awhile, go through this feedback solicitation process again to get their impressions of how your relationships with them have changed.

Taking a Personal Interest in Your People

When building a manager-employee relationship, it is often worthwhile to take an interest in employees' personal concerns, as well as their work-oriented concerns. Getting to know your employees' personal concerns will help you understand why they perform as they do and will let them know that you care about them as individuals, which can improve their performance.

Over the next few months, use the following guidelines to demonstrate a personal interest in your employees. However, it's best to take a gradual approach to getting to know your employees; a sudden, intense expression of interest may look like you are prying into their personal lives.

- Take time for informal chats with employees in the hallways or during brief, unscheduled visits. Ask about their personal interests — family, hobbies, goals. Follow up by occasionally inquiring about their current concerns.

- Share some of your personal interests. Employees will feel more comfortable sharing their interests with you if they feel that you are willing to reveal information about yourself.

- Consider arranging occasional social events, such as lunches or department parties, where you can discuss mutual interests other than business.

- If employees wish to discuss personal problems, be willing to listen. Take care, however, not to take on roles for which you may not be professionally trained, such as that of financial or family counselor.

Finally, respect the confidentiality of employees' personal concerns and avoid using shared personal information in a way that employees may see as traitorous. For example, if an employee is late to work, a comment such as, "I know you have small children you must take care of in the morning, but it's essential that you get to work on time," can make the employee regret that he or she opened up to you and reluctant to share personal information in the future.

Developing Effective Working Relationships with Peers

Positive, productive relationships with peers are important to ensure that you get the support, information, and resources you need to do your job well. If you want to improve your peer relationships, you must come across as a team member, not a competitor. This requires that you spend time on the relationship itself, not just on the work to be done. A good way to foster peer relationships is to be attentive to and interested in others. Your interest in them will encourage them to open up to you, volunteer information, and discuss issues. The following procedure is designed to help you initiate this mutual reinforcement:

As you work with your peers over the next week, ask yourself if you're emphasizing your tasks and opinions at the expense of team relationships. Take notes on your behavior and, at the end of the week, write a goal for yourself based on your self-assessment.

To improve relationships with peers:

1. Prepare a list of the peers with whom you work on a regular basis.

2. Using the following scale, rate the quality of your working relationship with each person on that list.

   1 = Work poorly together
   2 = Have an adequate working relationship
   3 = Work reasonably well together (room for improvement)
   4 = Work very well together

3. Identify the barriers or problems in the relationships. Determine what you can do to resolve these issues.

4. Set a date by which you can reasonably accomplish your goal of improving your working relationships with peers.

5. After this date, reevaluate each peer relationship.

As you become more relaxed, less intense, and more attentive to your peer relationships, monitor your peers' new willingness to volunteer information, provide feedback on your ideas and impact, and discuss issues with you. You'll know you're making progress when you start getting feedback from peers who have never offered it in the past.

Communicating with Colleagues in Other Departments

It can be difficult to work effectively with people you don't know well. Therefore, it's important to establish some type of contact with your associates in other units. The following guidelines provide suggestions for getting to know your peers in other units well enough to feel comfortable working with them:

1. Compile a list of employees from other units/departments with whom you have contact.

2. Identify the individuals on that list whom you don't know well.

3. Arrange an introductory meeting with each of these people. A lunch or coffee break would offer the desired relaxed, informal atmosphere.

4. Maintain contact with your peers in other units or departments. Pursue joint interests with them or simply call them periodically to stay in touch.

5. Update your list of contacts on a regular basis — say, every few months. As time permits, arrange informal get-togethers with these new colleagues, as well as with those whom you've already met.

Considering People's Feelings When Making Decisions

When a decision has the potential to affect a number of people, it is important that you consult with those involved to ensure that all needs are out on the table. While you may not be able to accommodate everyone's needs, consulting others will help you demonstrate concern and enhance others' commitment to your decisions. Use the following technique to involve others in decisions:

1. Allow enough time to gather input from those affected by the decision.

2. Solicit concerns, but also ideas for solutions, from others. As much as possible, incorporate reasonable solutions into your final decision.

3. If you can't accommodate some needs, let the people affected know why and be prepared to use active listening to deal with their reactions. Refer to the Listen to Others section for suggestions on developing your active listening skills.

4. Offer to further discuss people's reactions to your final decision.

Adopting a More Accepting View of Others

Tolerance of others requires insight into their strengths and weaknesses. This insight enables you to respond to both their "good" and "bad" points. Follow these tips for developing a more accepting view of individuals who "rub you the wrong way":

1. Identify two or three people with whom you find it difficult to work.

2. Over the next few weeks, concentrate on the positive aspects of working with them.

    *   List at least five positive characteristics of each individual.

    *   As you observe each person, be alert to what others see as his or her positive traits — the qualities that make that person likeable to his or her associates and friends.

3. Whenever you work with these individuals, concentrate on the strengths you've identified. Give compliments on the strong points, when appropriate. As you learn to focus on and appreciate their strengths, you will find yourself more tolerant of their weaknesses. Eventually, you'll find it easier to overlook the qualities that once made it difficult for you to work with these individuals.

Increasing the Quality of Relationships

The "winning by intimidation" style of interaction holds few benefits for anyone and almost always produces a hostile, uncooperative environment. The following guidelines are provided to help you pave the way for a cooperative work environment by increasing the amount of positive reinforcement you give to others. The accompanying chart can help you structure your information.

1. Over the next three weeks, keep track of the number of times you give positive feedback to other people. Also monitor the number of positive comments you get from others on your accomplishments.

2. Increase the number of positive comments you make to others.

   - Whenever you can honestly give others positive feedback for their good work, do so. Be especially careful to reinforce any actions that have positively affected you or your work area.

   - Set a goal to make a specific number of positive, rewarding comments each week to each colleague. (Pace yourself; don't make them all on Friday!)

3. Keep track of how many reinforcing comments you get in return and notice whether that number increases as your positive comments increase.

Individual's Name	Number of Positive Comments Given	Number of Positive Comments Received	Positive Feedback Goal	Reinforcing Comments Received in Return

Look for chances to work on projects where cooperative efforts are likely to result in win/win outcomes, which benefit everyone involved. Shared successes build relationships.

PART 3

Developing an Effective Working Relationship

Developing and Maintaining a Strong Relationship with Your Manager

The key to developing an effective working relationship with your manager involves understanding his or her style, strengths, and weaknesses; placing a high priority on helping the team be successful; treating your manager with respect; and showing commitment to a good relationship. The following suggestions can help you build a stronger relationship with your manager:

- Find out what your manager's professional and personal goals are, and help him or her to be successful in achieving them.

- Identify your manager's strengths and weaknesses, and use your skills to complement his or her skills.

- Be aware of style issues, such as the following, and work with them:
  - Does your manager want to hear about ideas in writing or in person first?
  - When is your manager most likely to be open to informal conversation? Before 8:00 a.m., after 5:00 p.m., at lunch time?
  - What does your manager want to know about?
  - How open does he or she want dialogue to be?
  - What will get you into trouble?

- If your manager is a big-picture person, present an overview of the problem rather than stating the small details of the problem.

- If your manager sees limited options, give specific alternatives without being insulting.

- Show concern and interest in your manager if he or she values that approach.

- Be open, direct, and respectful.

Minimizing Defensiveness in Interactions

Defensiveness (the tendency to be protective when others give us feedback) is an obstacle to be reckoned with in almost all instances of interpersonal communication. It's an especially difficult barrier when it affects your ability to open yourself up to your manager and accept helpful feedback. When you receive negative feedback:

1. Thank the person for the feedback.

2. Paraphrase the feedback so that he or she knows that you heard it and understand its importance.

3. Say what you think about the feedback. Discuss your point of view.

4. Come to an agreement about what you will do.

Learning to think of negative feedback as suggestions for dealing with particular situations — rather than as personal criticism — will increase your effectiveness and make you open to receiving valuable information. The guidelines that follow can help you learn how to use your manager's feedback to your advantage:

- Make an effort to check your response patterns for phrases like "Yes, but . . ." and eliminate them from your speech. Whenever you catch yourself assuming this defensive posture, stop talking and listen rather than justify.

- When you are feeling defensive, stop and ask yourself a fixed set of rational/analytical questions, such as the following, to help diminish your defensiveness:
  - Do I understand exactly what is being said?
  - Is the criticism about a topic or behavior I could do something about if I wanted to?
  - What would happen if I acted on the feedback?

- Act on the advice given. If your manager simply made a judgment, ask for coaching. Devise a plan and timetable for implementing his or her suggestions.

- Think of other times when people's advice helped you improve your work performance. When the advice included criticism, did the benefits of your improvement outweigh the unpleasantness of the criticism?

- Ask for time to think about the feedback before you respond. Consider the feedback rationally before you prepare a response.

As your resistance to criticism diminishes, you will come to think of it less as a sign of defeat than as a tool for improving your interactions with others.

Voicing Disagreement with Your Manager

Many people find disagreeing with their manager to be an unpleasant and difficult part of their jobs. If you are hesitant to express disagreement with your manager or to deliver "bad news," follow these guidelines for developing a plan to voice disagreement in a confident, straightforward manner:

1. Talk with your manager about how disagreement between the two of you, in general, can best be handled.

2. Before approaching your manager with a topic that may produce disagreement, think through your reasons for your position. Be prepared to state them logically and calmly during the discussion. Think of ways to resist becoming defensive about your position or quickly deferring to your manager's position. Vividly picture the scene in your mind, imagining both your manager's expression of his or her opinion and your statement of your case. Doing this can help you take a more positive, unwavering stand during the actual discussion.

3. Acknowledge your understanding of your manager's point of view.

4. Instead of criticizing your manager's point of view, state your own.

5. Work out the differences collaboratively when possible.

6. If your manager does not agree with your point of view, recognize when to stop trying to convince him or her. A "graceful withdrawal" is helpful. If you are "right," it will likely become obvious over time.

Increasing Feedback from Your Manager

Your manager is a valuable source of the feedback you need for self-improvement. Unfortunately, many people's fear of criticism causes them to miss opportunities to receive their manager's evaluation. The following guidelines can help you actively seek feedback:

1. Select an area in which you feel you need improvement — preferably, one in which you've received criticism in the past.

2. Prepare a plan for increasing your proficiency in that area. Sources of information include readings in the area of skill development, and friends and colleagues who are reasonably familiar with your work skills and habits.

3. Present your plan to your manager, informing him or her that you will be devoting time to it over the next month. Ask for

comments or suggestions on the plan, and request feedback on the area which you're trying to improve.

4. At the end of the month, review your progress with your manager. Show your appreciation for his or her input by pointing to specific outcomes that resulted from it.

Giving Feedback to Your Manager

The most satisfying relationships are built on two-way communication. Therefore, giving feedback to your manager — both positive and negative — is an important skill to develop. Most managers want to hear positive feedback; however, it's more difficult for some managers to hear negative feedback.

To give feedback to your manager:

1. Determine the risks of giving feedback. Recall what happened in the past when you or others gave feedback to your manager. Also consider the consequences if you do not give the feedback.

2. Think about the type of feedback that has been effective in the past.

3. Ask your manager if he or she is willing to hear some feedback.

4. Whenever possible, state the feedback in positive, objective terms: describe the situation, your manager's behavior, and the impact the behavior had on you. Avoid using inflammatory language or assigning motives.

5. Express your feelings, especially the more vulnerable ones, such as feeling hurt, ignored, not respected, and so forth.

6. Actively listen to your manager's response.

7. Specify what you want when you are asking for a behavior change.

8. Thank your manager for listening to the feedback.

RECOMMENDED READINGS

The publications listed here were selected for their content and suitability to a managerial audience.

People Smarts

Alessandra, Tony, and O'Conner, Michael J., San Diego: Pfeiffer & Company, 1994
ISBN: 0-89384-421-7
The authors introduce the "platinum rule": treat others the way they want to be treated and both parties win. Since everyone is unique, your goal is to adapt your approach to meet the different needs and priorities of the people you deal with. This book is helpful in identifying behavioral styles and learning how to adjust your behavior to increase trust, credibility, and cooperation.

The Human Touch

Arnold, William W., and Plas, Jeanne M., New York: John Wiley & Sons, 1993
ISBN: 0-471-57291-8
Arnold, the president of a leading medical center, stresses the crucial role of each individual in the organization and uses basic values, common sense, accessibility, and respect to increase productivity and profits. His account of providing person-centered leadership shows how to combine tough performance standards with the courage to be human.

Leaders: The Strategies for Taking Charge

Bennis, Warren, and Nanus, Bert, New York: Harper & Row, 1986
ISBN: 0-06-091336-3
The authors describe the essential qualities of effective leadership, addressing how to empower employees, incorporate creativity and innovation, communicate effectively, and create a vision.

Stewardship: Choosing Service Over Self-Interest

Block, Peter, San Francisco: Berrett-Koehler, 1993
ISBN: 1-881052-28-1
Block advocates replacing the traditional management tools of control and consistency with partnership and choice at all levels for employees as well as customers. His book is a practical resource to guiding your organization through a redistribution of power.

Influence Without Authority	**Cohen, Allan R., and Bradford, David F.,** New York: John Wiley & Sons, 1991 ISBN: 0-471-54894-4 The authors present a very readable, practical method for creating change and partnership in contemporary organizations. Their book demonstrates how to skillfully form mutually advantageous relationships.
Human Relations in Organizations (5th ed.)	**Costley, Dan L., and Todd, Ralph,** St. Paul: West Publishing, 1993 ISBN: 0-314-02689-4 This book focuses on the behavior of individuals in organizations. Its emphasis is on the skills needed for effective leadership including the abilities to communicate, understand human needs, cope with conflict and frustration, motivate others, use authority, and increase group productivity.
Conversationally Speaking	**Garner, Alan,** Los Angeles: Lowell House, 1991 ISBN: 0-929923-72-3 Garner's practical, concise book outlines strategies that teach the reader to start conversations, ask the kinds of questions that promote conversation, avoid behavior that invites rejection, issue invitations that are likely to be accepted, achieve deeper levels of understanding, handle criticism constructively, resist manipulation, become more confident in social situations, and listen so that others will be encouraged to talk.
Beyond the Trust Gap	**Horton, Thomas R., and Reid, Peter C.,** Burr Ridge, IL: Irwin Professional Publishing, 1991 ISBN: 1-55623-269-1 The authors suggest that downsizings, mergers, and acquisitions have ruptured relations between managers and their employees and created a "trust gap." This book offers guidelines for regaining credibility with middle managers in order to develop the speed and productivity needed to succeed in the competitive world economy.

Making Organizations Competitive

Kilmann, Ralph H., Kilmann, Ines, and Associates, San Francisco: Jossey-Bass, 1990
ISBN: 1-55542-285-3
This book shows how managers can make their organizations more responsive, creative, and flexible by building strong strategic alliances among groups that traditionally have not seen each other as partners. The authors offer practical techniques for coordinating competitive policies among diverse functions within an organization, establishing collaborative relationships with outside companies, and forging productive relationships between groups that have traditionally been adversarial.

The Clash of Cultures: Managers Managing Professionals

Raelin, Joseph A., New York: McGraw-Hill, 1992
ISBN: 0-07-103316-5
This book examines the relationships between managers and professionals such as engineers, nurses, doctors, lawyers, teachers, accountants, and so forth. The author contends that standard management practices are no longer sufficient when working with professionals. Specific techniques and methods for minimizing and managing conflict between professionals and corporate managers are provided.

SUGGESTED SEMINARS

The seminars listed here were selected for their appeal to a managerial audience. The reputation of the vendor, the quality of their seminar offerings, and the specific seminar content were considered in the selection process.

Because of the dynamic nature of the seminar marketplace, some seminars may have been upgraded or replaced, and others may no longer be offered. Likewise, costs and locations may have changed since this listing was compiled. We recommend that you contact the vendor directly for updated and additional information.

Working With Others

Participants in this workshop learn three critical areas of management: gaining peak performance from workers, leading work groups, and handling interpersonal relationships.
Length: 4 days; Cost: CD $1,775 + GST
Location: Niagara-on-the-Lake, Ontario, Canada
Center for Creative Leadership
One Leadership Place, P.O. Box 26300
Greensboro, NC 27438-6300
Telephone: 910/545-2810

Emerging Leaders

This program, designed for current and future leaders, addresses the evaluation, building, and sustaining of leadership excellence. Participants will assess and develop their leadership excellence with regard to four areas: personal, people, business, and work.
Length: 5 days; Cost: Call vendor
Location: Call vendor
Personnel Decisions International
2000 Plaza VII Tower, 45 South Seventh Street
Minneapolis, MN 55402-1608
Telephone: 800/633-4410

Individual Coaching Services

This customized coaching program helps people develop critical skills such as leadership, interpersonal, communication, and organizational influence skills. Through a tailored assessment to diagnose developmental needs, one-on-one skills training, and state-of-the-art techniques for behavior change, participants gain powerful self-insight and successfully learn new skills and behaviors to make them stronger performers.
Length: Call vendor; Cost: Call vendor
Locations: Call vendor
Personnel Decisions International
2000 Plaza VII Tower, 45 South Seventh Street
Minneapolis, MN 55402-1608
Telephone: 800/633-4410

Leadership Through People Skills

This seminar is designed to teach participants the practical skills it takes to become leader-managers, turn vision into reality, empower people with the freedom to act competently and confidently, and manage in all directions — upward with the boss, laterally with coworkers, and downward with direct reports.
Length: 3 1/2 days; Cost: $1,245
Location: St. Louis
Psychological Associates, Inc.
8201 Maryland Avenue, St. Louis, MO 63105
Telephone: 800/345-6525

People Styles

This seminar provides methods for analyzing work relationships through the social styles concept and offers specific skills that decrease interpersonal tension.
Length: 2 days; Cost: $750
Locations: Cazenovia, NY; San Francisco
Ridge Associates, Inc.
5 Ledyard Avenue, Cazenovia, NY 13035
Telephone: 315/655-3393

Trust and Teamwork

This seminar teaches specific skills necessary to bring compassion and accountability to the workplace. Experiential in nature, the program focuses on creating a more collaborative, open, and trusting work environment. Participants will examine their own communication styles, learn to manage their credibility, create collaboration, and learn constructive confrontation skills.
Length: 2 days; Cost: $595
Locations: Call vendor
The Atlanta Consulting Group
1600 Parkwood Circle, Suite 200, Atlanta, GA 30339
Telephone: 800/852-8224

How to Work More Effectively With People

This workshop is designed to teach managers how to develop positive relationships; why self-esteem and self-confidence are such important elements in human motivation and performance; and how to tune in to the needs of others. Participants also learn to understand and manage frustration, defensiveness, anger, hostility, and insensitivity in themselves and others.
Length: 2 days; Cost: $695
Location: Madison, WI
University of Wisconsin-Madison
Management Institute, Grainger Hall
975 University Avenue, Madison, WI 53706-1323
Telephone: 800/348-8964

DISPLAY ORGANIZATIONAL SAVVY

In an organizational context, the term savvy means understanding the structure, politics, and personalities involved in the organization and being able to exercise this knowledge in practical and productive ways.

Managers display organizational savvy in a variety of ways. Included in this repertoire of "savvy skills" are the abilities to:

- Understand the agendas and perspectives of others to establish mutually beneficial objectives.

- Recognize which battles are worth fighting and when it is time to compromise.

- Effectively balance personal needs — and those of one's group — with the needs of the broader organization.

- Develop effective give-and-take relationships with key individuals in the organization, both vertically and laterally.

- Be seen as committed to the organization and the people in it, rather than out for oneself.

Knowing how your organization operates is essential to the development of organizational savvy. The Organizational Knowledge chapter of this Handbook provides suggestions for developing a deeper understanding of how your organization is run.

The information and guidelines presented in this two-part section are designed to help you develop both organizational and personal savvy.

Part 1: Developing Organizational Savvy

- Involving the Right People at the Right Time
- Achieving Results through Formal and Informal Channels
- Fostering Effective Give-and-Take Relationships
- Understanding the Perspectives and Agendas of Others
- Knowing When to "Fight" and When to Compromise

Part 2: Developing Personal Savvy

- Knowing When to Lead and When to Follow
- Anticipating Others' Reactions or Positions Accurately
- Developing Timing
- Committing Oneself to the Organization

Valuable Tips

- Remember, "The right message at the wrong time is the wrong message."

- Compare a list of the organization's priorities with a list of your group's objectives. Keep objectives that are related to organizational priorities at the top of your "To accomplish" list, and try to eliminate objectives that are not related to organizational priorities.

- Identify a peer or a higher-level manager who is effective at involving others, observe his or her methods, and adopt them if possible.

- Exclude disruptive or unsupportive people from your projects by offering tactful ways for these people to "bow out."

- Seek out a resident "expert" to act as your mentor. This person can describe the formal rules of the company, and introduce you to the informal network as well.

- Maintain a policy of "no surprises" by relating both the good and the bad news to your manager or others who need to know.

- Keep key players informed of your project's status.

- Recognize that your peers can be valuable resources.

- Strengthen your personal allegiance to coworkers at all levels of your organization by treating them with respect and consideration.

- When you think that you may have to compromise on your agenda, classify your issues into "can drop," "nice to have," and "must have" categories. This will give you some flexibility for negotiation.

- Make a list of the resources you can offer to others; then, when someone asks you for help, you will know which resources you have available.

- Take time to listen to others' requests for assistance; even if you cannot help them directly, you may be able to suggest someone who can.

- Find effective ways to say "no" to a request for assistance from another without jeopardizing his or her future support.

- To understand others' perspectives, set aside your own agenda and listen to other people's ideas and rationales.

- Ask your manager or a respected peer for feedback on your reputation in the "fight/compromise" arena; use the feedback to modify your behavior.

- When faced with possible resistance, consider pre-selling your agenda to a couple of key players.

- Analyze the costs of pushing your agenda to the exclusion of others' agendas: If you "win," will you receive cooperation from the "losers" in the future?

- Learn to recognize when others are resisting your agenda by observing both their verbal and nonverbal behaviors.

- Willingly share leadership responsibilities with peers.

- Think about your audience's needs, concerns, and perspectives. Consider how people are likely to react to your message and, whenever possible, position your message in a way that appeals to them and avoids a strong negative reaction.

- Express criticism tactfully.

- Avoid delivering personal criticism in public.

- Make a list of where key players stand on particular issues for future reference.

- Before presenting a new idea or action plan, list the people whose support you will need. Attempt to discover where each person "stands" in relation to your proposal — pro, con, or neutral — and formulate a plan to handle each.

- Demonstrate your commitment to the organization in tangible ways: by your willingness to "go the extra mile" when necessary; by attending company social functions; and by supporting the organization's values, goals, and mission.

PART 1

Involving the Right People at the Right Time

Developing Organizational Savvy

Almost every manager has experienced a situation similar to this: The top management of a multinational corporation decided to streamline sales reporting by networking its field offices to a new computer system installed at headquarters and training the sales force to input data to the system. An executive task force was formed to discuss the purpose of the system and the desired results. A project team was then formed to act on the task force's recommendations. After the system was designed, the general manager in charge of field sales was asked to give his input. The general manager was annoyed that he had not been consulted during the design phase and refused to give his full cooperation. When the system was finally implemented, many of the salespeople resisted using it, claiming that it was too complicated.

This project seemingly had everything going for it — strong support from upper management, a defined need, and a dedicated project team. But it was doomed to fail because it lacked the support of key individuals — the salespeople. Even well-planned, strongly supported projects can fail if the wrong people are involved, or if the right people are involved at the wrong time. Identifying whose support you need — and at what level in the organization — is essential to the successful completion of most projects.

Knowing whom to involve — and when — maximizes your opportunities for success and positive recognition. The following tips can help you involve the right people at the right time:

- Determine whose support you will need to get your idea approved and implemented effectively. This typically means that end users and customers need to be involved early.

- Before presenting an idea at a meeting, run it by someone whose opinion you value. Ask this person to critique the idea and your presentation. What are the strengths and weaknesses of your idea? Also ask whose support you will need, and try to cover those players in your plan before you present it publicly.

- When putting together a task force or project team, ask members who else should be included. Invite others to sit in on meetings when you are discussing a topic that affects them, even if they aren't regular members of the committee. Send minutes of action items to interested parties for their information.

- Talk with key individuals who will be affected by your project. Ask who among their peers or higher management would support it and who would oppose it.

- Identify a peer or a higher-level manager who is effective at involving others.
  - Observe how this person determines who should be involved in what situations, as well as how he or she involves those people.
  - Write down the methods you observe.
  - Arrange a time to discuss these methods with the "expert."
  - Ask this person to give you feedback and suggestions on the people you involve in your next project.

- If you think a particular individual should be involved, offer him or her the opportunity. You will not only reduce the chances of overlooking someone important, but also get further insights into the appropriate people to involve in future projects.

- Because involvement generally means commitment, include people whose support you need in the planning and development phases of the project. If you anticipate that a particular person's involvement may be seriously disruptive to the team:
  - Offer to keep the person "in the loop," stressing the time he or she will save by not attending the meetings.
  - Involve the person on a one-on-one basis by asking him or her to be your advisor.
  - Assign the person to another project requiring his or her expertise to keep involvement at a minimum.

- Don't be afraid to exclude a person who would be ineffective or disruptive to the team.
  - If you really need the person's support, think of a way to get it without involving him or her as a member of the team.
  - If you don't need the person's support, keep him or her informed to the degree necessary as you go along.

Achieving Results through Formal and Informal Channels

Most work in an organization gets done by using both formal channels and informal networks. The key to accomplishing your objectives is to identify and follow the formal process. But you also want to cut through the red tape and expedite the formal process by tapping into the informal networks of your organization.

USING FORMAL CHANNELS TO ACHIEVE RESULTS

Every organization has a few "loose cannons." These are people who act independently, without considering the effects they may have on others. They bypass formal organizational channels, seizing whatever means they can to accomplish their own agendas. Such people rarely progress far in an organization because they lack the support of key players. Successful people use both formal and informal channels to achieve their goals.

To earn the respect and support both of your peers and managers, learn to use the formal structures in your organization to help you achieve your goals. Following these suggestions can help you use formal channels more effectively:

- Seek out a resident "expert" to act as your mentor. This person can describe the formal rules, and clue you in to the unwritten rules of the organization as well.

- To clarify your organization's structure, get to know your peers cross-functionally. Find out what they do and what processes or rules they follow, especially those that may have an impact on you or your group.
  - Be aware that different divisions or groups have different operating philosophies: Some are more traditional and operate mostly by the book, while others are more entrepreneurial and encourage employees to try new ideas and approaches. Get a feel for other groups' operating philosophies and procedures.
  - Keep a file of the people you contact, so you will know whom to call when you need advice or support.

- When functions are created or reorganized, spend some time talking with the people involved. What are their new responsibilities? How can you work together most effectively to get things accomplished?

- Keep your manager informed of what is going on in your department. Ask how he or she would like to be kept informed of progress or setbacks. Maintain a policy of "no surprises" by relating both the good and the bad news. (Your manager will appreciate hearing the bad news from you instead of from someone else.)

- Study the goals and strategies of your organization and identify how your work and the work of your group supports those goals and strategies. Use that linkage to help support your agenda.

USING INFORMAL CHANNELS TO ACHIEVE RESULTS

All organizations have informal networks that have developed to supplement, and in some cases to bypass, the formal channels. Networks serve a number of purposes — their members share information, resources, and ideas; solve problems; support one another; and gain influence within the organization. The Leverage Networks section of this Handbook provides an in-depth look at how to cultivate both internal and external networks to increase your managerial effectiveness.

Much of the work of an organization gets done through these informal channels. In fact, disregarding informal channels can not only make your job more difficult and frustrating, but can actually create obstacles when you need support. In addition, the manager who uses only formal channels to get things done may sense a "distancing" from others, resulting in delayed or formal responses, even on trivial matters.

To access the informal networks in your organization:

- Ask an experienced person to act as your coach or mentor. (This can be the same person who coached you in the formal structure, or you may want to choose someone different to act as your networking mentor.) Ask this person:
  - Who are the people who can "make things happen" in each group?
  - Who holds the positional power within each functional area? This person may be — and often is — different from the person who makes things happen.
  - Who are the key players in a particular group? What are the dynamics of that group?
  - What is important to the key players?
  - Of whom do you have to be careful?
  - What ways have you found to effectively shortcut the formal system? What are the likely consequences, if any, if you bypass the formal system?

- Connect with the informal communications system by making it your job to keep people informed.
  - Be honest and straightforward with people.
  - Tell them what you can, and explain the reasons when you cannot.
  - Create opportunities to communicate with people throughout the organization so you can hear perspectives and rumors about your group and correct any misinformation.

- Develop relationships with individuals throughout the organization. Take note of who has influence and the support of their peers at all levels of the organization. Get to know these people by setting up an informal meeting, such as lunch, or by working on a project together. Note that face-to-face contact is essential in developing these relationships. Trying to save time by calling the person or sending a memo will not help you build a mutually supportive relationship.

Fostering Effective Give-and-Take Relationships

Projects often require more resources than a single manager possesses. Sometimes the only way to complete a project successfully is to work with other managers to "borrow" or "lend" personnel, expertise, or financial resources.

The ability to work cooperatively with other managers who have different skills and objectives — and to avoid, whenever possible, the "turf battles" that are common in many organizations — is a skill that helps savvy managers hurdle seemingly insurmountable obstacles with apparent ease. Building give-and-take relationships requires both compromise and responsiveness on your part. By conceding relatively unimportant points and offering your own resources to others when feasible, you can create and maintain "quid pro quo" relationships that will serve you well.

Use the following guidelines to help build effective give-and-take relationships:

- Identify the resources you can offer to others. Then, when someone approaches you for help, state your resources up front. This demonstrates your willingness to be helpful.

- Make sure you understand exactly what the other person is requesting by asking questions and investigating the issues before agreeing to help. If possible, write down and agree upon the resources you will contribute.

- When you think that compromise may be required, classify your issues into these three categories:
  - Issues that can definitely be dropped or tabled without penalty to you. When negotiating, use these issues first as conciliatory gestures.
  - "Nice to have, but not essential" issues. These should be your next line of defense.
  - "Must have" issues. Hold out the longest for these.

- Keep in touch with people, so you can volunteer to help when needed. This proactivity shows real awareness and concern for others. It builds solid relationships.

- Resist the urge to go over the head of a person when he or she does not help you. This tactic will alienate the person whose support you will need in the future. Instead:
  - Believe he or she does want to help, but really does not have the time or resources.
  - Make your request again, emphasizing your common goals or the importance of the need.
  - Give the person direct feedback about the impact of his or her refusal on your ongoing relationship if lack of cooperation or give-and-take is frequent.

- When you can't offer assistance directly, advise the person making the request how he or she can get help. Sometimes you will not have the time or resources to help. Giving suggestions about other possible resources at least shows you are concerned.

- Don't be "too busy" to listen to another's requests; this can brand you as a manager who "uses" others, a reputation that can hurt you. Other managers may not want to work with or promote individuals who do not know how to *give* as well as take.

  If you truly are too busy to help, the following tips can help you say "no" without jeopardizing the relationship or future support:
  - Consider the importance of the task you are being asked to perform. Is it an integral part of your organization's major goals?
  - If it is not, suggest someone else who could help.
  - If it is, make sure there is no possible way you can take it on before you decline. Look for ways to rearrange your current priorities to allow you to accommodate the request. Or try to identify a peer or someone who reports to you who could temporarily or permanently assume one of your other responsibilities.
  - Strive to build a reputation for helping others when it is essential.

Understanding the Perspectives and Agendas of Others

The meeting has already gone an hour over its scheduled time. The participants are restless, eager to close the discussion, make a decision, and leave. But Jane Smith refuses to end the discussion until she's restated her position at least five more times. By now, everyone else has identified the areas of agreement and disagreement and is ready to tackle the problems. If Jane had only taken a few minutes to listen, instead of relentlessly promoting her own agenda, she might have realized an hour ago that no one was arguing her main points. The participants could have hammered out an agenda that everyone could at least live with.

Sound familiar? Jane Smiths abound in the corporate world, wasting time arguing moot points, obstructing processes, and alienating themselves from their colleagues. By taking the time to understand other people's agendas and perspectives, Jane could have increased her effectiveness on the job and gained the respect of her peers and higher-level managers.

Demonstrating your willingness to look at all sides of an issue to arrive at goals that are mutually beneficial can increase your chances of achieving personal, group, and organizational goals. The following tips can help you learn to see others' viewpoints and establish mutually beneficial goals:

- Listen to the other person's presentation and/or explanation of his or her agenda.
  - Ask clarifying questions to ensure understanding.
  - Be able to clearly explain the agenda to an uninvolved third party before assuming that you completely understand the other person's issues.

- Set aside your own agenda long enough to really listen to the other people's ideas and understand their rationales. (You may discover that your positions aren't so far apart after all.)
  - Be flexible. Realize that every situation is different, and every group has different dynamics.
  - Listen carefully, assessing the situation and the dynamics, and modify your position accordingly.

- Air people's ideas, using a roundtable discussion in which:
  - One person shares his or her ideas and answers questions for clarification only (no criticisms or arguments are allowed).
  - When all questions have been answered, the next person shares his or her ideas, and so on.
  - Disagreements or modifications can be discussed only after everyone has shared ideas and answered clarifying questions.

- Ask each person to list what he or she wants to accomplish during a given meeting, project, and so forth. Pool the lists, identify similar objectives, and work to resolve areas of difference.

- Facilitate a brainstorming session to identify the objectives that others would like to accomplish.
  - Observe the rules of brainstorming: everyone contributes, all suggestions are considered valuable, and no ideas are critiqued until everyone has had a chance to give input.
  - Look for ways to incorporate the majority of the objectives into your action plans.

Knowing When to "Fight" and When to Compromise

Managers who have to win every battle, even at the expense of others, reduce their overall effectiveness as well as their influence in the organization. Because they are so busy championing their own agendas, they may not be aware of the needs or agendas of others. Or, if they are aware of them, these managers tend to ignore the agendas that are contrary to their own.

You can increase your influence and foster greater cooperation by learning when it is appropriate to assert your agenda and when to set it aside for negotiation. The following guidelines can help:

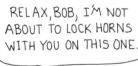

RELAX, BOB, I'M NOT ABOUT TO LOCK HORNS WITH YOU ON THIS ONE.

- Analyze the costs of pushing your agenda to the exclusion of others' agendas. If you "win," will you receive the cooperation of the "losers," whose help you may need to accomplish your goal? Will you be serving your personal needs at the expense of the team's or the organization's goals? Will you develop a negative reputation as a result of your need to win every point?

- Ask your manager or a respected peer for feedback on your reputation in the "fight/compromise" arena. Do you fight too many battles? Do you fight the wrong battles, but not the "right" ones? Are you viewed as stubborn and unwilling to compromise? Or as being too willing to give in at the first sign of resistance?

  This type of feedback can give you insight into how others view your willingness to find solutions through cooperative efforts. It may also help you find more effective ways to successfully promote your ideas and objectives.

- Consider pre-selling your agenda to a couple of key players. Ask to meet one-on-one with these individuals, and explain your position. If you can gain their support in advance, you may be able to avoid later conflict with less influential players.

- Recognize when others are resisting your agenda by observing both their verbal and nonverbal behaviors. (Are some members of the group more argumentative — or quieter — than usual? Are one or more people leaning back from the table with their arms crossed, or avoiding eye contact with you, or doodling when they should be listening?) Often, the harder you push an agenda on unwilling partners, the stronger they will resist.
  - Stop, and focus on understanding the concerns raised. Say, "Help me understand your concerns."
  - View the concerns as problems to be solved.

- Be aware of others' needs and goals before you assert your agenda. Do your homework by finding out the issues and concerns of key decision makers ahead of time.

- After your initial presentation, get feedback before continuing to push your agenda. Getting others' reactions — both positive and negative — opens the way for compromise and agreement.

- Don't concede immediately if you meet resistance. Instead, be willing to discuss and consider compromises.
  - Invite the others to ask you questions.
  - Answer the questions directly, without trying to slip in another "plug."
  - Know that your sincere willingness to listen to other points of view not only builds respect and trust, but it also gives more weight to your agenda.

- Before presenting your agenda to others, identify the areas in which you are willing to compromise. By anticipating resistance and having ready compromises, you can maintain control of the situation while negotiating.

- Look for a role model, someone who always seems to get the majority of his or her agenda accomplished even in the face of resistance — yet who continues to maintain strong working relationships with the resisters.
  - Observe the methods this person uses and adapt them to your personal style.
  - Ask for feedback from your role model whenever possible.

PART 2

Knowing When to Lead and When to Follow

Developing Personal Savvy

In reality, effective managers must be able to both lead and follow. Knowing when to take charge to make things happen is an essential characteristic for a manager, regardless of position or personal ambitions. However, a manager must also be able to follow, particularly when working on a project for his or her manager. Managers are less likely to promote those who refused to follow their directions than they are those who proved that they could lead their own people and still listen to their manager.

Learning when to lead and when to follow can strengthen your personal reputation and standing in the organization. The following suggestions can help you determine when it is wise to lead and when it is wiser to follow:

- Examine the situation you are in. Who is involved?
  - If the majority are upper-level managers, be prepared to follow. This does not mean, however, that you shouldn't share your ideas.
  - If, on the other hand, the majority are employees or peers, be ready to assert your leadership. Understanding the dynamics of the situation will help you choose the appropriate response.

- Identify the owner of the project or action plan.
  - When you are the owner, take on the leadership role without hesitation.
  - When others are the owners, make sure you know who is running the show. An upper-level manager in the background may not appreciate your attempt to take charge.

- Be willing to share leadership responsibilities with peers. If you have a project that is too big to handle alone or if someone else's contributions would be particularly valuable in a leadership role, offer to co-lead the project with another. By splitting the responsibilities, you show initiative, situational leadership skills, and a willingness to work with others to accomplish a common goal.

- When you are in a follower position, look for opportunities to shine. If the project needs a task leader or subgroup chairperson, offer to assume the role. Demonstrating the ability to lead and follow simultaneously shows your manager that you are a confident, competent contributor.

Anticipating Others' Reactions or Positions Accurately

Knowing in advance how people are likely to respond to your agendas or action plans is essential for your success. Being prepared for reactions or resistance ensures a stronger presentation and defense of your position. For example, if you know that your manager feels strongly about a particular topic, you can present ideas related to that topic in a way that will show their alignment with your manager's position.

Accurately anticipating others' reactions shows your respect for them and allows you more flexibility to compromise. The following methods can help you discover other players' "hot buttons":

- Regularly discuss general positions on work-related topics with your colleagues.
  - Invite others to lunch or coffee break for this purpose.
  - Afterward, write down what you learn so you will remember where others stand on particular issues, what their needs, goals, and agendas are, and so forth.

- Before presenting a new idea or action plan, make a list of the people to whom you will be submitting your agenda.
  - Use a grid like the following to determine where each person is likely to stand in relation to your proposal or agenda. For each person who you think is likely to block your objectives, briefly indicate why.
  - Determine whose support you need to have. Talk with others or review your past experience with these "must haves" to determine what you need to do to win them over.

Support	Block	Neutral

- Identify peers or higher-level managers who seem knowledgeable about others' positions.
  - Watch them closely, noting the methods they use to answer objections or questions.
  - Incorporate these methods into your next presentation.
  - Ask for feedback from the people involved, as well as from the people you have chosen as models.

Developing Timing   Asking for resources during budget cuts, criticizing someone's work after he or she stayed up all night to finish a project, and pointing out that you had warned someone of a result that just occurred are all examples of poor timing.

Some people are so concerned with demonstrating they were right, or so sure they know the best way, or simply oblivious to what others think and feel, that they shoot themselves in the foot with poor timing. These people are often labeled abrasive or insensitive.

To combat poor timing, try these suggestions:

- Before delivering your message, think: "How will others feel if I say that?" or "What will others think of me if I say this?"

- Be aware that timing is important, not just the "rightness" of the message.

- View your comments or requests in the context of what is going on. For example:
  - Commenting that Total Quality Management is just a new fad to a leader committed to TQM is not sensitive.
  - Commenting that the organization is not really committed to diversity at a meeting announcing a new diversity program will not be well received.
  - Disagreeing with an idea just to generate discussion or analysis is not always a useful way to encourage dialogue.

Committing Oneself to the Organization

People who are self-promoting, concerned only with what they and their group are doing, are focused on the short term.

On the other hand, people who have organizational savvy are seen as committed to the organization and the people in it. They are willing to "go the extra mile" for others and to get the job done. To demonstrate your commitment to the organization:

- Persevere when the going gets tough.

- Help others when they need assistance.

- Allow others to save face when they need help, but don't broadcast your generosity.

- Show honest, genuine concern about the people in the organization.

- Share credit for your accomplishments.

RECOMMENDED READINGS

The publications listed here were selected for their content and suitability to a managerial audience.

Networking Smart

Baker, Wayne E., New York: McGraw-Hill, 1994
ISBN: 0-07-005092-9
Baker defines networking as building and managing relationships productively both inside and outside the organization. His book offers practical theories and techniques you can use to create thoughtful, powerful networks with customers, suppliers, and even competitors.

Getting Things Done When You Are Not In Charge

Bellman, Geoffrey M., San Francisco: Berrett-Koehler, 1992
ISBN: 1-881052-02-8
Bellman's book is intended as a guide for those who want to successfully bring about change in their organization without the advantage of formal power. It offers practical approaches for effectively enlisting key players and earning the respect of management. Bellman presents insights on leadership, teamwork, empowerment, and organizational politics.

Influence Without Authority

Cohen, Allan R., and Bradford, David F., New York: John Wiley & Sons, 1991
ISBN: 0-471-54894-4
The authors present a very readable, practical method for creating change and partnership in contemporary organizations. Their book demonstrates how to skillfully form mutually advantageous relationships.

Beware the Naked Man Who Offers You His Shirt

Mackay, Harvey, New York: Ivy Books, 1991
ISBN: 0-8041-0583-9
This book provides tools to help managers deliver the quality and excellence necessary to compete in today's fast-moving global environment. It includes "how to's," insights, and self-tests.

The New Partnership

Melohn, Tom, Essex Junction, VT: Oliver Wight, 1994
ISBN: 0-939246-57-0
The author tells how he took a mediocre company and turned it into a success story with significantly increased sales, productivity, and profits. Melohn contends that every company can accomplish this by following several basic principles: trust and respect your employees, give recognition when due, promote teamwork, and keep your organization lean and efficient.

Cross-Functional Teams

Parker, Glenn M., San Francisco: Jossey-Bass, 1994
ISBN: 1-55542-609-3
Parker's book shows how teams comprised of individuals from different departments can achieve success, especially when the task is complex and requires speed, creativity, and special customer attention. Also included are suggestions on how to lead, appraise, reward, and best utilize cross-functional teams.

Discovering Common Ground

Weisbord, Marvin R., San Francisco: Berrett-Koehler, 1993
ISBN: 1-881052-08-7
The author explains a highly successful new way for organizations of all types to apply global thinking and democratic values to achieve rapid whole systems improvement. "Future searches" bring people with diverse interests together to create shared vision and collaborative action.

SUGGESTED
SEMINARS

The seminars listed here were selected for their appeal to a managerial audience. The reputation of the vendor, the quality of their seminar offerings, and the specific seminar content were considered in the selection process.

Because of the dynamic nature of the seminar marketplace, some seminars may have been upgraded or replaced, and others may no longer be offered. Likewise, costs and locations may have changed since this listing was compiled. We recommend that you contact the vendor directly for updated and additional information.

The Empowered Manager: Developing Positive Political Skills

This seminar presents empowerment as a business strategy that will enable managers to do more with less. Topics include maintaining a high quality of work life in an increasingly competitive marketplace, developing a vision, and examining ways of building alliances.
Length: 3 days; Cost: $1,200
Locations: Call vendor
Designed Learning, Inc.
1009 Park Avenue, Plainfield, NJ 07060
Telephone: 908/754-5102

Individual Coaching Services

This customized coaching program helps people develop critical skills such as leadership, interpersonal, communication, and organizational influence skills. Through a tailored assessment to diagnose developmental needs, one-on-one skills training, and state-of-the-art techniques for behavior change, participants gain powerful self-insight and successfully learn new skills and behaviors to make them stronger performers.
Length: Call vendor; Cost: Call vendor
Locations: Call vendor
Personnel Decisions International
2000 Plaza VII Tower, 45 South Seventh Street
Minneapolis, MN 55402-1608
Telephone: 800/633-4410

Positive Power and Influence Program

The program focuses on developing and refining the skills required to influence people and events while building and maintaining beneficial relationships. It covers assessing which influencing styles you use, overuse, misuse, or avoid; refining present skills and developing alternative styles; and applying the appropriate influence style to a given situation.
Length: 3-4 days; Cost: $950 - $1,250
Locations: Call vendor
Situation Management Systems, Inc.
195 Hanover Street, Hanover, MA 02339-2294
Telephone: 617/826-4433

Producing Results With Others II

This program helps participants recognize how their behavior comes across to others and how to adapt it. The program covers: recognizing the importance of versatility when working with others, understanding the difference between productive and nonproductive tension, and anticipating and modifying behavior in order to avoid miscommunication.
Length: 2 days; Cost: $750
Locations: Call vendor
The Tracom Corporation
3773 Cherry Creek North Drive, Suite 950
Denver, CO 80209
Telephone: 800/221-2321

LEVERAGE NETWORKS

Networks are composed of people, both internal and external to the organization, who provide one another with information, support, advice, and practical assistance to accomplish individual or group goals. Every organization has many networks, because people need to rely on one another for help to perform their jobs effectively. Networks exist to serve and support that interdependence.

Networks sometimes appear to arise almost spontaneously. They are formed by the people you work with every day, the people with whom you have shared common experiences. At other times, networks are carefully based on criteria such as influence, skills, experience, position, and so on.

Building and nurturing your network is an ongoing process. This section presents information and guidelines to help you facilitate this process. It includes:

- Recognizing the Value of Networks
- Identifying the People to Include in Your Network
- Building Your Network
- Establishing Networks Outside Your Organization
- Strengthening Your Network
- Leveraging Networks to Get Things Done
- Maintaining Your Network

Valuable Tips

- Recognize the reciprocal nature of networks. Members provide support to one another. That support may consist of information, ideas, resources, or influence.

- Develop a systematic approach to networking. Analyze what you need in a network and what you can offer other members.

- Be sincerely interested in other people and their success. Networks are based on mutual interest and genuine concern.

- Draw a "map" of your potential network. Include the names and titles of both lateral and vertical employees.

- Assess your current "networking" status by identifying the people in your own group and in other groups who have helped you. Also determine how often your colleagues ask for your support, and how often you ask for their support.

- Get to know higher-level managers in your group by volunteering to act as a resource or to work on a committee or special project.

- Ask a knowledgeable person in your group to act as your mentor. This person can tell you who has influence or special expertise in the organization, and may be willing to introduce you to these people.

- Get to know managers and professionals at levels below yours who are close to the day-to-day functioning of the organization.

- Recognize that nonworking hours can often be the best time to develop your network. Attend company social events to informally meet peers and higher-level managers from other groups.

- Treat other network members with respect.

- Work on developing the interpersonal skills that will help you gain the support of others.

- Join professional organizations to meet others in your industry.

- Read professional journals to keep current on new developments.

- Regularly touch base with network members to maintain your relationships. If you contact network members only when you need help, your relationships may be strained.

LEVERAGE NETWORKS

Recognizing the Value of Networks

In today's business world, even highly placed managers are not totally self-sufficient; they need the support, cooperation, and goodwill of their managers, peers, and employees to accomplish their goals. In most organizations, effective managers at all levels are adept at working both the "streets" and the "alleys." The streets are the formal avenues by which work is accomplished — in other words, the organization's formal chain of command and its written policies. The alleys are the informal avenues — the networks — that enable managers to marshal the resources they need to get things done.

Managers who are comfortable working only the streets can get bogged down in time-consuming procedures. They may also be viewed by their colleagues as strictly "by the book" people who are to be avoided if you want to get anything done quickly. On the other hand, managers who bypass the streets and operate only in the alleys may not be appreciated or trusted by upper-level management. Finding the right balance between the two is essential to your success. This balance will vary depending on a number of factors, including the organization itself, your functional area, and your position. See the Display Organizational Savvy section of this Handbook for suggestions on how to work effectively within both the formal and informal channels of your organization.

To find out how "networked" you are, answer the following questions:

EVALUATION CHECKLIST *(Circle the appropriate response.)*

Do you have a clear idea of what you *need* from a network?	**Yes/No**
Have you analyzed what you have to *offer* other members of a network (for instance, skills, knowledge, information, or influence)?	**Yes/No**
Do your colleagues contact you frequently for advice or support?	**Yes/No**
Do you make an effort to get together with colleagues on an informal but regular basis?	**Yes/No**
Do you volunteer to sit on task forces or committees to get to know higher-level managers and peers from other functional areas?	**Yes/No**

Have you established a good working relationship
with at least one key member of each function or
area on which you must rely to get things done? **Yes/No**

Do you periodically attend professional conferences
and make contacts with other key people in your
industry? In other industries? **Yes/No**

Are you an active member of at least one
professional association? **Yes/No**

Do you regularly attend company social events? **Yes/No**

If you answered "yes" to most of these questions, you're well on
your way to being networked. This section may provide you with
some additional ideas for working your networks more effectively.
If you answered "no" to most of the questions, ask yourself why.
Are you new to the organization? Do you feel uncomfortable with
the idea of networking? Are you unsure about how to get started?
The suggestions presented in this section can help you learn how
to work the "alleys" as well as the "streets."

Identifying the People to Include in Your Network

Organizations don't bequeath networks to their employees.
Networks are developed by individuals who stand to benefit from
their mutual association or who are concerned about one another.

It takes time and effort to identify appropriate contacts and to
develop relationships with these people. Consider the following
suggestions for developing a systematic approach to networking
that can help ease your entry into existing networks or build new
networks to meet your needs:

- Identify your needs. Whose support, advice, or cooperation do
  you need or want? Whom do you particularly want to help?

- Analyze how things typically get done in your organization —
  through formal or informal channels? If formal, are you well
  versed in the formal structure? If informal, who are the key
  people who can play a role in supporting your efforts?

- Identify the people in your organization who have been
  successful in achieving results and influencing others. How
  well do you know and relate to these people? Find out how they
  established and use their networks.

- Determine what you have to offer a network. Do you have
  special knowledge or expertise needed by others in a network?
  Can you help get an idea accepted by key people in the

organization? Do you have personnel or other resources that you can lend to another department temporarily? Do you personally have time to help? Can you access other resources for network members?

- Draw a physical "map" of your potential network. Include both lateral individuals (your peers in other departments) and vertical individuals (peers and upper- and lower-level managers in your own department). Along with the names of these people, list their functional responsibilities, the ways in which they can support you, and the support you can offer them.

- Develop a plan to contact these people to build rapport. Your initial contact should be an informal, face-to-face meeting (lunch, coffee break, dropping by the person's office, etc.) for the purpose of identifying common interests and needs. Following this meeting, stay in regular contact via phone, lunch, informative notes, and so on.

Building Your Network

Most managers who consistently achieve results or successfully coordinate efforts across functions have already established a strong network and laid the groundwork for gaining cooperation and support.

The following suggestions can help you begin to build beneficial network relationships:

- Identify the managers above you who are able to influence others and accomplish their goals. Talk with these managers and/or their employees about your team's objectives and how they fit with the company's overall mission. Determine what linkages, if any, exist between your responsibilities and theirs. Discuss these common goals and ways that you can help each other. If appropriate, volunteer to act as a resource to the manager and/or the team.

- Volunteer to serve on a committee or work on a special project to get to know higher-level managers. This way, they will have a chance to experience your skills, reliability, and enthusiasm firsthand. Look for opportunities to maintain these relationships after the committee or project work is done.

- Identify the people who hold positions similar to yours. Choose one or two who share common job concerns and problems, and meet with them informally to ask for and share ideas for resolving problems and expediting work flow.

- Identify a person who "knows the ropes" and would be willing to act as your mentor. This person can provide valuable information about key people in other functional areas: who has the authority or the influence to get things done, who can provide advice or political support, who has experience or skills in an area relevant to yours. This person may also be willing to personally introduce you to these people.

- Volunteer to serve on cross-functional committees to get to know managers in other areas. Make an effort to contact these people once your involvement with the committee has ended.

- Get to know other key managers and professionals at levels below yours in the organization. These people are closer to the day-to-day functioning of the organization and can offer a different perspective on how things get done most efficiently. In addition, their cooperation may be essential to you in accomplishing your own goals.

- Attend company social events to meet managers and peers from other functional areas. Company picnics, award banquets, open houses, and company-sponsored charity events are excellent ways to informally meet people from other areas, and provide a basis for future contacts.

Establishing Networks Outside Your Organization

Your peers in other organizations within your industry or profession can offer a different kind of networking support. They can provide new information and perspectives, and share how they handled problems or concerns similar to yours.

To develop a network of professionals outside your organization, consider these suggestions:

- Call key people in your field to ask for information, discuss an idea, or ask for advice. Most people like to help out and share ideas.

- Join one or more industry or professional associations. Attend meetings, conferences, and seminars. Work on program committees. Actively involve yourself in the group so you can get to know people. Spend time with those with whom you have interests in common and begin to develop a personal relationship beyond the professional association.

- Read professional newsletters and trade journals. These publications can keep you up-to-date on new developments in your field, and they often provide the names of people you may want to contact.

- Join (or form) a group of professionals from other organizations that gets together informally to exchange information on technical advances and discuss issues of common interest.

Strengthening Your Network

Networks are based on common needs, similar interests, and reciprocal relationships. Networking involves giving and sharing as well as getting help. The following activities can help you strengthen your network:

- Invite a respected colleague to lunch. Outline several of the issues you are currently dealing with and discuss how you are handling them. Ask the person for suggestions. Your objective is to create an open dialogue in which you both feel comfortable discussing common experiences and problems.
  - If the lunch goes well, increase your contact with that person through additional lunches, phone calls, and so forth. If you come across information of mutual interest, pass it along with a note.
  - As your relationship develops, this colleague may ask you to support an idea or plan. If you think that the idea or plan is feasible, actively support it. If you sense problem areas, explain what they are and recommend changes. Look for a resolution so that you can wholeheartedly support the other person's position. If, in the end, you cannot provide the requested support, explain your reasons. Reassure the person that you value his or her ideas and would like to help at a future time.
  - Call or stop by regularly just to talk. These casual encounters and frequent contacts without "wanting something" demonstrate your sincere interest in the other person.

- Recognize the give-and-take nature of networks, and offer to help others by sharing your ideas, time, resources, and so forth.

- Establish trust by speaking highly of your colleagues to others and by maintaining confidentiality regarding sensitive information.

Leveraging Networks to Get Things Done

Networks exist to get things done in the most effective and efficient way. Without a network, you may find yourself lacking critical support or cooperation from others when you most need it. But how do you go about "working" a network when you need assistance? Basically, you simply ask for it. Remember, networks are founded on the premise that the relationships are reciprocal: "I'll help you now; you'll help me in the future."

The following suggestions can help you leverage your networks for maximum benefit:

- Develop an information exchange among network members, if one does not already exist.
  - Arrange for periodic get-togethers during which network members can discuss new ideas, express their perspectives about particular issues, and seek input.
  - Take note of where each person "stands" on issues of concern to you and your group. This will help you identify the people who are supportive of your position and those who may need to be "courted."

- If you need practical assistance — such as advice or input on a proposal, another person's time, or priority for your project — state your needs in person to the individual whose help you need. Be prepared to negotiate if the other person cannot provide the assistance that you need.

- If you need support or backing from several people, think about the best way to present your position so that others will view it as mutually beneficial.
  - Meet individually with each person to discuss your position. Be open to questions, and give direct answers to clarify your needs.
  - Again, be prepared to negotiate if others cannot totally support your position.

- Treat other network members with respect. Ask for another's help, never demand it. Keep in mind that strong networks are built on mutual respect and common goals.

- Vary your approach depending on the individual. Effective managers use a whole array of interpersonal skills to gain the support or assistance of others: direct requests, motivation, recognition, diplomacy, encouragement, influence, and praise. What works well with one person may not work with another.

Maintaining Your Network

Networks are dynamic. Once you've developed a relationship, you can't just sit back and say, "Well, I've done *my* job. Now I'll wait for something to happen." It's important to nurture your network by contacting people periodically, helping when you can, and building linkages between what you and other network members are doing. With proper attention, your network will grow as the years go by. New people will join, others may play less prominent roles as your mutual interests decrease, and still others will become long-lasting friends.

To maintain your network:

- Develop strategies for staying involved. Keep in touch regularly by telephone (once every month or two). Even better, arrange to have lunch or informal get-togethers as often as possible.

- Show concern and provide help without being asked when you know that a colleague is swamped or is facing unexpected difficulties.

- Realize that asking for help after having no contact for a long time may feel like manipulation to others. A colleague who hasn't heard from you in several years may not be responsive to your requests for support. Although it takes time and effort to maintain regular contact, the benefits of doing so are well worth the investment.

RECOMMENDED READINGS

The publications listed here were selected for their content and suitability to a managerial audience.

Great Connections: Small Talk and Networking for Business People

Baber, Anne, and Waymon, Lynne, Manassas Park, VA: Impact Publications, 1991
ISBN: 0-942710-48-7
This book provides techniques for making connections and enhancing business and individual career success. Some of the techniques and areas covered by this book's many examples, worksheets, and guidelines are: how to use business cards effectively, how to generate sales leads and referrals, how to start and end conversations, and how to best utilize business meetings and conventions.

Networking Smart

Baker, Wayne E., New York: McGraw-Hill, 1994
ISBN: 0-07-005092-9
Baker defines networking as building and managing relationships productively both inside and outside the organization. His book offers practical theories and techniques you can use to create thoughtful, powerful networks with customers, suppliers, and even competitors.

Success Runs in Our Race: The Complete Guide to Effective Networking in the African-American Community

Fraser, George, New York: William Morrow & Company, 1994
ISBN: 0-688-12915-3
This book is filled with tips, ideas, strategies, and methods members of the African-American community can use to effectively network and achieve success in business or other endeavors. Also included are anecdotes and profiles of successful African-Americans.

The Age of the Network

Lipnack, Jessica, and Stamps, Jeffrey, Essex Junction, VT: Oliver Wight, 1994
ISBN: 0-939246-71-6
This book offers managers and teams a practical way to reinvent their companies without losing the value and knowledge that is inherent in their current organizational structure. Included are techniques designed to create an organization that is fast, agile, and contains highly interconnected relationships. In creating a network of teams, the authors stress, among other things, the need to establish a clear purpose and to create communication links.

The TeamNet Factor: Bringing the Power of Boundary Crossing Into the Heart of Your Business

Lipnack, Jessica, and Stamps, Jeffrey, Essex Junction, VT: Oliver Wight, 1993
ISBN: 0-939246-34-1
The authors use their experience as networking consultants to show companies how to be innovative and build teams that cross company boundaries rather than building strictly internal teams. The book contends that networking and team-building with other companies are essential to becoming more competitive and successful.

Cross-Functional Teams

Parker, Glenn M., San Francisco: Jossey-Bass, 1994
ISBN: 1-55542-609-3
Parker's book shows how teams comprised of individuals from different departments can achieve success, especially when the task is complex and requires speed, creativity, and special customer attention. Also included are suggestions on how to lead, appraise, reward, and best utilize cross-functional teams.

SUGGESTED SEMINARS

The seminars listed here were selected for their appeal to a managerial audience. The reputation of the vendor, the quality of their seminar offerings, and the specific seminar content were considered in the selection process.

Because of the dynamic nature of the seminar marketplace, some seminars may have been upgraded or replaced, and others may no longer be offered. Likewise, costs and locations may have changed since this listing was compiled. We recommend that you contact the vendor directly for updated and additional information.

Cross-Functional Communication: Strategies for Workplace Effectiveness

This highly interactive seminar shows participants how to develop win/win professional relationships that lead to organizational effectiveness.
Length: 3 days; Cost: $1,200
Locations: Call vendor
American Management Association
P.O. Box 319, Saranac Lake, NY 12983
Telephone: 800/262-9699

The Empowered Manager: Developing Positive Political Skills

This seminar presents empowerment as a business strategy that will enable managers to do more with less. Topics include maintaining a high quality of work life in an increasingly competitive marketplace, developing a vision, and examining ways of building alliances.
Length: 3 days; Cost: $1,200
Locations: Call vendor
Designed Learning, Inc.
1009 Park Avenue, Plainfield, NJ 07060
Telephone: 908/754-5102

Positive Power and Influence Program

The program focuses on developing and refining the skills required to influence people and events while building and maintaining beneficial relationships. It covers assessing which influencing styles you use, overuse, misuse, or avoid; refining present skills and developing alternative styles; and applying the appropriate influence style to a given situation.
Length: 3-4 days; Cost: $950 - $1,250
Locations: Call vendor
Situation Management Systems, Inc.
195 Hanover Street, Hanover, MA 02339-2294
Telephone: 617/826-4433

How to Influence Without Direct Authority

Participants in this workshop examine characteristics and skills of influential people to understand the sources of their informal power. They analyze situations requiring influence and learn how to build effective relationships upward, downward, and laterally. They also learn practical influential strategies; trust-building skills; and the tools of team building, persuasion, conflict management, and negotiation.
Length: 3 days; Cost: $850
Location: Madison, WI
University of Wisconsin-Madison
Management Institute, Grainger Hall
975 University Avenue, Madison, WI 53706-1323
Telephone: 800/348-8964

VALUE DIVERSITY

The work force is rich in diversity, which means both opportunity and challenge for managers. *Diversity* refers to a broad range of differences among people in terms of country of origin, age, gender, race, cultural heritage, lifestyle, education, physical ability, first language, and other factors.

Valuing diversity means viewing differences as assets rather than liabilities, seeing stereotypes for what they are, and getting beyond prejudices to appreciate differences. *Managing* diversity means utilizing those differences in the work force to accomplish organizational goals, finding the balance between developing shared organizational values and valuing diversity, and challenging assumptions that limit opportunities.

Today, as well as in the future, maximizing diversity is a critical business issue. Business challenges are escalating. Different approaches are needed. The market has changed. The work force is different. Organizations that manage diversity well are the ones that will be able to respond to these changes and remain competitive.

This section provides insights and guidelines for effectively managing diversity, including:

Part 1: Valuing Diversity — Working to Change Attitudes

- Assessing Yourself
- Increasing Your Sensitivity to Issues of Diversity

Part 2: Managing Diversity — Working to Change Behavior

- Creating an Environment of Acceptance
- Confronting Prejudging Behavior
- Confronting Intolerant Behavior
- Balancing the Need for Shared Values
- Utilizing the Full Potential of All Employees
- Recruiting and Promoting Diversity
- Assisting People from Diverse Backgrounds to Succeed

Part 3: Organizational Efforts — Working to Make Systemic Changes

- Assessing Organizational Readiness
- Accommodating the Needs of a Diverse Work Force
- Making It Happen
- Staying on Course

Part 4: Evaluating Progress

Valuable Tips

- Actively solicit input from a wide variety of people and functions.

- Involve diverse groups in solving problems and developing opportunities.

- Challenge assumptions that limit opportunities.

- Seek to understand diversity from a global, not just a national, perspective.

- When asking someone to explain a point of view different from your own, be sure to say that your intention is to *understand* that person's viewpoint, not to have him or her justify it.

- Stand up and speak out when others are not valued or their ideas or views are not taken into account.

- Identify your customer base. Then examine your organizational strategies and practices to make sure they reflect your actual customer base.

- Be sensitive to the fact that some people want their differences to be recognized while others do not.

- Watch any tendencies to joke about differences.

- Talk openly about the tension between the need to value and accept others and the desire for shared organizational values.

- Give feedback openly and respectfully to those whose different behaviors and values affect their credibility and effectiveness.

- Become a mentor to an individual whose background and experiences are different from your own.

- Broaden your view of diversity beyond just race or gender issues.

- Educate yourself about your own cultural values and background.

- Look at issues and opportunities from others' viewpoints before making decisions.

- Talk frankly and openly about the amount of time it may take to change the organization's acceptance of people who are different.

- Confront people directly about their prejudiced behavior or comments, but allow them a way to change without "losing face."

- Challenge organizational policies and practices that may be exclusionary.

- Recognize that people who are in the minority in one group are in the majority somewhere else.

- Build a support network with colleagues who are interested in valuing diversity.

- Use the Myers-Briggs Type Indicator to learn new ways of understanding some of the many differences among people, such as learning styles, social styles, and so forth.

- Continually monitor your automatic thoughts and language for unexamined assumptions and stereotypical responses.

- View educational videos, such as the *Valuing Diversity* film series produced by Copeland Griggs Productions of San Francisco.

- Learn more about other cultures and their values through travel, books, films, and by attending local cultural events and celebrations.

- Review suggestions in the Manage Disagreements section to learn ways to handle conflicts that may arise.

PART 1	# Valuing Diversity — Working to Change Attitudes

Assessing Yourself

The first step in learning to value diversity is to understand your own values and beliefs. It is important to see how these beliefs make you different and to recognize that others may not see them as "right" or as completely understandable as you do. The suggestions that follow will help you accurately assess your own attitudes, assumptions, and feelings about people who are different from you. These attitudes, assumptions, and feelings can affect your managerial effectiveness.

- Connect with and value your own culture. Expand your definition of culture to include educational background, economic status, religious affiliation, gender, rural versus urban focus, and so on. Begin to assess how your background translates into your own lifestyle, values, and world view.

- Over the next few weeks, examine the assumptions you make about others. Such assumptions are based on both external, easily identifiable differences, as well as more subtle, invisible differences. Some people find it difficult to acknowledge that their assumptions and cultural beliefs significantly affect how they see other people.

  Consider the following example:

  > A manager walks past the office reception area and sees two black men laughing. He concludes that they do not take their jobs as managers seriously. Next, he passes two women talking to each other at the mail station and assumes they are gossiping. Just before he reaches his office, he passes two white men talking and chuckling, and thinks nothing of it.

  > This manager has made assumptions without listening to the actual conversations. Instead, he has used external differences to draw conclusions.

  Making assumptions such as those in the example is often an automatic process, not a deliberate one — which is why it is so difficult to catch.

- Examine the language you use. For example, recognize that the word "minority" is a relative term that can be devaluing as well as inaccurate.

- Think about how it feels to be different by remembering times when you felt that you were in the minority. For example, you may have been in a situation where you were the only male, the only monolingual person, the only German, or the only older person. Examine how you felt and its impact on your behavior.

- Evaluate how you view people who disagree with you. Do you try to understand the basis for their views? Do you question them respectfully? Do you work toward mutual understanding, or simply try to convince them that you are right?

Increasing Your Sensitivity to Issues of Diversity

It's important for managers to push themselves beyond their current environment and interactions to develop their knowledge of and sensitivity to issues of diversity. Doing so can help you more fully understand, appreciate, and maximize the talents of others. It can also help you find ways to change the environment to encourage the full participation of all employees. The more you understand others' values and assumptions, the more you will know about their motivators. Consider these suggestions:

- Establish relationships with people who are different from you. Although it's a natural tendency for people to surround themselves with others like them, connecting with people of different backgrounds will help you learn about the unique contributions others have to offer.

- Ask people from a variety of backgrounds for help in understanding their experiences, perspectives, and culture. Seek to understand the individual, rather than seeing the person as a representative of a group.

- Volunteer for an organization where you are in the minority.

- Participate in community programs that focus on learning about and valuing different cultures, races, religions, ethnic backgrounds, and political ideologies.

- Make a list of your heroes and heroines in music, sports, theater, politics, business, science, and so on. Examine your list for its diversity. Compare it with the lists of others to learn about their heroes and heroines.

- Consider your actions or your group's work processes from the point of view of a different function.

- Consider the difficulties you might face if you were physically challenged.

- Learn about the contributions of older people and people with a visual or hearing impairment. Evaluate how their contributions have helped us all.

PART 2

Creating an Environment of Acceptance

WE WORK SO WELL TOGETHER, YET WE HAVE SUCH DIFFERENT BACKGROUNDS.

Confronting Prejudging Behavior

Managing Diversity — Working to Change Behavior

Creating an environment of acceptance goes beyond simply tolerating people who are different. It means actively welcoming and involving them. People take cues from the environment about how well they are accepted. For example, actively enlisting and involving people versus merely responding if they ask to be involved give two very different messages.

The following suggestions can help you and others create a more accepting environment:

- Develop an atmosphere in which it is safe for all employees to ask for help. In this environment, a person is not seen as weak if he or she requests assistance.

- Actively seek information from people from a variety of backgrounds, and include them in decision making and problem solving.

- Include people who are different from you in informal gatherings by inviting them to be part of work-related activities, such as going to lunch or attending organizational social events.

Because of our prejudgments, we often see others and interpret their behavior through a framework that does not allow us to get to know the individual. As a result, we sometimes limit the opportunities we may give them.

For example, we might assume that the 55-year-old, long-term employee would not be interested in an overseas assignment that would uproot him or her late in his or her career. Or, we may see a male employee's request to leave work in time to pick up his children from daycare as a sign that he either is not career-minded or is an unusually caring parent. These examples are prejudgments based on assumptions about people.

Take the lead in examining your own prejudgments while challenging others about theirs. The following steps can help you do this:

1. Begin by confronting your own prejudgments. You may believe that you have none, but that is unlikely. Prejudgments are a shorthand way of thinking and can be based on cultural values, experiences, or stereotypes. They may include beliefs such as:

   - Men are less sensitive and less considerate than women.

   - Accountants are "bean counters" who can't see beyond numbers.

   - French people are arrogant.

   - System analysts can't communicate their work clearly to others.

   - Black people are good athletes.

   - Older workers have a hard time learning new technologies and don't want to.

   - Gay people are very neat.

   - Women are less committed to their business careers than men.

   - Japanese people aren't creative.

   - Immigrants rely on free benefits.

2. Become aware of these prejudgments by listening to feedback from others, through diversity training, or simply by questioning your own assumptions. Notice the impact your behavior has on others. Do you:

   - Have higher career aspirations for your male employees than for your female employees?

   - Give less feedback to people of a different race for fear of being accused of racism or discrimination?

   - Shy away from talking with employees who do not speak your language well?

3. Challenge your prejudgments. Take the time to get to know people. Work to eliminate the prejudgments that are hurtful and unfair to others.

4. Model behavior that is inclusive, respectful, and not prejudging. By including a wide variety of people in your world, you can more easily serve as a model to others.

Confronting Intolerant Behavior

Challenge others' prejudgments. Nurture respect and interpersonal sensitivity. As a manager, you have the opportunity and the responsibility to take the lead in defining what behavior is acceptable in the workplace. Your actions to discourage and refuse to accept racist, sexist, ethnocentric, and other insensitive comments and behaviors that attack the self-respect of others will strongly influence the conduct of your group.

At times, it can be difficult for people to directly confront this negative behavior, particularly if they are part of the group being put down, for fear of being regarded as too sensitive. Others hope that if they ignore the behavior, it will just go away. Such behavior usually does not go away, and people continue to be hurt, embarrassed, or alienated. Still others will agree with those who make the comments, not realizing the damage they do.

Recognize the difference between expressions of differing beliefs or opinions and deliberately hurtful comments or "humorous" sarcasm that is damaging to others. The following approach may help you do so:

1. If the comment is subtle or you think the person truly does not understand its impact, ask the person for the evidence or rationale for his or her belief. Then summarize his or her point of view, and discuss the impact of the comment on others and, when useful, on your perception of him or her.

2. If the remark is an obvious put-down, simply say, "That's not appropriate," or "Comments like that are not welcome here." Then change the subject. This approach communicates that you believe the statement is inaccurate and is not open to debate.

3. If the person defends his or her behavior, simply reassert its inappropriateness. Your goal is not to humiliate the person, but to stop the comments. Tell the person that you realize he or she did not intend to be hurtful or unfair, but that he or she is responsible for changing the behavior.

4. If the comments continue or form a consistent pattern of behavior, treat the behavior as an on-the-job performance issue because it affects the morale of the group.

5. Realize that more controversial subjects will be more difficult (and more important) to speak out on. Demonstrate your leadership by clearly refusing to tolerate labeling and other prejudicial behavior.

Balancing the Need for Shared Values

Shared values are essential for successful organizations. Without some shared values, a team does not pull in the same direction. Yet successful organizations also value diversity. Effective leaders must struggle with the issue of how to include and respect diversity and at the same time develop a consensus on core values.

For example, some people on a team may like to work closely with others, while others do not. Or, some team members may want to work 10 to 12 hours a day, while others do not. To be effective, you and your team need to work out how much difference helps the team and how much is divisive and nonproductive. The following process can help you do that:

1. Plan team-building exercises to explore the balance between diversity and shared values for your team. Before the first session, ask each person to do the following:

   - Identify what he or she believes to be the shared values of the group. Examples may be: "We put customers first," "We proactively help one another in crunches," "We value quick, efficient analysis," and so on.

   - List differences in values perceived within the group. For example, some may value direct, no-nonsense feedback, while others prefer feedback that is cautious and polite. Some may value training and like to be brought along gradually, while others value quick learning and risk taking.

2. At the team-building session, post the statements of shared values that each person generated. Discuss these, and come to consensus on the shared values of the team.

3. Then discuss the differences in values:

   - Reach consensus on what the differences are.

   - Talk about the impact of these differences. Determine how the group can accept differences whenever possible. Many times, the shared values are so strong or the business issues so great that people find they can live with the differences and not have their work negatively affected.

   - If the differences are affecting the work of the group, discuss how to manage the situation. For example, you may have a team where most members believe in supporting decisions, while others believe it is all right to oppose decisions and even to go their own way. One way the team might manage that situation is by requiring consensus.

4. Discuss the team's need for both divergent and convergent thinking. Ensure that you gather divergent opinions for creative ideas and solutions during problem solving, but strive for consensus when you need to cooperate, take action, or form a team.

Create a new space for working together at the intersection of the values and background of each worker. Individuals retain their unique perspectives and values but move together to synthesize an environment where work can happen. This common ground is a dynamic atmosphere of exchange, consensus, and new ways of thinking.

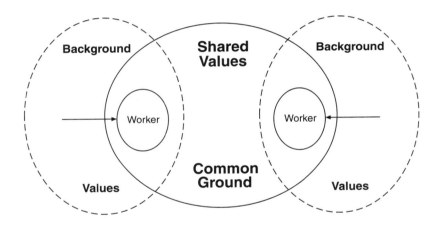

A key to working with issues of shared values and diversity is to talk openly about the issues, respect all points of view, and work cooperatively to solve problems and create understanding. A second key is to help people see how their lack of "buy-in" to shared values has a negative impact on the work, the group, and the success of the endeavor.

Utilizing the Full Potential of All Employees

Some managers assume that being different is a deficit. They may display their discomfort and judgmental attitude by their actions and body language. Others may operate as if differences in race, culture, background, and ways of working do not exist among their employees, treating them all exactly the same. An effective manager, however, recognizes the value of having a diverse team by maximizing the full potential of all employees and building on complementary skills, backgrounds, and cultural knowledge. The following suggestions can help you utilize your employees' potential:

- Recognize different learning styles, and explore with your team or work group ways to use these styles advantageously. A mixture of styles usually yields a richer, more innovative outcome. Examples of differences in learning styles and approaches include:
  - A structured, time-efficient approach to projects versus a less structured and more creative approach.
  - A focus on details versus a focus on the big picture.
  - A preference for bouncing ideas and strategies off others versus a desire to work in solitude.
  - A preference for individual projects versus a preference for group involvement.

- Include employees from a variety of backgrounds and experience in your problem-solving and decision-making processes. Use differences as a way of gaining a broader range of ideas and perspectives. Research shows that heterogeneous groups are significantly more effective problem solvers than homogeneous groups.

- Use cross-functional and multi-level groups to solve problems, spot opportunities, and go beyond conventional ideas and solutions.

- Focus on, talk about, and read about the value of diversity. Create the mindset that the involvement of employees representing a broad base of experience is an asset to the organization.

- Challenge your assumptions about others. For example, don't assume that an employee who uses a wheelchair cannot do a particular job where mobility is an essential element. Ask the employee if he or she can handle the job requirements, and, if not, ask if there is a reasonable accommodation that the organization can make to assist him or her. [Note: In the United States, the Americans with Disabilities Act prohibits a manager from discussing an applicant's disability before a job offer is made.]

- Take risks. For example, suppose a foreign national is the most qualified person for a job, but you are concerned about the negative reaction of some customers. Instead of selecting someone else, determine how you can address the discomfort of those customers and help the person be successful.

Recruiting and Promoting Diversity

Successful recruitment of people from diverse backgrounds is not an overnight process. It involves long-term, concerted effort with others throughout your organization. To help you with this process, try some of the following ideas:

- Develop specific strategies to increase your flow of applicants from a variety of backgrounds. For example, if you commonly recruit students from certain colleges, ensure that the student populations represent a diversity of backgrounds. Consider using other colleges, business schools, or graduate programs.

- Use internships to bring more diverse people into your organization or work group and help them gain on-the-job experience and skills.

- Be willing to hire employees with nontraditional backgrounds and skills.

- Use referrals from employees within your organization to help you identify promising candidates for recruitment. Pay attention to the diversity of this informal network.

- Attempt to bring in more than one person of a particular group so that they can support each other emotionally.

Hiring is the first step, but retaining, developing, and promoting the employees you hire is a critical second step. The following suggestions can help you with this step:

- Look at the career paths and opportunities in your area with as open a mind as possible. Aggressively attempt to eliminate intentional or unintentional discrimination or favoritism.

- Describe to all of your employees the specific promotional routes and the skills required for them to get there.

- Look for opportunities to develop employees from diverse backgrounds and to prepare them for positions of responsibility in your organization. Tell them about the options in their present careers, as well as other career opportunities within the organization.

Assisting People from Diverse Backgrounds to Succeed

Proactive managers fully understand the need to invest in the talent of people from a diversity of backgrounds. They recognize and seek to develop the skills of all employees, not just those who they think fit the traditional and dominant culture of the organization. They are willing to take risks in hiring, training, and coaching.

Evaluate what you need to do to help employees from different backgrounds succeed in the organization. Consider these suggestions:

- Most organizations have informal networks that utilize "tried and true" employees for new projects or work opportunities. The work of these employees is known, and they are regularly called upon when such opportunities arise. Help propel new employees into these informal networks by actively promoting their talents and their potential.

- Implement an informal mentor or buddy system, especially for new employees. Pair each new employee with a more experienced person who can help the new employee adjust to the organization and the work group.

- Help all employees understand the unwritten rules of the organization.

- Be flexible; recognize that each employee is an individual and that his or her training needs will be unique.

- Assign diverse employees to cross-organizational teams and task forces, thus increasing their exposure to employees in other divisions and departments in the organization. Let them know you will support them when they need help.

- Give people feedback to help them achieve success in the organization. Help people use their differences effectively and not alienate others.

- Re-examine how you have traditionally judged the characteristics or qualities you look for in high-potential employees.

- Help employees deal with frustrations stemming from their perception of slow progress toward acceptance. Listen.

- Recognize and confront aspects of your organizational culture that keep capable employees from being fully included and successful within your organization.

PART 3

Organizational Efforts — Working to Make Systemic Changes

Assessing Organizational Readiness

Before you embark on a plan to significantly change your organization's approach to diversity, it is wise to assess the organization's readiness. Assessing readiness for a "valuing diversity initiative" allows you to determine the best timing and level of change you want to pursue. To examine your organization's readiness, answer the following questions:

- Do employees and top management see a connection between efforts to value differences and the success of the business?

- Are your operating officers and managers "on board?"

- Is the organization already very diverse?

- Does the organization's power structure include a mix of people from diverse backgrounds? Countries?

- Is acceptance of differences part of the corporate language?

Use your answers to these questions to guide your pursuit of systemic changes. Initiatives that promote valuing diversity are more successful when they are seen as a business necessity. Therefore, it is important to establish this belief.

Accommodating the Needs of a Diverse Work Force

To seriously address the needs of a diverse work force, an organization must have systems and policies that are sensitive to and accommodate those needs. Following are some ideas and issues to consider:

- Explore the possibilities of flexible work hours, compressed work weeks, part-time hours, job sharing, and working from home.

- Develop a method for deciding in what language to conduct a particular meeting.

- If English is the organization's language, facilitate people learning the language.

- Expand options for childcare programs.

- Offer flexible benefits packages.

- Promote programs designed to actively recruit and retain older workers (for example, opportunities for upward and lateral mobility, close monitoring of hours to avoid adverse Social Security ramifications, and so forth).

- Eliminate unnecessary job requirements (for instance, too high a level of education).

- Evaluate the holidays your organization officially recognizes and celebrates to see whether they accommodate a diverse work force.

- Show sensitivity in your physical work environment (for example, display artwork representing a variety of cultures).

Making It Happen   Systemic changes do not happen overnight. But keep in mind that, even though you may not be able to change your entire organization so that it more consistently values diversity, you can influence its direction and provide a model in your department or area. Consider the following steps:

- Clarify your organization's operating image and philosophy. For example, assess your customer base, both current and potential.
  - Do your products and services communicate an awareness of and commitment to all segments of the market that could benefit from them?
  - Do your marketing and advertising materials represent your philosophy of valuing diversity?

- Clearly impart your vision for a diverse workplace to others through organizational meetings and forums.

- Form an officially recognized and supported steering committee to address issues of diversity. Invite team members who represent a diversity of backgrounds to join the committee.

- Study other companies. What strategies do they employ that can be brought into your organization?

- Promote and value diversity by involving all team members in your organization's surveys, task forces, steering committees, and specific training programs.

- Recognize that strong emotions may be generated by the organization's move toward a more inclusive environment.

- Implement training programs that focus on the organization's commitment to promoting diversity in the workplace (programs designed to develop a greater awareness of and sensitivity to differences). When delivering workshops and other training, pace the delivery of new information and allow time for discussion and debriefing.

- Celebrate differences through team-building activities.

- Hold managers accountable for making the necessary changes through formal channels such as performance reviews and departmental goals.

- Model the acceptance and use of differences to address issues.

Staying on Course

Your efforts to manage diversity can easily stir powerful emotions within your organization. Those who have stifled feelings of frustration for years may suddenly voice their rage. Some may see a diversity program as the beginning of a "quota" plan that will advance others' careers at the expense of their own.

To be effective, you must keep sight of the overall goal — to value the individual — and communicate it clearly and repeatedly. Valuing diversity is *a means of* valuing the individual. Managing diversity is the same as managing well, that is, appreciating individuals for their unique strengths and developing them. Consider the following:

- Clearly communicate that diversity refers to everyone. Use a broad definition of diversity in your discussions: age, profession, parental status, rural/urban, lifestyle, and so on.

- Use an exercise based on Taylor Cox, Jr.'s concept of "culture identity structure."

  1. Begin by thinking of all the groups with which you identify. Use the broad definition mentioned above. Weigh each group identity, considering how important it is to your self-identity.

  2. Draw a circle.

  3. Divide the circle into pie-shaped slices. Assign each slice to a group identity you value. Give more important identities larger slices; give less important ones smaller slices. For example, a person may strongly identify with both a profession and an age group, but not equally. By increasing the size of either slice, he or she indicates that it is more important than the other.

  4. Have others perform the same exercise.

  5. Compare your identity pie with theirs. Note the similarities and differences. Note how the same group identity can be of different size and importance from person to person. Think about and discuss with coworkers the implications of your similarities and differences. What are the advantages and the challenges?

Use the awareness created by your exercise to widen acceptance of diversity initiatives. Let it demonstrate your desire to include everyone in the definition of diversity. People who might otherwise consider themselves irrelevant to the discussion can feel they are full participants, while those who consider themselves overlooked can have their voices heard.

- Make sure everyone is aware of his or her own world view. Draw on people's travel experiences as a way of illustrating their personal perspectives.

- Balance your discussion of background with attention to individuality. Background is important to understanding a person, but individuals are more than just members of a group. Recognize that it's just as possible to alienate by accentuating differences as by discrediting them.

- Be clear about your intent. Some people won't want their differences recognized at all. Others may see your overtures to underrepresented groups as threatening. Make sure your message always returns to the central issue — how to recognize and enable each person's unique talents.

- Avoid the "blame game." Some people have suffered through poorly conducted diversity programs and may already be defensive. Some role-playing discussions devolve into turn-the-tables retribution. Finger-pointing provokes backlash and resentment.

- Follow through. Letting the issue slide will allow your attempts at inclusion to be dismissed as part of a passing trend, leading to negative feelings on all sides.

PART 4   Evaluating Progress

The success of any plan requires continuous improvement. To ensure the effectiveness of your efforts to value, promote, and maximize diversity, establish baseline measures or benchmarks to evaluate your progress. Then monitor the progress toward your goals on an ongoing basis. Keep in mind that this is often a long-term change effort. Consider using the following evaluation measures:

- Develop a greater understanding of the current attitudes and experiences of your employees through focus groups, attitude surveys, individual conversations, and exit interviews. Share feedback on results with all employees.

- Research the demographics of your organization as a whole and its individual departments. Determine what level of diversity already exists in your work group and your organization.

- Examine personnel records to compare your organization's current level of diversity with what you would like it to be in the future.
  - Notice who gets hired at different levels in your organization.
  - Determine whether promotion and advancement opportunities are equal for all employees.
  - Pay attention to terminations and the reasons behind them. Do people from a diversity of backgrounds stay with your organization? Are there certain work groups that tend to have unusually high or low retention rates?

- Pay attention to organization publications such as employee newsletters. Do they reflect a diversity of ideas, cultures, and perspectives?

- Scrutinize organizational policies and programs to uncover any possible unfairness or barriers that may exist.

- Develop other organization-specific measures to monitor progress toward your goal of valuing and maximizing diversity.

- Ask for feedback about your ability to develop strong shared values and your acceptance of diversity among the staff. Listen to and act on it appropriately and in a timely manner.

- Strive to continuously improve your ability to maximize diversity and value the individual.

RECOMMENDED READINGS

The publications listed here were selected for their content and suitability to a managerial audience.

Cultural Diversity in Organizations

Cox, Taylor, Jr., San Francisco: Berrett-Koehler, 1993
ISBN: 1-881052-19-2
The author presents a framework for understanding multiple group identities that shape each person's self-concept. All employees bring their diversity with them into the workplace where they interact with the needs and motivations of other group members and with the goals and processes of the organization. Understanding this complexity affects how well it is managed, both for accomplishing the goals of the individuals and the whole organization.

Managing a Diverse Workforce

Fernandez, John P., New York: The Free Press, 1991
ISBN: 0-669-26903-4
The author suggests that a manager's ability to get employees of different genders and of different ethnic and cultural backgrounds to work together effectively may be the crucial ingredient for corporate success in the future. Eye-opening and practical, this book provides managers with the sound guidance they need to recruit, retrain, and fully utilize workers.

Differences That Work

Gentile, Mary C., New York: McGraw-Hill, 1994
ISBN: 0-07-103581-8
This book is a discussion about issues of diversity in the workplace and establishes a framework in which diversity can be constructively debated. The focus of this book is that diversity is not a problem, but rather it can be a resource that makes companies more productive and successful.

Bridging Differences: Effective Intergroup Communication

Gudykunst, William B., Newbury Park, CA: Sage Publications, 1994
ISBN: 0-8039-5646-0
This book is useful to anyone who works with people from different cultural and ethnic backgrounds. The author shows how stereotypes lead to ineffective communication, including misinterpretation of messages we receive from members of cultural and ethnic groups different from our own.

Managing Workforce 2000: Gaining the Diversity Advantage

Jamieson, David, and O'Mara, Julie, San Francisco: Jossey-Bass, 1991
ISBN: 1-55542-264-0
This sensitive and timely book provides a useful framework for understanding the multiple dimensions of diversity and designing practical strategies to manage the opportunities diversity creates. Successful approaches are demonstrated by numerous examples from Fortune 500 companies.

The New Leaders: Guidelines on Leadership Diversity in America

Morrison, Ann M., San Francisco: Jossey-Bass, 1992
ISBN: 1-55542-459-7
This book covers: why diversity at the management level is important to organizations; the barriers operating today that keep women and people of color out of the executive suite; the practices used by progressive organizations to achieve diversity; and the elements of these practices that make them effective. The author also describes a step-by-step approach to designing and carrying out a diversity strategy.

Beyond Race and Gender

Thomas, R. Roosevelt, Jr., New York: AMACOM, 1991
ISBN: 0-8144-7807-7
This book outlines a model of management that goes beyond affirmative action programs of the past to an action plan for transforming the roots of corporate culture to reflect diversity.

SUGGESTED SEMINARS

The seminars listed here were selected for their appeal to a managerial audience. The reputation of the vendor, the quality of their seminar offerings, and the specific seminar content were considered in the selection process.

Because of the dynamic nature of the seminar marketplace, some seminars may have been upgraded or replaced, and others may no longer be offered. Likewise, costs and locations may have changed since this listing was compiled. We recommend that you contact the vendor directly for updated and additional information.

A Simulation in Managing Diversity

This program is designed to guide participants in examining their understanding of managing diversity within the context of organizational change. Participants will acquire personal, group, function/task, hierarchy, and community identities. These variables will surface in the simulation and managers will be faced with managing diverse employees. Each participant will have a distinct part to play in entering an organization and becoming a fully utilized employee.
Length: 2 days; Cost: $975
Location: Atlanta
American Institute for Managing Diversity, Inc.
Morehouse College, Box 83
351-55 Westview Drive S.W., Atlanta, GA 30314
Telephone: 404/756-1170

Diversity and Corporate Culture

This workshop provides participants with the skills and strategies to plan and implement long-range corporate cultural change for managing diversity. Participants will increase their ability to diagnose corporate culture within the context of managing diversity and identify changes that will facilitate the implementation of a managing diversity initiative.
Length: 3 days; Cost: $1,425
Locations: Call vendor
American Institute for Managing Diversity, Inc.
Morehouse College, Box 83
351-55 Westview Drive S.W., Atlanta, GA 30314
Telephone: 404/756-1170

Introduction to Cultural Audits

This program will walk participants through a step-by-step process of preparing, conducting, analyzing, and presenting the results of a cultural audit within their own organization.
Length: 2-1/2 days; Cost: $1,495
Locations: Call vendor
American Institute for Managing Diversity, Inc.
Morehouse College, Box 83
351-55 Westview Drive S.W., Atlanta, GA 30314
Telephone: 404/756-1170

Launching Managing Diversity

This workshop is designed to increase participants' ability to understand the impact of a managing diversity initiative on organizational culture and systems; give their organizations a competitive advantage by increasing productivity and efficiency through cutting-edge concepts; and enhance the success of existing change strategies and total quality management.
Length: 2 days; Cost: $950
Locations: Call vendor
American Institute for Managing Diversity, Inc.
Morehouse College, Box 83
351-55 Westview Drive S.W., Atlanta, GA 30314
Telephone: 404/756-1170

Linking Managing Diversity With Other Large-Scale Change Initiatives

This program is designed to provide participants with the opportunity to fully explore how a grasp of the concepts of managing diversity can be invaluable in understanding the hindering and facilitating factors in implementation of large-scale change processes.
Length: 2 days; Cost: $950
Locations: Call vendor
American Institute for Managing Diversity, Inc.
Morehouse College, Box 83
351-55 Westview Drive S.W., Atlanta, GA 30314
Telephone: 404/756-1170

Developing High Performing Culturally Diverse Organizations

Participants in this seminar explore the positive power of cultural differences through understanding and valuing themselves; understanding their effect on others; gaining knowledge about cultural diversity and the change process; learning how fully utilizing cultural diversity in the workplace can assist in the accomplishment of the organization's goals; and developing skills to assist the organization in a strategic cultural exchange.
Length: 6 days; Cost: $1,145
Location: Safety Harbor, FL
NTL Institute
1240 North Pitt Street, Suite 100
Alexandria, VA 22314-1403
Telephone: 800/777-5227

Managing the Multicultural Workforce: A Bottom Line Issue

This program is designed as a training program for managers to help them understand and respond to the changing management requirements of a culturally diverse work force. Topics include: understanding and valuing culturally diverse employees as a key business strategy; providing a framework for cultural value comparison; and identifying and practicing skills for influencing employees (flexibility, tolerance for ambiguity, overcoming stereotypes, conflict resolution, and trust building).
Length: 5 days; Cost: $835
Location: Washington, DC
NTL Institute
1240 North Pitt Street, Suite 100
Alexandria, VA 22314-1403
Telephone: 800/777-5227

Foundations of Intercultural Communication

This program uses a highly interactive learning environment to foster an awareness and appreciation of cultural differences in both the international and domestic arenas.
Length: 3 days; Cost: Call vendor
Location: Portland, OR
The Intercultural Communication Institute
8835 S.W. Canyon Lane, Suite 238, Portland, OR 97225
Telephone: 503/297-4622

MANAGE DISAGREEMENTS

Conflict is part of any dynamic business organization. It arises because people care and want to do their jobs well. Conflict is beneficial when the focus is on finding the best solution. It becomes destructive when the focus is on people and "winning."

Conflict arises because of limited resources; differing goals, responsibilities, and priorities; and differing ideas or interpretations. Conflict is especially difficult when it does not produce mutually satisfying solutions and it becomes personal.

As a manager, your goal should be to avoid "win/lose" situations and to ensure productive resolution of conflict. Effectively working through conflict results in stronger working relationships and encourages creative solutions, while handling conflict inappropriately results in damaged relationships and inhibits the expression of valuable opinions.

This section suggests ways to develop conflict management skills in the following areas:

- Improving Your Conflict Management Style
- Using Active Listening to Reduce Conflict
- Discussing the Real Reasons Underlying the Problem
- Dealing with Conflict Collaboratively
- Working toward Win/Win Solutions
- Minimizing Recurrent Conflict
- Resolving Conflict Among Your Employees

Valuable Tips

- Put yourself in the other person's situation and imagine how you would feel and react. Look at the other side before defending your own.

- Approach conflict situations as opportunities to strengthen interpersonal relationships.

- At the beginning of a conflict discussion, express your desire for a resolution that is acceptable to both or all of you.

- Ask the person, "What is the minimum you will accept? What would you prefer?"

- Restate the positions held by those on both sides of a conflict to ensure that the conflict is not just a misunderstanding and to show that you understand the others' perspectives.

- Encourage people to depersonalize the conflict; look at it as a conflict of ideas or approaches, rather than of people.

- Don't lecture about why you are right. Simply state your point of view.

- Bring conflict into the open without feeling that your leadership is threatened. When people disagree with you, analyze the reasons for their positions.

- Seek feedback from peers in both formal and informal situations about your effectiveness in handling interpersonal conflict.

- Ask a neutral third party to help you and the conflicting party talk through the problem.

- Allow others to vent their anger. Venting frustrations allows people to set them aside while you work through the conflict.

- Clearly tell the other person the things you both agree on before dealing with the points of disagreement. This approach provides a positive starting point by building bridges between people.

- If the other person feels like he or she is losing something or that you are being unfair, listen to what the person is saying; don't try to convince the person that he or she is wrong.

- Attack problems, not people.

- If a conflict escalates, call for a time out. Reconvene when both people have reduced tension to a productive level and have regained their perspective.

- Be willing to give and take in dealing with tough conflicts.

- Instead of showing your frustration with the conflict, *talk* about it.

- Be willing to confront others when you feel they have made an error.

- When a conflict situation arises, discuss it with your manager. When you have handled it, seek feedback from him or her about how successful you were.

Improving Your Conflict Management Style

To improve the effectiveness of your conflict management style, take the following steps:

1. Over the next few weeks, keep track of situations involving interpersonal conflict or tension, both on and off the job. Record your observations in a notebook, indicating the cause of the conflict, what occurred during the conflict situation, and the outcome of the conflict.

2. At the end of this period, analyze your observations to determine if they form a pattern. Which of the following describes you in a typical conflict situation?

   • Withdrawn — you avoid conflict as much as possible.

   • Agreeable — you usually allow the other party to win.

   • Disagreeable or aggressive — you promote win/lose situations.

   • Constructive — you work toward collaboration.

3. Based on your analysis, decide whether you want to change your conflict resolution style and, if you do, prepare a plan of action. Readings in the area of conflict management and discussions with friends, respected colleagues, and family members can provide additional ideas.

4. Implement your plan. Read it over at least once a week to reinforce your intentions.

5. After you have incorporated your plan into your conflict resolution style, record conflict situations you encounter for several more weeks. Compare the results of your new style with those of your old style to determine if you are able to reach satisfactory agreements with fewer negative repercussions.

Using Active Listening to Reduce Conflict

Too often, the parties involved in an argument spend most of their time talking instead of listening. When one person is speaking, the other is busy preparing a rebuttal or thinking of additional ways to support his or her viewpoint, rather than listening to what is being said.

In addition, most people immediately judge the statements of others — either to agree or to disagree. Frequently, the listener judges a statement from his or her point of view without considering the other person's perspective. Thus, true listening is not occurring; people hear what they expect or want to hear, rather than what the speaker intends to communicate.

Both of these behaviors can cause disagreements to escalate into arguments. When neither person stops to listen, there is a good chance that agreement will be delayed or prevented altogether. In addition, when emotions run high, people may say or do things they later regret. Over the next month, each time you sense that an argument is about to begin, switch from a defensive position to the listening mode. To accomplish this switch, try a technique called active listening:

1. Listen carefully to what the speaker is saying. Give the speaker your full attention, without thinking about how you are going to respond, and without judging the speaker's statements. Show that you are really listening through nonverbal behavior such as leaning forward, raising your eyebrows, nodding your head, and so forth.

2. Get the speaker to clarify his or her position by asking open-ended questions starting with phrases such as:

    *   Tell me about...

    *   Explain...

    *   How do you feel about...

    *   Describe...

    *   What...

    Avoid close-ended questions that can be answered "yes" or "no" — questions that start with words such as "is," "are," "could," "would," "do," "did," and "should."

3. Periodically paraphrase what the speaker has said to ensure that you understand what was meant and to let the speaker know that you are really listening. In doing so, reflect the feeling as well as the content of the message. Use phrases like, "As I understand it, your position is..." or "You seem to be concerned about..." If the speaker disagrees with your paraphrase, ask him or her to clarify the statement.

4. Determine whether your interpretations are becoming more accurate as the discussion progresses. Good listening should be rewarded with comments such as, "That's exactly what I meant" and "That's right! I think you understand my problem."

5. Avoid interrupting the speaker. Mentally tally the number of times you interrupt a speaker, and eliminate such interruptions by the end of the month.

If you are effectively applying active listening skills, your conflict situations will become less intense, and people will likely become more open to listening to your point of view and compromising. You will find that you are involved in more constructive debates and fewer destructive arguments. For additional suggestions on developing your active listening skills, read the Listen to Others section of this Handbook.

Discussing the Real Reasons Underlying the Problem

Many conflicts have multiple sources. It is difficult to arrive at a long-lasting solution unless you deal with all of the real causes of the problem. Another challenge in conflict resolution is that people do not always clearly know what their issues are.

The following suggestions can help you uncover the real reasons underlying a conflict:

- The next time you are discussing a problem, notice the layering or multiple issues involved. Becoming more aware of this will remind you to look for it.

- In a conflict situation, listen carefully. If you hear hints of underlying issues, ask about them. For example, you might say, "I wonder if you are angry because I got the assignment, and not you?" Or you can observe, "It seems that there might be something else bothering you." These types of questions or observations, quietly stated, can open the door for additional information.

- When you think you know the issues, summarize your understanding of them and ask if that accurately summarizes *all* of the person's concerns.

- When you are having difficulty reaching agreement on a problem, suggest to the other person, "I wonder if we have all of the issues out on the table." Then both of you can rethink and discuss any additional issues that are uncovered.

Dealing with Conflict Collaboratively

Collaborative problem solving is the most effective way to deal with conflict. Yet it can be challenging to continually keep the discussion moving forward. To deal with conflict collaboratively, try the following process:

1. Ask to meet with the other person in a nonthreatening place, such as his or her office or a conference room.

2. Begin the session with a statement defining the purpose of the meeting — something like, "Jim, I asked to meet with you today to discuss the disagreement you and I are having over the Fox contract. I want to work something out with you that we're both comfortable with."

3. Use active listening skills to draw out information from the other person and to help pinpoint the real source of the disagreement.

4. Treat the other person with respect. It takes willpower to fight the gravitational pull toward disrespect and negative emotional reactions when you are in disagreement.

5. When you have pinpointed the problem, together investigate alternative solutions. Remain nonjudgmental, and search for at least five possibilities.

6. Together, evaluate the possibilities you've both generated, listing pros and cons. Remember, the goal is to work with the other party to find the best solution for both of you.

7. Once you have evaluated the alternatives, commit to a solution with the other person.

8. At this point, clearly state the solution and develop a plan to execute it. List the specific action steps, assign responsibility, and set specific completion dates for each step. It's important that the plan be specific and that each step be measurable and attainable.

9. Develop a plan for future follow-up meetings or discussions to evaluate how things are going. Provide positive feedback when things are working well.

Working Toward Win/Win Solutions

Successful negotiation engages people, especially those who have ongoing interaction, in seeking and identifying a solution satisfactory to all. When both sides are open to winning on some points and compromising or losing on others, they are more likely to arrive at a solution they can accept and support. When a clear winner and a clear loser emerge from a negotiation session, hard feelings are likely to result. The "loser" may undermine the solution, and it is possible that no one will "win" in the long run.

To develop a win/win style:

1. Carefully monitor your tendencies to want to win. Look for positions proposed by the other person that you could live with.

Seek an outcome that includes some of the items you want and some of the items the other person wants.

2. During a disagreement, find a common goal on which you both agree and keep focusing on that goal. Tackle the disagreement after identifying areas of agreement. Remember to attack the problem, not the person.

3. After a disagreement, write down your analysis of what took place. Recall both of your initial positions and compare them with the outcome. Note the extent to which both sides compromised and the extent to which both sides "won."

While you may want to work toward a win/win outcome, you could find yourself in a conflict with someone who approaches situations from a win/lose perspective. In these cases, you may feel like you have to protect yourself. The result of such defensiveness, though, is that you can fall into win/lose behavior yourself. To better deal with such situations, use the following suggestions:

- Be aware of when you're falling into a win/lose mode. Catch yourself.

- Challenge the other person on your perception of his or her behavior. For example, you might say, "It seems to me that you want to resolve this in a way that benefits your group and that you don't care about the impact on my people." By checking out this perception and confronting it directly, you may find that you were wrong, or that after the clarification the person stops the behavior. If you confirm your initial feeling on the matter, resist the temptation to "get" the other person.

- Continue to strive to resolve the conflict in a win/win style, but also be prepared to find another solution that doesn't require the cooperation of the other person.

Minimizing Recurrent Conflict

Recurrent conflict can have damaging repercussions on a work unit's efforts. To minimize this type of conflict, follow these guidelines:

1. List the two or three people or departments who tend to "lock horns" on the job.

2. For each source of conflict, determine its cause. For example, does the conflict arise because people require the same resources at the same time? Or because people have different philosophies about how the operation should be conducted?

3. Next, analyze the problem from each perspective. Be as objective as possible, and try to understand the other people's reasons for behaving as they do.

4. Decide if it is necessary to meet. If it is, begin the discussion by stating your goal — to reduce the conflict so that work can be accomplished more efficiently. Then ask the other people to describe the problems from their perspectives. Because you initiated the conflict resolution process, it is important that you take steps to manage any tension that arises.

5. Once both sides have stated their problems, move into the problem-solving mode to determine ways to work together to minimize conflict in the future. In this phase, it is important that both sides remain open to compromise.

6. If all concerned are able to reach consensus on ways to reduce conflict, agree to meet periodically in the future to discuss progress and any problems that arise. Face-to-face discussions will help keep conflict from escalating.

Resolving Conflict Among Your Employees

Handling conflict between employees is a sensitive issue. While it's important not to interfere too much, your intervention may be necessary at times. The following guidelines will help you choose an appropriate and productive level of involvement:

1. Get feedback from your employees on your current level of involvement in their conflicts. Are you involved too much, or not enough?

2. Whenever possible, encourage your people to resolve their conflicts themselves and not come to you for a resolution. If an employee is reluctant to do so, coach him or her on how to deal with the other person to resolve the conflict. If necessary, role-play a conflict resolution situation with the employee to allow him or her to practice.

3. When conflict arises that does require your intervention (such that the employees cannot resolve it themselves), follow this procedure:

   • Help the individuals involved define the problem in specific, observable terms.

   • Ensure that each person listens to the other.

   • Help them identify areas of agreement.

- Have them brainstorm alternative approaches and determine viable solutions.

- Create a problem-resolution plan. If they are unable to do this cooperatively, it may be necessary for you to step in and determine the best course of action.

- Set up future meetings during which they can discuss how things are going and whether the chosen approach is working.

RECOMMENDED READINGS	The publications listed here were selected for their content and suitability to a managerial audience.
Human Relations in Organizations (5th ed.)	**Costley, Dan L., and Todd, Ralph,** St. Paul, MN: West Publishing, 1993 ISBN: 0-314-02689-4 This book focuses on the behavior of individuals in organizations. Its emphasis is on the skills needed for effective leadership including the abilities to communicate, understand human needs, cope with conflict and frustration, motivate others, use authority, and increase group productivity.
Power and Influence	**Dilenschneider, Robert L.,** Englewood Cliffs, NJ: Prentice-Hall, 1991 ISBN: 0-13-683327-6 The author, a proven master at turning corporate crises into corporate opportunities, explains how to become an "influential manager," how to influence the marketplace, and how to deal with crises.
Getting to Yes: Negotiating Agreement Without Giving In	**Fisher, Roger, and Ury, William,** New York: Penguin Books, 1991 ISBN: 0-14-015735-2 The authors provide a straightforward, universally applicable method for negotiating personal and professional disputes without getting taken and without getting nasty. The authors offer the reader a concise, step-by-step, proven strategy for coming to mutually acceptable agreements in every sort of conflict.
Credibility: How Leaders Gain and Lose It	**Kouzes, James M., and Posner, Barry Z.,** San Francisco: Jossey-Bass, 1993 ISBN: 1-55542-550-X In this book Kouzes and Posner, the leadership experts, show why leadership is fundamentally a relationship with credibility as the cornerstone. By providing rich examples, they show how leaders can encourage greater initiative, risk taking, and productivity by demonstrating trust in employees and resolving conflicts on the basis of principles, not positions.

The Clash of Cultures: Managers Managing Professionals

Raelin, Joseph A., New York: McGraw-Hill, 1992
ISBN: 0-07-103316-5
This book examines the relationships between managers and professionals such as engineers, nurses, doctors, lawyers, teachers, accountants, and so forth. The author contends that standard management practices are no longer sufficient when working with professionals. Specific techniques and methods for minimizing and managing conflict between professionals and corporate managers are provided.

Learning to Manage Conflict

Tjosvold, Dean, New York: The Free Press, 1993
ISBN: 0-02-932491-2
The author holds that not only is conflict inevitable, but it is beneficial. Learning how to manage conflict is essential for success in both personal and business relationships. The author introduces a technique called "cooperative conflict" where the parties in conflict learn to look for common goals and then work together to achieve those goals.

Getting Past No: Negotiating Your Way From Confrontation to Cooperation

Ury, William L., New York: Bantam Books, 1993
ISBN: 0-553-37131-2
Ury, co-author of the best-seller *Getting to Yes*, tells in this book how to deal with difficult negotiators by winning them over rather than simply winning. The book details a proven five-step strategy for handling tough negotiators and the challenging situations they present. By using these techniques, you will learn how to settle difficult negotiations amicably.

Discovering Common Ground

Weisbord, Marvin R., San Francisco: Berrett-Koehler, 1993
ISBN: 1-881052-08-7
The author explains a highly successful new way for organizations of all types to apply global thinking and democratic values to achieve rapid whole systems improvement. "Future searches" bring people with diverse interests together to create shared vision and collaborative action.

SUGGESTED SEMINARS

The seminars listed here were selected for their appeal to a managerial audience. The reputation of the vendor, the quality of their seminar offerings, and the specific seminar content were considered in the selection process.

Because of the dynamic nature of the seminar marketplace, some seminars may have been upgraded or replaced, and others may no longer be offered. Likewise, costs and locations may have changed since this listing was compiled. We recommend that you contact the vendor directly for updated and additional information.

Team Building and Conflict Management

In this seminar, participants learn to effectively: monitor group interaction; contribute to the team process as either a team leader or team member; maintain positive working relationships with other team members; and turn destructive conflict into constructive conflict.
Length: 1 day; Cost: $350
Location: New York
Arthur Andersen & Company
1345 Avenue of the Americas, New York, NY 10105
Telephone: 212/708-8080

Managing Differences and Agreement: Making Conflict Work for You

This seminar is designed to teach managers multiple options for successfully managing the opposition, conflict, clashes, discord, and other disagreements that arise when working with individuals and within teams. The program creates the confidence to take the lead in resolving differences, increasingly participants' personal effectiveness and ability to influence the performance of others.
Length: 3 days; Cost: $850
Locations: Call vendor
Designed Learning, Inc.
1009 Park Avenue, Plainfield, NJ 07060
Telephone: 908/754-5102

Communication Workshop: Learning by Doing

Through structured practice, participants learn to improve communication, practice skills involved in communicating and listening, understand problems of organizational communication, explore the effect of stress on interpersonal communication, practice giving and receiving feedback, and gain greater awareness of one's own communication style and impact on others.
Length: 6 days; Cost: $1,245
Location: Bethel, ME
NTL Institute
1240 North Pitt Street, Suite 100
Alexandria, VA 22314-1403
Telephone: 800/777-5227

Targeted Leadership Coaching

Participants in this program work one-on-one with a personal coach who provides a challenging, yet supportive and positive environment for learning and development. The training focuses on learning the competencies, including skills, tactics, strategies, and principles, to increase participants' performance in their own career setting.
Length: 4 or 5 half-day sessions; Cost: Call vendor
Locations: Call vendor
Personnel Decisions International
2000 Plaza VII Tower, 45 South Seventh Street
Minneapolis, MN 55402-1608
Telephone: 800/633-4410

People Skills

This seminar teaches the participant the skills involved in listening, reaching agreement, confronting problems, and managing conflict. Private coaching in instant-replay video sessions helps participants develop their skills and monitor their progress.
Length: 4 days; Cost: $1,100
Location: Cazenovia, NY; San Francisco
Ridge Associates, Inc.
5 Ledyard Avenue, Cazenovia, NY 13035
Telephone: 315/655-3393

Trust and Teamwork

This seminar teaches specific skills necessary to bring compassion and accountability to the workplace. Experiential in nature, the program focuses on creating a more collaborative, open, and trusting work environment. Participants will examine their own communication styles, learn to manage their credibility, create collaboration, and learn constructive confrontation skills.
Length: 2 days; Cost: $595
Locations: Call vendor
The Atlanta Consulting Group
1600 Parkwood Circle, Suite 200, Atlanta, GA 30339
Telephone: 800/852-8224

Achieving Performance Targets

Using a behavior-based feedback tool, this program is designed to help participants develop the skills necessary to effectively manage interpersonal tension. The program covers dealing with tension in others and with personal tension, listening skills, feedback skills, effective confrontation, and conflict resolution.
Length: 2 days; Cost: $595
Locations: Call vendor
The Tracom Corporation
3773 Cherry Creek North Drive, Suite 950
Denver, CO 80209
Telephone: 800/221-2321

LEADERSHIP SKILLS

LEADERSHIP SKILLS

Leadership: the ability to make things happen by encouraging and channeling the contributions of others, taking a stand on and addressing important issues, and acting as a catalyst for change and continuous improvement.

In the past, leadership was simpler. Yesterday's managers could demand performance. Today's managers are faced with a more educated and democratically oriented workforce. Problems and opportunities are complex and challenging.

As a result, today's manager must encourage and apply the contributions of all of the company's human resources, both individually and in groups. You need the creativity and resourcefulness of everyone to find solutions and the commitment of all employees to implement these solutions effectively.

This chapter contains developmental activities in the following seven major areas of leadership skills identified as essential to managerial success:

Provide Direction: Fosters the development of a common vision; provides clear direction and priorities; clarifies roles and responsibilities.

Lead Courageously: Steps forward to address difficult issues; puts self on the line to deal with important problems; stands firm when necessary.

Influence Others: Asserts own ideas and persuades others; gains support and commitment from others; mobilizes people to take action.

Foster Teamwork: Builds effective teams committed to organizational goals; fosters collaboration among team members and among teams; uses teams to address relevant issues.

Motivate Others: Encourages and empowers others to achieve; establishes challenging performance standards; creates enthusiasm, a feeling of investment, and a desire to excel.

Coach and Develop Others: Accurately assesses strengths and development needs of employees; gives timely, specific feedback and helpful coaching; provides challenging assignments and opportunities for development.

Champion Change: Challenges the status quo and champions new initiatives; acts as a catalyst of change and stimulates others to change; paves the way for needed changes; manages implementation effectively.

PROVIDE DIRECTION

The hallmark of an effective leader is clear focus and direction. Successful leaders operate with a vision of where they are going, and they use this vision to inspire their people and their organization.

Some leaders generate this vision and direction from within themselves and then develop support for it within their organization. Others work with their teams to create a vision together. In either case, it is this clear vision and focused direction that allow leaders to align and direct the energy and resources of the organization to achieve desired goals.

Successful managers align their vision with that of the larger organization of which they are a part. They then work with their team to identify the mission and goals of the team, out of which come the roles and responsibilities of each individual. This process helps ensure that each individual's objectives and decisions support the larger vision and eliminates many activities that are counterproductive.

This section provides suggestions on how to create and communicate your vision for your area to clarify each person's responsibilities in creating that vision. It addresses the issues of:

- Fostering the Development of a Common Vision

- Providing Direction and Defining Priorities

- Clarifying Roles and Responsibilities

- Linking the Team's Mission to That of the Organization

- Making the Team's Mission and Strategies Clear to Others

Valuable Tips

- Use your employees or management team to help create and update your vision, mission, and strategies on a yearly basis.

- Communicate your vision, mission, and strategies — and the rationale behind them — throughout the organization.

- Remember that effective leaders focus on the "right stuff."

- Make sure your direction is customer focused.

- Clearly communicate departmental objectives and solicit input from your employees on what they can do to help achieve them.

- Be willing to set priorities.

- Meet with employees to show them how their contributions support the goals of the organization.

- Periodically ask your employees for their vision of where they see their jobs and the department going. Use their ideas to update the vision statement when appropriate.

- Make sure that new employees receive a copy of the department's vision and mission statements and that their role in meeting these is clear.

- Meet with people who are skilled in translating broad strategies into day-to-day activities to get their ideas on how to provide good direction to your people.

- Consider having annual off-site meetings with your entire department to discuss performance in the past year and goals for the upcoming year.

Fostering the Development of a Common Vision

The foundation of an effective organization and team is a common vision and mission that is understood and accepted by everyone.

A vision is a statement of the future state that is desired. Each part of the organization should have its own vision of how it will contribute to the overall vision of the organization.

An organization and its parts also need a mission. A mission statement clarifies the organization's present state by defining:

- What business it is in
- What the boundaries of the business are
- Who its customers are
- How departments and individuals work together
- What needs to be accomplished
- How success is measured

Your team's vision and mission will focus its energy, clarify its goals, and set priorities in place. It will also help you and your team to reach agreement on team members' roles and the team's direction.

As the leader of a team, it is your responsibility to initiate the creation or refinement of your team's vision and mission. To do so, consider this process:

1. Set aside time for you and your team to meet about this. A two-day off-site meeting is commonly used for this purpose.

2. Before the meeting, analyze the internal and external factors affecting your business. At the beginning of the meeting, present and discuss these factors. Factors to consider include:

External	*Internal*
Competition	Strengths and weaknesses
Resources	Financial picture
Market	Talent pool
Vendors and suppliers	Quality processes
Customers	Organizational culture
Legislation/regulation	Management style
Global issues	

3. Next, use a visualization process to create individual visions.

   - Have team members visualize the way your business/team will look in five years. Ask them questions such as:

          - What is our business?
          - Who are our customers?
          - What is the team doing?
          - Who does the team consist of?
          - How is the work being done?
          - Where is the work being done?

- Have each team member write down what he or she saw or thought of in the visualization exercise.

- Share individual visions with the group without judgment.

4. Identify common themes and write them into draft statements. Compare these themes with your current vision statement.

5. Obtain agreement on the draft.

6. Focus next on the mission. Ask the question, "What business are we in?" Come to consensus on this question.

7. Identify strategies for achieving your mission and vision. Select the strategies most likely to lead to success.

8. Identify the "critical success factors" necessary to accomplish your mission and vision. Critical success factors are key activities the team needs to do, and do right, in order to achieve your vision and mission. Review your analysis (second step) to assist in identifying the factors.

9. Share your vision, mission, and strategies with others in your organization.

10. Make certain that everyone on the team knows and tracks the team's critical success factors.

Creating and refining your vision and mission and identifying the critical success factors will provide focus for your team. Periodically revisit your vision and mission to ensure that it is current; changes both internal and external to the organization may spur a need for fine tuning. Also review your team's efforts to ensure that they are pointed in the direction of your defined mission and critical success factors.

Providing Direction and Defining Priorities

People are most productive when they have a clear idea of what is expected of them, both on a daily basis and over the longer term. Being clear about organizational priorities enables employees to make appropriate decisions about the most important issues to tackle. You can take steps to clearly communicate the overall direction of a team to both current and new team members.

For current team members:

I'M SORRY I RUSHED OUT OF THE MEETING THIS MORNING, BUT I THOUGHT WE NEEDED TO MOVE ON THIS QUICKLY.

- Work with your staff to set team and individual goals and objectives that will lead toward the achievement of the mission.

- Communicate priorities to the team. Informing people of priorities or deciding the priorities with them enables your staff to make decisions without having to consult you when conflicting demands arise.

- Hold periodic update meetings to review the group's progress against goals and to determine whether a change in direction is necessary. For example, if the priority at the beginning of the year was to increase sales, but expenses increased dramatically at mid-year, you may decide to place more emphasis on reducing expenses.

- Use role negotiation to clarify responsibilities, as well as to provide a powerful and effective team-building experience. To negotiate team roles:
  - Find uninterrupted time for your team to meet.
  - Have an objective person facilitate the meeting if emotions are heightened.
  - Have each team member share specific expectations of other team members. If helpful, structure the sharing of expectations by having people describe what they'd like the others to do more of, less of, or the same as they currently are doing. The resulting discussion can be an effective catalyst to clear the air and build a commitment to a common purpose.

- Discuss priorities and expectations during each person's performance review and yearly goal-setting sessions. Measure employees' progress against goals and reward them for their contributions to the success of the group.

For new team members:

- As soon as possible, meet with new employees to discuss your expectations and those of the company, and to identify their expectations. Help the employee prioritize duties to give the job focus and to build support for the vision and mission.

- Hold biweekly update meetings during the first two months to monitor progress, revisit direction, and discuss new priorities.

- Clearly explain team relationships, what to expect, and who is responsible for what; take the time to orient the new member to the environment.

- Establish some short-term goals for the new employee's first several months.

Clarifying Roles and Responsibilities

Clarifying responsibilities increases ownership, alleviates conflicts, and eliminates unnecessary ambiguity. Furthermore, letting other areas know who is responsible for what allows your area to be more responsive to customer needs and can keep things from "falling through the cracks." Role clarification is an ongoing process in a dynamic organization. The following tips can help your team members clarify their roles and responsibilities:

- Use job descriptions to convey specific responsibilities to employees and interested others. If you don't have job descriptions for positions in your area, work with your human resources representative and your employees to put these together. Review them every couple of years to make sure that they are still up to date.

- Meet on a regular basis with your employees to discuss their current perceptions of their roles and the work they do. Discuss similarities to and differences from your expectations.

- When there are differences in role expectations among your employees, work with them to resolve the differences.

- Where there are voids in responsibilities, work with your team to identify ways to cover the responsibilities. When team consensus is not possible or not appropriate, make a decision and let the team know the rationale for your decision.

Linking the Team's Mission to That of the Organization

Sometimes employees are unclear about how their work ties into the organization; or they may be asked to do things that seem meaningless or unimportant. Tying individual goals and tasks to the organization's objectives can help employees view their assignments as important. Your contribution as an effective manager is to ensure that you and your people plan and act in a manner consistent with what the organization intends to accomplish. The following guidelines can help:

- Before you establish your department's goals and objectives, ask your boss for input on his or her goals and objectives. Then determine how your team can support them.

- When setting new objectives, help your employees see how these contribute to the group and to the organization as a whole. For example, explain how the group's task contributes to profitability.

- Groom some employees as spokespersons to represent your area at company-wide meetings. Rotate this assignment if possible. Giving employees a chance to talk about their area's work and hear from others is an excellent way for staff members to see how their work fits into the overall picture.

- During department meetings, take time to explain how the work group is measuring up against the overall objectives of the company. For example, if one of the organization's goals is customer responsiveness, give your staff feedback you have received from customers and others about your group's responsiveness.

- Revisit your plans and objectives to ensure that they are consistent with the organization's overall objectives. Review individual development plans and performance appraisal criteria to ensure that they, too, are consistent with the company's top priorities.

Making the Team's Mission and Strategies Clear to Others

Once you have a mission in place for your team, communicate it to others who are important to the success of your group. Doing so will help you gain the understanding and support you need to get your job done. The following suggestions can help you communicate your mission:

- When communicating your team's vision and mission, use specific, "real-life" examples to make the vision and mission clear and captivating to others. Explain exactly how they link to the overall objectives of the organization.

- Post your vision and mission so that people who enter your work area can see them. Talk about them often.

- When proposing strategies to other areas, clearly state your purpose and rationale for the actions you propose. Whenever possible, link your proposals to organization-wide initiatives.

- Keep your manager abreast of your group's progress in fulfilling the team mission. If you turn in status reports, include a section on how well your group is doing against the mission. If possible, include "hard data" (for example, dollar figures, specific feedback, production numbers) to support your comments.

Making your team's mission and strategy clear to others is a process, not an event. Continue to communicate with and update others on your team's progress with respect to the mission, and also communicate any changes the team has made to its vision or mission.

RECOMMENDED READINGS

The publications listed here were selected for their content and suitability to a managerial audience.

The Northbound Train: Finding the Purpose, Setting the Direction, Shaping the Destiny of Your Organization

Albrecht, Karl, New York: AMACOM, 1994
ISBN: 0-8144-0233-X
This comprehensive book explores future trends in the business world and what successful companies will have to concentrate on to survive and prosper. Albrecht can help you create a vision for your company based on creating value for the customer.

Managing by Storying Around

Armstrong, David, New York: Doubleday, 1992
ISBN: 0-385-42154-0
Armstrong has taken one of the oldest forms of communication — storytelling — and turned it into a powerful management tool. His method is simple and timeless yet effective for imparting information from rules and training to policies.

Competing for the Future

Hamel, Gary, and Prahalad, C.K., Boston: Harvard Business School Press, 1994
ISBN: 0-87584-416-2
The authors postulate that managers in today's most successful firms are more interested in creating new competitive space than positioning themselves in the existing market. Companies need to develop foresight by not only looking at the possible, but influencing the direction their industry is taking. This book shows how to develop stretch goals and build core competencies to create advantages and new markets for the future.

Playing For Keeps

Harmon, Frederick G., New York: John Wiley & Sons, 1996
ISBN: 0-471-59847-X
Based on case studies of large, international corporations, the author contends that every organization has its own set of "core values" that drive the way the organization conducts business. Provided are methods for measuring and implementing values, as well as tools that will help managers understand how to make the most of the relationship between personal goals and corporate goals.

Vision in Action

Tregoe, Benjamin B.; Zimmerman, John W.; Smith, Ronald A.; and Tobia, Peter M., New York: Simon & Schuster, 1990
ISBN: 0-671-70643-8
The authors focus on two central and related themes: 1) how to take the strategic direction formulated by top management and translate that direction into reality, and 2) how to go about achieving the participation necessary for implementing the vision.

Organizational Capability

Ulrich, Dave, and Lake, Dale, New York: John Wiley & Sons, 1990
ISBN: 0-471-61807-1
The authors go beyond the premise that the people of a company are its most important asset by introducing a concept they call "organizational capability." This concept is meant to help organizations realize their potential for competing from the inside out. Based on the authors' extensive research and first-hand experience with clients, this book offers both a strategic overview of organizational capability and precise guidelines for putting it into action.

SUGGESTED SEMINARS

The seminars listed here were selected for their appeal to a managerial audience. The reputation of the vendor, the quality of their seminar offerings, and the specific seminar content were considered in the selection process.

Because of the dynamic nature of the seminar marketplace, some seminars may have been upgraded or replaced, and others may no longer be offered. Likewise, costs and locations may have changed since this listing was compiled. We recommend that you contact the vendor directly for updated and additional information.

Leadership and Teamwork

The purpose of this seminar is to increase participants' ability to unify a team and to provide participants with comprehensive personal feedback. Key components include: resolving conflict and managing differences; defining, demonstrating, and mediating values for effective teamwork; and motivating and facilitating superior team performance on the job.
Length: 3 days; Cost: $2,300
Locations: Call vendor
Center for Creative Leadership
One Leadership Place, P.O. Box 26300
Greensboro, NC 27438-6300
Telephone: 910/545-2810

The Empowered Manager: Developing Positive Political Skills

This seminar presents empowerment as a business strategy that will enable managers to do more with less. Topics include maintaining a high quality of work life in an increasingly competitive marketplace, developing a vision, and examining ways of building alliances.
Length: 3 days; Cost: $1,200
Locations: Call vendor
Designed Learning, Inc.
1009 Park Avenue, Plainfield, NJ 07060
Telephone: 908/754-5102

Leadership and Mastery

This program is offered to executives and senior and middle managers. Its purpose is to challenge leaders to rethink and reawaken the potential of their own organizations. During the program, participants will work with advanced concepts of organizational and personal effectiveness. The program presumes that participants have management skills and experience.
Length: 3 days; Cost: $2,450
Locations: Call vendor
Innovation Associates, Inc.
3 Speen Street, Suite 140, Framingham, MA 01701
Telephone: 508/879-8301

Facilitative Leadership: Tapping the Power of Participation

In this seminar, participants learn how to: encourage team participation by focusing on process, results, and relationships; appropriately involve people in problem solving and decision making; design meetings, project plans, and change strategies that people support and understand; and develop a personal plan for continuously improving themselves as leaders.
Length: 3 days; Cost: $1,125
Locations: Call vendor
Interaction Associates, Inc.
600 Townsend Street, Suite 550, San Francisco, CA 94103
Telephone: 415/241-8000

Project Management

This hands-on, results-oriented program will assist managers in completing projects on schedule, within budget, and with the desired results by: clarifying project goals, specifying the needed resources, scheduling the project and assigning responsibility for completing tasks, monitoring and modifying the project during implementation, and evaluating the success of the project.
Length: 3 days; Cost: $1,095
Locations: Call vendor
Kepner Tregoe
Research Road, P.O. Box 704, Princeton, NJ 08542
Telephone: 800/537-6378

Impact Leadership

Participants in this workshop will learn more about their assets as a leader, understand their organization and its changes, learn how to enlist others in their vision, and establish their own leadership agenda. Working alone and in small groups, participants will identify leadership opportunities, set priorities, plan action steps, mark the milestones to achieving their vision, and set goals to continue developing their personal and interpersonal leadership.
Length: 5-1/2 days; Cost: $4,150
Locations: Call vendor
Personnel Decisions International
2000 Plaza VII Tower, 45 South Seventh Street
Minneapolis, MN 55402-1608
Telephone: 800/633-4410

Leadership Through People Skills

This seminar is designed to teach participants the practical skills it takes to become leader-managers, turn vision into reality, empower people with the freedom to act competently and confidently, and manage in all directions — upward with the boss, laterally with coworkers, and downward with direct reports.
Length: 3-1/2 days; Cost: $1,245
Location: St. Louis
Psychological Associates, Inc.
8201 Maryland Avenue, St. Louis, MO 63105
Telephone: 800/345-6525

Management of Managers: Leadership, Change, and Renewal

This program is designed to enable managers to become more effective and to derive more personal satisfaction from their corporate positions. Participants will review their current level of management proficiency, explore new techniques in managerial leadership, develop plans for renewing those leadership roles, and implement improvements for themselves and their organization.
Length: 12 days; Cost: $6,450
Location: Dallas
Southern Methodist University, Executive Development
Edwin J. Cox School of Business
Dallas, TX 75275-0333
Telephone: 214/768-3549

The Leadership Challenge Workshop

This seminar is an intensive program on the leadership practices required to get extraordinary things done. It strengthens individuals' abilities and self-confidence to lead others in challenging situations. It is based on the award-winning book *The Leadership Challenge* by Jim Kouzes.
Length: 2-1/2 days; Cost: $1,800
Location: Monterey, CA
TPG/Learning Systems
The Tom Peters Group
555 Hamilton Avenue, Suite 300, Palo Alto, CA 94301
Telephone: 800/333-8878

LEAD COURAGEOUSLY

Today's environment demands that leaders make decisions that involve risk, and take their stand in the face of ambiguity or adversity. Managers who lead courageously confront problems directly and take action based on what they believe is right. They win the respect and commitment of others by standing up for what they believe; making tough decisions despite ambiguity; by supporting others who make difficult decisions; and by following issues through to completion in spite of adversity.

The suggestions in this section cover the following topics:

- Clarifying What Is Important to You
- Taking a Stand for Your Values
- Demonstrating Managerial Courage
- Driving Hard on the Right Issues
- Taking a Stand to Resolve Important Issues
- Confronting Problems Promptly
- Being Decisive
- Challenging Others to Make Tough Choices

Valuable Tips

- Identify your most deeply held convictions. Use those convictions to guide your leadership.

- Give people the feedback they need even when it may be difficult.

- Openly acknowledge that your stand may be unpopular, and then explain why it is important for others to consider your point of view.

- Stand behind your people and back their decisions.

- Say "no" clearly and explain why.

- Attack problems, not people.

- Identify the people in your organization whose courage you most admire. Talk with them and learn how they act on their convictions.

- Talk with decision makers about how they arrived at their decisions and how they dealt with people's reactions. Incorporate some of their ideas and strategies.

- Use simple, clear language when communicating your position.

- When you see a need or problem that you wish someone would address, ask yourself if *you* could be doing something about it.

- In meetings, verbalize your concerns so they can be openly discussed.

- Determine if one of your veteran staff members has a chronic performance problem that no one has really addressed. Then deal with it.

- Identify the upper-level manager you find most intimidating or critical and make a conscious effort to be candid with this person during your next encounter.

- Honestly determine if you tend to avoid passing negative information upward.

- Report on both your successes and your failures with equal candor.

- Look at your staff and decide if you are spending more energy protecting them than holding them accountable.

- Step forward with a position of principle even when there is ambiguity regarding the facts.

LEAD COURAGEOUSLY

- Take calculated risks. Ask yourself, "What is the worst thing that could happen?" and then decide if proceeding is worth the risk.

- After speaking up for what you believe is important, be gracious whether your ideas are accepted or rejected.

- Remember that being a manager is not a popularity contest. You may not always be liked, but you should be respected.

- Show the courage to let your people learn from their mistakes.

- Believe that you have the power to make a difference, and accept the responsibility of trying.

- Read books or watch movies that exemplify true courage in others. They can inspire you to strengthen your courage in dealing with work-related issues.

Clarifying What Is Important to You

Championing something that you believe is right or important requires conviction. It's not always easy to go against the mainstream or to choose the more disruptive course of action. Therefore, knowing what is most important to you will strengthen your convictions and values.

To clarify what is really important to you:

- Carefully consider the following questions. Then write down your answers and file them in a place where you can review and update them regularly.
  - What is most important to me?
  - What do I value the most?
  - What is worth "fighting" or standing up for?
  - On which of my values will I never compromise?

- Develop a leadership creed that captures the essence of what leadership is to you. Share your creed with others. Periodically evaluate whether you are leading your team in a way that is consistent with your beliefs.

- Think about the legacy you want to leave your team and your organization. When you leave, what things or qualities do you want to be remembered for? Evaluate what you are currently doing, and make whatever changes are feasible or most realistic.

Taking a Stand for Your Values

Identifying what is most important to you establishes the foundation for leading courageously when it matters. Try the following suggestions to bolster your leadership courage:

- When facing a difficult dilemma or decision, examine it against your deeply held convictions and values. This will give you direction.

- Look for situations in which others may be overly concerned about taking a stand, but where you strongly believe in the "rightness" of your position based on your convictions. Make your rationale and position clear to others.

- Actively look for opportunities to stand up for what you believe. Push visibly and openly for the kind of involvement that supports your values.

Demonstrating Managerial Courage

Managers are often faced with situations in which taking the most appropriate course of action carries with it a backlash of complaints, problems, and negative reactions. It requires courage to take action in these situations. If others perceive you as lacking courage, try the following:

- Support your people when they make tough choices, particularly when people complain to you. Endorse your employees' decisions when appropriate.

- Confront tough issues head on. In the long run, no one benefits by ignoring issues that must be addressed and resolved. You can show respect and concern for people by confronting tough issues, not by ignoring them.

- Say "no" when necessary. Don't procrastinate or "soften the blow" by being tentative. When it's best for the organization to refuse a request, clearly explain to those involved why you cannot support them.

- When you are reluctant to make a change, ask yourself what is behind your resistance. If the answer is that you are afraid of change, push yourself to make the transition. Recognize that change is very difficult, but that being a willing champion of a new directive may be just what the organization needs.

- When facing a tough decision, such as trimming the budget or downsizing, carefully analyze various alternatives, get others' input, and settle on the course of action that meets the criteria you deem important. Then, when you communicate your decision, you will have the background and data to support your actions.

- Don't forget the "people" side of making tough decisions. Be prepared to deal with others' reactions and to direct people to resources that will help them deal with the impact of the decision.

- Don't be a "yes person" to upper management. Decide what is important and stand up for it. Most upper-level managers are not impressed by people who will not stand up for what they believe is important.

- Identify one risk you are afraid to take. Carefully analyze its potential benefits and negative consequences. Figure out what you would do if the worst-case scenario occurred. Then reevaluate whether you can take the risk.

Driving Hard on the Right Issues

Remember the old adage "choose your battles carefully" when you are deciding how best to spend your energies. You can't possibly do everything, but it is especially critical for you to address the issues that get in the way of, or further the development of, your mission. Following these guidelines can help you focus on what's important:

- When faced with a number of issues that need your attention, use the following criteria to decide which to handle first:
  - Does this issue involve my core values?
  - Does this issue impede my group in some way?
  - Is this issue a roadblock in the critical path to the achievement of our team's or organization's goals?
  - Will this issue damage important relationships?
  - For whom is this an important issue?
  - Is this issue important for now or for the future?

  Answering "yes" to any of these questions probably means you should address the issue. Ask yourself, "What will happen if I don't address the issue?"

- Ask your direct reports, peers, customers, and your manager what they believe are the critical issues on which you should focus.

- Determine the critical paths for your group. Address the issues and problems that block or hinder the success of the group.

- Think ahead. What are the critical issues that must be addressed for success in the future?

- If you turn an issue over to someone else, follow up and follow through. Ask for updates, progress reports, and problems, and let others know that you are on top of the issue.

Taking a Stand to Resolve Important Issues

Taking a stand and pushing to resolve important issues require clear communication, a strong emphasis on paying attention to and working with others, persistence, and the courage of your convictions.

When asserting your position, be wary of using tentative language like, "I might be persuaded to… " or "I'm not sure that it's the best way…" Instead, use firm, assertive language to state your position. Even if you are not ready to make a decision, explain this clearly to others (for example, "From the data I have, I am not comfortable making a decision at this time.").

- Listen carefully to reactions from others. Acknowledge their points of view and, when possible, incorporate them into your thinking or plans.

- Make an effort to help others see the issue from your point of view.

- Focus simultaneously on the stand you are taking and on trying to resolve the problem cooperatively whenever possible.

- Before you take a stand, decide how strongly and long you are willing to push or stand firm. What is your bottom line? How can you compromise? Then, pay attention to the impact of your behavior so that you can accurately monitor its effect on others.

- Follow issues through to completion. Persisting at problem solving sends a strong message that you want issues resolved as quickly as possible, and that you are willing to do what is necessary to bring problems to closure.

- Be gracious whether your ideas are accepted or rejected.

- When people ask you to be their advocate or to take a stand on a particular issue, listen carefully. Decide what you will do, and then get back to the person with the results. If you disagree with the request and cannot give your support, clearly explain your rationale.

Confronting Problems Promptly

When important individual or team issues come to your attention, it is critical to respond quickly. Addressing problems keeps them from growing and conveys the message to your team that you are willing to tackle tough issues.

To ensure that you confront problems in a timely way, try these suggestions:

- When you learn of an issue that has the potential to affect your group, take steps to look into it as quickly as possible. This may take the form of informal meetings with others affected by the issue, or a more formal investigation of the problem.

- If others come to you with a problem, let them know what you plan to do. Saying nothing may lead others to conclude that you are unconcerned or afraid to address the problem.

- Set goals for solving the problem. For example, set deadlines for investigating the problem and implementing the solution.

Record these benchmarks on your calendar and adhere to them as closely as possible.

- Hold periodic update meetings as a way to catch problems before they get too big. Listen for information suggesting that people are having a hard time getting support and resources, and take steps to resolve these problems.

- If a problem recurs, it's likely that the root source has not yet been addressed. If you find that you are dealing with the same problem over and over, take some time to determine what solutions have not worked in the past, and why, and what could be done to solve the issue permanently.

- If you procrastinate on certain issues, identify the reasons why you are reluctant to move ahead quickly. People procrastinate for a variety of reasons, including:
  - Lack of information
  - Unclear course of action
  - Lack of time to think through the issue
  - Fear of the negative consequences of acting on the problem

  Once you have identified your reasons for procrastinating, substitute decisive behaviors for indecisive ones. For example, if you lack information, quickly begin steps to get the information you need. If the course of action is unclear, get input from others on possible action steps and make a decision about how to proceed.

- Deal with "people problems" when they occur. Managers lose the respect of their peers and employees when they are not willing to deal with people who are negatively affecting the team's success or morale.

Being Decisive

Indecisiveness may result in the perception that you cannot make tough choices or take a stand on issues. The following process may help you increase your decisiveness:

1. Make a list of the major areas in which you have decision-making responsibility (for instance, capital expenditures, staffing, delegating, and policy making).

2. Identify the areas in which you tend to divert responsibility for decision making.

3. Analyze your concerns about making the decision. Find common patterns. For example, you may be uncomfortable making decisions involving technical areas with which you are

unfamiliar, or you may delay making decisions on issues important to your manager.

4. Consider whether any of the following indecisive behaviors apply to you. Then try the suggested action to become more decisive.

- If you have difficulty determining which of several alternatives is best, don't go to others for a decision. Instead, make yourself choose one of the options and develop a rationale for why that alternative is best. Only then should you seek input. Tell others your alternatives and your recommendation, and then ask for their opinions.

- If you turn to others immediately, before you've formulated options, ask yourself why. Do you need more information? If so, gather the facts you need and formulate alternatives on your own.

- If you tend to procrastinate on deadlines, make a commitment to arrive at a major decision by a certain date. For minor decisions, make your judgments within a few minutes.

- If you have a tendency to second-guess yourself, stand by your decision once you have made it. Avoid reopening the decision-making process unless new information strongly indicates a need for reconsideration.

- If you tend to push your decision-making responsibilities upward, get into the habit of presenting recommendations, rather than problems, to your manager.

- If others see you as indecisive because you use tentative language when describing your ideas, try tape recording yourself as you state your decisions and/or get feedback from others on the style with which you communicate your ideas.

- If you have lost touch with what is important to you, ask yourself, "What is more important to me in this situation? What do I care about the most?" The answers may lead you to your decision.

- If you are concerned that taking a stand will cause others to dislike you, remind yourself that it is impossible for everyone to like you, and that even if people don't like you, they may like your ideas. On the other hand, when people reject your ideas, this doesn't mean that they are rejecting you.

- If you look for approval before implementing your decisions, ask yourself whether this approval is really necessary. Consistently seeking approval can give others the impression that you lack confidence. If you are unclear about when you can make decisions independently, meet with your manager to discuss your span of control — where you can make decisions independently and where you need to seek approval.

Challenging Others to Make Tough Choices

As employees grow in capability and responsibility, they encounter situations in which they must make difficult decisions. Sometimes they turn to their manager to make these types of decisions for them.

To help employees develop confidence in their ability to make tough decisions, try these suggestions:

- Resist taking responsibility for your employees' decisions. In areas that are clearly their domain, lend your expertise, but stop short of making the decision for them. By coaching people to take responsibility, you are building their skills and helping them to rely less and less on you.

- The amount of guidance you give your employees may vary depending upon their level of expertise and experience. Gauge your coaching appropriately — provide more for less experienced people, and less for those who have been on the job longer.

- Recognize employees' independent decision making and initiative. Even when employees make poor decisions, take the time to reward their initiative. Then talk through what went wrong and suggest ways to do it differently in the future.

- Model risk taking. When appropriate, talk through problems with your employees and describe how you arrived at the decision you chose. Discuss the risks involved and the issues you considered in deciding to make the tough decision.

RECOMMENDED READINGS

The publications listed here were selected for their content and suitability to a managerial audience.

Crossing the Minefield

Barner, Robert W., New York: AMACOM, 1994
ISBN: 0-8144-0241-0
To be successful in competitive and changing times, you and your team need to know how to stay motivated, energized, and efficient. This book provides strategies for accomplishing this now, rather than later when your team has become stagnant. You will learn how to: help your staff manage stress, respond quickly to demands from customers and your company, focus your efforts, inspire team members, streamline your team, and reenergize yourself to meet new challenges.

Leadership When the Heat's On

Cox, Danny, and Hoover, John, New York: McGraw-Hill, 1992
ISBN: 0-07-013267-4
The authors contend that leadership is about making a positive difference in the lives of those around you. This book is a guide on how to be the best possible leader, especially during times of change and uncertainty.

The Confident Decision Maker

Dawson, Roger, New York: William Morrow & Company, 1992
ISBN: 0-688-11564-0
Dawson's book explains the core of confident, effective, systematic decision making. Practice his methods for identifying, analyzing, and responding to problems and opportunities, and achieve success through confident choices.

On Leadership

Gardner, John W., New York: The Free Press, 1993
ISBN: 0-02-911312-1
This renowned author takes the reader through a discussion of all aspects of leadership, including: the nature of leadership, the qualities and attributes of a leader, and how an individual becomes an effective leader. The author argues that leadership is the "release of human possibilities" and is a fundamental ideal in our society.

Leadership

Hughes, Richard L.; Ginnett, Robert C.; and Curphy, Gordon J., Burr Ridge, IL: Irwin Professional Publishing, 1992
ISBN: 0-256-10278-3
This textbook proceeds from the premise that leadership is a process, not a position. The authors look at how leadership develops and is measured, leadership as an art as well as a science, and how leadership is related to other concepts, such as power and influence. The book proposes a simple framework for conceptualizing leadership, composed of the Leader, the Followers, and the Situation.

If It Ain't Broke...BREAK IT

Kriegel, Robert J., and Patler, Louis, New York: Warner Books, 1992
ISBN: 0-446-39359-2
The authors contend that conventional business wisdom cannot help you keep pace in these rapidly changing times. Their book will help you unlock the creative thinker inside; work smarter, not harder; and explore new and different paths.

Leading Change

O'Toole, James, San Francisco: Jossey-Bass, 1995
ISBN: 1-55542-608-5
The corporate leader who sets out to command or manipulate employees to lead them through change is, says the author, doomed to failure. Change has been and always will be resisted. The only way to overcome that resistance is to use leadership based on moral values of integrity, trust, and an unwavering commitment to doing what is best for your employees. Also explored are why corporate culture and the status quo conspire to defeat change.

Authentic Leadership

Terry, Robert W., San Francisco: Jossey-Bass, 1993
ISBN: 1-55542-547-X
The author contends that the core principle of leadership is authenticity and that leadership is essential to success. The book begins by introducing the reader to concepts of leadership and is complete with resources and techniques that one can use to further everyday leadership actions.

SUGGESTED SEMINARS

The seminars listed here were selected for their appeal to a managerial audience. The reputation of the vendor, the quality of their seminar offerings, and the specific seminar content were considered in the selection process.

Because of the dynamic nature of the seminar marketplace, some seminars may have been upgraded or replaced, and others may no longer be offered. Likewise, costs and locations may have changed since this listing was compiled. We recommend that you contact the vendor directly for updated and additional information.

Assertiveness Training for Managers

This seminar is designed to teach participants effective assertiveness techniques. Topics include: managing assertively, achieving your objectives, resolving conflicts, and developing a self-improvement plan.
Length: 3 days; Cost: $1,260
Locations: Call vendor
American Management Association
P.O. Box 319, Saranac Lake, NY 12983
Telephone: 800/262-9699

LeaderLab®

LeaderLab® is a two-session program designed to encourage and enable leaders to take more effective actions in their leadership situations. Goals of the program include examining the challenges of leadership in the 21st century; developing an individual learning process which includes analysis, implementation, and evaluation; developing a vision for leadership; and implementing and achieving lasting behavioral change.
Length: 10 days; Cost: $7,300
Locations: Call vendor
Center for Creative Leadership
One Leadership Place, P.O. Box 26300
Greensboro, NC 27438-6300
Telephone: 910/545-2810

Covey Leadership Week

This is a personal experience teaching skills and tools used to create conditions necessary in building trust and empowerment within organizations. This course emphasizes character and explores the distinction between leadership and management.
Length: 5 days; Cost: $3,900 plus meals & lodging
Locations: Call vendor
Covey Leadership Center
3507 North University Avenue, Suite 100, Provo, UT 84606
Telephone: 800/331-7716

Leadership and Mastery

This program is offered to executives and senior and middle managers. Its purpose is to challenge leaders to rethink and reawaken the potential of their own organizations. During the program, participants will work with advanced concepts of organizational and personal effectiveness. The program presumes that participants have management skills and experience.
Length: 3 days; Cost: $2,450
Locations: Call vendor
Innovation Associates, Inc.
3 Speen Street, Suite 140, Framingham, MA 01701
Telephone: 508/879-8301

Developing the Organizational and Personal Self

This program is based on the premise that success is based on self-awareness. Given that, topics include: boundaries; reintegration; acceptance of ourselves; removing self-diminishing myths and behaviors; improving interactions with others; and speaking more clearly, directly, and candidly.
Length: 6 days; Cost: $1,345
Location: Burlington, VT
NTL Institute
1240 North Pitt Street, Suite 100
Alexandria, VA 22314-1403
Telephone: 800/777-5227

Impact Leadership

Participants in this workshop will learn more about their assets as a leader, understand their organization and its changes, learn how to enlist others in their vision, and establish their own leadership agenda. Working alone and in small groups, participants will identify leadership opportunities, set priorities, plan action steps, mark the milestones to achieving their vision, and set goals to continue developing their personal and interpersonal leadership.
Length: 5-1/2 days; Cost: $4,150
Locations: Call vendor
Personnel Decisions International
2000 Plaza VII Tower, 45 South Seventh Street
Minneapolis, MN 55402-1608
Telephone: 800/633-4410

The Executive Development Center

This program is designed to capture the complex skills and dynamic challenges of the general manager's role. For new and prospective executives, it provides a realistic preview of the demands, issues, and daily activities they will face. For experienced executives, it provides an opportunity to renew and refine skills and personal operating style.
Length: 4 days; Cost: $6,800
Locations: Call vendor
Personnel Decisions International
2000 Plaza VII Tower, 45 South Seventh Street
Minneapolis, MN 55402-1608
Telephone: 800/633-4410

The Management Development Center

This program helps managers assess their strengths and development needs in a wide range of managerial and leadership skill areas. Participants are engaged in a realistic simulation of the manager's job. The program provides an opportunity to receive immediate feedback and individualized coaching from fellow managers and highly trained management consultants. A summary report outlining development suggestions and a follow-up development discussion are included.
Length: 3 days; Cost: $4,600
Locations: Call vendor
Personnel Decisions International
2000 Plaza VII Tower, 45 South Seventh Street
Minneapolis, MN 55402-1608
Telephone: 800/633-4410

People Skills

This seminar teaches the participant the skills involved in listening, reaching agreement, confronting problems, and managing conflict. Private coaching in instant-replay video sessions helps participants develop their skills and monitor their progress.
Length: 4 days; Cost: $1,100
Locations: Cazenovia, NY; San Francisco
Ridge Associates, Inc.
5 Ledyard Avenue, Cazenovia, NY 13035
Telephone: 315/655-3393

Positive Power and Influence Program

The program focuses on developing and refining the skills required to influence people and events while building and maintaining beneficial relationships. It covers assessing which influencing styles you use, overuse, misuse, or avoid; refining present skills and developing alternative styles; and applying the appropriate influence style to a given situation.
Length: 3-4 days; Cost: $950 - $1,250
Locations: Call vendor
Situation Management Systems, Inc.
195 Hanover Street, Hanover, MA 02339-2294
Telephone: 617/826-4433

The Leadership Challenge Workshop

This seminar is an intensive program on the leadership practices required to get extraordinary things done. It strengthens individuals' abilities and self-confidence to lead others in challenging situations. It is based on the award-winning book *The Leadership Challenge* by Jim Kouzes.
Length: 2-1/2 days; Cost: $1,800
Location: Monterey, CA
TPG/Learning Systems
The Tom Peters Group
555 Hamilton Avenue, Suite 300, Palo Alto, CA 94301
Telephone: 800/333-8878

Leadership and Decision Making in Organizations

This seminar is designed to help senior managers increase their leadership potential. Through lecture, assessment instruments, and active participation and feedback, participants learn to extend their skills in understanding leadership styles, conflict resolution, decision making, and interpersonal communications.
Length: 4 days; Cost: $3,200
Location: New Haven, CT
Yale University
School of Management, Executive Programs
Box 208200, New Haven, CT 06520-8200
Telephone: 203/432-6038

INFLUENCE OTHERS

Leadership has taken on new meaning and greater challenges in the last decade. Influencing is a critical skill in today's environment, in which you must work with so many people to do your job. No longer can you order things to be done; no longer are problems so simple that everyone agrees on one solution.

Looking into the next century, it appears that leaders in business and industry will continue to encounter situations that will demand increasingly sophisticated skills to get others to endorse their initiatives. Influencing skills, then, will continue to be critical management assets.

This section provides suggestions for developing the following skill areas:

- Increasing Your Leadership Impact
- Improving Leadership through Feedback
- Becoming More Assertive
- Giving Compelling Reasons for Ideas
- Winning Support from Others
- Negotiating Persuasively
- Getting Others to Take Action
- Commanding Attention and Respect in Groups
- Influencing the Decisions of Upper Management

Valuable Tips

- Use a variety of techniques to influence others. View influencing as a problem to be solved. Brainstorm as many ways as possible to influence a particular person.

- Seek assignments that give you an opportunity to lead a group or influence others.

- Be one of the first people to offer ideas in meetings (if you usually let others take the lead).

- Encourage your employees to come to you with ideas, and then support the implementation of ideas you see as viable.

- Don't back down quickly when challenged. Instead, restate your position clearly to ensure that others understand your perspective.

- Prepare for your next meeting by looking over the agenda and thinking about the contributions you can make.

- Informally talk with your peers and your manager about their goals and concerns. Use this information when you need to link your ideas to their needs.

- Observe people in your organization who are highly influential, and try out the techniques that seem to work for them.

- Ask your peers for feedback on how persuasive and influential you are. Ask them for suggestions on what you could do to be more influential.

- Attend a leadership training program such as those offered by Personnel Decisions International, and apply the principles with your own people.

- Practice being more forceful in situations such as community meetings where the costs, risks, and implications are not as great as they are at work.

- Continuously ask yourself how your goals and tasks fit into the broader goals of the organization, and communicate this to others.

- Create a clear vision of the kind of leader you want to be — and then live it.

- Be willing to take the ideas of your people to the next higher level and support them enthusiastically. Give credit where credit is due.

- View yourself as a leader.

- Identify the behaviors that you believe are critical to success in your organization, and then lead by example.

- Adopt a "can-do" attitude and approach challenges from a problem-solving perspective. Look for alternative solutions, rather than focusing on why things can't be done.

- Use one of the "360-degree" feedback instruments offered by Personnel Decisions to get feedback on your leadership skills from your manager, peers, and direct reports.

- Initiate new ideas, objectives, and projects with your manager and with your people.

Increasing Your Leadership Impact

The ability to command the attention of others is necessary for effective leadership. If you suspect that your impact is low, there are several things you can do:

- When you meet with individuals and groups, stand up quickly and introduce yourself, if necessary.

- With employees, be firm and direct when stating expectations or confronting poor performance. Don't dilute your comments with phrases such as "...don't you think?", "It seems to me...," "Maybe I'm wrong, but...," etc. You can be firm and direct without being abrasive or disrespectful.

- If you are uncomfortable stating your point of view directly, consider enrolling in an assertiveness training course to build your skills and develop your confidence in presenting your opinions more forcefully.

- Pay attention to your vocal qualities when giving direction or feedback to others. If you tend to be soft-spoken, work on delivering your message in a more forceful and confident tone.

- Videotape yourself in a leadership role-play situation. Watch the tape to gain further insight into your strengths and development needs. Ask a trusted colleague to watch the tape and give you constructive feedback.

Improving Leadership through Feedback

Most managers do not have clear perceptions of their leadership style and their impact on others. Some feedback can be gained through observing others' reactions and through the feedback others provide in formal and informal settings. In-depth feedback is often helpful, yet others may be hesitant to provide it unless you actively solicit it. Ways to obtain this feedback are outlined in the following guidelines:

- Ask several individuals you trust and respect to give you feedback by answering specific questions, such as:
  - How would you describe my leadership style?
  - What do you feel I do particularly well as a leader? In what areas do I need work?
  - To what extent do I tend to be oriented more toward the work tasks than toward the people doing the work? Do I need to change my emphasis in any way?
  - In areas such as motivating others, managing meetings or groups, coaching my employees, delegating, handling crises, and so forth, have you observed specific situations in which I could have performed better?

You may also wish to ask the same people to provide feedback in the future as you take steps to improve your leadership skills.

- Use a formal instrument (questionnaire or rating scale) to obtain ratings of your performance in a number of areas. Some instruments ask for the input of the concerned individual only; others solicit feedback from direct reports, peers, and/or managers. When completed, these instruments summarize the ratings and provide you with feedback and suggestions for improvement.

  Professionally designed instruments of this type are available from Personnel Decisions International, 2000 Plaza VII Tower, 45 South Seventh Street, Minneapolis, MN 55402.

- Attend a seminar or assessment center designed to provide personal feedback on leadership behavior.

  The Impact Leadership program offered by Personnel Decisions helps managers learn and effectively apply the skills and strategies of leadership through the blending of assessment instruments and exercises, training experiences, and feedback.

- Informally and periodically ask your people, "What can I do to be more helpful and effective?" Show openness and listen carefully to what they tell you.

Becoming More Assertive

People who lack assertiveness skills are often overlooked, and thus have trouble getting their ideas accepted. The ability to present your point of view without offending others, even if you believe that others will disagree, is critical if you want to have an impact on your staff and on the organization. Try these suggestions to strengthen your assertiveness skills:

- If you sometimes have a hard time being assertive because you aren't sure how to phrase your message, use the following techniques to help you frame a strong, direct message:
  - State your observations first. Observations are facts, things that can be seen, heard, or taken in through your senses. Observations differ from opinions in that opinions are your perspectives or beliefs. For example, "You were 15 minutes late for our meeting" is a fact. "You were inconsiderate in coming in late" is an opinion. Facts are objective, cannot be argued, and help the other person understand what you are saying.

- After you state your observations, state your thoughts and feelings about the situation. Preface these statements with "I" to indicate that they are your thoughts and your feelings. For example, "I was frustrated when you were late because it resulted in 15 minutes of unproductive time for the group members."
- Finally, state what you want the other person to do. Make statements about your needs, rather than solutions. Stating needs opens the door to generating many alternative solutions, while stating solutions can close the door.

For example, "I would like you to be on time for meetings" is a statement of needs. A solution is "I will call you five minutes before meetings start to make sure you will be on time." The first statement naturally leads to discussion of options for how to meet the need, while the second statement closes off discussion of other options and places the responsibility for the problem on you.

- Use appropriate nonverbal communication to deliver an effective, assertive message (for example, steady eye contact, serious expression, firm voice, moderate rate of speech). Avoid aggressive gestures and a rigid posture.

- Practice putting together assertive messages before delivering them to others. Role-play them in your mind or actively practice saying them to a trusted colleague.

- Listen to the other person's response to your message. He or she may not be pleased with what you have to say, and it is important for you to hear the other person out. Check the Listen to Others section of this Handbook for some tips.

- Address concerns as soon as you can; delaying communication can escalate to conflict. If you're rattled about something, however, it may be better to remove yourself from the situation for a time. Calm down so that you can express yourself more clearly with assertive control of your intended message.

- Clarify with yourself and others when you are being assertive versus when you are being aggressive. Some people are afraid of being assertive because they perceive their behavior as aggressive, when in fact it is not.

Giving Compelling Reasons for Ideas

People are persuaded by different things. Some people are impressed by a strong, logical argument, while others are swayed by a forceful, impassioned explanation. To be most compelling, adapt your persuasive style to suit your audience. The following suggestions can help:

1. Before presenting your ideas, study your audience.

    *   What is important to your audience? What are their main concerns vis-à-vis your message?

    *   How will your message benefit your audience? What will they get out of accepting your ideas?

    *   Speak with some of the people who will be key to getting your ideas accepted. Get their input on how to approach others from whom you need support.

2. Prepare your argument beforehand. Jot down the three most important points you want to make. Be ready to address the concerns you uncover during the investigation process.

3. Give a brief synopsis of the information you will be discussing before you actually present your ideas. For example, "I've asked everyone to meet today to talk about next year's marketing strategy. I have three points I wish to make, and then I would be interested in getting your input."

4. When delivering your ideas, pay attention to the reaction of your audience. Do they appear engaged? Are they asking questions? Look for signs that they are interested in what you are saying and want to know more.

It's important not only to present the facts, but also to give your perspective on why you believe your ideas are valid. Refer to your beliefs, but also to the concerns of the audience; clearly relate the benefits of your proposal to their concerns.

Winning Support from Others

Gaining support from others is a skill that takes time and practice to hone. Good ideas are often not enough to get others to accept your point of view. If you find that you have a hard time getting support for your ideas, try the following:

*   Ask someone you trust in your organization to give you input on your ability to be persuasive. Have this person watch you in situations where you are attempting to gain others' support. Get feedback on how you came across and what you could have done differently.

- If you feel comfortable, ask for feedback from the people who did not give you their support. What were their concerns? What could you have done that would have swayed them?

- Observe a person in your organization who seems particularly skilled at gaining agreement from others. What techniques does this person use? What does this person do if he or she runs into roadblocks? How does this person state his or her argument? What in particular appeals to you when you listen to this person?

  From your observations, incorporate some of the effective techniques into your influencing behaviors and see how they work for you.

- Before presenting your idea to a group, explain it to a few trusted colleagues. Get their input on its feasibility, and encourage them to challenge you on the various aspects of the idea. Use this information to analyze parts of the process you might not have considered.

- Be aware that your speaking style directly affects how convincing you can be. Record yourself as you practice presenting your idea and analyze how you sound. Ask yourself the following questions:
  - Are my tone of voice and inflection consistent with the meaning of my words and the intention of my message?
  - Does the pace of my speech facilitate understanding?
  - Is the level of my enthusiasm and liveliness appropriate for the topic and setting?
  - Do I express myself in language that is clear enough for others to easily understand what I'm saying?

- If you want others to support your efforts, reciprocate by supporting their ideas and objectives whenever possible.

- For additional suggestions for gaining support, see the sections on Organizational Savvy and Leveraging Networks.

Negotiating Persuasively

Effective negotiation depends on a number of factors: preparation, knowledge of the other person's position and needs, and creativity in coming up with alternative solutions, to name just a few. One key to becoming a persuasive negotiator is to clearly specify how your objectives will benefit the other party or parties involved. The following techniques can help you improve your negotiation skills:

- Before going into a session where you will be presenting your point of view, spend some time thinking about and investigating the other person's position and needs. What is important to them? What are their goals? What can you do for them? The answers to these kinds of questions will give you the information you need to frame your argument during the discussion.

- Talk with others who have dealt with the people with whom you will be negotiating. Find out what has and has not worked in the past.

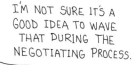

- Know what you want from three perspectives:
  - What is absolutely necessary
  - What is ideal
  - What you would be willing to give up

- Go in with the perspective that the other side is your ally rather than your enemy. Thinking about dealing with an ally can help you look for solutions that benefit both of you.

- While in the negotiation meeting, listen carefully to what the other person is saying. Try to discern the needs behind the requests they make. If you successfully identify their needs, you can better generate a number of alternatives from which you both can benefit. For example, if your colleague wants an extension on a deadline, work with him or her to figure out what needs would be served by extending the deadline (for instance, the need for more inspection of the product, the need to support other projects at the same time). Once you have identified the needs, generate alternative strategies for meeting the needs of both of you, and select the best one.

- Refrain from getting into a "win/lose" discussion where the only alternatives are for one of you to benefit and one of you to lose out. If the discussion reaches that point, note this fact to the others and communicate your desire for both of you to get something out of the agreement you reach.

- Identify someone in your organization who is skilled at getting others to go along with his or her initiatives. Observe this person and, if possible, meet to discuss how he or she approaches negotiation and what you can do to improve your techniques.

- During the negotiation session:
  - Draw out information from the other person using open-

ended questions (questions that call for more than "yes" or "no") to facilitate dialogue.

- Identify the issue or problem in terms of needs, not solutions.
- Maintain the perspective that your power, at a minimum, equals that of the other person. This will help you state your needs more confidently. If you begin to feel overpowered, ask yourself why, and do something to regain power. For example, if you are presented with new facts, draw out the other person until you have a clear understanding of this information or, if appropriate, postpone the meeting and take time to get up to speed before you meet again.
- Seek common ground. Finding areas of agreement is often the critical first step in achieving win/win outcomes.
- Minimize time pressures. Decreasing the importance of a deadline can give you more power to hold out for what you believe you want/need.
- Avoid becoming overly emotional or defensive.
- Prepare for the possibility that no decision will be reached by creating a list of actions you can take if you fail to reach agreement.
- Don't be too committed to reaching an agreement quickly. There may be alternatives which are not readily apparent.

Getting Others to Take Action

There are many ways to compel others to take action, but the most effective strategies result in people willingly and eagerly acting on your initiatives. If you find that you consistently have a hard time getting others to get moving, consider the following:

- Clarify and communicate your vision. The more clear and compelling your vision, the easier it is for others to understand and endorse it. To increase others' investment in and drive to achieve your vision, involve them in the process of developing it. Also, think about what is important to the people you want to involve, and adapt your approach to appeal to the needs of these people.

- Show your enthusiasm. The more excited and energetic you are about meeting your goals, the more committed others are likely to be in supporting you. Display your enthusiasm by conveying how important your goals are to you and how pleased you are that people are willing to pitch in and work with you. Continue to link people's efforts to the overall objective. In big and small ways, celebrate when you reach milestones.

- State positive expectations. Research shows that conveying positive expectations about what others can achieve can lead to better performance than when negative expectations are communicated — what is commonly called the "self-fulfilling prophecy." When you are seeking the cooperation of others, approach them with the expectation that they will be cooperative. Chances are that this approach will lead to increased cooperation.

- Provide rewards. People are typically more willing to cooperate when they perceive that they will benefit from the effort they put in. As a manager, you can offer tangible rewards (bonuses, salary increases, promotions) to your employees. When these rewards are not appropriate or when you do not have the authority to offer them, use your creativity to come up with other ways people will benefit from helping you out.

  Help employees see the intangible rewards they may receive for supporting you. For example, it may be that contributing to your project will increase others' exposure to upper management, help them develop particular skills, add variety to their jobs, allow them to work with a diverse group of people, and so forth. It works best if you can identify benefits that meet the individual needs and values of the people you are turning to for support.

Commanding Attention and Respect in Groups

Group situations are an excellent opportunity for you to demonstrate your leadership qualities and to have an impact on a large number of people. Take advantage of these opportunities by trying the following:

- Increase the level of your contributions in groups by making suggestions more often.

- In addition to speaking up more often, develop forcefulness in stating your opinions. Don't hesitate to voice your thoughts or to label them as your own. Take steps to ensure that other group members take your contributions seriously and consider them when making decisions.

- Use effective eye contact and speak to all individuals in the group.

- Increase your impact by preparing for meetings beforehand. Having the facts and figures may help you to be more forceful in stating your opinions.

- Summarize opinions frequently to build understanding.

- Look for opportunities to lead groups. Volunteer to lead a task force or project group, and try some new techniques to increase your impact. To get a feel for how effective your techniques are, ask people for feedback on how you are directing the group.

Influencing the Decisions of Upper Management

One of the most important areas in which to focus your influencing efforts is upper management. Getting the attention of your manager and his or her peers and other higher-level managers is a critical skill. Follow these guidelines:

- When you propose an action to upper management, be clear about how it will benefit the organization, for instance, how your idea will help solve a problem, save money, increase return on investment, and so forth. Don't leave people to draw these conclusions on their own.

- Periodically meet with your manager to let him or her know what you are doing and to hear about the issues which concern upper management.

- When you recognize that a decision from upper management might have a negative impact on your area, let your manager know. Again, be clear with your manager about the impact the decision will have by citing tangible consequences.

- Carefully watch what is important to upper management. Look for ways to spot opportunities important to the company. Strategize with your boss.

- Be willing to make concessions in your area when appropriate. People's trust in you is enhanced when your motives appear directed at benefitting the entire organization. Upper management will be more willing to give you what you want if they see that you have a balanced perspective about what is best for your area and what is best for the company.

RECOMMENDED READINGS

The publications listed here were selected for their content and suitability to a managerial audience.

Negotiating Rationally

Bazerman, Max H., and Neale, Margaret A., New York: The Free Press, 1992
ISBN: 0-02-901985-0
Knowing how to negotiate is important for success in many situations, both in business and in personal life. The authors suggest that increased emphasis has been placed on the skill of negotiating. Several trends occurring in business necessitate effective negotiating skills: work force mobility, corporate restructuring, diversified work force, service sector economy, renegotiation, and move to a global marketplace.

Getting Things Done When You Are Not In Charge

Bellman, Geoffrey M., San Francisco: Berrett-Koehler, 1992
ISBN: 1-881052-02-8
Bellman's book is intended as a guide for those who want to successfully bring about change in their organization without the advantage of formal power. It offers practical approaches for effectively enlisting key players and earning the respect of management. Bellman presents insights on leadership, teamwork, empowerment, and organizational politics.

Roger Dawson's Secrets of Power Negotiating

Dawson, Roger, Hawthorne, NJ: The Career Press, 1995
ISBN: 1-56414-153-5
Negotiating is necessary in all aspects of life from personal and social relationships to business interactions. Dawson is a speaker and author who has done extensive study on tactics involved in successful negotiation. The driving forces behind negotiation, the elements of power that control negotiating situations, methods of analyzing personality styles and adapting to them, and negotiating with individuals from different cultures are all discussed.

You've Got to Be Believed to Be Heard

Decker, Bert, New York: St. Martin's Press, 1993
ISBN: 0-312-09949-5
In this book, Decker shows you what he has learned through experience and extensive research — how to effectively and confidently reach, persuade, and motivate with the spoken word. The key to personal impact is to win the emotional trust of your audience. This book gives examples and specific how-to exercises to help you build a foundation that will transform the way you speak and listen.

On Power	**Dilenschneider, Robert L.,** New York: HarperBusiness, 1994 ISBN: 0-88730-652-7 Equating power with leadership enables Dilenschneider to develop unusual principles of executive success. His book covers, step by step, the foundation of power, its attainment, and its many manifestations.
Power and Influence	**Dilenschneider, Robert L.,** Englewood Cliffs, NJ: Prentice-Hall, 1991 ISBN: 0-13-683327-6 The author, a proven master at turning corporate crises into corporate opportunities, explains how to become an "influential manager," how to influence the marketplace, and how to deal with crises.
Getting to Yes: Negotiating Agreement Without Giving In	**Fisher, Roger, and Ury, William,** New York: Penguin Books, 1991 ISBN: 0-14-015735-2 The authors provide a straightforward, universally applicable method for negotiating personal and professional disputes without getting taken and without getting nasty. The authors offer the reader a concise, step-by-step, proven strategy for coming to mutually acceptable agreements in every sort of conflict.
I Can See You Naked	**Hoff, Ron,** Kansas City, MO: Andrews and McMeel, 1992 ISBN: 0-8362-8008-3 This book provides countless techniques on how to make fearless and successful presentations in every possible situation. Some of the issues involved in making presentations include: the basic elements of an effective presentation, dealing with nervousness, handling questions, how to make your presentation interesting, how to gear your presentation to a particular audience, and learning from your mistakes.
Assertiveness: A Positive Process	**Hopson, Barrie, and Scally, Mike,** San Diego: Pfeiffer & Company, 1993 ISBN: 0-89384-214-1 This workbook describes what assertiveness means and teaches you how to become assertive. It also provides examples of the main types of behaviors: assertive, aggressive, and unassertive. The author contends that becoming more assertive will help you succeed.

Field Guide to Negotiation	**Kennedy, Gavin,** New York: McGraw-Hill, 1994 ISBN: 0-07-103579-6 This book is one of a series that provides essential tools and concepts for today's manager. Included is a glossary that clarifies tactics, theories, ploys, and the details of the art of negotiating.
Managing with Power	**Pfeffer, Jeffrey,** Boston: Harvard Business School Press, 1994 ISBN: 0-87584-440-5 The author contends that power is the means which allows managers to set agendas and influence others to achieve results. This book examines the use and misuse of power and provides specific examples of how the effective use of power can result in success without building resentment.
Assertiveness Skills	**Shelton, Nelda, and Burton, Sharon,** Boston: Business One-Irwin/Mirror Press, 1993 ISBN: 1-55623-857-6 This book is designed to help individuals approach and respond to work situations confidently and positively without becoming aggressive. The author teaches how to become more productive and content in the workplace by using specific assertiveness techniques.
Persuasive Business Speaking	**Snyder, Elayne,** New York: AMACOM, 1990 ISBN: 0-8144-7722-4 The author offers straightforward advice for business speakers: be prepared, be brief, be interesting, and be seated. Her book provides a concise but complete guide for formulating a focused speech and projecting an executive image.

SUGGESTED
SEMINARS

The seminars listed here were selected for their appeal to a managerial audience. The reputation of the vendor, the quality of their seminar offerings, and the specific seminar content were considered in the selection process.

Because of the dynamic nature of the seminar marketplace, some seminars may have been upgraded or replaced, and others may no longer be offered. Likewise, costs and locations may have changed since this listing was compiled. We recommend that you contact the vendor directly for updated and additional information.

Assertiveness Training for Managers

This seminar is designed to teach participants effective assertiveness techniques. Topics include: managing assertively, achieving your objectives, resolving conflicts, and developing a self-improvement plan.
Length: 3 days; Cost: $1,260
Locations: Call vendor
American Management Association
P.O. Box 319, Saranac Lake, NY 12983
Telephone: 800/262-9699

Successfully Managing People

This program teaches participants skills and positive methods of dealing effectively with people at all levels. Topics include: how values and beliefs control behavior; how to enhance your reputation and increase your personal power; how to manage yourself and others; and how to manage so that people's values and needs are met.
Length: 3 days; Cost: $1,260
Locations: Call vendor
American Management Association
P.O. Box 319, Saranac Lake, NY 12983
Telephone: 800/262-9699

Effective Negotiating

This program covers: using hidden leverage, identifying strengths and weaknesses, determining what your opponent really wants, building long-term relationships, personal negotiating, setting and achieving your targets, developing an awareness of how other cultures negotiate, dealing with deadlocks, and guarding against tricks and subtleties.
Length: 2 days; Cost: $695
Locations: Call vendor
Karrass Seminars
1633 Stanford Street, Santa Monica, CA 90404
Telephone: 310/453-1806

On Leadership

This program has three objectives: to teach executives the basic principles of human behavior, to give them practice in applying these principles to enhance their leadership roles and resolve organizational problems, and to provide them with a reliable basis for making their own critical evaluations of various psychological techniques in management.
Length: 5 days; Cost: $4,350
Location: Bedford, MA
Levinson Institute, Inc.
404 Wyman Street, Suite 400, Waltham, MA 02154
Telephone: 800/290-5735

Targeted Leadership Coaching

Participants in this program work one-on-one with a personal coach who provides a challenging, yet supportive and positive environment for learning and development. The training focuses on learning core competencies, including skills, tactics, strategies, and principles, to increase participants' performance in their own career setting.
Length: 4 or 5 half-day sessions; Cost: Call vendor
Locations: Call vendor
Personnel Decisions International
2000 Plaza VII Tower, 45 South Seventh Street
Minneapolis, MN 55402-1608
Telephone: 800/633-4410

Positive Power and Influence Program

The program focuses on developing and refining the skills required to influence people and events while building and maintaining beneficial relationships. It covers assessing which influencing styles you use, overuse, misuse, or avoid; refining present skills and developing alternative styles; and applying the appropriate influence style to a given situation.
Length: 3-4 days; Cost: $950 - $1,250
Locations: Call vendor
Situation Management Systems, Inc.
195 Hanover Street, Hanover, MA 02339-2294
Telephone: 617/826-4433

How to Influence Without Direct Authority

Participants in this workshop examine characteristics and skills of influential people to understand the sources of their informal power. They analyze situations requiring influence and learn how to build effective relationships upward, downward, and laterally. They also learn practical influential strategies; trust-building skills; and the tools of team building, persuasion, conflict management, and negotiation.
Length: 3 days; Cost: $850
Location: Madison, WI
University of Wisconsin-Madison
Management Institute, Grainger Hall
975 University Avenue, Madison, WI 53706-1323
Telephone: 800/348-8964

Persuasion and Influencing Skills

This program is designed to increase participants' ability to sell their ideas, motivate individuals, and establish their credibility. Participants will practice creating rapport and negotiating effectively, using new tools and knowledge about the influence process.
Length: 3 days; Cost: $1,250
Location: Nashville, TN
Vanderbilt University
Owen Graduate School of Management
Executive Programs, 410 21st Avenue South, Suite 100
Nashville, TN 37203
Telephone: 615/322-2513

FOSTER TEAMWORK

The synergy that comes from putting employees together to form teams to solve problems, make decisions, and take action is power that organizations can harness for greater success. In these increasingly complex, changing times for business and industry, teams can supply more creative solutions and more powerful support for the organization. With an effective team, "the whole is greater than the sum of the parts."

Whether the team is a permanent work group or a temporary task force, however, creating such teams and leading them to success requires skill and finesse on the part of the team leader.

This three-part section provides suggestions to help managers foster successful teamwork.

Part 1: Creating an Environment Conducive to Teamwork

- Recognizing Management's Impact on Teamwork
- Building a Team Environment

Part 2: Building Your Team Leader Skills

- Building a Team
- Valuing the Contributions of All Team Members
- Encouraging Interaction among Group Members
- Increasing Interdependence Within Your Team
- Discouraging "We versus They" Thinking
- Involving Others in Shaping Plans and Decisions
- Acknowledging and Celebrating Team Accomplishments
- Evaluating Your Effectiveness as a Team Member

Part 3: Developing Team Problem-Solving and Decision-Making Skills

- Deciding When to Use a Team Approach
- Improving Your Team Decision-Making Process
- Seeking Appropriate Input before Making Decisions
- Improving Your Group Facilitation Skills

Valuable Tips

- Schedule an annual retreat to build team spirit and commitment to goals.

- Assess your decision-making style, paying attention to the extent to which you solicit others' ideas. Look for opportunities to use a more participative approach.

- Make a list of the key strengths and limitations of each person on your team. Find ways to utilize the strengths.

- Find ways to involve quiet team members without embarrassing them. Try using open-ended questions and reflective listening to draw out quieter members of your team.

- Use active-listening skills to acknowledge, summarize, and reinforce the contributions of your team members.

- Avoid premature judgment of others' ideas and suggestions.

- Strive for win/win solutions.

- Reward team accomplishment.

- Value and show appreciation to your administrative and support staff, not just your "line" or professional people.

- Celebrate as a team.

- Pull your people together as a group to solve problems.

- Foster an environment of trust by ensuring that all criticism is constructive and is focused on individuals' behaviors, not personalities.

- Use your team to develop the group's vision, mission, and goals.

- Share success with team members.

- Show your trust by sharing information beyond what is necessary.

- Have fun while working.

PART 1

Recognizing Management's Impact on Teamwork

Creating an Environment Conducive to Teamwork

How successful an organization is at effectively utilizing teamwork largely depends on the attitudes, directives, and policies that come from the management team. Your actions and the policies you develop affect teamwork both within your work unit as well as throughout your organization. To enhance the team environment in your work unit, use the following guidelines:

- Provide a structure conducive to teamwork. Too much hierarchy, whether formal or informal, can impede teamwork.

- Encourage cooperation, rather than competition, between different work units. Make sure groups set their goals in harmony with one another and that the goals are mutually supportive.

- Provide the necessary resources for team success (for example, proper staffing, up-to-date information, and so forth).

- Give work teams the authority to act upon their team decisions.

- Include an appraisal of team performance, in addition to individual performance, as a part of your performance management system.

- Reward successful team contributions, as well as individual contributions.

- Show by example how to be both an effective team leader and team member.

- Link the team directly with customers so members know the customers' requirements firsthand.

Building a Team Environment

Just as plants need a certain environment for maximum growth (an appropriate amount of sun and water, proper pruning, enough soil), teams need certain "ingredients" in their environment to function in the best way possible. Building an environment conducive to maximum team functioning is not a one-time event; rather, it involves an ongoing effort and process on your and your team's part.

To begin building a healthier team environment, ask yourself the following questions. The questions to which you answer "no" are the areas of opportunity for you to improve your present team environment.

EVALUATION CHECKLIST *(Circle the appropriate response.)*

Do the members of my team trust me and each other?	**Yes/No**
Are my actions consistent with my words?	**Yes/No**
Are my team members and I honest with one another? Is information readily shared?	**Yes/No**
Do I keep my commitments to team members? Do they keep commitments to each other?	**Yes/No**
Do my team and I listen effectively to one another?	**Yes/No**
Do we address disagreements and other conflicts proactively and responsively?	**Yes/No**
Do we value differences (for instance, do we value introverted members to the same degree as extroverted members)?	**Yes/No**
Is my work environment inclusive, engaging, and empowering (versus exclusive, controlling, and patronizing)?	**Yes/No**
Do I foster cooperation and information sharing with other departments?	**Yes/No**
Does my team have fun at work? Do we celebrate together as a team?	**Yes/No**

Ask your team members the same questions, and then discuss their responses.

PART 2

Building a Team

Building Your Team Leader Skills

It's important that the employees in your unit, division, and functional area work together with a team spirit to maximize the ultimate success of your team. Building a team attitude means managing your employees in a way that fosters teamwork instead of individual gain. Teamwork takes time to build and requires practice and effort on the part of both the manager and the employees. However, once you start the process, it gains momentum, like a ball rolling down a hill.

For your team members to work well together, your team needs a clear idea of why it is a team and must agree about how to work together. To accomplish this:

1. Define the team mission and vision with the team through strategic planning or team-building sessions. As part of the process, get input from all team members for the greatest buy-in. Discuss differences of opinion, and work to achieve consensus.

2. Next, define and clarify roles and responsibilities. Provide opportunities for team members to clarify and negotiate roles and relationships with one another. To empower your team, allow team members to work out responsibilities and roles among themselves and report their recommendations to you.

3. Ask your staff to evaluate the effectiveness of the team. Discussion criteria can include strengths and weaknesses in:

   - Clarity of purpose

   - Communication

   - Problem solving

   - Decision making

   - Change

   - Customer focus

   - Quality of work

   - Conflict resolution

   - Work processes

   - Feedback

4. Set performance goals based on team accomplishments and how well members work together as a team.

5. Help team members understand one another better. Share information about work being done. Discuss work histories, specific skills, successes, and talents. Help team members to understand, appreciate, and use differences among themselves to arrive at better solutions and to do better work.

6. If team members seem to resonate to some kind of group identity, reinforce that element of communality among them.

Valuing the Contributions of All Team Members

All members of the team — those who have more complex and highly compensated jobs as well as those whose responsibilities are more straightforward — are important to the success of the organization. For all members of the team to feel valued and worthwhile, there must be a pervasive attitude that everyone's work is important. Following are some ways to foster that attitude:

- Value the work that everyone does. Some people really do not value administrative work; others value only line, not staff, work; some believe particular functions are more "key" to business success; and others value work only if it is intellectually complex. Your team will function more smoothly if no one is considered better or more important than anyone else. Eliminate the symbols that make one group or type of employee appear to be more important than others.

- Provide verbal recognition for everyone's contributions.

- Include team members at all levels in as much planning, decision making, and problem solving as possible. If direct involvement is not appropriate, at least discuss the impact the decision will have on work load.

- When you want input from the team, ask for comments and suggestions from everyone. Don't treat your administrative people differently than you treat other professional employees.

- Give your staff feedback if you see any of them devaluing members of the team.

- Reinforce and recognize the attainment of goals. Praise the accomplishments of less visible employees as often as those of employees who are more in the spotlight.

- Be especially attentive to comments from less assertive individuals who may not feel comfortable or experienced in contributing ideas and opinions in a group.

Encouraging Interaction among Group Members

Interactions in group meetings typically take one of three forms:

- The group is largely silent, with the leader doing most of the talking.

- Group members interact with the leader.

- Group members interact with one another.

The third form represents the most effective type of interaction. When group members interact, the resources of all members are used most fully, and problem solving is promoted. Following are ways to encourage group interaction:

- Send out an agenda in advance of the meeting that indicates what group members should be prepared to discuss.

- When deciding where to sit at the meeting, choose a place that deemphasizes your leadership role. For example, sit at the side of a table instead of at the head.

- Establish the norm of group interaction immediately upon formation of the team. You might use a round-robin approach and ask each member to introduce themselves and discuss their expertise relevant to the team task or to express their opinions of the team task.

- Invite team members to respond to each other's comments. For example, you might ask, "Is there anything anyone else would like to ask Georgia about this position?"

- Avoid interrupting others. By interrupting, you redirect attention to yourself and your role as the director of the discussion.

- Use nonverbal behavior to direct team members' comments away from you and toward other team members. For example, a team member responding to a comment made by another team member might look to you for your reaction rather than at the other team member. Avoid reacting and look toward the team member who made the original comment.

- Redirect comments that are inappropriately directed to you. For example, you might say, "That sounds like a comment on Tom's position. What do you think, Tom?"

- Before the team meeting, ask one of the other team members to lead the discussion on a particular topic.

- During the meeting, ask team members to lead the discussion of particular points. Occasionally, you can better facilitate team interaction by temporarily having others serve as group leader.

Increasing Interdependence Within Your Team

Interdependence involves the concept that you and your team can accomplish more by working together than you could by working individually (in other words, the concept of "one plus one equals three").

If you tend to be competitive to the point where your actions destroy cooperation, your independence should be tempered to achieve the *inter*dependence necessary for constructive teamwork. The following suggestions will help you increase your interdependence:

1. Interdependence begins with the belief that dependence on others is not a sign of weakness. If you doubt that cooperating with others can enable you to achieve more than you could alone, you will have difficulty increasing your interdependence.

2. Next, determine the degree to which you are competitive at the expense of cooperation. Analyze your behavior in meetings and try to gauge the impact of your competitive behavior on the outcomes. Watch for the following tendencies:

   • Pushing your own ideas rather than listening to the ideas of others or compromising.

   • Withdrawing from the group psychologically or physically if your ideas are not accepted.

   • Behaving in a way that creates a win/lose situation.

3. If you observe these tendencies in your behavior, try the following:

   • Look for any suggestions or viewpoints of others that you agree with or can support.

   • Balance offering your ideas with accepting others' ideas to build a sense of shared commitment to group outcomes.

   • If you find yourself withdrawing, use this as a cue to begin striving for a compromise position.

   • Share credit with others.

   • Support the team decision once it is made.

4. Evaluate the effects of your new behaviors. Notice if others are becoming more supportive and enthusiastic about implementing shared decisions than they were about decisions made as a result of your aggressiveness. You may wish to ask others to help you evaluate the effects of your behavior.

Discouraging "We versus They" Thinking

Promoting teamwork among groups across an organization is essential to create an environment where people pursue common goals. To discourage "we versus they" thinking and increase efficient communication and collaboration across groups, consider the following:

• Build teamwork among different groups through formal committees. For example, management committees (which may include nonmanagerial employees) can be used to build teamwork and a sense of common purpose across all work groups represented, and can engage the team in a collaborative process.

- When making decisions using people from a variety of teams, avoid voting for decisions. Instead, strive for consensus. Voting is not likely to produce a true team decision.

- Avoid labeling and stereotyping (for instance, referring to accountants as "bean counters"). Respect for other groups and professions is critical to promoting teamwork among different groups.

- Encourage everyone involved to speak a common language. To avoid alienating outside groups, educate them and help them to understand the "lingo" of the team. Language that leaves others in the dark results in blocked communication, confusion, and disinterest.

- Evaluate your employees on their willingness and ability to work as part of a team in the organization. Encourage them to develop relationships throughout the organization, not just within their own functional area.

Involving Others in Shaping Plans and Decisions

People who assist in the planning and decision making are likely to be more invested in the successful execution of those plans and decisions. Engage all your team members in the development of your team's mission, strategy, and goals. When working on projects involving other functions, involve representatives from all affected areas. Following is a technique for involving others:

1. Identify everyone who should be involved. Check with others to be sure that you haven't missed anyone.

2. Meet with these people and give them the big picture of what is happening. Ask for the help you want from them. Clarity about your purpose is important. You may want to:

   - Simply inform people about the plan.

   - Show how your plan will affect them.

   - Get help in identifying the problem or opportunity.

   - Have them determine a course of action.

3. Conduct the meeting so that you get the input you need and the team feels involved in the process. Develop a plan to keep the team informed.

With the team members' mutual investment in the objective, you will be better able to get others to buy into your goal.

Acknowledging and Celebrating Team Accomplishments

Acknowledging and celebrating team accomplishments is a powerful way to recognize your team efforts and to keep motivation and momentum going. Following are some suggestions for celebrating team accomplishments:

- Make it a point to tell your team in staff meetings that you appreciate their contributions. Be specific about what they have done well.

- Publicly acknowledge good team performance in meetings and other company communication vehicles such as company newsletters.

- Let your team know that their efforts make a difference by recognizing them through a personal memo, a note on the bulletin board, an apple on their desk, or other creative ways.

- Incorporate into the performance appraisal process objectives that evaluate effective team involvement and behaviors.

- Keep team members informed about the team's performance (for example, share sales figures).

- Organize special get-togethers such as team lunches, barbecues, breakfasts, or coffee and rolls, upon successful completion of projects.

- Consider instituting a formal awards program with certificates, plaques, a traveling trophy, or other awards to honor teams for their work. When presenting the award, explain the specific efforts of the team and how they worked together to achieve an objective or complete a successful project.

Evaluating Your Effectiveness as a Team Member

Part of being an effective team *leader* involves being an effective team *member*. How effective are you in team situations? Do you contribute too much? Too little? Does the impact you have on a team depend on the circumstances? In developing a plan for improving your team skills, sharpen your awareness of how you currently function as a team member. The following process can help you develop this insight:

1. For the next several months, keep a record of your contributions in committees, meetings, informal team gatherings, and other team settings. Also keep track of ideas,

plans, and solutions that you could have contributed but did not.

2. Determine your overall impact in each situation. Did you contribute a great deal? Very little? Was the effect of your participation positive, negative, or neutral?

3. Evaluate and determine the reasons for your performance. For example, reasons for positive contributions might include:

   - Good preparation

   - Knowledge of the area

   - Interest in the topic

   - Feeling at ease with other team members (other members expected and/or welcomed contributions, the opinions of other members warranted responses/rebuttals, other members were quiet, and so forth)

   - Willingness to listen to others

   Reasons for ineffective performance might include:

   - Lack of preparation

   - Lack of knowledge of the subject

   - Lack of interest in the topic

   - Discomfort with other team members (shyness, intimidation due to their status levels, other members were too vocal)

   - Tendency to participate in situations in which you are the formal leader, but to hold back in other situations

   - Tendency to contribute, but if your ideas are not accepted, you immediately let them drop

   Closely scrutinize your attitudes and behavior in team situations. Add to the lists above to gain a clearer understanding of your level of effectiveness in team situations.

4. Ask a trusted coworker or manager to observe and critique your performance in team settings. Analyze that person's feedback in relation to the analysis you conducted in step 3 to determine patterns or tendencies that impede effective team performance. Realize that the first step of making a change is to understand the reasons behind your effectiveness and ineffectiveness in team situations.

5. Develop an action plan for positive change.

PART 3

Deciding When to Use a Team Approach

Developing Team Problem-Solving and Decision-Making Skills

Team leaders need to decide when and to what degree to use a team approach for decision making and problem solving. In general, the higher the level of commitment and buy-in your team members show, and the more creative, varied, and informative the input and opinions they offer, the more important a team approach for solving problems becomes.

When team members are involved in problem solving and decision making, they are more likely to accept the final decision and to feel ownership and shared responsibility for the success of the overall goal. Furthermore, the quality of decisions and problem solutions is greater because the group process generates a variety of perspectives and opinions that lead to more creative, effective results.

A team approach to problem solving and decision making tends to work best when:

- Full acceptance of the decision is necessary for effective implementation.

- Information from more than one person is required to make the decision.

- A high-quality result is desired.

- A creative solution is needed.

- The decision does not need to be made quickly.

A team approach may not be appropriate or desirable when:

- The decision involves a routine or simple task.

- The decision needs to be made quickly.

- The majority of the team members are likely to agree.

- Consensus or buy-in is not important.

- Compliance is fairly absolute.

Consider the following suggestions to increase your use of team problem solving:

- Write down all the decisions you have made in the last month. Assess the quality and the acceptance of your decisions. Analyze whether your final outcome would have benefitted from some type of team approach. Look for trends such as avoiding team involvement on certain kinds of problems or decisions.

- Think about the meetings you have conducted in the last month. Looking at the decision-making and problem-solving processes involved, what is the ratio of the number of times you directed them to the number of times you facilitated them? If you tend to underutilize the facilitation process, increase your use of it by allowing others more input into problem solutions. Learn additional skills on how to be an effective facilitator. On occasion, turn over facilitation of a problem-solving or decision-making effort to one of your team members.

- Seek feedback from your employees, manager, and peers. Ask for their perceptions of when you have effectively used a team approach to solve problems and when you have missed opportunities to do so.

- Identify other managers who effectively use a team approach to solve problems. Use them as role models. Observe what they do that makes them effective, and ask them for tips on how you might improve your own approach.

Improving Your Team Decision-Making Process

When a group has problems making decisions, it is usually because its members are confused or in disagreement about one or more of the following:

- What decision they are trying to make

- Who should be involved in making the decision

- How individuals should be involved (as information sources or decision makers, for instance)

- When the decision must be made

You can increase the effectiveness of group problem solving by asking the following questions before each session:

1. What is the problem we are trying to solve? The problem-solving process involves five parts:

   - Defining the problem

   - Generating alternatives

   - Selecting an alternative

   - Implementing a plan

   - Evaluating the plan

Before the team attempts to generate ideas, it is important that members fully understand the problem to be solved.

2. Who should be involved in this decision? Consider the following:

   • Who possesses the knowledge to ensure that the decision is logical and sound?

   • Who will be involved in implementing the decision?

   • Who must approve the decision? Approval may be easier to obtain if those in authority are invited to participate in the decision-making process.

3. How should each person be involved? Group members may be involved directly (actually make the decisions) or consulted (provide information or opinions). Clarify in advance the roles your group members will play in the process.

4. When will the decision be made? Set a time frame so people know when the decision will be made.

Seeking Appropriate Input before Making Decisions

Rarely can important decisions be made without input from others. Managers need to solicit input before making decisions for a variety of reasons: to obtain critical input, to build commitment in others, to develop others, to show respect for others' opinions, and to foster open communication and problem sharing. The following guidelines suggest ways to solicit input for the decision-making process:

• When you first learn that you must make a decision, determine who has the information you need to make a good decision, who you need to involve to get buy-in, and who you think should be involved.

• You can involve others in any phase of the process: defining the problem or opportunity, identifying other ways of looking at the problem, generating optional approaches, selecting criteria for making a final decision, making the final call, or planning implementation. You may involve everyone in every phase or engage different people in each, depending on the decisions and input needed.

• Options for soliciting input include:
  - One-to-one conversations
  - Group discussions

- Memos requesting input
- Electronic mail discussion (internal communications on computer)

• When appropriate, pull people together as a group so that individuals can work together to define the opportunities, goals, and best course of action.

• If you anticipate that people will have difficulty working together, talk with them individually first to solicit their cooperation. Deal respectfully with their concerns. Develop supporters in the group who will help you keep it focused and working constructively. Be clear about what you want, particularly with those you will rely upon as supporters.

• When interviewing others to gain information for problem solving, use open-ended questions and active listening. (See the Listen to Others section of this Handbook.) Take care not to judge others' suggestions or to convey, verbally or non-verbally, that you disapprove of their ideas. If you do not remain open to the information you solicit, others will sense that their input is not really important and will stop communicating with you.

Improving Your Group Facilitation Skills

To develop skills that will enable you to more effectively facilitate group problem-solving sessions, follow these suggestions when you lead such sessions during the next few months. Watch the groups you lead for signs of increased participation and the generation of more and better solution alternatives.

• As the group leader, facilitate, rather than direct, the group discussion. Group interaction allows the resources of all members to be used most fully.

• Use active listening skills to draw out the ideas and creativity of others. Be careful to reserve your judgment and provide ample opportunity for others to develop their ideas.

• Protect minority opinion. The most obvious or popular suggestions are not always the best. To ensure that innovative suggestions are given full consideration, provide those who propose minority solutions with an environment in which they feel comfortable voicing their ideas.

• Encourage sessions that are problem-oriented rather than solution-oriented. Too often, participants in problem-solving sessions jump immediately into the generation of solutions before the problem is fully defined; this process leads to solutions that may solve only part of the problem — or the wrong problem. To ensure adequate emphasis on problem definition, use a sequential structure (for example, "We will spend 15 minutes on problem definition, then 20 minutes on the generation of solution alternatives.").

- Use brainstorming techniques to generate alternate solutions. When brainstorming, group members strive for quantity rather than quality, piggyback on the ideas of others, and avoid judging alternatives. This approach results in increased quality of the ultimate decisions and greater creativity in problem solving. Refer to the Innovate section of this Handbook for additional guidelines on brainstorming.

- Look for a second solution after a first solution is arrived at to encourage additional creative approaches.

Group members should be informed of the steps you will take to improve group problem solving and your reasons for taking these steps. For example, you might start the session by saying, "Today I'm going to help the discussion along but not participate in or direct it. I'll try to protect minority opinion so that the full range of alternatives will be presented and encourage group interaction to ensure that we all benefit from each individual's experience."

RECOMMENDED READINGS

The publications listed here were selected for their content and suitability to a managerial audience.

Tips for Teams

Fisher, Kimball; Rayner, Steven; and Belgard, William, New York: McGraw-Hill, 1995
ISBN: 0-07-021224-4
Designed by a team, this book is a guide for overcoming obstacles and achieving success with teams on a day-to-day basis. Specific strategies are provided to: overcome resistance; resolve disagreements among team members; handle strong personalities; gain support of management, customers, and suppliers; and establish a winning strategy from day one.

Bridging Differences: Effective Intergroup Communication

Gudykunst, William B., Newbury Park, CA: Sage Publications, 1994
ISBN: 0-8039-5646-0
This book is useful to anyone who works with people from different cultural and ethnic backgrounds. The author shows how stereotypes lead to ineffective communication, including misinterpretation of messages we receive from members of cultural and ethnic groups different from our own.

The Wisdom of Teams

Katzenbach, J.R., and Smith, D.K., Boston: Harvard Business School Press, 1993
ISBN: 0-87584-367-0
The authors show that the team approach to business organization is key to achieving high performance and organizing proper and effective teams. By using thought-provoking examples, the authors give recommendations and techniques that will allow your company to utilize team-building to best suit its needs.

Self-Directed Work Teams

Orsburn, Jack D.; Moran, Linda; Musselwhite, Ed; Zenga, John H., Burr Ridge, IL: Irwin Professional Publishing, 1990
ISBN: 1-55623-341-8
This book discusses how self-directed work teams, when used effectively, can dramatically increase a company's productivity and quality. The authors deal specifically with the "why, what, and how" of this business technique, as well as methods of increasing productivity and improving quality.

*Don't Fire Them,
Fire Them Up: A
Maverick's Guide to
Motivating Yourself
and Your Team*

Pacetta, Frank, and Gittness, Roger, New York: Simon &
Schuster, 1994
ISBN: 0-671-86949-3
The authors, drawing on successful experience at a Xerox district
office, show how to build and motivate an organization to increase
productivity and sales. The book shows how to build trust, create
loyalty, and generate enthusiasm in order to create a successful
business team.

*Leading the
Transition*

Pike, Wilbur L., III, New York: Quality Resources, 1995
ISBN: 0-527-76247-4
Team-based decision making is the key to effective and productive
work. However, many problems arise in the transition between a
hierarchical approach and a team-based approach. This book is a
guide for managers on how to bridge the gap between the upper-
management hierarchy and the team-based work groups.
Management's role in other transition issues, such as work force
diversity, attitudes, and education, are also discussed.

*Why Teams Don't
Work*

Robbins, Harvey, and Finley, Michael, Princeton, NJ:
Peterson's/Pacesetter Books, 1995
ISBN: 1-56079-497-6
While teams strive to be efficient, creative, and innovative, some
teams fail either because of contention or other cross-purposes.
The most common problems with team-building are: personality
conflicts, confused goals of the team, confused roles of the team
members, and poor leadership. The book provides strategies for
dealing with these and other problems and will show you how to
guide a team from its beginnings through its successful formation.

The Team Handbook

Scholtes, Peter R., Madison, WI: Joiner Associates, Inc., 1993
ISBN: 0-9622264-0-8
The author presents a "how to" guide designed to help project
teams succeed in improving quality and productivity. Through
illustrations and worksheets, this handbook shows organizations
how to implement many quality improvement principles and is
targeted for all members of project teams.

The Skilled Facilitator

Schwarz, Roger M., San Francisco: Jossey-Bass, 1994
ISBN: 1-55542-638-7
This book is a guide for all facilitators and managers on how to successfully lead a group toward creative resolutions of the tasks before them. The book tells how to deal with all types of problems and situations that may arise in the course of group interaction.

Team-Based Organizations

Shonk, James H., Burr Ridge, IL: Irwin Professional Publishing, 1992
ISBN: 1-55623-703-0
The benefits of effective teamwork are well documented. Shonk's book will help you decide whether or not teaming is right for your company. It will then help you determine what type of teams to create, how to support them, how to make the conversion to teamwork, and how to manage the team-based organization once it's up and running.

Organizational Capability

Ulrich, Dave, and Lake, Dale, New York: John Wiley & Sons, 1990
ISBN: 0-471-61807-1
The authors go beyond the premise that the people of a company are its most important asset by introducing a concept they call "organizational capability." This concept is meant to help organizations realize their potential for competing from the inside out. Based on the authors' extensive research and first-hand experience with clients, this book offers both a strategic overview of organizational capability and precise guidelines for putting it into action.

Leadership Trapeze

Wilson, Jeanne M.; George, Jill; Welling, Richard S.; and Byham, William C., San Francisco: Jossey-Bass, 1994
ISBN: 1-55542-613-1
Managers are often confronted with the problem of how to provide leadership to self-directed work teams. The authors contend that it is essential that managers know when to abandon old leadership practices and when to adopt new ones. This book shows managers how to start, support, and sustain teams while providing innovative leadership.

SUGGESTED
SEMINARS

The seminars listed here were selected for their appeal to a managerial audience. The reputation of the vendor, the quality of their seminar offerings, and the specific seminar content were considered in the selection process.

Because of the dynamic nature of the seminar marketplace, some seminars may have been upgraded or replaced, and others may no longer be offered. Likewise, costs and locations may have changed since this listing was compiled. We recommend that you contact the vendor directly for updated and additional information.

Team Building and Conflict Management

In this seminar, participants learn to effectively: monitor group interaction, contribute to the team process as either a team leader or team member, maintain positive working relationships with other team members, and turn destructive conflict into constructive conflict.
Length: 1 day; Cost: $350
Location: New York
Arthur Andersen & Company
1345 Avenue of the Americas, New York, NY 10105
Telephone: 212/708-8080

The Changing Role of the Manager

This course will help managers meet the challenge of leading in a participative work environment. Participants will learn to identify skills, systems, and processes needed to build a participative work environment; negotiate across organizational boundaries; resolve conflicts; and manage personal and organizational resistance to change.
Length: 3 days; Cost: $995
Locations: Call vendor
Association for Quality and Participation
801-B West 8th Street, Cincinnati, OH 45203
Telephone: 800/733-3310

Leadership and Teamwork

The purpose of this seminar is to increase the participant's ability to unify a team and to provide participants with comprehensive personal feedback. Key components include: resolving conflict and managing differences; defining, demonstrating, and mediating values for effective teamwork; and motivating and facilitating superior team performance on the job.
Length: 3 days; Cost: $2,300
Locations: Call vendor
Center for Creative Leadership
One Leadership Place, P.O. Box 26300
Greensboro, NC 27438-6300
Telephone: 910/545-2810

Facilitative Leadership: Tapping the Power of Participation

In this seminar, participants learn how to: encourage team participation by focusing on process, results, and relationships; appropriately involve people in problem solving and decision making; design meetings, project plans, and change strategies that people support and understand; and develop a personal plan for continuously improving themselves as leaders.
Length: 3 days; Cost: $1,125
Locations: Call vendor
Interaction Associates, Inc.
600 Townsend Street, Suite 550, San Francisco, CA 94103
Telephone: 415/241-8000

Teams in Action

This workshop will teach participants to determine the root causes of poor team performance and develop strategies for improvement; facilitate team discussions; mediate conflict; generate synergy and creativity; exchange feedback to build trust and improve performance; and evaluate their effectiveness as a team member.
Length: 2 days; Cost: $825
Locations: Call vendor
Interaction Associates, Inc.
600 Townsend Street, Suite 550, San Francisco, CA 94103
Telephone: 415/241-8000

Beyond Teams

This workshop will equip participants with concepts and applications that will help them establish the most effective organizational structures and the most effective use of teams. Topics include: the importance of accountability in hierarchical systems, "effectiveness" versus "outputs" as the criterion for measurement, the ways to organize work, whether a team is appropriate or not, and naturally occurring managerial layers.
Length: 5 days; Cost: $4,350
Location: Bedford, MA
Levinson Institute, Inc.
404 Wyman Street, Suite 400, Waltham, MA 02154
Telephone: 800/290-5735

Team Builder

After attending this workshop, participants will be better able to understand the three critical success factors for building a high-performing team, assess the current level of their team's performance, develop the skills and behavior sets for leading or facilitating their team, build their team from formation stage to a higher performance level, and develop a plan to move their team forward.
Length: 3 days; Cost: $995
Locations: Call vendor
Personnel Decisions International
2000 Plaza VII Tower, 45 South Seventh Street
Minneapolis, MN 55402-1608
Telephone: 800/633-4410

Leadership and Teamwork

This course is designed for all levels of management who want to increase their effectiveness as team leaders, team members, and team builders. Participants will learn how to build a balanced team whose members work well together, assess each team member's strengths and development needs, and discover their own team-building effectiveness.
Length: 3 days; Cost: $2,000
Locations: Call vendor
The Leadership Development Center
4541 Prospect Road, Suite 102, Peoria, IL 61614-6529
Telephone: 309/685-1900

Orchestrating Team Performance

This program uses experiential exercises to help participants understand the different stages of team development and formation, teach the most effective leadership style for each stage, and build skills to improve team effectiveness.
Length: 3-4 days; Cost: $895
Locations: Call vendor
The Tracom Corporation
3773 Cherry Creek North Drive, Suite 950
Denver, CO 80209
Telephone: 800/221-2321

Group Facilitation: Practice, Practice, Practice

This program is designed to enable the participants to enhance group facilitation skills and knowledge, increase knowledge of intervention theory, broaden their repertoire of interventions, and increase their awareness of their intervention style.
Length: 2 days; Cost: $545
Locations: Call vendor
University Associates
8380 Miramar Mall, Suite 232, San Diego, CA 92121
Telephone: 619/552-8901

Understanding Group Dynamics

Participants in this highly interactive seminar will learn how to: recognize the phases of group development; assess and diagnose group functioning; determine the effects of group norms and standards on members' behavior; and set goals and make decisions in groups.
Length: 3 days; Cost: $765
Locations: Call vendor
University Associates
8380 Miramar Mall, Suite 232, San Diego, CA 92121
Telephone: 619/552-8901

MOTIVATE OTHERS

Imagine that one of your most capable employees has reached a "productivity plateau." For the past month, she's seemed bored with her job and has done only what's needed to get by. Nor has she shown any interest in a promotion you discussed with her six months ago. You're not sure what the problem is, but it's obvious that her motivation level has dropped.

There may be many reasons why this employee's motivation has waned. Among the areas to consider: She is unclear about what is expected of her; she has not been receiving regular feedback about her performance; she has "outgrown" her current job but is uncertain about her skills for the promotion; she lacks a sense of achievement; her responsibilities have evolved into a mismatch with her skills.

This section provides guidelines for handling motivation-related issues like the one described above. It examines the importance of:

- Using Basic Principles of Motivation
- Learning Motivation Approaches from Colleagues
- Establishing High Standards of Performance
- Conveying the Attitude That Everyone's Work Is Important
- Conveying Trust in People's Competence to Do Their Jobs
- Inspiring People to Excel
- Creating an Enjoyable Work Environment
- Enriching Jobs to Increase Motivation
- Rewarding People for Good Performance
- Individualizing Your Approach to Motivation
- Creating a High-Performance Environment
- Conveying Enthusiasm about Department Objectives

Valuable Tips

- Encourage employees to set ambitious goals. Reward effort and achievement.

- Serve as an example to others by performing at a high level of excellence.

- Give credit where credit is due.

- Communicate the achievements of your unit and your employees to higher-level management in a visible and positive way, showing pride in, and support for, your people.

- Use your employees as sounding boards in areas where they have expertise.

- Know what aspects of the job excite your employees, and then provide them with opportunities to pursue these activities.

- When interviewing prospective employees, talk about your expectations for excellence.

- Identify the behaviors that you feel are critical to success in your organization, and then lead by example.

- Learn what rewards your employees value that you can provide.

- Notice the good work people are doing and talk about it to them and to others outside your area.

- Establish a "group identity" and work at building pride in group membership — "esprit de corps."

- Recognize that some people may be happier outside your organization, and encourage their departure for their good and the good of the people remaining.

- Give recognition to people who strive for excellence and improve quality.

- "Go to bat" for your employees.

- When seeking to change the behavior of employees, specify both the current and the desired behavior, and identify the positive and negative consequences of each.

- Find ways to enrich the jobs of your employees by increasing their authority or span of control.

- Don't ask your people to do things that you are not willing to do yourself.

MOTIVATE OTHERS

Using Basic Principles of Motivation

The subject of motivation in the work environment is one on which volumes of information have been compiled, countless books written, and research studies conducted. Thus, the following summary of these principles is abbreviated. These key principles, however, can help guide managers who are learning to establish a motivational climate.

- Employees are likely to perform more effectively when they know what is expected of them. This principle stresses the importance of setting clear objectives, ensuring that employees know their responsibilities, and clarifying expectations.

- Employees are likely to perform more effectively when they receive feedback on and reinforcement of their performance.

- Managers can improve the motivational climate by removing barriers to employee motivation. Ask your people to identify what makes their job difficult to do. Identify any "dissatisfiers," such as lack of recognition, perceptions of inequity or unfairness, or dissatisfaction with the physical working conditions. Then promptly address these issues.

- Additional factors that influence motivation include an employee's:
  - Sense of achievement
  - Match between responsibilities and abilities
  - Opportunities for advancement
  - Opportunities for personal growth

  As a manager, you have a great influence on an employee's ability to attain these factors.

Many managers believe they have no impact on the motivation of others because motivation occurs within an individual, or because they have no control over some of the factors that affect employee satisfaction, such as working conditions and benefits. However, as the preceding principles point out, managers play a major role in distributing many of the rewards employees seek, and in eliminating many of the barriers to satisfaction that employees encounter.

Learning Motivation Approaches from Colleagues

Colleagues who are recognized for their ability to create a motivational environment can be excellent sources of learning for you. They can provide guidelines on which you can base your own behavior. To benefit from their experience, follow these suggestions:

1. Arrange to attend meetings led by these colleagues. Take note of the behaviors that are effective in bringing about the desired results. In addition, meet with these people outside the meetings to discuss approaches they have found effective.

2. Develop a plan to try out some of these people's approaches with your employees. For your first attempt, choose a relatively simple approach with which you are comfortable; this will improve your chances of success on your first try.

3. After implementing your plan, watch for improvement in your department's motivational climate. Seek feedback from others on the results of your innovations.

As you come closer to approximating the behavior of your role models, you will also come closer to attaining a motivational climate similar to those established by your models.

Establishing High Standards of Performance

As a manager, it is important that you clearly define performance standards for employees. Employees need to know what performance level is expected, what performance is below standards, and what it takes to achieve high standards of performance.

The most convenient time to set performance expectations is during the employee's annual performance review or at the beginning of a new business planning cycle. Prepare for this discussion by doing the following:

1. Identify what you would consider "stretch objectives" for the employee, that is, the goals for performance that exceed the job requirements and are challenging, yet attainable. Things to consider: giving the employee more decision-making authority, adding responsibilities, taking on supervisory roles, increasing productivity goals.

2. Consider also the requirements for satisfactory performance relative to the employee's tenure, experience, and expertise.

3. Discuss your expectations with your employee, taking into account his or her perspective and any information you may have overlooked that would affect standards of performance. The more input employees have in setting performance expectations, the more likely they will be to "buy into" the standards upon which you agree.

4. With your employee, come to consensus on performance standards that meet and exceed expectations. Document your decisions.

5. Clarify the rewards for performance with the employee.

6. Meet periodically to discuss progress. If appropriate, revise expectations while keeping goals challenging.

Conveying the Attitude That Everyone's Work Is Important

Employees' responsibilities vary in terms of complexity and breadth. However, each person plays a critical role in the success of your area. It is important to convey the attitude that everyone's work is important.

• Meet with your employees individually and show them how their responsibilities fit into the department and organization.

• At staff meetings, highlight how various employees are contributing to positive results.

• Frequently reinforce effective performance, emphasizing how it affects you and the rest of the organization.

• Heighten the exposure of people performing "low visibility" responsibilities. For example, when recounting a successful project, explain how the accuracy and timeliness of the typist contributed to efficiency and quality.

• Discourage actions that minimize the contributions of others. For example, when coordinating project planning meetings, include the staff responsible for typing, collating, and proofing, to help them see how their work will affect the overall project.

Conveying Trust in People's Competence to Do Their Jobs

Managers are often caught in the difficult position of assigning tasks to employees even though the manager may believe that he or she can do the job the best. In these situations, the manager may follow the employees' work very closely, conveying the impression that he or she does not have confidence in their ability to do the job.

To become more comfortable with an employee's alternative ways of approaching and performing a given task:

1. Identify the standards of performance for the task. Consider which outcomes are acceptable or unacceptable, and which outcomes reflect outstanding performance. Explicitly convey to your employee what is necessary to accomplish the task. Research has shown that the more explicitly task goals and criteria are presented, the more likely they are to be met.

2. Next, allow time for the employee to respond to what you have said. Ask for the employee's perspective and ideas on how to

accomplish the job. Express your confidence in the employee's ability to do the job.

3. Decide on a course of action with the employee and, depending on the employee's expertise and the task complexity, follow up as he or she is performing the task (for example, follow up more closely for less experienced employees, less closely for more experienced employees).

4. As the employee gains experience, grant the additional leeway he or she has earned. Resist taking over when things go wrong; instead, coach the employee on how to correct the mistake.

5. Identify the areas of the job where the employee is particularly skilled. Then fully delegate to the employee on those areas.

Inspiring People to Excel

Managers can create an environment of energy and enthusiasm by fostering optimistic, positive attitudes about people and their work in the organization. To inspire your people to excel, try the following suggestions:

- Model excellence and enthusiasm in what you do.

- When negative feelings or attitudes come to your attention, bring them into the open. Meet with the people in your area who seem to be experiencing low morale, and discuss the issues. Let people air their feelings, but also bring the discussion around to what can be done to improve the situation. Express optimism that things can be different.

- Watch that you or others do not get into the habit of making statements like, "You just can't win," or "Things will never change." Empathize with the perspective that it may be difficult to make things better, but point out the issues that suggest that problems can be overcome. Reward attempts to increase the effectiveness of your work group.

- When evaluating ideas, spend as much time on the positive aspects of the ideas as you do on the negative. Make it a rule to consider the positive facets of the idea before looking at the negative ones.

- Openly recognize attempts to go beyond what is expected. In particular, reward people who overcome difficult obstacles and achieve strong results.

- Expect your people to excel. Just as negative expectations can be a self-fulfilling prophecy, the same is true of positive expectations.

Creating an Enjoyable Work Environment

Creating a work environment where people enjoy what they do is critical to maintaining an energized and creative work team. People are more motivated in situations where they can combine hard work with fun.

- Examine your own attitude about work and fun. Do you believe that work should be fun? If not, it will be very difficult to create an environment where others can have fun. Some things to think about:
  - People spend more time in work-related activities than in any other activity in their lives.
  - American workers are demonstrating a decreasing willingness to sacrifice other areas of their lives for work.
  - The sense of loyalty to the organization is weaker now than it once was.
  - Studies show that people who try to make work fun actually have more fun at work.

  All of these factors suggest that the more enjoyable and rewarding work is, the more satisfied people will be.

- Try the following suggestions to help make work more fun for your employees:
  - Create situations where people can get to know each other. (Some ideas: interdepartmental meetings, parties, brainstorming sessions, celebrations.)
  - Smile more.
  - Organize company-sponsored events such as volunteer opportunities in the community or sports activities.
  - Be a model of how to laugh at oneself. Be willing to admit to and see the humor in your mistakes.
  - Focus on "small wins" in addition to the big ones.
  - Talk about and celebrate successes.
  - Give people recognition for their efforts.

Enriching Jobs to Increase Motivation

Job enrichment — changing jobs to make them more satisfying — is a technique that can lead to higher quality work. Following is a list of ideas from which you can choose:

- Add new tasks to the job to widen the variety of skills used in performing the job. This can increase motivation by reducing boredom.

- Increase your employees' authority and accountability. Give your employees full decision-making responsibility in areas for which your approval was formerly required.

- Increase your employees' visibility. For example, an employee who formerly prepared reports for your signature might now submit reports under his or her own signature.

- Give employees the opportunity to attend conferences or meetings as the company representative.

- Increase the meaningfulness of assigned tasks. An employee who previously completed only a portion of a task might be permitted to handle the entire task alone or with others to have the satisfaction of producing a total product.

- Increase the amount of feedback on performance. Feedback can be provided by you — the manager — or by the employees themselves. For example, a machine repairperson can keep a tally of the number of "call-back" service calls received on the equipment serviced.

- Periodically assign special projects to provide challenge and visibility.

Rewarding People for Good Performance

One primary factor in productivity is the reinforcement employees receive for their behaviors. If employees receive consistently positive reinforcement for desirable behaviors, productivity levels will tend to be high. If, on the other hand, employees perceive that unproductive behaviors are rewarded or — even worse — that productive behaviors are punished, productivity will tend to be low.

If your employees are not meeting your expectations, one approach is to determine whether something in the work environment is reinforcing their behaviors inappropriately. The following process can help:

1. Determine the consequences of current behavior using the following Behavior/Consequences matrix.

    - In Box A, list the positive consequences the employee experiences as a result of engaging in desirable behaviors.

    - In Box B, list the adverse consequences of engaging in desirable behaviors.

    - In Box C, list the positive consequences of engaging in undesirable behaviors.

CONSEQUENCES

	Positive	Negative
Desirable	A	B
Undesirable	C	D

CURRENT BEHAVIOR

- In Box D, list the negative consequences of engaging in undesirable behaviors.

Consider these consequences from the employee's perspective, not your own. Consequences that you label as negative from your perspective are positive from the employee's point of view — or they wouldn't continue. For example, from your point of view, the consequence of an employee's leaving early is that work is not completed on time; from the employee's point of view, the only consequence may be that he or she has more time for personal pursuits.

2. Identify the consequences that need to be changed to improve the behavior. Do this by determining how to remove the positive consequences of undesirable behaviors and create positive consequences for desirable behaviors.

3. Discuss the desired goals with the employee, putting them in behavioral, observable terms.

4. Catch employees "doing something right." Then make sure that you give positive feedback.

5. Once the desired behavior is performed, reward it immediately. Positive consequences increase the probability that the behavior will occur again. Possible reinforcers include:

- Monetary rewards

- Promotions

- Increased autonomy

- Increased responsibility

- Visibility in the organization

- Access to additional resources

- Recognition from the team

- Flexibility in time schedules

- Opportunity to present their successes, such as speak at a technical symposium or present at a conference

Individualizing Your Approach to Motivation

Individuals vary in how they value various rewards. The following guidelines will help you gear your motivational techniques to the individual employees in your work group:

Write each employee's name on a separate sheet of paper. Use these sheets of paper as follows:

1. List the needs and corresponding rewards you believe to be most relevant to each employee, based on your current knowledge of that employee.

2. Initiate a discussion with each employee to learn, directly from the source, what that employee perceives his or her needs to be. Compare the list supplied by the employee with the list of your perceptions to determine your level of sensitivity to employee requirements.

3. Observe employees over time and add to or alter your list of requirements. For example, you would change the list of requirements if you discovered that employees did not mention certain needs because they thought them inappropriate (for example, employees who consider it inappropriate to indicate that they require frequent recognition), or if you found that employees mentioned certain needs they do not have but believe you expect them to have (for example, employees who are not interested in advancement but who believe they will be penalized for lack of ambition should this fact become known).

4. In addition, observe employees to determine the optimum timing for rewards. For example, some employees may appreciate frequent encouragement and recognition throughout a project, while others may prefer to receive these rewards upon project completion.

5. Most importantly, develop and implement a list of ways in which you can provide the rewards that influence employees' individual motivation levels.

GREAT JOB, JENKINS! AS A REWARD, I'D LIKE YOU TO PREPARE THE OTHER 65 REPORTS.

To further develop your skills:

- Seek feedback on your motivational abilities from colleagues skilled in this area. If appropriate, arrange for coaching to improve your skills.

- Observe skilled colleagues in action and incorporate their approaches into your own program.

As you change the way you deal with employee motivation, watch for signs of improvement in the motivation level of your department.

Creating a High-Performance Environment

A high-performance environment is one in which:

- The focus is clear

- The work is challenging

- People feel appreciated

- Barriers to accomplishing work are at a minimum

- Resources are available

- People help and support one another

To create this environment, identify your employees' perception of "what exists today" and "what is needed." Ask your employees the following questions to gain a clearer understanding of your current environment and what action is needed to develop a high-performance environment:

- What have you done in the last six months that you are most proud of?

- What is challenging about your work? What challenges do you like?

- From what sources do you get a sense of job satisfaction?

- Who appreciates the job you do? Where do you get your recognition?

- What has motivated you in the past to work harder?

- What obstacles exist to doing your work?

- What resources are or are not available for you to do your job?

- Whom can you count on in a crunch?

- Where do you get support?

Conveying Enthusiasm about Department Objectives

Managers may assume that their commitment to department objectives and deadlines will automatically be communicated to employees. To some extent, that's true. However, using the following techniques can help ensure that your employees recognize your commitment:

- Emphasize your own commitment to the department and organization, and praise the commitment demonstrated by your staff.

- When you assign new projects to your employees, take the time to explain how the project fits in with overall department objectives. When employees understand how their work contributes to the whole, their commitment to it increases.

- Make it a point to regularly reinforce the importance of each individual's contributions and their value to overall department objectives.

- Remind your employees often that the success of the department or team is key to the success of the organization.

RECOMMENDED READINGS

The publications listed here were selected for their content and suitability to a managerial audience.

People Smarts

Alessandra, Tony, and O'Conner, Michael J., San Diego: Pfeiffer & Company, 1994
ISBN: 0-89384-421-7
The authors introduce the "platinum rule": treat others the way they want to be treated and both parties win. Since everyone is unique, your goal is to adapt your approach to meet the different needs and priorities of the people you deal with. This book is helpful in identifying behavioral styles and learning how to adjust your behavior to increase trust, credibility, and cooperation.

Principle-Centered Leadership

Covey, Stephen R., New York: Summit Books, 1991
ISBN: 0-671-74910-2
The author describes how the goals of excellence and total quality express an innate human need for personal, interpersonal, and organizational improvement. Covey discusses the key to managing expectations, the six conditions of effectiveness, how to understand people's potential rather than just their behavior, and the patterns of organizational excellence.

Bringing Out the Best in People

Daniels, Aubrey C., New York: McGraw-Hill, 1993
ISBN: 0-07-015358-2
This book teaches the principles of positive reinforcement that can help managers get top performance from their people. It shows precisely how to pinpoint, measure, and provide feedback on the specific behaviors and results that you want. Daniels' book guides you toward continuous quality improvement by using positive consequences.

Leadership Jazz

De Pree, Max, New York: Doubleday, 1992
ISBN: 0-385-42018-8
De Pree draws a compelling parallel between leadership and jazz — both art forms in which freedom and technique, improvisation and rules, and inspiration and restraint must be precisely and expertly blended. He shows how human values form the basis of extraordinary leadership.

Patterns of High Performance

Fletcher, Jerry L., San Francisco: Berrett-Koehler, 1993
ISBN: 1-881052-33-8
A High Performance Pattern is the distinctive sequence of steps people naturally follow when they are at their best. Each individual has a distinctive pattern and this book seeks to help the reader discover what that pattern is and how to best utilize it. Included are techniques on how to revitalize tasks, find new ways of working in difficult situations, change the focus of a group for better efficiency, and get critical projects back on track. These various High Performance Patterns are described and examined though sixteen case studies.

Reaching The Peak Performance Zone

Kushel, Gerald, New York: AMACOM, 1994
ISBN: 0-8144-0222-4
This book contends that the difference between outstanding and average work is an internal drive to achieve peak performance. Managers who are peak performers can encourage and teach others how to reach the peak performance zone. Peak performers are self-motivated people who freely accept the blame when things go wrong and who work energetically simply because they want to. The author provides a step-by-step method for motivating others to become peak performers.

Developing High-Performance People

Mink, Oscar G.; Keith, Owen Q.; and Mink, Barbara P.,
Reading, MA: Addison-Wesley, 1993
ISBN: 0-201-56313-4
This book addresses the managerial skills needed in the current business environment which emphasizes self-managed work teams, empowerment of employees, and organizational learning. It shows how to build trust and involvement with employees in order to help them achieve maximum effectiveness.

1001 Ways to Reward Employees

Nelson, Bob, New York: Workman Publishing, 1993
ISBN: 1-56305-339-X
Nelson reminds us of an essential management principle: the people who work for you are motivated by recognition. His book offers rewards of every conceivable type for every conceivable situation.

Don't Fire Them, Fire Them Up: A Maverick's Guide to Motivating Yourself and Your Team

Pacetta, Frank, and Gittness, Roger, New York: Simon & Schuster, 1994
ISBN: 0-671-86949-3
The authors, drawing on successful experience at a Xerox district office, show how to build and motivate an organization to increase productivity and sales. The book shows how to build trust, create loyalty, and generate enthusiasm in order to create a successful business team.

SUGGESTED SEMINARS

The seminars listed here were selected for their appeal to a managerial audience. The reputation of the vendor, the quality of their seminar offerings, and the specific seminar content were considered in the selection process.

Because of the dynamic nature of the seminar marketplace, some seminars may have been upgraded or replaced, and others may no longer be offered. Likewise, costs and locations may have changed since this listing was compiled. We recommend that you contact the vendor directly for updated and additional information.

Motivating Others: Bringing Out the Best in Your People

This program includes evaluating the participant's own degree of motivation, setting employees up for success, communicating directly and openly, providing feedback that motivates, and creating an atmosphere that allows people to flourish.
Length: 3 days; Cost: $1,145
Locations: Call vendor
American Management Association
P.O. Box 319, Saranac Lake, NY 12983
Telephone: 800/262-9699

Situational Leadership II® for Managers

This seminar introduces Ken Blanchard's Situational Leadership II® principles. The seminar uses a variety of case studies, instruments, and video programs to help participants gain insight into their leadership style and learn how to use the Situational Leadership II® model to improve their managerial effectiveness.
Length: 3 days; Cost: $895
Locations: Call vendor
Blanchard Training and Development
125 State Place, Escondido, CA 92029
Telephone: 800/728-6000

Working With Others

Participants in this workshop learn three critical areas of management: gaining peak performance from workers, leading work groups, and handling interpersonal relationships.
Length: 4 days; Cost: CD $1,775 + GST
Location: Niagara-on-the-Lake, Ontario, Canada
Center for Creative Leadership
One Leadership Place, P.O. Box 26300
Greensboro, NC 27438-6300
Telephone: 910/545-2810

Toward Understanding Human Behavior and Motivation

Participants in this seminar gain an understanding of human behavior and motivation, take a critical look at their own strengths and weaknesses as executives, and evolve plans for putting what they learn to work in their professional and personal lives.
Length: 5 days; Cost: Call vendor
Locations: Call vendor
Menninger Management Institute
P.O. Box 829, Topeka, KS 66601-0829
Telephone: 800/288-5357

Emerging Leaders

This program, designed for current and future leaders, addresses the evaluation, building, and sustaining of leadership excellence. Participants will assess and develop their leadership excellence with regard to four areas: personal, people, business, and work.
Length: 5 days; Cost: Call vendor
Location: Call vendor
Personnel Decisions International
2000 Plaza VII Tower, 45 South Seventh Street
Minneapolis, MN 55402-1608
Telephone: 800/633-4410

Improving Performance Management

At this workshop, managers learn how to gain individual and team commitment to improving performance and how to create a powerful learning environment. Participants will learn how to use a four-phase performance management model, clarify performance expectations, strengthen their planning process, and understand the link between pay and performance.
Length: 3 days; Cost: $850
Location: Madison, WI
University of Wisconsin-Madison
Management Institute, Grainger Hall
975 University Avenue, Madison, WI 53706-1323
Telephone: 800/348-8964

The Disney Approach: A Management Seminar

This seminar gives the participant an opportunity to discover the methods that the Disney management team uses to successfully select, train, motivate, and communicate to its people. Through the study of the successful Disney approach, participants also learn how to create a quality service theme and setting, how to deliver quality service, and how to put quality service into action.
Length: 2 days; Cost: $1,289
Location: Lake Buena Vista, FL
Walt Disney World
Disney University Seminars, P.O. Box 10093
Lake Buena Vista, FL 32830-0093
Telephone: 407/824-4855

COACH AND DEVELOP OTHERS

Just as technical research and development is essential for continued excellence and a competitive edge, so must coaching and development become the leader's focal point for leveraging the organization's human capital. Coaching others is no longer limited to your direct reports. In a learning organization, everyone must be prepared to learn from and coach anyone. Coaching depends not on hierarchy, but on who has the opportunity to create a learning experience.

The continuum of development ranges from helping poor performers improve to leveraging the strengths of longer-term employees to capitalizing on high-potential employees by keeping them challenged and "stretching" their current skills. Supporting the development efforts of others contributes to individual productivity and to the productivity of the team as a whole. Coaching is not a one-way street where you have all the answers, but rather a partnership where both people share responsibility.

The guidelines presented in this section take you through a number of phases, from new-hire employee orientation to grooming experienced employees for advancement.

Part 1: Developing Your Employees

- Emulating the Characteristics of Effective Coaches
- Improving Your Employee Orientation Program
- Training New Employees
- Identifying Others' Strengths and Development Needs
- Providing Ongoing Coaching
- Providing Developmental Challenges for Your Staff
- Tapping the Talent of Administrative Personnel
- Creating Developmental Assignments
- Preparing Employees to Represent You at Meetings
- Providing Books or Audio/Video Tapes
- Using Training Programs to Develop Your Employees
- Preparing Effective Development Plans

Part 2: Delivering High-Impact Feedback

- Establishing an Environment Conducive to Feedback
- Giving Others Positive Feedback
- Tempering Premature Criticism
- Providing Constructive Criticism
- Conducting a Debriefing Session

Part 3: Addressing Employee Performance Problems

- Analyzing Performance Problems
- Coaching Employees with Performance Problems

Part 4: Grooming Employees for Advancement

- Teaching Skills to Others
- Showing an Interest in Employees' Careers
- Providing Information on Career Opportunities in the Organization
- Increasing Employees' Exposure to the Total Organization
- Developing a Replacement

Valuable Tips

- Give positive recognition to people immediately.

- Meet individually with your employees to discuss their career goals and identify the skills they need to achieve these goals.

- Identify the weakest performer on your staff. Decide whether you think this person has the ability to perform adequately. If so, develop a program to bring him or her up to speed.

- Ask yourself, "What must people do to get positive feedback from me?" Evaluate your expectations.

- Don't hesitate to confront poor performance as soon as you notice it. Give feedback and begin constructive action to help.

- Maintain a development file on each of your employees. Keep track of successes, failures, development needs, and how you have agreed to help. Use this file during the performance review process.

- Help others learn from mistakes.

- Communicate current and future organizational needs and how they relate to the development priorities of individuals on your team.

- Focus your feedback on people's behavior. Be more descriptive and less evaluative in your feedback.

- Remember that people master tasks in small steps. Help your employees become competent by building from small to larger responsibilities.

- Recognize development efforts, not just results.

- Find ways for others to capitalize on and further develop their areas of strength.

- Help your employees build their skills by having each employee work on improving one development need and enhancing one strength at a time. Be specific about the steps he or she can take to meet his or her goals.

- Be a role model for development by openly pursuing learning and taking risks.

- Be alert to articles and development tips that could be of help to others; pass them on to appropriate individuals.

- Create your own development handbook of ideas especially suited to your company and function in the organization. Ask your employees to read this handbook and identify one or two suggestions they'd like to tackle.

- Allocate resources for development, including money, time, and consultation.

- Meet with your employees individually to identify what you can do to help them be more effective in their jobs.

- Identify the one or two employees most likely to replace you, and begin grooming them for your responsibilities.

- Rotate people through key positions to develop their general management capabilities.

- Let your employees stand in for you. Send them to meetings in your place.

- Encourage a "continuous improvement" mindset that allows rewards for mistakes and accompanying efforts to improve.

PART 1

Emulating the Characteristics of Effective Coaches

Developing Your Employees

Effective coaches are developed, not born. They have, over time, acquired the skills and attitudes to create an environment that nurtures learning and development. To become a more effective coach, review the following attributes to identify areas in which you are strong, as well as aspects of your coaching style that need improvement.

Effective coaches:

- Base the coaching relationship on trust, not similarity.

- Are optimists about human nature.

- Meet people where they are.

- Give people opportunities to take risks and learn from their mistakes.

- Listen more than they talk.

- Are patient, and are willing to find the "coachable" moment.

- Speak candidly, but dispense their message in the right size dose.

- Cultivate personal accountability and ownership.

- Approach resistance and reluctance to change with curiosity.

- Know their own strengths and limitations.

- Are continuous learners.

Improving Your Employee Orientation Program

New employees' formal and informal orientation to your organization and department will be one of their first and most powerful impressions of what they can expect. Hence, the quality of your orientation program has an impact on how well new employees perform on the job, how well they get along with their coworkers, their job satisfaction, and even their eventual career progress within the organization. To develop an effective orientation program, follow these suggestions:

- Evaluate your current program. The orientation program should provide employees with at least the following information:
  - A detailed presentation or reference guide of the organization's policies, work rules, and employee benefits

- General information about the day-to-day routine (location of rest rooms and lunchrooms, how to use telephones and copy machines, obtaining supplies, and so forth)
- A description of the organization's history, purpose, and products/services, and a discussion of how the employee's job contributes to the overall purpose
- The "musts" for survival and success (for example, mandatory attendance at financial planning meetings is expected of all managers with budget responsibility and accountability)
- Specific information about the work, people, and relationships in the new employee's area

- Survey all employees to get suggestions for improving the organization's employee orientation program. Ask them what they think new employees need in order to function comfortably and effectively.

- Ask new hires to help you evaluate the effectiveness of your program by providing feedback at designated points — such as two weeks, one month, and two months — after their hire dates.

- Assign an experienced employee as a sponsor for each new employee. Let the new hire know that this person will be available to answer any questions.

- Realize that it is your responsibility to see that new employees receive an effective orientation to their jobs, your department, and the organization. Decide which parts of the orientation you need to do and which parts would be appropriate to delegate to others.

- Conduct orientation for all levels of employees.

Training New Employees

Too often, the training of new employees is forgotten in the day-to-day rush to get the job done. It's possible, however, to develop a program that takes minimal time to administer, yet effectively integrates new people into your department. To develop such a program, build the following elements into your training program for new hires:

- Provide orientation. View orientation as the first step in the training program.

- Establish a support network. New employees should be introduced to the more experienced employees who will provide general support and assistance during your absence. Inform the experienced employees of their responsibilities in this area.

- Establish an environment that is conducive to learning. Newcomers usually have a variety of concerns. Let them know that you don't expect them to absorb everything the first time around, that you realize mistakes will be made, and that you encourage their questions.

- Provide on-the-job training experiences. A mix of on-the-job and formal training experiences will help new employees integrate their new knowledge and enable them to feel that they are contributing to the goals of the department. The sooner you start them making a contribution to the group, the more excited and motivated they will be.

- Encourage feedback from experienced employees. Feedback from experienced employees will help you determine the areas in which new employees require more training.

- Create a manual of training materials. Keep a record of the training procedures used to train new hires. After several employees have been trained, identify the procedures that have proven most effective and include them in a training manual. As the manual becomes more specific and complete, you will be able to delegate more and more training-related tasks to your employees.

Identifying Others' Strengths and Development Needs

Recognizing your employees' areas of strength and weakness helps you coach and develop your staff more effectively. To increase your understanding:

1. List the areas of competency that compose the individual's job. For each area, list the specific, behavioral actions that demonstrate competency. Identify the most important skills that are necessary for successful performance.

2. Compare the individual's observable performance with the desired behaviors, using a rating scale from 1 (low) to 5 (high).

3. Ask your employee to do the same evaluation.

4. Discuss your ratings with your employee to ensure that you are in agreement about the person's skills. If you disagree on any ratings, negotiate differences until you reach agreement.

When you want an objective view of your employees' strengths and development needs, use a development assessment process conducted by an experienced assessment organization. Match your analysis with that of the organizational psychologists who are trained to identify management skills.

Also, if applicable, volunteer to be trained as an assessor in your organization's assessment center. This training will increase your ability to assess strengths accurately and build a stronger team.

Providing Ongoing Coaching

Coaching is one of the most powerful ways to help employees grow. The first step in establishing an effective coaching effort is to determine the specific coaching needs of the employee.

To determine an employee's coaching needs, use your ongoing assessment of each of your employee's:

- Needs identified in individual discussions with the employee

- Improvements necessary in their current job

- Performance appraisal results

- Skills needed for future responsibilities

Keep in mind that employees typically need coaching in the following general areas:

- People skills

- Organizational savvy skills

- Technical problem-solving skills

Review the areas of coaching that you are providing to your employees to make certain you touch on their specific needs. Then follow this procedure to establish an effective, ongoing coaching effort:

1. Discuss methods for improvement. Identify the behaviors that are effective and those to be avoided in the area you are addressing. When possible, use examples of the employee's past behaviors.

2. Determine the most appropriate situations or settings for observing the employee's behavior and set aside time for regular observation.

3. Observe the employee's behavior. Watch for effective and ineffective behaviors; people learn more quickly if you point out what they do right, as well as what they do wrong. Take notes, including specific examples.

4. Give immediate feedback whenever possible. The more immediate the feedback, the more powerful it will be. Focus on specific, concrete behaviors. Whenever you point out an ineffective behavior, be sure to describe the correct behavior that should replace it.

5. Tailor your coaching to individual employees. Consider the following:

   • Ask the employee to critique his or her work or your own.

   • Ask the employee to present several alternatives and to explain the positives and negatives in terms of problem solving or impact on people.

   • Have the employee practice or role-play.

   • Tell stories that illustrate learning points for the employee.

   • Ask the employee to develop a strategy for getting the necessary support for a project.

Providing Developmental Challenges for Your Staff

One of the most powerful motivators for employees is the opportunity to work on challenging assignments and stretch their capabilities. It's tempting to always give the most challenging and crucial assignments to proven performers, but it's important to provide development opportunities for *all* employees.

To assess the way you currently assign projects:

1. Examine current and past assignments in your department. For each project, ask yourself:

   • How difficult was this project to complete?

   • How crucial was this project?

   • Who was assigned to this project?

   • Why was this individual assigned?

2. Now look at each employee's history, asking yourself:

   • Does this person often perform the same tasks repeatedly, or often take on new responsibilities?

   • Have I given this person opportunities to try new things and develop or enhance his or her skills?

   • Does this person indicate a desire for more challenging assignments?

- Does this person have the potential to handle more challenging work? If so, what skills, resources, or experiences would help him or her tap this potential?

3. Now look at the overall picture of the group. If you see that some employees are not being challenged by their current assignments, look for ways to provide the skills, resources, and experiences that will allow them to handle more challenging work. Then assign that work to them.

Tapping the Talent of Administrative Personnel

There is often a gulf between administrative personnel and professional or technical workers. Many times talent among the administrative ranks remains untapped. Maximize your talent pool by utilizing the skills of your administrative people. When you give assignments to an employee outside your organization's recognized professional staff, proactively support the employee by:

- Expressing confidence in the person to others

- Mentioning the experience that the person had that convinced you to give him or her the assignment

- Confronting active detractors

- Being available as a sounding board for the person

Don't let a person's title or role prevent you from tapping his or her talent and potential skills.

Creating Developmental Assignments

Effectively developing your people means being creative and proactive about the assignments you give them. Following are some suggestions for assignments:

- Put one of your people in charge of a cross-functional task force to give him or her exposure to other functions, an understanding of interrelationships, and an opportunity to build relationships and work on complex issues.

- Have your employees represent your organization at conferences and symposiums.

- Put them in situations where they have to perform a "fix-it" function to get experience managing change, analyzing business problems, and tackling tough assignments.

- Give them a temporary lateral assignment that forces them to see the business from an alternative perspective.

- Assign them to projects that require them to interface with your boss to provide exposure and experience working with higher-level managers.

- Give them assignments that thrust them beyond their zone of comfort.

- Have an employee represent you at a meeting and give a formal presentation on findings or results.

- Delegate complete responsibility for managing the execution of a complex project from start to finish.

- Assign them to mentor a new or inexperienced employee, which will require them to learn how to coach, explain things, and support people.

- Have them manage a highly talented employee, which will challenge their own expertise and coaching skill.

- Put them in charge of a project that has met with a high degree of resistance or conflict to provide practice in handling conflict, negotiating, influencing others, and building support.

- Have them manage a poor performer.

- Have them manage and be responsible for a part of your budget.

- Put them in charge of a cost containment project.

- Assign them formal training responsibility for others.

Preparing Employees to Represent You at Meetings

By training employees to represent you at meetings, you accomplish two goals: 1) you expose your employees to a wider range of organizational activities, and 2) you free yourself to devote time to your own growth. The following procedure will help you prepare your employees to represent you:

1. Identify employees who possess the necessary skills to represent you at meetings. Look for qualities such as:

   - Knowledge of the subject areas typically addressed at meetings

   - The ability to participate in problem-solving and negotiation sessions

   - Maturity, in terms of projecting the appropriate image

   - Interest in assuming managerial responsibilities

2. Over the next few months, determine, for each meeting, if it would be appropriate for one of your selected employees to accompany you. If so, prepare your employee for the meeting by explaining:

   - The purpose of the meeting

   - The personalities and politics involved

   - Your role in the meeting

   - Your expectations of him or her

3. After the meeting, discuss it with the employee. Carefully explain any unanticipated events or reactions to events.

4. After your employee has accompanied you to several meetings, send him or her as your replacement. Be sure that you provide appropriate coaching before the meeting and that your employee understands the degree of authority he or she has when acting as your representative.

5. After each meeting, discuss the events of the meeting with your employee and provide feedback when appropriate.

Whenever you delegate your responsibilities for leading meetings, it's important that you consider the needs of the others who will be attending the meetings. Take care that, in sending a replacement, you don't negatively affect the outcome of the meeting.

Providing Books or Audio/Video Tapes

The most powerful development opportunities occur on the job, but there may be a need to supplement that learning with other ideas, information, or background. Often one can augment development efforts by reading a book, listening to an audiotape, or watching a videotape. To ensure the maximum benefit from this form of learning, consider the following suggestions:

- Choose resources that are current and timely. Check the Recommended Readings listed at the end of each chapter of this Handbook, spend some time browsing the bookshelves in a large bookstore known for having a good business selection, or get recommendations from colleagues or friends.

- Read or review several books on the same topic to ensure that what you are recommending represents a broad view of the topic.

- Discuss the specific learning objectives before the person begins the book or tape. Is the need for general ideas or specific facts? If this preparation has been done, the person will be more aware when the information sought appears in the book or tape.

- Ensure that what has been learned is used as soon as possible. When the person finishes the book or tape, have him or her review the learning objectives. The person should solidify the learning by writing it out or by making a presentation about the book or tape to his or her manager or peers. Be sure that what was learned is put into practice on the job.

Using Training Programs to Develop Your Employees

Training programs can be a good way to learn a skill or to supplement on-the-job experiences. Moreover, you can take steps to maximize their impact and get the most from your training dollars.

- To select a training program for an employee, determine:
  - The specific development objectives for the employee
  - The results you hope to obtain

- Share these ideas with your employee and discuss possible programs or seminars. Involving your employee in the decision will be likely to increase his or her interest and willingness to participate in the seminar.

This Handbook is a valuable reference for defining options for training programs. The most effective seminars are those that:

- Focus on specific skill areas (for instance, selection interviewing, developing employees' time management skills).

- Include skills practice during the seminar.

- Provide feedback on how participants implement the skill. Videotaped role playing can be an excellent vehicle for providing this feedback.

If the training objective is to gain broader feedback on a range of skills, consider a more comprehensive development program designed to give participants in-depth feedback about their strengths and weaknesses as assessed over a two- to six-day period.

After selecting the appropriate program, consider the optimum time to enroll the employee in the seminar. To ensure transfer of skills to the job, have the employee attend the seminar just before he or she needs to apply the skill on the job. For example, if the skill is selection interviewing, have your employee attend the program just before he or she is scheduled to do some selection interviewing on the job.

When the employee has completed the program, take time to debrief him or her on what was learned and what specifically will be done differently on the job. You may wish to have your employee make a presentation about the course to peers so that they can also benefit from the training. As a coach, give the employee ample opportunities to use the new skills and reinforce these skills so that the training results in lasting behavior change.

Preparing Effective Development Plans

Partnering with employees about their development works best. This means that you work with employees to make certain the development plans are specific, practical, and addressing important current and future needs, and that you provide ongoing feedback. Ask your employees to write their own plans and then review them, or prepare them jointly.

When reviewing the development plans of your employees, be sure to consider the following features of a successful plan:

- *Specificity*. Goals and activities should be stated specifically and concretely so that both you and the employee know when objectives have been attained. Be sure to describe the skills or knowledge to be gained as a result of the assigned activity.

- *Limited focus*. Include no more than three major development areas in the plan.

- *Commitment*. Employees are more likely to be committed to goals they choose and plans they develop, yet the goals and plans must fit in with your objectives and those of your team. In addition, you must be committed to providing the opportunities and resources needed by the employee to fulfill the plan; otherwise, development plans become another source of bureaucratic busywork.

- *Small, reasonable steps*. Because people learn in small steps, expecting too much too soon can discourage progress. Divide development activities into small steps that lead to an ultimate goal.

- *On-the-job opportunities*. The most powerful development occurs on the job. It's important that managers and employees use job responsibilities as opportunities for development.

- *Support and feedback*. Provide support in the form of financial resources, time, feedback, reinforcement, encouragement, and other forms of coaching. Tailor your support to the individual's learning style.

- *Specified time frames for accomplishment.* Employees must have an established time frame for each task. Schedule target dates for completion and checkpoints for progress review.

- *Adequate variety.* Employees will be more enthusiastic about their plans if they include a variety of activities. Take care to provide a mix of on-the-job activities, readings, course work, evaluations, and other activities identified by the employee.

PART 2

Establishing an Environment Conducive to Feedback

Delivering High-Impact Feedback

Feedback is essential to employee development. It not only helps employees correct mistakes before they become habits, but it also reinforces positive behaviors, encourages the development of desirable work habits, and helps employees achieve their goals.

For feedback to be effective, it must be given in a safe, collaborative climate that is conducive to learning. Use the following guidelines to create such an environment:

- Explain your purpose. Let others know that your purpose is to help them, whether that is to help them develop, be more effective, understand others' perceptions, or make better choices.

- Establish trust. To demonstrate your trustworthiness, let those you coach know what to expect from the feedback process, do what you say you will do, and act with their best interest in mind.

- Work to *really* understand the people you coach. Pay attention to what they say and how they say it, and ask questions to discover their view of the world. Then make sure they feel understood, accepted, and validated in their own views.

- Invite people to shape the feedback process. Feedback is threatening or intimidating to some people because they see the coach as having all the power. Balance the power by sharing some of the decisions and control with the person you're coaching.

- Be genuine. Let your own personality, insights, observations, and self-disclosures add depth and richness to the feedback you give others.

- Treat feedback as information, not as a value judgment. Present feedback in a neutral way, rather than labeling the behavior or the person.

Feedback's impact depends not only on the climate in which it is given, but also on its timing. To be effective, feedback must be well timed (for example, not given when you are angry) and, as many studies have shown, timely. Regular feedback is key to the development of employees' skills. To help ensure that you provide feedback regularly:

- Establish mechanisms for reviewing your employees' performance on a regular basis. For example, you might set a goal to review their work at least once every two weeks.

- Communicate your willingness to provide feedback. This will encourage employees to consult you for advice before they take action that could be erroneous.

- Follow up quickly with feedback when you see improvements. Recognition of improvement is essential to change performance.

- Give corrective feedback when appropriate. Foster the belief among your team that talking about mistakes and learning from them is a way to encourage responsible risk taking and self-development.

For additional information, see the following sections: Giving Others Positive Feedback and Providing Constructive Criticism.

Giving Others Positive Feedback

Positive feedback is a powerful motivator when it is specific and behavioral. Global compliments, while encouraging, are too broad to be effective in maintaining or improving employees' performance. In giving individuals positive feedback, you recognize and appreciate the contribution of others. It is important to give positive feedback to your manager and peers, as well as to those who report to you.

To make your positive feedback specific and behavioral:

- Describe the behavior you are recognizing, such as meeting a deadline, surpassing productivity projections, or participating more fully in a meeting.

- Emphasize the impact of the behavior so that the person can clearly see why you believe it is important. You can talk about the impact on you, the job, the organization, the team, and so forth.

- Let the person know exactly what behaviors to continue. For example, "I'm delighted that you found a solution to that design problem and beat the deadline by two days," is more effective than "You did a good job on this project."

- Develop a habit of looking for and commending specific positive behaviors; such reinforcement will increase the incidence of those behaviors.

Tempering Premature Criticism

People learn by making mistakes. If you create an environment in which employees fear criticism whenever they try new tasks or skills, your department will soon become stagnant. Over the next several months, use the following techniques to counteract a tendency to criticize prematurely:

- Become results-oriented. Your employees may use methods that are different from yours but just as effective. Keep an open mind about new approaches if the results are there.

- Stop yourself from jumping to conclusions. Gather and consider all the facts before you criticize. Mistakes may be due to miscommunication or conditions outside the employees' control.

- Remember that your position as manager makes some employees extremely sensitive to your criticism. Thus, employees may overestimate the significance of offhand remarks or minor criticisms.

- If you tend to be perfectionistic with your own work, check to see if you approach other people's work in the same way. Temper perfectionistic criticism by focusing only on what is most important, recognizing effort, and acknowledging good work.

- Consider the sensitivity level of individual employees before delivering criticism. A frown may be all it takes to let one employee know that he or she has made a mistake, while another employee may require a blunt statement of the problem.

- If you become so personally involved with an employee that you can no longer be objective in your criticism, ask your boss or a trusted peer for help. A different approach to solving the problem, rather than more criticism, may be the answer.

Providing Constructive Criticism

It's usually easy to identify performance issues, but it's not always as easy to communicate negative feedback effectively and constructively. How you deliver criticism can make the difference between continued decline or an improvement in the employee's performance. The following guidelines can help you provide constructive criticism:

- Respect the person's need for privacy. Your reaction to a person's behavior or performance should be between you and the person.

- Give feedback that is specific and behavioral, rather than general and judgmental. Describe the behavior in objective and specific terms. Focus on the work, not on the person. Saying, "You're getting lazy," is much more likely to arouse defensiveness than saying, "You've missed the last two deadlines."

- Next, describe the behavior's impact on you, the team, or the attainment of the person's goals.

- Express your observations calmly. Make sure you are emotionally in control before you deliver negative feedback. Criticism offered when you are angry or upset may come out more harshly than you intended and have lasting negative effects.

- Avoid overwhelming the person with too much feedback all at once. Focus on relevant and important observations. Read the person's nonverbal cues to know whether you need to reposition a point, provide support, process their feelings and reactions, or move to the next topic.

- Let the person present his or her side of the problem, engage in a dialogue, and avoid any tendency to lecture.

- Focus on the future and, through your discussions, identify the specific behavioral change that is required. Offer useful suggestions for preventing similar mistakes in the future.

- Clearly identify the payoff or positive outcome of the desired behavior. This emphasizes the positive and helps motivate employees to change.

- Provide the appropriate balance of positive and negative feedback. When your comments are negative, offer to help the person improve, and express your hope for his or her success.

- Express empathy when you perceive discouragement. Acknowledge that change does not happen overnight and can be difficult at times.

Conducting a Debriefing Session

A debriefing session is a way to discuss an event or an assignment after the fact. Debriefing is critically important when you are coaching someone to learn a new skill because it helps the person synthesize and solidify his or her learning. Keep these points in mind when conducting debriefing sessions:

- Jointly plan what the person hopes to learn or practice before the event or assignment. This sets the stage for a good debriefing session.

- When debriefing, focus on both ends of the spectrum. Discuss what went well and what didn't. When talking about what didn't go well, engage the person in a discussion about what he or she can do differently in the future.

- Make sure the debriefing session encourages open communication. The session should synthesize what was learned, not pass judgment.

- Use effective, open-ended questions to help the person fully realize what he or she learned from the experience.

- A good debriefing session covers both what the person learned and the next steps in the development process. Use the session to reflect on what happened and to translate that learning into new situations or opportunities.

PART 3

Analyzing Performance Problems

Addressing Employee Performance Problems

Misdiagnosis of an employee performance problem can have serious consequences. To develop your ability to correctly determine the cause of a problem, use the following checklist the next few times a performance problem arises. The checklist addresses four of the most common causes of problem performance and will help you determine the most appropriate course of action.

EVALUATION CHECKLIST (*Circle the appropriate response.*)

Lack of Clear Communication   Comments

1. Does the person know the problem exists? (If not, it may resolve itself when brought to the employee's attention.)   **Yes/No**

2. Have I clearly communicated my **Yes/No**
   expectations concerning the
   employee's performance?

3. Did the employee clearly understand **Yes/No**
   my expectations? (To answer this
   question, ask the person to state
   his or her interpretation.)

Situational Constraints   Comments

Do any of the following obstacles outside of the
employee's control affect his or her performance?

- Lack of resources   **Yes/No**

- Lack of authority   **Yes/No**

- Conflicting directives   **Yes/No**

- Lack of time   **Yes/No**

- Other (Describe:_____)   **Yes/No**

Deficient Skills, Knowledge, or Abilities   Comments

1. Do I have evidence that this person **Yes/No**
   has the necessary abilities, knowledge,
   and skills to do this job?

2. Has the employee performed this task **Yes/No**
   adequately in the past?

3. Does the employee have the knowledge **Yes/No**
   or aptitude required to improve
   performance?

4. Is training available for employees **Yes/No**
   who have the required aptitude but
   not the required skills?

Inappropriate Consequences of Behavior   Comments

1. Do existing policies reward poor **Yes/No**
   performance or punish good
   performance?

2. Have I done what is necessary to **Yes/No**
   change policies that produce
   inappropriate consequences?

Coaching Employees with Performance Problems

When employee performance requires improvement, the coaching you provide can make the difference between success and failure. Follow this procedure, starting with a minor problem. When you're comfortable with the process, move on to more serious cases.

1. Get the employee's agreement that a problem exists. In some cases, this step is easy; employees are already aware that there are problems with their work and are ready to take steps necessary to resolve these problems. In other cases, however, this step may require a great deal of discussion.

2. Discuss alternate solutions. At this point, emphasize the quantity of solutions rather than the quality. Encourage the employee to generate alternatives; he or she will be more likely to accept a self-prescribed solution.

3. Evaluate all the alternatives generated to determine the best way to solve the problem. Mutually agree on the steps to be taken and when each will be taken.

4. Make sure the employee understands that the responsibility for correction and change is in his or her hands, not in yours. State that you can support improvements by giving effective feedback and encouragement and that you will make every effort to do so. Also encourage him or her to seek support and to solicit feedback from trusted colleagues.

5. Follow up on employee performance. When monitoring the employee's actions, be sure to recognize and reinforce any improvements in behavior — especially in the beginning — until the employee has incorporated these improvements into his or her routine.

PART 4

Teaching Skills to Others

Grooming Employees for Advancement

Passing a skill on to others is a great way to ensure that you know it. Teaching someone else requires that you spend some time dissecting what you do and developing a plan to convey your knowledge. When teaching, keep these things in mind:

- Put together a teaching plan. Organize what needs to be taught and the best way to teach it. Is the skill better passed on by lecture-type discussions, role plays, or hands-on demonstrations?

- Ask the person to describe what he or she would like to learn. Also, investigate what learning style works best for the person.

Does he or she learn best from listening or reading, from seeing something done, or from doing? Use the information you get to develop your teaching plan.

- Some skills may be effectively passed on by having a person observe you using the skill. For example, if you want to pass on your skill at negotiating persuasively, invite the person you want to teach to observe you in action. After the negotiating session, have the person tell you what he or she learned.

- Ensure that your skill was actually passed on. Ask the person to describe what he or she learned. Have the person give examples of how he or she will apply the skill. Observe the person using the skill and give feedback. Schedule future checkpoints to answer questions or to give more training.

- Be open to learning something from the person you are teaching. Listen carefully to the questions the person asks as well as his or her reaction after practicing the skill. An added bonus when teaching could be that you learned something new.

Showing an Interest in Employees' Careers

Effective employee development depends, in part, on an understanding of employees' career goals. You can get a better idea of where to focus developmental activities if you communicate regularly with employees about their careers. This regular communication is necessary because people change focus and goals throughout their work careers.

Schedule periodic individual discussions with your employees to review their career goals. Address such issues as:

- What are their goals?

- What skills must they develop to reach their goals?

- What opportunities for job expansion or promotion exist?

- What do you see that supports or contradicts these goals?

- Are their goals realistic, considering their skill potential and position within the organization?

- Are their career goals challenging enough, given their demonstrated potential?

- What can you and the organization do to help employees achieve their career goals?

Build development plans with employees that take the answers to these questions into consideration, and provide regular feedback on progress toward career goals.

Providing Information on Career Opportunities in the Organization

An organization that "grows" employees from one job into another is making powerful use of its human resources. When employees are aware of their opportunities for advancement, broadening, and enrichment, and know what they must do to make these happen, their commitment to the organization is enhanced and solidified. You can contribute to this commitment by providing appropriate career information to your employees. The following technique can help:

1. Encourage your employees to share their career goals with you. When you know their goals, you can help them focus their efforts.

2. Provide as much information as you can about positions within the organization that may be consistent with each employee's goals. Communicate skill requirements, additional education needs, and experiences that would help to qualify the individual for the new position. If you are unfamiliar with the requirements of a particular job, suggest that the employee interview those who either currently hold the job or know more about its requirements. Be sure to contact the people to whom you refer an employee and ask for their cooperation.

3. Discuss with employees what they have learned about various positions and how their current skills and experience fit with the options they have identified. Be careful to focus on enrichment, broadening, and mastery in their current job, in addition to advancement.

4. If you agree that an employee has the potential to reach his or her goal, together create a development plan for that goal.

5. If you see an employee's goal as unrealistic given current skill levels, point out where you see discrepancies and suggest other, more realistic alternatives. Make specific suggestions if you can; if not, refer the individual to others in the organization who can help.

It is easy to focus solely on advancement when discussing career opportunities with your employees. Career development, however, involves much more than just advancement. Consider the following vehicles of career development.

- *Mastery*: achieving expertise in all facets of one's current job and maintaining it over time. Mastery might include full depth and breadth of a skill in the present job, up-to-date knowledge of job-related information, or significant contributions and accomplishments in the current position.

- *Enrichment*: expanding or changing responsibilities in one's current job. Enrichment might occur by taking on new responsibilities that broaden the current job, completing a training program in the same or related area, or shifting work emphasis.

- *Broadening*: transferring one's base of functions through a job change, without moving to a more complex level. Broadening includes changing job skills and knowledge, applying skills in new and different ways, or changing tracks to create greater opportunity for advancement.

- *Balance*: shifting gears in a way that de-emphasizes the complexity or intensity of the job. Balance might mean working reduced hours for a while to achieve balance between career and family life, to acquire further education, or to take a less intense role for other reasons.

- *Enterprise*: creating an entirely new application of one's skills, knowledge, or experience, which transforms the nature of the work. This might include designing a new program or position within the organization, or moving outside it.

Increasing Employees' Exposure to the Total Organization

By giving employees opportunities to become familiar with other areas in your organization, you accomplish several goals. Your employees:

- Become more versatile. If the need arises, they can assist in areas outside their specialties, including assisting you with your responsibilities.

- Better understand how their regular job duties contribute to the organization's overall goals.

- Gain increased awareness of career opportunities within the organization, which allows them to participate in setting their career goals.

Use the following procedure to begin a program for increasing an employee's exposure to the organization:

1. Meet with the individual to identify ways in which he or she can increase organizational exposure. Begin by listing several

examples of opportunities, such as serving on task forces, taking on a job rotation, attending organizational events, and acting as a liaison with other related departments.

Then ask the individual to identify two or three ways in which he or she could increase contact with others outside the department. Record these ideas on the following chart:

Ways to Increase Contact	Time Limits	Degree of Authority	Feedback Requirements

2. Next, work together to fill in the remaining boxes on the chart. Determine how much time the employee should spend on the activity, the degree of authority the employee will have in representing your department, and the feedback you expect from the employee.

3. Give the employee a completed copy of the chart and retain one for your records.

4. Periodically review the plans to determine if modifications — events added or removed, authority increased, and so forth — are necessary.

Developing a Replacement

Grooming a replacement for your position is important because: 1) it will be difficult for you to advance in your organization if no one has been trained to replace you, and 2) a trained replacement can ensure continuity in the organization's work flow.

The best way to groom a replacement is to select an individual with high potential to serve as your assistant. This method effectively helps the assistant develop the knowledge, skills, and attitudes required. In addition, this person can serve as your stand-in when you are away.

Ideally, the person you select will possess the basic skills required to assume your position and will have a position such as yours as a career goal. Following are suggestions for helping to ensure the success of the individual you choose as your assistant:

- Transfer responsibilities gradually, adding one at a time and allowing time for that task to be mastered before another is added. Allow the individual to be completely responsible for assigned tasks; stay away from these responsibilities yourself. Encourage your assistant to ask for additional responsibilities as soon as he or she can handle them.

- Encourage your assistant to think things through alone. Insist that problems and possible solutions be thoroughly considered before they are brought to you.

- Hold your assistant accountable for what you have delegated. Check on progress periodically and provide feedback. Ask for progress reports that include the current status of assignments, difficulties encountered, and methods used to solve problems and make decisions.

- Support your assistant's decisions. Consider your assistant's directives as important as your own and provide support if criticism arises. If it becomes necessary to reverse a decision your assistant has made, talk to the individual privately and let him or her announce the reversal.

- Let your assistant know that you expect a certain number of mistakes on new responsibilities, but that the mistakes should be admitted and promptly corrected.

- Keep your assistant apprised of your plans so that he or she can make intelligent decisions during your absence.

These suggestions represent the ideal development situation. Undoubtedly, at times you will find one or more of the guidelines impractical, inadvisable, or even impossible to follow. In general, however, adhering to these principles whenever possible will promote the successful growth of your successor.

You will have met your goal of developing a replacement when you can recommend your assistant as your successor with no major reservations.

RECOMMENDED READINGS

The publications listed here were selected for their content and suitability to a managerial audience.

Working Wisdom

Aubrey, Robert, and Cohen, Paul M., San Francisco: Jossey-Bass, 1995
ISBN: 0-7879-0058-3
Making sense of accumulated knowledge is called wisdom. The teaching of wisdom requires an ongoing, active, one-on-one relationship between teacher and learner. Managers can help make learning happen through what the authors call the five skills of wisdom: accompanying, catalyzing, sowing, showing, and harvesting.

Bringing Out the Best in People

Daniels, Aubrey C., New York: McGraw-Hill, 1993
ISBN: 0-07-015358-2
This book teaches the principles of positive reinforcement that can help managers get top performance from their people. It shows precisely how to pinpoint, measure, and provide feedback on the specific behaviors and results that you want. Daniels' book guides you toward continuous quality improvement by using positive consequences.

Structured On-The-Job Training

Jacobs, Ronald L., and Jones, Michael J., San Francisco: Berrett-Koehler, 1995
ISBN: 1-881052-20-6
This book addresses the problem of effective on-the-job training which is not always relevant to the job. On-the-job training is often informal, incomplete, and an extra burden on colleagues. The answer is structured on-the-job training, and the authors present a step-by-step plan for preparing, delivering, and evaluating structured on-the-job training.

Reaching The Peak Performance Zone

Kushel, Gerald, New York: AMACOM, 1994
ISBN: 0-8144-0222-4
This book contends that the difference between outstanding and average work is an internal drive to achieve peak performance. Managers who are peak performers can encourage and teach others how to reach the peak performance zone. Peak performers are self-motivated people who freely accept the blame when things go wrong and who work energetically simply because they want to. The author provides a step-by-step method for motivating others to become peak performers.

The Corporate Coach: How to Build a Team of Loyal Customers and Happy Employees

Miller, James B., and Brown, Paul B., New York: HarperBusiness, 1994
ISBN: 0-88730-685-3
The authors liken running a successful company to coaching a winning team. Their book shows how to empower people at every level, and give them opportunities to develop, improve, and be creative.

Developing High-Performance People

Mink, Oscar G.; Keith, Owen Q.; and Mink, Barbara P., Reading, MA: Addison-Wesley, 1993
ISBN: 0-201-56313-4
This book addresses the managerial skills needed in the current business environment which emphasizes self-managed work teams, empowerment of employees, and organizational learning. It shows how to build trust and involvement with employees in order to help them achieve maximum effectiveness.

Development FIRST: Strategies for Self-Development

Peterson, David B., and Hicks, Mary Dee, Minneapolis: Personnel Decisions International, 1995
ISBN: 0-938529-13-7
Development FIRST is the first in a series of books dealing with practical approaches to individual and team development within the changing corporate environment. Its five concise development strategies enable users to plan and execute their own development in a busy, demanding world.

The Art of Advice: How to Give It and How to Take It

Salacuse, Jeswald W., New York: Times Books, 1994
ISBN: 0-8129-2102-X
Giving and taking advice is an essential task in modern life, and in fact, few companies make significant decisions without consulting an advisor. The author contends that giving advice is an art and provides techniques for effectively communicating your knowledge when you are called upon to give advice.

Analysis for Improving Performance

Swanson, Richard A., San Francisco: Berrett-Koehler, 1994
ISBN: 1-881052-48-6
Augmented by exercises, examples, worksheets, and forms, this book helps organizations lay the foundation for successful performance programs and real improvement. Clear steps help define the problem and the desired outcome. The diagnosis includes specific interventions required to meet the goal.

SUGGESTED SEMINARS

The seminars listed here were selected for their appeal to a managerial audience. The reputation of the vendor, the quality of their seminar offerings, and the specific seminar content were considered in the selection process.

Because of the dynamic nature of the seminar marketplace, some seminars may have been upgraded or replaced, and others may no longer be offered. Likewise, costs and locations may have changed since this listing was compiled. We recommend that you contact the vendor directly for updated and additional information.

Leadership Development: How to Cultivate In-House Talent

This workshop takes a step-by-step, systematic approach to establishing a successful leadership development program. Participants will explore the full scope of training, education, development, work experiences, and career planning activities.
Length: 2 days; Cost: $1,380
Locations: Call vendor
American Management Association
P.O. Box 319, Saranac Lake, NY 12983
Telephone: 800/262-9699

Situational Leadership II® for Managers

This seminar introduces Ken Blanchard's Situational Leadership II® principles. The seminar uses a variety of case studies, instruments, and video programs to help participants gain insight into their leadership style and learn how to use the Situational Leadership II® model to improve their managerial effectiveness.
Length: 3 days; Cost: $895
Locations: Call vendor
Blanchard Training and Development
125 State Place, Escondido, CA 92029
Telephone: 800/728-6000

Foundations of Leadership

This workshop is designed to assist first-level and middle-level managers with three areas of critical development: evaluating interpersonal effectiveness, understanding basic leadership principles, and developing the potential of others.
Length: 3 days; Cost: $2,200
Locations: Call vendor
Center for Creative Leadership
One Leadership Place, P.O. Box 26300
Greensboro, NC 27438-6300
Telephone: 910/545-2810

Communicating for Improved Performance

Participants in this seminar learn to identify and agree upon the "real" problem with employees and then provide the coaching and counseling necessary to improve performance.
Length: 2 days; Cost: $1,150
Locations: Call vendor
Communispond, Inc.
300 Park Avenue, 22nd Floor, New York, NY 10022
Telephone: 212/486-2300

Internal Consulting

Participants in this workshop will get state-of-the-art diagnostic tools to identify the strengths and development needs of managers, teams, and organizations, and will take part in a realistic simulation which provides an opportunity to practice diagnosing from this new perspective.
Length: 3 days; Cost: $1,095
Locations: Call vendor
Personnel Decisions International
2000 Plaza VII Tower, 45 South Seventh Street
Minneapolis, MN 55402-1608
Telephone: 800/633-4410

Manager as Coach

During this interactive workshop, managers gain insight and skills into why and how to coach employees. The workshop's dual focus equips today's busy managers to take advantage of both informal on-the-job coaching opportunities and more formal one-on-one development discussions. Through experiential activities, case studies, role plays, and on-the-job applications, managers actually practice the four-step coaching model and the skills that will increase their impact as a coach. The reward is a clearer grasp of the coaching role and the power to tap into the motivation and job satisfaction of each employee.
Length: 2 days; Cost: Call vendor
Locations: Call vendor
Personnel Decisions International
2000 Plaza VII Tower, 45 South Seventh Street
Minneapolis, MN 55402-1608
Telephone: 800/633-4410

People Skills

This seminar teaches the participant the skills involved in listening, reaching agreement, confronting problems, and managing conflict. Private coaching in instant-replay video sessions helps participants develop their skills and monitor their progress.
Length: 4 days; Cost: $1,100
Locations: Cazenovia, NY; San Francisco
Ridge Associates, Inc.
5 Ledyard Avenue, Cazenovia, NY 13035
Telephone: 315/655-3393

Effective Managerial Coaching and Counseling

This program is designed to help participants distinguish between coaching and counseling situations; to aid them in applying managerial coaching and counseling techniques appropriately and effectively; and to explore coaching and counseling as it relates to organizational growth and success.
Length: 3 days; Cost: $1,950
Location: Ann Arbor, MI
University of Michigan Business School
Executive Education Center, Ann Arbor, MI 48109-1234
Telephone: 313/763-1000

CHAMPION CHANGE

Companies stagnate if they don't change to embrace new technologies, meet market demands, respond to employee needs, or create new business opportunities. Effective leaders seek out, initiate, support, and manage needed change; they are "change champions." They see opportunities for improvement and motivate their staff to seek and implement productive changes.

Your willingness and ability to initiate and champion change, to use your people in planning and implementing change, and to coordinate change efforts in the organization will determine your effectiveness as a manager in today's competitive business environment.

This section provides suggestions to help you initiate, implement, and champion change in your organization.

Part 1: Understanding the Change Process

- Assessing Your Own Reactions to Change
- Understanding Resistance to Change
- Addressing Resistance to Change

Part 2: Managing Change

- Knowing the Steps of Change Management
- Planning the Change
- Gaining the Commitment of Key Individuals
- Determining Readiness for Change
- Setting Up Needed Systems and Structures
- Involving Others in the Change Process
- Communicating the Change
- Following Up on the Change
- Implementing Organizational Change

Part 3: Championing Change

- Championing New Initiatives
- Viewing Change from a Big-Picture Perspective
- Motivating People to Welcome Change
- Stimulating Others to Make Changes and Improvements

Valuable Tips

- Always involve the people who will be affected by change in the planning and implementation process.

- When planning change, ensure that objectives, responsibilities, and time frames are defined and clearly communicated to people.

- During times of broad organizational change, be available to your people and share whatever information you can.

- Tell people what you think the change will mean for them, and then listen to their reactions.

- Listen to and ask for a lot of advice in change situations.

- Use a multifunctional task group to identify opportunities for change.

- Expect resistance to change; develop strategies to deal with it.

- Prepare your staff to expect changes; continuous improvement means change.

- Develop transition plans.

- Allow people to talk about their feelings, especially when they feel they are losing something due to change.

- Treat resistance to change as a problem to solve, not as a character flaw.

- Seek projects that require initiating and planning change within your organization.

- Meet with someone who has implemented change successfully. Discuss the steps he or she took throughout the change process. Review your own plans for change with this person, and ask for feedback.

- Communicate your vision of the change to others so they can more easily understand and buy into the change.

- Identify the change champions in your organization and work with them to support and initiate change.

- Find early successes and recognize them.

- Hold feedback meetings to allow employees to express their feelings about how the change is going.

- Through books or courses, learn about a change model that can help you understand how people change and, therefore, better manage change.

- Educate others about change and how people typically react to it.

- See work on transitions and change as part of the primary responsibilities of the people concerned, and for which compensation and other rewards should be allocated.

PART 1

Assessing Your Own Reactions to Change

Understanding the Change Process

To effectively manage change, it's important to understand your own reactions to change. The following process can help you evaluate how you typically react to change:

1. Think about past changes (both positive and negative) that you have encountered on the job, in your career, and in your personal life. Recall how you felt during each of these changes. Were you anxious? Angry? Excited?

2. Analyze the causes of your reactions to change.

   - For those times when you reacted negatively, identify the causes of your anxiety, discomfort, or other negative reactions.

   - For those times when you reacted positively, identify the factors surrounding the change that resulted in positive reactions.

3. Evaluate what you did to successfully manage the change. What worked well? Remember these successful strategies when facing change in the future.

Understanding Resistance to Change

People grow throughout their lives, yet also retain some degree of predictability, stability, and habitual behavior. People need both growth and stability to thrive. Resistance to changing from that stable, comfortable state to something unknown is predictable and to be expected. Yet, this resistance is also a signal to managers to delve more deeply into employees' attitudes toward proposed changes.

People *resist* change when:

- They believe it is unnecessary or will make the situation worse. Employees at lower levels in the organization often believe that upper-level managers don't know "what the real world is like."

- They fear that the change will mean personal loss — of security, money, status, friends, freedom, and so forth.

- They don't like the way the change was introduced.

- They had no input into the decision.

- The change was a surprise.

- They are not confident that the change will succeed.

- They feel manipulated because the changes were kept secret during the planning stage.

- The timing of the change was poor.

- They subscribe to the belief that "If it's not broken, don't fix it."

- They believe that you don't have the necessary resources to implement the change.

People *support* change when:

- They expect that it will result in some personal gain.

- They expect a new challenge as a result.

- They believe that the change makes sense and is the right thing to do.

- They were given an opportunity to provide input into the change.

- They respect the person who is championing the change.

- They believe it is the right time for the change.

Addressing Resistance to Change

People vary in their reactions to change. Some welcome the novelty and the variety of the change, while others fear the change and resist letting go of the status quo. Ambivalence is also common; people can both welcome and resist the same change. As a manager, it's important for you to make a special effort to assess and deal with people's individual reactions to change.

One of the first steps in dealing with resistance to change is to develop an attitude that resistance is neither good nor bad. In fact, signs of resistance can serve as a warning signal that opportunities exist to improve the change effort or implementation process.

Use the following steps when working through resistance to change:

1. Encourage people to openly express their thoughts and feelings about the change.

2. When resistance occurs, listen carefully. Employees who are feeling resistant don't want to hear a lengthy explanation of why the change is necessary. Instead, work to understand the resistance by exploring their concerns and by taking their feelings and concerns seriously.

3. Once you understand the specific concerns, bring people together to discuss and deal with the perceived problems. The following suggestions can help facilitate this process:

Reason for resistance	Recommended action
Loss of something important	Listen and allow the person to talk and grieve about the loss.
Belief that the change is not a good idea; sees no need for the change	Identify the specific problems anticipated. Involve the person in making it work. Educate the person about the rationale for the change; give him or her direct access to the information you used to determine the change (for example, visit a company that is implementing the process).
Anger about lack of involvement in the decision-making process	Let the person vent his or her feelings; involve the person in future decision making when possible.
Lack of skills or confidence	Provide training.
Concern about more work	Recognize extra work. Involve the person in deciding how to temporarily reduce or limit other work.

4. Recognize that it takes time to work through reactions to change.

PART 2

Knowing the Steps of Change Management

Managing Change

Managing change means managing the conditions and activities that move an organization from its present state to some desired future state. Without careful management, a much needed change can fall by the wayside.

To manage change well:

1. Know the current situation. Investigate how things stand by talking with people at all levels of the organization.

2. Develop a clear picture of where the organization needs to go. This vision should be based on the concrete factors that prompted the initiation of the change.

3. Set specific goals and dates by which to achieve that vision. Whenever possible, get input from the people affected by the change.

4. Outline the transition state in detail. This is a specific and unique state that needs to be managed in itself.

5. Determine what needs to be done to achieve the desired change. The organization's subsystems of people, structure, technology, and tasks need to be directed to be compatible with the change.

6. Develop and execute the plan for managing the transition state.

Planning the Change

Spend some time examining the change. Keep in mind where the change originated. Is it being mandated from above? Is it an idea of your own that you are trying to sell to those above you as well as to your team? Is it an idea for improvement that one of your employees has suggested? Realize that your strategy for planning and implementing the change will vary for each situation. The following guidelines can help you create a plan for managing a specific change:

- Take time to chart out the steps involved in implementing the change. Look for ways to improve the implementation process.

- Determine the best way to coordinate the change activities with day-to-day activities. For example, a sales representative may use time during a regularly scheduled customer meeting to inform the customer of the changes taking place, rather than scheduling a separate meeting for this purpose.

- Acknowledge and plan for lower production rates during the change, from the point at which the change is introduced to the point at which employees begin to accept the new way of doing things.

- Consider all the possible consequences of the change by analyzing "what if" scenarios. Based on this exercise, prepare several possible approaches to the types of problems that could occur.

- Think about how the change process may affect other aspects of the group's normal work activities. Keep a calendar large enough to chart simultaneous projects and corresponding time lines. Ensure that personnel and resources are distributed according to need.

- Pay particular attention to how the change will affect currently established work relationships. Minimize disruption to these relationships whenever possible.

Gaining the Commitment of Key Individuals

Successful change efforts require the commitment and support of key individuals in the organization to plan the change, manage the transition, and implement the change. The following steps can assist you in gaining this commitment:

1. Determine whose active support you need at each stage of the process.

2. Decide what critical mass is needed to provide the energy and momentum for the change to occur.

3. Develop a strategy to get the necessary people on board. You might meet with each person individually to explain the rationale for the change, the potential benefits, and the implementation plans. Or, if this is not possible, form a committee composed of key individuals (or their representatives) to discuss the proposed change, get members' input, and gain their support for the change.

4. Actively monitor the process of gaining commitment from all the necessary players and maintaining their support throughout the change process.

Determining Readiness for Change

Prior to planning or implementing a change, determine the readiness or openness of the change. The change will likely get voluntary support if the dissatisfaction with "what is" is great or if the change itself is seen as desirable.

You will increase the readiness for change if you make the problem with "what is" more clear or obvious, or show that the change is a desirable one.

You can:

- Use customer feedback to indicate the severity of problems.

- Provide data on the costs of the problems.

- Show what is possible by giving specific examples.

- Clearly show the benefits to the individual, team, organization, or customers.

- Involve the people affected by the change in looking at options and in making the decision.

Setting Up Needed Systems and Structures

For change to happen efficiently in both the short term and the long term, supporting structures and systems must be designed and implemented. Consider using the following approaches the next time you embark on a change effort:

- Try a zero-based approach, which essentially asks the question, "If we did not have any systems, structures, policies, and procedures in place, how would we create them from scratch to support the new vision?" This model requires you to look at the vision or goal of the change effort and build systems and structures from the ground up.

- Assess your current systems and structures by doing the following:

  1. List all of the current policies and procedures, and other formal and informal systems, that could affect the change effort.

  2. Analyze the current structure of your organization and team. Look at both the structure of your team and the way in which your team interacts (both formally and informally) with other teams in the organization. Does the structure (for example, job descriptions, compensation, geographic location, reporting relationships, etc.) support the change?

  3. Scrutinize each of these factors carefully in light of the new change. Ask yourself and your team, "Does this practice or procedure serve our new goal?" Eliminate unnecessary practices, modify those practices that are still helpful but out-of-date, and design new structures that will work for you.

For example, if your change effort is focused on producing a quality product, a measurement of units per person or team may run counter to your goal. Through your analysis, you may determine that a new productivity measure is needed, or you may decide to modify the current one by adding a variable to address production problems.

Involving Others in the Change Process

To maximize buy-in, minimize resistance, and make the change work, involve others in the process. When employees feel that they are valued participants in planning and implementing the change, they are more likely to be motivated toward successful completion. To get others involved, try these suggestions:

- Examine how decisions will be made during the change process. Make sure that the decision-making process involves the appropriate people.

- Make a list of all individuals who should be involved. Recognize that the people involved will differ as you move through the various stages of the change process.

- Involve the people on the front lines early in the change planning process. While the role of the leader is to provide the vision, or big picture, of where the organization is going, how to get there is often best determined by the people who are "in the trenches" day after day.

- Solicit and use input from your team, peers, and manager when planning your change effort. Indicate up front that you cannot guarantee that every suggestion will be implemented, but that you will genuinely try to include as many ideas as possible.

- Whenever possible, involve your employees in the process of establishing time frames for implementation.

- Ask employees from the areas affected by the change to serve as experts in determining the steps needed for change.

- If the change requires a new procedure, ask for volunteers to test out the change. Solicit their feedback on what is working well, where the problem areas are, and how to work out any difficulties.

- When you use an employee's suggestion, publicly and privately recognize that employee.

- Once the change has been implemented, use your employees as an ongoing barometer of what is working well and what is not working well. Ask them to suggest improvements.

Communicating the Change

Lack of communication often hinders the change process. The uncertainties and anxieties that employees feel when they are not adequately informed often lead to unproductive behavior and a lack of support for the change. To minimize stress and maximize productivity, make a conscious effort to increase communication whenever changes affect your area.

Consider using the following process to communicate a change:

1. Call a meeting of all individuals affected by the change. Describe how the change will help the organization and the department to succeed. Give the group the same information that convinced you the change was necessary. After explaining the big picture, describe how the employees will be affected by the change.

2. If the change means significant loss, don't sugarcoat the message and pretend that it's good news. Just deliver the message, including the support you will provide during the transition period. Be straightforward and honest about the implications of the change.

3. Welcome questions and comments. Giving employees a chance to voice their concerns and listen to the concerns of others can ultimately help them accept the change.

4. Communicate your vision of the change; then, whenever possible, have those affected by the change create the implementation plan.

5. Use active listening skills to encourage input and show that you have heard and understood the comments and concerns raised by others. See the Listen to Others section of this Handbook for suggestions on developing active listening skills.

6. Finally, emphasize to your employees that you will be available and willing to answer any questions they may have. Increase your exposure through "management by walking around."

Following Up on the Change

Close follow-up during the transition period and after the change has been implemented serves as a check that everything is going smoothly and proceeding according to plan. Follow-up also helps you identify problems you didn't anticipate.

Set aside time in your weekly schedule for follow-up, and require regular verbal or written updates from key personnel. Compare status reports with the objectives of the change effort. You may find that you need to revise your plan once the process has started.

Implementing Organizational Change

To effect large scale organizational change, upper management must lead and orchestrate the change. High-level visibility and support for and commitment to the change are absolutely necessary for successful implementation. Work with your managers to provide the support they need to successfully implement the change at their levels.

As change moves down through the organization, help your employees to understand the role they play in the organization and to view it as important. If your employees are able to see the value of their contributions to the organization, they are more likely to feel a strong desire to see the organization succeed.

Following these guidelines can help smooth the way for successful organization-wide change:

- Give people the same information that made you decide that the change was necessary.

- Be straightforward, honest, and thorough in describing all aspects of the change process, including both its positive and negative implications.

- Recognize that if you tell people only what they need to know, you aren't telling them enough. Tell your employees as much as you can as soon as you can, including the bad news and your concerns, to prevent them from hearing it through the grapevine.

- Be more available to your people, even though you may experience increased demands and work pressures during this time.
  - Establish an open door policy. This does not mean that you must be available at all times but, rather, that you set aside regular blocks of time for discussing employee concerns and questions.
  - If you must be out of the office for long periods of time, set up a message system so that you can reach others and they can reach you.
  - Increase your exposure through "management by walking around." Initiate contacts, particularly with those employees with whom you have little contact, to provide information and listen to their concerns.

- Throughout the change process, touch base with your people, your peers, and other groups regarding their information needs. Talk with others about any surprises they have had and any additional information they would like. Then develop methods for communicating this type of information in the future.

- Implement formal communication procedures such as the following to further enhance participation during change:
  - Hold periodic staff meetings to share information about new developments. Invite your entire staff.
  - Establish a departmental bulletin board to keep people up-to-date on the changes taking place.
  - Route memos regarding the change when the contents would be of interest to others.

PART 3

Championing New Initiatives

Championing Change

Successful leaders reach beyond their everyday assignments and responsibilities by identifying and championing new initiatives and improvements within their organization. Consider the following suggestions to improve your ability to champion new ideas:

- Identify the one or two changes that will have the greatest impact on your strategic vision, and champion these changes.

- Create a clear, compelling vision of the change you want. Articulate what it is and why it is necessary.

- Identify the people who can help make the change a reality, and determine how to get their support and cooperation.

- Take the initiative to share your ideas, conclusions, and reasons for excitement and commitment with others. Explain what's in it for them.

- Whenever you can, eliminate barriers in the organization that interfere with your initiatives. Strive to bring organizational systems into line with your change. For example, make certain that the promotion system fits with the performance appraisal system. People should be promoted based on the same criteria by which they are evaluated.

- When you believe that a problem is impossible to overcome, stop yourself from thinking negative thoughts that may shut down your resourcefulness. Take a break from the project and return to it later with a fresh perspective.

- Be willing to take a stand on your issues and ideas, even when they are in opposition to others' points of view.

- If the organization is not ready for your idea, "plant seeds."

Plan a strategy to get the necessary support over time. Many changes take years to germinate and grow.

Viewing Change from a Big-Picture Perspective

Taking a big-picture perspective is critical when you are planning and implementing change. If your plans for change are not coordinated with the functions of other departments or the organization as a whole, if they fail to address potential obstacles and problems, or if they fail to consider future trends in the marketplace, they are likely to cause more harm than good.

The following suggestions can help you achieve the overall perspective necessary for effectively planning change:

- Study the long-range plan for your organization or division and consider its implications for your department. Keep this information in mind whenever you develop plans or make decisions.

- Develop a vision of where you would like to see your department in five years. Ask yourself:
  - What major goals and objectives do I want to achieve?
  - What will my operations look like?
  - What new directions do I see my department taking?

  Record your thoughts and ideas on paper and begin developing a long-range plan for making these changes happen.

- Keep in close contact with individuals in other functional areas of your organization. Facilitate greater coordination and communication with these other areas so that you can stay up-to-date on their operations and future plans. Make a special effort to enhance coordination when changes are occurring in your area or in other areas of the organization.

- Whenever you develop a plan or solve a major problem, analyze the problem, solution, and implementation process in long-range terms. Carefully think about the future, and force yourself to move from the details to the big picture.

Motivating People to Welcome Change

More and more change is occurring every day. Organizations often need to move quickly to maximize opportunities. Employees who are prepared to expect and welcome change will be one step ahead of the pack. Use the following suggestions to prepare your staff to expect change and learn to adapt quickly:

- Prepare your organization to expect change as a part of doing business and being successful. To do this:
  - Build in the expectation of continuous improvement. Ask

employees about improvements they have identified. Make it a clear expectation that spotting opportunities is part of their job.

- On an annual basis, identify old assumptions that are out-of-date, changes in the external environment (for example, with competitors, the market, the economy), and opportunities for change.
- Frequently reinforce effective performance during the change period.

- In presenting change, take care to emphasize the benefits of the change. When approaching individuals, support the change on the basis of what you know is important to them. Don't be manipulative, but, when possible, let people know how the change will help them.

- Demonstrate your own enthusiasm and commitment to the change. When your commitment is obvious to your employees, their motivation and involvement in the success of the change effort are likely to increase.

- Celebrate and communicate successes — even small ones!

- Teach people to remember their successes with change as a way to build up their resilience.

- Coach your staff on what they need to do to make the change work; knowing these strategies provides employees with their own resource bank for dealing with future changes.

Stimulating Others to Make Changes and Improvements

Successful change doesn't happen by itself; it requires focus and ongoing, conscious effort. Given the opportunity, many people will backslide into that comfortable prechange state. To keep the momentum going, try these suggestions to encourage others to promote change and improvement:

- Set the expectation that people will make improvements and initiate change by modeling these behaviors yourself.

- Welcome and encourage improvements. Talk about good ideas people have had. Celebrate the successes.

- Don't "shoot the messenger" who tells you about problems. Ask for solutions.

- As part of performance planning, set goals for changes and improvements that employees will make.

- Encourage and require the measurement of work processes so that improvement can be charted and seen by others.

- Help others understand both organizational and personal barriers to change. Part 1 of this section describes typical barriers and resistance to change. Attempt to reduce or eliminate these barriers.

- Recognize and reward people who are making improvements in their effectiveness and behavior on the job. Changes that receive positive reinforcement are likely to be maintained.

- Support and encourage others who are attempting to make changes. Help them recognize that change takes time and backsliding is common, but progress is still possible.

- Support people during stressful times. Be aware that behavioral change is especially fragile and that stress often leads to the resumption of old behaviors.

- Model the norms, values, and behaviors expected as a result of the change. Be an example for others to follow.

RECOMMENDED READINGS

The publications listed here were selected for their content and suitability to a managerial audience.

Managing the Whirlwind

Annison, Michael H., Englewood, CO: Medical Group Management Association, 1993
ISBN: 1-56829-029-2
The author provides strategies for successfully adapting to rapidly changing markets by taking advantage of technology and other information management techniques. The book shows how to make quality the top priority in order to succeed in a customer-centered society.

Knowledge for Action: A Guide to Overcoming Barriers to Organizational Change

Argyris, Chris, San Francisco: Jossey-Bass, 1993
ISBN: 1-55542-519-4
This book provides a step-by-step method for assessing a company's capacity to learn, analyze data, and design techniques that will make the company more innovative. The author contends that actionable knowledge is that which tests the validity of the research methods themselves. The book provides tools for effectively utilizing this knowledge.

Reengineering Management

Champy, James, New York: HarperCollins, 1995
ISBN: 0-88730-698-5
This book contends that corporate reengineering often stops at the upper level of a corporation leaving managerial levels unchanged. The author provides managers the tools to lead, organize, inspire, measure, and reward the work that reengineering creates. Management processes must focus on mobilizing, enabling, defining, measuring, and communicating in order for reengineering to remain a continuous and successful process.

Managing for the Future

Drucker, Peter F., New York: NAL-Dutton, 1992
ISBN: 0-525-93414-6
The author provides five "gauges" for best measuring how your company's operation is running: market position, innovation, productivity, liquidity, and profitability. This book examines what true leadership looks like and the keys to successful research. Drucker's goal is to get you to think critically about what every idea means for you and your company.

The Reengineering Revolution	**Hammer, Michael, and Stanton, Steven A.,** New York: HarperCollins, 1995 ISBN: 0-88730-736-1 In *Reengineering the Corporation*, Michael Hammer introduced reengineering and now in this handbook he offers practical guidance on essential elements of reengineering. Specifically addressed are the most dangerous mistakes in reengineering and how to avoid them, how to assess whether management is truly committed to reengineering, how smaller companies can benefit from reengineering, and how to overcome the greatest obstacle to reengineering — overcoming people's resistance to change.
The Age of Paradox	**Handy, Charles,** Boston: Harvard Business School Press, 1994 ISBN: 0-87584-425-1 Handy suggests that in order to live and succeed in a rapidly changing world, we must organize in our minds the confusion generated by these changes before we can do anything about them. Managing business, family, education, money, and relationships are just some of the many topics covered. Through a discussion of these topics, strategies for maintaining a sense of continuity and direction, and for balancing personal and professional responsibilities, are provided.
If It Ain't Broke...BREAK IT	**Kriegel, Robert J., and Patler, Louis,** New York: Warner Books, 1992 ISBN: 0-446-39359-2 The authors contend that conventional business wisdom cannot help you keep pace in these rapidly changing times. Their book will help you unlock the creative thinker inside; work smarter, not harder; and explore new and different paths.
Mastering the Winds of Change	**Olesen, Erik,** New York: HarperBusiness, 1994 ISBN: 0-88730-692-6 This author, consultant, and therapist witnessed how stressful change is for most people and organizations, yet recognized that some extraordinary people seem to thrive in it. He surveyed high achievers and prominent people to define the specific strategies they use to deal with change and learned that coping skills help you overcome obstacles, discover new opportunities, build confidence, and learn from mistakes.

Leading Change

O'Toole, James, San Francisco: Jossey-Bass, 1995
ISBN: 1-55542-608-5
The corporate leader who sets out to command or manipulate employees to lead them through change is, says the author, doomed to failure. Change has been and always will be resisted. The only way to overcome that resistance is to use leadership based on moral values of integrity, trust, and an unwavering commitment to doing what is best for your employees. Also explored are why corporate culture and the status quo conspire to defeat change.

Overwhelmed: Coping with Life's Ups and Downs

Schlossberg, Nancy K., New York: Lexington Books, 1994
ISBN: 0-02-927896-1
The author has studied people in transition and developed a model for coping more effectively with the disruptions, expected or unexpected, that everyone faces. The transition model is also useful to organizations in the process of restructuring and can help affected people learn how to negotiate unwanted change. A companion to the book is the *Transition Coping Guide*, a self-scoring questionnaire which helps individuals or groups take stock of critical resources and provides ways to think about change more creatively. For further information, or to order the *Transition Coping Guide* published by Personnel Decisions International, call 800/633-4410.

Control Your Destiny or Someone Else Will

Tichy, Noel M., and Sherman, Stratford, New York: HarperBusiness, 1994
ISBN: 0-88730-670-5
This book is a blow-by-blow account of how Jack Welch transformed GE into the successful company it is today. Welch's six rules to live by will teach you the advantages of shifting power in your company from the managers to the people who do the work.

SUGGESTED SEMINARS

The seminars listed here were selected for their appeal to a managerial audience. The reputation of the vendor, the quality of their seminar offerings, and the specific seminar content were considered in the selection process.

Because of the dynamic nature of the seminar marketplace, some seminars may have been upgraded or replaced, and others may no longer be offered. Likewise, costs and locations may have changed since this listing was compiled. We recommend that you contact the vendor directly for updated and additional information.

Effecting Change

The purpose of this seminar is to develop a vision, strategy, and plan for effecting empowered change in organizations. Major goals of the program include: learning and applying a change leadership model for bringing about change, examining change as a personal and organizational process, learning to manage resistance and build the commitment of others, and developing a clear plan to successfully implement a change project.
Length: 3 days; Cost: $2,200
Locations: Call vendor
Center for Creative Leadership
One Leadership Place, P.O. Box 26300
Greensboro, NC 27438-6300
Telephone: 910/545-2810

Leadership and Change

This workshop teaches participants how to develop and successfully implement positive change that improves business results. Topics include: improving skills to make real change happen, building on strengths to initiate and manage change efforts, becoming more adept at implementing lasting improvements, and increasing ability to enhance mindsets around personal and organizational change.
Length: 3 days; Cost: $1,100
Locations: Call vendor
LMA, Inc.
54 Melendy Road, P.O. Box 140, Milford, NH 03055
Telephone: 603/672-0355

Building Resilient Organizations for Turbulent Times

Participants in the program learn how to assess the human and organizational impact of major change, identify critical implementation problems that must be addressed for a change to succeed, measure the strength of resistance to the change, and develop effective strategies for the implementation process.
Length: 3 days; Cost: $1,250
Location: Atlanta
ODR, Inc.
2900 Chamblee-Tucker Road, Building 16
Atlanta, GA 30341
Telephone: 404/455-7145

Managing Innovation

This program will teach participants how to: analyze strategies for managing innovation, explore ways to encourage innovation and change, assess the process of innovation within their organizations, and develop an action plan to improve that process.
Length: 3 days; Cost: $2,875
Location: Stanford, CA
Stanford Continuing Education Executive Programs
Stanford Alumni Association, Bowman Alumni House
Stanford, CA 94305-4005
Telephone: 415/723-2027

Facilitating Organizational Change

Participants in this seminar will learn: how to anticipate and reduce resistance to change efforts, techniques to help manage transitional states, how attitudes toward change can impact ability to implement change efforts, and models that will enhance understanding or an ability to guide a change effort.
Length: 2 days; Cost: $545
Locations: Call vendor
University Associates
8380 Miramar Mall, Suite 232, San Diego, CA 92121
Telephone: 619/552-8901

Managing Organizational Change

This seminar shows change as a natural process that can be continuously nurtured within organizations. Through simulations, case studies, group presentations, and videotapes, participants develop and practice the skills needed to recognize, adjust to, and facilitate change.
Length: 5 days; Cost: $4,550
Location: Philadelphia
University of Pennsylvania, The Wharton School
Aresty Institute of Executive Education
Steinberg Conference Center, 255 South 38th Street
Philadelphia, PA 19104-6359
Telephone: 800/255-3932

Managing Change in the Turbulent Workplace

This program is designed to help participants gain new understanding of the change process and its emotional after-effects. A new, practical model for managing change provides step-by-step guidelines for preparing, implementing, adapting, and learning.
Length: 3 days; Cost: $850
Location: Madison, WI
University of Wisconsin-Madison
Management Institute, Grainger Hall
975 University Avenue, Madison, WI 53706-1323
Telephone: 800/348-8964

MOTIVATION SKILLS

MOTIVATION SKILLS

A manager's level of motivation acts as the energy or fuel that enables him or her to achieve results and be successful. While it is important to have an adequate and consistent source of energy, or motivation, how you use those energy reserves is equally important.

A manager who effectively uses his or her energy sets high standards of motivation, focuses energy on the most critical issues, and works hard to achieve results and move beyond challenges and obstacles.

Motivated and successful managers have a positive effect on others. They serve as role models for the drive and enthusiasm needed to be effective in their organizations.

This chapter provides development activities in the following two areas of motivation skills:

Drive for Results: Drives for results and success; conveys a sense of urgency and drives issues to closure; persists despite obstacles and opposition.

Show Work Commitment: Sets high standards of performance; pursues aggressive goals and works hard to achieve them.

DRIVE FOR RESULTS

While hard work is usually a precursor to success, the *results* that a manager achieves have as great an impact as the work that produced his or her success.

Effective leaders focus on achieving results through and with others. They are concerned with accomplishment and with providing useful services, products, or advice. Effective leaders persistently go after goals and measure their success in terms of results achieved.

This section will help you and your team focus and commit to attaining results.

- Strengthening Your Sense of Purpose

- Putting a Top Priority on Getting Results

- Conveying a Sense of Urgency When Appropriate

- Persisting in the Face of Difficulties

- Bringing Issues to Closure

- Displaying a High Energy Level

Valuable Tips

- Demonstrate clear purpose, enthusiasm, and commitment to your employees. Be a role model.

- Show your enthusiasm for the organization through your commitments and actions.

- Be persistent.

- Adopt a "can-do" attitude, and approach challenges from a problem-solving perspective.

- Take on extra work to help the organization meet its objectives.

- Focus on results, not just on activities or long hours.

- Work to eliminate the need to seek unnecessary permission or approval.

- Get involved in activities that make you feel excited and alive, both at work and in your personal life.

- Undertake a daily exercise program to increase your energy level and endurance.

- Talk with people in higher management levels about their roles and what it takes to be successful.

- Avoid negative self-talk and increase positive self-talk.

- Take calculated risks to demonstrate your orientation to action.

- Review progress on your goals and objectives regularly and often.

- Identify the "critical path" and then remove the obstacles that get in its way.

- Reinforce yourself with rewards for achieving goals.

- Involve employees in setting departmental goals and objectives. Keep them informed of results.

- Recognize and reward employees for their contribution to your success and the success of the team.

- After your *first* reading of each in-basket item, take as much action as possible on that item. Avoid the temptation to set things aside.

- Refrain from saying "it can't be done," and focus on how you can make it happen.

Strengthening Your Sense of Purpose

Effective leaders persistently focus on what is important to the organization and work to achieve those goals. To drive for results in this way, and to develop the persistence sometimes needed, you must be firmly committed to the results.

To strengthen your sense of purpose, consider these suggestions:

- Determine what is most important to you. What results do you value and believe in?

- Examine the meaning and importance of achieving your group's vision for yourself and for your team.

- Write your own personal statement of the results to which you are committed and in which you will invest your time and energy.

Putting a Top Priority on Getting Results

Getting results is important for your organization's bottom line. You may be perceived as not putting a high priority on getting results because of the nature of your job (some staff work is seen as less results-oriented), because of work style differences between yourself and others, or because you are not clearly focused on results. To be seen as driving for results:

- Make sure that your team has measurable goals and objectives. Then focus on results, not activity.

- Monitor the results of your group frequently. Indicate satisfaction when they meet or exceed their goals and dissatisfaction when they do not.

- Challenge yourself and others to do better without minimizing what you or they have already accomplished.

- Focus team efforts on high-payoff activities and goals that others, such as your management team, deem important and critical.

- Keep others informed about what you and your group are doing.

- Check to see if your concerns about people, accuracy, quality, and so on, are seen as not putting a priority on getting results. Ask for feedback about this. Find a way to make these concerns compatible with achieving strong results.

- Recognize that in order to attain quality results you need quality processes to get you there.

- Tell your people how their efforts contribute to the bottom line and to organizational success. Discuss organizational results and what you and your team are or are not doing to impact those results.

- Persistently work to resolve differences and solve problems.

Conveying a Sense of Urgency When Appropriate

Some people do not convey a sense of urgency at all, and others around them may become nervous that deadlines will not be achieved. Still others may give the impression that *everything* is urgent and must be addressed immediately.

The following points will help you analyze the sense of urgency you convey and address areas you may wish to work on:

- Think about the key projects and tasks you have been working on in your department over the last three months. Analyze whether you have conveyed an appropriate amount of urgency on these projects:
  - Did you not convey enough urgency?
  - Did you convey too much urgency on too many projects, so that direction to your staff was unclear?
  - Did you convey a sense of urgency on your own projects but not on the projects of others?
  - Did you demonstrate a sense of urgency on only certain kinds of tasks or issues (for example, did you fail to demonstrate urgency in resolving interpersonal issues)?

- Seek feedback from others. Ask for their perceptions of your communication of urgency on projects and tasks. Solicit specific information about when you have displayed appropriate urgency, when you have shown inappropriate urgency, and any patterns they have observed.

- Determine which of your projects are urgent and which are less urgent. Doing so will enable you and others to focus on a limited set of priorities. Communicating great urgency and importance on everything you're involved in creates unnecessary brush fires.

- When you are working on a key project, tell your employees that the project is a top priority so that they understand what counts for you.

- Follow up on the progress of the project and continue to convey the urgency appropriate to its priority.

- If you or your employees tend to procrastinate and wait until the last minute to complete a task, set checkpoints ahead of the actual deadline. Thus, you and your employees will have the time to ensure that the final product is of high quality and will avoid placing unnecessary pressure on others.

- Identify a role model. Look for a manager who shows an appropriate amount of urgency for important projects and tasks and less urgency on less important projects. Ask the manager how he or she prioritizes projects, how he or she specifically shows a sense of urgency (both verbally and nonverbally), and what strategies have worked well.

Persisting in the Face of Difficulties

Some work is simply difficult to do. It takes time, is complex, is intellectually challenging, or is politically complicated. Yet successful people are persistent, even on tasks such as these.

Despite evidence to the contrary, persistence does not mean banging one's head on an obstacle until one or the other gives way. It does mean finding and applying strategies that will move you forward. When you find that your progress toward your objectives is impeded, consider the following:

- After working on a strategy for a while with no success, consider that lack of success a signal. You may need to develop another approach.

- If you cannot solve the problem yourself, determine who can help you to look at it objectively and brainstorm possible solutions.

- Put the project aside for the time being. Sometimes a little "incubating time" will help you discover an obvious solution at a later date. Or sometimes an obstacle will disappear if you leave it for a while.

- Set reasonable expectations about the amount of effort and time things will take. In new areas, ask more experienced people for help in setting expectations. Know yourself — do you typically underestimate? Overestimate?

Bringing Issues to Closure

Nothing saps energy faster than constantly dealing with the same old problems. Don't let yourself be pulled down by these nagging issues. Resolve recurring issues by initiating action and encouraging others to get things done. The following suggestions can help you move toward closure:

- Get the people involved together in a room and insist on resolution. Give all parties a chance to air their views. List the issues on a board or flipchart. Identify the areas of agreement, and then facilitate a discussion to resolve the areas of disagreement. If necessary, seek a neutral third party to intervene and negotiate or arbitrate a solution.

- Demonstrate by your own conflict management behavior that diversity of opinion is valuable in decision making, but that to get results, the issues must be resolved.

- Rely on the people who do the work to find the best way to accomplish tasks. Allow them to do what they know best — their jobs — and then hold them accountable.

Displaying a High Energy Level

If you find it difficult to maintain high energy on the job, you may want to assess your fitness level. Consider:

- Nutrition. Examine your eating habits. If you typically rush out of the house without breakfast and eat lunch on the run, you may not be getting the balanced diet you need to sustain energy on the job.

- Exercise. Regular physical exercise, whether it is a brisk evening walk or an intense workout, can go a long way toward making you feel energetic and alert all day.

- Sleep. While the amount of sleep needed varies with each individual, you may need more or less than you're getting right now. Examine your sleeping pattern and decide what is the right amount for you.

- Stretch breaks. Long periods of intense work effort can create lethargy and drowsiness. Break up these sessions with short "stretch breaks." Take a short walk outside, or do some simple calisthenics to relieve tension and relax stiff muscles.

You may consider yourself to be busy or have energy, but others may not share this perception. You may be a low-key person among hard-charging drivers. You may be accomplishing a lot without working 12 hours a day, but others may not see it. If so:

- Talk to others about your priorities and your investment in your work. Doing so will show your commitment.

- Share what you are doing and accomplishing.

RECOMMENDED READINGS

The publications listed here were selected for their content and suitability to a managerial audience.

Crossing the Minefield

Barner, Robert W., New York: AMACOM, 1994
ISBN: 0-8144-0241-0
To be successful in competitive and changing times you and your team need to know how to stay motivated, energized, and efficient. This book provides strategies to implement for accomplishing this now rather than later when your team has become stagnant. Among the things you will learn is how to: help your staff manage stress, respond quickly to demands from customers and your company, focus your efforts, inspire team members, streamline your team, and reenergize yourself to meet new challenges.

Patterns of High Performance

Fletcher, Jerry L., San Francisco: Berrett-Koehler, 1993
ISBN: 1-881052-33-8
A High Performance Pattern is the distinctive sequence of steps people naturally follow when they are at their best. Each individual has a distinctive pattern and this book seeks to help the reader discover what that pattern is and how to best utilize it. Included are techniques on how to revitalize tasks, find new ways of working in difficult situations, change the focus of a group for better efficiency, and get critical projects back on track. These various High Performance Patterns are described and examined though sixteen case studies.

The Disney Touch

Grover, Ron, Burr Ridge, IL: Irwin Professional Publishing, 1991
ISBN: 1-55623-385-X
This book is a behind-the-scenes account of how Disney went from a company rooted in the past to one of today's most successful organizations. The author uses extensive interviews with Disney executives to chronicle this turnaround story.

Competing Against Time

Stalk, George, Jr., and Hout, Thomas M., New York: The Free Press, 1990
ISBN: 0-02-915291-7
The authors contend that time is the equivalent of money, productivity, and quality. With many detailed examples from companies that have put time-based strategies in place, the authors describe exactly how reducing production time can make the critical difference between success and failure.

SUGGESTED SEMINARS

The seminars listed here were selected for their appeal to a managerial audience. The reputation of the vendor, the quality of their seminar offerings, and the specific seminar content were considered in the selection process.

Because of the dynamic nature of the seminar marketplace, some seminars may have been upgraded or replaced, and others may no longer be offered. Likewise, costs and locations may have changed since this listing was compiled. We recommend that you contact the vendor directly for updated and additional information.

Managing Emotion in the Workplace: Maintaining High Performance Under Pressure

Participants in this workshop will learn to identify their personal trigger points, develop techniques for staying calm in tense situations, receive criticism in a positive manner, and re-energize themselves at the end of the workday.
Length: 2 days; Cost: $1,085
Locations: Call vendor
American Management Association
P.O. Box 319, Saranac Lake, NY 12983
Telephone: 800/262-9699

The Seven Habits of Highly Effective People

This program is based on the fundamental, yet critical, principles of interpersonal relationships outlined in Stephen R. Covey's book, *The Seven Habits of Highly Effective People*. The program is based on the premise that effective leadership starts from the inside out and is designed to heighten the participant's total leadership potential.
Length: 3 days; Cost: $1,495
Locations: Call vendor
Covey Leadership Center
3507 North University Avenue, Suite 100, Provo, UT 84606
Telephone: 800/331-7716

Creating Results

This workshop focuses on three important areas: organizational "street smarts," self-empowerment, and positive influence skills. Participants will learn to feel more confident in taking risks, increase their productivity, establish better partnerships, develop flexibility to influence effectively, and implement projects to create desired results.
Length: 3 days; Cost: $900
Locations: Call vendor
LMA, Inc.
54 Melendy Road, P.O. Box 140, Milford, NH 03055
Telephone: 603/672-0355

SHOW WORK COMMITMENT

Organizations look for individuals who are committed and willing to invest themselves in their work. Committed managers set high standards of performance, pursue aggressive goals, and work hard to achieve them. Managers who display a commitment to work take pride in their work and place work high on their priority list.

Yet sometimes managers may get bogged down by repetitive tasks and long hours, and find it difficult to maintain enthusiasm for and commitment to their jobs. Changing priorities, recurring problems, budget constraints, and lack of promotional opportunities can cause frustration and sap one's energy.

If, for whatever reason, you find your commitment level lower than you want, you can use the suggestions in this section to strengthen your commitment to work.

- Defining Your Priorities
- Setting High Personal Standards of Performance
- Making Your Job More Interesting
- Seeking Out New Work Challenges
- Readily Putting in Extra Time and Effort
- Initiating Activities Without Being Told to Do So
- Committing to Your Organization

Valuable Tips

- Think through your values to determine how committed you are to them. Ask yourself how you can change your job or work behavior to align more closely with your values.

- Take the initiative to go beyond what is expected.

- Buy some of your company's stock. Then do your part to make it grow.

- Look for the opportunity to do something extraordinary.

- Seek and generate additional challenges and let people know that you are looking for increased responsibility and personal growth.

- Ask yourself what you need to do to feel excited about work.

- Share your personal values and goals with your manager, peers, family, and friends.

- Invest more energy in your job and increase your commitment by gaining experiences in various management areas through job rotation or management development seminars.

- To develop your work motivation, identify the outcomes you want from a job.

- Volunteer for a lateral job in another functional area to gain experience and add challenge to your work.

- Discuss the satisfaction you expect from your career with company associates, your family, and friends.

- Be willing to sacrifice in the short term for long-term gains in the welfare of your organization.

- Buy a set of motivational tapes and listen to them when commuting to and from the office.

- Consider returning to school to acquire new knowledge and stimulate your interest in your chosen profession or to explore another career.

- Show initiative by suggesting new ways to make or save money for your organization.

Defining Your Priorities

What do you consider to be your life's work? What do you want from your work or career? Successful managers usually work hard, but they do not have to be workaholics.

Managers can better focus on work and personal priorities when they have first clarified their own values. Once you have a clear picture of what is important to you, you can choose activities that are consistent with those values.

Your values and priorities may change over the course of your lifetime. Periodically use the following process to help you define your values and align your priorities:

1. Define and write down your life values, goals, and priorities. Consider the following questions to help you identify them:

   - Who and what are most important to me?

   - What do I want out of life?

   - What is my life's work?

   - What does getting up and going to work each day make possible in my life (in other words, what am I able to have, do, or be as a result of my work)?

   - How would I live if money were not an issue?

   - What do I want to accomplish in my lifetime?

   - What kind of leader do I want to be?

   - What do I want to contribute and accomplish at work?

   - What do I consider worth "fighting for"?

   - What balance do I want between my work and home life?

2. Discuss your values and priorities with family, friends, and work colleagues. Listen to their comments and feedback. Others can see you from a different perspective than you see yourself. They can often confirm a hunch or point out a blind spot.

3. Compare your values with the ways in which you spend your time, energy, and money. Analyze whether your allocations of time, money, and energy are consistent with your values and priorities.

4. Determine what, if any, changes you would like to make. Ask yourself what the consequences of not changing would be.

5. If appropriate, create an action plan for change. You may find that instituting your changes will mean that you have to make some sacrifices. In addition, you may experience a feeling of loss of the "old way of doing things." Realize that people change in evolutionary, not revolutionary, ways.

Setting High Personal Standards of Performance

Although recognition, increased status, and other rewards are important, your own satisfaction with your performance is the ultimate and longer lasting reward. These guidelines will help you develop high standards for your performance:

1. Analyze your work and set your own objectives using the following procedure:

   - Write down your five most important responsibilities.

   - Describe the characteristics of superior performance in each area.

   - Describe the characteristics of performance that are not acceptable in each area.

   - Using these extremes, set personal standards for yourself in each area. Make your standards challenging, yet attainable.

   Use a chart such as the following to help you structure your analysis.

Most Important Duties	Superior Performance	Not Acceptable Performance	Personal Standards
1.			
2.			
3.			
4.			
5.			

2. On a regular basis, monitor your performance as it relates to your personal standards.

3. Take time to congratulate and reward yourself when you accomplish a goal or meet a standard, and enjoy the feelings of personal accomplishment that go with these achievements.

4. After six months, compare your own assessment of your work with the feedback and recognition you receive from others to see how accurate your self-assessment is.

Although recognition and support from others are important, your personal assessment of your achievements should become increasingly important as a source of reward. It can help you emphasize task accomplishment and continuous improvement in your work instead of focusing too heavily on status and recognition.

Making Your Job More Interesting

If you've held a job for so long that many of your assignments have become routine, you may have difficulty developing and maintaining enthusiasm for your work. Instead of looking at your work as an obligation, redefine your work activities into tasks that engage you, hold your attention, and leave you in a positive state of mind. Following is a method you can try for revitalizing your job and regaining your enthusiasm:

1. Make a list of your job duties. Then identify the tasks that have become so routine that they no longer interest you. To regain your enthusiasm for these tasks:

   - Ask yourself whether you are performing them with maximum efficiency. Is your method the best possible method for performing each task? Generate several ideas for improving the accomplishment of each task, such as eliminating a step or adding a step that will improve the end product.

   - Consider whether the tasks should be delegated. Routine tasks usually provide excellent opportunities for preparing an employee for advancement. What seems routine to you may be challenging for an employee.

2. Prepare a job description for an improved version of your job. Include any current tasks that you find stimulating, and list additional, related tasks that you would like to be given the opportunity to perform.

   When you have finished your description of your ideal job, set it aside for a day or two. Then review it to determine if the modifications you would like to make are realistic. Eliminate unrealistic changes from your description.

3. As a final step, show your description to your manager and negotiate any major changes. Then implement the changes gradually.

  • Change your schedule so that you alternate between high-interest and low-interest tasks. This will allow you to avoid large blocks of time spent on unpleasant duties.

  • Be patient and tenacious. The time between promotions and job changes typically increases as you move up in an organization. Instead of waiting for others to give you new duties when you master a current one, take it upon yourself to find additional challenges while ensuring that you perform those duties that tend to be less interesting at a consistently high level of excellence. Performing well in *all* aspects of your job is the best route for increasing the chances that you'll be rewarded with interesting work in the future.

After a month or two, evaluate the changes you made based on these suggestions. Determine whether they are helping you change your overall attitude toward your job and resulting in improved job performance.

Seeking Out New Work Challenges

The initiative you take in seeking out new work challenges demonstrates your commitment to the organization and increases the variety and scope of your job. The following suggestions can get you started:

  • Talk with your manager about your desire to broaden the range of your responsibilities. Indicate your interests and ideas. Make sure that you have mastered all of the duties of your job, not just the fun ones, before you ask for more.

  • Identify issues critical to your organization's success in the future, and develop expertise in those areas. Talk about the knowledge and skills you have, and watch for opportunities to demonstrate their usefulness.

  • Identify projects or assignments that are of interest to you, but for which you are not currently responsible.

  • Consider volunteering for special projects, task forces, or a lateral move in a different functional area of the organization to gain experience and add challenge to your work.

- Be realistic about what you can handle. Consider your strengths and weaknesses, and set your goals accordingly. Don't try to take on too much at one time.

Readily Putting in Extra Time and Effort

Undoubtedly there will be times when you are required to make an extra effort to complete a project or get caught up on your routine responsibilities. When such situations arise, it is important that you be responsible and tenacious. The following suggestions can help you deal with these situations effectively:

- Whenever possible, do what needs to be done.

- When you are not able to stay late, find out how you can nevertheless meet the commitment. It may mean borrowing help from others, working at home, redefining the project, or becoming more creative in freeing up your time.

- When you are asked to work longer hours, do so willingly. If you cannot put in the extra time, clearly explain why, show your concern, and assist in finding someone who can help. With your manager, find a solution; with your peers, you may want to give suggestions.

- Track the hours you work beyond your optimal number (each person seems to have a range of hours he or she is comfortable working). If you frequently work beyond the optimal number for you, check to see how your experience fits with that of others in the organization. You may discover that you need to hire more people, reprioritize, eliminate work, delegate more, or become more comfortable with the number of extra hours.

- If some people have the perception that you do not put in extra time and effort, you may need to work with them to help them see how productive you are during the hours you work. Some people pay more attention to the number of hours worked than they do to the results achieved.

- Look at the long-term consequences that working extended hours will bring. "Going the extra mile" shows others that you are willing to do whatever it takes to get the job done. As a consequence, you will likely find yourself involved in many interesting and challenging projects. On the other hand, working extended hours may be keeping you from other important goals and priorities you have set for yourself outside of work. You will need to decide which takes priority and accept the consequences of that decision.

I'VE ENJOYED OUR DISCUSSION ABOUT GOING THE EXTRA MILE... BUT YOU MISSED MY EXIT BACK THERE.

Initiating Activities without Being Told to Do So

Taking the initiative regarding activities and responsibilities demonstrates your commitment to the organization and increases the variety and challenge of your job. Use the following suggestions to initiate more activities and assignments in your job:

- Talk with your manager about your desire to broaden your range of responsibilities. Indicate your interests and then discuss possible action steps.

- Watch for opportunities to help out in other departments, as well as in your own. This will give you greater exposure to other areas and will help to build your reputation as a team player.

- Don't wait for assignments — simply decide what needs to be done in your area of responsibility and do it.

- Take the initiative to propose solutions to problems outside your area, and determine how to provide that input to those directly responsible without alienating them.

- Identify opportunities for improvement and work to address these opportunities.

- Adopt the view that your responsibility goes beyond your specific job accountabilities to include identifying and seizing opportunities.

Committing to Your Organization

When you start working for an organization, you make both an explicit and an implicit contract with that organization. The explicit contract involves the description of the work you will do or the position you will hold. In addition to this basic explicit contract, there may be other explicit components, such as the availability of training or growth opportunities.

Beyond the explicit contract there is an implicit one. Implicit contracts vary, but they are critical to one's motivation, commitment, and sense of job satisfaction. It is the implicit contract that many have had — that "if I do a good job, I will continue to have employment and increased opportunities" — that has been so affected by recent downsizings in the United States. Some believe that this contract has been broken.

The belief that "it's my company's responsibility to keep me interested and challenged by a variety of new and exciting tasks" is another kind of implicit contract. Employees who subscribe to this belief typically do not stay for the long haul.

While it is wise to look out for yourself and your interests in the long run, being committed to your work and your organization is essential for your success on the job, for generating confidence and trust, and for developing cooperative work relationships with others. Because, in the end, people are not impressed by and do not trust people who are merely out for themselves.

The following strategies can help you make a personal commitment to your work and organization:

- Pledge to yourself that you are committed to your organization. This is a personal and private agreement with yourself that can help guide you through organizational life's ups and downs.

- Work to strengthen your commitment during both good times and bad. It's easy to lose faith when you don't get the promotion or bonus you expected, when you get a poor performance review, or when your manager or organization makes a decision that you consider poor. Your commitment is put to the test at these times. How strong will it be?

- Make a commitment to yourself that you will do all that you can to help your fellow employees, your customers, and your company's leaders.

RECOMMENDED READINGS

The publications listed here were selected for their content and suitability to a managerial audience.

The Empowered Manager

Block, Peter, San Francisco: Jossey-Bass, 1991
ISBN: 1-55542-265-9
This book is written for executives involved in running an organization and for managers caught in a bureaucratic mode of thinking. Block offers practical ways for executives and managers to take more responsibility for making positive changes in the organization and developing an entrepreneurial spirit in themselves and in members of their work teams.

Principle-Centered Leadership

Covey, Stephen R., New York: Summit Books, 1991
ISBN: 0-671-74910-2
The author describes how the goals of excellence and total quality express an innate human need for personal, interpersonal, and organizational improvement. Covey discusses the key to managing expectations, the six conditions of effectiveness, how to understand people's potential rather than just their behavior, and the patterns of organizational excellence.

The Seven Habits of Highly Effective People

Covey, Stephen R., New York: Simon & Schuster, 1989
ISBN: 0-671-66398-4
Covey presents a holistic, integrated, principle-centered approach for solving personal and professional problems. His principles provide the security to adapt to change and the wisdom and power to take advantage of the opportunities that change creates.

Thinking for a Living

Marshall, Ray, and Tucker, Marc, New York: BasicBooks, 1993
ISBN: 0-465-08557-1
The authors contend that in order for the United States to compete with foreign companies in the global marketplace, both schools and the workplace need restructuring. Students and workers alike need to be trained how to think conceptually, communicate effectively, and work independently. Companies must then allow their employees to utilize these skills.

The New Dynamics of Winning

Waitley, Denis, New York: William Morrow & Company, 1993
ISBN: 0-688-11562-4
The author, drawing on his knowledge of sports psychology and consulting experiences in both business and athletics, shows how to achieve a championship mentality and success in business. The author presents his seven rules for winners, the five most prevalent self-destructive beliefs, and how to use stress to your advantage.

SUGGESTED SEMINARS

The seminars listed here were selected for their appeal to a managerial audience. The reputation of the vendor, the quality of their seminar offerings, and the specific seminar content were considered in the selection process.

Because of the dynamic nature of the seminar marketplace, some seminars may have been upgraded or replaced, and others may no longer be offered. Likewise, costs and locations may have changed since this listing was compiled. We recommend that you contact the vendor directly for updated and additional information.

Leadership at the Peak

This workshop is designed to help top executives examine their leadership styles and strengths through an intense program of learning, discussion, and feedback. Participants will conduct a self-assessment and use this assessment to create specific developmental goals. They will also share experiences and ideas with other top-level managers who understand the stress and demands of leadership and gain new insights and fresh perspectives on topics important to their organization.
Length: 5 days; Cost: $7,000
Locations: Colorado Springs, CO
Center for Creative Leadership
One Leadership Place, P.O. Box 26300
Greensboro, NC 27438-6300
Telephone: 910/545-2810

The Seven Habits of Highly Effective People

This program is based on the fundamental, yet critical, principles of interpersonal relationships outlined in Stephen R. Covey's book, *The Seven Habits of Highly Effective People.* The program is based on the premise that effective leadership starts from the inside out and is designed to heighten the participant's total leadership potential.
Length: 3 days; Cost: $1,495
Locations: Call vendor
Covey Leadership Center
3507 North University Avenue, Suite 100, Provo, UT 84606
Telephone: 800/331-7716

Increasing Human Effectiveness

This program, taught in a relaxed lecture/discussion format, provides participants with the tools that will enable them to tap the wellspring of potential that exists within them.
Length: 2 days; Cost: $395
Locations: Call vendor
Edge Learning Institute
2217 North 30th Street, Suite 200, Tacoma, WA 98403
Telephone: 800/858-1484

Management of Managers: Leadership, Change, and Renewal

This program is designed to enable managers to become more effective and to derive more personal satisfaction from their corporate positions. Participants will review their current level of management proficiency, explore new techniques in managerial leadership, develop plans for renewing those leadership roles, and implement improvements for the betterment of themselves and their organization.
Length: 12 days; Cost: $6,450
Location: Dallas
Southern Methodist University
Executive Development, Edwin J. Cox School of Business
Dallas, TX 75275-0333
Telephone: 214/768-3549

ORGANIZATIONAL KNOWLEDGE

ORGANIZATIONAL KNOWLEDGE

Managers are challenged to keep pace with increasing amounts of new and updated information relating to their profession, industry, and competition, to name a few. The world's information base doubles every few years. Methods and strategies for conducting business in organizations and the marketplace have become more complex.

This chapter explains how increasing your knowledge of your organizational and industrial practices and trends can help you improve your professional competence and increase your contributions to your organization. It contains development suggestions for the following three skills areas:

Use Financial and Quantitative Data: Establishes realistic budgets; uses financial and quantitative information effectively to manage.

Use Technical/Functional Expertise: Possesses up-to-date knowledge in the profession and industry; is regarded as an expert in the technical/functional area; accesses and uses other expert and technological resources when appropriate.

Know the Business: Shows understanding of issues relevant to the broad organization and business; keeps that knowledge up-to-date; has and uses cross-functional knowledge.

USE FINANCIAL AND QUANTITATIVE DATA

As a manager, it is important for you to have a "bottom-line" focus and to demonstrate an understanding of the financial and quantitative aspects of your business. This section presents strategies for becoming more comfortable with and effectively utilizing quantitative information in managing your area.

- Increasing Your Familiarity with the Financial System
- Establishing and Maintaining a Realistic Budget
- Using Quantitative Information to Manage
- Using Microcomputers and Software Programs
- Analyzing Reports Quickly
- Using Statistical and Quantitative Information
- Improving Your Math Skills
- Presenting Business Data for Planning and Decision Making
- Improving Data Submitted by Your Employees
- Improving Others' Perceptions of Your Quantitative Skills

Valuable Tips

- Meet with a controller or financial accounting person in your organization to discuss the information you most need to understand to do your job better.

- Talk with department heads in the finance and accounting functions about their responsibilities, how they fit into the overall picture of the company, and how they can help you.

- To understand budget items, go to the department or plant and "walk the floor" so you know the origin of each line item.

- Read one of the many books available on "finance for nonfinancial managers."

- Ask an accounting friend to explain the annual report of your own and one other organization.

- Develop and maintain a detailed household budget.

- Learn to compute ratios such as return-on-investment (ROI) on a calculator by using data available to you in your job.

- Assemble a mock portfolio of stocks based on financial reports, and track their progress weekly.

- Develop a spreadsheet for your department by using a personal computer and a spreadsheet software package.

- Take a course at a local college to address math anxiety.

- Ask for special assignments or additional duties that will require more financial and quantitative knowledge.

- Avoid getting bogged down in data by determining the two or three most important implications of the data.

- Track performance progress on a quantitative level when appropriate.

- Back your decisions with quantitative logic whenever possible.

- Find ways to quantitatively measure the effectiveness of each important work process.

- When reading financial reports, review the numbers and ask yourself whether the data supports the conclusions.

Increasing Your Familiarity with the Financial System

Every organization must have sound financial control in order to survive. Your development in the area of finance can help you prepare for advancement and do your part to maintain your organization's financial system. Following are suggestions for increasing your familiarity with the financial aspects of your organization:

- Learn to read and analyze financial statements. With the help of reference materials or a knowledgeable colleague, study them and look for trends. Predict the impact of your department's tasks, decisions, and outcomes on overall financial results. Then discuss your perceptions with someone in the organization who is knowledgeable about financial report analysis.

- Become involved in the budgeting process. If you don't currently participate in your organization's budgeting process, ask your manager if it would be possible for you to become involved. As you begin the budgeting cycle, ask your manager and peers for their perspective on the process and how your department's budget fits in with that of the total organization.

- Learn your organization's system of financial reporting. Obtain coaching from someone who understands your organization's system of financial reports. Your manager or someone from the accounting department would be a likely choice. Ask your coach to explain:
  - The purpose of each report in the system
  - Who is responsible for the completion of each report
  - Which reports are incorporated into other reports
  - How often each report is updated
  - The process by which each report is updated

- Explore other perspectives on financial reporting. Talk with people from outside your unit to obtain their perspectives on the financial reporting system. Ask these people to explain their jobs, their views of your department, how your department fits in with the rest of the organization, and which financial skills would be most important to you as you assume advanced responsibilities.

- Develop your analytical skills. People who are uncomfortable with numbers tend to skip over them when reading reports. If that is something you do, force yourself to go through the numbers and ask yourself whether the data supports the conclusions of the reports. Look for inaccurate or missing data.

In doing so, you will begin to notice situations in which the conclusions are not adequately supported by data.

- Develop measurable goals for each area of your business. Track actual progress against your objectives. Practice analyzing this data to see what information it provides.

Establishing and Maintaining a Realistic Budget

It's important for you to understand the budgeting and planning process for your area and how it fits in with the total organization. If you are not already involved in the budgeting process, approach your manager to see how you can become involved.

A budget should be based on realistic premises, rather than on overly optimistic projections. Use the following guidelines to help you create and maintain a realistic budget:

1. Before beginning the budget process, review your strategic plan, identify goals and objectives, and determine the resources needed to achieve those objectives.

2. Carefully assess what resources you have and what additional resources you will need during the period to be covered.

3. Review the past and present budgets to determine what significant variations exist and whether they should be taken into account in the preparation of the new budget.

4. Meet with the controller or finance group to gain a better understanding of how your departmental budget fits into the organization's budgeting process as a whole. In addition, ask him or her to share concerns about budget items or areas where departments typically build in cushions. Request any historical information or report summaries which could aid the process.

5. Develop contingency plans for possible conditions of slower growth or business contraction. Ask yourself and your employees the question, "Given a substantial retrenchment, what can we give up, stop doing, or defer?"

6. Assign responsibility for the preparation of subdepartmental budgets to the people responsible for particular projects or budget areas. Provide adequate instructions to people working with you to prepare their portion of the budget.

7. Compile all subdepartmental budgets, reconcile differences, and make sure that the overall budget includes general costs for items such as supplies, staff personnel, management, and other overhead.

8. Establish a schedule for periodic budget reviews. Compare your budget to actual numbers and, if necessary, make midcourse corrections to expenditure levels in order to meet the budget.

Using Quantitative Information to Manage

When people think of quantitative information, financial data is usually what comes to mind. While quantitative information is often financial in nature, it can also be any numerical information that provides a way to measure results. Quality programs and continuous improvement require measurement.

- If you do not currently measure the work processes in your group, begin doing so. Determine which information is important to have and then agree upon relevant criteria to measure against (for example, clear goals, customer compliments, number of performance reviews conducted on time) and useful measurement tools.

- Make a list of the major types of decisions in which you are involved during the year. For each decision area, note the kind of quantitative or financial data you need to make your decisions or support your conclusions. For example, the total number of work hours projected for the year is a number often used to justify the hiring of additional staff. Savings in labor dollars and projected work hours per machine can be used to justify the purchase of equipment. Based on your analysis of the type of information required, create a plan to collect and use the information.

- Find ways to measure the intangibles of your business. Look from the outside in — not from the inside out — by analyzing the customer's, supplier's, or vendor's point of view. Keep in mind both internal and external customers and suppliers as you do this analysis.

- Review your reports and recommendations with your manager to determine whether they can be improved with quantitative data.

- With the help of your manager, identify a project in your organization that requires a close working relationship with financial or accounting managers.

Using Micro-computers and Software Programs

More and more managers are using microcomputers and software programs in financial and quantitative analysis. Following are suggestions to help you gain familiarity with microcomputers and spreadsheet programs:

- Visit a computer store to learn about microcomputers and software programs. Most stores offer informational literature on the machines and programs they carry. Often, salespeople will give demonstrations of the capabilities of the machines and programs. Some stores even offer seminars at little or no cost.

- Obtain coaching from a person experienced in using microcomputers for financial/quantitative analysis. You'll be surprised at the number of people who will be glad to share their knowledge with you once you have expressed an interest.

- If your organization has a computer information center, contact that area to find out what services are available to you and your team for supporting your use of microcomputers.

- If, through your study of microcomputers and software, you find that there are tools that could help you perform your job, learn to use these tools. For example, you could use spreadsheet programs for:
  - Cash flow
  - Sales forecasts
  - Budget forecasts
  - Breakeven analysis
  - Staffing projections

Database programs can be used to create any type of report that requires the listing and sorting of data. For example, a database program can be used to log customer comments. Information such as type of comment, frequency of comment, and department or division of comment can be easily generated.

New software programs are literally being introduced to the marketplace daily. Being computer literate is a must in today's competitive marketplace. To keep your managerial skills current, continue to build on your knowledge and use of computers.

Analyzing Reports Quickly

Financial reports, budget information, and other computer reports are usually structured to meet the needs of a wide variety of people within the organization. As a result, they often contain far more information than any one person in the organization requires.

A second common problem with computer-generated data involves the readability of the data. When the users of a report are not involved in its design, the data may not be laid out in as readable a fashion as possible.

In an ideal world, you could attack these problems at their roots by asking for reports tailored to meet your needs and by suggesting computer program modifications to make the reports easier to read. These solutions, however, can involve considerable time and expense for the organization as a whole. If making computer modifications to tailor these reports is cost prohibitive, you can use the following process to help you analyze financial information more quickly:

1. Identify the departmental or organizational reports you have difficulty using efficiently. If you work with numerous reports, select a subset of reports that have one or more of the following characteristics:

   • Most important to your job

   • Used most frequently

   • Most difficult to analyze

2. Ask your manager or a peer adept at reading the reports to go over them with you, focusing on the items of importance for you and your department.

3. Compare the key items on each report with the same items on earlier versions of the report. Correlate the differences among the items to what has been happening in your department or business.

4. Create a "crib sheet" for each report that contains definitions of key items and a step-by-step procedure for analyzing the report.

Using Statistical and Quantitative Information

Managers are often barraged by periodic computer reports and summaries, some of which contain valuable information for the operation of the department and some that do not. To determine the difference, you need to clearly understand the information contained in these reports. Follow these guidelines each time a computer report appears in your in-basket:

1. Take the report back to the department from which it came and have someone thoroughly explain the report to you.

2. Make notations on any information in the report that is relevant to projects in your department. The report may contain helpful feedback for monitoring the achievement of your departmental or organizational goals.

3. File the report and your notes on it for quick reference should you need to read it at a later date.

Improving Your Math Skills

Many people avoid financial and statistical analysis because their math skills are inadequate. Some have become "rusty" at math because years have elapsed since they learned the concepts. Some took too few math classes in school. Others have decided that they don't have the ability to learn math skills (these people are said to have "math blocks" or "math anxiety"). If your math skills are deficient, for whatever reason, improving them will help you become more comfortable with quantitative data. The following suggestions will help you develop your skills:

GET A GRIP ON YOUR MATH ANXIETY, ED. THEY'RE JUST FLASH CARDS.

- Overcoming math anxiety. If you have math anxiety, you may not believe you can understand mathematics enough to use financial and quantitative information. Fortunately, because so many people have the same problem, many training programs have been designed that can help you overcome your anxiety. Survey the course and seminar catalogs of your local university and community colleges. Look for a program geared toward people with math anxiety or one that diagnoses skill levels so that you can be placed in the appropriate class.

- Brushing up or learning new skills. If you need a math review or want to learn new math skills, survey the catalogs of your local university and community colleges for courses that meet your needs. Many managers take such courses as business math, managerial accounting, advanced math, and statistical analysis. You might wish to buy one of the numerous programmed learning texts on the subject of your choice. If you choose this option, be sure to set a deadline for finishing each section of the book to help prevent procrastination in finishing the program.

Presenting Business Data for Planning and Decision Making

Managers who have difficulty understanding data, especially financial or statistical information, may also find it difficult to organize such data well for planning or decision making. To increase your competence in presenting business data, take advantage of opportunities to practice this skill. Try the following:

1. Evaluate your audience's comfort with the data and your goals.

   - Do they need the data? Why?

   - What do you want them to do with the data?

2. If people are concerned only with your conclusions, present the conclusions and have the data available for questions.

3. If you want the group to draw conclusions from the data:

   - Clearly explain and label each piece of data.

   - Avoid presenting column after column of numbers; make the presentation visually easy to read by providing summaries when appropriate.

   - Use software packages to present data in visual form (for example, pie charts, graphs, sequential presentation).

4. Practice your presentation of data. Calibrate what is comfortable and useful to your audience.

In addition, watch how other sources present business data effectively, and look for opportunities for feedback on your presentation style. For example:

- Become involved in meetings where the discussion focuses on financial and other statistical business issues. Study how others effectively present, assess, challenge, and gain an understanding of the quantitative information presented. Incorporate their effective strategies into your own presentations.

- Before committing to a major financial decision, prepare a written analysis of your decision. Then consult with a competent finance person to get additional input on how the decision might affect earnings. Ask for feedback on how you have organized and presented your data.

Improving Data Submitted by Your Employees

In many cases, employees submit financial and statistical reports or forecasts to their managers who, in turn, use them in preparing reports that they submit to their managers. In such instances, the employees' reports may lack data, include inaccurate data, or contain unrealistic forecasts. To improve the accuracy of your reports and to develop the report-writing abilities of your people, try the following activities:

- Instead of asking your employees to submit their reports directly to you, hold a review meeting at the time of submittal. Ask employees to make transparencies of their reports and to present them to the staff as a group. Ask group members to comment on problem areas they observe.

- Ask your people to assist you in compiling your reports to help them understand the ultimate purpose of the reports. Rotate this assignment among qualified employees each preparation period so that, eventually, your entire staff will be qualified to prepare the data.

- Focus on one major area of expense control each reporting period. Meet with your employees as a group to discuss ways in which expense control can be improved.

Improving Others' Perceptions of Your Quantitative Skills

While you may think of yourself as having strong financial and quantitative skills, others may have the opposite perception. Possibly you are in a staff function and, by nature of your position, others view you as spending money without making money. Or possibly you haven't given others an opportunity to observe your quantitative analysis skills. To improve this potentially inaccurate perception by others, try the following:

- Set specific goals for yourself and your area, and then measure progress toward these goals in a quantitative fashion. When reporting your team's progress to others, be sure to include your measured quantitative progress with your verbal or written reports.

- Constantly watch for opportunities to show quantitative reasoning for your decisions. For example, if you are a staff manager and are attempting to convince line managers that greater employee diversity is needed in your work force, talk to them in their language and focus on the bottom line. Indicate the potential dollar cost of a lawsuit, as well as the benefits of increasing diversity among the organization's employee group.

- Talk to a manager skilled in quantitative analysis, and solicit his or her suggestions on how you can demonstrate your financial and quantitative skills to others.

RECOMMENDED READINGS

The publications listed here were selected for their content and suitability to a managerial audience.

The McGraw-Hill 36-Hour Course in Finance for Nonfinancial Managers

Cooke, Robert A., New York: McGraw-Hill, 1992
ISBN: 0-07-012538-4
This book is a helpful guide for nonfinancial managers on financial reporting and budgeting that is applicable for day-to-day operations. In addition, there are clear explanations of all major financial topics as well as exercises designed to help you apply the material presented.

Finance and Accounting for Nonfinancial Managers (3rd ed.)

Droms, William G., Reading, MA: Addison-Wesley, 1990
ISBN: 0-201-52366-3
This book is specifically designed to appeal to managers and other professionals who are relatively untrained in the areas of accounting and finance but now feel the need to become better versed in this area for continued professional growth. The book provides an understanding of those basic concepts in finance and accounting necessary for analysis and proper use of information.

Statistics for the 21st Century

Duncan, Joseph, and Gross, Andrew, Burr Ridge, IL: Irwin Professional Publishing, 1995
ISBN: 0-7863-0328-X
This is a guide for understanding and analyzing the multitude of statistics currently available. It takes a critical look at the reliability of these statistics. For example, the reliability of most statistics depends on who compiles them and how they are used. This guide will help you discern which statistics are worthwhile and helpful to your business.

Guide to Total Cost Management

Ernst & Young, New York: John Wiley & Sons, 1992
ISBN: 0-471-55877-X
Total Cost Management is a set of tools, developed by the Big Six accounting firm of Ernst & Young, for identifying and keeping business costs down. This desktop guide addresses, in nontechnical language, how companies can make better decisions with regard to costs of products, services, and investments in everyday business operations.

Corporate Game: A Computer Adventure for Developing Business Decision-Making Skills

Rye, David E., New York: McGraw-Hill, 1993
ISBN: 0-07-911763-5
You're given a million dollars to launch a company and one year to make it successful. Rye's book and accompanying software painlessly teach economics, marketing, manufacturing, and how these disciplines interact.

NumberWise: How to Analyze Figures for Smart Decisions

Thomsett, Michael C., New York: AMACOM, 1992
ISBN: 0-8144-5038-5
Thomsett's book is directed at an audience that lacks a financial background or education. It teaches how to analyze the numerical aspects of a problem that will lead to a numbers-oriented solution. *NumberWise* lays out specific, practical steps to take toward sound financial detail that can support your proposals.

Almanac of Business and Industrial Financial Ratios

Troy, Leo, Englewood Cliffs, NJ: Prentice-Hall, 1995
ISBN: 0-13-349531-0
The data for benchmarking a company's financial performance are provided in this vital resource. Included are fifty performance ratios for firms in the same industry and of the same asset size. The numbers cover operation revenues and costs, liquidity ratios, profitability ratios, and many more.

SUGGESTED SEMINARS

The seminars listed here were selected for their appeal to a managerial audience. The reputation of the vendor, the quality of their seminar offerings, and the specific seminar content were considered in the selection process.

Because of the dynamic nature of the seminar marketplace, some seminars may have been upgraded or replaced, and others may no longer be offered. Likewise, costs and locations may have changed since this listing was compiled. We recommend that you contact the vendor directly for updated and additional information.

Basic Budgeting for Nonfinancial Managers

From the basics of budgeting through planning and implementation, participants in this workshop will develop the capability to identify the costs and characteristics of different budgeting systems.
Length: 2-1/2 days; Cost: $1,145
Locations: Call vendor
American Management Association
P.O. Box 319, Saranac Lake, NY 12983
Telephone: 800/262-9699

Finance and Accounting for the Non-Financial Executive

This program provides an overview of the financial tools and techniques needed in an increasingly complex business environment. Particular emphasis is placed on understanding financial performance measures and the role the measures play in the planning and control of business operations.
Length: 6 days; Cost: $4,250
Location: Harriman, NY
Columbia University
Graduate School of Business, 2880 Broadway, 4th Floor
New York, NY 10025-6989
Telephone: 212/854-3395

Basic Financial Strategies for Decision Makers

This program is designed for managers who need to build a foundation for understanding the studies, analyses, recommendations, and financial strategies used by their organizations.
Length: 1 week; Cost: $4,100
Location: Durham, NC
Duke University, The Fuqua School of Business
Office of Executive Education, Durham, NC 27706
Telephone: 800/372-3932

Finance and Accounting for Nonfinancial Managers

In this seminar, participants will learn to: comprehend basic accounting principles; understand how finance and accounting are used in internal control and external reporting; read and understand financial statements; perform basic financial analyses; evaluate performance; develop pro forma financial statements as part of budgeting; and evaluate major capital investment decisions.
Length: 4 days; Cost: $1,400
Location: Houston
Rice University
Jesse H. Jones Graduate School of Administration
Office of Executive Development, P.O. Box 1892
Houston, TX 77251-1892
Telephone: 713/527-6060

Financial Seminar for Non-Financial Managers

Topics explored in this seminar include: understanding financial reports; using ratios in financial analysis; interrelating key financial variables; forecasting financial requirements; and financial leveraging. Participants will develop an understanding of the fundamentals of finance; learn the latest techniques of financial analysis; and explore the use of these techniques in making strategy and policy decisions.
Length: 3 days; Cost: $2,200
Location: Stanford, CA
Stanford Continuing Education Executive Programs
Stanford Alumni Association, Bowman Alumni House
Stanford, CA 94305-4005
Telephone: 415/723-2027

Finance for the Non-Financial Manager

This program is designed to help participants improve communication with people in financial areas, develop financial policy, and better understand the impact of financial decisions on the organization's profitability.
Length: 5 days; Cost: $4,300
Location: Ann Arbor, MI
University of Michigan Business School
Executive Education Center, Ann Arbor, MI 48109-1234
Telephone: 313/763-1000

Integrating Finance and Marketing: A Strategic Framework

This seminar helps managers develop techniques for integrating finance and marketing concerns; gain the ability to assess the costs and benefits of various marketing strategies; better understand the key determinants of profitability; explore how successful companies were able to achieve their successes, and learn how to better use financial information to assess performance.

Length: 5 days; Cost: $4,550
Location: Philadelphia

**University of Pennsylvania, The Wharton School
Aresty Institute of Executive Education, Steinberg
Conference Center, 255 South 38th Street
Philadelphia, PA 19104-6359
Telephone: 800/255-3932**

USE TECHNICAL/FUNCTIONAL EXPERTISE

In the past, it was often possible for workers to train for specific jobs and to hold those jobs for the rest of their working lives. Now, however, the world of business changes quickly and dramatically. As a result, it is not uncommon for people to hold many different positions during their professional careers as some jobs become obsolete and new ones take their place. It is particularly important for organizational leaders to keep pace with this information explosion. Organizations must be able to respond quickly to rapidly changing market needs and technology advances if they are to survive in today's fast-paced, competitive world.

Although managers may not need to strive for the same high level of technical knowledge and skill as that of their staff, at a minimum they must have sufficient knowledge to make sound hiring and capital resource decisions, and to address training and development needs.

This section explains how increasing your technical or functional knowledge of industry practices and trends, and keeping up to date on technology innovations, can help you improve your professional competence as well as your promotional opportunities. It includes information on leveraging computer resources to maximize organizational effectiveness.

Part 1: Increasing and Using Your Knowledge

- Understanding the Requirements of Your Job
- Increasing Your Knowledge of Specific Job Areas
- Increasing Your Knowledge of Functional Areas
- Relying Effectively on Your Own Expertise
- Using Your Expertise to Resolve Technical Problems
- Keeping Up to Date on Technical Developments
- Staying Informed about Industry Practices
- Presenting Technical Information Clearly

Part 2: Recognizing the Value of Computers

Part 3: Exploring New Technology

- Investigating Technology Options
- Defining Your Needs
- Researching the Alternatives
- Evaluating the Options

Part 4: Utilizing Computer Technology
- Making the Best Use of Your Organization's Computer Technology
- Increasing Your Computer Skills

Valuable Tips

- Have lunch with a colleague to discuss innovations in your mutual areas of interest.

- Lay out a career plan specifying the moves that will help you acquire the functional, occupational, or technical knowledge needed to achieve your goals.

- Work for someone who is particularly competent in a field you want to learn.

- Seek a job rotation to a lateral position in your function in another department, or to a lateral position in a different function.

- Develop one or more specialty areas where you will be considered the expert in your organization.

- Ask your managers, both immediate and higher, to identify the most important job assignments you need to maximize your knowledge.

- List the three emerging technological advances most likely to have an impact on your field and develop an action plan to address these areas.

- Hire people whose superior technical knowledge will challenge you.

- Ask your employees to give you feedback on your three strongest and three weakest technical areas.

- Identify a mentor outside your chain of command.

- Read the latest books in your field. Look for research on new ideas and developments.

- Discuss with people in other functional areas their job responsibilities and satisfactions, and consider a functional change for yourself.

- Interact with people in different managerial functions.

- Ask for task force and project assignments in functional areas other than your own.

- Volunteer to take on a technically challenging project.

- Consider taking a pay cut in order to acquire broader knowledge and lay the foundation for rapid pay growth in the future.

- Meet people in your industry upon whom you can call for advice.

- Write a journal article in your field.

- Join a professional association related to your area of expertise. Attend meetings, get involved in program committees, and attend conferences and seminars.

- Build an informal network of peers in similar organizations through which you can exchange ideas and discuss issues relevant to technical advances in your field.

- Ask for more detailed updates from your people when they are working on highly technical tasks so that you can gain a better understanding of the subject matter.

- Teach a class in your area of technical expertise.

PART 1

Understanding the Requirements of Your Job

Increasing and Using Your Knowledge

Your job has many aspects. To perform at your full potential, you need to clearly understand the requirements and objectives of your position. This can be accomplished by using the following procedure:

1. Read through previous job descriptions or objectives for your position to get a feel for the required responsibilities and how they have changed over the years.

2. Describe the purpose of your current role in the organization.

   • Why does your position exist?

   • What would be the effect if it didn't exist?

   • How do you see your position's role or mission changing over the next year?

3. Detail the three to seven key result areas in which effective performance is critical. Focus on these critical few areas, rather than on the trivial many.

4. Identify indicators for measuring performance in each key result area. For example, in sales it might be revenues; in customer service it might be average time responding to customer complaints.

5. Set specific objectives for each indicator. An example might be: "Respond to 95 percent of customer complaints within 24 hours, and 100 percent within 48 hours."

6. Meet with your manager to get his or her input into your objectives. Get your manager's assurance that your objectives cover the key areas of your job, and get his or her agreement on the level of performance your objectives represent.

7. Share your objectives with your employees and others in the organization with whom you work closely.

8. Periodically review your performance against your objectives, and update your objectives when necessary.

Increasing Your Knowledge of Specific Job Areas

Many positions, especially those held early in one's career, require knowledge in specific technical areas. Some areas of technical knowledge relate to an individual's specific function in the organization. For example, a financial manager would have specialized technical knowledge about the task of analyzing and managing an organization's finances.

Other positions require knowledge about specific products or specialized techniques. For example, a person who supervises programmer analysts should keep informed of state-of-the-art developments in both systems technology and specific applications.

Although the type of required technical knowledge varies from one position to the next, some sources of information can provide general knowledge. The following suggestions apply to a cross section of positions:

- Read manuals, books, articles, research publications, and specialized technical literature that contain information about areas related to your job.

- Take courses offered by your organization, local universities or community colleges, or adult education programs.

- Seek opportunities to observe, work with, and get feedback from individuals (your supervisor, a colleague, or someone from another part of the company) who are highly skilled in your specific job area.

- Request assignments and tasks that will broaden or increase your technical knowledge. Depending on your job and the knowledge you want to acquire, these assignments may involve more difficult tasks, a greater variety of tasks, new categories of tasks, or areas of greater specialization. Whenever possible, arrange to receive coaching and feedback on your performance of these assignments.

- Solicit feedback on your performance — either your overall performance or your way of handling specific activities or situations. You may want to ask for a more formal appraisal (by your manager) or several informal ones (by colleagues or your employees).

Increasing Your Knowledge of Functional Areas

Many positions are part of a broad functional area. Operations may include engineering, design, assembly, material distribution, production planning, and plant management. Employees advance in their careers as they move from specialized positions to jobs in broader functional areas.

The following guidelines for professional development within a functional area are similar to those for increasing one's technical knowledge; they simply take a broader view. Instead of focusing on your specific position, concentrate on the functional area.

Again, the development possibilities depend on the functional area and on the organization itself.

- Observe the actions and practices of those in positions similar or related to yours within your functional area. You may want to ask them if you can work with them on tasks, interview them formally or informally to learn their secrets for success, or associate with them more often to develop a relationship.

- Request job assignments that increase your breadth of experience.

- Talk with individuals, both inside and outside your organization, who have expertise in particular areas. Look upon committees, task forces, and department meetings as chances to increase your understanding of functional areas.

- Read reports and documents that describe procedures, practices, and other information related to your functional area.

- Attend courses and seminars that can give you a broader perspective of how your position fits into the functional area.

- Join professional organizations. For example, a materials manager might want to get involved in a professional organization that encompasses additional areas of manufacturing.

Relying Effectively on Your Own Expertise

If you are uncomfortable relying on your expertise at times, you may turn to others for help in areas where they expect you to be knowledgeable. This behavior could indicate a need to further develop your skills in some areas. The following procedure can help you determine where you may lack the skills you need to perform more independently:

1. For one month, keep a log of problems related to lack of expertise that you encounter on the job.

2. After one month, study your log, paying attention to:

   - The types of problems you most frequently have

   - The people to whom you go most often for help or advice

3. Determine what knowledge or skills these people possess that you may lack.

4. Prepare a development plan to address these weaker areas, particularly those that cause you to seek help most frequently.

Using Your Expertise to Resolve Technical Problems

One indication of your technical expertise is the extent to which others come to you with questions or ask for your help in resolving technical problems. The following techniques can help you increase your expertise and ensure that coworkers benefit from your knowledge:

- Let others know what you know. Mention your work and its results. Many people are overly concerned or embarrassed about appearing superior; as a result, others are not familiar with their skills.

- Talk with people about their work and offer helpful suggestions. Take care that the suggestions are seen as helpful, rather than as meddling.

- Deliberately develop expertise in an area if you do not have it.

- When people come to you with questions, be supportive. Work with them to solve the problem, instead of solving the problem for them. When they leave your office, they should feel good about asking for help, rather than foolish or incompetent because they were unable to resolve the problem independently.

- Examine how you give advice when others come to you for help. Take care to not act "superior" because you know the answer. Also avoid using jargon; or, if you use it, explain the terms.

- Offer to serve as a sounding board for others if they run into technical difficulties, and ask them to do the same for you.

- Over the next two weeks, keep track of the number of times people come to you with questions about projects they are working on. After two weeks, if this number seems low, go out and talk to others in your area about their current projects. Show a genuine interest in their work and, if appropriate, mention projects of a similar nature that you are working on or have completed.

- To chart your long-term progress, periodically monitor the number of times people come to you with technical questions.

Keeping Up to Date on Technical Developments

Keeping up to date with the technical advancements in your field is important for your own and your organization's continued growth and development. Following are some suggestions on resources to consult and activities to pursue to help you do this:

- Build an informal network of peers in similar organizations through which you exchange ideas and discuss issues relevant to technical advances in your field.

- Aim to take on at least one new project each year that will challenge you to search out new ideas and information.

- Attend conferences on your professional specialty. Consult professional or organizational newsletters for information on these conferences.

- Offer to present a paper at a conference on a project you've completed or on some other technical aspect of your work.

- Become a program chairperson for your professional organization's conventions or conferences.

- Subscribe to trade journals and professional publications.

Staying Informed about Industry Practices

Industry practices or standards can change. What was considered the norm as you started your career may no longer hold true. To stay informed about the practices and standards in your industry:

- Join one or more industry or professional associations. Attend meetings, conferences, and seminars. Work on program committees. Actively involve yourself in the group.

- Read professional newsletters and trade journals. These publications can keep you up to date on new developments in your field.

- Join (or form) a group of professionals from other organizations that gets together informally to exchange information on technical advances and discuss issues of common interest. Such affiliations can be based on any number of common bonds — type of business, organization size, manufacturing processes, market, and so on.

- Attend university and industry association educational events to keep abreast of developments.

- Visit other companies and talk with people in similar functions and with their customers. After each visit, detail what you have learned for yourself.

Presenting Technical Information Clearly

Every function has its own jargon and complex terms. Confusion, frustration, and misunderstandings occur when technical terminology is not explained. Many people will hesitate to ask for clarification. Thus, it's important to adopt the habit of speaking in clear, simple language and explaining any technical terms you have to use. The following suggestions will help you communicate technical information clearly:

- Identify your audience. If it consists primarily of people with relevant technical expertise, your use of technical terms and concepts is appropriate, even desirable. The more diverse the group, however, the fewer such terms you should use.

- Consider how much detail you need to communicate. Is the entire piece likely to be read? If not, open with an "executive summary" that is a page or less in length. This frees the reader from wading through inessential details before getting to the "meat" of the document. If you can't avoid using technical terms in a document intended for wide distribution, you may want to:
  - Define the terms.
  - Provide a context that makes their meanings apparent.
  - Have your manager or a trusted colleague read your document and then review it for the clarity of the message.

- When talking with people about technical information, give illustrations and examples to which your audience can relate.

- Ask others to tell you when you have lapsed into using technical terminology without clarifying the terms.

PART 2

Recognizing the Value of Computers

The soaring rate of computer use in the business world is a testament to the computer's value as a business tool. More than 25 million computers have been brought into the U.S. workplace since 1983, as managers and executives increasingly recognize the power of the computer as a leadership tool. Because computers allow users to quickly access, filter through, and analyze information, they are invaluable in helping to manage the complexity of today's business world.

As a business tool, the computer has virtually limitless benefits. Computer technology allows you to, among other things, streamline operations, manage complex information, make business forecasts, manage your time, and communicate more efficiently.

Computers can also enhance your managerial effectiveness by allowing you to improve teamwork and group thinking through better communication, track performance against goals more accurately and efficiently, keep people focused on the most important numbers and goals, and pass on new knowledge and skills.

Because computers put information into the right hands and give people the information they need to think and act on their own, they also foster a more empowering environment.

The types of information you can access via the computer and the methods by which you can analyze and distribute the data are also limitless. Typical examples of the type of information to which computers provide quick access include:

- Company information, such as sales figures, profit margins, inventory data, performance against goals, cost data, and operational data from various functions and sites

- Market information, such as economic trends, demographic data, and competitor information

- Customer information, such as customer satisfaction surveys, customer profiles, contacts, addresses, and information on past business

Various programs allow you to access and work with this information in a number of different ways. Among these applications are:

- Text programs, such as word processing and desktop publishing

- Numbers programs, such as statistics packages, spreadsheet programs, inventory control systems, and decision-support programs

- Image tools, such as graphics packages, presentation generators, design programs, and drawing programs

- Time organizers, such as calendars, schedulers, project management programs, and account management programs

- Communications tools, such as electronic mail, on-line conferencing, and networked file-sharing applications

- Information programs, such as internal database management programs and external databases accessed through bulletin boards, the Internet, or commercial on-line services, such as CompuServe and America Online

Because of their power and range of capabilities, computers can significantly contribute to your capabilities as a manager. By capitalizing on this powerful tool, you can increase your effectiveness as a manager and enhance your organization's success.

PART 3

Investigating Technology Options

Exploring New Technology

With the rapid ongoing advancements in computer technology and the wide range of existing programs, a manager must be continually on the lookout for useful new programs and systems. Whether you are in an organization that already uses computers extensively or in a small company that has not yet begun to use computers widely, you can benefit by keeping up to date on available technology and its potential uses in your organization.

If you are not in a position to select computer technology for your organization, find out how these decisions are made and talk with the individuals who make them. Most organizations have an Information Services or Systems (IS) expert or department that evaluates computer and other communication needs and finds the technology to meet those needs. If your company has an IS expert, meet with that person to discuss your needs. The IS expert can determine whether your needs will be best met by existing commercial products, a commercial system that the IS department modifies, a new system that the IS department builds itself, or a combination.

If your organization does not have an IS expert or department and you are in a position to purchase software for your organization, the following procedures can help you evaluate your needs and find the technology to meet them. If you do not have a great deal of computer knowledge, seek the help of someone in your organization who does, or set up a task force to work on these issues. You might also consider hiring an outside consultant.

Whether you make the decisions on your own or provide input to others, the following steps can help you become better informed about computer technology and your organization's needs for it.

Defining Your Needs

When defining your needs, ask questions such as:

- What are your information needs? What type of data do you need? How will you use the information? Who will use it? How frequently do they need it, and how current must it be?

- What are your process needs? How could automation improve your processes? What type of quality checks would be helpful?

- What are your technology requirements? What computer technology is your company currently using? How many users will there be? Will it be necessary to be networked internally and/or externally?

Once you have a list of your requirements and needs, prioritize and rank them to establish a set of criteria to use in the selection process.

Researching the Alternatives

Using your criteria, investigate the technology available to meet them. The following resources can help you:

- Periodicals such as *PC World* or *Computer World*

- Vendors for specific computer brands

- Multi-application and platform vendors

- Catalogs such as *Data Source*

- Information on the Internet or commercial on-line services

- CD ROM services

- Technical consultants

You can also gain valuable input by talking to people in positions similar to yours in other companies about the technology they use.

Evaluating the Options

Once you have a thorough list of available software packages that could potentially meet your needs, take these additional steps to narrow the list:

1. Call vendors for more detailed information about each package, and compare this information with your criteria. Select about five packages for further evaluation.

2. Set up vendor demonstrations, and make reference calls to companies using those programs. Then narrow your list to two or three packages.

3. If possible, you may want to visit companies where the technology is being used before you make your final decision.

While it is unlikely that any one program or system will completely meet all your requirements, these steps will help you find the product that best meets your most important needs.

PART 4

Making the Best Use of Your Organization's Computer Technology

Utilizing Computer Technology

It is likely that your organization is already using computer technology to some extent. By capitalizing on these existing computer resources, you can make significant improvements in your area with no added cost to the organization.

To investigate available resources, begin by assessing your needs. The questions listed in Part 3, Defining your Needs can help you identify your needs. If your company has an Information Services or Systems (IS) department, meet with someone in that area. This person can help you pinpoint your needs and explore available options.

If others in your organization are known for making good use of computer resources, seek input from them. Discuss your needs and ask for advice on how you can be as effective.

Your peers can also be a good source of information. Ask them about the computer technology they use and how it benefits them. You may want to set up a formal task force or group discussion on how to use computer resources more effectively. You are likely to learn a great deal from others' experiences.

Increasing Your Computer Skills

The widespread use of personal computers in the home and workplace is a recent development, beginning in the early 1980s and rapidly increasing in the early 1990s. Experts expect this growth rate to soar in the late 1990s and early 2000s, as a wide range of microprocessor devices and a comprehensive telecommunications grid are developed and integrated into all aspects of our lives. By the year 2020, it is expected that the microprocessor and computer will be completely absorbed into society, dramatically changing the way we live, work, and communicate.

Unlike the youngest members of today's work force, who have grown up with computer technology, some managers have had limited experience with the computer. They may have never had to use a computer, or they may be reluctant to try, preferring to do things as they always have. Those who do use computers may be using only a few basic applications, rather than exploring the many ways that computer technology could make their work easier. Because of the prevalence of the computer in today's workplace and the complete integration of computer technology anticipated in the near future, however, computer expertise is becoming not only a valuable tool, but a necessity in the business world.

Whether you have no computer experience or are simply interested in learning a new program, the following suggestions can help you enhance your expertise:

- If you have some computer knowledge and prefer to work independently, you may want to train yourself by reading the manuals written for your software or by using the on-line tutorial and help screens. Most software packages come with an on-line reference tool that includes step-by-step procedures you can follow as you work, as well as examples, demonstrations, and reference information about the program's functions.

- Look at a bookstore or library for one of the many books available which provide various levels of training on particular computer programs. These can be very helpful, particularly if you are interested in learning at your own pace.

- If you need more extensive training, contact the software vendor or an independent computer training company for individual or class lessons. These lessons may be conducted at the vendor's or training company's location, or you may be able to bring a trainer to your work site. When setting up training, make sure you clearly specify your needs and current level of experience.

- Ask for coaching from someone in your company who is known for his or her computer expertise. If your organization has an Information Systems or Services (IS) department or expert, begin there. In most organizations, the IS expert is responsible for assessing computer and other communication needs, determining what technology best fits those needs, and providing the training and support to use the technology.

- Before deciding on a particular trainer or coach, interview the individual to ensure that the training methods and resources fit with your particular needs and learning style. Also make sure your trainer begins by providing a comprehensive basic understanding of computer technology, rather than merely asking you what you want to know. Once you have this foundation, you can begin working on practical applications and hands-on assignments.

- If you have never used computers and are reluctant to begin, start by talking to people about their learning experiences and the benefits they have gained from computer technology. You can find out about the learning methods that worked best for others, and you may gain comfort in seeing that others went through the same learning process. Hearing how computers have helped others may also increase your motivation to learn.

Whichever learning method you choose, be sure to set aside a specific time each day or week to practice what you have learned. Focus on increasing your skills gradually, rather than trying to learn everything at once. Even after you have learned the basic applications you need, continue to experiment with the computer on your own.

RECOMMENDED READINGS

The publications listed here were selected for their content and suitability to a managerial audience.

TechnoTrends: Twenty-four Technologies That Will Revolutionize Our Lives

Burrus, Daniel, and Gittness, Roger, New York: HarperBusiness, 1994
ISBN: 0-88730-700-0
The authors argue that in order to be effective and competitive, companies must avail themselves of the latest technological innovations. This book is a guide on how to recognize these innovations and apply them effectively to increase productivity and efficiency.

Trend Tracking

Celente, Gerald, New York: Warner Books, 1991
ISBN: 0-446-39287-1
Celente teaches a foolproof system for identifying and tracking trends, and shows how to transform them into opportunity and profits. Learn to monitor current events that form future trends and make connections between seemingly unrelated fields.

2020 Vision

Davis, Stan, and Davidson, Bill, New York: Simon & Schuster, 1992
ISBN: 0-671-77815-3
This book argues that in order to compete successfully in world markets, the United States must adapt to a new reality of continuous technological innovation, and that being first and/or early with a new product is more important than being efficient. The author suggests actions the United States must take if it is to prosper in this new reality.

Management of Information Technology

Frenzel, Carroll W., Boston: Boyd & Fraser, 1992
ISBN: 0-87835-508-1
Frenzel examines issues involved in information technology from all levels of management. The book deals with: information asset management, people management, long- and short-range planning, and managing expectations. Also included are examples of how new technology is currently influencing business and industry.

Megamedia Shakeout

Maney, Kevin, New York: John Wiley & Sons, 1995
ISBN: 0-471-10719-0
The term megamedia describes new technology and capabilities in the communications industry that will lead the world into the twenty-first century. Megamedia is often described in broad concepts or individual products as: information superhighway, multimedia, wireless communication, or digital technology. This book discusses the technology soon to be in place, as well as the companies and people making it happen.

The Popcorn Report: Faith Popcorn on the Future of Your Company, Your World, Your Life

Popcorn, Faith, New York: HarperBusiness, 1992
ISBN: 0-88730-594-6
Popcorn has proven her ability to successfully make predictions on what new products, markets, and businesses will be profitable in the future. This updated book predicts future trends, products, and habits both in the workplace and at home, and shows how to profit from these future innovations.

Paradigm Shift

Tapscot, Don, and Caston, Art, New York: McGraw-Hill, 1993
ISBN: 0-07-062857-2
This book explains how to take advantage of new technology in order to change your organization into a responsive and competitive company ready to take advantage of new opportunities. It shows managers and professionals with little technological background how to take action to achieve immediate benefits from this technology and how to transform their organization for long-term growth. The techniques offered here are the result of extensive research into more than 4,500 businesses and governmental organizations.

SUGGESTED SEMINARS

The seminars listed below were chosen for their general scope and interest. Because of the highly specialized nature of the information specific to many occupational and technical areas, a comprehensive list of available seminars would be beyond the scope of this Handbook. For information about courses dealing with your area of expertise, contact your local library, professional/trade association, or university. There are also many courses available at community colleges and trade schools.

Effective Presentations Skills for Technical Professionals

Participants in this program will develop the skills necessary to be effective when making presentations to technical and/or nontechnical audiences and when communicating complex technical concepts.
Length: 3 days; Cost: $1,200
Locations: Call vendor
American Management Association
P.O. Box 319, Saranac Lake, NY 12983
Telephone: 800/262-9699

Managing Information Technology

In this program, participants will learn how information technology is impacting organizations and individuals today and its anticipated future impact. Participants will learn how to utilize a broad range of software applications, integrate information technology into their own work activities, and make various types of software work together.
Length: 3 days; Cost: $1,050
Location: Houston
Rice University, Jesse H. Jones Graduate School of Administration, Office of Executive Development
P.O. Box 1892, Houston, TX 77251-1892
Telephone: 713/527-6060

Technology Forecasting Workshop

This interactive seminar is for managers and professionals involved in planning for new technologies and markets. It is a combination of formal instruction, group discussion, and practical exercises designed to teach people how to conduct and assess technology forecasts and to integrate them into organizational planning.
Length: 3 days; Cost: $995
Location: Austin
Technology Futures, Inc.
11709 Boulder Lane, Austin, TX 78726
Telephone: 800/835-3887

Program for Technology Managers

This program is designed to help participants communicate effectively about technology and innovation across functional areas, help the organization understand the strategic significance of technology and innovation, and successfully manage strategic alliances among corporations for new technology development.
Length: 2 weeks; Cost: $7,600
Location: Chapel Hill, NC
University of North Carolina at Chapel Hill
Kenan-Flagler Business School, Executive Education
Campus Box 3445, Chapel Hill, NC 27599-3445
Telephone: 800/862-3932

KNOW THE BUSINESS

To operate successfully in today's business environment, managers need to know far more than just how to do their own jobs. As you know, decisions made in one part of an organization significantly affect other parts of the business.

Effective leaders understand these interrelationships. They know the role each function plays in the success of the business, and they ensure that their team works with other teams and functions.

Successful managers also understand their industry, including its key success factors, the competition, and expected future developments and challenges. They know how their organization stacks up against the competition and they develop strategies to maximize and enhance this position.

This section suggests ways to develop your knowledge of how your organization operates and its place within the larger context of the industry and the marketplace:

- Understanding the Organization
- Knowing How the Business Operates
- Understanding the Competition
- Analyzing Impacts on the Business
- Using Cross-Disciplinary Knowledge Effectively

Organizational Knowledge

Valuable Tips

- Ask someone who seems particularly savvy about the organization to be your mentor. Ask your manager to suggest someone who could be helpful in this role.

- Read your company's corporate history to understand how the business has developed and changed.

- Study a company-wide organization chart to get a "big picture" of the business as a whole and to understand how the various functions relate to each other.

- Build an informal network with peers in other functional areas to learn more about the work they do.

- Look for opportunities to lunch and socialize with others outside the normal work environment, or perhaps after hours when informal "bull sessions" about the organization take place.

- Read publications such as *Business Week, Fortune,* and the *Wall Street Journal* to keep on top of business developments. Consider any implications these developments might have for you or your company.

- Volunteer to serve on a task force that is dealing with a problem relevant to the company's future.

- If your organization is implementing a total quality management program or some other broad-based effort, volunteer to serve on the steering committee or task force to broaden your perspective and to meet peers from other functional areas.

- Get to know several people in the sales organization. Salespeople can be good sources of information about the competition and marketing strengths and weaknesses.

- Develop benchmarks for the key success factors in your industry and your organization.

- Seek opportunities to learn about other disciplines or functions that interact with your group. Attend a course or seminar for nonexperts at a local college.

- Read as many internal publications as you can, including newsletters and technical publications from other departments.

- Ask your peers how the work of your group affects them.

- When your group tries to solve a problem, ask what other parts of the company have a stake in the outcome. Find out whether your group has received input from these stakeholders.

Understanding the Organization

To succeed as a manager, you need to understand your organization's mission, goals, strategies, strengths, and weaknesses — in other words, the larger framework within which your management responsibilities lie. This knowledge will also enable you to help your employees develop a similar understanding of the organization.

To increase your knowledge of the organization:

- Do your homework before you decide to join an organization or transfer to a new division within your company, and then ask a lot of questions: about the mission, strategies, structure, culture, and management style. You can learn a great deal by asking the right questions.

- Initiate a meeting or lunch with a seasoned manager. Ask this person to share his or her knowledge of the organization's history, explain the evolution of the company's mission, and describe the origin of the company's strengths and weaknesses. Ask about the key success factors for the business. Ask a lot of questions to help you understand what has happened and why.

- Read books or articles written about the company to develop a historical perspective of the organization.

- Obtain a copy of your organization's vision and mission statements, if you are not already familiar with them. If you have any questions, ask your manager to explain. Once you have a clear understanding of the vision and mission, look for opportunities to communicate them to your employees.

- Involve employees in identifying several things the team can do that will contribute directly to achieving the corporate mission.

- Be sure that you and your people attend company meetings in which results and strategies are discussed.

- Ask your manager to fill you in on corporate planning sessions that he or she has attended. Get his or her perspective on the company's strategies, goals, strengths, and weaknesses.

- Read your organization's annual report, particularly the CEO's message to stockholders. This message typically includes a clear statement of company goals, recent progress toward longer term objectives, and future challenges.

- Ask your manager to use you as a "stand-in" when he or she is unable to attend key meetings.

- Ask your stockbroker to send you research reports on your company prepared by industry analysts.

- Contact your corporate communications department to obtain recent newspaper or magazine articles that profile or discuss your company. Also be on the lookout for corporate advertising, specialized brochures, and so forth.

- Get a recent copy of your company's executive briefing to security analysts, published in *Wall Street Transcripts,* from your corporate communications department. This document can give you an overview of the organization's future direction and goals.

- Develop a contact with someone in your organization's corporate planning and development department to learn more about strategic issues and new developments.

- List three things you can do personally to help the organization overcome its weaknesses, and list three things you can do to make the organization's strengths even greater.

- Identify the most troublesome organizational problem that affects your job. Chair a task force to address the problem.

Knowing How the Business Operates

One indicator of managerial effectiveness is the manager's understanding of how other parts of the organization function. Rather than narrowly focusing on their own functional or geographic area, effective managers make it their business to develop a wide-angle perspective of the company as a whole.

How can you gain a working knowledge of what other groups do in your company? The following suggestions can help you develop a better understanding of how your business is run:

- Meet informally with your peers in other functional areas. For example, stroll through other functional areas after work looking for people with whom to strike up a conversation. Ask them to describe their job responsibilities, how their areas operate, and important issues they are currently dealing with. Most people love to talk about what they do — especially to an interested listener. Develop an informal relationship with some of these people and talk on the phone with them at least every month.

- Become an "armchair traveler" by reading internal and external publications that deal with your organization. Company newsletters are especially useful for providing information about what other subsidiaries or divisions around the country are doing, including special accomplishments, products under development, new contracts, project completions, and management promotions.

- Compile a list of the things you would like to find out about the organization that would help you perform more effectively. Seek individuals or documents that can provide the information you need.

- Study available documents that describe strategic plans, goals, and operating philosophy for the organization as a whole, or for specific divisions or departments.

- Broaden your contacts within the organization. Joining informal clubs, playing on one of the company's sports teams, attending company social events, and making a list of people you've met on work assignments are all good ways to start increasing your contacts in other areas of the company. See the Leverage Networks section of this Handbook for additional suggestions.

- Read job descriptions for your position and for others in your group. If they are available, also read job descriptions for the heads of your division and functional area, and for those of related functional areas.

Understanding the Competition

Developing a thorough understanding of your competitors' strengths and weaknesses requires significant knowledge of the competition's products, strategies, and philosophies. The following activities can help you increase that knowledge:

- Ask your customers for their evaluation of how your organization measures up to the competition.

- Obtain competitors' promotional literature to learn more about their products or services.

- Ask your stockbroker for copies of analysts' reports on your competitors.

- Attend conferences and trade shows to stay current with what the competition is doing.

- Obtain a copy of *How to Find Information about Companies: Corporate Intelligence Sourcebook,* published by Washington Researchers Publishing. This book lists resources and suggests ways to obtain information. It should be available at the library, or it may be ordered through some trade journals.

- Create a detailed profile of each competitor. These profiles will form the basis from which to develop strategies for gaining competitive advantage. Include the following factors in your profile:
  - Quality and price of competitor's products or services compared with similar products/services offered by your company
  - Market share
  - Marketing strategies and targeted markets
  - Level of innovation and/or amount of money spent on R&D
  - Level of service provided to support products
  - Reputation in the industry
  - Corporate leaders — their strategies and philosophies
  - Strengths and weaknesses

- Join one or more professional associations. Get to know people with whom you can share information about the competition. It can be especially useful to meet people from other geographical areas, because they may be more willing to share information if they don't see you as a direct competitor.

Analyzing Impacts on the Business

Your business or organization operates within a particular environment that has an impact on its success. To know the business, effective leaders understand these environmental factors, strategize ways to deal with them, and capitalize on the opportunities they offer.

To analyze and understand the external factors that affect your group, consider the following questions:

- Who are your five to ten top competitors? Review these competitors' profiles to understand what they are doing and to identify opportunities or potential problems.

- What impact does technology have on your:
  - Products or services?
  - Work processes?
  - Quality?
  - Hiring qualifications?

IT'S TO REMIND ME THAT THE BUSINESS IS ALWAYS CHANGING.

- How will changing demographics affect your work force, products and services, marketing strategies, and so forth?

- What is the impact of the global economy on your business? What are the threats? Where are the opportunities?

- What is the impact of job regulations locally, nationally, and internationally? How do you manage a worldwide organization that must deal with local rules and regulations?

To gather information and learn about the strategies used by others:

- Get involved in one or more industry associations. Your involvement might consist of reading association journals, attending meetings and seminars, and/or volunteering to serve on a program, membership, or steering committee.

- Join groups that get together on a formal or an informal basis to exchange information and explore common issues. These affiliations can be based on any number of common bonds — type of business, organization size, manufacturing processes, market niche, and so on.

  Some groups form because of geographical proximity; others form because their members want to associate with people who are in similar businesses but who serve a completely different market area. This latter practice promotes information exchange without the threat of competition.

- Look for books, publications, and research information on practices and trends in industry categories that are related to your own. Associations, government publications, universities, and libraries are good sources of these documents.

- If your organization is a member of the American Management Association, look for AMA publications, workshops, and/or conferences that deal specifically with your industry or with broad industry trends.

Using Cross-Disciplinary Knowledge Effectively

Today's business challenges tend to be complex. Few developments or changes involve just one function or one area of knowledge. For example, the design and implementation of a new computerized inventory system to speed up distribution, and thereby improve customer service, requires the input of people with different types of expertise — systems designers, programmers, inventory managers, distribution personnel, customers, other users, and systems trainers.

At the very least, having a basic knowledge of what people in other functions do can help you put together more effective teams and coordinate their efforts to maximum advantage. The preceding example illustrates the need to develop some cross-functional or cross-disciplinary knowledge, as well as the importance of maintaining good working relationships with peers who have expertise in other areas.

To develop your understanding of other disciplines that interact with or affect your group:

- Make a determined effort to learn the business from the perspectives of people in other functional areas. Take advantage of the times when you're working with experts in other fields. Begin to learn their disciplines from them. Ask these experts to recommend books or other resources that will help you learn the rudiments of the subject.

- Bring together cross-disciplinary teams when you are working on complex or recurring problems or pursuing business opportunities. Provide an open forum to enable experts in other areas to contribute their ideas to the team.

- In looking at your career goals, decide whether you are interested in progressing up the ranks of your own functional area, or through the business as a whole. If you are interested in general management, be sure to take on some cross-functional assignments. Discuss with your manager how you can pursue cross-functional opportunities, and gain his or her support in reaching this goal.

- Take courses in subjects that interest you. Most universities offer courses for nonexperts in a number of areas. Enroll in a finance course for nonfinancial managers, a course in human resource management for operations managers, a course in quality management, and so on.

- Read general management journals and publications such as *Harvard Business Review*.

RECOMMENDED READINGS

The publications listed here were selected for their content and suitability to a managerial audience.

Corporate Lifecycles

Adizes, Ichak, Englewood Cliffs, NJ: Prentice-Hall, 1990
ISBN: 0-13-174426-7
The author describes the behavior of an organization throughout various stages in its "life cycle" and provides tools for analyzing the changes in behavior during an organization's growth. The author also introduces a process for changing organizational behavior as well as organizational cultures and their performance.

Benchmarking for Best Practices

Bogan, Christopher E., and English, Michael J., New York: McGraw-Hill, 1994
ISBN: 0-07-006375-3
The strategies provided in this guide address all aspects of identifying the best business practices and adapting them into a benchmarking program. The author teaches how to: sell benchmarking to all levels of an organization, design a benchmarking program that will ensure success upon implementation, integrate benchmarking into other initiatives, and encourage innovation by adapting proven practices. Examples from some of the world's most successful companies help demonstrate how best practices benchmarking works.

TechnoTrends: Twenty-four Technologies That Will Revolutionize Our Lives

Burrus, Daniel, and Gittness, Roger, New York: HarperBusiness, 1994
ISBN: 0-88730-700-0
The authors argue that in order to be effective and competitive, companies must avail themselves of the latest technological innovations. This book is a guide on how to recognize these innovations and apply them effectively to increase productivity and efficiency.

The Monster Under the Bed

Davis, Stan, and Botkin, Jim, New York: Simon & Schuster, 1994
ISBN: 0-671-87107-2
The knowledge industry is changing the way business is conducted and it will dominate the global marketplace. This book makes several observations about business's role as purveyor of knowledge to customers, employees, and eventually to schools, including: the increasing role of business in education, the idea that learning is a continuous process, and the notion that any business can become a knowledge business.

Competing for the Future	**Hamel, Gary, and Prahalad, C.K.,** Boston: Harvard Business School Press, 1994 ISBN: 0-87584-416-2 The authors postulate that managers in today's most successful firms are more interested in creating new competitive space than positioning themselves in the existing market. Companies need to develop foresight by not only looking at the possible, but influencing the direction their industry is taking. This book shows how to develop stretch goals and build core competencies to create advantages and new markets for the future.
Marketing 2000 and Beyond	**Lazar, William; La Barbera, Priscilla; MacLachlan, James M.; and Smith, Allen E.,** Chicago: American Marketing Association, 1990 ISBN: 0-87757-198-8 These authors reveal emerging market opportunities and shifts in target markets. They identify profitable market segments, the kinds of products and services to produce, and the direction a firm should take to position them. Insights and thoughts from recognized CEOs, leading futurists, and academicians are also discussed.
The TeamNet Factor: Bringing the Power of Boundary Crossing Into the Heart of Your Business	**Lipnack, Jessica, and Stamps, Jeffrey,** Essex Junction, VT: Oliver Wight, 1993 ISBN: 0-939246-34-1 The authors use their experience as networking consultants to show companies how to be innovative and build teams that cross company boundaries rather than building strictly internal teams. The book contends that networking and team building with other companies are essential to becoming more competitive and successful.
Simplicity Wins	**McKinsey and Company, Inc.,** Boston: Harvard Business School Press, 1995 ISBN: 0-87584-504-5 An in-depth study of thirty-nine machinery component manufacturing companies in Germany found firms that were significantly more successful than their competitors in terms of cost, time, and quality. All these firms had one thing in common: simplification of management, organization, and procedures. Included are lessons on: dropping marginal products and customers, buying standard parts and making unique parts in-house, integrating the process, grouping functions, and simplifying operations without computerized automation.

The Competitive Advantage of Nations

Porter, Michael E., New York: The Free Press, 1990
ISBN: 0-02-925361-6
Based on extensive research, the author identifies elements that create a national, competitive advantage in an industry. The book further identifies the stages of competitive development through which entire economies advance and decline. Porter combines this research with the ideas presented in his previous works and explores how industries become competitive in a global marketplace.

SUGGESTED SEMINARS

The seminars listed here were selected for their appeal to a managerial audience. The reputation of the vendor, the quality of their seminar offerings, and the specific seminar content were considered in the selection process.

Because of the dynamic nature of the seminar marketplace, some seminars may have been upgraded or replaced, and others may no longer be offered. Likewise, costs and locations may have changed since this listing was compiled. We recommend that you contact the vendor directly for updated and additional information.

Competitive Strategy: How to Develop Marketing Plans, Strategies, and Tactics

This program is designed to give participants an expanded market point of view for attaining and sustaining a distinct competitive advantage.
Length: 3 days; Cost: $1,495
Locations: Call vendor
American Management Association
P.O. Box 319, Saranac Lake, NY 12983
Telephone: 800/262-9699

Business Strategy

This program teaches a systematic but creative approach to the planning and effective implementation of strategy in a wide variety of organizations. Key topics include: competitive analysis; industry dynamics; process and product innovation; pitfalls in applying strategic tools; and human resource factors in strategy.
Length: 2 weeks; Cost: Call vendor
Location: Harriman, NY
Columbia University
Graduate School of Business, 2880 Broadway, 4th Floor
New York, NY 10025-6989
Telephone: 212/854-3395

Program for Manager Development

This seminar is designed to improve the managerial performance of high potential executives and prepare them for future leadership in their organizations; to provide each participant with a better understanding of the need for close integration of the functional areas of marketing, operations, human resources, research and development, and finance; and to give each participant an understanding of external and internal forces that affect the achievement of corporate goals.
Length: 2 weeks; Cost: $7,800
Location: Durham, NC
Duke University, The Fuqua School of Business
Office of Executive Education, Durham, NC 27706
Telephone: 800/372-3932

Strategic Marketing Management

This program is designed for experienced managers with significant marketing responsibility. Topics covered include: key elements of marketing strategy; processes of marketing analysis, planning, and control; organizational design as it relates to the marketing function; implementation of marketing plans; and the relationship of marketing to overall business and corporate strategy.
Length: 2 weeks; Cost: $9,000
Location: Boston
Harvard Business School
Executive Education Programs, Soldiers Field-Glass Hall
Boston, MA 02163-9986
Telephone: 800/427-5577

Systems Thinking: A Language for Learning and Action™

This seminar will teach managers how to apply systems thinking. The seminar is designed to increase participants' natural inclination to think systematically. During the seminar, participants will practice communicating critical business issues from a systematic point of view, learn to talk convincingly about root causes, and develop alternative actions for desired changes.
Length: 3 days; Cost: $1,995
Locations: Call vendor
Innovation Associates, Inc.
3 Speen Street, Suite 140, Framingham, MA 01701
Telephone: 508/879-8301

Meeting the Mid-Management Challenge: Developing Cross-Functional Skills in High-Potential Managers

This program has been designed to provide middle managers with a foundation of theory and practice in key areas of business management in preparation for advancement in their organization. Special attention is paid to developing cross-functional skills.
Length: 6 days; Cost: $3,650
Location: Dallas
Southern Methodist University
Executive Development, Edwin L. Cox School of Business
Dallas, TX 75275-0333
Telephone: 214/768-3549

Marketing for the Non-Marketing Manager

The program is designed to provide participants with a clear understanding of the marketing function and enable managers to work more effectively with the marketing team; to strengthen participants' knowledge and perception of how various factors enter into the marketing decision; and to explore the interrelationship of company objectives, the marketing environment, and marketing planning and strategy.
Length: 5 days; Cost: $4,300
Location: Ann Arbor, MI
University of Michigan Business School
Executive Education Center, Ann Arbor, MI 48109-1234
Telephone: 313/763-1000

Integrating Finance and Marketing: A Strategic Framework

This seminar helps managers develop techniques for integrating finance and marketing concerns, gain the ability to assess the costs and benefits of various marketing strategies, better understand the key determinants of profitability, explore how successful companies were able to achieve their successes, and learn how to better use financial information to assess performance.
Length: 5 days; Cost: $4,550
Location: Philadelphia
University of Pennsylvania, The Wharton School
Aresty Institute of Executive Education, Steinberg
Conference Center, 255 South 38th Street
Philadelphia, PA 19104-6359
Telephone: 800/255-3932

ORGANIZATIONAL STRATEGY SKILLS

ORGANIZATIONAL STRATEGY SKILLS

As the world and our work environment continue to change, the strategies and priorities of organizations and managers must address and grow with these changes.

Most companies are becoming global enterprises, or at least must learn to "think global." The competition in today's marketplace requires continuous improvement in products and services, increased focus on meeting customers' needs and providing superior customer service, and the wise expenditure of resources. We also know that businesses must increasingly be managed in an ecologically sound manner. Finally, companies must also maximize profitability for both the short and long term, which requires prudent long-term thinking.

This chapter presents suggestions for improving your skills in the following five organizational strategy areas:

Manage Profitability: Emphasizes the need to contribute to the organization's profitability; makes decisions that enhance the organization's financial position.

Commit to Quality: Emphasizes the need to deliver quality products and/or services; defines standards for quality and evaluates products, processes, and/or services against those standards; manages quality.

Focus on Customer Needs: Anticipates customer needs; takes action to meet customer needs; continually searches for ways to increase customer satisfaction.

Promote Corporate Citizenship: Fosters wise use of scarce resources; works on community issues relevant to the business; devotes time and effort to future resources.

Recognize Global Implications: Seeks to understand issues, trends, and perspectives of various cultures and countries; recognizes that what works in one's own country will not necessarily work in another; addresses cultural and geographic differences in strategies and approaches.

MANAGE PROFITABILITY

Profits are essential for any business. Unless there is a sufficient profit margin, the business cannot exist. The jobs it provides, the products and services it delivers, and the contributions it makes to the community would cease.

All managers play a role in an organization's overall profitability. Some managers are responsible for generating revenue, others are responsible for making products or delivering services, and still others are responsible for helping the line functions do their jobs.

To be a successful manager, you need to manage your financial responsibilities. This is much more complex than just increasing revenue and keeping costs low — it also means managing assets and liabilities.

To manage profitability, you need to understand how the organization makes money and your unit's role in that process. You may need to set financial goals, work with sales and marketing to determine pricing and volume, determine whether and when to make capital expenditures, identify ways to reduce costs, justify investments, and so on.

This section provides guidelines and suggestions for effectively managing profitability, including:

- Understanding Financial Management
- Setting Challenging Financial Goals
- Managing Against Your Financial Goals
- Looking for Ways to Reduce Costs
- Pursuing Ways to Increase Revenue
- Analyzing and Justifying Capital Expenditures
- Involving Employees in Financial Management
- Managing the Perception of Your Profitability Management

Valuable Tips

- Ensure that everyone who is responsible for meeting the stated financial goals knows what these goals are and what they are expected to deliver.

- Include the people responsible for meeting the goals in the process of developing them, to the degree that this is possible.

- Talk with people who have been successful forecasters and "money managers" to find out what they do.

- Learn to use computer software packages to forecast and monitor budgets.

- Look for customer needs that you could be meeting but currently are not. Develop a plan for meeting these needs with additional or expanded products and services.

- Look for breakthrough opportunities that will dramatically generate new returns, rather than just settling for extensions of the past. Find at least one of these opportunities.

- Talk with an expert in your accounting or finance department about establishing and managing a budget.

- Set budget goals that will challenge you and your staff.

- Become familiar with all of the details of your budget — past and present — and analyze how they are related.

- Look at your organization's history. Talk with long-term employees to get an explanation of what happened, and why, from a financial perspective.

- In setting and managing budgets, focus on three to five "make or break" areas that will determine whether you are financially successful.

- Learn the details of the operational areas that contribute to your budget. Talk with the heads of those units to understand how each area fits into the whole.

- Understand how you'll need to work across departments to achieve your goals.

- Develop an effective working relationship with your information systems area. Work with them to create the budget-monitoring reports that give you the exact information you need. Have these reports generated on a schedule that will be most useful to you. Be clear about what you need.

- Become cost-conscious. Ask others to justify expenditures. Be on the lookout for ways to cut costs.

- Use zero-based budgeting methods to develop your budget.

- Take a course on the basics of marketing to learn how to generate more revenue.

- Understand that increasing sales volume does not necessarily mean increasing profitability.

- Talk with the people who market and sell your products and services to gather their ideas for expanding the market.

- Regularly read publications such as the *Wall Street Journal* that focus on the financial aspects of business. Read publications in your industry and look for ideas that will work in your organization.

- With your peers, start an informal support group to help each other learn about, and more effectively perform, financial management tasks.

- Ask yourself, "If this were my own business, what would I do?"

- Involve your staff as much as possible in every aspect of the budgeting process.

- Educate your staff on the budget-setting and monitoring process. As you teach, so will you learn.

- Ask yourself, "If I could pocket 50 percent of every dollar I cut from expenses or added to revenue, where would I cut or add?"

- Don't accept things as they are unless you are comfortable with both the process and the results of the numbers for which you are responsible.

Understanding Financial Management

Sometimes the biggest obstacle to effective financial management is simply a manager's lack of understanding of financial terms and processes. Often just learning the basic financial principles allows managers to use financial processes and reports and thus improve their work unit's profitability. Here are some suggestions for learning the basics of financial management:

- Take a course or workshop in financial management for nonfinancial managers, or read one of the many books available on this topic.

- Meet with your manager or a peer who has expertise in financial management. Ask him or her to teach you the basics of how to manage profitability.

- Get to know someone in your accounting or finance department who can help you understand the basic principles of setting and managing budgets. Ask that person how to use your organization's budget process, financial reports, and ratios to better manage for profitability.

- Become involved in the development of a new product or project your company is considering. Sit in on the financial discussions and perform your own financial evaluation of the budget, including cost and revenue projections, to see whether it makes sense to move ahead. Ask a financial manager to review your assessment.

Setting Challenging Financial Goals

The first step in managing for profitability is establishing financial goals and a budget that is realistic, yet challenging, in its profit objectives. You may have the responsibility of actually setting goals, or you may give input to others for goal setting and budgeting. The following ideas will help you set financial goals:

- Remember that financial goals, like other goals, should be attainable, yet should contain an element of challenge that encourages people to "perform beyond the norm."

- Ask your manager for his or her expectations of your budget. Ask him or her to assess the range of financial goals and identify any that are too pessimistic or overly optimistic. Use this input to help you develop your goals.

- Realize that financial goals are budgets, and budgets are built on details. So analyze the details of past budgets for your area. Compare projections with actual figures, and look for trends that will have an impact on your forecasts. Assess how past performance has affected the current financial status of your work unit. Use this information to help you identify a profit goal that is aggressive, yet attainable.

- Document the assumptions upon which you based your goals.

- Talk with the sales and marketing people who sell your products or services. Find out their expectations for the coming period.

- To learn the bigger picture, ask to see the current and past budgets into which your budget fits. Understand how the performance of your business unit affects other units. Examine both the projections and the actuals. Look for trends in how costs and revenues are managed — especially as they relate to your area. Find out what happened and why.

Managing Against Your Financial Goals

Once you have established your financial goals, your next responsibility is to manage effectively so that you stay on course and come as close as possible to achieving them. To help you do this, follow this process:

1. Identify the three to five key cost and revenue areas that will make or break your financial goals. To do so:

   - Get to know the operations of the areas that make up your costs and provide your revenues. Talk with the people who know how these areas operate, the impacts they have, and the ways in which they are affected by other forces.

   - Ask your manager, your employees and, if appropriate, your peers for their opinions on which of your budget items are the key ones.

2. Determine how frequently you need to see reports comparing budget projections and actuals. A produce warehouse manager, for example, might need to see daily reports because of the perishable nature of the product. A company experiencing an extremely tight cash flow, or one with a lot of cash flowing in, might also need to see daily reports. On the other hand, a stable department that experiences little fluctuation may be fine with monthly reports.

   Successful companies have quick turnaround of financial information to enable their managers to track where they are against budget.

3. Once you have determined the best reporting period for you, work with your information systems department to design a report (or reports) that will provide you with the information

you need. Make sure that these reports focus on the three to five key areas that you have identified and that they include the information you need to know.

It's important to develop a positive working relationship with the accounting and information services departments. Take the initiative to build this positive relationship. Explain how you plan to use the information you need and be clear about the reports and information you want.

4. When you receive the reports you requested, monitor them carefully to see how your budget is working.

5. Plan in advance how you will handle significant changes in your budget projections. For each of your key "make or break" areas, have some ideas ready in case these areas do not go according to plan.

6. Conduct formal quarterly reviews. Use the reviews to track status and progress against goals, understand what is happening, and make changes in assumptions and forecasts if necessary. Involve the team in the process, when appropriate, to share information and discover opportunities to work together to maximize use of resources.

Looking for Ways to Reduce Costs

Becoming cost-conscious and continually looking for ways to reduce costs is one way that you can manage for greater profitability. Although you are undoubtedly aware that long-term goals and strategies sometimes require expenditures that won't contribute to short-term profits, for the most part it is helpful to look for ways to reduce costs wherever you can. Here are some suggestions to help you become more aware of ways to reduce costs:

*   Develop your budget from the perspective of zero-based budgeting. That is, for every expense line item in your budget, start with a budget of zero dollars and add budget amounts only as far as you can justify that cost. Be able to discuss the impact or expected results of the expenditures and what will be lost if the money is not spent.

    By looking to justify every line item, you may discover some items that are not necessary at all and others that do not need to be as large as they have been. This zero-based approach forces you to examine what you want to spend and make certain that the return is worth it. In addition to finding ways to reduce costs, this approach may result in a decision to increase costs in a certain area, because you expect the increased costs to produce a higher return.

- Examine the four or five largest expenditures in your budget to see:
  - Exactly what you are getting for your money
  - Whether there is a more cost-effective way to obtain that product or service

- Systematically analyze each work process your staff performs. Become familiar with every step of the process, and evaluate whether it is being performed in the most efficient way. By looking at all aspects of the process, you may find a number of inefficiencies that, if corrected, could reduce costs.

- Research the cost of using supplies that do not meet your specifications. Work with suppliers who will deliver exactly what you need, when you need it.

Pursuing Ways to Increase Revenue

As you know, you can increase revenue by increasing sales or by increasing the price of your products or services. However, increasing sales without concern for profit margins or increasing prices without knowing the impact on sales is both shortsighted and naive.

The primary responsibility for sales and pricing belongs to the sales and marketing departments. It is important to understand this process and monitor what you are getting, especially if you have overall responsibility for the business unit.

In addition, managers these days also are concerned with internal suppliers and customers. Many managers are internal suppliers and, in turn, are also customers. You sell to your internal customers and set prices. Many of the same principles of selling and pricing are involved internally as well as externally.

INCREASING VOLUME

To help you determine whether increasing volume is the most appropriate way to increase revenue, follow these suggestions:

- Take a course or workshop in the basics of marketing. Select one that is particularly appropriate for the product or service you sell. If your direct customers are internal, rather than external, choose a course that focuses on marketing internally.

- Learn more about your customers — their needs, and how they use your products and services — by talking with your sales and marketing people. Determine how you can modify or improve the product or service, improve distribution and customer service, and in any other way increase the product's value to your customer.

- Talk with your customers and people in your marketing or sales area to identify new ways to use the product or service or to expand the product line so that the same product can serve a larger customer base. If you proceed with a product expansion, analyze the costs required for research and development, production, and marketing to ensure that your investment is justified by the return.

- If your direct customers are internal groups, find out whether they are utilizing your products or services, or going to outside vendors. If it is the latter, work with them to identify their needs and discover why they are choosing an external vendor. Then develop a proposal that meets these customers' needs, or work to restructure your pricing so that it is more competitive. Ask them to give your group a chance at providing the product or service.

- Talk with the people who market and sell your product or service and find out how it is being sold. Ask these individuals how they would increase the volume of sales and profitability if they could implement any plan they wished.

- Keep on top of marketing and sales trends in your industry. Read trade journals and industry reports. Join a professional association or one of its special interest groups that will provide you with sales and marketing ideas for your product or service.

ESTABLISHING PROFITABLE UNIT PRICES

Sales and marketing personnel are responsible for setting pricing. Yet if you are responsible for the business unit, you will want to understand the process. You should know enough so that you can challenge assumptions made in developing the pricing strategies and generate new thinking within the group. Challenging assumptions doesn't mean that you should cease to rely on the judgment of the experts on your staff. Rather, it often leads to healthy debate that maximizes opportunities and creative approaches.

- Talk with your sales and marketing people to learn their pricing strategies.

- Look for an assignment on a committee or task force whose role is to examine your department's or organization's pricing structure.

- Seek the advice of managers in your organization who are known for their effective pricing strategies. Find out how they analyze the costs of producing a product or service and how they determine unit prices.

- Find out the price of your competitors' products and services. Obtain this information from your marketing department if your customers are external. If your direct customers are internal, ask them what they pay for your competitors' products and services, or conduct your own survey of your competition's pricing.

- Learn how to set a unit price that incorporates all of the research and development and other "hidden" costs necessary to produce your product or service; the actual production costs could be just the tip of the iceberg.

Analyzing and Justifying Capital Expenditures

Managing profitability includes spending money wisely. When you or your employees have identified capital expenditures that are believed necessary, conduct a thorough analysis of actual total costs and expected benefits. Include the following in your analysis:

- Cost of identifying vendors or suppliers

- Actual capital cost itself

- Cost of implementation or change, including training needed

- Intangible costs, including stress and inconvenience

- Expected benefits, both tangible and intangible

- Cost or impact of not making the expenditure

Ask your staff to make this kind of analysis for all capital expenditures, so that you can make more informed decisions.

Involving Employees in Financial Management

Your employees can be your best allies in increasing the profitability of the area for which you are financially responsible. Involving your staff members in every aspect of the budgeting process to which they can contribute can yield many ideas for improving profitability. Following are suggested ways to increase your staff's involvement in the financial management of your work unit:

- Communicate frequently and openly about financial matters. Provide as much information as will be helpful to your staff. See the Communication Skills chapter in this Handbook for suggestions on improving communication with your employees.

- Consistently stress the importance of improving profitability. Observe your communications with your staff. If profitability does not receive as much focus as it should, make it a priority.

- Educate your staff on the budgeting process. Explain how costs and revenues are forecast, and what happens when projections do not match actuals. Encourage them to question and probe further.

- When developing your budget, involve your staff as much as possible. Assign those who are responsible for each line item to generate the numbers for that item for the upcoming year. They are most likely to know where the opportunities lie.

- When you are required to reduce your budget, involve your staff as much as possible. Call an impromptu meeting to brainstorm cost reductions or revenue increases. Take all suggestions into consideration, and incorporate as many as you can.

- Make a game of finding ways to reduce costs or increase revenues. Encourage your staff (and yourself) to take the perspective that if they could figure out how to reduce costs or increase revenues, they would personally pocket 50 percent of the additional profit. Track the results, and give small awards to those who were the top "profiteers" in this game.

- Always follow up with your staff on any of their suggestions that you use in the financial management process. Make sure they know that their input is seriously considered and used whenever feasible.

Managing the Perception of Your Profitability Management

Some managers believe that they already are managing aggressive financial goals, but others may not share that perception. If this situation occurs, first collect additional information by answering these questions:

- How do your goals compare with others in the organization?

- How aware are others of your attention to the organization's bottom line?

- What's the perception of the opportunities available to you for contributing to profitability?

- How does what you do in your area compare to how other managers approach their financial responsibilities?

This analysis will identify the areas of discrepancy between you and others. Then you can determine a plan of action that may include:

- Stretching your group more

- Educating others

- Providing more financial information

- Becoming more comfortable holding people accountable for aggressive numbers

RECOMMENDED READINGS

The publications listed here were selected for their content and suitability to a managerial audience.

The McGraw-Hill 36-Hour Course in Finance for Nonfinancial Managers

Cooke, Robert A., New York: McGraw-Hill, 1992
ISBN: 0-07-012538-4
This book is a helpful guide for nonfinancial managers on financial reporting and budgeting that is applicable for day-to-day operations. In addition, there are clear explanations of all major financial topics, as well as exercises designed to help you apply the material presented.

2020 Vision

Davis, Stan, and Davidson, Bill, New York: Simon & Schuster, 1992
ISBN: 0-671-77815-3
This book argues that in order to compete successfully in world markets, the United States must adapt to a new reality of continuous technological innovation, and that being first and/or early with a new product is more important than being efficient. The author suggests actions the United States must take if it is to prosper in this new reality.

Guide to Total Cost Management

Ernst & Young, New York: John Wiley & Sons, 1992
ISBN: 0-471-55877-X
Total Cost Management is a set of tools, developed by the Big Six accounting firm of Ernst & Young, for identifying and keeping business costs down. This desktop guide addresses, in nontechnical language, how companies can make better decisions with regard to costs of products, services, and investments in everyday business operations.

Cut The Fat, Not The Muscle

Kobert, Norman, Englewood Cliffs, NJ: Prentice-Hall, 1995
ISBN: 0-13-292443-9
This book provides strategies for analyzing ways to cut costs, rather than simply discharging employees and cutting costs indiscriminately. To make smart cost-cutting decisions a company needs to: find out where its core business lies, work closely with suppliers to reduce costs, train employees in cost reduction, find where the true costs are, and use ratios to measure profitability and maximize the use of assets. Throughout the book, Kobert provides strategies for engaging in this detailed analysis.

The Healthy Company: Eight Strategies to Develop People, Productivity, and Profits

Rosen, Robert H., and Berger, Lisa, New York: Perigee Books, 1992
ISBN: 0-87477-708-9
Relying on extensive research, the authors provide strategies for making your company "healthy." The key to a healthy company is having healthy employees who are committed to their work for more reasons than simply money. This book gives specific suggestions and comments from successful executives for making employees and the company healthy and profitable.

Developing Products in Half the Time

Smith, Preston G., and Reinertsen, Donald G., New York: Van Nostrand Reinhold, 1991
ISBN: 0-442-00243-2
Since quality and productivity are essential elements of today's business climate, the authors contend that the key to being successful is producing products as quickly as possible. This book takes the reader through the entire development process and provides specific management techniques that will enable a company to get products on the market quickly, but with the requisite high level of quality.

Competing Against Time

Stalk, George, Jr., and Hout, Thomas M., New York: The Free Press, 1990
ISBN: 0-02-915291-7
The authors contend that time is the equivalent of money, productivity, and quality. With many detailed examples from companies that have put time-based strategies in place, the authors describe exactly how reducing production time can make the critical difference between success and failure.

Downsizing

Tomasko, Robert M., New York: AMACOM, 1990
ISBN: 0-8144-7734-8
This book is an important resource for managers faced with restructuring their organizations and striking a balance between the strategic, the practical, and the humane. It provides a practical, tough-minded, and original analysis of how to make corporate structures lean and effective.

SUGGESTED SEMINARS

The seminars listed here were selected for their appeal to a managerial audience. The reputation of the vendor, the quality of their seminar offerings, and the specific seminar content were considered in the selection process.

Because of the dynamic nature of the seminar marketplace, some seminars may have been upgraded or replaced, and others may no longer be offered. Likewise, costs and locations may have changed since this listing was compiled. We recommend that you contact the vendor directly for updated and additional information.

Competitive Strategy: How to Develop Marketing Plans, Strategies, and Tactics

This program is designed to give participants an expanded market point of view for attaining and sustaining a distinct competitive advantage.
Length: 3 days; Cost: $1,495
Locations: Call vendor
American Management Association
P.O. Box 319, Saranac Lake, NY 12983
Telephone: 800/262-9699

Finance and Accounting for the Non-Financial Executive

This program provides an overview of the financial tools and techniques needed in an increasingly complex business environment. Particular emphasis is placed on understanding financial performance measures and the role the measures play in the planning and control of business operations.
Length: 6 days; Cost: $4,250
Location: Harriman, NY
Columbia University
Graduate School of Business, 2880 Broadway, 4th Floor
New York, NY 10025-6989
Telephone: 212/854-3395

Strategic Financial Planning

This program focuses on the selection, design, and evaluation of strategies that create and enhance shareholder value. It is aimed at all executives with profit responsibility as well as officers in finance and strategic planning.
Length: 2 days; Cost: $1,900
Location: Evanston, IL
Northwestern University
J.L. Kellogg Graduate School of Management, Executive Programs, James L. Allen Center, 2169 Sheridan Road
Evanston, IL 60208-2800
Telephone: 708/864-9270

Creating Strategic Leverage

This workshop provides the missing link between strategy theory and the operating decisions business managers make every day. Participants will learn to identify and exploit opportunities in any given market; avoid common mistakes such as putting money into low leverage areas; translate common planning tools, such as Porter's Five Forces, into actionable programs; refocus resources from current tactical problems to future opportunities; and drive strategic thinking throughout the organization.
Length: 2 days; Cost: $1,295
Locations: Call vendor
SLC Consultants, Inc.
Suite 1400, 30 West Monroe Street, Chicago, IL 60603
Telephone: 312/346-7797

COMMIT TO QUALITY

The quality revolution is sweeping through organizations around the world. The desire for quality is nothing new for many organizations, but success in delivery has been mixed. Now, however, global competition and increasing customer expectations have brought the quest for quality to the forefront.

Traditionally, quality efforts have focused on the end product by emphasizing the detection and correction of defects. Today's approaches view quality as encompassing the entire process — from raw materials to final delivery to the customer.

Beginning with Total Quality Management (TQM), these approaches have gone under many different names. No universal term has emerged, yet many approaches share a common set of assumptions and processes that are referred to here as *Continuous Quality Improvement* (CQI). In addition, a more recent approach that focuses on the radical change of processes is known as *reengineering*.

For quality to be realized, every step in the process must be performed to the highest possible standard. An effective quality approach generally includes a focus on:

- The customer's requirements

- Continuous improvement

- Measurement

- Shared responsibility by everyone, with total commitment from management

- A systems perspective, with an emphasis on process

This three-part section on quality addresses the following topics:

Part 1: Understanding Continuous Quality Improvement

- Defining Continuous Quality Improvement
- Understanding Quality Principles
- Understanding Deming's Principles
- Understanding Juran's Principles
- Understanding the Baldrige National Quality Award Criteria (USA)
- Understanding ISO 9000: International Standards for Quality

Part 2: Implementing Continuous Quality Improvement

- Starting Continuous Quality Improvement
- Focusing on Customer Requirements
- Building Quality into Each Process
- Taking a Systems Perspective
- Developing Criteria for Quality
- Measuring Quality
- Developing Quality Partnerships with Vendors and Suppliers
- Instituting Continuous Improvement
- Celebrating Quality Improvement

Part 3: Reengineering Processes

- Understanding Reengineering Principles
- Creating a Reengineering Strategy
- Applying Reengineering Principles

Valuable Tips

- Read one of the many books available on the subject of quality management.

- Take one step at a time, and don't expect to transform your organization in a year — building a quality management environment takes many years.

- Focus quality improvement on the *entire* organization. The easiest improvements will occur in operations — either production or services. But product innovation, administrative functions, sales, and other infrastructures must also improve, or excess capacity will cause many short-term problems.

- Contract with a consultant who can help your organization select which model to implement and decide how to carry out the implementation.

- Focus on the process as the key to quality improvement.

- Keep the issue of quality alive among your coworkers, upward, downward, and sideways. Take on a leadership role consistent with your belief in and dedication to CQI principles.

- Document and develop criteria for all work processes; the ability to measure is the key.

- Gather information from customers. Set up continual lines of communication with both your internal and external customers. Invite their complaints, comments, and suggestions.

- Gather information on employees' perceptions of the organization's cultural and systemic barriers and supports to their achievement of quality.

- Generate and nurture an open environment in the workplace so that people feel free to discuss issues of quality honestly and to raise problems without fear of retribution.

- Engage your employees as problem-solvers for the problems they are experiencing.

- Focus on improving organizational systems and developing effective work processes, not on "fixing" people. Ineffective systems, rather than individuals, cause most organizational problems.

- Join your local chapter and/or the national organization of the American Society for Quality Control (ASQC), American Society for Training and Development (ASTD), and other professional associations that provide educational opportunities and support systems for organizations implementing CQI.

PART 1

**Defining
Continuous Quality
Improvement**

Understanding Continuous Quality Improvement

In the past, quality has focused only on the final output. Today, however, CQI includes managing *all* of the processes involved in conducting your business. Continuous Quality Improvement:

- Defines quality in terms of what the customer wants and needs

- Is driven by customer requirements, not specifications determined by internal groups

- Views quality as everyone's responsibility

- Recognizes that poor quality is expensive and that high quality has a good return on investment

- Makes quality the priority; believes that high quality and good service result in business success

- Emphasizes the continuing quest to improve processes

- Focuses on developing effective work processes, not on "fixing" unmotivated people or poor performers

- Forges strategic alliances with vendors, suppliers, and distributors

- Drives decision making down to the lowest level possible

- Uses employees working in cross-functional groups to solve problems

- Focuses on continuous improvement, believing that there will always be ways to improve how processes are performed

- Uses process-specific tools to determine the stability of the process and whether improvements are being made

- Requires total commitment from management

- Maximizes the system, rather than an individual process, to avoid suboptimizing the system

- Requires an open system with extensive communication upward, downward, and sideways, without fear of recrimination

- Relies on the education, training, and development of individual employees and teams

Understanding Quality Principles

Many names are linked with quality principles. W. Edwards Deming, Joseph M. Juran, Armand Feigenbaum, and Kauru Ishikawa are all associated with the early quality movement in Japan during the 1940s and 1950s. In the 1980s, the work of Genichi Taguchi, Phil Crosby, Tom Peters, Robert H. Waterman, and William Ouchi gained popularity in the United States.

Today, while there is little agreement, people associate ongoing efforts related to quality with Peter Senge, Margaret Wheatley, Michael Hammer, Alan P. Rummler, Philip B. Brache, and many others. Further, the emphasis on quality in the 1980s led the U.S. Congress to approve the Malcolm Baldrige National Quality Award. Several states followed with their own awards, usually based on the same criteria as the Baldrige Award.

Because of space limitations, this section presents the principles of only a few of these leaders in the quality movement.

Understanding Deming's Principles

W. Edwards Deming, one of the initiators of the quality movement, created a theory of management based on his beliefs about managing quality. For the most part, Deming is silent about how to implement his philosophy. Rather, he challenges organizations to figure out for themselves how to apply his principles to their own needs and structure.

The foundation of Deming's management theory consists of the following 14 points of quality management:

1. Create constancy of purpose toward improvement of product and service, with the aims of becoming competitive, staying in business, and providing jobs.

2. Adopt the new philosophy. We are in a new economic age. Western managers must awaken to the challenge, learn their responsibilities, and take on leadership for change.

3. Cease dependence on inspection to achieve quality. Eliminate the need for inspection on a mass basis by building quality into the product in the first place.

4. End the practice of awarding business on the basis of a price tag. Instead, minimize total cost. Move toward a single supplier for any one item, based on a long-term relationship of loyalty and trust.

5. Improve constantly and forever the system of production and service, to improve quality and productivity and thus constantly decrease costs.

6. Institute training on the job.

7. Institute leadership. The aim of leadership should be to help people, machines, and gadgets do a better job. Leadership of management is in need of overhaul, as well as leadership of production workers.

8. Drive out fear, so that everyone may work effectively for the company.

9. Break down barriers between departments. People in research, design, sales, and production must work as a team to foresee problems of production and use that may arise with the product or service.

10. Eliminate slogans, exhortations, and targets for the work force asking for zero defects and new levels of productivity.

11. a. Eliminate work standards (quotas) on the factory floor. Substitute leadership.

    b. Eliminate management by objective. Eliminate management by numbers or numerical goals. Substitute leadership.

12. a. Remove barriers that rob the hourly worker of his or her right to pride of workmanship. The responsibility of supervisors must be changed from sheer numbers to quality.

    b. Remove barriers that rob people in management and in engineering of their right to pride of workmanship. This means, among other things, abolishment of the annual or merit rating, management by objective, or management by the numbers.

13. Institute a vigorous program of education and self-improvement.

14. Put everyone in the company to work to accomplish the transformation. The transformation is everyone's job.

A very useful exercise for an organization, a team, or a department is to determine what it would mean if each point were implemented and what it would take to implement each point. Such an exercise can help a group identify its strengths and its areas of opportunity.

Understanding Juran's Principles

Like Deming, Joseph M. Juran was actively involved in the quality transformation that occurred in Japan following World War II. Unlike Deming, Juran focuses his approach on the improvement of specific processes, with an explicit implementation process consisting of three basic managerial processes (called the Trilogy): quality improvement, quality planning, and quality control.

For the first process of the Trilogy, *quality improvement*, Juran outlines nine responsibilities for upper management:

1. Create awareness of the need and opportunity for improvement. (Juran sees the need for major improvements in business processes.)

2. Mandate quality improvement; make it a part of every job description.

3. Create the infrastructure: Establish a quality council; select projects for improvement; appoint teams; provide facilitators.

4. Provide training in how to improve quality.

5. Review progress regularly.

6. Give recognition to the winning teams.

7. Propagandize the results.

8. Revise the reward system to reinforce the rate of improvement.

9. Maintain momentum by enlarging the business plan to include goals for quality improvement.

For the second process, *quality planning*, Juran provides five steps:

1. Identify the customers. Anyone who will be affected is a customer, whether external or internal.

2. Determine the customers' needs.

3. Create product features that can meet the customers' needs.

4. Create processes that are capable of producing the product features under operating conditions.

5. Transfer the processes to the operating forces.

Finally, Juran adds three more steps, creating the feedback mechanism he calls *quality control*:

1. Evaluate actual performance.

2. Compare the actual with the goal.

3. Take action on the difference.

Understanding the Baldrige National Quality Award Criteria (USA)

Many U.S. organizations use the Baldrige Award criteria or similar quality award programs sponsored by individual states to compete for awards and recognition. They also use such structures as practical auditing devices for their company-wide quality efforts. Scores are helpful in pointing out the strengths and weaknesses of the company in relation to the given criteria. For your information, the Baldrige categories of quality criteria are listed here. Revised annually, this is the set prepared for 1995.

1.0 Leadership
    1.1 Senior Executive Leadership
    1.2 Leadership System and Organization
    1.3 Public Responsibility and Corporate Citizenship
2.0 Information and Analysis
    2.1 Management of Information and Data
    2.2 Competitive Comparisons and Benchmarking
    2.3 Analysis and Use of Company-Level Data
3.0 Strategic Planning
    3.1 Strategy Development
    3.2 Strategy Deployment
4.0 Human Resource Development and Management
    4.1 Human Resource Planning and Evaluation
    4.2 High Performance Work Systems
    4.3 Employee Education, Training, and Development
    4.4 Employee Well-Being and Satisfaction
5.0 Process Management
    5.1 Design and Introduction of Products and Services
    5.2 Process Management: Product and Service Production and Delivery
    5.3 Process Management: Support Services
    5.4 Management of Supplier Performance
6.0 Business Results
    6.1 Product and Service Quality Results
    6.2 Company Operational and Financial Results
    6.3 Supplier Performance Results

7.0 Customer Focus and Satisfaction
    7.1 Customer and Market Knowledge
    7.2 Customer Relationship Management
    7.3 Customer Satisfaction Determination
    7.4 Customer Satisfaction Results
    7.5 Customer Satisfaction Comparison

The program gives the greatest weight to the Business Results and the Customer Focus and Satisfaction categories, each of which accounts for 25 percent of the total points. The more detailed award criteria are available without cost from:

Malcolm Baldrige National Quality Award
National Institute of Standards and Technology
Administration Building, Room A537
Route 270 and Quince Orchard Road
Gaithersburg, MD 20899-0001
Telephone: 301/975-2036
Fax: 301/948-3716

Understanding ISO 9000: International Standards for Quality

For companies doing business worldwide, international standards are becoming more of an issue. The International Organization for Standardization (ISO), with headquarters in Geneva, Switzerland, oversees more than 90,000 standards through nearly 200 technical committees affecting international commerce in goods and services. It certifies applicant organization sites that meet the appropriate set of criteria.

As of 1995, ISO 9000 compliance is mandatory for some government contracts and for certain products in the European Community Economic Union, where well over 50,000 sites have been certified. To ensure alignment, many organizations are requesting that their suppliers become certified. U.S. site certifications, 2,000 by 1994 and increasing rapidly, are proving useful for public relations and marketing, as well as for proof of compliance.

The ISO 9000 standards are minimal, basically requiring that companies document their quality management practices, whatever those practices may be. As with the Baldrige, these standards apply to an all-encompassing range of categories, including: management responsibility; quality system; contract review; design control; document control; purchasing; purchaser supplied product; product identification and traceability; process control; inspection and testing; inspection, measuring, and test equipment; inspection and test status; control of nonconforming product; corrective action; handling, storage, packaging, and delivery; quality records; internal quality audits; training; servicing; and statistical techniques.

"ISO does not bring one single element of business management into play that a well-managed company isn't doing anyway," says Roy Richardson, former vice president of quality management systems for Graco Inc. "But the effectiveness of our business processes is being enhanced tremendously."

PART 2

Starting Continuous Quality Improvement

Implementing Continuous Quality Improvement

Many organizations are incorporating elements of Continuous Quality Improvement (CQI) into their business practices. To whatever degree works best for your organization, use the following suggestions to help you begin or enhance your quality efforts wisely:

- Visit companies in related industries to learn what they are doing, what has worked for them, what hasn't worked, and why.

- Learn the practices of companies that have been recognized for their quality efforts, such as winners of the Malcolm Baldrige National Quality Award or another quality award.

- Ask your suppliers and customers about their quality improvement efforts.

- Read extensively about CQI theory and case studies; many books and articles have been written about CQI.

- Involve top management in learning about CQI, perhaps by inviting them to participate with you in the steps outlined earlier.

- Build a consensus among key players in the organization that CQI is necessary, and develop a strategy to adopt or create a CQI process.

- Be aware that CQI works best from the top down, but that you can always begin with your span of control.

- Attend conferences on quality conducted by quality experts to gain familiarity with approaches that others have used successfully.

- Invite quality consultants in to talk about their CQI processes.

Focusing on Customer Requirements

Before you can implement CQI, you must create your own definition of quality in your organization. For example, quality may be any or all of the following:

- Achieve customer satisfaction by meeting customers' requirements.

- Surpass customer expectations in delivering your services.

- Deliver outstanding products and services that meet and anticipate customer needs.

To determine your definition of quality and to establish measures of success, work with your customers. For some groups, customers are other people and groups within the organization (internal customers); for others, customers are external to the organization. Furthermore, in a quality-focused environment, managers consider their direct reports to be their customers — the direct reports are the recipients of the manager's services. Regardless of whether your customers are internal or external, the same principles apply.

To determine your customers' requirements, ask them questions that elicit the following kinds of information:

- The purpose and use of the product or service

- Specifications about the product or the service itself

- Service requirements

- Cost considerations

- Delivery issues

- Previous problems or concerns (see the Focus on Customer Needs section for specific questions)

- Anticipated future needs

- Appearance requirements, if applicable

With the customer, identify both the key requirements and the "nice to have, but not essential" features. Then manage with the intention of meeting both sets of requirements.

You, alone, cannot determine whether you successfully met these requirements. You must also involve your customers in making this determination. A wide range of options is available for doing this:

- Customer focus groups

- Customer interviews

- Customer follow-up telephone calls

- Customer surveys

- Analysis of warranty requests

- Tabulation of compliments and complaints received

- Repeat business

- Referrals

Such measures allow you to revisit your customers' requirements, thus creating an unending cycle of: determining customer requirements, leading to products and services intended to meet these requirements, and leading to determining whether the requirements were met.

Building Quality into Each Process

CQI requires that quality be the focus of each step of each process. The outcome cannot be quality when any step in any process does not incorporate the principles of quality. To assist in building quality into each step of each process, take the following actions:

1. Create cross-functional teams to study and recommend ways to build quality into all steps. The charter of these teams should include identifying the work processes involved in each product or service — that is, what is involved in finally getting the product or service to the customer. This is usually done by documenting each process, often using flow-charting techniques in addition to narrative outlines.

2. Next, have the teams clarify and document each part of the work process in terms of what the customers' requirements are:

   - What is needed to meet the customers' requirements?

   - What is the most useful process?

   - How can we measure whether we are meeting our customers' requirements for this process?

3. As the final product of a specific quality improvement focus, have each team develop clearly defined work processes with specific objectives, standards, and procedures for measuring success.

Do not attempt to "improve" processes until these steps have been followed, no matter how tempting it might be. Until documentation with measurement is in place, it is impossible to know whether any change is, in fact, an improvement, or whether you are simply tampering with the system.

Taking a Systems Perspective

All of its processes together comprise an organization's total system. Any team attempting to improve a process must understand the total system and how the process fits into that system. Without that understanding, improvements in one process may actually decrease the quality present in another process. For example, making improvements to increase sales, without comparable improvements in the ability of operations to produce, may increase pressure on production so that quality actually diminishes. This is called *suboptimization*. Consider the following actual incident:

> A refrigerator manufacturer wanted to reduce production costs. It gave the purchasing department incentives for improving (decreasing) the cost of products used in manufacturing. Purchasing was able to locate a vendor willing to sell hinges at a price considerably less than the current vendor's. The company switched to the new vendor, reducing costs from $.15 to $.03 per hinge, a 500 percent decrease. However, it didn't take long to discover that the hinges did not last through the warranty period. As a result, the company had to hire a number of maintenance people to go out and replace all of the hinges. The company ended up with losses in the millions of dollars over a relatively minor, but faulty, part.

This is a perfect example of suboptimization.

Whenever any change is made in a process, it is imperative that all other processes in the system be examined to determine the impact this change will have on them.

Further, there is almost universal agreement that 85 percent or more of the problems in any organization are the result of the system, not the individuals within the system. A systems perspective, then, begins with the assumption that, when a problem arises, it is because something is wrong with a process in a system. Only after thorough examination of the processes is it cost-effective to look at individuals to determine whether training, transfer, or outplacement is needed.

The same is true for recognition and compensation systems. When it appears that one person is consistently outperforming his or her peers, always ask the question, "What is there in the system that allows this person to perform so well?" Answering this question may identify process changes that would help others in the system become equally productive.

Developing Criteria for Quality

Specifications in a quality environment are driven by customer requirements and are influenced by the competition. Where competition is minimal, it may be enough to simply meet the requirements of the customer, as long as you keep close tabs on those needs and on the competition. In highly competitive environments, however, you must go beyond the requirements and surpass your competitors in ways that your customers value. If you are not proactive in going beyond expectations, you can be sure that your competitors will be.

Because the quality of the end product or service depends on the quality at all steps along the way, specifications should be developed for each step in the process. However, this can be done only if the resulting standards or goals are valid. For a goal to be valid:

1. Data must be derived from a system in a state of statistical control. (That is, it must be shown with historical measurement that the process is stable.)

2. Valid methodology must be used. (That is, it can't just be a manager's wish that profits will grow 20 percent annually; a method for accomplishing this goal must be developed.)

3. Employees must be able to meet the goal or develop a plan capable of meeting the goal. (That is, the goal must be attainable.)

Unless these three criteria are in place, you will not be able to develop quality standards or goals. To implement these criteria, use the suggestions under Measuring Quality in this section.

Measuring Quality

Measuring your work against defined standards is essential to the quality process. *What* you measure is determined by your documentation of each process. *How* you measure this is determined by the techniques that will give you practical, useful information about how well each step in the process is being performed.

To help your measurement practices and techniques truly support your quality processes, you and your team can:

- Get exposure to a variety of quality measurement techniques and tools (known as statistical process control, or SPC) through reading and attending seminars or workshops. These tools include pareto charts, run charts, control charts, and so forth.

- Select measurement strategies that are user friendly and appropriate for the process.

- Be sure to measure the *right* criteria in the *right* way; make sure the processes and measures are customer focused.

- Measure frequently.

- Use both quantitative and qualitative data.

- Make the results visible.

- Present the results in a way that people can easily understand.

- Focus on the key measures for effectiveness; don't overwhelm people with too much data.

- Use the results.

- Train people on measurement techniques.

- Have employees analyze and present their own results and next steps. Evaluation is not your responsibility; it belongs to the people doing the work process.

Developing Quality Partnerships with Vendors and Suppliers

Vendors and suppliers are the beginning of a quality process. As their customer, you have a right to require that they use quality processes in their work for you. To help you develop quality partnerships with your suppliers, use the following guidelines:

- Determine your requirements for quality and service from your vendors, and communicate those needs.

- Share your customers' requirements for your products and services with the vendors and suppliers who will be contributing goods or services to the creation of those products.

- Select vendors on the basis of quality, not just price.

- Develop partnerships, and even strategic alliances, with your vendors and suppliers so you can count on each other. Let them know that, if they deliver quality and good service, you will give them your business.

- If a competitor of your vendor presents a better offer, give your vendor a chance to respond.

- If your vendors do not have a quality process in place, invite them to participate in your training programs. Work with them to help them implement their own quality plan.

- Don't accept a lack of quality from your vendors. If they are not committed to a quality system and are unwilling to begin one, work with your team, the organization, and the industry to develop options for other vendors.

Instituting Continuous Improvement

Quality and service standards and expectations are moving targets. What is considered exceptional quality today will be routinely expected tomorrow — an excellent rationale for continuous improvement.

Consider a three-pronged approach to continuous improvement:

- Fix problems immediately upon discovery.

- Prevent problems.

- Improve processes.

You'll probably be doing all of the above all of the time, with sometimes the same and sometimes different processes. The prevention and, better yet, the *preclusion* of problems is a goal in itself. Nevertheless, the ultimate goal of quality management goes as far beyond mere avoidance of errors, defects, and problems as you can take it. Quality management encourages breakthrough thinking on new ways to both surprise and please the customer. To do that, you must decrease the number of preventive interventions. Here's an example of some guidelines for doing so:

1. When a problem occurs, determine whether it has happened before and if it will happen again. If the answer is "yes" or "maybe," form a team to examine why it may happen again. The team should focus on three to five levels of "why" to identify clearly the steps in the evolution of the problem.

    Example: A customer does not get a requested nonsmoking hotel room.

    Ask: Has this happened before? (Answer: Yes, about two times per day.)

    Will it happen again? (Answer: Most likely.)

    Examine why: Level 1: The hotel did not know the customer wanted a nonsmoking room.

    Level 2: There was no record of the request in the computer.

Level 3: There was nothing in the special comments section on the computer screen.

Often, simply asking "why" will identify causes and suggest options.

2. To focus on prevention, have the team look at the cause of the problem and ask how it could have happened, or, if it's a recurring problem, how it *can* happen.

Example: To continue with the previous example, asking how the problem happened might generate the following responses:

- Reservations clerk did not know of the request.
- Customer only *thinks* he or she made the request.
- No nonsmoking rooms were available.
- Travel agency did not tell the hotel.
- Customer's secretary did not tell the travel agency.
- Hotel did not put the request into the computer.

3. Next, the team should determine an improvement plan that addresses each possible cause.

Example: Some possible improvement plans for the problem with reserving nonsmoking rooms might be:

- Survey customers or use available data to determine an adequate percentage of nonsmoking rooms.
- Standardize the procedure of requesting nonsmoking or smoking rooms when reservations are made.
- Develop frequent-customer profiles that include room preferences.
- Put a section on the reservation card that specifically asks for smoking preference, rather than just including it in the special comments section.
- Give travel agencies a list of what you need to know from them.
- Educate travel agents through industry meetings about the importance of asking for smoking preference.

Celebrating Quality Improvement

For quality management to work over the long term, it must be institutionalized. Top management and organizational systems and processes must support it. In addition, quality champions and the improvements they make must be recognized and rewarded. To celebrate quality improvement:

- Make successes visible.

- Ask quality teams to present their work at company-wide gatherings.

- Make a videotape that documents the quality improvement and the team's role in it, and distribute it to employees, customers, vendors, and stockholders.

- Celebrate efforts as well as successes.

- Provide feedback to employees on an ongoing basis; don't save it up for an annual performance review or an organization-wide meeting. When an individual or a team does something well, let them know immediately.

- Be cautious about providing public statements or recognitions. Everyone in a process has a supplier and a customer. Everyone in that process determines the success or failure of that process.

PART 3

Understanding Reengineering Principles

Reengineering Processes

As organizations pursue sustained customer satisfaction, they continue to evolve new quality management approaches and related change efforts. These approaches offer a great variety of methods and tools for documenting, measuring, streamlining, improving, and transforming business processes.

While not all of these approaches are compatible, they do all share a focus on systems. Peter Senge, for instance, outlines the kind of systems thinking that allows individuals and teams in the "learning organization" to transform processes across their whole enterprise and all markets. Transitioning from quality theory into the study of complex systems, Margaret Wheatley brings models of creative, systems-sensitive leadership. Michael Treacy and others identify *value,* which is key to quality thinking, as the new live wire in business. They are shifting the primary metric from quality control statistics to the quantified value chain.

Meanwhile, use of the "re-" approaches is spreading: reinventing, rethinking, and, most significant, Michael Hammer's and James

Champy's *reengineering* the organization. All more or less radical, these systemic restructurings stress the fundamental transformation of basic processes and work relationships, rather than their continuous, incremental improvement.

As a result of management change efforts in "total quality," "continuous quality improvement," Baldrige Award criteria, ISO 9000 requirements, cycle time reduction, and related systemic approaches, the structure of many workplaces has shifted from functional organization to process organization. Because process organization allows a business to act faster and more seamlessly in dynamic environments, it is clearly a more adaptive structure than the functional divisions that breed bureaucracy, redundancy, and intra-organizational competition.

Like W. Edwards Deming, however, today's proponents of systemic change do not ignore the people — the teams — who create, fuel, and manage the process, who create and add the value. You, the manager, are there to support the people and their processes, and to create an environment where both can be continuously improved or, where necessary, fundamentally transformed.

Whatever quality philosophy and methods best fit your business and its goals, keep in mind the exhortations of systems visionary and futurist Stan Davis:

- Understand first that your business is something quite distinct from your organization.

- Apply original thinking to identify the business you are in, the stage of your business's life cycle, and its historical economy, lest you improve, design, redesign, and reengineer processes for the wrong business or era.

- Committing to quality means scoping out the long term while keeping your eye on the fast ball.

Creating a Reengineering Strategy

To create an effective reengineering approach, you need to examine:

- Customer satisfaction, measured and anticipated

- Your business's processes and systems

- Your business's economic and historical contexts

- How added value in efforts and results are measured

- How everyone's knowledge is developed and used

- Process organization and teamwork

Start it right. Follow these guidelines for a successful strategy:

1. **Work to understand, along with others in your organization, what your basic business is.** This is not a frivolous exercise. If, for instance, your company manufactures refrigerators, the basic business you are in is food preservation, not refrigerator production. Shifting your perspective in this way allows your people to better see the quality needs of the business, as well as to better generate ideas for innovative, even breakthrough, products and services.

2. **Help people throughout the organization learn who your customer was, is, and will be.** Gather all the information available on your customers and their preference patterns. Give this data new shape in light of new strategy and new process organization possibilities.

3. **Help clarify in the organization what your organization wants to accomplish in a change effort.** Articulate goals clearly and specifically. Communicate them repeatedly through various vehicles.

4. **Acquaint yourself with some of the current bestsellers, older classics, and other books** and articles that call for systemic change and process organization. Get a good sense of what's available, and of what companies have tried, with what success, and lessons learned.

5. **Identify some models and related methods of organizational transformation and process improvement** that are relevant to your business and its goals.

6. **Help top management and others determine which approach or combination of approaches best serves** the short-term needs of your business and which ones serve its long-term needs.

7. **Obtain, as early as you can and from as many people in the organization as you can, information and input** about the needs for systemic and process change that they see in the business, most specifically in customer and vendor relationships.

8. **Understand, and help others to understand, that as much merit as any quality methodology may have in**

itself, only the people can transform the organization.
The methodology and the quality tools you choose are there to
help your people. It is their commitment, shared knowledge,
and openness to change that will create success.

9. **Develop specific implementation plans with the people
   involved in the processes to be changed.** Implementation
   and execution are where the real work of change lies. Get the
   people who will do the work engaged in designing the work.

10. **Build into processes noninvasive ways of keeping in
    touch with customers.** Encourage people to be imaginative
    in identifying how and where to collect information as part of
    other core processes that touch the customer. Document and
    measure, wherever you can, customer perceptions of given
    products, services, and their various features.

11. **Use benchmarking and other measurement techniques**
    not as ends in themselves, but as ongoing feedback that helps
    regulate how you keep improving processes. Think of your
    quality metrics as the levers and oars of your navigation.

12. **Keep learning the process of managing process change.**
    Engage your team throughout but take responsibility for the
    communications, resources, and overall coordination the team
    needs to carry out the details. See that these things happen
    according to an expected schedule. Use meetings efficiently
    and sparingly, observing some agreed-upon set of meeting
    ground rules.

13. **Be alert for opportunities to develop learning and
    leadership throughout the organization.** Quality is a
    team effort. As Deming says, "The transformation is
    everybody's job." Help get everybody and their potential
    involved.

14. **Demonstrate your commitment to quality in your
    attention and actions.** Mission statements, stated
    principles, and outlined goals play a definite role, and in some
    undertakings, may even be necessary. But they are never
    sufficient. Automatic pilot won't guide change efforts; decisions
    won't manage the system. Roll up your sleeves and help
    execute. Successful quality strategies are more about walk
    than talk.

Applying Reengineering Principles

As you undertake reengineering efforts, keep these principles in mind:

- Define quality from the point of view and experience of the customer.

- Stress the continuing nature of improvement in relation to known customer satisfaction.

- Look to the long-term success of the business.

- Build relationships with customers.

- Forge strategic alliances with vendors, suppliers, and distributors.

- Show that low quality is expensive, high quality a good return on investment.

- Maximize whole systems rather than individual processes in those systems.

- Use documentation and statistical tools to determine stability in a system and to measure improvements.

- Reconfigure functional work groups into cross-functional teams.

- Drive decision making and leadership potential down and through the organization.

- Develop open communications and learning up, down, and across the organization without fear of recrimination.

- Focus more on systemic causes of problems than on individual performance per se.

- Require the support of top management.

- Tend to evolve, branch out, and blend into other strategies for organizational transformation.

Periodically review your efforts against these qualities.

RECOMMENDED READINGS

The publications listed here were selected for their content and suitability to a managerial audience.

Breakthrough Process Redesign

Adair, Charlene B., and Murray, Bruce A., New York: AMACOM, 1994
ISBN: 0-8144-5031-8
The authors provide a clear guide to total quality improvement. Their method integrates redesign with customer value, corporate goals, leadership, and innovation.

Beyond Quality

Bowles, Jerry, and Hammond, Joshua, Berkeley, CA: Berkeley, 1992
ISBN: 0-425-13408-3
The authors outline a step-by-step process for implementing continuous improvement strategies. They provide examples of the efforts of the American corporation to improve quality, discuss why quality control is merely the first step in the continuous improvement process, explain the importance of CEO involvement and support, and suggest additional criteria above and beyond those outlined by the Malcolm Baldrige National Quality Award.

Baldrige Award Winning Quality (5th ed.)

Brown, Mark Graham, New York: Quality Resources, 1995
ISBN: 0-527-76294-6
This publication is a useful guidebook for those applying for the Malcolm Baldrige National Quality Award, as well as for those interested in using the criteria to plan, guide, and assess their total quality management effort. The author explains the ninety-nine areas that comprise the seven major categories of the Baldrige Award criteria and recommends strategies on how to fulfill the requirements in each of these areas.

Business Process Benchmarking

Camp, Robert C., Milwaukee, WI: ASQC Quality Press, 1995
ISBN: 0-87389-296-8
Benchmarking should be used to improve business processes and not only to solve narrow operational problems. Camp offers a ten-step plan adapted for evaluating processes and also shows managers how to establish, support, and sustain benchmarking. Six case studies and seven appendices on resources conclude this detailed and authoritative guide.

Firing on All Cylinders: The Service/Quality System for High Powered Corporate Performance	**Clemmer, Jim, and Sheehy, Barry,** Burr Ridge, IL: Irwin Professional Publishing, 1992 ISBN: 1-55623-704-9 This book is a guide for all businesses and organizations on how to improve their service and quality in order to succeed in a competitive and demanding market. The authors describe the twelve "cylinders" that make up the Achieve Service/Quality System and provide examples of how effective use of these cylinders results in exceptional service and quality.
The Death and Life of the American Quality Movement	**Cole, Robert E.,** New York: Oxford University Press, 1995 ISBN: 0-19-509206-6 In this series of fifteen essays, noted experts demonstrate that Total Quality Management remains of vital importance for an organization's continued success. They identify seven key elements of a successful quality initiative: provide leadership from management; focus on meeting customer needs; emphasize the quality of business processes; decentralize decision making; implement cross-functional management; continuously improve while developing breakthrough strategies; and create an effective reward system.
The Monster Under the Bed	**Davis, Stan, and Botkin, Jim,** New York: Simon & Schuster, 1994 ISBN: 0-671-87107-2 The knowledge industry is changing the way business is conducted and it will dominate the global marketplace. This book makes several observations about business's role as purveyor of knowledge to customers, employees, and eventually to schools, including: the increasing role of business in education, the idea that learning is a continuous process, and the notion that any business can become a knowledge business.
Deming's Profound Changes	**Delavigne, Kenneth T., and Robertson, J. Daniel,** Englewood Cliffs, NJ: Prentice-Hall, 1994 ISBN: 0-13-292690-3 This book is designed to help the reader understand the differences between traditional management practices and those taught by Dr. W. Edwards Deming. The authors trace, over the past century, the development of various management techniques and the effect on organizations.

Out of the Crisis

Deming, W. Edwards, Cambridge, MA: MIT, Center for Advanced Engineering Study, 1986
ISBN: 0-911379-01-0
In this, his classic text, Deming explains, with illustrations and graphs, what he believes managers have been doing wrong, informs them what they must do differently, and shows them "Deming's way out of the crisis."

Statistics for the 21st Century

Duncan, Joseph, and Gross, Andrew, Burr Ridge, IL: Irwin Professional Publishing, 1995
ISBN: 0-7863-0328-X
This is a guide for understanding and analyzing the multitude of statistics currently available. It takes a critical look at the reliability of these statistics. For example, the reliability of most statistics depends on who compiles them and how they are used. This guide will help you discern which statistics are worthwhile and helpful to your business.

Reengineering the Corporation

Hammer, Michael, and Champy, James, New York: HarperBusiness, 1993
ISBN: 0-88730-640-3
In the current business environment of global competition, companies must abandon outdated notions of how the work is done and ensure that processes and procedures are efficient and effective. This book provides a roadmap for the reengineering journey, showing how to focus on your larger objectives, not minute tasks.

The Reengineering Revolution

Hammer, Michael, and Stanton, Steven A., New York: HarperCollins, 1995
ISBN: 0-88730-736-1
In *Reengineering the Corporation*, Michael Hammer introduced reengineering and now in this handbook he offers practical guidance on essential elements of reengineering. Specifically addressed are the most dangerous mistakes in reengineering and how to avoid them, how to assess whether management is truly committed to reengineering, how smaller companies can benefit from reengineering, and how to overcome the greatest obstacle to reengineering which is people's resistance to change.

Creating High Performance Organizations	**Lawler, Edward E., III.; Mohrman, Susan Albers; and Ledford, Gerald E., Jr.,** San Francisco: Jossey Bass, 1995 ISBN: 0-7879-0171-7 This book presents the results of an extensive study on the adoption and impact of total quality management and employee involvement practices on the largest U.S. companies. The authors explain the type of practices service and manufacturing firms have implemented, the results they have achieved, and how management practices have changed since 1990.
The ISO 9000 Quality Manual Developer	**Novack, Janet,** Englewood Cliffs, NJ: Prentice-Hall, 1995 ISBN: 0-13-215477-3 This book is a tool for understanding the ISO 9000 quality standard requirements, evaluating your organization against this standard, and developing strategies for meeting the requirements. Also included is a diskette that contains policies for initiating the ISO 9000 quality standard.
Manufacturing Renaissance	**Pisano, Gary P., and Hayes, Robert H.,** Boston: Harvard Business School Press, 1995 ISBN: 0-87584-610-6 This collection of twenty *Harvard Business Review* articles explores how to gain a competitive advantage through a manufacturing strategy based on flexibility, responsiveness, innovation, and customer service. One article details how to reorganize the factory in order to achieve greater flexibility. Another describes four stages of manufacturing effectiveness culminating with the production process actually generating new opportunities for other functions.
Commit to Quality	**Townsend, Patrick L.,** New York: John Wiley & Sons, 1990 ISBN: 0-471-52018-7 Townsend focuses on quality processes specifically for service industries. Those he describes combine concepts from participative management, quality aids, and value analysis. He also delineates strategies for enlisting employee support, providing insights into the leadership principles necessary for the process to succeed.

The Discipline of Market Leaders

Treacy, Michael, and Wiersma, Fred, Reading, MA: Addison-Wesley, 1995
ISBN: 0-201-40648-9
This book seeks to answer the question of why some companies provide much better prices and services to their customers. Companies that are market leaders have focused attention and resources on different things. Market leaders chose to excel in one of the customer "value disciplines:" best cost, best product, or best solution. Focusing on one of these disciplines means knowing which one to choose, designing your organization around it, and offering better value year after year.

Deming Management at Work

Walton, Mary, New York: Perigee Books, 1991
ISBN: 0-399-51685-9
Walton outlines how to apply Deming's management methods using examples, quotations, and stories. This guide serves as a practical, accessible introduction to this system-wide quality management approach.

Leadership and The New Science

Wheatley, Margaret J., San Francisco: Berrett-Koehler, 1992
ISBN: 1-881052-44-3
The author contends that "new sciences" such as discoveries in quantum physics, chaos theory, and biology provide insights into how people organize their work and life. The book discusses issues affecting all organizations: order, change, autonomy, control, structure, planning, and innovation. Descriptions of new scientific discoveries are also included.

SUGGESTED SEMINARS

The seminars listed here were selected for their appeal to a managerial audience. The reputation of the vendor, the quality of their seminar offerings, and the specific seminar content were considered in the selection process.

Because of the dynamic nature of the seminar marketplace, some seminars may have been upgraded or replaced, and others may no longer be offered. Likewise, costs and locations may have changed since this listing was compiled. We recommend that you contact the vendor directly for updated and additional information.

How to Plan and Implement a Total Quality Management Program

This program presents a corporate approach to quality as an across-the-board strategic priority. Participants will learn about the principles of Total Quality Management, a four-phase approach to Total Quality Management, variation reduction techniques, and the impact of design on quality. The relationship of TQM to the Malcolm Baldrige National Quality Award and ISO 9000 is also examined.
Length: 3 days; Cost: $1,800
Locations: Call vendor
American Management Association
P.O. Box 319, Saranac Lake, NY 12983
Telephone: 800/262-9699

ISO-9000: Certification and Continuous Improvement — How to Integrate ISO-9000 Into Your Business Strategy for World-Class Performance

This program covers the certification process for ISO 9000 and its rewards once achieved. Participants will learn steps for implementation, what problems to avoid, and how to maximize benefits to decision-making and competitiveness. The relationship to the Malcolm Baldrige National Quality Award is also discussed.
Length: 2 days; Cost: $1,380
Locations: Call vendor
American Management Association
P.O. Box 319, Saranac Lake, NY 12983
Telephone: 800/262-9699

Process Improvement Through Work Redesign

This course focuses on implementing process improvement efforts and leads to creating new tasks for individuals and teams, as well as new opportunities for customer involvement.
Length: 2 days; Cost: $695
Locations: Call vendor
Association for Quality and Participation
801-B West 8th Street, Cincinnati, OH 45203
Telephone: 800/733-3310

Partners in Quality

This program addresses the "soft side" of Total Quality while focusing on both internal and external customer/supplier relationships. Through a simulation and an assessment instrument, participants diagnose the quality of their interactions with customers and suppliers. They develop skills to create an environment of trust, integrity, and caring between customers and suppliers; formulate plans to make positive changes in key partnerships; and develop a strategy for tracking improvements that occur.

Length: 2 days; Cost: $595
Location: Atlanta
**The Atlanta Consulting Group
1600 Parkwood Circle, Suite 200, Atlanta, GA 30339
Telephone: 800/852-8224**

Strategic Quality Planning

In this highly interactive workshop, participants learn how to incorporate quality goals into strategic business plans. This seminar defines the actions required to integrate your quality efforts with your business objectives.

Length: 2 days; Cost: $995
Locations: Call vendor
**Juran Institute, Inc.
11 River Road, P.O. Box 811, Wilton, CT 06897-0811
Telephone: 800/338-7726**

Creating World Class Quality: A Strategic Evaluation

This program is targeted to upper-level management and other key staff members with involvement in quality. The seminar outlines the initiatives that leadership must take as it seeks to move aggressively toward installing a corporate-wide quality improvement process.

Length: 6 days; Cost: $3,650
Location: Evanston, IL
**Northwestern University
J.L. Kellogg Graduate School of Management, Executive Programs, James L. Allen Center, 2169 Sheridan Road
Evanston, IL 60208-2800
Telephone: 708/864-9270**

Management Today and Tomorrow: How it Must Change

This seminar is designed to familiarize managers with Dr. W. Edwards Deming's philosophy and methodology. Topics include: Deming's fourteen points; the failure of adversarial competition; the interrelationships between people, leadership, and environment; management of stable and unstable systems; training and leadership; operational definitions; and profound knowledge for transformation.

Length: 4 days; Cost: $995
Location: Marina del Rey, CA
Quality Enhancement Seminars, Inc.
1081 Westwood Boulevard, Suite 217
Los Angeles, CA 90024
Telephone: 800/574-5544

Strategic Quality Management Program

This program is designed to provide a framework from which to manage an organization using strategic quality management. Topics include: strategic quality management; leadership and change; customer satisfaction and feedback into improvement activities; improving processes; human resource management; cost of quality and performance measures; ISO 9000; and construction of a quality plan.

Length: 5 days; Cost: $4,300
Location: Ann Arbor, MI
University of Michigan Business School
Executive Education Center, Ann Arbor, MI 48109-1234
Telephone: 313/763-1000

Managing Service: Reengineering for Customer Satisfaction

This program is for managers who believe that a critical "product" advantage lies in the quality of the organization's customer service. The program examines significant implications of providing a service orientation from management, marketing, financial, and strategic perspectives. It also discusses concrete steps to improve your organization's customer service.

Length: 5 days; Cost: $4,550
Location: Philadelphia
University of Pennsylvania, The Wharton School
Aresty Institute of Executive Education, Steinberg
Conference Center, 255 South 38th Street
Philadelphia, PA 19104-6359
Telephone: 800/255-3932

FOCUS ON CUSTOMER NEEDS

Customer focus is the cornerstone of business success. Your customers may be external to the organization, or they may be internal, such as the functional groups or other business groups you serve. Customer focus includes — but goes beyond — customer service. It means listening to customers; identifying, meeting, and exceeding their needs; and anticipating their future needs. It means aligning what you do and how you do it with what the customers need, not with what the organization wants.

This section on customer focus includes suggestions on the following topics:

Part 1: Understanding the Customer

- Defining Your Customer Base
- Recognizing Customer Needs
- Encouraging and Listening to Feedback

Part 2: Developing and Implementing Customer Focus

- Developing a Strategy
- Delivering on Customer Commitments
- Recovering from Mistakes
- Removing Barriers to Customer Service
- Soliciting Employee Feedback and Suggestions
- Practicing What You Preach

Part 3: Improving Your Customer Service Team

- Communicating Your Customer Service Statement
- Hiring the Right People
- Training for Superior Customer Service
- Rewarding Excellent Customer Service

Valuable Tips

- Examine everything you do against the criterion "Does this contribute to meeting customer needs?" or "What value does this add to the customer?"

- List the needs you believe your customers have. Then ask your customers what their needs are. Note the differences.

- Personally take time every day to ask customers, "How are we doing?" *Actively* listen to what they say. Communicate these findings to the appropriate people in your organization. Distribute customer feedback and information.

- Develop standards for the products and services that meet or surpass customer requirements.

- Look "outside in," not "inside out" — look at things from your customer's viewpoint.

- Conduct focus groups with customers to determine what they see as your strengths and weaknesses. What improvements do they recommend?

- Interview customers who have stopped using your products or services. Find out their reasons. Discover what you can do to win them back.

- Interview or conduct focus groups with potential customers who do not use your products or services.

- Don't assume that your customers have the same criteria for evaluation as you do. Find out what is important to them.

- Develop your vision and quality goals in terms of exceeding your customers' expectations.

- Treat your internal customers with the same care and respect as you treat your external customers.

- As a manager, consider your staff to be your customers.

- Use cross-functional teams to improve work processes to more clearly meet customer requirements.

- Develop a customer satisfaction survey and send it to your customers. Use the results to improve your service. Use a feedback instrument for teams.

- Keep a file of newspaper clippings, trade and business journals, annual reports, and marketing research on each of your customers to stay in touch with their business.

- Meet with your front-line people to discuss how you can be more supportive of their efforts with customers.

- Benchmark organizations that have a reputation for focusing on customers.

- Listen to the questions new people ask about your work processes, service, and so forth.

- Reward staff members who consistently provide good customer service.

- Eliminate excess paperwork from your complaint-resolution process.

- Create a "Customer Pleaser of the Month/Week/Day" board to publicly recognize those staff members who provide excellent customer service.

- Provide special training for all employees on customer service. Include tips on how to handle difficult customers and how to carry out service-related company policies and work processes.

- Fully explain and communicate your commitment to high standards of customer service to your employees. Then be a role model.

- Handle the paperwork necessary for complaint resolution after the customer has left.

- One week after a complaint has been resolved, call the customer to check up on his or her satisfaction level.

- Provide a suggestion box for employees and customers to submit their ideas on improving customer service.

- Reserve one hour a week to identify ideas for improving customer service.

- Review feedback from customers.

- Develop a process to track the trends in feedback from customers.

- Create a monthly internal newsletter that includes:
  - Tips on dealing with difficult customers
  - Customer focused policies and procedures
  - Summaries of current customer service readings
  - Recognition of excellent customer service

- Have lunch with internal customers and listen to their needs.

- When hiring, look for good customer service qualities, such as: maturity, positive outlook, tolerance, outgoing personality, and friendliness.

- Use a team concept for your customer relations or service people. A client is more likely to find someone they relate to when there are choices.

PART 1

**Defining Your
Customer Base**

Understanding the Customer

Satisfied customers are the key focus of successful organizations. They fuel success and growth. Every organization has both internal and external customers. External customers purchase your products and services, and internal customers are your employees and the functional groups you serve.

The first step in developing a customer focus is to identify your customers. The following suggestions will help you define your customer base:

1. List all of the constituencies or the people you need to satisfy in your job. Include both internal and external customers and the product or service you provide to each. Also include the people who *think* you should satisfy them.

2. Once you have identified particular individuals or groups as customers, determine the specific expectations these customers have of you. (Rather than assuming you know, ask.) Be sure to include internal customer expectations as well as external customer expectations.

3. Periodically update your list of customers and their expectations.

**Recognizing
Customer Needs**

Countless organizations have attempted to meet their own perceptions of their customers' needs and expectations, rather than asking customers directly about their needs and expectations. They may have provided 15 options in a product, whereas the customers wanted one or two options that worked reliably. To accurately identify your customers' needs:

- Survey your customers. Make the survey simple, but ensure that it generates specific information about your ability to satisfy. Include such questions as:
  - What do you like about our product/service? (Easy to use, inexpensive, reliable, doesn't break, choice of colors, or adapts to my individual needs)
  - What do you like about our competitors' product/service?
  - What service qualities are important to you? (Efficiency, no-hassle return, friendliness, reliability, or 800 number)
  - Why did you buy from us? (Convenience, good reputation, salesperson, or better product/service than competitor)
  - Tell us about a time when you received poor service. What happened? How can we handle it better in the future?

- Personally call 30 customers and ask how satisfied they were with your product or service. Ask for specifics, and also inquire about aspects with which they were dissatisfied.

- Conduct focus groups with your customers.

- Conduct focus groups with your organization's front line people. Ask them to define their customers and those customers' expectations and requirements for doing business. Then develop and implement a plan to meet your customers' desires more fully.

- Make complaining easy. Provide a suggestion box so that customers can anonymously evaluate your performance.

- Answer the following questions:
  - What patterns emerged from our customer satisfaction research?
  - Why are our customers using our product or service?
  - What other customers can we serve?
  - Why don't we have their business?
  - How can we attract that business?
  - What customer needs are not being met by our company?

- To anticipate customer needs, research your customers' industries to keep up-to-date with their business.

- Keep a file of clippings on every customer or customer group. Investigate the following resources:
  - Trade and business journals
  - Annual reports
  - Newspapers
  - Market research reports

Encouraging and Listening to Feedback

It's sometimes hard to listen to critical comments. But it's essential to listen, take the comments seriously, and not become defensive when customers tell you something you don't want to hear. To encourage and be more receptive to customers' feedback:

- Provide formal and informal ways for customers, both internal and external, to give you feedback without fear of retribution.

- Spend time on the front line yourself.

- Ask people: "How are we doing? How can we improve?"

- As you listen to others, ensure that you are *listening,* not trying to sell or convince them. Refer to the Listen to Others section of this Handbook for suggestions on improving your listening skills.

- React in a positive way to any information from customers.

- Focus on the problem presented, not on the person.

- Treat customers' perceptions as reality; for them, they are reality.

- Check back regularly to see how things are going after you have responded to a customer's comment.

- Clarify the indirect messages (the subtext) of any feedback you receive by asking questions.

PART 2 Developing and Implementing Customer Focus

Developing a Strategy

Once you understand what is important to your current and potential customer base, determine clear strategies for implementing a strong customer focus. These strategies should specify how the organization will meet both present and anticipated needs of the customer. The strategies need to be specific to your organization. Consider the following:

- Examine everything that is done against the criteria, "Does this contribute to meeting your customer needs?"

- Review your mission statement to ensure it includes helping customers solve problems.

- Establish partnerships with customers.

- Invite customers, suppliers, and distributors to develop effective work processes with you.

- Create simplified purchase agreements (contracts) that make doing business with your organization understandable and easy.

- Involve customers in designing new products.

- Work with customers to conduct beta tests of new products.

- Define and use a structured process to funnel customer feedback into decision making for product enhancements and product development.

- Develop a customer service function.

- Hire people specifically oriented to customer service.

- Solicit and use customer feedback.

- Get more or different people involved with customers.

- Create site licensing agreements that are easy for your customers to administer.

- Establish a help desk and staff it with knowledgeable people.

- Establish simplified and easy procedures for ordering products from faxing to e-mail.

- Provide a vehicle for feedback from your customers, such as a response section on your home page on the World Wide Web.

- Leverage information and resources by making them available on-line to your customers.

- Create contingency plans for maintaining customer service when the unexpected happens.

- Examine the flexibility and adaptability of your service systems to see if they meet unique or different customer needs.

- Stay ahead of the demand for service that sales creates by building sufficient infrastructure.

Delivering on Customer Commitments

Customers want, and deserve, quick action. They want to deal with an employee who has all of the supplies, paperwork, and information necessary to competently and expeditiously help them. They also expect and deserve efficient follow-through, with no exceptions, on the commitments you have made to them.

1. Always deliver by the agreed-upon date. Customers expect to receive your product or service as promised. The only exception to this rule is to deliver early.

2. Measure your performance. Establish a tracking system to determine turnaround times, and to identify where the process gets tied up, and why. Find effective ways to remove these roadblocks and inefficiencies.

3. Recognize and reward individuals or teams who consistently meet delivery dates.

4. Provide the necessary resources for service employees. Keep this information at their fingertips for quick access. For example, place copies of policies and procedures under each counter.

5. Eliminate as many trips as possible to obtain supervisor approval. Provide your employees parameters within which to work, and then give them the latitude to "flex" with each customer's needs. Employees can then give the customer some options and thus increase the customer's feelings of being accommodated. Ideally, employees should be empowered to do whatever possible to satisfy customers.

Recovering from Mistakes

At some point, every organization is bound to make mistakes in the delivery and the quality of its product or service. How you deal with mistakes and complaints, however, can make or break a valued customer relationship. The following process can help you rectify mistakes and, in most cases, retain the customer's business:

1. Empathize with the customer; let the person know that you understand he or she is upset.

2. Take responsibility for the mistake; don't blame another employee for the problem.

3. Atone for the mistake; give the customer a little extra in return for the trouble.

4. Expedite the recovery process as quickly as possible.

5. Follow up with the customer to assure his or her satisfaction.

A good recovery can solidify, rather than weaken, a relationship with a customer. Statistics show that customers are more likely to patronize a business that has successfully rectified a problem than those with whom they have never registered a complaint.

Removing Barriers to Customer Service

Your employees may be committed to providing exceptional customer service, but may be unable to do so because organizational or departmental constraints prohibit them from "going the extra mile." Make every attempt to remove the barriers that get in the way of giving your customers top-notch service. Common barriers and possible solutions include:

Barrier	*Possible Solution*
Excess paperwork and red tape for front-line employees and customers.	Eliminate excess paperwork from your complaint-resolution process. Whenever possible, handle necessary paperwork after the customer leaves.
Front-line employees lack the authority to make decisions to satisfy unhappy customers.	Let front-line employees make the necessary decisions to satisfy your customers, even if it means you must change or make exceptions to your current policies.
Satisfaction with the status quo.	Raise your expectations. Anticipate customer needs. Know and communicate what your competitors are doing.
Belief that you have a corner on the marketplace.	Recognize that the nature of today's marketplace is dynamic and competitive. Ask what you can do to go beyond what the competition is doing, and then do it.
Concerns that the customer will engage in a legal battle or try to take advantage of lenient customer service policies.	Determine the parameters of what constitutes a legitimate customer complaint and any sensitive issues that may make you legally vulnerable. Train your staff on ways to identify and handle legally sensitive issues.
Front-line workers are overstressed from constantly putting out fires and the heavy workload.	Acknowledge that customer service work is stressful. Let your front line know that their efforts are valued and respected. Initiate a stress management program. Rotate job assignments to give employees "recharge" time.

Soliciting Employee Feedback and Suggestions

Front-line personnel (customer service representatives, receptionists, salespeople, service technicians, telemarketers, and so forth) can provide exceptional feedback on service because they meet customers face to face, every day. They have valuable information about which products people return and what the customer is really saying and feeling about your service. To tap this resource:

- Meet weekly with your staff to discuss complaints and the products customers returned most often.

- Provide a suggestion box for employees' ideas on improving customer service.

- Demonstrate that you take your employees' input seriously by acting on their comments and suggestions.

- Recognize the varying priorities of different groups/ departments, such as design and manufacturing or marketing and accounting, and how these priorities may affect delivery of customer service. Identify ways to gain commitment to total customer service from all groups.

- Use e-mail or groupware to gather information from employees about what customers are saying or feeling about service.

- Hold regular interdepartmental meetings to get a broader perspective.

- Recognize the value of feedback by acknowledging employees' contributions at department meetings or organization-wide meetings.

- Create a "think tank" room where the setting (from music to special furniture to art) encourages people to open up and share their creative energy.

- Use brainstorming sessions with employees to find creative, intuitive solutions to customer problems.

Practicing What You Preach

Showing employees how to focus on customer needs is a good way to teach and motivate them to do it. Treating your employees as your internal customers can provide this model. Try these suggestions to model effective customer service behaviors:

- Be friendly and respectful toward your employees.

- Manage by walking around; be visible and available.

- Involve senior management; set an example for the whole organization.

- Show genuine concern for and commitment to customer service; pitch in and help to resolve customer service issues and complaints.

- Be responsive; return calls or messages from employees within 24 hours.

- Consider your employees your customers. Ask them what you can do to improve their job satisfaction.

- Anticipate and deliver on the needs of your employees.

- Recognize that the human needs of your employees (for trust, respect, understanding, and appreciation) are the same as those of your customers.

- Send through your body language, dress, voice, and energy level the same positive attitude you want your employees to send to customers.

- Provide cross training to employees to increase their abilities to solve problems on their own.

PART 3

Communicating Your Customer Service Statement

Improving Your Customer Service Team

A team that has a shared goal of providing superior service and that talks about how to continue achieving this goal is more likely to deliver higher levels of customer service. Communicating this goal to all levels of your organization serves to focus all team efforts on the same expectations and standards for customer service.

To effectively communicate your commitment to customer service:

- Create a statement that encompasses your service commitment. Define it in terms of both employee and customer expectations. Make it a snappy catchphrase that's easy to remember. For example, Target Stores' motto is "Fast, Fun and Friendly."

- Put your service motto on posters and place them strategically throughout halls and open areas frequented by front-line customer service people.

- Show how each job is an important link in the chain of meeting customer needs. Consider using Michael Porter's value chain assessment to demonstrate this. Communicate that no matter what the job is, it is valued and important.

- Stress the benefits of the team's efforts not only for the entire organization, but also for them as individuals. For example, tie in the fact that better customer service means better business, and thus stronger job security.

- Continually update what you know about customers. Share this information with everyone, especially those who have a lot of customer contact.

- Make certain that employees at all levels view customer focus as their priority, not just the job of customer service people.

Hiring the Right People

It is wise to begin your efforts to improve customer service with the people you hire. To focus your efforts, determine the specific requirements of the job. Incorporate the information you have solicited from your customers on their needs and expectations, and then target your interview questions to identify these attributes.

Characteristics important for good customer service include:

- Oral communication skills

- Cooperation and teamwork

- Even-tempered disposition

- Sensitivity to and concern for others

- Problem-solving and decision-making skills

- Enthusiasm and energy

- Flexibility and adaptability

Use behavioral interviewing techniques to predict how a candidate will behave on the job. During the interviews, ask candidates for specific, real-life examples that demonstrate a strong service orientation. Identify the specific skills needed and use these as part of your selection process. More detailed tips on formulating an interview can be found in the Structure and Staff section of this Handbook.

Training for Superior Customer Service

Once you've selected the best candidates, get them off to the right start with a strong orientation and comprehensive training. The benefits of thoroughly orienting and training your employees include: fewer mistakes, improved customer service, higher levels of productivity, and happier employees.

The following suggestions will help you provide new employees with effective orientation and training experiences:

- Begin with a brief overview of your customer vision and strategies. Outline your customer service expectations.

- Design and present a fast-paced, energized program.

- During the training, treat employees the way you expect customers to be treated.

- Make the orientation fun. People who enjoy their training will more likely enjoy the job and thus treat customers better.

- Include your service motto throughout the orientation and training materials; see Communicating Your Customer Service Statement earlier in this section.

- Use praise and encouragement to build your new employees' confidence. Show them the effort you took to hire the best. Tell them, "You're in this job because we believe in you!"

- Walk employees through various ways to handle difficult customers. Model techniques for dealing with these tough cases. Get employees involved in their training by allowing them to role-play various scenarios. Then give them a chance to critique how they handled the "customer."

Rewarding Excellent Customer Service

No matter how competent and self-confident they are, all employees like to know that their efforts are recognized and appreciated by management. Most managers agree that the best way to motivate employees to perform better is to reward their efforts — both verbally and tangibly. Consider implementing the following suggestions to show your appreciation to employees who provide outstanding customer service:

- Realize that positive reinforcement often works best when it is linked to specific rewards. Remember, not everyone is motivated by the same thing — vary your rewards to fit the individual.

- Create avenues for recognizing superior performers. For example, initiate a public recognition of the "service employee of the month."

- Obtain feedback from the people "in the know" — your customers. One way to get this valuable information is by using evaluation cards. Place these cards near the service desk, or have service employees hand them out. Encourage customers to make an evaluation. This feedback can then be used in performance appraisals and for giving rewards for good service.

- Create performance-standard expectations to measure everyone. Communicate these standards to your employees.

RECOMMENDED READINGS

The publications listed here were selected for their content and suitability to a managerial audience.

Managing Knock Your Socks Off Service

Bell, Chip R., and Zemke, Ron, New York: AMACOM, 1992
ISBN: 0-8144-7784-4
This is a practical, hands-on guide on how to hire the right people, train them, reward them, celebrate their successes, and gain their commitment. It is an instructional blueprint for keeping you ahead of the competition by ensuring that each member of your organization values good service.

Sustaining Knock Your Socks Off Service

Connellan, Thomas K., and Zemke, Ron, New York: AMACOM, 1993
ISBN: 0-8144-7824-7
This book is a guide on how to effectively sustain service initiatives through the long term. By using numerous examples, the authors instruct companies and individuals on how to continue serving the customer long after the first implementation of a customer service initiative.

High Performance Sales Organizations

Corcoran, Kevin J.; Petersen, Laura K.; Baitch, Daniel B.; and Barrett, Mark F., Burr Ridge, IL: Irwin Professional Publishing, 1995
ISBN: 0-7863-0352-2
This book discusses how organizations can achieve competitive advantage, increase customer loyalty, and improve profitability in a highly competitive marketplace. Strategies and methods are provided that will allow your organization to immediately: exceed customers' expectations; develop a sales plan that will allow your organization to be more competitive; train your sales staff to successfully implement the sales plan; and coordinate your sales, marketing, and service initiatives to maximize profitability.

The Monster Under the Bed

Davis, Stan, and Botkin, Jim, New York: Simon & Schuster, 1994
ISBN: 0-671-87107-2
The knowledge industry is changing the way business is conducted and it will dominate the global marketplace. This book makes several observations about business's role as purveyor of knowledge to customers, employees, and eventually to schools, including: the increasing role of business in education, the idea that learning is a continuous process, and the notion that any business can become a knowledge business.

Fabled Service

Sanders, Betsy, San Diego: Pfeiffer & Company, 1995
ISBN: 0-89384-270-2
The author is a former vice president and general manager of Nordstrom's Southern California division and led that region to annual revenues of $1 billion. The key to that success was a policy of exemplary service which made Nordstrom's a benchmark for service in the industry. "Fabulous service," says Sanders, "is quite simply ordinary people doing ordinary things extraordinarily well." By teaching the importance of attentive and caring service, simple acts have extraordinary outcomes.

Customers for Life

Sewell, Carl, and Brown, Paul B., New York: Pocket Books, 1991
ISBN: 0-671-74795-9
This book is a practical guide to customer service. It is organized into a series of short, well-focused chapters: how to "underpromise and overdeliver," how to see what the customer sees, how to turn employees into "service superstars," why there is no such thing as "after hours," and the importance of measuring absolutely everything that is done.

Teamwork for Customers

Tjosvold, Dean, San Francisco: Jossey-Bass, 1992
ISBN: 1-55542-491-0
Loyal and satisfied customers are essential to business success. This book guides companies toward becoming customer driven organizations through the use of teams and an overall customer-oriented attitude. Also included are examples of how to effectively deal with customer complaints.

The Discipline of Market Leaders

Treacy, Michael, and Wiersma, Fred, Reading, MA: Addison-Wesley, 1995
ISBN: 0-201-40648-9
This book seeks to answer the question of why some companies provide much better prices and services to their customers. Companies that are market leaders have focused attention and resources on different things. Market leaders chose to excel in one of the customer value disciplines: best cost, best product, or best solution. Focusing on one of these disciplines means knowing which one to choose, designing your organization around it, and offering better value year after year.

Upside-Down Marketing

Walther, George R., New York: McGraw-Hill, 1994
ISBN: 0-07-068047-7
The author presents methods whereby a company can reach out to customers whose buying activity has slowed or stopped completely. By getting feedback from these customers, a company will be able to identify and correct problems that will make these customers once again loyal purchasers. Included are specific strategies for calculating the "lifetime value" of a customer, turning angry customers into satisfied ones, soliciting feedback, analyzing customer needs, and utilizing new technology to speed up response time.

The Customer Driven Company

Whiteley, Richard C., Reading, MA: Addison-Wesley, 1993
ISBN: 0-201-60813-8
The author suggests that one of the keys to a satisfied customer is that customer service is defined by the customer. This book provides a step-by-step method for companies that wish to become customer-driven organizations and teaches companies how to satisfy their customers every time.

Stop Selling Start Partnering

Wilson, Larry, Essex Junction, VT: Oliver Wight, 1994
ISBN: 0-939246-74-0
This book provides a new approach for finding and keeping customers through developing powerful, long-lasting partnerships. Through advice, anecdotes, and personal experiences, the author shows managers, executives, and salespeople how to deliver real value to customers. Salespeople are encouraged to abandon the practice of "power selling" and instead develop partnership relationships with customers which will extend long into the future.

SUGGESTED SEMINARS

The seminars listed here were selected for their appeal to a managerial audience. The reputation of the vendor, the quality of their seminar offerings, and the specific seminar content were considered in the selection process.

Because of the dynamic nature of the seminar marketplace, some seminars may have been upgraded or replaced, and others may no longer be offered. Likewise, costs and locations may have changed since this listing was compiled. We recommend that you contact the vendor directly for updated and additional information.

Becoming Customer Driven

This program is designed for managers from all functional areas who need to increase their strategic understanding of what it takes to enhance the value of the customer relationship.
Length: Call vendor; Cost: Call vendor
Location: Durham, NC
**Duke University, The Fuqua School of Business
Office of Executive Education, Durham, NC 27706
Telephone: 800/372-3932**

Achieving Breakthrough Service

This program is designed for senior managers of multilocation organizations engaged in the delivery of services. It focuses on the development of analytic and implementation-oriented skills in customer assessment, positioning, operating system design, and human resource management.
Length: 2 weeks; Cost: $9,000
Location: Boston
**Harvard Business School
Executive Education Programs, Soldiers Field-Glass Hall
Boston, MA 02163-9986
Telephone: 800/427-5577**

Partners in Quality

This program addresses the "soft side" of Total Quality while focusing on both internal and external customer/supplier relationships. Through a simulation and an assessment instrument, participants diagnose the quality of their interactions with customers and suppliers. They develop skills to create an environment of trust, integrity, and caring between customers and suppliers; formulate plans to make positive changes in key partnerships; and develop a strategy for tracking improvements that occur.
Length: 2 days; Cost: $595
Location: Atlanta
The Atlanta Consulting Group
1600 Parkwood Circle, Suite 200, Atlanta, GA 30339
Telephone: 800/852-8224

Achieving Service Excellence

This seminar is designed for anyone in an organization who serves internal or external customers. It teaches the participants to understand how their customers define high-quality service and how to deliver excellent service, deal with customer relationships, improve teamwork, and close gaps in service quality.
Length: 2 days; Cost: Call vendor
Location: Boston
The Forum Corporation
One Exchange Place, Boston, MA 02109
Telephone: 800/367-8611

Coaching for Service Excellence

This seminar helps managers of the customer contact people who have attended or plan to attend the Achieving Service Excellence Program. It helps managers develop the skills necessary to improve customer focus in their work units and build superior relationships with customers.
Length: 1 day; Cost: Call vendor
Location: Boston
The Forum Corporation
One Exchange Place, Boston, MA 02109
Telephone: 800/367-8611

Leadership

This seminar is designed for middle- to senior-level managers of people or projects. During this session, managers learn the skills necessary to shape and support their organization's customer-focused culture.
Length: 3 days; Cost: Call vendor
Location: Boston
The Forum Corporation
One Exchange Place, Boston, MA 02109
Telephone: 800/367-8611

Customer Satisfaction: Management Strategies and Tactics

In this seminar, participants will learn how customer satisfaction affects customer loyalty; the firm's market share and corporate profitability; why companies fail to meet customer needs; and a framework for identifying potential problems.
Length: 2 days; Cost: $1,145
Location: Chicago
University of Chicago, Center for Continuing Studies
5835 South Kimbark Avenue, Chicago, IL 60637
Telephone: 312/702-1724

Managing Service: Reengineering for Customer Satisfaction

This program is for managers who believe that a critical "product" advantage lies in the quality of the organization's customer service. The program examines significant implications of providing a service orientation from management, marketing, financial, and strategic perspectives. It also discusses concrete steps to improve your organization's customer service.
Length: 5 days; Cost: $4,550
Location: Philadelphia
University of Pennsylvania, The Wharton School
Aresty Institute of Executive Education, Steinberg
Conference Center, 255 South 38th Street
Philadelphia, PA 19104-6359
Telephone: 800/255-3932

Measuring Customer Satisfaction

This seminar covers the fundamentals of a comprehensive customer satisfaction program from the design of a customer satisfaction survey to evaluation.
Length: 2 days; Cost: $950
Location: Nashville, TN
Vanderbilt University
Owen Graduate School of Management, Executive
Programs, 410 21st Avenue South, Suite 100
Nashville, TN 37203
Telephone: 615/322-2513

PROMOTE CORPORATE CITIZENSHIP

Effective leaders are usually good stewards who make wise and careful use of all resources — personal time and energy, material and physical resources, and other people. They take a holistic view of the community and the business enterprise, recognizing that what happens in one arena inevitably affects the other.

Another mark of good leaders — particularly upper-level managers — is that they champion corporate citizenship, both for altruistic reasons and because it enhances their corporation's reputation.

Many leaders exhibit an altruism that prompts them to reach beyond their own particular organizational responsibilities. The most admired leaders are those who are committed to causes beyond their personal egos and who find small and large ways to contribute to the communities to which they belong.

In an earlier time, stewardship and corporate citizenship may have been thought to be a nice sentiment, but unnecessary. In today's global society, economy, and environment, it is a necessity. This section offers suggestions that can help you strengthen your commitment to stewardship and corporate citizenship.

- Developing Collaboration between Business and Community
- Understanding Community Issues Relevant to the Business
- Seeking Alternatives to Business Practices Harmful to the Environment
- Encouraging Responsible Use of Resources
- Supporting Efforts to Improve Stewardship
- Contributing to Community Organizations
- Addressing Current and Future Work Force Issues

Valuable Tips

- With your staff, brainstorm ways to conserve energy and resources.

- Join with other business communities to revitalize part of your city. Some companies regularly contribute a certain amount of pretax revenue to community improvement.

- Initiate and support recycling efforts in your organization.

- Develop strategies to eliminate or reduce the harmful impact your organization's products or processes may have on the environment.

- Maintain a big picture perspective of how your organization and your community can work together. Identify ways in which you can share resources.

- Find out from the building supervisor what opportunities are available for recycling paper, glass, plastic, and aluminum in your offices.

- Reduce the amount of colored paper you use. The dyes are harmful to the environment, and the large amounts of bleach used to de-ink the paper pollute our water supply.

- Use fluorescent lights in your office; they consume less energy and last considerably longer than incandescent lights.

- Read *50 Simple Things Your Business Can Do to Save the Earth* by the Earthworks Group.

- Work cooperatively with environmental groups to protect environmental resources.

- Volunteer some of your time to community organizations; encourage your employees to do likewise.

- Gain a better understanding of, and get involved in, local government.

- Read *Workforce 2000* to gain a better understanding of future work force implications.

- Become involved in education to increase the quality of applicants.

- Sponsor work projects with your team, such as working with the elderly in your community or mentoring high school students.

Developing Collaboration between Business and Community

Increasingly, businesses and communities are finding it mutually beneficial to work together to conserve resources and promote educational and community-support programs.

Effective business leaders see across organizational boundaries. They seek and create opportunities for cooperation, collaboration, and synergy between and among various business and community entities. To help you develop collaboration between business and the community, consider the following:

- Find an area where your organization can use and complement the resources of a community agency. For example, many communities have excellent resources in childcare, family counseling, and drug and alcohol rehabilitation. You can use the community resources available and build your organization's programs around those resources.

- Get to know political and community leaders in your area. Learn about and better understand their issues and concerns. Use both formal and informal opportunities to share your perspective on issues of mutual interest.

- Work with local schools. Offer to speak in classrooms. Invite school administrators, instructors, and students into your work environment and share some of the opportunities, common threads, needs, and constraints your organization faces. Offer internship and scholarship opportunities.

- Create or sponsor a speakers' bureau of people who are able to talk about issues of concern to the organization, industry, and community. Offer to send speakers to groups with common interests and concerns. Service groups are often interested in this type of opportunity, and they can be an excellent source of referral.

- Show commitment to the community by making efforts to ensure that your employee demographics are representative of the community.

- When you have products, services, or office supplies that are no longer needed, donate them to a local agency or charitable organization. Your old lobby chair may be someone else's prize office furnishing.

Understanding Community Issues Relevant to the Business

Every organization operates within a community and is affected by many internal and external factors associated with that community. Successful leaders are frequently active in addressing the community issues that have an impact on their business or profession. Others work on community issues simply because they're concerned and want to contribute their talents.

Initiatives and efforts that benefit both your organization and the community can be worth your serious consideration. Following are some actions to consider:

- Read publications such as those published by the Citizens League, Chamber of Commerce, and other civic and neighborhood groups. Check out the "State of the City" and "State of the State" reports to identify strengths and weaknesses of the areas in which you do business.

- Note projections made by demographers and various organizations regarding the future.

- Be aware of future projects planned in the community and their likely impacts on your business.

- Identify the community factors that help and hurt your business. Examples include:
  - Quality of schools
  - Level of violence
  - Status of housing
  - Traffic and overall infrastructure
  - Business climate, including taxation policies
  - Overall amenities

- Listen to the community critics to identify problems that need attention.

- Encourage your people to serve in the community.

Seeking Alternatives to Business Practices Harmful to the Environment

Your organization may use or produce products or processes that may be harmful to the environment. To develop your awareness in this area:

- Learn about the products and processes your organization uses. Follow up on environmental reports that have been done on your products, or see that such reports are produced. Use your own people as well as independent agencies to look at the environmental impact of your operations. By using a variety of information sources, you will get a more accurate reading on the risks involved.

- If you determine that your products or processes may be harmful to the environment, set up a task force to learn about and open the way for alternative methods. Countless examples exist of business leaders who have identified safer production methods for their organizations.

- Bring your scientists and engineers together to work on reducing the potential negative impact that your products or processes may have on the environment.

- Link environmental efforts with your organization's overall objectives. In the short term, the use of products and processes harmful to the environment may generate a high financial return. Over the long term, however, this is not the case.

Encouraging Responsible Use of Resources

The "greening" of businesses has had a significant positive impact on the environment. Resource conservation efforts are good for the physical environment as well for public relations, employee morale, and the financial bottom line. To encourage your organization to be more responsive to resource conservation, consider the following:

- Create a recycling task force with staff members. Brainstorm recycling ideas and put decisions into action.

- Provide containers for recycling in offices, work areas, lounges, and break rooms.

- Reduce the amount of paper you use by copying documents on both sides of the paper and by using voice mail and electronic mail in lieu of internal memos. Use erasable boards rather than paper flipcharts for presentations.

- Conserve energy in your office space by turning off lights when you will be gone for more than ten minutes. In addition, use fluorescent lights in your office space. They use less energy and last longer than incandescent lights.

- Work with the facilities department to identify energy conservation methods available, and implement the relevant, cost-effective measures.

- Invite an energy expert (inside or outside the company) to talk with your staff about personal conservation measures that can be taken at work and at home.

- Include tips on recycling and waste reduction in departmental and organizational newsletters and other communications.

I'M TRYING TO MAKE MY OFFICE AS ENVIRONMENTALLY FRIENDLY AS POSSIBLE.

Supporting Efforts to Improve Stewardship

Stewardship involves the effective and efficient use of all human, financial, and material resources of businesses and community agencies. Stewardship begins with a mindset, a perspective that looks for ways of effectively and efficiently using resources.

Good leaders are good stewards of the organization's resources. If they are not, the enterprise eventually could suffer. Some steps you can take to promote good stewardship include the following:

- Evaluate your personal stewardship.
  - Identify one or more ways in which you could be more effective or efficient in your work, and make a change that will produce improvement.
  - Are you giving satisfactory amounts of time, money, and energy to your important personal, relationship, community, and career priorities? Personal stewardship involves maintaining an adequate life balance, in which all areas receive appropriate attention (not *equal* attention).

- Review your staff to see if their capabilities are being fully utilized and if there are other contributions they could and would like to make. Ask your people to identify activities, practices, or procedures that hinder their work. Make improvements wherever possible.

- Encourage others to be good stewards of their own energy, talents, and time.

- Look for opportunities to improve the stewardship of any community organizations that you work with. Are their people well used? Is an adequate percentage of funds and other material resources going to the group being served?

- Overall, minimize the negative environmental impact of your activities.

Contributing to Community Organizations

Part of effective corporate citizenship is contributing in an altruistic manner to organizations that improve the quality of life in your community, regardless of any positive impact on your business.

Contributions can take a variety of forms; at times they may involve financial support, while at other times they may involve donating your time, energy, and skills to an endeavor. Following are some activities you might consider:

- Join and participate in an active service organization. If your schedule prohibits regular attendance, you may wish to work on a special project within a service club.

- Identify organizations that have a significant positive impact on your community, and periodically contribute money to them.

- As a way of passing on inspiration and encouragement to future leaders, contribute your time (for example, as a board member or a volunteer) to a youth, athletic, or cultural endeavor.

- Seek an elective or appointive political or community position. Many such positions (such as school board, city council, planning commission) can be coordinated for a period of time even with a demanding career.

- Become knowledgeable and active in local politics.

- Match employees' financial contributions to civic organizations.

- Support the involvement of your people in community service.

Addressing Current and Future Work Force Issues

Changes in the makeup of the work force are requiring businesses to examine their participation in shaping that work force. Effective managers also want to ensure that they can find, hire, and retain qualified people who will work toward the organization's success. The following guidelines can help you address the present and future work force needs of your team and your organization:

- Review your organization's strategic plan for the future. Identify the implications for human resources.
  - How will the organization change in the next 5, 10, 15 years?
  - What qualifications and experience will be necessary?
  - How do we educate, train, and prepare people for changing job and skill demands?
  - What are the retention and hiring projections by level?
  - What does the succession plan call for?

- Identify the impact of the education crisis on your future work force.
  - What is the competence level required for new hires?
  - How do your feeder schools measure up?
  - What needs to be done?

RECOMMENDED READINGS

The publications listed here were selected for their content and suitability to a managerial audience.

Workplace 2000

Boyett, Joseph H., and Conn, Henry P., New York: NAL-Dutton, 1992
ISBN: 0-452-26804-4
The authors provide a blueprint for the future as well as a survival manual for companies facing relentless global competition. Their book offers valuable personal guidance and charts the education, skills, and attitudes that will be required of future workers.

Prosperity Without Pollution

Hirschhorn, Joel S., and Oldenburg, Kirsten U., New York: Van Nostrand Reinhold, 1991
ISBN: 0-442-00225-4
The authors explain why and how preventive environmental strategies are more effective and cost-saving than remedial efforts. They also offer scientific data and practical examples in which ecology and economy are combined.

The E-Factor: The Bottom-Line Approach to Environmentally Responsible Business

Makower, Joel, New York: NAL-Dutton, 1994
ISBN: 0-452-27190-8
This book outlines the environmental issues confronting companies and how they can become more aware and responsive to these environmental issues and legislative initiatives. The author shows how reducing waste and maximizing resources will make companies more competitive and profitable over the long term.

Transforming the Crisis-Prone Organization

Pauchant, Thierry C., and Mitroff, Ian I., San Francisco: Jossey-Bass, 1992
ISBN: 1-55542-407-4
This book provides strategies for preventing crises and tragedies that may be attributable to your organization and managing those that do occur. The authors' recommendations are based on five hundred interviews with crisis management professionals, as well as examples of techniques used in major environmental crises such as the Exxon oil spill in Alaska and the Union Carbide chemical incident in Bhopal, India.

50 Simple Things
Your Business Can
Do to Save the Earth

The Earthworks Group, Berkeley, CA: Earthworks Press, 1991
ISBN: 1-879682-02-8
The authors of this book recognize the realities of business, that it is not possible to change well-honed products and processes overnight to protect the environment and still function as a business. They do, however, offer practical suggestions on how to become more environmentally responsible corporate citizens which they believe will give businesses a competitive advantage in the marketplace of the future.

SUGGESTED SEMINARS

The seminars listed here were selected for their appeal to a managerial audience. The reputation of the vendor, the quality of their seminar offerings, and the specific seminar content were considered in the selection process.

Because of the dynamic nature of the seminar marketplace, some seminars may have been upgraded or replaced, and others may no longer be offered. Likewise, costs and locations may have changed since this listing was compiled. We recommend that you contact the vendor directly for updated and additional information.

New Developments in Managing Diversity

This workshop is designed to provide participants with the most up-to-date thinking, strategies, and approaches in the Institute's work with managing diversity. The information presented will give participants the opportunity to benchmark their managing diversity efforts and to incorporate new information into their strategies.
Length: 1 day; Cost: Call vendor
Location: Washington, D.C.
American Institute for Managing Diversity, Inc.
Morehouse College, Box 83, 351-55 Westview Drive S.W.
Atlanta, GA 30314
Telephone: 404/756-1170

Executive Seminar

This values-based seminar brings together leaders from the public, private, and other sectors to enhance their qualities of vision and integrity. Classic readings from Plato to Jefferson support a discussion of the forces at work in society and the global community. Participants will examine the origins of many current business issues to acquire new perspectives as they manage change in their organizations.
Length: 1 week; Cost: $4,700
Location: Aspen, CO
The Aspen Institute
1000 North Third Street, Aspen, CO 81611
Telephone: 303/544-7952

Tuck Executive Program

This program is designed for senior managers. An intensive program, it integrates the study of the major business disciplines within the context of general strategic management. The curriculum also examines important issues in the international environment confronting managers of complex organizations. Corporate governance, public policy issues, and business ethics receive substantive attention.
Length: 4 weeks; Cost: $17,500
Location: Hanover, NH
Dartmouth College
The Amos Tuck School of Business Administration
Office of Executive Education, 100 Tuck Hall
Hanover, NH 03755-9050
Telephone: 603/646-2839

Globalization: Merging Strategy with Action

Corporate strategy, human resource management, cross-cultural communication, and operations management all have special characteristics in a globally competitive industry. Participants learn how to become better managers in a world where competition is global, complex, and intense.
Length: 1 week; Cost: $4,000
Location: Glendale, AZ
Thunderbird
American Graduate School of International Management
Thunderbird Executive Training Center
15249 N. 59th Ave., Glendale, AZ 85306-9904
Telephone: 602/978-7820

Can You Compete with 21st Century, Inc.?: A New Paradigm for Managing Your Business Under Environmental Constraints

This interdisciplinary seminar revolves around a hypothetical corporation, 21st Century, Inc., that has dealt successfully with environmental issues. By exploring the challenges facing this organization, participants will learn how change in corporate strategy, culture, and decision making can achieve profitable and sustainable growth.
Length: 2-1/2 days; Cost: $1,125
Location: Nashville, TN
Vanderbilt University
Vanderbilt Center for Environmental Management
Studies, Owen Graduate School of Management
Executive Programs, 410 21st Avenue South, Suite 100
Nashville, TN 37203
Telephone: 615/322-2513

RECOGNIZE GLOBAL IMPLICATIONS

Increasingly we are becoming citizens of the world, and our organizations are becoming global ones. Our organizations may be full members of the global business community, or be affected by the global economy. Whether a company is operating as a total global organization, manufacturing in other countries, sourcing materials from other parts of the world, actively marketing its products internationally, or facing the need to address competition from abroad, the global economy affects its business.

The ability to operate within this global economy is becoming increasingly more important for managers at all levels. To successfully lead in this global economy, it is essential to understand the profound impact of the global economy on your business, and to become increasingly knowledgeable about conducting business within this global community. It is also imperative to be able to work with people from other cultures, know how to conduct business and manage employees in other cultures, and be able to continually position your organization to compete successfully in the international marketplace.

This section provides guidelines and suggestions for effectively recognizing global implications in your business and for developing the skills to manage those implications. It includes:

Part 1: Developing and Strengthening Your Global Perspective

- Analyzing the Globalization of Your Business
- Expanding Your International Mindset
- Learning the Business Practices of Other Cultures
- Developing an Understanding of How World Events Affect Your Business

Part 2: Preparing Yourself for the Global Future

- Assessing Your Future Global Skills
- Stretching Your Imagination to View Possibilities
- Keeping Up with Technology
- Anticipating Trends and Their Impact on Your Organization

Part 3: Working with Other Cultures

- Understanding Culture
- Understanding Cultural Impact
- Developing Cross-cultural Knowledge
- Bridging Cultures

Part 4: Developing International Business Savvy

- Understanding Your Global Position
- Working Your Globalization Strategy
- Conducting Business in Other Countries
- Marketing Products and Services Internationally
- Managing Employees in Other Countries

Valuable Tips

- Analyze the degree to which your business is affected by the global economy.

- Become aware of the natural, common business practices in your own country that are viewed differently in other countries.

- Try to understand other people's ideas from their point of view, rather than making judgments based on your own perspective or culture.

- Ask for coaching from people within your organization who know the culture of the country you'll be working in.

- Research the country's laws that affect how you do business in that country.

- Analyze the ways in which your organization is a global organization.

- Recognize that it can take more effort to build a trusting relationship with people from another country.

- Remember that you can respect other points of view without agreeing with them.

- Encourage discussion of international business within your organization, including wrestling with the difficult issues of how to handle differing business practices and cultural norms and values.

- Talk with the organization's technology experts periodically to learn what they are working on, the advances they expect in their areas in the future, and their current challenges.

- Talk to expatriates about their experiences.

- Build bridges together. Talk openly about how each person sees the situation and how you can create the bridge to a new understanding and new ways of working.

- Learn the language of the country in which you work.

- Get in tune with trends in the industry, your organization, and the global landscape. Continually explore how these changes might affect your business. Create and take advantage of developing business opportunities.

- Get to know people from other cultures who work in your organization.

- Identify communications technology that will facilitate the global coordination you need to have.

- Identify what needs to be global — sourcing, manufacturing, distribution, marketing, sales, and so on.

- Determine a set of organization core values to communicate throughout the organization to build a common language and a way of doing business with one another.

- Before you work in another country, learn all you can about its language, culture, values, and customs.

- Study how your competition sells its products internationally.

- Develop contacts internationally, and discuss the market, demographics, and cultural norms of their countries.

- When another person is talking, listen carefully to hear his or her values and beliefs. Check out your understanding respectfully and nonconfrontationally, even if the values you hear are very different from your own.

- In international meetings, communicate clearly and completely. Check the accuracy of your assumptions.

- When dealing with foreign associates, be aware of cultural differences in social and business norms and learn how to modify your behavior when necessary.

- Take a course in cross-cultural studies to understand culture and its impact on people.

- Determine the appropriate global/local balance.

- Study the business practices of successful multinational businesses. Compare these practices with your organization's values and practices. Identify those practices that are similar and that are different, and the reasons why.

- Remember that individuals see themselves as both members of their culture and different from it. Do not assume that all people from a particular culture are a particular way.

- Define your company's "global market" (the countries with which your company does business or would like to do business). Determine how your company's products can meet the needs of the people in the countries you identified.

PART 1

Analyzing the Globalization of Your Business

Developing and Strengthening Your Global Perspective

Businesses and industries are becoming more global every year. Your customers may be on various continents, your raw materials may come from other parts of the world, new technologies may originate in other countries, or your business may be partially owned by foreign investors.

A useful first step in recognizing global implications is to understand the degree to which, and the ways in which, your organization is part of the global economy.

Talk with international experts and knowledgeable managers about the international components of your business, including:

- What percentage of revenues and profits come from foreign markets?

- In which markets are future growth expected? Are these markets domestic or foreign?

- Who are your suppliers? From inside or outside your country? Who do you anticipate your suppliers will be in the future? Where will they be located?

- Where is manufacturing now? In the future? What is the current and future impact on the business of the manufacturing location(s)?

- Who are your primary domestic and foreign competitors now? In the future? What would be the impact of a change in competitors?

- Is your company owned or partially owned by foreign investors? What is the impact? What changes do you anticipate?

- Where is your technology developed and supplied currently? In the future?

- What percentage of your organization is located in other countries? Which countries?

- What percentage of your work force and managers are foreign nationals?

- What percentage of managers are managing outside their country of origin?

You can conduct this analysis in a number of ways:

- Conduct it yourself with the knowledge you currently have. If you are an experienced manager with some global knowledge, this process may help determine in which areas you need additional help.

- Use your team to gather the information, share it, and draw conclusions together. This approach would capitalize on the expertise of others, plus develop shared knowledge and consensus.

- Ask a team or task force to gather the information, analyze it, and develop recommendations. The task force can present the information to you and/or the other teams in the organization.

This analysis will enable you to spot opportunities and potential problems.

Expanding Your International Mindset

No matter how involved you are in international business — whether you manage a foreign subsidiary or simply need to be aware of how world events could affect your industry — the first step is to expand your own mindset about what it means to think globally. The following suggestions can help you move beyond a domestic business focus:

- Learn how others view your country and its role in the world and in the global economy.

- Keep an open mind in all situations. Step back and observe your feelings, opinions, and assessments about international events or other countries' cultural norms. Before making a judgment, look at other viewpoints and objectively consider the merits of those viewpoints. Not only will this allow you to broaden your mindset about the complexity of the world, but it will also help you to learn specific practices of other cultures.

- Identify people in your organization from other cultures. Discuss both business and social topics with them. Aim to see things from their perspective. Deliberately look for differences in the way they would handle and interpret different situations. Then look for similarities.

- If you work, or even vacation, in another country, record your observations in a journal. What surprises you? What is similar? What is hard to understand?

- Talk and spend time with people from other cultures.

- Rotate staff whenever possible to give people exposure to other cultures. Think creatively, so that the opportunities are available to people other than managers and executives.

- Stay abreast of world events by reading newspapers and magazines daily. Develop the habit of asking yourself how specific events will affect you and your business.

- Join or start a discussion group that analyzes world events, and monitors and predicts the impact of those events on people, governments, and business.

- Read newspapers from other countries. Notice the difference in emphasis and interpretation in the different newspapers. Each country's media typically will have an underlying cultural interpretation of events.

- Take a course in world economics that provides an overview of the major world economic systems and how they interact. In particular, watch for examples of how economic events in one system can affect other systems.

- Keep in mind that understanding does not require agreement or approval. Expect to find customs or viewpoints with which you disagree, but still need to understand.

- Examine how other cultures differ from and are similar to your own. Choose one country a month and learn all you can about that country, comparing and contrasting it with your own. Study both its social and cultural norms with objectivity.

Learning the Business Practices of Other Cultures

In the United States, businesspeople exchange business cards with hardly a glance at what's on them. In Japan, it's expected that upon receiving someone's business card, you will study it carefully, acknowledge having received it, and perhaps make a comment or ask a polite question about it. During a meeting, you would put the card, along with those of the others at the meeting, in front of you. Such treatment of the business card shows that you respect the individual who gave it to you.

Business practices, as an extension of the culture of a country, vary widely throughout the world. To effectively conduct business with individuals of another country, it's essential to understand the key differences in how business is practiced in the other country versus your own. The following guidelines present ways for you to increase that understanding:

- Observe or study the business practices of successful multinational businesses. Identify the similarities and differences among the practices and the reasons for them. Compare these practices with your organization's values and practices.

- Talk to expatriates about their experiences. What did they learn about themselves, their culture, the culture of others? What were their frustrations? Their greatest successes? What would they do differently? What should others know?

- Benchmark global businesses.

- Take an expatriate assignment. Whether of a short- or long-term duration, an expatriate assignment will allow you to "live" cultural differences and their effects on business, not just read and theorize about them.

- Learn enough of the language of the country to be able to use the basic forms of introductions, greetings, and similar exchanges that are used by businesspeople in that country.

- Join an organizational task force or project team working with global issues. Working through a real-life business issue is an "action learning" opportunity. Reflect on what you are learning as you work on the assignment.

- Identify people within your organization, industry, or network who are from the country you're researching. Ask them to tell you about the business practices of that country. Find out both how *to* behave and how *not* to behave.

- Ask a consulting firm that specializes in cross-cultural training for business to teach you the business practices of the countries in which you are or will be doing business. This is particularly useful after you have acquired a more general and conceptual understanding of the culture.

- If your organization has an office in the country you're researching, travel to that office and spend some time with its staff. Observe them as they work with their customers and other business associates. Pay attention to how they behave, what procedures they follow, and what kinds of customs they observe. Note the level of formality and informality, the atmosphere of the meetings, and who leads in any meeting.

- Develop a list of questions to ask and topics to cover about business practices. Role-play several situations with the office staff to make sure you are practicing the customs correctly.

- Attend orientations and briefings held by government agencies about doing business in particular countries.

Developing an Understanding of How World Events Affect Your Business

Whether your business has been involved in the global marketplace for years or has had no contact with other countries (other than as sources of potential competition), your business is affected by world events. The more you understand how world events affect your business, the better prepared you will be to minimize the negative impact and capitalize on the positive.

To further your understanding of the impact that world events can have on your business, consider these suggestions:

- Ask yourself how specific international events, particularly economic developments, will affect your organization or your industry. If you don't know the answers, discuss the events with others in your organization or your network. Ask for the opinions of coworkers from other countries.

- Develop your own perspective of business in the global economy. Watch for patterns and predictors. For example, if a major corporation shifts its national base of production, what kind of fallout can be expected for the industry worldwide and for your organization's place in it?

- Anticipate and interpret world events and their impact on your organization and industry.

- Talk with the informal historians in your organization. Ask how major events in the past, such as a fire, major labor strike, war, or natural disaster, affected the organization. This information will help you anticipate some of the effects of major world events on your organization.

- Attend conferences hosted by government agencies that assist organizations interested in international trade. Even if your organization is already trading internationally, these conferences can give you additional insights into how world events are currently affecting the marketplace.

- Allocate a certain amount of time daily or weekly for reading books, periodicals, and other literature that address the global market and evolving world trends.

- Ask experts in international business to help you understand the interaction between world events, global business, and your business.

PART 2	**Preparing Yourself for the Global Future**
Assessing Your Future Global Skills	

As you look to the future, anticipate that competition, complexity, and the pace of business will increase. Competitors will emerge. Old alliances will crumble, and new ones will develop. An increase in competition and in collaboration will occur simultaneously, often with the same organizations.

Technology will make it possible to accomplish almost everything differently. New organizational structures will arise and will as quickly change. People will need to manage highly complex webs of relationships and to develop relationships with different people.

To manage within this competitive environment, you will need to develop a passion for learning, an ability to analyze and synthesize a large amount of disparate information, a willingness and ability to negotiate and work out extraordinarily complex relationships among people and organizations, skills to keep up with and ahead of technology, and the ability to manage complex and changing systems.

To assess your future global skills, consider the degree to which each of the following describes you, using a scale of L = low, M = medium, and H = high:

___ Able to learn information quickly

___ Able to synthesize disparate information

___ Fascinated with learning and understanding

___ Able to master new ways of working quickly

___ Constantly learning

___ Comfortable with using communication technology such as voice mail, computer electronic mail, video conferencing, the Internet, and so forth

___ Experiment with new things

___ Follow emerging communication technology

___ Keep up to date with technology

___ Imagine applications of new technology

___ Able to negotiate difficult and complex relationships

___ Speak at least two languages

___ Enjoy learning about different cultures

__ Expert at orchestrating change

__ See challenges as exhilarating and fun

__ Have lots of energy

After you assess yourself, ask those who work with you about their points of view on your skills.

Stretching Your Imagination to View Possibilities

A global manager cannot allow him- or herself to become trapped by what currently exists or is currently possible. Challenge yourself and your team to do or discuss the following:

- Think of the current constraints within which your team or business operates. If those constraints were gone, what could you do?

- Identify your current greatest business challenge. What could happen if this were eliminated?

- Consider an entirely different way in which the organization could be structured. What would be the consequences?

- If your present distribution channels disappeared, what would you do?

- If your current sources of material disappeared, what would you do?

- Suppose your staff members were all from different parts of the world. How would your staff be different?

- If you could increase sales by 250 percent in one year, what would be the consequences?

- How would it be different if the teams reporting to you really were self-managed teams?

- What would happen if you could reduce the time it takes to do your job by 50 percent? What would you do with the time?

Meet with your staff and select one of the above situations that would help stretch your imaginations. Select a topic from the list, or develop another one, that taps into current problems or possibilities that would be useful to explore. After discussing the issues and ideas raised, determine what you learned from the experience and what you can apply to the current situation.

Keeping Up with Technology

Staying abreast of technological developments is critical. Technology is transforming the ways in which business is transacted. Advances in technology that affect your ability to communicate will make it easier and more feasible to manage globally. Manufacturing is becoming much more automated. Computers assist in product design. New products are created daily that were impossible five years ago because the technology did not exist.

In the future, whoever drives an industry's technology will emerge as the industry leader, as long as the organization does not fail on its other core competencies.

Effective global managers, whether or not they are in technical positions, need to keep up with technological advances to understand what is possible. To accomplish this:

- Talk with the organization's technology experts periodically to learn what they are working on, the advances they expect in the future, and their current challenges.

- Identify the current barriers to technological advances in your organization. Develop strategies to eliminate or reduce those barriers.

- Establish technology symposiums if your organization does not sponsor them already. Technology symposiums provide an opportunity for the technical people in the organization to learn what each other is doing.

- Attend your organization's technology symposiums. Listen for ideas that could change the way you do business.

- Join informal conversations about technology.

- Read science magazines that describe new findings in areas of your business. Also read about new developments currently unrelated to your business; in the future, these developments could easily migrate to your industry.

- Ask your communications and computer experts to present to you and your staff what they can do to improve communication globally.

- Ask your technology gurus to present to your staff their ideas about how your work will be done in the future.

- Ask your telephone company, computer vendor, and key software vendors to present to you and/or your staff their ideas about what will be possible in three to five years.

- Take part in beta testing of technology whenever appropriate. This will give you opportunities to see new products, as well as to talk informally with some of the developers.

Anticipating Trends and Their Impact on Your Organization

Continual analysis of your industry, global trends, and technological advances is important to anticipating the future. It is essential that organizations stay ahead of the competition.

- Dynamically monitor global business activities, both inside and outside the organization, to avoid being blind sided and to maximize opportunities.

- As you get in tune with trends in the industry, in your organization, and on the global landscape, forecast their effects on your business. Continually explore how these changes might affect your business. Create and take advantage of developing business opportunities.

- Watch the competition. What moves are they making in response to current trends? Are they somewhere you should be? Are they more experienced than you in particular markets? Learn from their successes and mistakes. How can you keep your organization from making the same mistakes? How can you learn from their successes to leapfrog them in the future?

- Actively develop your own perspective of business in the global economy. Watch for patterns and predictors. Anticipate and interpret world events.

- Shift your thinking from "where I do business" to "how I do business."

PART 3

Understanding Culture

Working with Other Cultures

Culture can be seen as collective patterns of thinking, feeling, and acting that distinguish one group from another. Culture, unlike an individual's traits, is learned, not inherited.

When you work with people of differing cultures, you will observe that similarities and differences occur because the people are members of different groups. Common group memberships that affect how people think, feel, and behave include national, regional, religious, and/or ethnic affiliation; gender; generation; social class; and corporate or organizational level.

Obviously, individuals within these various groups do not necessarily project the same or even consistent messages. In fact, they often are conflicting.

Determine the dimensions of culture that you encounter with the people with whom you work. These dimensions can be:

- *Rule Based or Relationship Based.* In a rule-based culture, people obey rules. An honorable person is one who keeps his or her word. Contracts and agreements are important.

  These societies tend to imply equality in that all persons falling under a rule or in a particular category should be treated the same. Not everyone may fall in the same category, though, which may be used to justify some different behavior toward different groups of people.

  Relationship-based cultures focus on exceptions. Decisions about what to do are based on the relationships between people. The closer the relationship, the more important it is to do what is best for the person. The emphasis is on relationships, not rules.

  Contracts can readily be changed, because the situation changes for people. For these cultures, trustworthy people honor the changing perspectives of one another.

  Relationship-based cultures believe that there are several perspectives on reality relative to each person. Rule-based cultures believe there is one reality.

- *Individual Focus or Group Focus.* Individual-focused cultures view the individual as having personal responsibility; he or she makes decisions and accepts responsibility. In group situations, individuals represent their respective groups and make decisions for them.

  With group-focused cultures, the group or team makes decisions and accepts joint responsibility. In a group, the delegate refers issues back to the group for the decisions.

- *Internal or External Control.* Cultures whose focus is internal control are flexible and adaptable. People of these cultures are willing to adapt in order to work harmoniously. They are comfortable with the waves and shifts and can adapt readily to the needs of others. Compromise is valued and respected.

External control-oriented cultures are more interested in controlling than adapting. People of these cultures admire people who fight for their point of view.

- *Time Management*. Some cultures see time as something that is controlled and managed. Meetings are set for a particular time and that is when they begin. Actions are time-based; if the time is up, the conversation is over.

  Other cultures adjust the time to fit the need of the situation. If you have something important to do, you do it. Even though there may be starting and ending times established for a meeting, interactions last as long as they need to. Time adjusts to the personal need; the person does not adjust to time.

- *Time Orientation — Past, Present, or Future*. Past-oriented cultures talk about the past, show respect for the past and for elders, are motivated to recapture the past, and view the present and future in relation to the past.

  Present-oriented cultures focus on the present. Relationships here and now are important. Activities of the moment are most important. Plans may be made, but it is not important that they are carried out.

  Future-oriented cultures center on the future — the possibilities, the hopes, the dreams. Planning and strategizing are critical. There is much interest in youth and the potential of the future. Lessons of the past are the past. The past and present are used to build the future.

- *Emotion Showing and Non-emotion Showing*. Cultures differ in terms of how much emotion their members show.

  In cultures in which the affect is low, people do not share what they think and feel. Physical contact is minimal. A cool, collected appearance is valued.

  In cultures that show emotion, heated, animated expression is admired. In these cultures, you know what people are thinking and feeling. Their expression is dramatic, and they touch and gesture expansively and often.

- *Achievement/Performance or Ascription*. In achievement-oriented cultures, the focus is on what the person or group does. Respect is accorded those who achieve.

  In ascription-oriented cultures, focus is on who you are and what your title is. Titles are used extensively. Respect for your superiors is seen as an indicator of your commitment to the group or organization.

- *Direct or Indirect.* In direct cultures, people are straightforward, to the point, and purposeful. Communication is direct and definitive. Principles are consistent and are independent of the situation or the people involved.

  People in indirect cultures relate in a roundabout way. Action is usually circuitous. Communication is indirect, tactful, and often ambiguous. Principles are less relevant than the situation and the context.

Talk with your staff and the people with whom you work about the different cultural approaches you have. Discuss with one another the assets and liabilities of each approach. Determine what each can do to help the other understand differing points of view when cultural differences are encountered.

Understanding Cultural Impact

Culture has a sometimes obvious, sometimes subtle effect on business processes such as problem solving, decision making, and communication. Knowing how these processes may be affected and staying alert to signs of these effects will help you work internationally.

- If a person objects to your statement of a problem or a solution, what are they really objecting to? It could be semantic — perhaps "problem" is too extreme a description for the situation from their point of view. Are they motivated to "solve" the "problem?" Some cultures value the acceptance of fate.

- Include people in the discussion of the situation before labeling it as a problem or an issue that needs a decision. You may see a need for change, but perhaps not everyone does.

- State a solution or change in terms of the desired state, the ultimate goal. Allow others to operationalize the goal in the best way possible for their culture. Agree on the end result; leave the means up to those who know best.

- Work with the strengths and needs of the people involved. Are they interested in facts or possibilities? Have them gather the information they feel is most pertinent, and put it all out on the table for the group to consider.

- Accept that implementation of ideas may take different amounts of time. Ask your internal experts to predict the timetables. Then work out deadlines that are reasonable for those who will take longer in implementation, but that don't hold up the rest.

- Assume differences until similarity is proven. Even if a person's words sound like those you want to hear, be patient and ensure that the understanding behind those words is the same.

- Always check out your assumptions.

- Understand that culture affects decision making and problem solving. For example, some cultures expect the executive to make certain decisions. Some cultures do not solve problems, they accept them.

- Identify the ways in which problem solving and decision making differ and are similar in the countries in which you are located.

Developing Cross-cultural Knowledge

To succeed in a global organization, managers need to know about their own culture and the cultures of people with whom they work or will work. It is essential to learn the key cultural customs and practices that will allow you to work together. Below are some suggestions for developing that cross-cultural knowledge:

- Identify people from other cultures in your organization or network. Ask them for insights about the similarities and differences between your culture and theirs. Identify cultural differences that could be problematic in conducting business. Make sure you also concentrate on the similarities.

- When you are in another country, record your observations in a journal. What surprises you? What is similar? What is different?

- Talk with and spend time with people from other cultures.

- Visit the country or countries on which you are focusing in your work. Talk with people. Learn the proper etiquette in that country. Learn about its social structures and norms. Seek to understand the local and business culture.

- Take a course in cross-cultural studies. Learn not only how specific countries differ from one another, but along what lines the cultures vary. Learn about similarities as well as differences.

- Rotate staff whenever possible so that people get exposure to other cultures.

- Participate in cross-cultural communication workshops or training to get a deeper understanding of the culture.

- Learn the language of the country in which you work.

- Encourage your staff to learn additional languages if they do not already know them. Make language proficiency a requirement for particular positions.

- Write to the embassies of the countries you're interested in and ask for information about the culture of each country, as well as its regional differences.

- Spend time with natives of foreign countries, discussing the differences and similarities of your respective backgrounds.

Bridging Cultures

Working successfully with other cultures requires bridging cultures. Bridging involves the continual interplay of two or more cultures or realities. It requires that people of differing cultures discover ways to work together that respect one another's culture, yet at the same time go beyond any one culture.

Bridging cultures is essential for successful global management. Without bridging, it is impossible to meet global and local needs. The organization will incorrectly identify market needs and solutions. To bridge cultures and communicate effectively:

- Do not assume that all people of a culture act or think in a particular way. No one wants to be seen as typically American, Chinese, French, and so forth.

- Challenge people who say, "The French (Italian, African, Indian, English) are like that." Statements like this are seen as offensive.

- When another person is talking, listen carefully to hear his or her values and beliefs. Check out your understanding respectfully and nonconfrontationally, even if the values you hear are very different from your own.

- Recognize that effective cross-cultural communication requires the interplay of the cultures or alternative realities. Cross-cultural communication requires that individuals be seen as individuals within the context of their culture.

- When you work with people, imagine their culture surrounding them. It is one of the influences on who they are and what they do. Also imagine your own culture surrounding you. You both need to step forward and meet in the space between the two cultures in which you are individuals, influenced by your cultures, yet part of the same cultural organization.

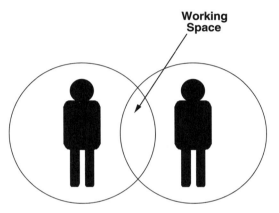

Working Space

- Build bridges together. Talk openly about how each sees the situation, and discuss how you can create the bridge to a new understanding and new ways of working.

- Periodically discuss what you have learned from each other. It is important that, if the organization has a majority culture, its members learn from people from the other cultures in the organization. Cross-cultural learning is a two-way street.

- Do not ask a person of one culture to represent the opinions of his or her culture. The person is an individual of the culture, not its representative. People in every culture have differing opinions. People in France or China or the United States are not all the same. It is very difficult to make any generalization that holds across a culture.

- If you are in a multinational organization, be aware that your global colleagues may not be truly representative of their cultures, because people who work in multinational companies become acculturated to the organization.

- Do not allow yourself or others to be intimidated by or become ineffective because of "cultural bullies." Some people protect themselves from others' influence or ideas by saying, "That doesn't work here," or "We have different values," when the real message is, "I do not like what you want to do."

- Do not become a cultural bully yourself. Do not assume your way is the best. Also do not assume your way is representative of your culture. It may simply be *your* way.

- Expect gaps in communication when you or others are not speaking your native languages. Phrase your questions carefully, so that you get accurate answers. Summarize what you hear.

- Talk slowly and remove idiomatic expressions. Clarify and rephrase often.

- It is most helpful if executive and management staffs are composed of people from the cultures in which the organization operates or wants to do business.

PART 4

Understanding Your Global Position

Developing International Business Savvy

To compete in the global economy, most organizations will find it necessary to increase their global position. To accomplish this, first determine what your current position is and then develop plans to address the issues. As you begin this analysis, determine the information you know and that which you need from the business or functional experts.

It is best to conduct this analysis with your team or to gather a task force to conduct the analysis with you so you do not unintentionally limit your information or analysis.

Be sure to look at the following areas in your analysis:

- Who in the industry has the greatest share of the global market?

- In which markets is future growth expected?

- Have foreign competitors targeted your primary markets as good ones to enter?

- Have foreign competitors targeted your industry as a good one to enter?

- Who are your primary domestic and foreign competitors now? In the future? What will be the impact of a change in competitors?

- What are the core factors of your success globally?

- What have been your limitations to success globally?

- Who in the industry is working with the toughest, most demanding customers?

- Who in the industry is introducing the most successful new products and line extensions?

- Who drives the development of technology necessary for your business — you or your competitors? Your supplier of technology?

- Who is in the position to redefine the industry?

- Who sets the standard in the industry for quality, customer service, manufacturing excellence, and technological advancement?

- What trade barriers protect your organization? What is their future?

- What political trends or events are occurring in the countries in which your business is located that may affect the company?

Through this analysis, determine which areas you must address now and which areas must be addressed in the future.

Working Your Globalization Strategy

Once you have determined how globalization affects you, create a vision of what that means. If you are in a global organization, take your lead from the corporate vision. If you are not, and you are one of the opinion- or decision-making leaders of the organization, you will want to create a vision for the new global organization and, most importantly, articulate the strategic imperative to become a global organization.

- Identify what needs to be global — sourcing, manufacturing, distribution, marketing, sales, and so forth.
  - Benchmark other organizations to learn effective ways to manage this function, business, or part of the business.
  - Start small, unless you are prepared or need a high-risk strategy because of the competitive threat. Test what works for you before you take the process all over the world.

- Determine the appropriate global/local balance.
  - Benchmark global management in other organizations. Understand their rationale for their particular kind of global management.
  - Present the alternative ways to manage globally.
  - Discuss the strengths and weaknesses of each approach.
  - Determine what you want to use for the present.

- Identify the criteria you will use to determine if the global management approach is working.

- Identify communications technology that will facilitate the global coordination you need to have.
  - Invite the organization's communication technology experts to a staff meeting to present you with options and possibilities.
  - Discuss your communication needs with potential internal and external providers.

- Determine your entry strategy if you are not already working in particular markets.

- Develop the partnerships (for example, translation firms, legal assistance, business partners) you need to work globally.

- To determine whether you should enter an alliance, understand your organization's core competencies and processes. Think very seriously before you decide to let another organization be responsible for one of your core competencies; normally, an organization should retain its core competencies and processes and use alliances to support other processes.

- Regularly review what is working, and identify problems. Develop plans to capitalize on what is working to address the problems.

- Determine a set of organization core values to communicate throughout the organization to build a common language and way of doing business with one another.
  - Use a global task force to develop the values.
  - Assure that the values do not reflect only one culture.
  - Ask high-level executives, preferably your CEO, to initially present the values and their rationale to the organization.
  - Get a commitment from the executive team to communicate, expect, and manage in accordance with the values.
  - Reinforce the values at every opportunity.
  - Use the values to build common direction and processes with your teams.

- Tell stories about successful global projects.

- Conduct the following analysis if you question the importance of becoming more globally oriented:
  - Are your competitors global players?
  - What are your competitors doing globally? Where are they?

What markets are they entering? What are they doing that you are not?

- From where will new competitors come? How will they compete against you?

    1. As a strategic planning learning experience, divide your staff into teams, with each team taking on the role of a particular competitor. Have the teams come to a meeting prepared to present how they will take 25 percent to 50 percent of your market share in the next three years.
    2. Ask each team to present its strategy. Have the other teams challenge the presentations and rationale.
    3. Debrief what you learned, and determine what to do as a result.

- What are your sources of raw materials? What are the chances of these sources staying the same for the next five years? How does the global economy affect your sources of raw materials?
- Where is manufacturing done? What are the chances that manufacturing locations or sources of labor will stay the same for the next five years?
- Where and who are your customers? Will they continue to provide large enough growth for the organization? From where may your future customers come?

Conducting Business in Other Countries

How you conduct business in other countries can be very different from how you do business in your own country. From knowing when to give gifts to understanding the protocol of negotiation, different customs can significantly affect your dealings with customers, distributors, suppliers, and colleagues in other countries. Recognizing and handling those differences can be the deciding factor in a successful international business effort. To help you conduct business internationally, try the following suggestions:

• Before you work in another country (or in your own country, with businesspeople from the foreign country), learn all you can about the cultural norms and customs of doing business in that country. For example, what is the cultural norm about coming to appointments on time? Where and when are decisions made? At the meeting at which they are discussed, or at dinner afterward?

• Remember, too, to take into account the *regional* differences within the country. Just as your own country has regional variations, so do all other countries. These regional differences can become pivotal when they affect business practices.

- Develop international contacts and discuss with them the market, demographics, perceptions, and so on, of the country and the region in which you plan to market your products or services.

- Learn about the national and local laws of the country that relate to your business involvement. For example, if you will be establishing a manufacturing plant in another country:
  - Are there national or local laws related to the use of local suppliers for the raw materials to be used?
  - What are the requirements about hiring local citizens?
  - Are there certification or licensing laws that your organization's employees or agents must comply with?
  - What limits, if any, exist on foreign/national composition of management ranks?
  - What are the anti-pollution laws?
  - What currencies are allowed for transacting business?

- Learn the differences between commissions and salaries in other countries.

- When you are in another country, hire a cultural guide. Check references, and hire a reputable and experienced coach. This should be someone who knows the language and who can coach you on proper conduct. Make it clear up front that you want feedback on your behavior. Your guide will be your teacher.

- Be as flexible as you can; let go of your agenda when necessary. Keep your goals in mind, but remember that the standards and business practices of the country in which you are doing business may require a different route to the achievement of those goals than you had in mind.

- Recognize that it can take more effort to build a trusting business relationship when you are working with people and businesses from a different culture.

- When checking with others for information about a specific country, don't rely on a single source of information. Use more than one source to avoid biased perceptions.

- When a plan you've developed does not work as expected, analyze the situation. Research what may have gone wrong from a cultural perspective.

- Recognize that goals and objectives for your staff need to reflect the local business practices and the cultural norms.

- When you select people to work internationally, choose individuals who are curious, flexible, and respectful of other cultures and customs. Provide these people with cultural training and ongoing support.

- Learn the 50 or so words that express respect, gratitude, appreciation, greeting, and empathy in the language in which you are working.

Marketing Products and Services Internationally

One of the biggest problems organizations face in their efforts to market products and services internationally is learning how to position and advertise the product so that it fits into the culture of a specific country. Cultural differences, language differences, and differences in what people value play a role in marketing products internationally. What plays well in New York City doesn't necessarily do well in Tokyo. The needs of the people of Paris differ from those in Lima, Peru.

The following suggestions can help you effectively position your products or services so that they appeal to the cultures involved:

- Identify and define your company's "global market" (for example, the countries with which your company does business or would like to do business). Determine how your company's products can meet the needs of the people in the countries you identified.

- Assess the countries with which you want to do business to determine what it takes to market and sell there. The following activities will help you do this:
  - Study how the competition sells its products internationally, and evaluate how successful their methods have been.
  - Look at publications from those countries to see how nationals advertise their products.
  - Know the economy of the country and how people purchase products. (For example, one organization found that in order to sell cough drops, they had to package the drops individually because consumers couldn't afford to buy a whole package.)
  - Travel to the countries to see for yourself how you might position your products and services.

- Look at your competitors.
  - Study your competitors and learn from their successes and mistakes.
  - Go where your competitors are not. Consider this strategy carefully, especially if you compete with top-notch organizations. To make this work, you need to know why they have not entered the market and be ready to be successful in it.
  - Notice whether your competition is in a particular market. If it isn't and you are usually first, there may be no problem. But if your competitor is usually first into a market and is not there, make certain you or someone knows why, and that those reasons have been taken into account in your plans for entering the market.
  - Go where your competitors are only when you know you have a competitive offering.

- Where are your future competitors? Consider entering markets in which you think you may have future competitors and gain market share before they actively enter that market.

- Carefully watch for assumptions about similarities to existing markets. Ask your staff to challenge assumptions.

- Understand your customers. Find out if there is a market for your products. For example, even though it's cheaper, the "huge economy size" will probably be a tough sell in countries where space is at a premium, both in stores and in homes.

- Question the impact of your product on customers. Will it help them? Are there any negative consequences for them?

- Add people to your staff who have personal experience in the foreign markets you plan to enter.

- Assign natives of the country to the team that is responsible for marketing the product in that country.

- Identify the best way to introduce your product or service or your new marketing campaign to the country involved. For example, one organization has set up symposiums to which it invites its key customers in each of the countries in which products are being introduced. An expert from headquarters is brought in to introduce the new product or campaign, which lends credibility and helps to gain the support of those key customers.

- Always remain open to making changes based on your own or other team members' increased understanding of the culture involved. Use internal and external experts as much as possible every step of the way.

Managing Employees in Other Countries

With the growth of multinational companies, more people are finding themselves managing staffs of people from other countries — either in that country, or remotely, from the organization's headquarters. The following suggestions are helpful in such situations:

- Recognize that the goals and objectives for your staff need to reflect the local business practices and the cultural values and norms. For example, U.S. nationals may be more concerned than others about getting personal credit for success, demonstrating their drive to succeed, or confronting unequal treatment. Some employees from U.S. companies and elsewhere may be willing to work late hours, because they believe it is important, while others believe that spending time with family is more important.

- When writing or interpreting policies, identify the desired outcome and the intention of the policy. Allow the local staff to fine-tune the specific procedures for carrying out the policy. This eliminates situations where the specifics of policies and procedures don't match the local work environment and thus are disregarded. It also encourages the involvement and buy-in of the local staff.

- Learn as much of the local language as you can, especially if you are working in the country involved. Your attempts to learn and use the language of the country will help you build trust and credibility with your staff.

- Learn all that you can about the social and business customs of the country. These customs apply as much to your staff as they do to your customers and business associates.

- Understand the educational system of the country. Typically, the American educational system tends to produce more specialists, while other countries' systems tend to produce more generalists. As a result, the division of tasks may be different — less specialized — in other countries than you might be accustomed to in your own country. For example, one company found that, in its German plant, one position handled the work that was divided among four different specialist positions in its American plants.

- Ask for assistance from your organization's human resources office or your manager about handling international staffs.

- What reputation does your organization have for treatment of employees? Is it consistent internationally?

- Recognize the holidays of the countries in which your business is located.

- Build or tap into a network of managers in your organization and industry, as well as in other organizations or industries, who have had similar experiences. Ask for their advice and support.

- Create different reward systems to accommodate cultural differences.

- Personnel practices differ. Decide how these issues should be handled on a country-by-country basis.

RECOMMENDED
READINGS

The publications listed here were selected for their content and suitability to a managerial audience.

Competitive Frontiers: Women Managers in a Global Economy

Adler, Nancy J., and Izraeli, Dafna N. (eds.), Cambridge, MA: Blackwell Publishers, 1994
ISBN: 1-55786-510-8
This book exposes the myths that have prevented many companies from fully utilizing talented women in their global work forces. It tells why equal opportunity makes sound business sense.

Business International's Global Management Desk Reference

Dreifus, Shirley B., New York: McGraw-Hill, 1992
ISBN: 0-07-009333-4
This book is a reference guide to understanding and capitalizing on opportunities emerging in the international marketplace. It is filled with tips and strategies for creating and developing an international organization that is effective at competing on the rapidly changing international scene.

Personal Engelska

Eisen, Adam, and Neld, Margareta, Stockholm, Sweden: Advanced Business Communication Sweden/PA Forum, 1993
ISBN: 91-88458-02-4
A handbook for Swedish individuals and companies, this book details the organizational and developmental structures of English-speaking companies, both British and American. Although the book is written for Swedish individuals, most of the substantive sections of the book are in English and provide insight into American and British business and culture from an outside perspective.

The Executive Guide to Asia-Pacific Communications

James, David, New York: Kodansha, 1995
ISBN: 1-56836-040-1
Topics include bridging cultures, guidelines for marketing, and background on key countries in the Asia-Pacific region. This book shows people doing business in this region what to do and what not to do to overcome cultural differences and achieve success in Asian and Pacific countries. Included are insightful tips to Asians on how to deal with Australians and North Americans.

International Dictionary of Management (4th ed.)	**Johannsen, Hano, and Page, G. Terry,** New York: Nichols Publishing, 1990 ISBN: 0-89397-358-0 This desk reference contains more than 6,000 entries that provide concise explanations of the major terms, techniques, and concepts being used in worldwide management circles. The entries cover several different aspects of management, including human resources, training, computerization, legal areas, and statistics.
International Management (2nd ed.)	**Killing, J. Peter; Beamish, Paul W.; Lecraw, Donald J.; and Crookell, Harold,** Burr Ridge, IL: Irwin Professional Publishing, 1993 ISBN: 0-256-11584-2 This book examines how firms become and remain international in scope. Through carefully selected, comprehensive case studies and integrated text material, this book links the internationalization process with multinational management.
The World in 2020	**McRea, Hamish,** Boston: Harvard Business School Press, 1995 ISBN: 0-87584-601-1 In looking at future trends, the author first looks at the world as it is today, as well as the major forces of world change, including demographics, the environment, trade, technology, and government. Capitalism, democracy, technology, and advanced communications are identified as key factors that will lead to increased global prosperity. Prosperous countries will be those that quickly and creatively adapt their strengths to meet the competition.
Globalwork	**O'Hara-Devereaux, Mary, and Johansen, Robert,** San Francisco: Jossey-Bass, 1994 ISBN: 1-55542-602-6 The authors, using research from the Institute for the Future, put forth a set of key competencies that managers need in order to be successful when conducting business on the international scene. The book describes both complex and basic strategies for dealing with global business issues ranging from communicating over several time zones to culturally based differences.

The Competitive Advantage of Nations	**Porter, Michael E.,** New York: The Free Press, 1990 ISBN: 0-02-925361-6 Based on extensive research, the author identifies elements that create a national, competitive advantage in an industry. The book further identifies the stages of competitive development through which entire economies advance and decline. Porter combines this research with the ideas presented in his previous works and explores how industries become competitive in a global marketplace.
Culture Clash	**Seelye, Ned H., and Seelye-James, Alan,** Lincolnwood, IL: NTC Business Books, 1995 ISBN: 0-8442-3304-8 Success in international business is about communicating across cultures. In global business, you must communicate in a way that is sensitive to different backgrounds, values, and ways of doing business. This book provides tips and taboos that will help you understand different cultures, overcome cultural barriers, and discover opportunities in mixed cultures both at home and abroad.
Head to Head: The Coming Economic Battle Among Japan, Europe, and America	**Thurow, Lester,** New York: William Morrow & Company, 1992 ISBN: 0-688-11150-5 With the demise of communism and the breakup of the Soviet Union, world competition has shifted from a military to an economic focus. The author examines the elements that provide strategic advantage in the current global environment. He then prescribes a course of action for a national structure that could ensure the continued competitiveness of the United States.
Riding the Waves of Culture	**Trompenaars, Fons,** Burr Ridge, IL: Irwin Professional Publishing, 1994 ISBN: 0-7863-0290-9 This book shows the emerging international manager how to build the skills, sensitivity, and cultural awareness needed to establish and sustain management effectiveness across cultural borders.
Total Global Strategy	**Yip, George S.,** Englewood Cliffs, NJ: Prentice-Hall, 1992 ISBN: 0-13-357658-2 The author contends that multinational companies are not changing fast enough to respond to the new reality of global competition. He conducted a five-year study of some of the world's largest multinational corporations. This book will enhance your global perspective and show you how to manage your business based on an integrated, worldwide strategic plan.

**SUGGESTED
SEMINARS**

The seminars listed here were selected for their appeal to a managerial audience. The reputation of the vendor, the quality of their seminar offerings, and the specific seminar content were considered in the selection process.

Because of the dynamic nature of the seminar marketplace, some seminars may have been upgraded or replaced, and others may no longer be offered. Likewise, costs and locations may have changed since this listing was compiled. We recommend that you contact the vendor directly for updated and additional information.

**International
Managers'
Programme**

The program's learning objectives include: encouraging participants to identify and apply their knowledge, experience, and skills to effectively manage in the international arena; developing the skills required to achieve results while managing key transitions, responsibilities, and operations; and enabling participants to broaden their horizons by involvement with similar caliber managers from global organizations.
Length: 2 weeks; Cost: £5,750 (+VAT)
Location: Berkhamsted, UK
**Ashridge Management College
Berkhamsted, Hertfordshire, HP4 1NS UK
Telephone: (+44) (0)1442 841015**

**The European
Management
Programme**

Program learning objectives include: learning to think in intercultural terms and adapt to new ways of working; developing the ability to think strategically from a European perspective, to acquire a better understanding of European political, financial, and social systems, and their effect on long-term corporate growth; and developing and practicing cross-cultural skills and communication in a multinational atmosphere.
Length: 10 days; Cost: 6,800 ECUs (excluding residential costs)
Locations: Berkhamsted, UK; Paris
**Ashridge Management College
Berkhamsted, Hertfordshire, HP4 1NS UK
Telephone: (+44) (0)1442 841015**

Executive Seminar

This values-based seminar brings together leaders from the public, private, and other sectors to enhance their qualities of vision and integrity. Classic readings from Plato to Jefferson support a discussion of the forces at work in society and the global community. Participants will examine the origins of many current business issues to acquire new perspectives as they manage change in their organizations.
Length: 1 week; Cost: $4,700
Location: Aspen, CO
The Aspen Institute
1000 North Third Street, Aspen, CO 81611
Telephone: 303/544-7952

Tuck Executive Program

This program is designed for senior managers. An intensive program, it integrates the study of the major business disciplines within the context of general strategic management. The curriculum also examines important issues in the international environment confronting managers of complex organizations. Corporate governance, public policy issues, and business ethics receive substantive attention.
Length: 4 weeks; Cost: $17,500
Location: Hanover, NH
Dartmouth College
The Amos Tuck School of Business Administration
Office of Executive Education, 100 Tuck Hall
Hanover, NH 03755-9050
Telephone: 603/646-2839

Managing for Market Success

This annually revised program is designed to provide a solid foundation in marketing. Participants will review and upgrade their skills in domestic and global marketing strategy; learn tools and concepts for effectively creating and carrying out their strategies; and expose themselves to other organizations' marketing methods through discussion and comparison of practices from a wide range of countries and industries.
Length: 2 weeks; Cost: 11,000 Swiss Francs
Location: Lausanne, Switzerland
International Institute for Management Development
Chemin de Bellerive 23, P.O. Box 915
CH-1001 Lausanne, Switzerland
Telephone: (41) 21/618 02 55

Networks and Alliances: The New Competitive Organization

This annually updated seminar concentrates on teaching the strategic use of alliances. Intended for anyone involved in management or planning, the program examines the purpose, structure, and spirit of good alliances with added focus on technology-driven partnerships and global strategies. Participants will share perspectives from a wide range of countries and industries.
Length: 5 days; Cost: 8,000 Swiss Francs
Location: Lausanne, Switzerland
International Institute for Management Development
Chemin de Bellerive 23, P.O. Box 915
CH-1001 Lausanne, Switzerland
Telephone: (41) 21/618 02 55

Foundations of Intercultural Communication

This program uses a highly interactive learning environment to foster an awareness and appreciation of cultural differences in both the international and domestic arenas.
Length: 3 days; Cost: Call vendor
Location: Portland, OR
The Intercultural Communication Institute
8835 S.W. Canyon Lane, Suite 238, Portland, OR 97225
Telephone: 503/297-4622

Financial Issues in Global Firms

This seminar is designed to give mid- and upper-level managers a working knowledge of the financial, accounting, and control issues that arise as an organization becomes global. Topics covered include management of foreign exchange and interest rate risk, capital expenditure analysis, international performance measurement, and control systems.
Length: 1 week; Cost: $4,000
Location: Glendale, AZ
Thunderbird
American Graduate School of International Management
Thunderbird Executive Training Center
15249 N. 59th Ave., Glendale, AZ 85306-9904
Telephone: 602/978-7820

Globalization: Merging Strategy with Action

Corporate strategy, human resource management, cross-cultural communication, and operations management all have special characteristics in a globally competitive industry. Participants learn how to become better managers in a world where competition is global, complex, and intense.
Length: 1 week; Cost: $4,000
Location: Glendale, AZ
Thunderbird
American Graduate School of International Management
Thunderbird Executive Training Center
15249 N. 59th Ave., Glendale, AZ 85306-9904
Telephone: 602/978-7820

Managing International Operations

This course is designed to provide participants with an understanding of the increasingly complex global competitive environment. They will learn to analyze the nature of global industries, competitors, and markets; to examine international finance and economics; and to gain sensitivity to cultural, economic, and governmental influences abroad.
Length: 5 days; Cost: $4,300
Location: Ann Arbor, MI
University of Michigan Business School
Executive Education Center, Ann Arbor, MI 48109-1234
Telephone: 313/763-1000

International Forum

This program includes an intensive exploration of global strategic issues. The Forum provides an opportunity for senior business leaders to test their thinking, their priorities, and their concerns with others having similar responsibilities but different perspectives.
Length: 5 days; Cost: $38,000
Locations: Call vendor
University of Pennsylvania, The Wharton School
Aresty Institute of Executive Education, Steinberg
Conference Center, 255 South 38th Street
Philadelphia, PA 19104-6359
Telephone: 800/255-3932

Advanced Management Program

This program is designed to help participants develop sound strategic thinking and decision-making skills and understand the organizational impact of financial analysis, market competition, government policies, legal issues, and other aspects of the business environment. This program explores changing social, political, and economic conditions at home and around the world and assesses their impact on business, both now and in the future.
Length: 5 weekends; Cost: $3,995
Location: Los Angeles
University of Southern California
Office of Executive Education, School of Business Administration, Davidson Conference Center, Room 111
Los Angeles, CA 90089-0871
Telephone: 213/740-8990

SELF-MANAGEMENT SKILLS

**SELF-
MANAGEMENT
SKILLS**

"Thriving" or "surviving" — which of these words describes you?

If you classify yourself as a survivor, you are probably experiencing problems with balance; you may feel that you are in a reactionary mode instead of basing your behavior and actions on your inner values and principles. You may be experiencing difficulty with finding a balance between your personal and work-related activities and between the needs of the organization, others, and yourself.

A person who thrives in a managerial position realizes that to effectively deal with the concerns of the organization and the people in it, one must also ensure that one's own needs receive attention. Thriving managers are flexible and adaptable. They establish balance in the areas of positive and negative stress, self-confidence, and self-acceptance. This means taking time to reflect on your own behavior to ensure congruency with principled and ethical leadership. It also means placing a high priority on learning and self-development.

This chapter covers the following three self-management skills areas:

Act with Integrity: Demonstrates principled leadership and sound business ethics; shows consistency among principles, values, and behavior; builds trust with others through own authenticity and follow-through on commitments.

Demonstrate Adaptability: Handles day-to-day work challenges confidently; is willing and able to adjust to multiple demands, shifting priorities, ambiguity, and rapid change; shows resilience in the face of constraints, frustrations, or adversity; demonstrates flexibility.

Develop Oneself: Learns from experience; actively pursues learning and self-development; seeks feedback and welcomes unsolicited feedback; modifies behavior in light of feedback.

ACT WITH INTEGRITY

At any level in your organization, you will occasionally find yourself in potentially compromising situations. How you deal with these situations is a measure of your integrity. How others view your effectiveness in dealing with sensitive situations will determine the level of trust they place in you.

Integrity involves the inherent knowledge of right and wrong, the ability to avoid the wrong, and the willingness to stand up for what is right. A macro perspective of integrity includes abiding by the laws set forth in our formal legal system, while micro perspectives of integrity include trusting employees with important assignments, showing fairness and candor in evaluating your employees' work, and showing consistency between your words and actions.

This three-part section will assist you in creating an atmosphere of trust and integrity.

Part 1: Establishing Trust and Integrity

- Evaluating Your Integrity
- Using Honest Communication to Enhance Your Integrity
- Making Realistic Promises and Keeping Them

Part 2: Working to Increase Your Integrity

- Modeling Ethical Behavior
- Working with Confidential and Private Information
- Making Ethical Decisions

Part 3: Developing Organization-Wide Ethics

- Protecting the Organization's Reputation
- Developing and Using a Written Code of Ethics

Valuable Tips

- Realize that establishing trust between you and your coworkers takes time. Building trust is a process, not an event.

- Make promises only if you plan to keep them.

- Openly discuss ethical issues.

- Follow up with those who question your decisions to understand their concerns and to explain the reasons for your decisions.

- Model your ethical beliefs through your behavior.

- Acknowledge courageous employees who have demonstrated high ethical standards or beliefs through their behavior.

- Read Barbara Toffler's *Managers Talk Ethics* with others in your organization, and discuss how the cases in the book may apply to your organization.

- Seek feedback on others' perceptions of your honesty and ethics.

- Work with leaders in your industry to resolve and communicate positions on ethical issues common to your industry.

- If you make a mistake, admit it.

- Be authentic. Seek opportunities to strengthen your self-insight, and then share who you are and what you believe and feel.

- Look for your company's written code of ethics, and apply it judiciously. If there is none, spearhead an effort to write one.

- Avoid "shooting the messenger" of bad news; you will thus allow problems to surface more easily.

- Protect confidential information. Respect the fact that others gave you information in confidence.

- Don't promise confidentiality if you are not certain that you can keep the information private.

- Stand up for others, especially your people, when they need your support.

- Resist the urge to rationalize away poor practices.

- Realize that a failure to meet deadlines is sometimes seen as lack of integrity by others.

ACT WITH INTEGRITY

- Behave in a way that is consistent with what you say — "walk your talk."

- If you receive feedback that you are seen as untrustworthy or unethical, ask for clarification. Instead of becoming defensive, work to understand the other person's point of view.

PART 1   Establishing Trust and Integrity

How does one go about building trust? By being consistent, communicating clearly and honestly, making (and keeping) realistic promises, protecting confidences, and treating others with respect. As you read this section, keep in mind that establishing trust takes time. Building a framework of trust and integrity is an involved and rewarding process, but it is a *process*, not an event.

Evaluating Your Integrity

As a manager, your effectiveness may be diminished if your staff or other coworkers think you lack integrity. They may be reluctant to entrust you with necessary confidential information, or they may be reluctant to bring up ethical dilemmas that your organization might be facing. To help you determine your current level of integrity, answer the following questions.

Do you consistently: *(Circle the appropriate response.)*

1. Make realistic promises and keep them?   **Yes/No**

2. Give honest answers to questions and challenges?   **Yes/No**

3. Protect confidential or sensitive information?   **Yes/No**

4. Admit when you've made a mistake?   **Yes/No**

5. Consider the trust and confidence of your coworkers to be important?   **Yes/No**

6. Make an effort to foster open, honest, and sincere communication?   **Yes/No**

7. Encourage others to question practices they cannot support?   **Yes/No**

8. Make use of your company's written code of ethics to guide you when making ethical decisions?   **Yes/No**

9. Demonstrate consistency between your words and actions?   **Yes/No**

10. Allow time for others to ask questions?   **Yes/No**

If you couldn't answer "yes" to most of these questions, you will find this section useful in helping you to establish and maintain an open and trusting environment. Even if you answered "yes" to most of these questions, the suggestions offered here are good reminders of what high-integrity behavior looks like. It's important for your staff to have the confidence in you to seek your counsel on ethical dilemmas and maintain a level of trust in your integrity.

Using Honest Communication to Enhance Your Integrity

One of the most effective ways of enhancing the trust that people place in you is through your daily communications with them. Use the following suggestions to help you to establish and maintain a high level of trust with your staff and others:

- Use open, sincere statements to clearly state your personal position, especially on ethical conduct. This is a simple way to directly communicate your integrity. By using your statements as a model for acceptable behavior, your staff will find it easier to conduct themselves in a similar fashion.

- When you make a mistake, admit it. This will encourage others to do the same, and the problems that stem from attempts to hide mistakes can be circumvented. Admitting your mistakes will also increase your credibility because it lets others know that they will not be severely punished for making mistakes. They will believe that you understand they are human, too.

- Give honest answers to questions and challenges. If others perceive you as not giving complete or honest answers, their level of trust in you will decline. Answering evasively can also damage your integrity. If you are not able to answer a challenge or question, state your reasons and strive to satisfy the questioner by dealing with the areas of concern that you *are* able to address.

- Sometimes communication is stifled when information is not provided. Attempt to keep your staff and others as informed as possible. Ask yourself:
  - Am I withholding information that others need?
  - Do I allow time to address questions and problems?
  - Do I give people only the information they need?

  If others think that you are keeping information from them, they will not be as likely to view you as trustworthy. Assure others that important issues can and will be addressed.

- Seek feedback from others on their perceptions of your honesty and ethical priorities. Use the following suggestions in soliciting feedback:
  - Talk to others in private.
  - Use active listening skills.
  - Respect another's perceptions of you as valid for that person.

- Use an objective third person if you feel the information is such that you will have a difficult time processing it objectively.
- Try to identify the origin of others' negative perceptions.

Correcting others' perceptions of you takes time and effort and requires rebuilding of relationships. Recheck others' perceptions of you periodically.

- Take time to think through your answers instead of responding too quickly. Some people mistrust quick answers.

Trust builds trust. Trust your staff. When you are open with them about information, ideas, and feelings, they are more likely to develop trust in you.

Making Realistic Promises and Keeping Them

Trust is also built on fulfilled promises. When promises are not made in earnest, but simply to buy time or to escape pressure, hard feelings and tarnished relationships often result. A deliberate failure to keep a promise without advance warning, follow-up, or apology can harm your credibility and may lead to major confrontations with others.

Following through on commitments is an essential component of building integrity. Appearing for meetings on time and completing assignments on schedule may seem like good organizational skills, but they are also measures of your integrity, reflecting your ability to make and keep promises.

The following guidelines can help you keep promises:

- Purchase a good time-organization system or have your secretary keep one for you. Attend the meetings you have committed to. Keep your appointments at the specified times. Allow yourself some lead time between appointments.

- Resist the urge to make empty promises to keep others off your back or to buy yourself time. These actions reflect negatively on your integrity.

- Avoid making statements that others may misinterpret as promises. For example, someone hearing "I'll try to read your report by Monday" might believe that you will be ready to discuss the report on Monday. Using clear and unambiguous statements will eliminate any confusion.

- Keep a tally of your implied or direct promises. Check whether you have followed through on each of these promises in a timely way. Examine the extent to which you deliver on your commitments. If appropriate, develop an action plan to improve your behavior.

PART 2

Modeling Ethical Behavior

Working to Increase Your Integrity

Modeling is one of the best ways to teach sound business ethics. By demonstrating consistency between what you say and what you do, your staff will have an effective role model to learn by. In addition, if people believe that you are honest and straightforward — that you take pains to "walk your talk" — they will be more inclined to trust you and to believe that their trust is well placed. Use the following pointers to help you effectively model ethical behavior:

- Actions speak louder than words. Set a good example for others by consistently engaging in solid ethical behavior.

- Keep both implicit and explicit promises. Broken promises can do considerable damage to relationships.

- Be aware of any internal conflicts you have, and recognize that you may telegraph mixed messages to others. This is confusing and, if frequent, can erode feelings of trust.

- Encourage the discussion of ethical considerations before decisions are made.

- Freely admit your mistakes. Encourage others to do the same.

- Stand up for what you believe is right.

- Reward behavior that upholds high ethical standards for your work group.

- Don't allow yourself to be swayed by what others would like you to say.

- Share the ethical dilemmas you have. Ask for input and help in determining how to handle them.

- Go beyond merely expressing concern for others and their struggles. Be available and approachable, and help out whenever possible.

Working with Confidential and Private Information

Managers often find themselves acting as caretakers of sensitive information. This "classified information" might consist of personnel records, compensation figures, proprietary technical information, or corporate "secrets." How you handle this information and to whom you choose to impart it reflect on your integrity as a manager. These suggestions can help you deal ethically with confidential information:

- Find out if your corporate code of ethics outlines any guidelines for handling sensitive information. Or see if there is a handbook that details common ethical concerns for your field. Referring to these documents when working in sensitive areas can be a good source of guidance.

- Read Barbara Toffler's *Managers Talk Ethics*. Talk with other managers to see if the ideas presented could be relevant to your company.

- Understand that your organization's culture determines the way in which confidentiality is addressed and maintained. If a situation demands an exception to these rules, use your best judgment to resolve the issue. Can you look at yourself in the mirror and say you are comfortable with your knowledge and the actions you took on it?

- Read Part 3 on Organization-Wide Ethics to resolve conflicts of personal and corporate interest.

Making Ethical Decisions

Undoubtedly, as a manager, you will be faced with ethical dilemmas when making decisions. Making ethical decisions and confronting practices that you cannot support can be a challenging, yet strengthening, process. Do you consistently consider and discuss with others the ethical considerations of decisions that are made? Are you willing to take a stand and speak up on decisions that you believe are wrong? When faced with such situations and decisions, ask yourself the following questions:

- What is the issue? How important are the consequences in the short term? In the long term?

- Are my needs, or the needs of those I report to or advise, keeping me from seeing the full reality of the problem?

- Is this situation harmful or dangerous to others? Is this information necessary to prevent something from happening that could damage the reputation of the company, my clients, or myself?

- If someone else came to me with this problem, how would I advise him or her to handle it?

- Will my action stand the test of time? Will I be glad that I ignored the problem or took the action I did a year from now?

- If this knowledge were taken to a higher level in the organization, would upper management approve of my actions?

- Would I be comfortable with my decision if it were broadcast on national television?

- Am I willing to be patient and not take immediate action? Do I act carefully, considering both the results I want to achieve and the actions required to achieve them?

- When I find myself in a situation in which I don't ethically know what to do, do I seek help? Do I inform and involve my manager?

Others in your organization probably have some of the same concerns that you do. Seek them out and support one another in your dilemmas. There is strength (and greater knowledge) in numbers.

PART 3

Protecting the Organization's Reputation

Developing Organization-Wide Ethics

A company's reputation is one of its best resources. If that reputation is tarnished for whatever reason — including unethical behavior by its managers or employees — the company's future can be jeopardized. To protect your organization's reputation, consider these suggestions:

- Represent yourself and your organization in the best way possible. Because you are a model of what your organization believes, people form an opinion of your organization based on your interactions with others.

- Be the embodiment of "quality" by acting ethically in all situations. Just as people associate quality products with organizations, so they associate ethical employees with organizations.

- Protect your organization's reputation by welcoming whistle-blowers. Persuade them to stay within the organization by thoroughly investigating their concerns, satisfying their doubts and complaints, and correcting the problems that they point out.

Developing and Using a Written Code of Ethics

Employees come from different backgrounds. What is considered right by one employee may be considered wrong by another. Ethical issues can be very complex, with no universally agreed-upon resolution. A written code of ethics can clarify expectations by spelling out the actions and behaviors that are acceptable and those that are not. A strong code of ethics includes a specific written policy and a culture that supports that policy.

An effective written policy:

- Incorporates business ethics with corporate strategy.

- Uses clear and specific wording.

- Spells out the rules by detailing standards, thus keeping misinterpretation to a minimum.

- Provides guidelines for dealing with vendors, competitors, and customers.

- Changes company rules and policies that do not support strong business and personal ethics.

It is up to top management to send a clear message to employees that good ethical behavior is the foundation of good business. It is up to each manager to send this message (through both words and actions) to his or her employees. The following suggestions can help you integrate ethical behaviors into your organization's standard operating procedures:

- Have each department discuss how its members can influence opinion about approaches to policy in your organization.

- Emphasize integrity, concern for people, and orientation to company values and policies in documents such as handbooks, policy statements, and job descriptions.

- Encourage and support firm action to be taken with employees at any level in response to wrongdoing.

- Unite your professional staff around goals related to developing and promoting a code of ethics.

- Provide training courses on dealing with ethical issues.

- Recruit people who share the company's values.

- Post your written code of ethics (or a summary of it) on bulletin boards.

- Create an ombudsperson or a telephone hotline number where employees can confidentially discuss ethical concerns and get answers and action.

RECOMMENDED READINGS

The publications listed here were selected for their content and suitability to a managerial audience.

Managing Corporate Ethics

Aguilar, Francis J., New York: Oxford University Press, 1994
ISBN: 0-19-508534-5
Based on extensive research, Aguilar's book shows managers how to create ethical programs that enhance corporate performance. It contains many practical, convincing, real-life examples of successful ethics programs.

Working Ethics

Brown, Marvin T., San Francisco: Jossey-Bass, 1990
ISBN: 1-55542-280-2
Ethics can be a powerful tool for better decision making and can create conditions that foster greater organizational effectiveness. The author explores components of an ethical decision-making process, addresses how to handle arguments constructively, and explains how to help create and develop organizations that make morally and socially responsible decisions.

A Rock and A Hard Place: How to Make Ethical Business Decisions When the Choices are Tough

Hodgson, Kent, New York: AMACOM, 1992
ISBN: 0-8144-5037-7
Decision making is arguably the most critical task in the current business environment, and Hodgson provides a system for making decisions that are responsible, practical, and defensible — decisions that are both ethical and better for business. The book offers illustrations, examples, and exercises that bring the process sharply into focus.

Beyond the Trust Gap

Horton, Thomas R., and Reid, Peter C., Burr Ridge, IL: Irwin Professional Publishing, 1991
ISBN: 1-55623-269-1
The authors suggest that downsizings, mergers, and acquisitions have ruptured relations between managers and their employees and created a "trust gap." This book offers guidelines for regaining credibility with middle managers in order to develop the speed and productivity needed to succeed in the competitive world economy.

Credibility: How Leaders Gain and Lose It

Kouzes, James M., and Posner, Barry Z., San Francisco: Jossey-Bass, 1993
ISBN: 1-55542-550-X
In this book Kouzes and Posner, the leadership experts, show why leadership is fundamentally a relationship with credibility as the cornerstone. By providing rich examples, they show how leaders can encourage greater initiative, risk taking, and productivity by demonstrating trust in employees and resolving conflicts on the basis of principles, not positions.

Leading Change

O'Toole, James, San Francisco: Jossey-Bass, 1995
ISBN: 1-55542-608-5
The corporate leader who sets out to command or manipulate employees to lead them through change is, says the author, doomed to failure. Change has been and always will be resisted. The only way to overcome that resistance is to use leadership based on moral values of integrity, trust, and an unwavering commitment to doing what is best for your employees. They also explore why corporate culture and the status quo conspire to defeat change.

Managers Talk Ethics

Toffler, Barbara Ley, New York: John Wiley & Sons, 1991
ISBN: 0-471-83022-4
The author presents techniques for enhancing an organization's ethical consciousness through the discussion of real-life ethical case studies that managers, ranging from the shop foreman to the chief executive officer, have faced on the job.

SUGGESTED
SEMINARS

The seminars listed here were selected for their appeal to a managerial audience. The reputation of the vendor, the quality of their seminar offerings, and the specific seminar content were considered in the selection process.

Because of the dynamic nature of the seminar marketplace, some seminars may have been upgraded or replaced, and others may no longer be offered. Likewise, costs and locations may have changed since this listing was compiled. We recommend that you contact the vendor directly for updated and additional information.

Covey Leadership Week

This personal experience teaches skills and tools used to create conditions necessary in building trust and empowerment within organizations. It emphasizes character and explores the distinction between leadership and management.
Length: 5 days; Cost: $3,900 (plus meals & lodging)
Locations: Call vendor
Covey Leadership Center
3507 North University Avenue, Suite 100, Provo, UT 84606
Telephone: 800/331-7716

Tuck Executive Program

This program is designed for senior managers. An intensive program, it integrates the study of the major business disciplines within the context of general strategic management. The curriculum also examines important issues in the international environment confronting managers of complex organizations. Corporate governance, public policy issues, and business ethics receive substantive attention.
Length: 4 weeks; Cost: $17,500
Location: Hanover, NH
Dartmouth College
The Amos Tuck School of Business Administration
Office of Executive Education, 100 Tuck Hall
Hanover, NH 03755-9050
Telephone: 603/646-2839

Developing the Organizational and Personal Self

This program is presented on the premise that success is based on self-awareness. Given that, topics include: boundaries; reintegration; acceptance of ourselves; removing self-diminishing myths and behaviors; improving interactions with others; and speaking more clearly, directly, and candidly.
Length: 6 days; Cost: $1,345
Location: Burlington, VT
NTL Institute
1240 North Pitt Street, Suite 100
Alexandria, VA 22314-1403
Telephone: 800/777-5227

Trust and Teamwork

This seminar teaches specific skills necessary to bring compassion and accountability to the workplace. Experiential in nature, the program focuses on creating a more collaborative, open, and trusting work environment. Participants will examine their own communication styles, learn to manage their credibility, create collaboration, and learn constructive confrontation skills.
Length: 2 days; Cost: $595
Locations: Call vendor
The Atlanta Consulting Group
1600 Parkwood Circle, Suite 200, Atlanta, GA 30339
Telephone: 800/852-8224

DEMONSTRATE ADAPTABILITY

In a changing world, it has become increasingly important for managers to be adaptable. This constant change is increasing the need to move quickly, deal with ambiguity, and accept change.

The person who thrives in a managerial position is comfortable with ambiguity and a fast pace, and has established balance between personal and work-related activities and between the needs of the organization, others, and self. This person knows that, to effectively deal with the concerns of the organization and the people in it, one must also ensure that one's own needs receive attention.

This section contains activities to help you develop balance in areas of positive and negative stress, self-confidence, and flexibility and adaptability.

Part 1: Coping with Stress

- Reducing Stress through Adequate Preparation
- Reducing Your Emotional Involvement in Stressful Situations
- Reducing Stress by Using Physical Coping Strategies
- Reducing Stress through Positive Self-Talk
- Using Support Groups to Cope with Stress
- Relaxing through Regulated Breathing Patterns
- Relaxing through Mental Imagery
- Coping with Stress by Managing Your Time
- Reducing Stress by Addressing Conflict

Part 2: Displaying Self-Confidence

- Projecting an Appropriate Degree of Self-Confidence
- Identifying Reasons for Lack of Self-Confidence
- Using Strengths to Increase Your Confidence
- Dealing Constructively with Your Mistakes
- Accepting Criticism Openly and Nondefensively

Part 3: Increasing Flexibility and Adaptability

- Increasing Your Flexibility When Interacting with Others
- Increasing Your Adaptability to Alternative Situations
- Working Effectively in Ambiguous Situations
- Handling Crisis Situations Effectively
- Demonstrating an Appropriate Level of Patience

Valuable Tips

- Develop your sense of humor. Learn not to take yourself too seriously.

- Live in the present. Avoid "fueling stress fires" by bemoaning the past or spinning your wheels about the future.

- Look for two or three quick and simple ways to relax and escape daily tensions.

- Set aside time for vigorous physical activity, and then do it.

- If you are overcommitted and expect to be great at everything, focus your energy on fewer areas and allow yourself to be average in less important matters.

- Expect things to turn out well.

- Accept and acknowledge your accomplishments as worthwhile.

- Have your manager put you in ambiguous situations and coach you on how to cope with them.

- Finish what you start. Anxiety can result from a lot of loose ends.

- Use the serenity prayer from Alcoholics Anonymous, "God grant me the serenity to accept the things I cannot change, the courage to change the things I can, and the wisdom to know the difference."

- Hold to simple truths.

- Establish and deepen nonwork friendships. "Let your hair down," be yourself, and talk about sensitive areas without being afraid.

- Decontaminate your leisure time. Set aside time to have fun and don't let work or thoughts about it intrude.

- Be aware of times when you are holding on to a solution or procedure because "that's the way it has always been done" instead of giving consideration to other viable alternatives.

- Broaden your family activities.

- Develop your assertiveness skills. Learn to say what you think and feel in ways which others can hear and understand.

- Express your frustration without blaming others.

- Set aside time for attending to the spiritual side of your life, and then do it.

- To control your temper, take ten slow, deep breaths through your nose before responding.

- Get organized and manage your time better to help reduce stress.

- Pay attention to your diet. Learn more about good nutrition and about drugs that can affect your stress level or sleep patterns.

- Don't "catastrophize" events at work. Problems are to be expected and are rarely catastrophic.

- Watch for habits of negative or self-defeating inner conversations or self-talk. Work at replacing them with positive inner dialogue.

- Get involved in enough other areas of your life to enhance your feelings of competence even when one area is going wrong.

- Be more willing to take personal criticism without showing resentment or anger.

- Recognize the potentially self-defeating aspects of your impatience.

PART 1

Reducing Stress Through Adequate Preparation

Coping With Stress

You probably know in advance when a situation is likely to be stressful for you. The following procedure will help you increase your confidence and reduce the stress you experience. The accompanying chart will help you structure your analysis.

1. Identify situations that cause stress.

2. For each situation, list all of the circumstances and responsibilities that make you feel particularly tense and pressured in that situation. Assume, for example, that the situation is a group meeting. Circumstances that often cause stress in meetings include:

    -   The need to speak in front of a group

    -   The presence of higher-level managers

    -   Lack of knowledge about the meeting topics

    -   Interpersonal conflict between you and another group member

3. Prepare for the worst. List the worst thing that could happen in each circumstance.

Situation: _____

Stressful Outcome	Worst Outcome	Methods of Coping

4. Take steps to prepare yourself for and cope with each stressful circumstance. For example, if interpersonal conflict between you and another group member causes you to feel stressed in a group situation, you could get together with that person before the meeting to iron out your differences in private.

Reducing Your Emotional Involvement in Stressful Situations

You may find times when you become too emotionally involved in stressful situations. The following suggestions will help you remove yourself emotionally from work-related problems so you can view them objectively and reduce your stress level:

1. First, learn to recognize your symptoms of excessive emotional involvement. Because it's difficult to be objective about one's own behavior, you may need help with this step. Ask a colleague to observe your behavior the next time you're involved in a stressful situation and to watch for signs of stress, such as clenched fists, irritability, and so forth. Afterward, ask your colleague to describe your behavior. As you listen to the description, take note of the behaviors that indicate increasing emotional involvement. Try to remember how you were feeling when you exhibited these behaviors.

2. The next time you're involved in a similar situation, monitor your behavior.

   - In situations involving only one or two people, be flexible in scheduling your time to help alleviate stress. At the first sign that you are becoming too emotionally involved, pull back and set the problem aside for a time. When you feel ready to review the problem objectively, return to it.

   - In situations where you can't set the problem aside, such as a group meeting, monitor your behavior as if you were an objective third party while you work on the problem. When you see yourself becoming too involved, talk yourself into calming down and becoming more objective. For example, if you find yourself getting angry, you might say to yourself: "I'm getting angry about this. I don't need to take it personally; I'll just step back a little and calm down."

3. Learn to laugh at yourself and take yourself less seriously.

Reducing Stress by Using Physical Coping Strategies

You probably are already aware of some of the ways in which your physical state affects your ability to handle stress. For example, most people realize that stressful situations are more difficult to cope with when they are tired. Following are additional areas in which your physical state affects your ability to cope with daily crises and demands:

- General physical fitness. When your body is not in good shape, it's less efficient in using available energy. To improve fitness, start a three-phase exercise plan that includes body flexibility, muscle strength, and cardiopulmonary endurance exercises. In addition to conditioning your body so that you're better able to cope with stress, physical exercise also helps discharge built-up stress energy. (Be sure to consult a physician before beginning an exercise program.)

- Use of drugs. Three types of drugs can reduce your ability to cope effectively with stress:

  - *Stimulants*. Stimulants act on the central nervous system to speed it up. Stimulants cause a rise in the heart rate, blood pressure, and body temperature. Stimulants can provide temporary energy that allows you to push beyond your normal level of endurance for short periods of time. Stimulants include common ones, such as caffeine, to dangerous ones, such as cocaine or methamphetamines. Stimulants can have very mild effects that cause few problems, or they can have dramatic, negative effects on your personality.

    Do not use illegal stimulants to help cope with stress. If you do, consult your Employee Assistance Program for help to stop their use.

    Monitor your intake of beverages with caffeine and over-the-counter preparations during times of stress. Observe whether you experience negative side effects, such as stomachaches, irritability, headaches, sleeplessness, and so forth. If you do, reduce or eliminate your intake.

  - *Alcohol*. Alcohol is a drug that your body must work extra hard to metabolize. Alcohol abuse also can have interpersonal and personal ramifications that create stress. If you are in the habit of consuming more than one beer, four ounces of wine, or one-and-a-half ounces of hard liquor a day, it's possible that your alcohol use is interfering with your ability to deal with stress. You may want to consider cutting down on your intake of alcohol.

  - *Nicotine*. Nicotine is a stimulant that reduces the body's ability to deal with pressure and stress. If you are smoking a large number of cigarettes each day, it's possible that your nicotine use is interfering with your ability to cope with stress. Consider gradually reducing the number of cigarettes you smoke each day.

Reducing Stress through Positive Self-Talk

Much of our stress comes from our attitudes — what we say to ourselves about the situations, trials, and challenges that confront us. Positive attitudes and positive, affirming ways of approaching situations will likely lead to positive short-term stress instead of negative chronic stress. To increase your positive mindset, try the following:

- Allow performance to be acceptable instead of needing it to be perfect. This may mean being comfortable with a job performed by one of your employees or learning when to "let go" of a project and declare it done.

- Avoid "black-and-white" thinking. This type of thinking often results in viewing performance as either a total success or a total failure. In reality, most performance falls somewhere in-between; increase your "gray" thinking.

- Focus on the positive things you do. Avoid "maximizing the negative" and "minimizing the positive." Dwelling on the negative and downplaying the positive will only increase stress and decrease self-esteem. Give yourself credit for positive experiences and avoid magnifying negative events.

- Watch the extent to which you personalize the outcome of situations. Personalizing involves seeing yourself as the primary cause of some negative external outcome that, in reality, you were not primarily responsible for.

- Think optimistically. Anticipating that things will not work out well can turn into a "self-fulfilling prophecy." Anticipating a positive outcome, in and of itself, will increase your chances of success, as well as your feeling of well-being.

Using Support Groups to Cope with Stress

When you're under pressure, other people can help alleviate your stress. Talking with others about problems can provide an outlet for stress energy. In addition, these people can help you generate solutions.

Thus, it's important to have a strong support network to turn to for both personal and work-related problems. The following procedure and accompanying chart will help you evaluate and build your support network:

1. Evaluate your support network for both your work and personal life. Using the chart which follows, list the people on whom you can rely in each situation listed.

2. Review your list and determine whether your network is adequate. Do you have people who can help you in each area?

3. For areas in which you require a stronger network, create a plan for building your network.

   - Ask trusted friends and coworkers where they've found support and help.

- Think of other ways in which you can build your network. For example:
  - To build a stronger network for support with work-related problems, think of people in your organization or other organizations who hold positions similar to yours. Professional organizations and meetings can be excellent places to meet these people.
  - To build a stronger network for support with personal problems, consider your church, community organizations, health clubs, and so forth.

Keep in mind that building long-lasting support relationships takes time and requires a lot of give-and-take.

WORK LIFE	People Who Can Provide Support	PERSONAL LIFE	People Who Can Provide Support
Information/ Training		Relaxation and Enjoyment	
Advice		Advice	
Relief From Overload		Relief from Overload	
Discussions of Issues/Values/ Problems		Companionship	
Other		Discussion of Problems/Sharing of Consequences	
Other		Romance	

Relaxing through Regulated Breathing Patterns

By slowing your breathing cycle, you lower your oxygen intake, which, in turn, slows the function of your body in general and leads to relaxation.

The breathing cycle of a normal adult ranges from 18 to 20 respirations per minute. It's possible to lower this rate to 10 to 14 breaths per minute. To do so, follow these steps:

1. Begin by paying attention to the *breath* leaving and entering your nostrils. Awareness of this pattern can help you lower your breathing cycle and make it smoother.

2. Next, pay attention to your *nostrils* during your breathing cycle (when inhaling and exhaling). Count each breath as it leaves your nostrils. Count to ten and then begin again very slowly, trying to breathe a little slower. As you do so, consciously begin to breathe gently and smoothly.

Whenever you are stressed, use this exercise to relax.

Relaxing through Mental Imagery

Mental imagery is very powerful. You can make yourself upset by imagining all of the possible negative aspects of a decision or an event. But you can also relax by using positive images. To relax through mental imagery, follow this procedure:

1. Find a comfortable place to sit or lie down. Then close your eyes and take four slow, deep breaths through your nose. Think of the place in which you relax as your personal sanctuary.

2. In your mind, construct a scene that is very pleasant and relaxing for you. This may be a scene from your past or an image you create just for this exercise. It is preferable that your chosen image not involve activity on the part of yourself or others. For example, you might picture yourself fishing on a beautiful, calm lake or sitting in a comfortable chair in front of a warm fire on a cold winter day.

The secret to using imagery is to develop as vivid a scenario as possible. Use all of your senses to imagine how it would feel to be in that situation — what it would look like, the sounds you would hear, and the diverse aromas in the air.

Set aside 5 minutes a day to take one of these "mental vacations."

Coping with Stress by Managing Your Time

If you are experiencing stress because you can't accomplish everything you need to accomplish or because you sometimes neglect high-priority items, effective time management can help reduce your stress level. To begin a time-management program, follow these guidelines:

1. Write down your five most important values or goals in your life.

2. Use a "time finder" to keep track of how you spend your time over the next week. A time finder is simply a grid with spaces

Activities

	Day 1	Day 2	Day 3	Day 4	Day 5	Day 6	Day 7
6:00 a.m.							
7:00 a.m.							
8:00 a.m.							
Etc....							
6:00 p.m							

for noting how you spend your time each hour of the day for seven days.

3. When the week is over, analyze the ways in which you spent your time. Identify the time spent on different areas of your life (work, family, leisure, spiritual, and so forth). If your time distribution is inconsistent with the values and goals you listed in the first step, it may be contributing to negative stress.

   Realize that if you spend little or no time on leisure activities, you're not allowing yourself opportunities to "charge your batteries" and recover from the demands placed on you.

4. Read through the Work Efficiently section of this Handbook and select the suggestions most applicable to your situation.

Reducing Stress by Addressing Conflict

Conflict is unavoidable in a dynamic organization. For those who are unable to deal with it constructively, conflict can create an emotional strain and cause stress. To deal with conflict on the job, follow these suggestions:

1. Analyze the way in which you currently deal with conflict. Over the next month, keep track of situations that involve interpersonal conflict or tension.

   • Note your reactions to these situations. Did you back down? Were you drawn into any win/lose confrontations?

- Keep track of the outcome of each situation. Were you satisfied with the result of the conflict and/or your behavior?

The following chart will help you monitor these situations.

Conflict Situation	Reactions	Outcome

2. Once you recognize sources of conflict and your current way of coping with them, apply the following guidelines each time you become involved in conflict:

   - Reduce antagonism by accepting that others' opinions are just as important to them as yours are to you. Accept the fact that some people will never be completely persuaded to accept your point of view, and be willing to compromise.

   - Present your opinions forcefully, but tactfully, without blaming others.

   - Investigate the other conflict management techniques presented in the Manage Disagreements section of this Handbook.

   - Evaluate the outcomes of conflict situations to determine if your new methods of handling conflict are reducing the amount of stress you feel.

3. Continue to improve your conflict management skills until you are comfortable with your performance in stressful situations.

PART 2

Projecting an Appropriate Degree of Self-Confidence

Displaying Self-Confidence

Effective leaders project a strong sense of self-confidence that instills confidence in others and promotes good "followership." Nonetheless, it's wise to temper one's self-confidence with some measure of humility to avoid seeming overly assured. Self-confidence without humility can be offensive.

- Talk about your accomplishments, but share credit for your successes.

- Look for opportunities to recognize the ideas and successes of others. As you listen during meetings, pick up on the suggestions made by others and support them.

- Willingly show your humanness by admitting when you have made a mistake. Also, all managers have weaknesses in some area. Being open about both your strengths and weaknesses will bring you closer to others, including your employees, and will make it easier for others to be open with you.

Identifying Reasons for Lack of Self-Confidence

To build a development plan to increase self-confidence, it is helpful to determine the reasons for your lack of confidence. The following guidelines can help you do this:

1. Over the next two weeks, pay attention to all situations in which you feel a lack of confidence. Write down what you are thinking to yourself at such times. Be certain to include any negative names, adjectives, or characteristics you apply to yourself. Following are examples of the types of statements that indicate lack of self-confidence:

   - "I just can't handle this kind of situation."

   - "I'm in way over my head; I don't have enough background in this area."

   - "I can never make them understand."

   - "I'm just not smart enough."

2. Next, analyze the thoughts you've recorded. Look for patterns that indicate particular areas of concern, including thoughts that:

   - Suggest that you believe you must be perfect

   - Are self-putdowns or negative self-talk

- Indicate that you expect impossible things of yourself, such as competence in every area of your life

- Refer to your lack of skills or abilities

3. For those thoughts that indicate a lack of confidence due to lack of skills, prepare a plan for increasing your skills. Be sure your plan includes a resolution to think positive thoughts about your increasing skills.

4. For areas in which you have unrealistic thoughts or put yourself down, use rational, positive statements, such as:

- "Nobody's perfect, and I shouldn't expect to be, either."

- "I'm not a terrible person just because I made a mistake."

- "Just because one person didn't like my idea doesn't mean it's a bad idea."

Gradually, as you increase your skills and think positive thoughts about yourself, you will find your self-confidence increasing.

Using Strengths to Increase Your Confidence

A lack of self-confidence can have negative effects on your career. It can keep you from actively seeking new responsibilities and leadership opportunities. In addition, it's difficult for others to have confidence in you if you lack confidence in yourself. Thus, it's important to curb any tendencies to be negative about yourself. The following ways of focusing on your accomplishments will help you establish this control:

- Keep a file of your accomplishments and successes — good performance evaluations, letters of commendation, your own descriptions of difficult and challenging situations in which you performed well. When you begin to doubt your competence, read through this file. Refer to your accomplishments at appropriate times when speaking with others about additional opportunities.

- Seek positive feedback from trusted managers, peers, direct reports, and friends when you feel a need for support.

- Be careful to balance your failures by giving equal consideration to your successes.

- Become involved in off-the-job activities that are rewarding and provide recognition. Again, refer to your successes, when appropriate, as you participate in these activities.

- Act as if you are confident. Then watch the results.

- In the United States, you will appear self-confident if you look people in the eye, have a firm handshake, and state your opinions clearly ("I think"; "I believe"). Do not make tentative statements, such as "I don't know, but..."

Dealing Constructively with Your Mistakes

Successful people experience failures and setbacks. Sometimes they make poor judgment calls. Successful people differ from unsuccessful people, however, in that they learn from these experiences. To make the most of a situation in which you find your personal or business plans thwarted, look at your failures and mistakes as learning opportunities and development experiences. The following guidelines will help you deal constructively with your setbacks:

- Consider a setback a learning experience. Review the events that led up to it, and assess your attitude and behavior at the time. Did you neglect to get buy-in from employees? Did you take a high-handed approach with others? Did you fail to do your homework? After you have assessed the situation, decide how you can change your attitude or behavior to achieve a more favorable outcome the next time.

- Focus on the process rather than the outcome. Thwarted plans may mean that you have neglected to build relationships with internal or external sources who are important to organizational goals. Focus not on the failed outcome, but on the conditions and causes of the setback. Consider in particular your relationship with individuals and groups who were an integral part of the situation.
  - Do you have a viable relationship with those involved?
  - Have you shown your trustworthiness?
  - Have you "walked your talk" and "lived your values"?

  Seek feedback from people who can comment on these questions to check the validity of your assumptions. Resolve to build or strengthen crucial relationships with others.

- Consider the situation a challenge. Rather than viewing the setback as a failure, look at it as an opportunity to think creatively. Brainstorm ways you can get around whatever obstacles it reflects.

- Confront errors. When you attempt something and fail, ask yourself, "What have I learned?" rather than kicking yourself or blaming someone else. Discovering the value in your mistakes will make you a better, smarter manager.

If you have not weathered setbacks in your organizational life, you probably have not taken many risks or stretched yourself by taking on tough and difficult goals. The key to organizational success over the long run is to take some calculated risks and use failures as opportunities to learn.

Accepting Criticism Openly and Nondefensively

In a world where things change rapidly, feedback is necessary to stay on track. Defensiveness, the tendency to be protective when others give feedback, is a common but troublesome characteristic. It results in your not hearing important feedback and in people feeling uncomfortable working with you. It is an especially difficult barrier when it affects your ability to be open to and accept helpful feedback.

Learn to think of negative feedback as positive suggestions on how you can do better, rather than as personal criticism. Doing so will increase your effectiveness and open you to valuable information. The following guidelines can help you use feedback to your advantage:

- Listen attentively to feedback until you are sure the speaker is finished. Ask if he or she is ready to hear your response.

- Check your response patterns for phrases such as "Yes, but..." and eliminate them from your speech. Whenever you catch yourself assuming this defensive posture, stop talking and listen, rather than justify.

- Be aware that when you are explaining your point of view, others may see this as defensive behavior.

- Paraphrase the feedback and demonstrate in other ways your understanding of what was said.

- Ask yourself a fixed set of rational/analytical questions, such as the following, to help reduce your defensiveness:
  - Do I understand exactly what is being said?
  - Is the criticism about a topic or behavior I could do something about if I wanted to?
  - What would happen if I acted on the feedback?

- Decide whether you want to change or if you need more information.

As your resistance to criticism diminishes, you will begin to think of such criticism as a tool for improving your interactions with others.

PART 3

Increasing Your Flexibility When Interacting with Others

Increasing Flexibility and Adaptability

If you are strongly opinionated, you may not spend enough time listening to what others are saying. Rather than listening to alternate approaches, you may tend to prepare rebuttals to argue your own case. This can cause others to see you as rigid and inflexible. Use the following exercises to increase your flexibility in this area:

- To ensure that you are listening in order to understand what another person is saying (rather than to strengthen your own position), concentrate on paraphrasing or summarizing the speaker's message. This will help focus your attention on the speaker and let the speaker know that you are tuned in to his or her message.

- If you have difficulty seeing the value of another person's viewpoint, mentally reverse sides to see if you can come up with ideas that support that person's position. While your goal is not necessarily to accept the opposite view as your final opinion, understanding another person's thinking may enhance your own ideas and make you appear less rigid.

- Ask trusted coworkers to provide feedback on situations in which others think you tend to be overly opinionated or rigid in your thinking. Most people have specific "problem areas." Recognizing the fact that you are becoming inflexible is the first step in changing.

- If you are seen as strong-minded, ask others for their opinion before you state yours. When sharing your opinion, preface your statements with words such as, "In my opinion…" or "I think…"

Increasing Your Adaptability to Alternative Solutions

If your typical response to a problem is to immediately generate a specific solution or to hold on to a solution or procedure because "that's the way it's always been done," you may find it difficult to give adequate consideration to other possibilities. This tendency can decrease the quality of your decisions. To reduce this tendency, follow these guidelines:

- When you approach a problem, remind yourself that there are many possible solutions to any given management problem and that you must be willing to consider the unique facts about the situation before making a final decision.

- Watch for "snap" reactions. Rather than assuming that the first alternative that enters your mind is the best solution, consider other options.

- Consciously delay making a final decision. Gather more information so you can gain a thorough understanding of several possible solutions and their unique benefits and draw-backs. Once you understand the solutions, weed out those that are least appropriate, using facts to substantiate your decisions.

- Look for opportunities to combine the best features of several solutions to improve the quality of your final decision.

- Adopt the philosophy, "If it works, make it better."

Working Effectively in Ambiguous Situations

The ability to think on your feet is essential in positions of increasing responsibility. If you are ill-at-ease in situations where you do not know exactly what is expected of you or in which there is no clear leader or structure, the following suggestions will help you learn to cope:

- Examine times when you have been in ambiguous situations. It might have been a situation in which your responsibilities were not clearly established. Consider your response. Did you tend to sit back and wait for someone else to take the lead, or did you step forward to help establish a structure? Set a goal to expand your range of behavior. For example, begin to take actions to provide yourself with more structure.

- Rather than avoiding unstructured situations — such as unstructured problem-solving groups or task forces — seek them out as opportunities for demonstrating your leadership abilities. Ask trusted participants to give you feedback about your performance and suggestions for how you could be more effective.

- Ask your manager to thrust you into ambiguous situations and then ask him or her to give you feedback on your performance.

Some people see ambiguity as an opportunity for applying creative approaches to issues, while many others view it as irritating, stressful, and unnecessary. To learn to benefit from ambiguity, first understand what you do not like about it, what you could like about it, and why it makes you less effective. Use the following technique for changing your behavior in ambiguous situations:

1. Identify key past and current ambiguous situations. How have you behaved? Did you:

   • Try to get control of what was happening?

   • Wait for others to make clear what was expected?

   • Worry about whether the decision was right?

   • Wonder when things would become clear?

2. Examine how you felt about these situations. Did you feel:

   • Angry about a lack of direction?

   • Hurt or angry about not being involved in the decision?

   • Anxious that the course of action may not work?

3. In today's business environment, it is important to be comfortable with ambiguity. Plan to adopt more useful behaviors in future ambiguous situations. Some ways to do this might include the following:

   • Change your own expectations; don't expect to have all the information when you make a decision.

   • Expect that things will change.

   • Recall how you have weathered ambiguous situations well in the past, and use those strategies.

   • Ask others what they do to cope.

   • Volunteer for projects and activities that will give you practice working under ambiguous conditions.

   • Watch and talk with people who you believe handle ambiguity well.

Handling Crisis Situations Effectively

How do you react when a work emergency is brought to your attention? In crisis situations, keep a cool head and evaluate the seriousness of the situation before reacting. If you find that you tend to react too quickly to crises and make decisions without getting all the facts, you may want to try this technique:

1. Make it a practice to discuss the situation with your manager, a peer, or affected employees before making a decision.

2. Together, gather all the facts and evaluate the seriousness of the situation. Give the situation a crisis rating from 1 (can wait) to 10 (urgent, immediate attention required).

3. Together, brainstorm alternative courses of action. Select the alternative that best addresses the situation.

This technique can help you put the crisis in perspective and decide if you absolutely must drop everything to react to it. The result of your evaluation may be that you have more time to address the situation than you thought, or that what you initially identified as a crisis may be a small problem — or no problem at all.

Demonstrating an Appropriate Level of Patience

Patience with others requires active effort on your part to accept and understand their experience and point of view. To become more patient with people:

- Seek feedback from others regarding recent occasions in which you did not demonstrate an appropriate level of patience.
  - Don't try to justify or explain your behavior. Listen intently and take notes about what they observed.
  - Later, analyze the circumstances and try to identify themes in your impatience.
  - Attempt to identify situations in which you tend to lose your patience. Do you lose patience when you are overwhelmed? Do you express impatience with slow learners?

- To control your impatience, change your perspective by thinking more accepting thoughts (for example, "I have the time," "If I wait, I'll understand," or "This will pass"). Temporarily leave the situation if you cannot refrain from saying something inappropriate.

- Look carefully at the strengths and development needs of others to gain insight into their behavior and to increase your tolerance of it. Be attentive to the qualities that make a particular person likable and valuable; then concentrate on his or her strengths. As you learn to focus on and appreciate the strengths of others, you will find yourself more tolerant of their weaknesses.

- Avoid interrupting others when they are talking.

- Consciously refrain from immediate judgment or criticism of others' ideas and concerns. Instead, ask open-ended questions to understand their issues more fully. Recognize that what may not be an issue to you may be a valid concern to others.

RECOMMENDED READINGS

The publications listed here were selected for their content and suitability to a managerial audience.

Crossing the Minefield

Barner, Robert W., New York: AMACOM, 1994
ISBN: 0-8144-0241-0
To be successful in competitive and changing times you and your team need to know how to stay motivated, energized, and efficient. This book provides strategies to implement for accomplishing this now rather than later when your team has become stagnant. Among the things you will learn is how to: help your staff manage stress, respond quickly to demands from customers and your company, focus your efforts, inspire team members, streamline your team, and reenergize yourself to meet new challenges.

Self-Defeating Behaviors

Cudney, Milton R., and Hardy, Robert E., San Francisco: HarperSanFrancisco, 1991
ISBN: 0-06-250169-0
The authors provide proven methods for understanding and eliminating habitual destructive behaviors. The book examines the source and pattern of destructive, self-defeating behaviors and provides practical solutions for overcoming and abandoning these destructive cycles.

A Change of Heart: Converting Your Stresses to Strengths

Eliot, Robert S., M.D., New York: Bantam Books, 1994
ISBN: 0-553-07117-3
Dr. Eliot and his colleagues at the Institute of Stress Medicine have identified the prime stressors that affect people today. This book offers practical, time-tested techniques to turn stresses to strengths by attitude adjustment, having values, practicing good time management, eating well, and exercising. It also involves channeling your energy more productively.

Controlling Stress in the Workplace

Gatto, Rex P., San Diego: Pfeiffer & Company, 1993
ISBN: 0-89384-218-4
Gatto provides a handbook on how to anticipate workplace stress and then move beyond it with specific techniques that will relieve the stress. In addition, the book will show you how to turn stress into a positive, productive force you can use.

The Age of Paradox

Handy, Charles, Boston: Harvard Business School Press, 1994
ISBN: 0-87584-425-1
Handy suggests that in order to live and succeed in a rapidly changing world, we must organize in our minds the confusion generated by these changes before we can do anything about them. Managing business, family, education, money, and relationships are just some of the many topics covered. Through a discussion of these topics, strategies are provided for maintaining a sense of continuity and direction, and for balancing personal and professional responsibilities.

Transitions: Positive Change in Your Life and Work

Hopson, Barrie, and Scally, Mike, San Diego: Pfeiffer & Company, 1993
ISBN: 0-89384-212-5
This workbook presents ideas of transition and change for your own self-development and will give you the tools to identify and cope with changes as they happen. It will enable you to identify the two types and seven stages of transition and to better understand the effect they have on your life.

Mastering the Winds of Change

Olesen, Erik, New York: HarperBusiness, 1994
ISBN: 0-88730-692-6
This author, consultant, and therapist witnessed how stressful change is for most people and organizations, yet recognized that some extraordinary people seem to thrive on it. He surveyed high achievers and prominent people to define the specific strategies they use to deal with change and learned that coping skills help you overcome obstacles, discover new opportunities, build confidence, and learn from mistakes.

Overwhelmed: Coping with Life's Ups and Downs

Schlossberg, Nancy K., New York: Lexington Books, 1994
ISBN: 0-02-927896-1
The author has studied people in transition and developed a model for coping more effectively with the disruptions, expected or unexpected, that everyone faces. The transition model is also useful to organizations in the process of restructuring and can help affected people learn how to negotiate unwanted change. A companion to the book is the *Transition Coping Guide*, a self-scoring questionnaire which helps individuals or groups take stock of critical resources and provides ways to think about change more creatively. For further information, or to order the *Transition Coping Guide* published by Personnel Decisions International, call 800/633-4410.

Managing the
Unknowable

Stacey, Ralph D., San Francisco: Jossey-Bass, 1992
ISBN: 1-55542-463-5
Defying conventional management norms, the author contends that accepting and welcoming instability inspires creativity and can result in successful outcomes. The book provides strategies and techniques for making companies ready and able to benefit from unstable situations.

SUGGESTED
SEMINARS

The seminars listed here were selected for their appeal to a managerial audience. The reputation of the vendor, the quality of their seminar offerings, and the specific seminar content were considered in the selection process.

Because of the dynamic nature of the seminar marketplace, some seminars may have been upgraded or replaced, and others may no longer be offered. Likewise, costs and locations may have changed since this listing was compiled. We recommend that you contact the vendor directly for updated and additional information.

Managing Emotion in the Workplace: Maintaining High Performance Under Pressure

Participants in this workshop will learn to identify their personal trigger points, develop techniques for staying calm in tense situations, receive criticism in a positive manner, and reenergize themselves at the end of the workday.
Length: 2 days; Cost: $1,085
Locations: Call vendor
**American Management Association
P.O. Box 319, Saranac Lake, NY 12983
Telephone: 800/262-9699**

Time and Stress Management

This seminar is designed for those who want to get maximum productivity from their time and are concerned about the effects of stress on their job performance and personal health. The techniques and concepts taught in this seminar enable participants to recognize the symptoms and effects of stress and to minimize their negative impact.
Length: 1 day; Cost: $350
Location: New York
**Arthur Andersen & Company
1345 Avenue of the Americas, New York, NY 10105
Telephone: 212/708-8080**

Centering for Individual and Professional Development

This program covers finding one's physical and mental point of equilibrium, obtaining greater clarity about oneself, and finding one's own "unique center."
Length: 7 days; Cost: $1,395
Locations: Bethel, ME; Northern California
**NTL Institute
1240 North Pitt Street, Suite 100
Alexandria, VA 22314-1403
Telephone: 800/777-5227**

Developing the Organizational and Personal Self

This program is presented on the premise that success is based on self-awareness. Given that, topics include: boundaries; reintegration; acceptance of ourselves; removing self-diminishing myths and behaviors; improving interactions with others; and speaking more clearly, directly, and candidly.
Length: 6 days; Cost: $1,345
Location: Burlington, VT
NTL Institute
1240 North Pitt Street, Suite 100
Alexandria, VA 22314-1403
Telephone: 800/777-5227

Individual Coaching Services

This customized coaching program helps people develop critical skills such as leadership, interpersonal, communication, and organizational influence skills. Through a tailored assessment to diagnose developmental needs, one-on-one skills training, and state-of-the-art techniques for behavior change, participants gain powerful self-insight and successfully learn new skills and behaviors to make them stronger performers.
Length: Call vendor; Cost: Call vendor
Locations: Call vendor
Personnel Decisions International
2000 Plaza VII Tower, 45 South Seventh Street
Minneapolis, MN 55402-1608
Telepone: 800/633-4410

The Leadership Challenge Workshop

This seminar is an intensive program on the leadership practices required to get extraordinary things done. It strengthens individuals' abilities and self-confidence to lead others in challenging situations. It is based on the award-winning book *The Leadership Challenge* by Jim Kouzes.
Length: 2-1/2 days; Cost: $1,800
Location: Monterey, CA
TPG/Learning Systems
The Tom Peters Group
555 Hamilton Avenue, Suite 300, Palo Alto, CA 94301
Telephone: 800/333-8878

How to Work More Effectively with People

This workshop is designed to teach managers how to develop positive relationships, why self-esteem and self-confidence are such important elements in human motivation and performance, and how to tune in to the needs of others. Participants also learn to understand and manage frustration, defensiveness, anger, hostility, and insensitivity in themselves and others.
Length: 2 days; Cost: $695
Location: Madison, WI
University of Wisconsin-Madison
Management Institute, Grainger Hall
975 University Avenue
Madison, WI 53706-1323
Telephone: 800/348-8964

DEVELOP ONESELF

As the pace of change continues to intensify in today's business environment, continued development of one's skills and knowledge is no longer optional. Success in one's career now requires a serious commitment to learning and self-development.

Effective learning is not an automatic process. Instead, it begins with a vision and a strategy, requires a commitment to lifelong learning, and involves continuing effort. The Development FIRST[1] model can help you proactively drive your development and establish a cycle of continuous learning. This model involves:

Focusing on your priorities
Implementing something every day
Reflecting on what happens
Seeking feedback and support
Transferring learning into next steps

Learning is like an insurance policy for success and survival in tomorrow's world. To help maintain your "policy" in good standing, consider the strategies and tactics for effective learning and self-development in this section, which use the Development FIRST model.

Part 1: Capitalizing on Opportunities for Learning

- Employing the Strategies of Successful Learners
- Broadening Your Learning Experiences
- Viewing Mistakes as Learning Opportunities
- Expanding the Scope of Your Knowledge Base
- Leveraging Your Areas of Strength

Part 2: Creating a Plan for Learning and Self-Development

- Analyzing Your Skills Portfolio
- Focusing on Your Development Objectives
- Creating a Plan for Personal Growth

Part 3: Implementing Your Development Plan

- Spending Time Each Day on Your Development
- Seizing On-the-Job Development Opportunities
- Involving Others in Your Development Efforts
- Seeking Honest Feedback from Others
- Eliminating Defensiveness When Receiving Feedback

---

[1] *Development FIRST*, David B. Peterson, Ph.D., and Mary Dee Hicks, Ph.D., Personnel Decisions International, 1995.

- Overcoming Barriers to Development
- Monitoring Your Progress
- Reflecting on What You Have Learned
- Transferring Learning into Next Steps

Valuable Tips

- Spend five minutes every day visualizing yourself attaining your goals.

- Find something you can learn from each person with whom you work.

- Do one thing every day, even if it is a small step, to move toward your goals.

- When you set goals, ensure that they reflect accomplishments you really want, not what others want or what you think you should want.

- Learn to look at negative feedback and criticism as potentially useful information that you need to understand more fully.

- Keep your goals in front of you at all times — for example, on a mirror at home, in your desk drawer, and so forth.

- Approach each day with the same sense of discovery that you had when you were a child.

- Decide on a clear-cut, long-range goal for yourself. Then establish what you will need to do and what attitudes you will need to have in order to achieve it.

- Take more risks.

- Limit your focus. Genuine progress on your two or three most important goals is more meaningful and rewarding than negligible progress on a dozen less critical fronts.

- Keep a list of the things that you want to learn in the next 5, 10, and 20 years.

- Make some form of public commitment to your goals so others will encourage you to reach them.

- When you make a mistake, learn from it.

- Examine what you do with the lessons you learn from feedback and experience. Observe how you change and adapt, based on these lessons.

- Keep track of lessons learned; refer to them periodically to reinforce your learning.

PART 1

Employing the Strategies of Successful Learners

Capitalizing on Opportunities for Learning

Sometimes learning just happens without much planning or forethought. Successful learners, however, actively pursue learning opportunities as a part of their everyday life. They take advantage of experiences and challenges, both great and small, to improve and become more effective managers. They view the learning process as fun and exciting.

Try the following suggestions to increase your "learning quotient:"

- Learn for the sake of gaining wisdom, not just knowledge.

- Commit to being a lifelong learner. Approach every situation by asking yourself, "What can I learn?"

- Break out of your normal routine. When you are locked into your comfortable habits, you are less able to adapt to changing situations. Search for innovative ways to approach the situations you deal with every day.

- Involve others in your learning pursuits. You can learn a great deal by:
  - Paying attention to other managers' successes
  - Modeling the behaviors and techniques of managers who are skilled in your weak areas
  - Seeking feedback from others
  - Getting input on a strategy or idea you have
  - Receiving encouragement and advice from supportive colleagues

  Unsuccessful learners often view learning and development as something they can achieve in a vacuum; successful learners view the involvement of others as their lifeline to learning.

- Hold a "postmortem" meeting (either alone or with your team, or both) at the completion of projects. Discuss what went well and what did not go well. Determine what you'd like to do differently and what successful strategies you'd like to replicate. Build this learning step into each of your projects.

- Confront problems instead of avoiding them. When you put off dealing with a problem situation, ask yourself why. Learn to lean into your areas of discomfort to improve your skills and knowledge.

Broadening Your Learning Experiences

Sometimes the not-so-obvious experiences turn out to offer the most powerful opportunities for learning. Training yourself to take advantage of a broad variety of experiences can accelerate your learning and development. To increase your opportunities for learning:

- Diversify. Get involved in a variety of experiences to maximize your development. High-quality learning most often comes from a wide range of life activities, not just a few.

- Admit your weaknesses and compensate for them by surrounding yourself with people who are skilled in areas where you are weak. For example, hire employees who have strengths that you lack. Not only can you learn from them, but your team will be more well rounded and synergistic.

- View your strengths as development opportunities. Typically, your greatest successes will come from leveraging your strengths. Broaden and improve your current strengths by finding new ways to use these skills, by teaching them to others, and by pursuing assignments that stretch your skills even further.

- Determine how effectively you handle your emotions by answering these questions:
  - Do I worry too much about what others think and, as a result, allow my actions to be unduly influenced by their opinions?
  - Do I tend to be out of touch with my emotions and take action without tuning in to my own feelings or considering the feelings of others?
  - Do I express too little or too much emotion?

  Successful learners effectively tune in to their emotions and use their emotions to help guide their decisions and enhance their effectiveness.

- Examine what you dislike about others. Sometimes what we dislike about others can provide insights about our own blind spots.

Viewing Mistakes as Learning Opportunities

Some people believe that learning is merely a matter of motivation. In reality, learning is a reflection of how people think. Viewing mistakes and failures as learning opportunities builds a foundation for further learning. Mistakes often prompt managers to look inward and evaluate their limitations and shortcomings, learning more about themselves in the process. Becoming aware of

your weaknesses is an important first step in developing and improving your skills.

Mistakes are only a problem if you repeat them or don't learn from them. Try the following suggestions to turn your mistakes into learning opportunities:

- The next time you attempt something and fail, ask yourself, "What have I learned?" Write down what you learned, as well as possible ways to do things differently the next time.

- Share your mistakes. You will find that talking through a mistake with others will increase your understanding of the situation. Solicit their suggestions and ideas on what you might do differently in the future. When you can openly share your mistakes with others, they will become more comfortable sharing their mistakes with you. You can also learn valuable lessons from others' mistakes.

- Focus on your role in the failure, rather than looking at what others did or didn't do. Avoid any temptation to blame others. Instead, examine what *you* did or failed to do so that you can learn from your actions to create more success in the future.

- When you make a mistake, ask yourself and others, if appropriate, if you have made a similar mistake in the past. You can gain powerful insights by studying patterns of behavior that have resulted in repeated mistakes, miscalculations, or misreadings of a situation.

- If you have not been stretched or challenged lately, ask yourself:
  - Am I challenging myself in my job and outside of work?
  - Am I requesting or hearing feedback from others?
  - Am I taking any risks?

Expanding the Scope of Your Knowledge Base

Today's continuous changes make many procedures and strategies obsolete in a short period of time. To keep pace and remain at the forefront, managers must pursue continuous learning to stay current with the advances in their own profession, as well as in other areas that have an impact on their business. To broaden the scope of your knowledge:

- Set aside a regular period of time each week for reading.
  - Read the major publications in your field and industry. Copy and save the most stimulating and relevant articles.
  - Read the latest books in your field.
  - Read articles and books outside your area of expertise.

- Search for one insight or application in everything you read. It is more beneficial to read one article and learn from it than to lightly skim five articles and take away nothing of substance. Work hard when you are reading by drawing conclusions and searching for meanings relevant to your development. Personal growth requires thought and energy. If you just wait for inspiration, your development will take much longer.

- Select an area of particular interest in your work, and research it thoroughly. Write an article for publication and present it as a topic at a seminar or symposium.

- Attend seminars, symposiums, and conferences that address new developments in your field. Afterward, ask yourself:
  - What does this information mean to me?
  - How does this information help me?
  - How can I transfer this knowledge or skill to my job?

- Be open to new ideas and innovations that you encounter in your readings and seminars. Determine whether you can implement them in your own area. Refine your ideas by discussing them with colleagues and staff.

- Acquire cross-functional knowledge by networking and talking with others about what is going on in their business units. Improve your understanding of how your function or group fits into the overall picture of the organization. For example, to maximize their effectiveness, marketing people need financial knowledge, financial professionals need to understand operations, and so on.

- Obtain knowledge that transcends your usual day-to-day experience. For example, a course in literature or the humanities can broaden your horizons and stimulate you to think beyond your usual frame of reference. A course in political science or world religion can expand your knowledge of different world views and increase your level of awareness about issues of diversity.

Leveraging Your Areas of Strength

People succeed because of what they do well. Often, people are so focused on improving their weak areas that they ignore their strengths. Yet it makes good sense to also look for ways to further capitalize on your strengths. Consider the following.

- Gain a greater understanding of your areas of strength by considering how you would answer the following questions in a job interview:

- Why should we hire you?
- What are you skilled at?
- What special qualities and abilities would you bring to our organization?
- What things have people praised you for?

- Redefine your current opportunities. First, identify parts of your job that you handle easily. Then add a new challenge by asking yourself:
  - How can I make this more strategic?
  - Can I teach this to others?
  - How can I streamline it and reduce cycle time?
  - How can I make it more effective?

- Seek experience in new, complex situations.

- Spend time with others who are more skilled than you.

- Benchmark yourself against the leaders in your field.

- Cross-train and pursue learning in related areas.

PART 2

Creating a Plan for Learning and Self-Development

Analyzing Your Skills Portfolio

Your ability to achieve your full potential requires that you have a good handle on both your strengths and your weaknesses. While personal insight is a good starting point for assessing your assets and deficits, including others will most likely increase the accuracy and objectivity of your skills assessment. In addition, your openness to others about your own strengths and development needs will likely lead to increased feedback and encouragement from them. Your employees will see you as someone who has to work on weak areas just as they do, and you will be a positive role model for them.

To analyze your strengths and weaknesses, consider these suggestions:

- Use a model to evaluate your strengths and weaknesses. If you evaluate yourself solely on your personal opinion of what it takes to be an effective manager, you may overlook some critical skills important for your job. Using a model of effective managerial performance will ensure that you address the total range of skills necessary for success. One model of managerial effectiveness is presented in the introductory chapter, Using This Handbook.

- Find out what others see as your strengths and development needs. To gather this information, you can use past performance appraisals; discussions with your manager, trusted peers, and direct reports; or input and feedback from others on your skills identified in the managerial model discussed in the previous paragraph. Compare this information with your own understanding of your strengths and weaknesses. Work to gain a greater understanding of the discrepancies.

- Look at where you have been successful and what you have done that has contributed to your success. Then look objectively at your skills in situations where you have not been as successful, and examine areas of skill deficit.

- Consider using a multi-rater or 360-degree feedback instrument to obtain comprehensive feedback on your skills from others. For information about The PROFILOR® feedback instrument, contact Client Relations, Personnel Decisions International, 2000 Plaza VII Tower, 45 South Seventh Street, Minneapolis, MN 55402-1608, 800/633-4410 or 612/339-0927.

- Share your perception of your strengths and development needs with others, including your manager and employees, and let them know that you are open to talking about their impact. Solicit and be open to the comments and insights of others.

Focusing on Your Development Objectives

Managers who have a vision for their development and a strategy for making that vision a reality are much more likely to succeed than those who are less directed in their development and personal growth. Once you have completed an accurate assessment of your skills, the next step is to select one or two high-priority goals based on what is most valuable to you and your organization. Consider the following process:

1. Create and define your vision, for both the short term and the long term. Ask yourself where you want to be and what you want to be doing 1, 5, 10, and 20 years from now. Also consider changes both within and outside the organization that are likely to take place during these time frames.

2. Determine what primary skills and additional competencies or experiences you will need to achieve your vision, both long term and short term. Compare this list with your current skill level. Note where gaps in skill and experience exist.

3. Identify one or two target areas in which improvement or experience is needed. Focus on areas of greatest priority and on areas where changes would be most beneficial to attaining your vision. When you determine development goals, choose those that demand you stretch yourself and take some risks. Also recognize that your strengths need to be developed and challenged.

4. For each goal, determine whether you need:

   - More information and knowledge

   - Practice in applying the knowledge and skills

   - Increased priority on using the skills you have

   - Communicating to others your existing expertise or skill that is currently underutilized

5. Write specific objectives addressing your needs in each goal area.

Creating a Plan for Personal Growth

While your vision and goals will define where you want your development to take you, an action plan will aid you in achieving your development objectives. True development does not have a beginning and an end, but instead is an ongoing process in which goals are achieved and simultaneously updated and revised.

Think of your development plan as you would any other project or business plan. Many of the same elements are required — goals, action steps, people involved, time frames for completion, and success or quality criteria. Use a format that makes sense to you so that you actually *use* the plan.

As you write your development plan, make sure you follow these guidelines for creating a successful plan:

- State objectives with a high degree of specificity. Specific, concrete goals will enable you to determine when you have achieved your objectives.

- Limit the focus. Include no more than three major areas in your plan.

- Lay out small, reasonable steps. Expecting too much too soon will discourage progress. Divide development activities into small steps that lead to your end goal.

- Include on-the-job activities. This is where the most powerful development occurs.

- Allow for feedback and support from others. Development occurs most readily with the help and involvement of others.

- Include deadlines. Schedule target dates for completion and checkpoints for progress review.

- Provide for a variety of activities. For example, include a mix of on-the-job activities, readings, course work, and evaluations.

- List your most likely barriers to development and strategies to overcome them.

- Include criteria for success so that you can effectively measure progress.

PART 3

Spending Time Each Day on Your Development

Implementing Your Development Plan

The easiest and most effective way to develop is to make it a regular part of your daily discipline. You are more likely to succeed if you chip away at your development in small, bite-sized pieces than if you attend one intensive training program a year. Consider the following suggestions for a daily development discipline:

- Make development routine. Set aside a regular time, such as at the beginning or end of each day, to act and reflect on your development goals.

- Link your goals with something you are already doing. Take a moment each day to examine the development opportunities that are right in front of you.

- Do old things in new ways. For example, use a team process for making a decision that you typically make on your own.

- Make the development process easy by setting reasonable expectations that do not require a huge up-front commitment.

- Experiment and take intelligent risks each day.

Seizing On-the-Job Development Opportunities

Some development opportunities present themselves without any effort on the part of the individual. On the other hand, managers who are committed to their own development actively look for key development assignments and experiences and take maximum advantage of each one. To do this yourself, consider taking the initiative in some of the following activities:

- Take on projects that help you develop a tolerance for ambiguity and uncertain outcomes.

EXCUSE ME – I BELIEVE THAT'S MY CAREER PATH YOU'RE STANDING IN.

- Push yourself to take on work for which you may lack some of the necessary skills, in order to improve those skills.

- Seek assignments that will use and stretch your strengths.

- Train others. A good way to hone your own skills is to teach them to someone else.

- Seek out big challenges if you want to be seen as someone who can do the job.

- Look for development opportunities that include "start-up" or "fix-it" situations to demonstrate that you can successfully tackle tough assignments.

- Get involved in, or offer to lead, a task force to develop your cross-functional knowledge.

- Volunteer for projects that require you to learn new information within tight time frames.

- Take on projects that are highly visible to others.

- Seek roles that will enable you to work with people outside your department with whom you have not worked before.

Involving Others in Your Development Efforts

Effective development rarely happens in isolation. Rather, successful learning occurs through a continuous process of feedback and support from others. Consider the following suggestions for involving others:

- Realize that no single person will fill all of your development and feedback needs. Thus, keep a diverse list of people who can support your development. Colleagues, direct reports, manager, team leaders, human resources staff, role models and mentors, and family and friends can all support your development in various ways.

- Involve others in testing your assumptions and conclusions to ensure that you are on the right track. Choose people who will give you candid feedback and encourage you to take risks.

- Ask others about significant events in their careers to get a better view of the experiences and challenges you are likely to face as you assume greater responsibility.

- Observe others who are skilled or savvy in the areas you are attempting to develop. When observing their behavior, note what they do well and what they don't do well. Integrate the positive aspects into your own behavior.

- Learn from people outside of work. Leaders from other professions or organizations, as well as community leaders, can serve as effective coaches and role models. They may be able to expose you to skills, styles, and techniques that you have not found in your current situation.

- Ask for support when you get frustrated or feel discouraged. Others can be a sounding board for you when you face barriers or slowed progress on your development goals.

Seeking Honest Feedback from Others

Getting personal feedback is like finding your location on a map. If you set out on a trip without a map, it is likely to take you much longer to reach your destination (if you reach it at all). Feedback works the same way. While it's important to know where you've been and what your destination or goal is, it's also critical to have an accurate picture of where you are now. Ongoing and frank feedback from others will allow you to continue to develop.

Many people are reluctant to give feedback, especially negative feedback. As a result, if you wait for others to offer their feedback, you may never get it. It's up to you to actively solicit the feedback you need to grow and develop. The following suggestions can help you do so:

- Before you solicit feedback from others, know what to ask for. Then ask questions that effectively uncover what you are trying to learn about yourself. For example, if you are just beginning to work on something, broad feedback is likely to be most helpful. Or, you may want feedback on different elements at different times. Let others know what feedback will be most helpful to you before they observe you so they know what to look for.

- Actively seek feedback from your manager on a continuing basis. He or she can be a valuable source of feedback for self-improvement. Ask for specific comments, suggestions, and feedback in areas you are attempting to improve.

- Encourage your direct reports and peers to provide feedback. Ask them how you can be more effective in your job. Also ask what you might change to help them be more effective in their jobs.

- Solicit feedback from others at the end of projects. Ask them what you did that was effective and what you did that was not effective. Once you have thought about the feedback and have decided how you'd like to do things differently the next time, ask them to observe you in this specific area on a future project and provide you with additional feedback.

- When someone gives you vague feedback (for example, "nice job"), either positive or negative, ask for specifics on what you did well or where your performance was lacking.

- Obtain comprehensive feedback on your skills using multi-rater or 360-degree feedback instruments available through Personnel Decisions International.

- After receiving feedback from others, ask yourself these questions:
  - Is the feedback valid and accurate?
  - Is the feedback important?
  - Do I want to change my behavior or approach? If yes, how can I change it?

- Express your appreciation to those who give you feedback. Then put relevant feedback to visible use. If others see that you act on the feedback you receive, they will be more willing to give you constructive, honest feedback in the future.

Eliminating Defensiveness When Receiving Feedback

Negative feedback often evokes automatic defensiveness from the recipient. It is common to stand up for ourselves in the midst of criticism. Defensiveness, however, stops others from giving you the feedback and information you need to improve your performance.

The following suggestions can help you fight the tendency to be defensive and keep feedback channels open:

- View defensiveness as your worst enemy. Don't argue, don't explain, and don't debate the feedback. If you become defensive, others will be reluctant to give you feedback in the future, and you will cut off information that is critical for meeting your goals.

- When you find yourself "explaining why" in response to feedback, immediately stop yourself. Explanations are often perceived as a defensive response.

- Use discretion when sharing your point of view. First, summarize the feedback to ensure that you fully heard and understood it. Second, share your point of view only if the other person is interested in hearing it.

- Ask trusted colleagues to tell you when you are coming across as defensive. Promptly eliminate or change the behavior they have labeled as defensive, even if you do not agree with their point of view. Their perception of your behavior is reality; it is what they believe to be true.

Overcoming Barriers to Development

Development is not easy. Our natural tendency is to return to the status quo. Therefore, it's important to anticipate barriers and obstacles to your development so that you are better prepared to overcome them. Consider the following suggestions:

- Show your development plans and goals to others. This will increase your commitment to attaining the goals and will help involve others in your development. Specifically ask for support and feedback in the areas you find toughest to master.

- Focus on a simpler process. Complexity can make the development process intimidating, rather than motivational.

- Lean into your discomfort, rather than getting trapped by procrastination and fear. Realize that change and development may feel uncertain or ambiguous at times, and remind yourself that this feeling is only temporary.

- Be patient and realize that *real* change takes time. Change will feel natural and easy only with persistence and practice.

- Record what happens when your progress begins to slip. Then look for the patterns and trends that caused you difficulty in those situations. Becoming aware of your typical barriers is the first step to overcoming them.

- Create reminders. For example, write your development goals where you will see them every day.

- Redefine failure and success by separating what you are *learning* from how you are *performing*. Ask "What have I just learned?" rather than "How did I just do?"

Monitoring Your Progress

In both their personal and professional lives, people are motivated by their progress toward goals. By establishing and monitoring your goals, you will be better able to gauge your progress, thereby feeling an increased sense of achievement. Follow these guidelines for monitoring your short-term goals:

1. At the beginning of each day or week, list the things you wish to accomplish and the dates by which you wish to accomplish them. Make sure that these activities move you in the

direction of your vision of your future. Then use this list as the basis for your daily activities.

2. Compare your actual accomplishments with your scheduled accomplishments. Determine whether you are satisfied with your achievements during the established time period.

3. If you would like to accomplish more during a given time period, gradually increase the demands you make on yourself by slowly adding activities to your list. Establish a pace that will enable you to attain your goals, and set interim dates so that all activities will be completed by the end of your chosen time period.

4. If you have difficulty achieving your goals, consider your use of time management techniques. Refer to the Work Efficiently section of this Handbook for suggestions on improving your time management skills.

5. Regularly evaluate your progress to determine whether your achievement level is satisfying your need to realize progress toward your goals.

Reflecting on What You Have Learned

Development and change require both action and reflection. Reflecting on what you have learned is the foundation for continued action in your development efforts. Focused reflection allows you to identify themes and patterns in your behavior to ensure that you continue to apply the lessons you have learned. It also helps you continuously challenge your assumptions so that you remain open to new learning. Consider the following suggestions for reflection:

*   Create a regular time for reflection. Take advantage of the following natural cycles for reflection:
    - Regular daily events, such as your commute to and from work, can be a good time to reflect on lessons of the day.
    - Periodic reviews, such as at the beginning of each month or quarter, provide an opportunity to consolidate your lessons.
    - Major events, such as completion of a long-term assignment, offer opportunities to debrief both on what went well and what needs improvement. Reflection at the mid-point of a large assignment also makes good sense, because you then still have a chance to make course corrections.

*   Learn from your successes by examining them and determining exactly what you did to succeed. Then look for opportunities to transfer your behaviors and skills to other situations.

- Be resilient and learn from your mistakes. Identify what was in your control and what wasn't. Then determine what you can do differently next time to increase your chances of a successful outcome. Seek the input of others to ensure your conclusions are on track.

- Tune in to your emotions. Use negative emotions to motivate you, to draw your attention to something that may need changing, or to identify areas of future growth. Also pay attention to positive emotions, such as feelings of satisfaction, and think about what you did to experience them.

- Consider keeping a learning log to track and document your lessons and your progress.

Transferring Learning into Next Steps

The learning process is a continuous one. So it's important to adapt and plan for continued growth. It's also important to acknowledge your accomplishments. Use the following suggestions to make your development a continuous process, rather than a one-time event:

- Take time to celebrate and acknowledge progress and accomplishment of a development objective. Personal recognition builds self-confidence and feelings of personal worth, and provides renewed energy for your continued growth.

- Create additional opportunities to apply what you have learned. Using your new skills will ensure that you keep them sharp and up to date.

- If your development efforts have not been successful, create a plan to make any necessary changes in your approach. Review your objectives and actions with others, and seek their candid feedback and advice.

- Take a break to recharge your batteries in preparation for your next development challenges and opportunities. Take stock of what development strategies and tactics worked best so you can apply these same successes in your future development efforts.

- Focus on new goals. Update your skills portfolio to include your newly developed skills. Then choose whether to focus on developing new goals or on achieving further mastery in those skill areas in which you are currently working.

RECOMMENDED READINGS

The publications listed here were selected for their content and suitability to a managerial audience.

The Seven Habits of Highly Effective People

Covey, Stephen R., New York: Simon & Schuster, 1989
ISBN: 0-671-66398-4
Covey presents a holistic, integrated, principle-centered approach for solving personal and professional problems. His principles provide the security to adapt to change and the wisdom and power to take advantage of the opportunities that change creates.

Small Decencies

Cowan, John, New York: HarperBusiness, 1992
ISBN: 0-88730-559-8
This book is a collection of essays on how to approach work and life from a more human perspective. Drawing on his vast work and life experiences, the author presents ways of incorporating "small decencies" into work and personal relationships which will in turn make life more meaningful.

Self-Defeating Behaviors

Cudney, Milton R., and Hardy, Robert E., San Francisco: HarperSanFrancisco, 1991
ISBN: 0-06-250169-0
The authors provide proven methods for understanding and eliminating habitual destructive behaviors. The book examines the source and pattern of destructive, self-defeating behaviors and provides practical solutions for overcoming and abandoning these destructive cycles.

Patterns of High Performance

Fletcher, Jerry L., San Francisco: Berrett-Koehler, 1993
ISBN: 1-881052-33-8
A High Performance Pattern is the distinctive sequence of steps people naturally follow when they are at their best. Each individual has a distinctive pattern and this book seeks to help the reader discover what that pattern is and how to best utilize it. Included are techniques on how to revitalize tasks, find new ways of working in difficult situations, change the focus of a group for better efficiency, and get critical projects back on track. These various High Performance Patterns are described and examined though sixteen case studies.

When Smart People Fail: Rebuilding Yourself for Success	**Hyatt, Carole, and Gottlieb, Linda,** New York: Penguin Books, 1993 ISBN: 0-14-017811-2 This book identifies the nine most common reasons people fail and the six stages of failure. The authors provide guidance for overcoming failure, "reinventing" yourself after failure, and harnessing your talents to achieve success in the future.
The Lessons of Experience	**McCall, Morgan W., Jr.; Lombardo, Michael M.; and Morrison, Ann M.,** Lexington, MA: Lexington Books, 1989 ISBN: 0-669-18095-5 This book has two primary purposes: 1) to advise managers that it is their responsibility to take charge of their development, and 2) to direct organizations how to better provide for developmental experiences for managers.
Development FIRST: Strategies for Self-Development	**Peterson, David B., and Hicks, Mary Dee,** Minneapolis: Personnel Decisions International, 1995 ISBN: 0-938529-13-7 *Development FIRST* is the first in a series of books dealing with practical approaches to individual and team development within the changing corporate environment. Its five concise development strategies enable users to plan and execute their own development in a busy, demanding world.
The Career Prescription	**Searing, Jill A., and Lovett, Anne B.,** Englewood Cliffs, NJ: Prentice-Hall, 1995 ISBN: 0-13-303322-8 It is necessary to bring more than just the minimum to a job if you want to keep the job or advance. This book is filled with real-life examples that illustrate strategies for protecting and advancing in your job. Also provided are examples of attitudes and practices to avoid. The authors' goal is to provide specific guidance on how to heal an ailing career and to control the direction of your career.
The Fifth Discipline: The Art of Practice of the Learning Organization	**Senge, Peter M.,** New York: Doubleday, 1990 ISBN: 0-385-26094-6 Senge offers the concept of the learning organization as an alternative to the traditional authoritarian hierarchy. He argues that people are the only long-term competitive advantage today, and that their potential lies in the knowledge they bring to the enterprise. Their value is maximized by continuous opportunity for lifelong learning.

SUGGESTED
SEMINARS

The seminars listed here were selected for their appeal to a managerial audience. The reputation of the vendor, the quality of their seminar offerings, and the specific seminar content were considered in the selection process.

Because of the dynamic nature of the seminar marketplace, some seminars may have been upgraded or replaced, and others may no longer be offered. Likewise, costs and locations may have changed since this listing was compiled. We recommend that you contact the vendor directly for updated and additional information.

Leadership at the Peak

This workshop is designed to help top executives examine their leadership styles and strengths through an intense program of learning, discussion, and feedback. Participants will conduct a self-assessment and use this assessment to create specific developmental goals. They will also share experiences and ideas with other top-level managers who understand the stress and demands of leadership and gain new insights and fresh perspectives on topics important to their organization.
Length: 5 days; Cost: $7,000
Locations: Colorado Springs, CO
Center for Creative Leadership
One Leadership Place, P.O. Box 26300
Greensboro, NC 27438-6300
Telephone: 910/545-2810

The Looking Glass Experience: Leadership in Action

Participants in this program gain sharper insights into their own strengths and weaknesses through feedback from their fellow participants and from Center staff, as well as through a feedback instrument completed by their coworkers back home.
Length: 5 days; Cost: $3,500
Locations: Call vendor
Center for Creative Leadership
One Leadership Place, P.O. Box 26300
Greensboro, NC 27438-6300
Telephone: 910/545-2810

**The Women's
Leadership
Program**

This program is designed to bring women executives together to focus on self-awareness and understanding, career enhancement, and an appreciation of gender difference.
Length: 5 days; Cost: $3,300
Locations: Call vendor
**Center for Creative Leadership
One Leadership Place, P.O. Box 26300
Greensboro, NC 27438-6300
Telephone: 910/545-2810**

**The Seven Habits
of Highly Effective
People**

This program is based on the fundamental, yet critical principles of interpersonal relationships outlined in Stephen R. Covey's book, *The Seven Habits of Highly Effective People.* The program is based on the premise that effective leadership starts from the inside out and is designed to heighten the participant's total leadership potential.
Length: 3 days; Cost: $1,495
Locations: Call vendor
**Covey Leadership Center
3507 North University Avenue, Suite 100, Provo, UT 84606
Telephone: 800/331-7716**

**Increasing Human
Effectiveness**

This program, taught in a relaxed lecture/discussion format, provides participants with the tools that will enable them to tap the wellspring of potential that exists within them.
Length: 2 days; Cost: $395
Locations: Call vendor
**Edge Learning Institute
2217 North 30th Street, Suite 200, Tacoma, WA 98403
Telephone: 800/858-1484**

**Toward
Understanding
Human Behavior
and Motivation**

Participants in this seminar gain an understanding of human behavior and motivation, take a critical look at their own strengths and weaknesses as executives, and evolve plans for putting what they learn to work in their professional and personal lives.
Length: 5 days; Cost: Call vendor
Locations: Call vendor
**Menninger Management Institute
P.O. Box 829, Topeka, KS 66601-0829
Telephone: 800/288-5357**

The Executive Development Center

This program is designed to capture the complex skills and dynamic challenges of the general manager's role. For new and prospective executives, it provides a realistic preview of the demands, issues, and daily activities they will face. For experienced executives, it provides an opportunity to renew and refine skills and personal operating style.
Length: 4 days; Cost: $6,800
Locations: Call vendor
Personnel Decisions International
2000 Plaza VII Tower, 45 South Seventh Street
Minneapolis, MN 55402-1608
Telephone: 800/633-4410

Targeted Leadership Coaching

Participants in this program work one-on-one with a personal coach who provides a challenging, yet supportive and positive environment for learning and development. The training focuses on learning the core competencies, including skills, tactics, strategies, and principles, to increase participants' performance in their own career setting.
Length: 4 or 5 half-day sessions; Cost: Call vendor
Locations: Call vendor
Personnel Decisions International
2000 Plaza VII Tower, 45 South Seventh Street
Minneapolis, MN 55402-1608
Telephone: 800/633-4410

The Management Development Center

This program helps managers assess their strengths and development needs in a wide range of managerial and leadership skill areas. Participants are engaged in a realistic simulation of the manager's job. The program provides an opportunity to receive immediate feedback and individualized coaching from fellow managers and highly trained management consultants. A summary report outlining development suggestions and a follow-up development discussion are included.
Length: 3 days; Cost: $4,600
Locations: Call vendor
Personnel Decisions International
2000 Plaza VII Tower, 45 South Seventh Street
Minneapolis, MN 55402-1608
Telephone: 800/633-4410

Management of Managers: Leadership, Change, and Renewal

This program is designed to enable managers to become more effective and to derive more personal satisfaction from their corporate positions. Participants will review their current level of management proficiency, explore new techniques in managerial leadership, develop plans for renewing those leadership roles, and implement improvements for the betterment of themselves and their organization.
Length: 12 days; Cost: $6,450
Location: Dallas
Southern Methodist University
Executive Development, Edwin J. Cox School of Business
Dallas, TX 75275-0333
Telephone: 214/768-3549

Producing Results With Others II

This program helps participants recognize how their behavior comes across to others and how to adapt it. The program covers: recognizing the importance of versatility when working with others, understanding the difference between productive and nonproductive tension, and anticipating and modifying behavior in order to avoid miscommunication.
Length: 2 days; Cost: $750
Locations: Call vendor
The Tracom Corporation
3773 Cherry Creek North Drive, Suite 950
Denver, CO 80209
Telephone: 800/221-2321

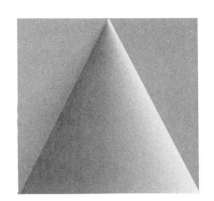

THINKING SKILLS

THINKING SKILLS

Managers need a strategic mindset to be successful in today's business environment. They also must be able to gather and process large amounts of information and then efficiently sift through masses of detail to obtain the facts required for sound decisions.

In addition, in this era of rapid change, managers must be creative and resourceful to keep ahead of the competition. And, to make the most of limited resources, they must be able to effectively balance creativity and resourcefulness — to decide whether to start from scratch or to build upon what already exists.

This chapter presents development activities in the following four areas of thinking skills:

Think Strategically: Considers a broad range of internal and external factors when solving problems and making decisions; identifies critical, high payoff strategies and prioritizes team efforts accordingly; uses information about the market and competitors in making decisions; recognizes strategic opportunities for success; adjusts actions and decisions for focus on critical strategic issues (for example, customers, quality, competition, and so forth).

Analyze Issues: Gathers relevant information systematically; considers a broad range of issues or factors; grasps complexities and perceives relationships among problems or issues; seeks input from others; uses accurate logic in analyses.

Use Sound Judgment: Makes timely and sound decisions; makes decisions under conditions of uncertainty.

Innovate: Generates new ideas; goes beyond the status quo; recognizes the need for new or modified approaches; brings perspectives and approaches together, combining them in creative ways.

THINK STRATEGICALLY

The real voyage of discovery consists not in seeking new lands but in seeing with new eyes.

— Marcel Proust

Effective leaders think strategically. They analyze opportunities and problems from a broad perspective and anticipate and plan for reactions from others. They focus team energies on those key activities that will have a significant impact on the organization. Strategic thinking is characterized by the ability to visualize what might or could be, as well as by a day-to-day strategic approach to issues and challenges.

Strategic thinking is required for, but not limited to, long-term strategic planning. Strategic planning is an event, while strategic thinking is a process and an approach. To use strategic thinking, a manager must first adopt a "strategic mindset," and then follow through on the approaches and opportunities he or she identifies.

This section provides suggestions that will help you to improve your strategic-thinking skills and use them to more effectively lead your team and manage your unit.

Part 1: Developing a Strategic Mindset

- Evaluating Your Strategic-Thinking Skills
- Enhancing Your Strategic Thinking
- Recognizing the Broad Implications of Issues
- Developing a Strategic Perspective of Your Own Area
- Seeing the Relationships
- Analyzing Factors Outside the Business

Part 2: Applying Strategic-Thinking Skills

- Identifying Key Strategic Opportunities
- Capitalizing on Strategic Opportunities
- Developing Strategic Alliances to Increase Competitive Advantage

Valuable Tips

- Read the *Wall Street Journal* and business magazines to learn about the strategies other organizations have implemented to enhance their competitive position. Determine which of these strategies could work well in your organization.

- Be flexible. Strategic opportunities may arise unexpectedly, and you need to be ready to quickly shift gears to pursue new goals.

- Avoid the temptation to find a quick fix when problems arise; instead, take a broad view of the problem by looking at all the options.

- Anticipate reactions to what you and your team plan to do. Strategize ways in which you can achieve your goals with the support of others, rather than create dissension with them.

- Research your company's major competitors and develop a detailed profile of each competitor.

- Ask your team to evaluate the main paradigms under which it operates to determine which are obsolete or restrictive.

- Learn to play chess.

- Volunteer to serve on a strategic planning committee or task force.

- Conduct an "environmental scan" of external opportunities and threats and internal organizational strengths and weaknesses that will affect your company's current or future strategies or competitive position.

- Get a fresh perspective on your company's (or your group's) strategies by looking at them from the viewpoint of a customer or a competitor.

- Learn more about other functional groups within the organization to understand how you affect one another.

- Invite the company's strategists to lunch. Ask them to explain what they do and how they do it.

- Take a course on creative thinking.

PART 1

Evaluating Your Strategic-Thinking Skills

Developing a Strategic Mindset

To evaluate your current strengths as a strategic thinker, answer "yes" or "no" to the following questions:

EVALUATION CHECKLIST *(Circle the appropriate response.)*

Do you anticipate others' concerns?	**Yes/No**
Do you strategize ways to get your ideas accepted?	**Yes/No**
Do you periodically assess your group's contribution to achieving corporate goals?	**Yes/No**
Do you and your staff brainstorm new ideas that could help the organization achieve competitive success?	**Yes/No**
Are you up-to-date on new developments or activities (for example, new products, new markets, cost-saving measures, etc.) occurring in other parts of your organization, as well as in your own?	**Yes/No**
Are you aware of the latest trends in your industry?	**Yes/No**
Can you list your major competitors' strengths and weaknesses?	**Yes/No**
Are you familiar with what customers (both internal and external) need and want in terms of products or services?	**Yes/No**
Do you spend time visualizing how the organization could increase its profit or market share?	**Yes/No**
Do you habitually consider how changing political and socioeconomic forces affect your work and your organization?	**Yes/No**

If you answered "yes" to most of these questions, you possess at least some of the skills or behaviors required of a strategic thinker. The suggestions presented in this section may help you improve those skills. If you answered "no" to most of the questions, this section can help you develop a strategic mindset.

Enhancing Your Strategic Thinking

Most managers who are considered good strategic thinkers possess the following traits:

- Curiosity

- Flexibility

- Future focus

- Positive outlook

- Openness to new ideas

- Breadth of knowledge and interests

In addition, they are able to exercise several types of thinking skills, including the following:

- *Critical thinking* — the ability to objectively analyze a situation and to evaluate the pros and cons and the implications of any course of action

- *Conceptual thinking* — the ability to grasp abstract ideas and to put the "pieces" together to form a coherent picture

- *Creative thinking* — the ability to generate options, visualize possibilities, and formulate new approaches

- *Intuitive thinking* — the ability to factor hunches into the decision-making equation without allowing them to dominate the final outcome

To increase your strategic-thinking skills:

- Challenge the paradigms (the assumptions and belief systems) you use, and create new paradigms to replace obsolete or restrictive ones. For example, the digital quartz watch challenged the paradigm that a watch had to have hands to tell time and mechanical parts to work. Some watch manufacturers lost the opportunity to capitalize on the new technology by not changing their watch paradigm.

  The paradigm that the purpose of quality control is to inspect products at the end of production (and that this is the only and best way to assure quality goods) is now obsolete. Ensuring quality at every step of the process is the new paradigm.

- Challenge the paradigms that relate to your business and to how you and your team approach work. What else is possible? How do you or your team restrict your options?

- Ask your team to identify the critical factors that block or hinder even greater performance, quality, or customer service. What prevents the team from achieving its potential? Which of these factors are considered to be "givens" (things the team believes will always exist)? Be aware that these "givens" are what your competitors will figure out how to change, so begin working on them *now*. Come up with solutions or alternatives.

- Realize that strategic thinking works with relationships, too. In working with others, think through how your plans will affect your colleagues, customers, employees, and so forth. Decide whether the impact on others matches your intent.

- Engage in "what-if" thinking. Consider: "If we do this, how will our competitors respond, what will our customers think, what impact will this have on our suppliers and distributors, or what will our next move be?"

- Think through future implications and weigh the benefits and risks associated with your actions.

- Continually look for alternative ways to work with people that will create better results and working relationships. In a particular situation, challenge yourself to identify three or four options and think about how the people involved will receive them.

- Constantly look for new ideas and new approaches.

- Learn to play chess, and apply the anticipatory thinking required in chess to your work.

- Watch Joel Barker's videotape, *Discovering the Future: The Power of Vision*[1], and discuss it with your team.

After you have practiced using strategic thinking, ask for feedback on your skills from your manager or from people who are known to be strong strategic thinkers.

Recognizing the Broad Implications of Issues

Managers who think strategically are able to see the big picture. When dealing with issues, they operate from a broad, long-term perspective, rather than taking a narrow view or focusing only on short-term implications.

To gain a broad perspective when issues arise:

1. Identify all the stakeholders potentially involved in the issue. Ask your team to review your list or to identify the stakeholders themselves.

2. In discussing the issue, probe beneath the surface; gather information from the different stakeholders.

---

[1]Charthouse International Learning Corporation, 221 River Ridge Circle, Burnsville, MN 55337, 800/328-3789.

3. Listen carefully to understand the underlying issues. Link the information you receive to help you more fully grasp the issue and understand the connections or interrelationships.

4. Define the problem from the perspective of each stakeholder.

5. To develop a more complete perspective, think of the implications of what you have learned.

6. Identify potential solutions or actions. When considering alternative actions, evaluate how they will affect each stakeholder. Think about whether the action being considered will help achieve your goals or those of the organization. Is it consistent with strategy? How will stakeholders react?

7. Use your team and the stakeholders to determine what will be needed for the solution to work. What are the pitfalls? How can potential problems be anticipated?

8. Communicate the decision, rationale, and plan to all of those who were involved in the process of identifying the issues.

Developing a Strategic Perspective of Your Own Area

Effective managers recognize the importance of looking at their own area from a strategic perspective. They know and capitalize on their organization's strengths. They consider the external factors that affect their organization. And they know what activities their group must do well in order to succeed.

It's critical to analyze your "organizational competencies" in order to better determine how to capitalize on the strengths and address the weaknesses of your organization. To look at the strengths and weaknesses of your group from a strategic perspective:

1. Make a list of the internal factors that affect your group. Involve your stakeholders in this identification process. These internal factors will include, but are not limited to:
   - Strategic goals
   - Stage of the business (growth, stabilization, downsizing)
   - Structure
   - Cooperation among groups
   - Competitive focus
   - Leadership style
   - Employee skills

2. Rate your group's strength (or lack thereof) in each area. Ask your stakeholders for input in this step.

3. Based on the analysis, focus your attention on leveraging strengths and capitalizing on opportunities. Develop strategies to anticipate threats and shore up weaknesses.

It's also important to consider the external factors that will affect your organization or group at a strategic level. Increase your awareness of external factors. Look at the current situation, then project into the future. Talk with experts and do research to gather this information. Meet with your customers directly. This type of analysis will enable you to identify opportunities and threats.

The external factors that may affect your group include:

- Resource availability
- Competition
- Environmental concerns
- Global marketplace
- Customer requirements
- Quality standards
- Regulations
- Technology advances
- Demographics of customers
- Suppliers/vendors
- Education

Finally, you will want to identify your organization's key success factors. These are the activities that need to be done — and done well — to achieve your goals. The following process can help you identify these key success factors:

1. Review history and conduct postmortems on key successes and failures. Determine which factors contributed to the successes. Evaluate these factors to see whether they are still critical to your success.

2. Ask each of your team members to list his or her primary job tasks or activities. These tasks and activities should be viewed from how they contribute to the goals of the team. For example, "answering customer calls in a way that makes them feel they are taken care of" is a better description of the activity than just "answering phones"; or, "providing accurate,

timely sales forecasts to marketing" is better for this purpose than just "forecasting sales."

3. Compile your team's lists into one master list. Add appropriate items from your review of past successes and failures. Then ask each team member to weigh the importance of each activity relative to your larger organization's strategic goals and the needs of your important stakeholders (*especially* including customers). Use a scale of 1 to 5, as follows:

   5 = absolutely necessary
   4 = critically important
   3 = important
   2 = preferred
   1 = not important

4. Review the rank-ordered list from others' perspectives. Would your customers agree with this priority? Would your manager or management team agree? How about your divisional or corporate executives? Does this prioritization support the strategic direction of your larger organization? Make any necessary changes to the list based on this review.

Keep your list of key success factors on hand at all times. Use it to help you make decisions from a more strategic point of view and ensure that your team is always keeping its focus on the "20 percent that makes 80 percent of the difference."

Also, whenever you propose something new, identify the key success factors for this new endeavor and determine how they will be achieved. Then you can manage the "right stuff."

Seeing the Relationships

No division or group in an organization operates autonomously. To develop a strategic perspective of how your group fits into the whole, start by learning how the various departments and functions within your organization are interrelated. The following activities can assist you in this process:

- Obtain a copy of your company's organization chart. Ask your manager or an experienced peer to explain the major functions of the other groups in the organization. Also ask how these groups affect what your group is doing, and vice versa.

- Get to know people in other functional groups by volunteering to serve on cross-functional teams or committees. Find out the strategies and goals of these groups. Compare your group's strategies and goals with those of other groups. Identify where there is a "fit," and where groups may be working at cross-purposes.

- Study the company's consolidated financial plan to determine how you and your group affect the goals of your operating unit. If helpful, take an accountant or planner to lunch and ask him or her to explain how your group goals, in terms of budgets and/or revenues, contribute to the big picture.

- Identify other groups or functions that might be helped or harmed if you exceed or fall short of your goals.

- Consider your company's strategy, and your piece of it, from the perspectives of your stockholders, your competitors, your customers, and your employees. Imagine how each of these groups would react if they studied your strategy.

Analyzing Factors Outside the Business

Effective strategists are forward thinkers, looking to the future to find opportunities and direction. To be a forward thinker, however, you can't focus only on the future. You also need to be aware of what has happened in the recent past and what is happening now, both within your own organization and outside the organization. For example, what strategies have your major competitors tried in the recent past that failed? This information can help your organization avoid the same mistakes.

The following suggestions can help you conduct an "environmental scan" of internal and external trends that could affect your current strategies or play a part in new strategies that you develop:

- Research the latest trends. Read industry reports, professional journals, and financial journals to learn about trends in the industry. As you read these publications, ask yourself:
  - What are the latest technical advances in the industry? Is my organization current with this technology or, better yet, in the forefront of its development?
  - Who needs this technology, and how will they use it? Are these people (or companies) part of our customer base?
  - Where is the greatest demand for these new products or services? Is the demand industry related, regional, or both?
  - If the demand is regional, do we have a presence in these areas?
  - How long is this particular trend likely to last? Could it be a "flash in the pan," to be quickly replaced by something new? Or is it more likely to become a standard product, something to be enhanced but not replaced any time soon?

- Analyze the competition. Identify your company's five to ten top competitors. Using corporate reports, industry analyses, and publications like *Standard and Poors* as resources, look at the following factors for each competitor:
  - Quality and price of competitor's products or services compared with similar products/services offered by your company
  - Marketing strategies and targeted markets
  - Level of innovation and/or amount of money spent on research and development
  - Level of service provided to support products
  - Reputation in the industry
  - Corporate leaders — their strategies and philosophies
  - Strengths and weaknesses

  Creating a detailed profile of each competitor will provide the basis from which to develop strategies for gaining competitive advantage.

- Analyze customer needs. Identify customer buying trends by studying internal customer satisfaction surveys and external industry reports on buying patterns. If such information is not available or up-to-date, suggest that your organization conduct a survey of current and potential customers to identify what they need and want in your products or services.

- Understand how government regulations may affect your organization. If your industry is subject to regulation by federal, state, or local agencies, make an effort to stay current with new or pending legislation. Read industry and government reports to learn more about specific regulations governing such areas as safety, quality standards, training, advertising/labeling, and pricing.

PART 2

Identifying Key Strategic Opportunities

Applying Strategic-Thinking Skills

Successful leaders focus the energy of their organization on the initiatives that will have the greatest strategic impact. This energy may be focused on leveraging strengths to gain market share, investing in a new technology that will pay off in the future, or any number of other initiatives. The key to strategic success is the ability to analyze the current situation, determine what you want, and mobilize resources in the critical areas to achieve these goals.

The first step in the process of achieving strategic goals is to identify key strategic opportunities. The following suggestions can help you do this:

- To improve your competitive position, work with your team to answer these questions:
  - Who are our customers?
  - What are their current needs?
  - What external trends are likely to shape their wants and needs in the near future? Where are the opportunities?
  - What products or services does our organization provide to meet these needs now?
  - What opportunities do we have to address existing or emerging needs?
  - How do our products and services compare with our competitors? What are our strengths and weaknesses?
  - What are our competitors doing differently now or are likely to do in the future to capitalize on these opportunities? (These are the threats.)
  - What competitive threats must we address?
  - How can we favorably differentiate ourselves from our competitors?

  After you and your team identify the opportunities, decide what strategies and actions will have the greatest impact. Remember that trying to do everything at once usually results in poor quality and a superficial approach. Keep your organization focused on the critical few activities that will make the biggest difference.

- Encourage team members to always analyze whether, and how, their proposed plans or actions will favorably affect the success of the organization. Ask them to be prepared to discuss the costs or risks of not doing anything.

- Identify what you can do in working with your manager, employees, customers, peers, and suppliers that will have the greatest impact on achieving your goals. Don't just assume that you know the answer — *ask* them! Focus your attention on what is most important to the key constituencies and individuals who help you to be successful.

Capitalizing on Strategic Opportunities

When a strategic opportunity arises, it's important first to recognize it as such and second to be able to do something about it quickly. Strategic opportunities can arise unexpectedly or you can identify them yourself. In either case, it will be to your benefit to be able to leverage your organization's strengths to take advantage of such opportunities.

The following suggestions can help you leverage the strengths of your team and other individuals and teams in your organization to make the most of strategic opportunities:

- Know the organizational competencies of your organization. Does it have a reputation for outstanding customer service? Is it known for innovative marketing or the top-notch quality of its products? Identify the divisions or groups responsible for providing these quality products or services.

  When a strategic opportunity arises, consider how these strengths can play a role in turning that opportunity into a win for your organization.

- Network with people in other parts of the organization so you can quickly get their support when opportunities arise. Get to know the key people who represent your organization's "strengths." Form alliances with these people. See the Leverage Networks section of this handbook for suggestions on developing network ties within your organization.

  When a strategic opportunity arises, determine whether others in your network can help you turn the opportunity into a success or whether you and your team can support their initiatives. If so, seek out their support and/or offer yours.

- Ask yourself and your team: "What do we do well? Something that, given the projected changes in customer needs, it makes sense to improve even more or go beyond our current capabilities?" For example, if your group is known for good service, how can you use that strength to develop new services or further solidify the strength?

  By identifying and enhancing these special strengths, you will be in a good position to use them to capitalize even further on a strategic opportunity that arises.

As you uncover strategic opportunities, map out in detail the steps required to pursue the opportunity, the resources needed, and the projected results. You are more likely to get "buy in" from your manager if you can present a well-researched plan for implementing your ideas.

**Developing
Strategic Alliances
to Increase
Competitive
Advantage**

An organization becomes more competitive in the marketplace when all of its people pull together in the same direction, rather than pulling in several different directions. This type of concerted effort requires clear communication among divisions and a clear directive from top management on what the organization's strategic goals are.

You can increase communication and knowledge among the various groups in your organization by doing the following:

- Identify your internal customers — those departments or functions that rely on you for service or information. List five ways that you could improve the quality of the service you provide to each of these customers. Take a representative of each department to lunch and show your list to that person. Ask for feedback on its accuracy.

- Identify groups within the organization that have impeded your group's efforts. Meet with key people in these groups and tactfully suggest ways that your groups could work together more effectively.

- Think about the external parties that do or could contribute to your competitive position. For example, in a research and development function, there may be related technologies that you don't have, but that could greatly increase your competitive position if you could build them into your products. This could be an opportunity for a third-party alliance. Another organization may have a strong distribution system in parts of the world where you do not. Again, this could be an opportunity for cooperation.

In creating these alliances, look for ways in which both parties will benefit. How can you position it so both parties benefit, and it is worth the risk? What issues would the alliance raise that need to be resolved or managed?

RECOMMENDED READINGS

The publications listed here were selected for their content and suitability to a managerial audience.

The Northbound Train: Finding the Purpose, Setting the Direction, Shaping the Destiny of Your Organization

Albrecht, Karl, New York: AMACOM, 1994
ISBN: 0-8144-0233-X
This comprehensive book explores future trends in the business world and what successful companies will have to concentrate on to survive and prosper. Albrecht can help you create a vision for your company based on creating value for the customer.

Applied Strategic Planning

Goodstein, Leonard; Nolan, Timothy; and Pfeiffer, J. William, New York: McGraw-Hill, 1993
ISBN: 0-07-024020-5
The authors show managers and CEOs how to identify and implement strategic objectives, emphasizing organizational culture, the integration of business and functional plans, and more. The book is full of charts, diagrams, and examples from the authors' consulting practice that will be helpful for strategic planning.

Competing for the Future

Hamel, Gary, and Prahalad, C.K., Boston: Harvard Business School Press, 1994
ISBN: 0-87584-416-2
The authors postulate that managers in today's most successful firms are more interested in creating new competitive space than positioning themselves in the existing market. Companies need to develop foresight by not only looking at the possible, but influencing the direction their industry is taking. This book shows how to develop stretch goals and build core competencies to create advantages and new markets for the future.

Reengineering the Corporation

Hammer, Michael, and Champy, James, New York: HarperBusiness, 1993
ISBN: 0-88730-640-3
In the current business environment of global competition, companies must abandon outdated notions of how the work is done and ensure that processes and procedures are efficient and effective. This book provides a roadmap for the reengineering journey, showing how to focus on your larger objectives, not minute tasks.

*Manufacturing
Renaissance*

Pisano, Gary P., and Hayes, Robert H., Boston: Harvard
Business School Press, 1995
ISBN: 0-87584-610-6
This collection of twenty Harvard Business Review articles
explores how to gain a competitive advantage through a
manufacturing strategy based on flexibility, responsiveness,
innovation, and customer service. One article details how to
reorganize the factory in order to achieve greater flexibility.
Another describes four stages of manufacturing effectiveness
culminating with the production process actually generating new
opportunities for other functions.

*The Competitive
Advantage of
Nations*

Porter, Michael E., New York: The Free Press, 1990
ISBN: 0-02-925361-6
Based on extensive research, the author identifies elements that
create a national, competitive advantage in an industry. The book
further identifies the stages of competitive development through
which entire economies advance and decline. Porter combines this
research with the ideas presented in his previous works and
explores how industries become competitive in a global
marketplace.

Competitive Strategy

Porter, Michael E., New York: The Free Press, 1980
ISBN: 0-02-925360-8
The author addresses major questions of vital concern to
managers and presents a comprehensive set of analytical
techniques for understanding a business and the behavior of its
competitors. The book presents techniques to anticipate and
prepare for, rather than simply react to, sudden competitor moves
or shifts in industry structure.

*Vision: How Leaders
Develop It, Share It,
and Sustain It*

Quigley, Joseph V., New York: McGraw-Hill, 1993
ISBN: 0-07-051084-9
This book has been widely endorsed by recognized leaders for its
approach to developing and implementing the vision and strategy
of a business. The author provides a specific method for
developing a company's strategic vision and putting it into
practice.

*Top Management
Strategy*

Schwartz, Peter, New York: Doubleday, 1991
ISBN: 0-385-26731-2
The author expounds on his proven technique of the "scenario"
approach to developing strategic vision within business. His book
is a guide to the practice of convergent thinking about divergent
futures.

Strategic Business Forecasting	**Shim, Jae K.; Siegel, Joel G.; and Liew, C.J.,** Chicago: Probus Publishing, 1994 ISBN: 1-55738-569-6 These three top experts outline forecasting methods for all corporate and financial activities. You can learn to develop accurate projections for everything from profits to expenses to help ensure the long-term success of your company.
The Transformational Leader	**Tichy, Noel M., and Devanna, Mary Anne,** New York: John Wiley & Sons, 1990 ISBN: 0-471-62334-2 Transformational leaders are a special breed capable of managing the kind of massive turnaround most companies will have to undergo to remain competitive. The book dissects their processes and provides specific, practical ideas for accomplishing transformation.

SUGGESTED SEMINARS	The seminars listed here were selected for their appeal to a managerial audience. The reputation of the vendor, the quality of their seminar offerings, and the specific seminar content were considered in the selection process.

Because of the dynamic nature of the seminar marketplace, some seminars may have been upgraded or replaced, and others may no longer be offered. Likewise, costs and locations may have changed since this listing was compiled. We recommend that you contact the vendor directly for updated and additional information.

Competitive Strategy: How to Develop Marketing Plans, Strategies, and Tactics

This program is designed to give participants an expanded market point of view for attaining and sustaining a distinct competitive advantage.
Length: 3 days; Cost: $1,495
Locations: Call vendor
American Management Association
P.O. Box 319, Saranac Lake, NY 12983
Telephone: 800/262-9699

Thinking and Managing Strategically

This program covers the strategic planning process: incorporating mission, goals and constituencies into planning; financial analysis; the human resource element; summing up strategic decisions; and the pitfalls and hallmarks of strategic planning.
Length: 3 days; Cost: $1,490
Locations: Call vendor
American Management Association
P.O. Box 319, Saranac Lake, NY 12983
Telephone: 800/262-9699

Business Strategy

This program teaches a systematic but creative approach to the planning and effective implementation of strategy in a wide variety of organizations. Key topics include: competitive analysis; industry dynamics; process and product innovation; pitfalls in applying strategic tools; and human resource factors in strategy.
Length: 2 weeks; Cost: Call vendor
Location: Harriman, NY
Columbia University
Graduate School of Business, 2880 Broadway, 4th Floor
New York, NY 10025-6989
Telephone: 212/854-3395

Tuck Executive Program

This program is designed for senior managers. An intensive program, it integrates the study of the major business disciplines within the context of general strategic management. The curriculum also examines important issues in the international environment confronting managers of complex organizations. Corporate governance, public policy issues, and business ethics receive substantive attention.
Length: 4 weeks; Cost: $17,500
Location: Hanover, NH
Dartmouth College
The Amos Tuck School of Business Administration
Office of Executive Education, 100 Tuck Hall
Hanover, NH 03755-9050
Telephone: 603/646-2839

Systems Thinking: A Language for Learning and Action™

This seminar will teach managers how to apply systems thinking. The seminar is designed to increase participants' natural inclination to think systematically. During the seminar, participants will practice communicating critical business issues from a systematic point of view, learn to talk convincingly about root causes, and develop alternative actions for desired changes.
Length: 3 days; Cost: $1,995
Locations: Call vendor
Innovation Associates, Inc.
3 Speen Street, Suite 140, Framingham, MA 01701
Telephone: 508/879-8301

Creating Strategic Leverage

This workshop provides the missing link between strategy theory and the operating decisions business managers make every day. Participants will learn to identify and exploit opportunities in any given market; avoid common mistakes, e.g., putting money into low leverage areas; translate common planning tools, such as Porter's Five Forces, into actionable programs; refocus resources from current tactical problems to future opportunities; and drive strategic thinking throughout the organization.
Length: 2 days; Cost: $1,295
Locations: Call vendor
SLC Consultants, Inc.
Suite 1400, 30 West Monroe Street, Chicago, IL 60603
Telephone: 312/346-7797

Applied Formulation and Implementation

In this program, participants will learn about the various roles in the design and implementation of an organization's strategic plan; how a successful planning team focuses on establishing priorities, self-examination, and confronting difficult choices; new ways to develop criteria for making and evaluating operating decisions; and how to ensure ongoing successful implementation of strategic plans.

Length: 3 days; Cost: $875
Locations: Call vendor
University Associates
8380 Miramar Mall, Suite 232, San Diego, CA 92121
Telephone: 619/552-8901

Strategy Formulation and Implementation

This program is designed for executives who are seeking new ways to approach their organization's strategic planning process. It explores a broad set of strategic management issues to provide executives with the knowledge of concepts and practical applications for long-range organizational planning, strategy formulation, and implementation.

Length: 6 days; Cost: $4,300
Location: Ann Arbor, MI
University of Michigan Business School
Executive Education Center, Ann Arbor, MI 48109-1234
Telephone: 313/763-1000

Strategic Thinking and Management for Competitive Advantage

This seminar will help managers use the planning process as an opportunity to step back and ask the right questions, learn new approaches, and question their organization's basic assumptions. They will learn to think strategically and use resources more effectively.

Length: 5 days; Cost: $4,550
Location: Philadelphia
University of Pennsylvania, The Wharton School
Aresty Institute of Executive Education, Steinberg Conference Center, 255 South 38th Street
Philadelphia, PA 19104-6359
Telephone: 800/255-3932

Advanced Management Program

This program is designed to help participants develop sound strategic thinking and decision-making skills and understand the organizational impact of financial analysis, market competition, government policies, legal issues, and other aspects of the business environment. This program explores changing social, political, and economic conditions at home and around the world and assesses their impact on business, both now and in the future.
Length: 5 weekends; Cost: $3,995
Location: Los Angeles
University of Southern California
Office of Executive Education
School of Business Administration
Davidson Conference Center, Room 111
Los Angeles, CA 90089-0871
Telephone: 213/740-8990

ANALYZE ISSUES

In today's fast-paced environment, managers are faced with a myriad of issues each day. Some of these issues are uncomplicated and call for straightforward solutions, but others are complex and require probing analysis before decisions can be made.

Systematic analysis is the foundation of good decision making. This section provides suggestions for improving your skill in analyzing issues systematically.

Part 1: Diagnosing Problems

- Defining the Issue
- Diagnosing Problems Efficiently
- Reducing Time Spent Collecting Unnecessary Data
- Preventing Problems by Analyzing Their Cause

Part 2: Identifying and Gathering Necessary Information

- Identifying Information Needed to Understand and Solve a Problem
- Using Print Resources to Obtain Information
- Interviewing Others to Obtain Information

Part 3: Analyzing the Alternatives

- Analyzing Problems from Different Points of View
- Recognizing and Coping with Complexity
- Obtaining Necessary Data Efficiently
- Learning New Information Quickly
- Applying Accurate Logic in Solving Problems
- Fine Tuning Inductive and Deductive Thinking Skills

Valuable Tips

- Identify the most important decision you have to make this quarter. Then start gathering the information you will need to make it.

- Write out the steps and information required for a future major decision. Get the input of others early.

- Recognize that often you will not have all the information you need to make a decision.

- Look for improved ways to collect and analyze data for your decisions.

- Allow yourself plenty of time to work on the big problems, and work on them in several sittings.

- Keep paper and pencil handy so that you can write down thoughts that occur while you are sleeping, taking a shower, running, and so on.

- Before making decisions, gather as much necessary information as possible without getting bogged down in detail.

- Review the Kepner-Tregoe process of problem solving and use it in defining problems.

- To search for alternative solutions to a problem, summarize the problem and then list all possible solutions before evaluating them.

- Ask for input from those closest to the problem.

- Reformulate or restate the problem in different words or from different perspectives to uncover alternative ways to define the problem.

- Ask your people their views on the pros and cons of an issue to identify different perspectives and to uncover potential conflicts or ambiguities that need further analysis.

- Acquire the habit of double-checking the data related to important decisions and actions to see if you have neglected salient details.

- Develop a checklist of details that need to be handled when making certain decisions.

- To avoid getting bogged down in detail, ask yourself how various items relate to your overall objectives.

- Identify the critical issues and investigate them fully.
- Keep a record of the problems that arise in your area. Then analyze them to identify interrelated themes and to look for root causes.

PART 1

Defining the Issue

Diagnosing Problems

The first critical step in analyzing an issue is to specify as clearly and succinctly as possible what the issue or problem is about. Taking time to clearly define the issue will save substantial time in the long run, because it will provide the framework for guiding you through subsequent steps of the analytical process. You will have a better sense of what information needs to be gathered and how it should be evaluated, as well as who should be involved in the process.

When you are confronted with an issue, define it by writing down brief responses to each of the following questions:

- What is the crux of this issue — what major questions, problems, challenges, or opportunities does this issue raise?

- What is the potential impact of this issue — does it have significant consequences or ramifications? If so, what are they?

- What other people and functions are likely to be affected by this issue?

- What do I or others expect to accomplish by resolving this issue?

Define the issue as a need or a problem, not as a solution. If your definition of the issue suggests a solution, you may overlook critical information and alternatives and end up jumping to unwarranted conclusions.

If the issue is complex or subtle, your responses to the questions above will be somewhat tentative. As you gather information about the issue, revise your initial responses to fit your increased awareness and understanding of the issue.

Diagnosing Problems Efficiently

The ability to quickly discover the source of a problem is helpful when you must solve problems under pressure. To cut down on the time wasted pursuing unlikely alternatives, follow these steps for the next few weeks until you are satisfied with your ability to quickly eliminate dead-end alternatives. The chart that follows will help you structure your analysis.

1. For each problem, generate a list of all possible causes in order of probability.

2. For each cause, rate its probability of being the main cause of the problem. Use a scale from 1 to 100, with 1 being the lowest probability.

3. For each cause, determine what must be done — what investigative steps need to be taken — to verify that it is the cause.

4. Rate the effort required to investigate whether the cause listed is the cause of the problem. Use a scale from 1 to 5, with 1 representing the least effort.

5. Balance the probability of the cause with the amount of investigation required. Based on this analysis, determine the order in which you will investigate the causes. Also identify any alternatives you can drop altogether.

6. Review your analysis with colleagues and ask for feedback. Adjust your investigation plan as appropriate.

Potential Cause	Probability of Cause (1-100)	Investigation Needed	Effort Required (1-5)	Order of Investigation
			1 2 3 4 5	
			1 2 3 4 5	
			1 2 3 4 5	
			1 2 3 4 5	
			1 2 3 4 5	

Reducing Time Spent Collecting Unnecessary Data

A second way to diagnose problems faster is to reduce the time you spend collecting unnecessary data — data that you don't really need but that you collect "just to make sure."

The next time you reach a tentative solution when solving a problem, answer these questions:

- What additional information could be collected?

- What information would make me feel better, but probably would not cause me to change my decision?

- What information is absolutely necessary?

After answering these questions, stop gathering information you've identified as unnecessary.

Preventing Problems by Analyzing Their Cause

Do you ever have days when it seems that you are constantly "fighting fires?" Although some problems are unavoidable, preventive measures can be taken to forestall many of them. If you find yourself in a constant state of crisis management, you may wish to complete the following exercise in preventive problem solving:

1. Over the next few weeks, keep a list of the unforeseen problem situations that require your attention. Although it may seem inconvenient at the time, the most important time to compile such a list is when you're inundated by a large number of unanticipated crises.

2. Look at the list. Do you see any themes? Are there any commonalities among the various situations?

3. For each problem on the list, ask yourself:

   - What was the cause of this problem?

   - Could this problem have been prevented?

   - If so, what action could have prevented the problem?

   - Who should have taken preventive action? Me? My employees? My manager?

   - What can be done to prevent the recurrence of this problem?

   It may help to use a model against which to analyze your problem. A model can help you analyze problems more quickly and compensate for blind spots that you might have in relation to the problem. For example, you may use the model for effective meetings presented in the Work Efficiently section of this Handbook to analyze your meetings and find opportunities for improvement.

4. If you don't see any themes at first, reexamine the problems and determine whether their causes can be grouped into general categories, such as inadequate oral communication, failure to delegate, lack of written follow-up, or lack of procedure standardization.

5. For areas in which either you or your employees require development, prepare and implement development plans.

PART 2

Identifying Information Needed to Understand and Solve a Problem

Identifying and Gathering Necessary Information

Getting the right information is essential to effectively solve problems. When you are confronted with a problem that needs resolving, your first step is to identify the information you need. Use the following process to help you do this:

1. Make a list of what you need to know in order to resolve the issue or problem effectively. List information that is important to resolving the issue; leave off the list information that can be easily accessed but is not important to the issue.

   Consider the following suggestions when listing your information needs:

   • Incorporate other viewpoints. For example, if other people or parts of the organization will be affected, you will need to know their perceptions. Get customer or supplier input when appropriate.

   • Build on past experience to avoid reinventing the wheel. Ask yourself:
   - Has the organization faced a similar issue in the past? If so, who was involved and how was it handled? What were the results?
   - How have other organizations handled similar issues?

   • Get input from experts inside or outside your organization.

2. Rank order the items on your list according to how critical they are to resolving the issue. To avoid wasting time collecting unnecessary or marginally useful information, pursue first the information that is likely to yield the most value. Recognize when information is difficult to access or will take an unreasonably long time to acquire, and gather only the data that is critical to your decision-making process.

3. Identify how and where you will gather the information. Your sources of information might include written materials, interviews, group discussions, questionnaires, or observation. The sources you use will depend to a large extent on your specific information needs.

   If you are not sure how to obtain the information you need, ask your manager or your people for ideas, or consult a peer who has handled a similar issue.

Using Print Resources to Obtain Information

Print resources may be relevant to many of the issues you face. These resources might include manuals, books, published periodicals, and statistical or financial reports. Recognize that the amount of research required to solve problems varies. Many issues require little research, while others can call for extensive research and information gathering. The following procedure can help you identify and obtain useful information when needed:

1. List several general problem areas in which you need additional information. List any resources of which you are already aware.

2. Ask your manager and colleagues to identify any resources they feel would be valuable, how the resources can be obtained, and the portions of these materials likely to be most helpful.

3. Determine which print resources will help you more effectively manage the projects for which you are responsible. In many situations, you will probably need access to certain reports for only a short period. For others, it may make sense to have your name added to a permanent mailing list.

4. As you read each section in the resource, ask yourself questions such as:

   • What is the key point to be gleaned from this section?

   • How does this information compare and contrast with information I have already gathered?

   • What are the implications for the issue I face?

5. On your list of resources, summarize the ways in which each resource is helpful. If the resource belongs to you, flag or highlight useful sections so that you can locate them easily when you need to refer to them. If you borrow a resource and find valuable content, make or acquire a copy so that you will have easy access to the information you need.

Interviewing Others to Obtain Information

When a problem arises, you will often need to gather information directly from someone else. For example, if an individual has a stake in the issue you are confronting, you will need to gain an understanding of his or her perspectives.

When interviewing others to gain information, you can use several techniques to increase your efficiency and effectiveness. These techniques are called structuring, active questioning, and active listening.

FIRST THE THIRTY DAY FORECAST, THEN THE CRACKERS.

- Structuring involves establishing an agenda for your interview to ensure that the interview stays on track and that you get the information you want.
  - Before you meet with the person you plan to interview, list the topics to discuss and the information you need from him or her.
  - Then, write down questions you can ask that will produce the desired information.
  - At the outset of your meeting, let the person know what you hope to accomplish by meeting with him or her.
  - In many instances, you may find it helpful to share your agenda, including the questions you plan to ask. The person is more likely to be able to give you the requested information if he or she knows what you need.

- Active questioning involves asking open-ended questions that require more than a one- or two-word response. Examples of active questions include those that begin with such phrases as "What do you think..." or "Tell me about..." Avoid questions that encourage passive responses — questions that begin with the words "did" or "is" and can be answered with a simple "yes" or "no." In addition to limiting the amount of information you gain, a string of closed questions usually results in an interview that seems more like an interrogation and tends to alienate the listener. On the other hand, active questions are effective for clarifying points and getting down to specifics.

- Active listening involves paying close attention to what the speaker is saying, rephrasing the speaker's comments, and then asking whether you have understood correctly. You may also wish to take notes and to summarize the interview by quickly reviewing your notes with the interviewee to determine if they are correct.

Keep an open mind when you are listening. Take care not to judge the speaker's suggestions or to convey, verbally or nonverbally, that you disapprove of the information you are receiving. If you do not remain open to the information you are soliciting, your speaker will sense that his or her input is not really appreciated and will stop trying to communicate with you.

You may find that several people have bits and pieces of information that you need. In such cases, it may be helpful to get a group of people together. These interviewing techniques — structuring, active questioning, and active listening — also work in group situations.

Additional information and tips on developing interviewing skills can be found in the Structure and Staff section of this Handbook.

PART 3

Analyzing Problems from Different Points of View

Analyzing the Alternatives

It is critical for you to examine problems and issues from different perspectives. Not only will this improve the quality of your decisions, but it is also likely to increase others' acceptance of your decisions because you can demonstrate that you have taken their interests and concerns into account.

The best approach frequently is to assemble representatives of each point of view (for example, different functions, levels, and so forth) and get their viewpoints firsthand. If that is not possible, try the following:

1. List all perspectives/points of view that have a bearing on the issue. Examples may include those of employees, customers, managers, suppliers, or the general public. Alternatively, the various perspectives might be defined as operations, finance, marketing, legal, and so on.

2. Look at the issue from each person's perspective. Put yourself in their place. How would they define the issue?

3. For each alternative you are considering, identify the pros and cons from each perspective. For example, what would employees gain and what would they lose? Which alternative would be preferable to them?

4. If your ideas appear feasible, present them to a trusted representative of each perspective and ask for feedback to see if you are on the right track.

Recognizing and Coping with Complexity

In organizations, issues do not occur in a vacuum. To understand issues, you need to look beyond their immediate dimensions. This doesn't mean that you need to make things more confusing than they are, but rather that you need to see how the issues are connected to one another. To gauge the complexity of an issue, review the subsection in Part I titled Defining the Issue. The greater the impact of the issue, and the more people and functions affected by the issue, the more complex the issue is likely to be.

When exploring an issue or opportunity, be aware that you are working in a system. That means that anything you do, even something that people like and agree with, will have an impact on others. Therefore, you need to look at your whole mode of operation in reference to your issue. For example, if you introduce a new, improved product, it will affect the sales of the old one. Or if you decide to distribute globally, you will need to consider your distribution channels and perhaps your supply channels as well.

To understand complex relationships surrounding an issue, consider the people involved, their goals, and their history with one another. It is important to approach this quest for understanding with an open mind. Recognize that two major barriers to understanding are the beliefs that "only the facts count" and that "nonsense is anything that doesn't make sense to me." To develop a better understanding of these relationships:

1. Ask the people involved to explain the relationships to you.

2. Ask others who you believe are insightful about people or organizations to discuss the issue with you.

3. Make a flowchart, map, or network chart to help you visualize the interrelationships and connections.

4. Test your hypotheses with others. You may want to model what will happen if a change is made. In some situations, schematic diagrams outlining the relationship between cause and effect will be effective. Modeling techniques are often facilitated by the use of computer software, which can graph interactions and calculate the quantitative aspects of these relationships.

5. Within the complexity, identify the critical path necessary to achieve your goals.

6. To make the most of complex relationships, find the commonalities and mutual goals that exist between people or groups, and leverage these for the benefit of the greater goal.

Obtaining Necessary Data Efficiently

Considering too much detail can prevent you from making timely decisions. To determine whether you typically look at the right amount of detail in decision making, use the following process to evaluate your use of detail:

1. Set a limit on your data-gathering time, and when you have reached that limit, make your decision.

2. Next, spend as much time as you normally would in gathering additional information. Then make your final decision. Compare your final decision to the preliminary one to determine if the extra time you spent was worthwhile.

3. Make several decisions in this manner, keeping track of the results each time you apply the process. Then evaluate your results to determine when you can reduce the amount of detail you collect before you make a decision.

You may want to repeat these steps to look for additional ways to reduce data-gathering time. Also, finding more efficient ways to collect data can speed up your process.

Learning New Information Quickly

To progress in an organization, you need to continue learning. Effective managers continue to gain knowledge and develop the necessary skills for their job and beyond. Their ability and willingness to do so also make them more valuable and promotable. Use the following suggestions to keep acquiring new knowledge and skills that will help you analyze issues and make decisions:

-   Determine your own most effective learning style. Some people learn best from courses or training programs; others learn best by example; still others by trial and error. Use the style that works best for you.

-   Through tapes, courses, or self-study, learn strategies to increase your comprehension ability.

-   Allow your people to teach you. Spend time with all of the people in your department who have the expertise and skills you need. Ask them questions.

-   Read professional publications that will bring you up to speed and keep you current with the technology in your field.

-   Spend one hour each day for 20 days developing a new knowledge or skill. Vary your way of doing this, but do it consistently. You'll be surprised at your rapid development.

-   Take a rapid reading or accelerated learning course and practice the recommended strategies.

-   Keep up on information related to your field, such as local, national, or world events; legislative and economic issues; and changing demographics.

Applying Accurate Logic in Solving Problems

Efficient and accurate decision making is a critical component of managerial effectiveness. The following guidelines will help to ensure that you are using accurate logic in your problem-solving efforts. These guidelines outline the topics discussed in this section of the Handbook.

1. Carefully identify and define the problem. Ask such questions as:

   - What is the situation?

   - What facts are known, and what is still unknown?

   - When does the problem occur, or not occur?

   - What opinions and feelings do people have about the situation?

   - What associated problems are present?

   - What assumptions were made that might need to be challenged?

   - What does the "real" problem seem to be?

2. Organize the data, input, and ideas in a format so that you can understand all of the different pieces of the puzzle and how they relate to each other.

3. Once the problem has been defined, investigate the situation further to identify the contributing factors. Include input from others to ensure that you are seeing the problem from different points of view.

4. Explore potential solutions and evaluate the pros and cons of each alternative. Weigh the alternatives in terms of solving the problem, and in terms of acceptance and support from those who need to implement the solution.

Fine Tuning Inductive and Deductive Thinking Skills

When you analyze issues and consider the pros and cons of various proposed solutions, you will be better able to make the best decisions if you check the logic you used to analyze and decide the issue.

People use two types of logic to reach conclusions: inductive and deductive. Inductive thinking moves from the specific to the general; in other words, given that we know facts A, B, and C, we can conclude X. Deductive thinking moves from the general to the specific; in other words, if X is true, then A, B, and C follow. You use both kinds of reasoning every day.

Regardless of whether you use an inductive or a deductive process to reach a conclusion, it's important to check your reasoning to make sure that it is logically sound. Try these suggestions:

- When you have facts and draw a conclusion from these facts, make sure that the facts really support the conclusion. Ask yourself if they point to any other conclusions.

- Check to be sure that your conclusion or generalization is really supported by the facts, and not just by your personal beliefs. Also double-check others' conclusions.

- When you come to a conclusion from a situation or series of events, check that the specifics really do logically follow or are the only options that make sense. For example, if quality is important to your customers, you may assume that you have to take particular actions to ensure quality. You'll need to evaluate whether these are your only options: Do they really follow?

Checking your own and others' logic is a useful and necessary skill if you want to do solid problem analysis.

RECOMMENDED READINGS

The publications listed here were selected for their content and suitability to a managerial audience.

Cut The Fat, Not The Muscle

Kobert, Norman, Englewood Cliffs, NJ: Prentice-Hall, 1995
ISBN: 0-13-292443-9
This book provides strategies for analyzing ways to cut costs, rather than simply discharging employees and cutting costs indiscriminately. To make smart cost-cutting decisions a company needs to: find out where its core business lies, work closely with suppliers to reduce costs, train employees in cost reduction, find where the true costs are, and use ratios to measure profitability and maximize the use of assets. Throughout the book, Kobert provides strategies for engaging in this detailed analysis.

Breakthrough Thinking: The Seven Principles of Creative Problem Solving

Nadler, Gerald, and Hibino, Shozo, Rocklin, CA: Prima Publishing, 1994
ISBN: 1-55958-421-1
This American/Japanese collaboration contains the results of the authors' ground-breaking studies on how the most intuitive and creative leaders and organizations solve problems. They show how to improve incorrect thinking, which they contend accounts for the failure of many enterprises.

Corporate Game: A Computer Adventure for Developing Business Decision-Making Skills

Rye, David E., New York: McGraw-Hill, 1993
ISBN: 0-07-911763-5
You're given a million dollars to launch a company, and one year to make it successful. Rye's book and accompanying software program painlessly teaches economics, marketing, manufacturing, and how these disciplines interact.

The Fifth Discipline Fieldbook

Senge, Peter; Kleiner, Art; et. al., New York: Doubleday, 1994
ISBN: 0-385-47256-0
This fieldbook takes Senge's theory regarding a learning organization and makes it practical. It is a pragmatic guide to creating an organization where collaboration is the lifeblood of every endeavor, and the tough questions are fearlessly asked.

Vision in Action

Tregoe, Benjamin B.; Zimmerman, John W.; Smith, Ronald A.; and Tobia, Peter M., New York: Simon & Schuster, 1990
ISBN: 0-671-70643-8
The authors focus on two central and related themes: 1) how to take the strategic direction formulated by top management and translate that direction into reality, and 2) how to go about achieving the participation necessary for implementing the vision.

SUGGESTED SEMINARS

The seminars listed here were selected for their appeal to a managerial audience. The reputation of the vendor, the quality of their seminar offerings, and the specific seminar content were considered in the selection process.

Because of the dynamic nature of the seminar marketplace, some seminars may have been upgraded or replaced, and others may no longer be offered. Likewise, costs and locations may have changed since this listing was compiled. We recommend that you contact the vendor directly for updated and additional information.

Critical Thinking: A New Paradigm for Peak Performance

This three-day workshop will teach managers how to build and expand their thinking skills, enable them to fully consider all sides of an issue, and anticipate a broader range of possibilities. It presents a holistic process which can be learned and applied to the day-to-day course of conducting business.
Length: 3 days; Cost: $1,200
Locations: Call vendor
American Management Association
P.O. Box 319, Saranac Lake, NY 12983
Telephone: 800/262-9699

Problem Solving and Decision Making

This program teaches participants how to strike a balance between logical soundness and intuition when making decisions. Topics include: differentiating between problem solving and decision making; balancing logic and experience with creativity; evaluating options; and setting up criteria to evaluate decisions and monitor results.
Length: 3 days; Cost: $1,260
Locations: Call vendor
American Management Association
P.O. Box 319, Saranac Lake, NY 12983
Telephone: 800/262-9699

Systems Thinking: A Language for Learning and Action™

This seminar will teach managers how to apply systems thinking. The seminar is designed to increase participants' natural inclination to think systematically. During the seminar, participants will practice communicating critical business issues from a systematic point of view, learn to talk convincingly about root causes, and develop alternative actions for desired changes.
Length: 3 days; Cost: $1,995
Locations: Call vendor
Innovation Associates, Inc.
3 Speen Street, Suite 140, Framingham, MA 01701
Telephone: 508/879-8301

Problem Solving and Decision Making

The key topics of this seminar include solving critical problems, making decisions when the choice among alternatives is not clear, anticipating potential problems and opportunities, managing complex issues, and applying proven principles to on-the-job concerns.
Length: 3 days; Cost: $1,095
Locations: Call vendor
Kepner Tregoe
Research Road, P.O. Box 704, Princeton, NJ 08542
Telephone: 800/537-6378

USE SOUND JUDGMENT

Sound judgment can be defined as good common sense combined with solid analysis, and business "smarts" mixed with more than a touch of concern for people. Sound judgment is based on an accurate and complete analysis of known information. It reflects a solid understanding of the business and its priorities, and factors both hard data and respect for "people concerns" into the analysis and decision-making process. It also requires weighing the known against the unknown, predicting benefits and costs, and weighing risks.

Based on research conducted by Personnel Decisions, sound judgment is one of the five skill areas considered by managers to be most important. It's one of the key factors you look for and work to develop in your people.

This section focuses on the decision-making part of exercising sound judgment and provides suggestions for overcoming the common pitfalls managers encounter in this area. The topics addressed in this section include:

Part 1: Making Decisions

- Defining a Sound Decision
- Analyzing Alternative Solutions
- Considering the Consequences of Decision Alternatives
- Testing the Practicality of Your Decisions
- Collaborating with Others in Decision Making

Part 2: Overcoming Problems in Decision Making

- Making Decisions in Complex Situations
- Making Decisions in the Face of Uncertainty
- Making Timely Decisions
- Overcoming Procrastination
- Curbing Impulsiveness
- Taking Responsibility for Decision Making

Valuable Tips

- Determine whether immediate action is required before making a hasty decision.

- Talk to colleagues about their approaches to difficult decisions. See what you can learn from their methods.

- Instead of choosing the first solution that presents itself, consider alternative solutions to a problem. Usually, there are more alternatives than you might imagine.

- Weigh the consequences of alternative solutions before making decisions.

- Be open to the possibility of changing your decisions when new information becomes available.

- If you "shoot from the hip," ask yourself what else you need to know before going with your first reaction.

- To become less impulsive in your decision making, ask your manager for feedback regarding inappropriate snap decisions you may have made in the past.

- Ask yourself, "What is the worst thing that could happen if I made this decision without more information?"

- Go to your manager with your analysis and a recommended solution, rather than with the problem.

- Use your best time of day for decision making and problem solving.

- If you tend to delay making decisions, push yourself by deciding quickly in low-risk decision areas. Set a time limit for making the decision that takes into account how much information is already available, how important the decision is, and the urgency of making the decision. Then push yourself to meet your deadline.

- Identify routine decisions that you or others can make easily or automatically.

- Be willing to accept risk in decision areas where you can't possibly improve your information analysis.

- Force yourself to move from details to the "big picture" to gain a broader perspective.

- Look at each issue from several angles to get a better perspective and improve your judgment.

- Put each issue and decision in the context of how it will affect all of the key constituents involved.

- Look for practical, workable solutions that will be easy to implement.

PART 1

Defining a Sound Decision

Making Decisions

A sound decision has the following characteristics:

- It is based on accurate analysis.

- It reflects a solid understanding of the business and its priorities.

- It incorporates the analysis of hard data and people's concerns.

- It weighs the pros and cons of alternatives.

- It involves the necessary people in the decision-making process.

Sound judgment means maximizing the positive outcomes and minimizing the negative ones. People with sound judgment make good calls in spite of time constraints, inadequate information, or the complexity of the issue.

Analyzing Alternative Solutions

Some problems are simple to resolve; they have one straightforward answer. For more complex problems, however, it is often advantageous to generate and look at a variety of solutions. Once you have generated a number of possible solutions, evaluate these alternatives objectively by measuring them against established criteria.

The following process can help you generate and analyze alternative solutions:

1. To generate alternative solutions:

   - Brainstorm possible solutions with others. See the Innovate section in this chapter for more information on brainstorming techniques.

   - Use idea-generating questions, such as: "If we had no resource limitations, what could we do?" or "Technical limitations aside, what would be the best solution?"

   - Find out how others have handled similar situations and use those ideas to stimulate alternatives.

2. Next, determine the criteria you will use to evaluate the possibilities, such as:

   - Strategic impact on the business

   - Acceptance

   - People resources

- Time

- Cost

- Available technology

- Impact on current operations

3. After you have generated alternative solutions and determined your criteria, use the following process to ensure that you evaluate all possible alternatives against the criteria for decision making. The chart that follows will help you to structure your analysis.

   - State the problem at the top of the chart.

   - Along the left side, record, in order of priority, the criteria you identified to evaluate your alternative solutions.

   - Write the alternative solutions across the top of the chart.

   - Using a scale from 1 to 5, determine the degree to which each solution meets the criteria you have listed, with 1 being "does not satisfy the criterion" and 5 being "satisfies the criterion very well."

PROBLEM: _____

Criteria	Solution: _____ _____	Solution: _____ _____	Solution: _____ _____

4. Choose the solution that most completely satisfies the important criteria. Then ask yourself the following questions:

   - How effectively does this alternative address the issue?

   - Can I combine this alternative with another to make it more effective?

   - What will this alternative cost to implement in terms of money, time, and people resources?

Considering the Consequences of Decision Alternatives

When making decisions, especially in complex or controversial areas, it's important to involve those who will be affected by the decisions as early as possible in the problem-solving process. Often, the reason that a solution doesn't work out is that it affects certain people so negatively that these people set out to change the solution. This is especially true when the people affected by the decision have not been involved in the decision-making process.

The following process can help you avoid this problem and analyze the consequences of a decision:

1. For each alternative you are considering, ask yourself how the decision will be accepted by:

   - Your employees

   - Your manager

   - Other departments

   - Informal leaders in the organization

   - People outside the organization (for example, vendors, customers)

2. Write down the pros and cons for each alternative according to who will support or resist the alternative. A chart similar to the following can help you structure your analysis:

Persons Affected	Alternative 1		Alternative 2		Alternative 3	
	Pros	Cons	Pros	Cons	Pros	Cons
Your employees						
Your manager						
Other departments						
Informal leaders						
Customers						

3. Analyze this information and use it to help you make your decision. However, don't choose the most acceptable or popular decision alternative unless it is also the best. Once you have made your decision, use this information to construct your implementation plan and to "sell" your decision and plan. Those who disagree the most will require the most attention in the selling and implementation phases.

Testing the Practicality of Your Decisions

In many cases, a solution that looks good on paper or sounds feasible at first does not work when implemented. Following are several ways to test the practicality of decisions to increase their probability of success:

- When making a decision, get into the habit of asking yourself whether it is workable. Consider the specifics of your situation. Think through all possible results of the decision to ensure that you've covered all your bases.

- Before making your final decision, put yourself in the shoes of those who will be affected by the solution; assess the impact of the decision on them and whether they are likely to accept it. Remember to consider individuals in other units who may be affected by the changes you initiate. These people can be as instrumental in determining the success of your plan as those within your own group.

- Ask people who are likely to be affected by your decisions for their opinions on the practicality of those decisions.

- Develop a sound implementation plan. Even good solutions can fail because of a poor implementation plan. A complete plan includes the correct sequence of steps and assigned responsibility for the success of each step. To test the practicality of your decision, as well as to create a good plan, get input from representatives of all groups or departments that will be affected. If you understand how best to implement the change from their points of view, you increase the likelihood that your plan will be accepted and supported.

- Identify potential problems and plan ways to deal with them.

Despite the most careful analysis and planning, there will be times when a seemingly sound solution proves unworkable. In such cases, it's important to be flexible enough to adapt your decisions or to discontinue efforts that are not working out. Be aware of this fact, and don't let these cases deter your future efforts to choose and implement the best solutions.

Collaborating with Others in Decision Making

Because many perspectives and ideas come into play in collaborative decision making, this approach often produces the best decisions. In addition, those who were involved in making the decision are more likely to be committed to carrying out the solution. Thus, the increased time required in the initial decision-making process is often regained during the implementation phase.

There are times, however, when group decision making is not appropriate. When decisions need to be made immediately, when the issue is confidential, or when buy-in is assured, collaborative decision making is not necessary.

The following steps will help you identify appropriate situations for collaborative decision making and get others involved in the process:

1. When you first learn that a decision must be made, determine if the decision is solely your own or if it should be made collaboratively. Collaborative decision making is useful when:

    -   Others have information that you need.

    -   The problem is complex or ambiguous, and others are needed to clarify and define the problem.

    -   Others are needed for implementation, and they want to be involved.

    -   The situation can be used to train others in problem analysis or decision making.

2. If you determine that the decision should be made collaboratively, use the group to define the problem, look for alternatives, determine criteria for making the decision, and/or actually make the decision. The group may be the same for each phase of the process, or you may want to use a larger group for getting input and a smaller group for making the decision.

    When using a collaborative approach to decision making, keep the following in mind:

    -   Involving others in the process can be done by consulting one-on-one, asking for written input, or through group meetings.

    -   Collaborative decision making can be effectively accomplished in well-run meetings, especially when the participants are informed of the issues in advance.

3. Ask the group to use consensus decision making rather than taking the majority view. Think of consensus as "Can I live with this?" rather than "Do I like this?"

For more suggestions on involving others in decision making, read the Foster Teamwork section in the Leadership Skills chapter of this Handbook.

PART 2

Making Decisions in Complex Situations

Overcoming Problems in Decision Making

Many problems are relatively simple. Others are much more complex or ambiguous. Sometimes, the problem or opportunity is not clear; at other times, there are many different ways to look at the issues. And with some problems, it is not possible to get definite information on which to base a solution.

To make effective decisions in these situations:

1. Gather together the people who have information or perspectives on the situation.

2. With these people, determine what is known and what needs to be known in order to make a decision. Separate the necessary information from the "nice to know" information. Then plan how to gather the additional information.

3. Once you have obtained the needed information, use it to define the problem or opportunity as clearly as possible. At this point, you may have multiple problem definitions.

4. Determine whether it is necessary to make a decision now. What are the advantages and possible negative consequences of making the decision now versus tabling it until a later date? Involve the stakeholders in this decision.

5. Generate alternatives if you decide to make a decision now. Look for alternatives that satisfy the multiple facets of the problem.

6. Develop criteria for judging the alternatives and selecting the best solution.

7. Make the decision and plan what you will do if the solution doesn't work out.

Making Decisions in the Face of Uncertainty

Every decision involves an element of risk. Sometimes, however, sound decisions or decision alternatives are discarded because they appear too risky or because the decision maker feels uncomfortable with unproven alternatives.

Calculated risk taking implies that a decision is made with a thorough understanding of the potential risks and benefits involved. The ability to recognize and take calculated risks is a skill required of all managers.

Following are some of the problems commonly experienced in the area of risk taking and suggestions for overcoming each type of problem:

- A need to gather too much data. Fact-finding is a necessary step in the decision-making process. It can, however, be carried to the point where valuable time is wasted. If you have a tendency to gather too much information to ensure that your decisions are well formulated:
  - Try making a decision at an earlier stage in the process.
  - Before all data has been collected, force yourself to make a decision and write it down.
  - Then analyze the additional data and make a final decision.
  - Compare your final decision with your preliminary one to determine whether the additional information was needed.

  If you consistently find that the additional data was not needed, begin making decisions based on less information.

- Lack of knowledge of the true risk level. At times, you may feel uneasy about the level of risk involved because you haven't clearly identified the pros and cons of each alternative. In such cases, write down each alternative and its associated risks and benefits. Then choose the one that provides the greatest benefit, even if it involves some risk.

- Discomfort with the consequences of risk taking. It's not unusual for people to become so uncomfortable about the possible consequences of a risky decision that their discomfort prevents them from taking risks altogether. If you tend to overemphasize the possible negative results of a decision, try the following:
  - Ask yourself, "What is the worst thing that could happen as a result of this decision? How much impact could this 'worst thing' have on me personally, on the organization, or on the work?" Determine what you could do if the worst-case scenario occurred.

- Develop a strategy for reducing risks. Some risks can be reduced by good planning.
- If you find yourself concentrating on the negative aspects of an alternative and deemphasizing its benefits, try substituting positive statements or thoughts for negative statements. This process will help you determine whether the negatives are really as strong as you thought or whether you have gotten yourself into a "rut" by placing too much emphasis on the drawbacks of the alternatives.

- Discomfort due to unknown risk factors. In some cases, you may have a vague feeling that a solution carries with it some unknown risks. Rather than allowing these feelings to keep you from trying the solution, attempt to understand what it is that bothers you. Discuss your feelings with someone who has greater insight or experience. Analyze your implementation process and determine the points at which the process could be halted — the "go/no go" decision points. Inform others of these points so they will not be surprised if you decide to discontinue the process at some point. Then, if the risk becomes too great, stop the process at one of these points.

- Discomfort in selected areas. If you analyze the various areas in which you must make decisions — hiring, capital expenditures, work flow, organizational structure, and advertising expenditures, to name a few — you will probably find that you are very comfortable with certain kinds of risks and less comfortable with others. In the areas to which you are risk-averse, work at being less cautious.

When dealing with areas of discomfort, turn to others in your organization who seem particularly skilled at making decisions that involve these kinds of risks. Talk with these individuals about how they take risk factors into account in their decisions, and study the way they make decisions. Then apply what you have learned from these people to your own decision-making process.

Making Timely Decisions

When managers do not make timely decisions, they may miss deadlines, hold up projects, waste resources, and frustrate others who are waiting for the decisions. In these situations, some managers want to be certain they have collected enough information; others, concerned about "being right," spend a lot of time on the analysis of that information. To be timely in decision making:

- Ask yourself:
  - What additional information could be collected? How long would it take to collect?
  - What information is absolutely necessary?
  - What information would make me feel better, but probably would not cause me to change my decision?

- Avoid "analysis paralysis." Set a deadline to complete your information analysis. Prioritize your greatest concerns and spend your analysis time on them.

- Rather than insisting on certainty in the decision, anticipate what you will do if problems arise.

- Once you've made a decision, stand by it. Avoid reopening the decision-making process unless new information strongly indicates the need for reconsideration.

Overcoming Procrastination

The opposite of impulsive decision making is procrastination. Most people do not procrastinate every time they make a decision; rather, they tend to delay decisions under certain circumstances. It's useful to identify those circumstances in which you tend to procrastinate and to determine how you can handle these situations in the future. The following suggestions should help:

1. Each time you find yourself delaying a decision, ask yourself the reason for the delay. Some of the more common reasons include:

   - Lack of information

   - Unclear course of action, especially in subjective matters

   - Lack of time for thought

   - Fear of negative consequences, such as anger on the part of those affected by the decision or having the decision prove unsuccessful

2. Once you determine why you procrastinate, begin to focus on finding a solution. Plan ways to substitute decisive behaviors for the delaying tactics you wish to eliminate. Following are some possible approaches:

   - For situations in which you lack information, use the information-gathering suggestions in the Analyze Issues section of this Handbook to acquire more data. Construct a plan for how you will gather the information, and implement your plan immediately.

- When a course of action is unclear, choose what appears to be the best plan and implement it on a temporary basis. A trial run of a plan may turn up unanticipated benefits or drawbacks. Even if the plan doesn't work, the trial run may produce alternatives that have more credibility than any that could be generated without the benefit of this experimentation.

- If you lack sufficient time for focused, concentrated thought, block out time on your schedule for decision making when you are confronted with a major issue. Quiet time is necessary to think effectively about issues and possible solutions. Many people find early morning or late in the day to be the most conducive time for thinking through issues and making important decisions.

- If you fear negative consequences in making a decision, face your fears. Seek the involvement of those you believe would resist your decision; a participative process is usually better in this kind of situation. If you are worried that your plan will fail and that your career may suffer as a consequence, inform your manager of the risks involved and ask for approval to proceed.

In almost all situations, it is helpful to designate a time frame for decision making. You may want to create a flowchart of the decision-making process, with deadlines for each part of it. You also might want to request the assistance of someone who can help ensure that you meet your deadlines.

Curbing Impulsiveness

If you often make decisions and later have to backtrack or you wish you'd waited until you had more information, you're making decisions impulsively. Knowing the reasons for your haste can help you temper this impulsiveness. Does one of the following apply to your situation?

- Do you feel pressured into making decisions that you are not ready to make? If so, learn to "buy time" in decision-making situations. When possible, tell the person applying the pressure that you need more time and why; then name a date by which you will announce your decision.

- Do you neglect to look at the consequences of not making a decision? Sometimes it is not feasible to get enough data within the time frame to feel secure. Yet, the consequences of not making decisions may be worse for the organization and the people involved than making a less than perfect decision would be.

- Do you make decisions emotionally, for instance, when you're upset or angry? If so, try waiting a few hours or "sleeping on it" to calm down. You can then judge whether the decision is really the best one or simply the one that seemed right at the time.

- Do you often sense that you are "leaping to a solution" because you have a desire for action? If so, create a decision-making plan that will result in action. Write down who will be involved in the decision-making process, the types of information you will need, the criteria you will use to judge solutions, and a time frame for action.

Taking Responsibility for Decision Making

Indecision can often result in a tendency to leave the decision making to someone else. If you tend to divert decision-making responsibility to others, try the following actions:

- Make a list of the major areas in which you have decision-making responsibility. Examples of such areas include capital expenditures, staffing, delegating, and policy making. Identify the areas in which you tend to divert responsibility by determining which of the following decision-making processes you usually use in each area:
  - Make decisions on your own.
  - Formulate alternatives, select what seems to be the best alternative, and then ask for the opinions of others.
  - Formulate alternatives, but have problems determine which is best.
  - Ask for others' opinions immediately.

  For example, you may feel comfortable making decisions on capital expenditures and often make decisions in this area on your own. You may feel less comfortable making policy decisions and may tend to ask for others' opinions immediately.

- If you have difficulty determining which of several alternatives is best, don't use that as a cue for going to others for a decision. Instead, choose one of the alternatives and spell out the reasons you chose that alternative as the best one. Only then should you seek input. Tell the other persons what your alternatives and recommendations are, and then ask for opinions.

- If you turn to others immediately, before you've even formulated any alternatives, ask yourself why. Do you need more information? If so, make that clear to others when you approach them. Ask for the information you need, gather the facts, and then formulate alternatives on your own.

- If you turn to others out of habit or because you are uncomfortable making decisions alone, formulate alternatives and make a recommendation on your own before seeking the help of others. This will help you break the habit and gain confidence in making decisions, especially if others agree with your recommendations.

- If you have a tendency to push your decision-making responsibilities upward, get into the habit of presenting recommended solutions rather than problems to your manager.

RECOMMENDED READINGS

The publications listed here were selected for their content and suitability to a managerial audience.

The Confident Decision Maker

Dawson, Roger, New York: William Morrow & Company, 1992
ISBN: 0-688-11564-0
Dawson's book explains the core of confident, effective, systematic decision making. Practice his methods for identifying, analyzing, and responding to problems and opportunities and achieve success through confident choices.

Managing for Results

Drucker, Peter F., New York: HarperBusiness, 1993
ISBN: 0-88730-614-4
The author holds that a successful business operation focuses on opportunities rather than problems. This book combines economic analysis with entrepreneurial initiatives in order to show the manager or individual how to move his or her enterprise forward.

Rules for Reaching Consensus

Saint, Steven, and Lawson, James R., San Diego: Pfeiffer & Company, 1994
ISBN: 0-89384-256-7
With the increased use of teams and collaborative work groups, a new method of decision making called collective decision making or consensus has emerged. This guide focuses on the steps to follow in order for a group to reach full agreement. Provided is a step-by-step approach to mastering consensus decision making which includes discussions on: common concerns about consensus, the consensus meeting, the preconsensus process, the rules of the consensus process, and tips for facilitators.

How to Meet, Think, and Work to Consensus

Tagliere, Daniel A., San Diego: Pfeiffer & Company, 1993
ISBN: 0-89384-225-7
Small groups and teams are essential to an organization's decision-making process. This book presents a method which makes meetings a productive and integral part of the work process. The author provides tools for improving the quality of decisions, solving problems, furthering creativity, and achieving reliable solutions through a collaborative team process.

Paradigm Shift   **Tapscot, Don, and Caston, Art,** New York: McGraw-Hill, 1993
ISBN: 0-07-062857-2
This book explains how to take advantage of new technology in
order to change your organization into a responsive and
competitive company ready to take advantage of new
opportunities. It shows managers and professionals with little
technological background how to take action to achieve immediate
benefits from this technology and how to transform their
organization for long-term growth. The techniques offered here
are the result of extensive research into more than 4,500
businesses and governmental organizations.

SUGGESTED SEMINARS

The seminars listed here were selected for their appeal to a managerial audience. The reputation of the vendor, the quality of their seminar offerings, and the specific seminar content were considered in the selection process.

Because of the dynamic nature of the seminar marketplace, some seminars may have been upgraded or replaced, and others may no longer be offered. Likewise, costs and locations may have changed since this listing was compiled. We recommend that you contact the vendor directly for updated and additional information.

Critical Thinking: A New Paradigm for Peak Performance

This three-day workshop will teach managers how to build and expand their thinking skills, enable them to fully consider all sides of an issue, and anticipate a broader range of possibilities. It presents a holistic process which can be learned and applied to the day-to-day course of conducting business.
Length: 3 days; Cost: $1,200
Locations: Call vendor
American Management Association
P.O. Box 319, Saranac Lake, NY 12983
Telephone: 800/262-9699

Problem Solving and Decision Making: Good Decisions, Good Solutions

This program teaches participants how to strike a balance between logical soundness and intuition when making decisions. Topics include: differentiating between problem solving and decision making; balancing logic and experience with creativity; evaluating options; and setting up criteria to evaluate decisions and monitor results.
Length: 3 days; Cost: $1,260
Locations: Call vendor
American Management Association
P.O. Box 319, Saranac Lake, NY 12983
Telephone: 800/262-9699

Problem Solving and Decision Making

The key topics of this seminar include solving critical problems, making decisions when the choice among alternatives is not clear, anticipating potential problems and opportunities, managing complex issues, and applying proven principles to on-the-job concerns.
Length: 3 days; Cost: $1,095
Locations: Call vendor
Kepner Tregoe
Research Road, P.O. Box 704, Princeton, NJ 08542
Telephone: 800/537-6378

Emerging Leaders

This program, designed for current and future leaders, addresses the evaluation, building, and sustaining of leadership excellence. Participants will assess and develop their leadership excellence with regard to four areas: personal, people, business, and work.
Length: 5 days; Cost: Call vendor
Location: Call vendor
Personnel Decisions International
2000 Plaza VII Tower, 45 South Seventh Street
Minneapolis, MN 55402-1608
Telephone: 800/633-4410

Advanced Management Program

This program is designed to help participants develop sound strategic thinking and decision-making skills and understand the organizational impact of financial analysis, market competition, government policies, legal issues, and other aspects of the business environment. This program explores changing social, political, and economic conditions at home and around the world and assesses their impact on business, both now and in the future.
Length: 5 weekends; Cost: $3,995
Locations: Los Angeles, CA
University of Southern California
Office of Executive Education
School of Business Administration
Davidson Conference Center, Room 111
Los Angeles, CA 90089-0871
Telephone: 213/740-8990

Leadership and Decision Making in Organizations

This seminar is designed to help senior managers increase their leadership potential. Through lecture, assessment instruments, and active participation and feedback, participants learn to extend their skills in understanding leadership styles, conflict resolution, decision making, and interpersonal communications.
Length: 4 days; Cost: $3,200
Locations: New Haven, CT
Yale University
School of Management, Executive Programs, Box 208200
New Haven, CT 06520-8200
Telephone: 203/432-6038

INNOVATE

The ability to generate creative solutions is essential in business today, when an organization's survival and success may depend on how quickly it can respond to a changing world. Creativity involves not only coming up with original and innovative solutions, but also being resourceful by taking what is and making it better.

Creativity is a process that requires commitment and effort. By developing your ability to come up with "new and improved" ideas, you can dramatically increase your value to the organization, helping to move it to a greater competitive position. By increasing the innovation of your people, you can improve the quantity and quality of the ideas coming out of your area.

This section is presented in two parts:

Part 1: Developing Personal Creativity

- Increasing Your Mental Flexibility
- Determining When to Use Creative Thinking
- Approaching Problems with Curiosity and Open-Mindedness
- Making Use of Existing Information
- Generating Innovative Ideas and Solutions
- Thinking Positively When Faced with Obstacles

Part 2: Encouraging Innovation in Others

- Encouraging Innovation in Your Department
- Using Logical and Intuitive Approaches
- Brainstorming
- Stimulating Creative Ideas in Others
- Challenging "The Way It Has Always Been Done"

Valuable Tips

- Suspend your critical judgment, that part of you that says, "It won't work."

- Talk about the situation with someone from a different discipline.

- Believe that you are an innovative person.

- Talk with others in the organization, colleagues outside the organization, and friends to see how they have addressed similar situations or problems.

- Be less conservative and take more risks in your decision making.

- Generate as many options as you can during both the problem identification phase and the generation-of-alternatives phase of the problem-solving process.

- If you run out of ideas, take a break. Later, redefine the problem and look at it from a different perspective.

- Fantasize a "different universe" with a different set of natural laws. Then ask yourself, "What possibilities exist for solving this problem?"

- Don't be satisfied with your first idea. Push yourself to generate other ideas before committing to one.

- Practice coming up with what may at first seem like "way out" ideas to get your "creative juices" flowing and reduce your self-criticism.

- Allow yourself quiet time.

- When considering alternatives, ask yourself and others "why not?" instead of "why?"

- Avoid premature censoring of ideas, and don't be concerned about whether ideas are flowing in a logical sequence.

- Use group idea-generation techniques, such as brainstorming.

- Keep a file titled "New Ideas." Each time you think of something innovative related to your job, write it down and file it.

- Read material different from the kind you typically read. For example, if you usually read journals in your field, read biographies of artists or research another field.

- Don't take yourself too seriously; a playful attitude is fundamental to creativity.

INNOVATE

- To further stimulate your creativity, try drawing out problems instead of writing them down.

- Recognize and take advantage of your "biorhythmic clock." Most people have a "best" time of the day when their creative juices flow more easily. Chart your creative times and set these hours aside for creative tasks.

- To loosen yourself up, try a warm-up activity, such as spending ten minutes enumerating solutions to questions like, "What can you do with a thousand paper clips?"

- Listen to music that gives you positive energy. An upbeat attitude can help you feel more creative.

- Daydream.

PART 1

Increasing Your Mental Flexibility

Developing Personal Creativity

Mental flexibility is the ability to adjust to new information and to consider a broad range of alternatives when solving problems. People who think inflexibly generally hold to policy, display rigidity in problem solving by discarding alternatives before thinking them through, and believe that each problem has only one right answer.

To become more flexible, follow these guidelines:

- Ask trusted coworkers to provide feedback on situations in which you tend to be overly opinionated or rigid in your thinking. Most people have specific "problem areas." Recognizing the fact that you are becoming inflexible is the first step in initiating change.

- Watch for "snap" reactions. Rather than assuming that the first alternative that enters your mind is the best solution, write down your first reaction, then consider other opinions.

- Once you have defined a problem and generated solutions, challenge yourself to think how you would defend the problem from the opposite point of view.

- Practice mental flexibility by doing brain teasers, such as the one presented later in this section, to help you get into the habit of challenging your assumptions.

Determining When to Use Creative Thinking

Before diving into a creative problem-solving process, it's important to first evaluate whether the situation or problem at hand would be best solved through a creative process or through more traditional means. Use the following guidelines to determine to what degree you should employ a creative-thinking process:

Use creative problem solving when:	*Use traditional problem solving when:*
• Problems keep recurring.	• Problems seldom recur.
• You want to do things differently.	• You want to do things better.
• Problems are ambiguous.	• Problems are well defined.
• You are not sure how to evaluate the problem.	• All essential criteria for evaluating the problem are known.

Use creative problem solving when:

- Facts are unknown; feelings abound.

- Causes are unknown.

- Unpredictable and risky solutions are acceptable.

- Something that has not been a problem becomes one.

- The standard "way it has always been done" is no longer working.

Use traditional problem solving when:

- Facts are central to the process.

- Causes are definite and defined.

- Corrective solutions are acceptable.

Approaching Problems with Curiosity and Open-Mindedness

Creative people engage in undisciplined, open-minded, and uncritical thinking in the initial stages of the problem-solving process. Remaining open-minded allows you to generate more alternatives. To increase your use of creative approaches, try the following suggestions:

- Realize that how you view a problem often corresponds to how you approach it. Develop a more positive mindset about problems. Examine what you've done in the past few weeks when faced with new problems. Did you look at these problems as unpleasant or disruptive, or as an adventure or a challenge?

- Look at your style to see if there are certain kinds of problems that excite you, that make you curious and enthusiastic, and others that are unappealing. What are the differences? Frame those problems that don't stimulate you in such a way that they resemble those that do.

- When generating ideas, spend more time in the initial stages of problem formulation. Broadly scan the alternatives, challenging yourself to view the problem from at least three different perspectives — for example, those of your customers, your suppliers, and your competitors. By spending more time defining the problem in a multitude of ways, you will be able to generate a broader range of possible solutions.

- Use the "W" questions (why, where, what, who, when, and how) more in approaching problems. They'll increase your understanding of the problem and its relation to other problems. These links can lead you to greater enthusiasm and satisfaction.

- Constantly expose yourself to new ideas and trends. Build your intellectual curiosity by developing your knowledge of the world around you. Get into the habit of reading newspapers and periodicals for current events, technical journals for new developments in your field, and books related to your work and life.

Making Use of Existing Information

Innovation does not necessarily require doing, making, or thinking something that did not exist before. For example, if your task is to create a training program, don't "reinvent the wheel" or copy those that already exist. This can be a waste of time or unethical. Instead, learn as much as you can about how others have done the task. Then use their ideas, along with your own, to design a unique but solid program that suits your particular needs.

To put this concept into practice, follow these guidelines:

1. Choose an area related to your job that you think would benefit from innovation, such as a time-consuming process that may be a bottleneck.

2. Obtain information about the situation from available resources.
   - Attend trade shows or conferences.
   - Talk with people who are knowledgeable in your chosen area and capitalize on their ideas. For instance, call your local university and talk with a subject-matter expert.
   - Talk with people who have dealt with the same issue and learn what they have done.

3. Analyze what you have learned to see what will work in your situation. Look at your resources and develop your implementation strategy. Convince others that your proposal will be an improvement. Then implement it.

Generating Innovative Ideas and Solutions

One of your challenges as a manager is to help your group "think outside the box" about the problems they encounter. Managers often need to take the lead in this activity by demonstrating alternative solutions that are possible and feasible. Consider the following suggestions for coming up with fresh perspectives and innovative approaches.

- Try the following "brain teaser" activity. Connect all of the nine dots using four consecutive straight lines. Follow these two requirements:
  - The end of one line must touch the beginning of the next.
  - When drawing the lines, don't lift your pen or pencil from the paper.

The answer appears at the end of this section.

- Think of yourself as a creative genius. One of the greatest impediments to creativity is believing that you aren't creative. Believing that you *are* creative will help you to *be* creative.

- Change your scene. A different physical environment may be all it takes to generate innovative ideas.

- Approach the problem differently. For example, instead of putting your problem on paper in written form, draw it out. Drawing can stimulate images, concepts, and intuition, while writing lends itself to facts, numbers, and logic. Chart your problem and illustrate different aspects of it; turn it into a motion picture in your mind.

- Engage in an activity that forces you to operate outside your comfort zone.

- Argue the other side. This may move you to commit to your original idea all the more strongly, or it may cause you to modify your idea or abandon it completely.

- Believe that a solution is possible. When you're faced with a problem, your confidence may wane. Snap out of it! Believe that every step you take will bring you closer to an effective solution.

- Turn your ideas into action. Be relentless about putting your ideas into practice. See what works and what doesn't. You'll not only enjoy what you've conjured up and exert a more positive influence, but you'll be more creative in the future.

- Form cross-functional teams. Involve people from other functions who have different styles from the rest of your team.

- View risk taking and failures as an exciting form of learning.

Thinking Positively When Faced with Obstacles

When you feel that a task is impossible or that an obstacle cannot be overcome, stop yourself from thinking these negative thoughts; they close down your mental processes and prevent you from being resourceful. You can overcome your feeling of being "stuck" by using the following techniques:

- Acknowledge that you are stuck; once you realize that your problem-solving processes are blocked, there are a number of techniques you can use to get past the block.

- Think positively. Instead of telling yourself that the task is impossible, tell yourself that you have reached a momentary impasse and that a solution does exist and will eventually come to you. Adopt a "can-do" attitude. Remind yourself that if the task were easy to solve, it wouldn't be a challenge.

- View the obstacle as an opportunity to find a new approach. You'll be in a much better position to create or improve methods when the current ones aren't working.

- Take a break from the problem and return to it later with a fresh perspective.

- Avoid censoring your ideas. Suspend your critical judgments until later.

- Conceptualize the problem, redefine it, and look at it from a different perspective.

- Imagine how the most resourceful person you know would react to the same situation.

- Don't hesitate to ask for help. When a new perspective on the problem is required, others may be able to help you develop this perspective. Seek ideas and suggestions from people with perspectives or backgrounds different from your own.

PART 2

Encouraging Innovation in Your Department

Encouraging Innovation in Others

Most people are reluctant to voice new ideas if they fear they will look foolish. To encourage innovation, create a climate in which individuals feel free to present their ideas without fear of criticism. To foster this type of climate over the next month, implement two or three techniques for generating new ideas in group discussion. Following are examples of these techniques:

- Set aside time at your regular staff meeting to discuss new, innovative ideas. Stress the fact that ideas need not be fully considered.

- Promote a climate in which people initially encourage, rather than criticize, new ideas. Ask people to first discuss what they like, rather than what they dislike, about an idea.

- Initiate two or three sessions dedicated to brainstorming on a particular issue or question. These need not be formal sessions; if a problem arises during a staff meeting, suggest that the group brainstorm to generate as many solutions as possible.

- Reward people for their ideas by thanking them and telling others about their good ideas. Champion their ideas and help them to implement them. Success and the belief that one's good ideas will be acted upon go a long way toward encouraging innovation.

- Foster the attitude that innovative thinking is a part of everyone's job, regardless of function and level of responsibility.

As people's fear of criticism diminishes, you will see your department's climate change and hear people voice more new ideas.

Using Logical and Intuitive Approaches

Both logical and intuitive thinking are necessary for creating the optimum climate for innovation. Logical thinking is a sequential process, while intuitive thinking tends to be holistic. Idea-stimulation techniques can also be classified in these ways. To maximize innovative solutions, make sure that you and your team members utilize both ways of thinking and generating ideas.

A logical, or linear, approach provides structure and a logical sequence of steps for generating alternative solutions. Following are some examples of linear approaches:

- Matrix analysis uses a two- or three-dimensional matrix to help identify where to look further for new ideas. For example, you might structure a matrix like the following to explore areas where opportunities exist for new ideas.

	Markets			
	A	B	C	D
1	✓	✓	✓	✓
2	✓	x	✓	x
3	✓	✓	✓	✓
4	x	✓	x	✓
5	✓	✓	x	✓

Technologies labels rows 1–5.

Key: ✓ = already have; x = opportunity exists

- Attribute listing is a simple process in which you define all of the attributes or components of a procedure or product that you wish to improve. Next, you look at each attribute for possible ways to improve it.

  For example, a telephone has the following attributes, in addition to many others:
  - Receiver
  - Casing or body of the phone
  - Mechanism for dialing

  Each of these attributes has been improved over the years, including:
  - Receivers have been improved with headsets, and even eliminated by speakerphones.
  - Heavy metals have been replaced by lightweight plastics that are available in a variety of decorative colors and styles.
  - Rotary dials have been replaced by touch pads with quick touch-tone dialing.

- Force-field analysis is a method for exploring the feasibility of possible solutions by identifying a solution's strong points and potential problem areas. This method can help you clarify your vision, identify strengths that can be used to their fullest potential, and pinpoint weaknesses that can be overcome or minimized.

  Using the following format, write an objective statement of the problem you wish to solve and then describe the factors blocking and the factors supporting a successful outcome.

PROBLEM DEFINITION: _____

_____

Blocking Factors   Supporting Factors

FORCES

Negative (-)		Positive (+)
1.	1.	
2.	2.	
3.	3.	

Once you have completed this chart, you can analyze the positive and negative forces to identify ways to strengthen the positive forces, weaken the negative forces, or add new positive forces.

- Reframing questions is a technique that helps you to view your problem from a different perspective. It involves asking questions about your problem in a way that helps you to examine it from a broader perspective and identify the less obvious aspects of the problem.

An example of a reframing question is, "What are the facts of this problem or situation, and how can each of these facts be challenged?" If you apply this question to a delivery problem, for example, you and your team may determine that one of the facts of the situation is that you must ship product, in full, to your customer on Tuesday mornings. By challenging this assumption, you might find that your customer would be equally, or more, satisfied with shipments on Tuesday evenings or Wednesday mornings, which would ease your delivery person's tight schedule.

- The design tree is a way to map ideas around a concept or idea that you wish to expand upon, such as a technology or a product. For example, if you are implementing a voice mail phone answering service, your design tree might begin like this:

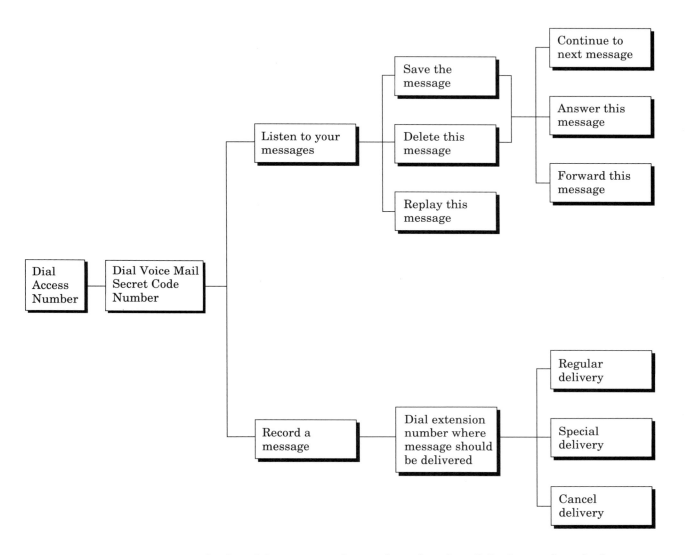

An intuitive approach, on the other hand, looks at the whole instead of the parts. Solutions are often arrived at in one larger step instead of a sequence of steps. Following are some examples of intuitive approaches:

- Imagery is a method of generating ideas by imagining experiences, scenes, or symbols. Aspects of nature, such as mountains, roads, trees, or darkness and lightness, can be used to clarify or depict aspects of a project or work process.

- Drawing is an effective way of bringing out intuitive processes through the communication of impressions and symbols, rather than words. Drawing can be used as a technique for putting imagery on paper.

- Analogies draw similarities or a parallel between two situations or things that would otherwise be dissimilar. This approach serves to make an unfamiliar situation or problem more understandable and can be used to discover new approaches and insights to problems. For example, the invention of Velcro™ was based on the analogy of burdock burrs clinging to clothing.

- Dreams — both daydreams and night dreams — may produce images and key words that can be creatively applied to real-world situations.

Brainstorming

I'LL HAVE YOU KNOW YOU'RE VIOLATING THE SPIRIT OF BRAINSTORMING!

When a number of people gather to solve a problem, their ideas can build on each other. This is especially true in an environment that encourages idea generation. To encourage the sharing of ideas in your organization, conduct brainstorming sessions, following these guidelines:

1. Organize an informal brainstorming session to discuss new approaches to persistent departmental problems or innovative applications of existing products and/or services. The purpose of the session should be to generate as many novel ideas as possible. Limit the number of participants to seven to nine to ensure the active participation of all members. Find a place to work that will be free of interruptions.

2. To create the proper environment, announce these ground rules at the beginning of the session:
   - The emphasis is on quantity rather than quality. Avoid blocking creative thinking with unnecessary concentration on detail. For the moment, implementation constraints should be ignored.
   - No criticism of ideas is allowed. All ideas will be evaluated at a later time.
   - People should feel free to add to already-suggested ideas or to combine ideas.

3. Set a time limit for the brainstorming to generate a sense of urgency.

4. Appoint a person to record *all* of the ideas, even ones that have been mentioned before. Use a flipchart so the ideas are in full view of the participants. Record the ideas in a nonsequential fashion to avoid favoring the first or last ideas presented.

5. Present a clear definition of the problem, remind participants

of the ground rules, and then let loose. Have fun. Laugh. As a leader, you are responsible for stopping criticism, preventing judgments, and trying to get everyone to participate.

6. At the end of the meeting, review the ideas. You can perform this review yourself, get other group members involved, or send the ideas to a preselected committee for evaluation. Your mission at this point is to identify the ideas that could actually be implemented.

When the group is comfortable with this process, you may want to invite individuals from different levels in your department or division to participate. A brainstorming session can serve as a communication bridge, helping people to work together as a team.

Stimulating Creative Ideas in Others

To switch from a corporate culture that endorses conformity and compliance to one that fosters creativity and initiative, you need to show that you support innovativeness in others. Try the following techniques for encouraging creativity in others:

- Allow time for ideas to brew before asking for a solution that can be implemented. Creativity typically is not produced on demand. People need to be given "think time"; some day-dreaming must be allowed.

- Provide challenges and permit freedom in how tasks are carried out. When employees bring problems to you, ask them to propose solutions to these problems. This will force them to tap into their own creative energy.

- Protect "idea" people. Creative people are often not popular. Others may feel threatened by their ideas for change. Their peers may regard them with suspicion, even hostility. Ensure that others understand why idea people are important. Idea generators need a champion and a cheerleader; give them the support they need.

- Tolerate failure. Recognize that creativity and risk taking go hand-in-hand. To maximize creativity, minimize the fear of taking risks.

- Recognize the people who suggest creative solutions by giving them both tangible rewards (adequate work space, budget, merit salary increases, or promotions) and intangible rewards (special attention, public credit for their ideas, or challenging tasks).

- Provide innovators with opportunities to network and to learn what others are doing by attending seminars, workshops, and professional meetings. Allow them to have contact with your customers and with others in the organization. In addition, involve them in committees, task forces, and quality circles.

Challenging "The Way It Has Always Been Done"

Managers can no longer accept "the way it has always been done" as an excuse to avoid making changes. They need, increasingly, to question status-quo assumptions. To break out of the "usual" way of doing things, try the following ideas:

- Challenge your employees to find ways of improving how work is done. Use various forums (staff meetings, private conversations, performance plans) to stimulate and reinforce the need to make continuous improvements.

- Eliminate organizational barriers to innovation. For example:
  - Remove policy barriers whenever possible. People are often encouraged to analyze their own suggestions in terms of existing procedures and policies; thus, they may be discouraged from proposing solutions contrary to current guidelines.
  - Reserve a portion of the budget for implementing innovations. Financial plans frequently do not allow for the cost of promoting an innovation.
  - Identify people who may have hidden agendas or motives for maintaining the status quo. Look for alternative ways to meet their needs.
  - Because specialists may overlook relationships outside their area of expertise, combine people from various areas when you are developing new ideas.
  - Do not overdirect, overobserve, or overreport. These activities will inhibit your employees' ability to be innovative.
  - Reward flexibility. "The way things have always been done" is often a refuge for the inflexible.

- Challenge statements that close off alternatives (for example, "It has to be done like this," "They'll never accept . . . ," or "We can't . . ."). Reward employees who have a "can-do" attitude.

- Support individuals who challenge assumptions and question the way things are done. Unfortunately, organizations typically reward those who avoid rocking the boat. Promote innovation and motivation by actively encouraging questions and positive challenges.

- Be open to the possibility of changing your decisions after you have made them. Listen to new information and gather new data about the solutions you have implemented. Based on this information, decide whether to revisit the decision-making process.

- Refer to the Champion Change section of this Handbook for additional tips on encouraging improvement in your area.

Here's the solution to the brain teaser:

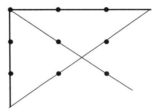

Notice that the problem can't be solved unless you draw outside of the structure. Most people erroneously assume that they are not allowed to draw outside the boundaries of the dots.

This same principle applies to problem solving on the job. Many effective solutions are those that require you to think outside the structure, or paradigm, of the situation.

RECOMMENDED READINGS

The publications listed here were selected for their content and suitability to a managerial audience.

Innovation On Demand

Fahden, Allen, Minneapolis: The Illiterati, 1993
ISBN: 0-9629663-1-2
Fahden outlines the four different types of innovators and how to get the best from them. In a practical, readable guide he shows how to unlock your creativity, how to get unstuck, and how to know when you've gone too far.

If It Ain't Broke...BREAK IT

Kriegel, Robert J., and Patler, Louis, New York: Warner Books, 1992
ISBN: 0-446-39359-2
The authors contend that conventional business wisdom cannot help you keep pace in these rapidly changing times. Their book will help you unlock the creative thinker inside; work smarter, not harder; and explore new and different paths.

The Creative Edge

Miller, William C., Reading, MA: Addison-Wesley, 1990
ISBN: 0-201-52401-5
This book is both a practical handbook of techniques and an inspirational work designed to help the reader develop creative skills and promote creativity within the organization. The author explains his model of creativity and innovation, and also addresses overcoming blocks to creativity, developing creative business strategies, and encouraging a creative organizational climate.

Liberation Management

Peters, Tom, New York: Fawcett Columbine, 1994
ISBN: 0-449-90888-7
Peters holds that in the "new economy" the most important work will be "brainwork." He shows how successful companies are replacing old hierarchical business structures with networks of small, autonomous, project-oriented teams.

The Fifth Discipline: The Art & Practice of the Learning Organization

Senge, Peter M., New York: Doubleday, 1990
ISBN: 0-385-26094-6
Senge offers the concept of the learning organization as an alternative to the traditional authoritarian hierarchy. He argues that people are the only long-term competitive advantage today, and that their potential lies in the knowledge they bring to the enterprise. Their value is maximized by continuous opportunity for lifelong learning.

The Fifth Discipline Fieldbook	**Senge, Peter; Kleiner, Art; et. al.,** New York: Doubleday, 1994 ISBN: 0-385-47256-0 This fieldbook takes Senge's theory regarding a learning organization and makes it practical. It is a pragmatic guide to creating an organization where collaboration is the lifeblood of every endeavor, and the tough questions are fearlessly asked.
Developing Products in Half the Time	**Smith, Preston G., and Reinersten, Donald G.,** New York: Van Nostrand Reinhold, 1991 ISBN: 0-442-00243-2 Since quality and productivity are essential elements of today's business climate, the authors contend that the key to being successful is producing products as quickly as possible. This book takes the reader through the entire development process and provides specific management techniques that will enable a company to get products on the market quickly, but with the requisite high level of quality.
Becoming a Learning Organization	**Swieringa, Joop, and Wierdsma, Andre,** Reading, MA: Addison-Wesley, 1993 ISBN: 0-201-62753-1 The authors contend that continual organizational development is essential for remaining competitive. This concise book extols the wisdom of learning from experience and teaches companies how to do it.
Mastering the Dynamics of Innovation	**Utterback, James M.,** New York: McGraw-Hill, 1994 ISBN: 0-07-103582-6 Through the use of historical examples of technological innovations and industry's use of them, the author shows businesses how to embrace and utilize innovation in order to succeed in a competitive marketplace. Understanding and harnessing new technological advances is essential to remaining competitive and this book gives insights into how to accomplish this.
A Whack on the Side of the Head	**Von Oech, Roger,** New York: Warner Books, 1993 ISBN: 0-446-77808-7 The author provides puzzles, exercises, metaphors, questions, stories, and tips to help you systematically break through your mental blocks and unlock your mind for creative thinking. This book will help you come up with new approaches to old problems.

***The Machine that
Changed the World***

Womack, James P., et al., New York: Rawson Associates, 1990
ISBN: 0-89256-350-8
This book is the result of an extensive study on the future of the
auto industry and describes the Japanese move from mass
production to lean production. Some of the basic principles of lean
production are: teamwork, communication, and efficient use of
resources. The authors argue that American business would do
well to adopt this innovative approach to production.

SUGGESTED SEMINARS

The seminars listed here were selected for their appeal to a managerial audience. The reputation of the vendor, the quality of their seminar offerings, and the specific seminar content were considered in the selection process.

Because of the dynamic nature of the seminar marketplace, some seminars may have been upgraded or replaced, and others may no longer be offered. Likewise, costs and locations may have changed since this listing was compiled. We recommend that you contact the vendor directly for updated and additional information.

Creativity and Innovation: Dynamic Solutions to Work-Related Challenges

Participants in this program will learn idea-generating techniques, discover how to build and develop creative teams, avoid the common mistakes that block creativity, identify the characteristics of creative thinkers, and return to the work setting with solutions to real-life challenges.
Length: 3 days; Cost: $1,200
Locations: Call vendor
American Management Association
P.O. Box 319, Saranac Lake, NY 12983
Telephone: 800/262-9699

Leadership for Technical Managers

This workshop is designed to build the critical skills needed to manage effectively and lead technical or cross-disciplinary teams responsible for product innovation and process development.
Length: 6 days; Cost: $3,400
Location: Greensboro, NC
Center for Creative Leadership
One Leadership Place, P.O. Box 26300
Greensboro, NC 27438-6300
Telephone: 910/545-2810

Managing Innovation

This program will teach participants how to: analyze strategies for managing innovation, explore ways to encourage innovation and change, assess the process of innovation within their organizations and develop an action plan to improve that process.
Length: 3 days; Cost: $2,875
Location: Stanford, CA
Stanford Continuing Education Executive Programs
Stanford Alumni Association, Bowman Alumni House
Stanford, CA 94305-4005
Telephone: 415/723-2027

Strategic Thinking and Management for Competitive Advantage

This seminar will help managers use the planning process as an opportunity to step back and ask the right questions, learn new approaches, and question their organization's basic assumptions. They will learn to think strategically and use resources more effectively.
Length: 5 days; Cost: $4,550
Location: Philadelphia
University of Pennsylvania, The Wharton School
Aresty Institute of Executive Education
Steinberg Conference Center, 255 South 38th Street
Philadelphia, PA 19104-6359
Telephone: 800/255-3932

The Disney Approach to Creative Leadership

This seminar is designed to expand the participant's understanding of how to foster creativity in the work environment. Topics include a discussion of creative processes that can be adapted to your organization, how to turn "dynamic tension" into creative reality, and how to balance creativity with expense and operational constraints.
Length: 3 days; Cost: $2,295
Location: Lake Buena Vista, FL
Walt Disney World
Disney University Seminars, P.O. Box 10093
Lake Buena Vista, FL 32830-0093
Telephone: 407/824-4855

International Resources

The following is a beginning list of resources available outside the United States. They have been organized according to The PROFILOR® factors. This list is by no means exhaustive. For further information on available resources in Europe, please contact Client Relations at PDI Europe, Avenue de Tervuren 12, 1040 Brussels, Belgium. Telephone: 32-2-732-91-27, Fax: 32-2-732-90-92. We welcome suggestions and input from you, our readers, of additional resources outside the U.S. that you have found to be valuable.

ADMINISTRATIVE SKILLS

**Advanced
Management
Programme**

This program is designed to improve managerial skills, professional competency, and those capabilities required to meet the demands of expanding responsibilities. It covers a variety of key areas including organizational behavior, operations management, management accounting and control, and financial management.
Length: 4 weeks; Cost: FF 72,000 (accommodations not included)
Location: Fontainebleau, France
INSEAD
O.B. Department, Blvd. de Constance, 77305 Fontainebleau Cédex, France
Telephone: (+33) 60 72 41 88

**Managing
Corporate
Resources**

This program improves managers' skills in allocating resources and using them efficiently. It develops participants' ability to appreciate and understand: the internal and external forces that affect the business, the industry, and themselves; the interaction of different functions within the organization; the structures and management systems required to ensure that the activities of the various functions are compatible and fit overall company strategy; and techniques to achieve effective management and implementation of strategy through people.
Length: 4 weeks; Cost: 20,000 (Swiss Francs)
Location: Lausanne, Switzerland
International Institute for Management Development
Chemin de Bellerive 23, P.O. Box 915, CH-1001
Lausanne, Switzerland
Telephone: (41) 21/618 01 11

Systems Thinking and Strategic Modelling

This program focuses on developing skills for systems thinking, the main strategic management problems, methods for building and using models, and communication. Participants consider case studies of organizations which have successfully used strategic modeling in a variety of settings.
Length: 6 days; Cost: £3,400
Location: London
London Business School
Sussex Place, Regent's Park, London, NW1 4SA, UK
Telephone: (+44) (0)171 262 5050

Managing Critical Resources

This management program is for managers whose positions require an understanding of other areas within the company, and who must plan and coordinate their function with these areas. It adds an international dimension to the executive's understanding of business practices and policies in an international context.
Length: 12 days; Cost: $7,500
Location: Cambridge, England
University of Virginia, Executive Programs
The Darden School Foundation, P.O. Box 6550
Charlottesville, VA 22907-6022
Telephone: 804/924-3000

COMMUNICATION SKILLS

Individual Coaching Services

This customized coaching program helps people develop critical skills such as leadership, interpersonal, communication, and organizational-influence skills. Through a tailored assessment to diagnose developmental needs, one-on-one skills training, and state-of-the-art techniques for behavior change, participants gain powerful self-insight and successfully learn new skills and behaviors to make them stronger performers.
Length: Call vendor; Cost: Call vendor
Locations: London, Brussels, Paris
Kerr Brown PDI
8 Hinde Street, London, W1M 5RG, UK
Telephone: (+44) (0)171 487 5776

INTERPERSONAL SKILLS

Working With Others

Participants in this workshop learn three critical areas of management: gaining peak performance from workers, leading work groups, and handling interpersonal relationships.
Length: 3 days; Cost: BEF 60,000 (+19.5% VAT for Belgian residents)
Location: Brussels
Center for Creative Leadership
Avenue Molière, 219, B-1060, Brussels, Belgium
Telephone: (+32) 2 346 42 01

Interpersonal Skills for Senior Managers

This program covers a range of subjects grouped into three areas: the employment process, the control process, and interaction. Subjects include coaching, recruitment and induction, motivation, designing and maintaining structures, teamwork, feedback skills, and managing diversity across different corporate and national cultures.
Length: 6 days; Cost: £3,650
Location: London
London Business School
Sussex Place, Regent's Park, London, NW1 4SA, UK
Telephone: (+44) (0)171 262 5050

Working With Others

This program (see above), developed by the Center for Creative Leadership, is also available under license at The Niagara Institute.
Length: 4 days; Cost: CD $1,775 + GST
Location: Niagara-on-the-Lake, Ontario, Canada
The Niagara Institute, 358 Mary Street
Niagara-on-the-Lake, Ontario, L0S 1J0, Canada
Telephone: 905/468-4271

LEADERSHIP SKILLS

Influencing Strategies and Skills

Individuals attending this program will develop their abilities to persuade and influence others by learning which approaches are appropriate for particular situations and building their confidence to handle a variety of scenarios where social influence is necessary.
Length: 5 days; Cost: £2,300 + VAT
Location: Berkhamsted, UK
Ashridge Management College
Berkhamsted, Hertfordshire, HP4 1NS, UK
Telephone: (+44) (0)1442 841015

Making Change Work

This short program is intended for middle- to senior-level managers who are responsible for managing and implementing organizational change. Participants will develop an action plan for undertaking a change project within their own organization. The principles and techniques learned will enable individuals to create the momentum for change, undertake and evaluate the process, and be equipped to manage continual change.
Length: 2 days; Cost: £1,300 + VAT
Location: Berkhamsted, UK
Ashridge Management College
Berkhamsted, Hertfordshire, HP4 1NS, UK
Telephone: (+44) (0)1442 841015

Compete to Win: Continuous Improvement

This integrated seminar combines a proven, structured approach to leadership with a customer-focused continuous improvement process. The seminar is designed to provide executives, managers, and supervisors with new, proven leadership skills that enable them to work more effectively through other people in the achievement of the organization's success.
Length: 2 days; Cost: CD $985 + GST
Location: Toronto
Gilmore and Associates, 150 Bloor Street West, Suite 340
Toronto, Ontario, M5S 2X9, Canada
Telephone: 416/926-1944

Leadership Development Program

This program is designed to offer middle- to upper-level managers an opportunity to stimulate their personal and professional growth while increasing their organizational effectiveness. Participants acquire a better understanding of their strengths and weaknesses, improve their ability to give constructive feedback to direct reports, and develop their leadership style and effectiveness.
Length: 6 days; Cost: BEF 160,000 (+19.5% VAT for Belgian residents)
Location: Brussels
Center for Creative Leadership
Avenue Molière, 219, B-1060, Brussels, Belgium
Telephone: (+32) 2 346 42 01

Leadership Development Program

This program (see above), developed by the Center for Creative Leadership, is also available under license at Ashridge Management College.
Length: 6 days; Cost: £3,900 + VAT
Location: Berkhamsted, UK
Ashridge Management College
Berkhamsted, Hertfordshire, HP4 1NS, UK
Telephone: (+44) (0)1442 841015

Leadership Development Program

This program (see above), developed by the Center for Creative Leadership, is also available under license at Monash Mt. Eliza Business School.
Length: 6 days; Cost: AD 4,975
Location: Mt. Eliza, Australia
Monash Mt. Eliza Business School
Kunyung Road
Mt. Eliza, Victoria 3930, Australia
Telephone: 61-3-787-4211

Leadership Development Program

This program (see above), developed by the Center for Creative Leadership, is also available under license at The Niagara Institute.
Length: 6 days; Cost: CD $4,400
Location: Niagara-on-the-Lake, Ontario, Canada
The Niagara Institute, 358 Mary Street
Niagara-on-the-Lake, Ontario, L0S 1J0, Canada
Telephone: 905/468-4271

Leadership Development Program

This program (see above), developed by the Center for Creative Leadership, is also available under license at Tecnología Administrativa Moderna (TEAM), S.C.
Length: 6 days; Cost: $3,900 (U.S.)
Location: Mexico City
Tecnología Administrativa Moderna (TEAM), S.C.
Avenida León Felipe 42
Álvaro Obregón
01049 México, D.F.
México
Telephone: 011-525-550-8878

THE Change Program — Making It Happen

This program focuses on the problems that face an organization when it embarks on a program of fundamental restructuring. Its specific objectives include examining the need for change, defining what is to be changed, and overcoming the most common obstacles.
Length: 2 weeks; Cost: 15,000 (Swiss Francs)
Location: Lausanne, Switzerland
International Institute for Management Development
Chemin de Bellerive 23, P.O. Box 915
CH-1001 Lausanne, Switzerland
Telephone: (41) 21/618 02 55

Leadership for Change: Understanding and Action

This program covers the role of the leader in the planning, implementation, and management of the change process. It provides participants with: skills necessary to analyze change, feedback on their own strengths as change managers, an understanding of change processes in other organizations, and a detailed plan for implementing change in their own organization.
Length: 6 days; Cost: £3,250
Location: London
London Business School
Sussex Place, Regent's Park, London, NW1 4SA, UK
Telephone: (+44) (0)171 262 5050

MOTIVATION SKILLS

Introduction to Management

This course is designed for new managers who want to acquire a basic understanding of the position. The program covers the manager's role, and identifies managerial strengths, the advantages of teams, and the process of adding value to the organization.
Length: 5 days; Cost: £2,150 + VAT
Location: Berkhamsted, UK
Ashridge Management College
Berkhamsted, Hertfordshire, HP4 1NS, UK
Telephone: (+44) (0)1442 841015

ORGANIZATIONAL KNOWLEDGE

Finance for Managers

This program is designed for managers at all levels who wish to gain a solid understanding of business finance and how financial techniques can be applied to improve the quality of decisions. Areas covered include: measuring business performance, financial planning, assessing your own and competitors' performance, cost and profitability analysis, and investment appraisal.
Length: 5 days; Cost: £1,990 + VAT
Location: Berkhamsted, UK
Ashridge Management College
Berkhamsted, Hertfordshire, HP4 1NS, UK
Telephone: (+44) (0)1442 841015

Marketing Management and Business Development

Intended for marketers and general managers, this program looks at integrating business strategies and plans in order to gain a more distinct market focus across the organization. Participants will learn to analyze business opportunities with the aim of increasing value to the customer, be confident in using marketing techniques, and be competent at producing and carrying out market strategies.
Length: 5 days; Cost: £4,600 + VAT
Location: Berkhamsted, UK
Ashridge Management College
Berkhamsted, Hertfordshire, HP4 1NS, UK
Telephone: (+44) (0)1442 841015

Strategic Human Resource Management

This program is aimed at senior managers who need to maximize their human resource contribution to the design of business strategy and realize corporate strategy through human resource management. The program covers strategy concepts, the role of human resource management in strategy implementation, the development of appropriate structures, the connections between human resource practices and strategy, and action planning.
Length: 5 days; Cost: £2,450 + VAT
Location: Berkhamsted, UK
Ashridge Management College
Berkhamsted, Hertfordshire, HP4 1NS, UK
Telephone: (+44) (0)1442 841015

Managing for Market Success

This annually revised program is designed to provide a solid foundation in marketing. Participants will review and upgrade their skills in domestic and global marketing strategy, learn tools and concepts for effectively creating and carrying out their strategies, and expose themselves to other organizations' marketing methods through discussion and comparison of practices from a wide range of countries and industries.
Length: 2 weeks; Cost: 11,000 (Swiss Francs)
Location: Lausanne, Switzerland
**International Institute for Management Development
Chemin de Bellerive 23, P.O. Box 915
CH-1001 Lausanne, Switzerland
Telephone: (41) 21/618 02 55**

Networks and Alliances: The New Competitive Organization

This annually updated seminar concentrates on teaching the strategic use of alliances. Intended for anyone involved in management or planning, the program examines the purpose, structure, and spirit of good alliances with added focus on technology-driven partnerships and global strategies. Participants will share perspectives from a wide range of countries and industries.
Length: 5 days; Cost: 8,000 (Swiss Francs)
Location: Lausanne, Switzerland
**International Institute for Management Development
Chemin de Bellerive 23, P.O. Box 915
CH-1001 Lausanne, Switzerland
Telephone: (41) 21/618 02 55**

Financial Seminar for Senior Managers

This course is intended for senior managers who do not have a financial background but need to gain an understanding of this area. Participants will learn how to undertake financial analyses in order to interpret financial statements, to identify problems, to improve profit performance, and to carry out project appraisals.
Length: 6 days; Cost: £3,250
Location: London
**London Business School
Sussex Place, Regent's Park, London, NW1 4SA, UK
Telephone: (+44) (0)171 262 5050**

ORGANIZATIONAL STRATEGY SKILLS

The European Management Programme

Program learning objectives include: learning to think in intercultural terms and adapt to new ways of working; developing the ability to think strategically from a European perspective, to acquire a better understanding of European political, financial, and social systems, and their effect on long-term corporate growth; and developing and practicing cross-cultural skills and communication in a multinational atmosphere.
Length: 10 days; Cost: 6,800 ECUs (excluding residential costs)
Locations: Berkhamsted, UK; Paris
Ashridge Management College
Berkhamsted, Hertfordshire, HP4 1NS, UK
Telephone: (+44) (0)1442 841015

International Managers' Programme

The program's learning objectives include: encouraging participants to identify and apply their knowledge, experience, and skills to effectively manage in the international arena; developing the skills required to achieve results while managing key transitions, responsibilities, and operations; and enabling participants to broaden their horizons by involvement with similar caliber managers from global organizations.
Length: 2 weeks; Cost: £5,750 +VAT
Location: Berkhamsted, UK
Ashridge Management College
Berkhamsted, Hertfordshire, HP4 1NS, UK
Telephone: (+44) (0)1442 841015

Strategy and Finance

Participants of this program will benefit their organization by learning techniques for conducting analyses regarding organizational issues such as competitive position, financial performance, and means of improvement. The course content includes: evaluating the determinants of profitability, assessing the attractiveness of a business area, and measuring competitor performance.
Length: 5 days; Cost: £2,600 + VAT
Location: Berkhamsted, UK
Ashridge Management College
Berkhamsted, Hertfordshire, HP4 1NS, UK
Telephone: (+44) (0)1442 841015

Managing Multinational Enterprise

The focus of this program is on the issues associated with multinational management and on general management responsibilities and tasks. The program concentrates on broad strategic and organizational issues and examines in-depth the problems encountered in formulating and implementing strategy for transnational operations. Topics covered include: achieving efficiency, promoting flexibility, providing for information sharing and collective learning, examining the executive's role, and creating organizational capacity for change.

Length: 2 weeks; Cost: FF 54,000 (accommodations not included)
Location: Fontainebleau, France
INSEAD
O.B. Department, Blvd. de Constance, 77305 Fontainebleau Cédex, France
Telephone: (+33) 60 72 41 88

SELF-MANAGEMENT SKILLS

Self-Managed Development Workshop

This program examines the principles and methods for self-managed development and provides a starting point for people to begin. This program benefits both the individual and the organization by providing more focused and relevant development programs and a heightened commitment to the process.

Length: 3 days; Cost: £1,300 + VAT
Location: Berkhamsted, UK
Ashridge Management College
Berkhamsted, Hertfordshire, HP4 1NS, UK
Telephone: (+44) (0)1442 841015

THINKING SKILLS

Developing Business Strategy

This is an intensive, two-day course which provides participants with a general overview of strategy and methods of strategy development. At the end of the program, participants will have an understanding of the strategy development process from analysis to implementation based on practical work related to their own business situations.

Length: 2 days; Cost: £1,300 + VAT
Location: Berkhamsted, UK
Ashridge Management College
Berkhamsted, Hertfordshire, HP4 1NS, UK
Telephone: (+44) (0)1442 841015

Directors' Strategy Programme

Designed for directors and senior managers, this course provides a practical understanding of the strategy development process. Participants will learn about the role and responsibilities of the director, how to influence the development of strategy, and how to develop strategies with an enduring competitive advantage.
Length: 5 days; Cost: £2,800 + VAT
Location: Berkhamsted, UK
Ashridge Management College
Berkhamsted, Hertfordshire, HP4 1NS, UK
Telephone: (+44) (0)1442 841015

Innovative Business Development

Participants will benefit from this program by increasing their flexibility and self-confidence, gaining insight into their own creativity, and learning strategies for influencing people. Other topics include: the innovation culture and creativity, the learning organization, and benchmarking for innovation.
Length: 5 days; Cost: £2,300 + VAT
Location: Berkhamsted, UK
Ashridge Management College
Berkhamsted, Hertfordshire, HP4 1NS, UK
Telephone: (+44) (0)1442 841015

Strategic Decisions

Designed for senior executives, this program enhances the quality of strategic decision making using both lectures and practical exercises. Topics covered include: strategic appraisal, financial appraisal, individual's roles in the decision process, decision-making styles, and decision process tools.
Length: 5 days; Cost: £2,800 + VAT
Location: Berkhamsted, UK
Ashridge Management College
Berkhamsted, Hertfordshire, HP4 1NS, UK
Telephone: (+44) (0)1442 841015

Strategic Management Programme

This comprehensive, three-week program is designed to help managers develop and instigate more effective strategies. Topics include: strategic analysis, competitive strategy, finance and strategy, corporate culture and strategy, models of leadership, and transferring strategy from theory to practice.
Length: 3 weeks (also available 10 + 5 days); Cost: £8,500 + VAT
Location: Berkhamsted, UK
Ashridge Management College
Berkhamsted, Hertfordshire, HP4 1NS, UK
Telephone: (+44) (0)1442 841015

Strategy in Action   Participants will learn methods for devising actionable strategies, competitor assessment, and strategic change. Also covered are the issues involved in building commitment to a strategy and obstacles which prevent strategic change.
Length: 5 days; Cost: £3,250
Location: London
London Business School
Sussex Place, Regent's Park, London, NW1 4SA, UK
Telephone: (+44) (0)171 262 5050

About Personnel Decisions International

Personnel Decisions International (PDI) is a firm of organizational psychologists and consultants specializing in assessment-based development of individuals and organizations. We use measurement and evaluation of individual and organizational characteristics as a foundation for services, products, and consulting that enhance effectiveness.

Founded in 1967, PDI has become an internationally recognized leader in applying behavioral sciences to building successful organizations. PDI delivers services with the highest professional standards to hundreds of corporations and organizations throughout the world, from Fortune 500 organizations to government agencies to new growing companies.

We promote close professional relationships with clients to better understand and meet their special needs. PDI's growth has been guided by a firm commitment to maintain and enhance the expertise our clients require. As a result, we have won a reputation for both professional excellence and practical results.

Assessment-based development is the specialty of more than 200 psychologists and consultants at Ph.D. and Masters levels. Our expertise spans many disciplines of psychology, a broad mix of corporate backgrounds, and practical business experience. This diversity of staff experience and professional credentials gives PDI a depth and breadth unique in our field.

Services, products, and consulting from Personnel Decisions International provide solutions to virtually every area of concern in human resource development:

- Assessment, for selection and promotion of the most qualified people for critical, key positions

- Management development, to build the effectiveness and leadership ability of managers and executives

- Organizational effectiveness, to maximize the potential of the entire group

- Career transitions and career development, to strengthen organizations and preserve individual dignity

For information on services and products, call or write Personnel Decisions International, 2000 Plaza VII Tower, 45 South Seventh Street, Minneapolis, Minnesota 55402-1608, USA. Telephone: 800/ 633-4410 or 612/339-0927.